Marketing of Agricultural Products

Marketing of Agricultural Products

FIFTH EDITION

Richard L. Kohls
Joseph N. Uhl

Purdue University

Macmillan Publishing Co., Inc.
NEW YORK

Collier Macmillan Publishers
LONDON

MACMILLAN PUBLISHING CO., INC.
866 THIRD AVENUE, NEW YORK, NEW YORK 10022

COLLIER MACMILLAN CANADA, LTD.

Library of Congress Cataloging in Publication Data

Kohls, Richard Louis, (date)
  Marketing of agricultural products.

  Includes bibliographies and index.
  1. Produce trade. 2. Produce trade—United States.
3. Farm produce—Marketing. I. Uhl, Joseph N., joint
author. II. Title.
HD9000.5.K57 1980   381'.41   78–20779
ISBN 0–02–365640–9 (Hardbound)
ISBN 0–02–979360–2 (International Edition)

PRINTING: 5 6 7 8   YEAR: 2 3 4 5 6

Preface

The fifth edition represents a substantial revision in this text, first published in 1955. As with previous revisions, the goal has been to keep the text up to date with the real world in which the students find themselves. More than ever before, the appropriate organization and functioning of the nation's food marketing system are of concern not only to those farmers and marketing-firm operators directly involved but to consumers and the general public as well.

This book, like the previous editions, is written for those who are beginning their study of the food marketing system. It is designed for the use of students who have had little or no previous contact with economics and those who have had elementary economics. The book presents the starting points for learning and discussion and leaves to the teacher the task of adjusting the levels of achievement to the particular class involved. To aid in this, footnote and bibliography references to other marketing research works are amply supplied. It is hoped that these will encourage further study or at least call attention to the immense volume of marketing literature that is now available.

Textbooks are not novels! However, it has been our pleasure over the years to hear the student's favorable comment on the readability of this book. Some of our colleagues have commented that it is too elementary and easy; this, however, we have accepted as a compliment rather than a criticism. In the final analysis texts should be written for students, not for our professional colleagues.

We do not claim that this is a complete text adequately covering all phases of marketing. The commodity chapters are only brief reviews of the system of the particular commodity. Many instructors use them largely as supplemental case studies to illustrate the wholeness of the marketing process. Entire books are written on many of the individual aspects of marketing discussed. The purpose here is to present as detailed and interesting a total picture as possible within one book of reasonable length. Many instructors will find it both necessary and desirable to supplement the text with additional material in particular areas they wish to stress.

The approach of this edition, like that of the others, is mixed—partly by function, partly by institutions, partly by market levels, and partly by commodities. Each of these approaches provides unique and complementary perspectives of the food marketing processes and problems. The book also blends descriptive, analytical and normative approaches to the food marketing system.

Part I, "The Framework of The Marketing Problem" has received further elaboration. There is additional material on the interrelatedness of food markets—particularly the complementarity of farm and middlemen marketing activities; the controversial nature and rationale of middlemen; and the criteria for evaluating food marketing performance. Part II, "Food Markets and Institutions" traces the food production and marketing process from input supply markets to the kitchen. A chapter on international trade in agricultural commodities has been added to highlight the increased importance of the world market. Part III, "Prices and Marketing Costs" contains revised chapters on food price analysis, food marketing competition, farm prices and marketing costs. There is also considerable new material in Part IV, "Functional and Organizational Issues," relating to integration, decentralization, market power, market development and the futures market. Part V, "Government and Food Marketing," describes the growing role of regulations and the changing nature of agricultural price and income policies. Part VI provides sub-sector analyses of several major commodities.

It is hoped that the addition of chapter previews, questions for discussion, and summaries will assist the student in grasping the fundamental marketing concepts presented in this edition. An annotated bibliography in Chapter 16 and the glossary have also been added to assist the student in understanding food marketing.

In any book that has an extended history such as this one, many people have made significant comments and suggestions. It would be impossible to recognize all of them. However, we do wish to recognize specifically the administrative support of Dr. Paul Farris, Head of the Department of Agricultural Economics at Purdue University. To our wives and families go our appreciation for both their help and patience.

R. L. K.
J. N. U.

Contents

PART I
The Framework of The Marketing Problem

1. INTRODUCTION TO FOOD MARKETING   **3**
What is Marketing? / The Food Marketing System / Marketing Is Complex and Costly / Marketing Defined / Marketing Is Productive / The Marketing Process / Growth and Role of Marketing / Historical Benchmarks In Food Marketing / Summary

ANALYZING AGRICULTURAL AND FOOD MARKETS   **22**
Approaches To The Study of Food Marketing / Analyzing Market Performance In The Food Industry / Food Marketing Efficiency / Consumers and Food Marketing / Food Marketing Trends and Issues / Summary

3. AGRICULTURAL PRODUCTION AND MARKETING   **48**
The Agricultural Plant / The Structure of U.S. Agriculture / Characteristics of the Product / Characteristics of Production / The Farm Marketing Problem / Farm Marketing Questions / The Farmer's Marketing Plan / Summary

PART II
Food Markets and Institutions

4. FOOD CONSUMPTION AND MARKETING   **73**
The Anatomy of Food Preferences / Food Consumption and Expenditure Patterns / The Demographics of Food Consumption / Income and Food Consumption / The Away-From-Home Food Market / Summary

5. FOOD PROCESSING AND MANUFACTURING   **92**
Innovation and Branding In Food Manufacturing / The Structure of Food Manufacturing / The Location of Food Processing / The Law of Market Areas / Problems of Food Processors / Summary

6. FOOD WHOLESALING AND RETAILING   **107**
Principal Changes in Food Wholesaling and Retailing / Food Whole-
saling / Food Retailing / Competition and Pricing In Food Retailing /
Marketing Implications of Retailing Developments / Food Shoppers'
Behavior / Summary

7. THE INTERNATIONAL MARKET FOR FOOD   **128**
Significance of Agricultural Trade / The Rationale for Trade / U.S.
Farm Product Exports / U.S. Food Imports / Agricultural Trade Pol-
icy / Summary

PART III
Prices and Marketing Costs

8. PRICE ANALYSIS AND THE EXCHANGE FUNCTION   **149**
Role of Prices in The Competitive Economy / Relative Prices and Food
Marketing Decisions / Supply and Demand Analysis / Applications
of Supply and Demand Analysis / The Supply-Demand Balance /
Marketing and The Law of One Price / Price Discovery / Summary

9. COMPETITION IN FOOD MARKETS   **184**
Perfect Competition / Monopoly–Monopsony / Oligopoly–Oligopsony / Monopolistic Competition / Competitive Conditions in Food
Markets / Usefulness of the Competitive Model / Workable Competition / Summary

10. THE BEHAVIOR OF FARM PRICES   **201**
Forces Influencing Farm Prices / Farm and Food Price Trends /
Commodity Price Fluctuations / Farm Prices and Costs Over the Busi-
ness Cycle / Agricultural Price Cycles / Seasonal Price Variations /
Farm Income and Prices / Summary

11. FOOD MARKETING COSTS   **220**
The Food Marketing Margin / The Food Marketing Bill / Cost Com-
ponents of the Marketing Bill / Farm-Retail Price Spreads / The
Farmer's Share / Interrelationships of the Marketing Margin and Food
Prices / The Future of Food Marketing Costs / Summary

PART IV
Functional and Organizational Issues

12. THE CHANGING ORGANIZATION OF FOOD MARKETS   **249**
Vertical Coordination In Food Markets / Specialization and Diversification in Food Markets / Decentralization of Food Markets / Inte-

Contents

19. STORAGE   **396**
Food Stocks, Carryover and Reserves / Storage Operations / Who Should Store? / Food Storage and Prices / Reducing Food Storage Costs / Summary

20. RISK MANAGEMENT AND THE FUTURES MARKET   **411**
Types of Market Risk / The Futures Market / Relationships Between Cash and Futures Prices / Hedging and Risk Management / Futures Market Participants / The Futures Market Controversies / Forward Contracts and Futures Contracts / Public Regulation of Futures Trading / Summary

PART V
Government and Food Marketing

21. GOVERNMENT PRICE, INCOME AND MARKETING PROGRAMS   **437**
Rationale For Government Market Intervention / The Evolution of U.S. Farm Price and Income Policy / The Development of Parity / Analysis of Farm Price and Income Support Programs / Impacts of Farm Programs On Marketing / Summary

22. FOOD MARKETING REGULATIONS   **452**
Issues In Market Regulation / Regulations to Maintain and Police Competition / Regulations To Control or Offset Monopoly Conditions / Regulations to Facilitate Trade and Provide Services / Regulations To Protect the Consumer / Regulations to Directly Affect Food Prices / Regulations to Foster Economic and Social Progress / The Regulatory Agencies / The Future of Food Marketing Regulations / Summary

PART VI
Commodity Marketing

23. LIVESTOCK AND MEAT MARKETING   **473**
Livestock Production / Growth of Specialized Feedlots / Livestock Products and Meat Consumption / Livestock Assembly Operations / Decentralization In The Livestock and Meat Packaging Industries / Meat Packing and Processing / Meat Wholesaling and Retailing / Standardization and Grading of Livestock and Meat / Livestock Marketing Problems / Summary

gration of Food Markets / Integration Into Farming / Future
nization of Food Markets / Summary

13. COOPERATIVES IN THE FOOD INDUSTRY
What Is A Cooperative? / Kinds of Cooperative Business / T
Cooperative Organization / History and Status of American Co
tion / Cooperation By Regions and Commodities / What M:
Successful Cooperative Association? / Problems of Modern Co
tives / Consumer Food Cooperatives / The Changing Role of C
atives / Summary

14. MARKET DEVELOPMENT AND DEMAND EXPANSION
Market Development In The Food Industry / Varieties of Fo
mand / Roles and Criticisms of Advertising / Advertising B
Marketing Firms / Farmers and Market Development / Exp
Nonfood Uses For Agricultural Products / Synthetics and Agric
Substitutes / Public Food Programs / Summary

15. MARKET AND BARGAINING POWER
Market Power In The Food Industry / Marketing Orders and
ments / Cooperative Bargaining Associations / Marketing Bc
Summary

16. MARKET INFORMATION
Roles of Market Information / Public and Private Food Mar
formation / Criteria For Evaluating Market Information / U
partment of Agriculture Information Programs / Problems of
News and Information / Criticisms of Market Information Prog
Information Users' Responsibilities / Summary / Append
notated Bibliography: Food Marketing Research, Information an

17. STANDARDIZATION AND GRADING
Standardization In The Food Industry / Food Quality Grad
Standards / Market Impacts of Standardization / Governme
Food Quality Standards / Objectives and Problems of Food (
Grading / Farmers and Uniform Grading / Marketing Agenc
Food Grading / Consumers and Food Grades / Summary

18. TRANSPORTATION
Transportation For The Food Industry / Alternative Modes of
portation / Transportation Regulation and Freight Rates /
Prices and Transportation Costs / Reducing The Food Transpo
Bill / Summary

24. **MILK AND DAIRY PRODUCT MARKETING**   **495**
Milk Production and Use / Products and Consumption / Country Assembly of Milk / Milk Pricing / Fluid Milk Channels / Processed Dairy Product Channels / Summary

25. **POULTRY AND EGG MARKETING**   **515**
Production Patterns / Poultry Products, Consumption, and Prices / Integration In The Poultry Industry / Poultry and Egg Marketing Channels / Industry Problems / Summary

26. **GRAIN MARKETING**   **534**
Grain Production and Uses / The Marketing Channels / Country Grain Buying and Merchandising / Grain Grading / Grain Storage / Structure and Competition In The Grain and Oilseed Product Industries / Summary

27. **COTTON AND TEXTILE MARKETING**   **553**
Cotton Production / Consumption Trends / Cotton Industry Structure / Cotton Trade / Cotton Marketing Margins and Prices / Problems In Cotton Marketing / Summary

28. **TOBACCO AND TOBACCO PRODUCT MARKETING**   **566**
Tobacco Production / Tobacco Consumption / Marketing Channels and Methods / Tobacco Trade / Supply Control and Price Support Programs / Tobacco Marketing Problems / Summary

Glossary   **583**

Index   **605**

PART I

The Framework of the Marketing Problem

CHAPTER 1

Introduction to Food Marketing

"TODAY, the process of meeting food and fiber needs involves much more than farming. It includes many activities beyond the farm gate—farm input supply, for example, as well as both marketing and processing of agricultural products."*

Preview

- This chapter describes the nature and role of the food marketing system.
- The food marketing system is shown to be a collection of channels, middlemen, and business activities which facilitate the physical distribution and economic exchange of the nation's food supply.
- The numbers of food marketing firms, the costs of food marketing, and the contributions of the food industry to the national economy are described.
- A definition of food marketing is given, highlighting the mutual interdependence of farmers and food marketing firms.
- The productive nature of food marketing is emphasized, and four varieties of marketing utilities are described.
- The growth and evolution of the food marketing system is traced to changing agricultural patterns and socioeconomic trends.
- The history of food marketing is examined.
- Key terms and concepts:
  agribusiness
  food marketing system
  market

  marketable surplus
  marketing
  marketing utility

---

* *The Food and Fiber System—How It Works,* U.S. Department of Agriculture, Agriculture Information Bulletin No. 383, March 1975.

Key terms and concepts (continued)

middlemen	specialization
social capital	value-added
sorting, assorting	

Beginning students of food marketing are somewhat like the seven blind men attempting to describe an elephant by touch. Each is familiar with some aspect of food marketing, yet few are acquainted with the process in its entirety. Farmers, consumers, food processors, wholesalers, and retailers all view food marketing from different perspectives. Our understanding of food marketing also is colored by past experiences and preconceptions. There is little wonder, then, that considerable confusion exists about food marketing— what it is, how it works, and its role in the food industry and the economy. Our first task is to describe the basic nature of food marketing. This will provide a framework for the more difficult task ahead, that of evaluating the food marketing process.

WHAT IS MARKETING?

Have you ever heard a group of farmers arguing over the relative merits of selling their livestock at the local auction as opposed to shipping them to a meat packer for sale on a carcass basis? Or in another situation these same farmers might be engaged in a heated discussion over the merits and ramifications of accepting the production and marketing contract being offered to egg producers in their area. If you have ever attended the meeting of a cooperative association, you might have heard the members debating whether or not to make a large investment to modernize their operations. In reading a single issue of your newspaper, you may have read about the large profits and growth of one food processing company and the bankruptcy of another. Still other news releases may be telling of the recent ban on certain food ingredients or the prosecution of a firm for misleading advertising. Or if the season is right, your television screen may be filled with candidates for political office who are proclaiming the need for an investigation of the high costs of food marketing or for action to improve the bargaining position of farmers against large food processing and retailing firms.

All of these are brief insights into the activities and conflicts involved in the marketing of agricultural products. Many different alternatives exist for getting the job done. There are different marketing channels, selling arrangements, and proposals for individual, group, or government action. There are firms that are successful and those that are not. There are continual changes in technology.

Watch a housewife shop in a modern supermarket. As she pushes her cart through the aisles, she picks and chooses from among literally thousands of different items. She may stop at the dairy case and select cheese from among dozens of different varieties. At the meat counter she is confronted not only by the various cuts of fresh meat but also by a tremendous variety of luncheon and precooked meats. Pushing on, she may pick up a can of frozen orange juice and a carton of frozen shrimp from the deep-freeze cabinet. At another rack she finds perhaps twenty to thirty different kinds of fresh produce. On her way out she may pick up a loaf of bread baked "just today." Or if she prefers to do her own baking, she can choose either ready-for-baking biscuits packed in a vacuum tin, or a box that contains all the dry ingredients ready for mixing. In all, she may choose from among over 9,000 items in a single store.

Listen to this housewife at the check-out counter. She makes no comment concerning the tremendous variety of goods at her disposal. Rather, she is more likely to make some bitter remark about her favorite brand of frozen peas being out of stock, or question why the new cake mix she saw advertised on television was not on the shelf. Then, with perhaps a parting remark about the high cost of food, she pays her bill and departs. This scene could take place in New York City or in a small Midwestern town. It could happen in the heat of summer or the cold of winter.

Here we see the end product—goods available for consumption—of the tremendous marketing organization of the country. Here also, in the housewife's casual acceptance of this vast array of foods at her disposal, we have the American consumer's vote of confidence that the system works.

THE FOOD MARKETING SYSTEM

Food marketing may be thought of as the connecting link—the bridge—between specialized food producers and consumers. It is both a physical distribution and an economic bridge designed to facilitate the movement and exchange of commodities from the farm to the fork.

A bird's-eye view of the food marketing system is shown in Figure 1-1. It is composed of alternative product flows (called marketing channels), a variety of firms (middlemen), and numerous business activities (referred to as marketing functions). Within this food marketing system a myriad of decisions are made which influence the quality, variety, and cost of the nation's food supply.

This book is about this food marketing system. It is called a *system* because it consists of interrelated component parts that contribute toward overall industry goals. The marketing system is also sometimes referred to as "the marketing machinery" or "the food distribution system."

This system plays two important roles in the food industry: the role of

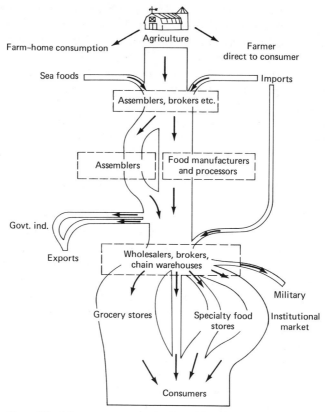

Figure 1-1. Flow of food from source to destinations. The thickness of the flow lines indicates proportionate volume for each channel. (U.S. Department of Agriculture)

physical distribution, which is concerned with the physical handling and transfer of foods as they move from producers to consumers, and the role of adding value to farm commodities and facilitating the exchange process between buyers and sellers. The latter, economic aspect of the food marketing system is less tangible than that of the physical distribution aspect, but no less important. Both the physical distribution and economic roles of markets will be examined and evaluated in this book.

MARKETING IS COMPLEX AND COSTLY

The system, which brings the vast array of food products together and places them at the disposal of over 215 million Americans and countless overseas customers, is complex, expensive, and a significant component of the national economy.

6

In 1978, the initial production of raw materials for these food products took place on 2.7 million U.S. farms. The marketing task begins here, on these diverse farms. Some farms produce small amounts of a great many commodities. Other specialized operations produce large amounts of only a single commodity. Farm products are not only perishable, but they vary in quality. Production is highly seasonal and geographically concentrated in areas that are often located some distance from consumers. Farm commodities must be collected, sorted, and swiftly moved to market, or stored for later use. These production and commodity characteristics give rise to the basic marketing activities, such as storage, transportation, processing, and the like. Few products make more stringent demands on their marketing systems.

There were almost 600,000 business establishments involved in food processing and distribution in 1973. This included 11,000 farm product assemblers and brokers, 28,000 food processing plants, 39,000 grocery product wholesalers, 268,000 retail food stores, and over 253,000 restaurants and public eating places.

The food marketing process is expensive. Two out of every three consumer dollars spent for food remain in the marketing system. In 1977, the food marketing firms' labor costs exceeded the value of commodities sold by farmers. Today, marketing costs have as great an influence on retail food prices as do the farm prices of foods. For example, grocery store prices rose 56 per cent over the 1972–1977 period. The 1972–1973 portion of this rise was primarily the result of increased farm commodity prices. However, fully 90 per cent of the $30 billion increase in consumer food expenditures over the 1974–1977 period was the result of rising food marketing costs. This situation alone warrants greater attention to the food marketing system on the part of consumers, farmers, and legislators.

The food marketing system has a substantial impact on the national economy. In 1976, food marketing activities employed 6.15 million workers on a full-time equivalent basis. Together, farming and food marketing are said to be related to one of every five American jobs. Consumers spent about 17 per cent of their after-tax income for food in the 1970–1977 period, and food and beverages accounted for 19 per cent of total consumer expenditures. The contributions of various agricultural and food marketing sectors to the national economy are shown in Table 1-1. Overall, farming and food marketing account for about one quarter of the U.S. gross national product.

MARKETING DEFINED

Marketing means different things to different people. To the consumer, marketing may refer to the weekly food shopping trip to the supermarket—the most visible tip of the food marketing iceberg. The farmer deals primarily with local farm product buyers, and may associate marketing with the loading

Table 1-1. Contributions of the Food and Fiber Sectors to the U.S. Economy, 1967.

	CONTRIBUTION TO THE GROSS NATIONAL PRODUCT	
FOOD AND FIBER SECTOR	BILLION DOLLARS	PER CENT
Farm supply goods & services	$ 49.1	14%
Farming	51.1	14
Food processing	83.7	23
Textiles and apparel manufacturing	34.9	9
Other manufacturing	53.6	15
Trade and transportation	82.7	23
Imports	8.5	2
Total, food and fiber industry	363.6	100%
Gross National Product	$1,520.5	24%

Source: *The Food and Fiber System—How It Works,* U.S. Department of Agriculture, Agricultural Information Bulletin No. 383, March 1975, p. 1.

of hogs into the pickup for the trip to market, or with the calling of local elevators to determine which is offering the highest price for grain. In contrast, food middlemen such as retailers, wholesalers, and processors may view marketing as a process for gaining competitive advantage over market rivals, improving sales and profits, and satisfying consumers. Each group has only a partial concept of the total food marketing process.

For our purposes, we will define food marketing as *the performance of all business activities involved in the flow of food products and services from the point of initial agricultural production until they are in the hands of consumers.* Several key points of this definition should be noted.

First, the definition does not limit marketing to all the nonfarm activities in the food industry nor to everything that happens to food after it leaves the farm gate. Because no product should ever be produced unless it has a market, marketing begins with production on the farm. The farm gate has become an increasingly ambiguous dividing line between farming and food marketing. More and more, farmers are performing many of the traditional food marketing functions on the farm. Through cooperatives and other arrangements, farmers are also extending their operations to off-farm marketing activities. At the same time, some food marketing firms are crossing over the farm gate to engage in farming. Hence, care must be taken in drawing a hard and fast line between farming and food marketing at the farm gate.

This definition of marketing also recognizes a mutual interdependence between farmers and food marketing middlemen. The food production process does not stop at the farm gate; the food marketing activities complement the agricultural production process. Although it is true that there would

8

be no food without farmers, it is also true that consumers rely on the food marketing system to complete the food production process begun on the farm. The relationship between farmers and food marketing firms is at the same time competitive and complementary.

Food marketing is neither a mechanical nor an automatic operation. The essence of marketing is management decision-making. All business activities involve interpersonal relations and decisions: What is the correct buying and selling price? Should you sell now or store for later sale? How much should be spent on advertising and new product development? Correct decisions to these questions influence the profit and loss statement. The quality of food marketing management decisions influences to a great extent the cost and efficiency of the food marketing system.

There is some debate about whether the farm supply industries should be included as part of the food marketing system. These supply markets can be considered a vital part—indeed the resource base—of the food industry. How well a farmer purchases in these input-procurement markets may influence his profits quite as much as how well he makes sales marketing decisions. Thus, we will, in this book, include the farm-input markets as part of the marketing system.

There are some economic conflicts involved in the food marketing system. Consumers are interested in securing the highest food value at the lowest possible price. Farmers want the highest possible returns from the sale of their products. Food marketing middlemen seek to earn the greatest profit possible. One of the primary tasks of the food marketing system is to reconcile these sometimes conflicting demands.

We will define a *market* as an arena for organizing and facilitating business activities and for answering the basic economic questions: what to produce, how much to produce, how to produce, and how to distribute production. A market may be defined by (1) a location (for example, the St. Louis market); (2) a product (for example, the grain market); (3) a time (for example, the May soybean market); or (4) a level of the market (for example, the retail food market). The choice of market definition depends on the problem to be analyzed. Sometimes it is desirable to study the farm price of corn in a local market; at other times it is necessary to analyze the world price of corn. The most observable features of a market are its pricing and exchange processes. Markets join together the various components of the food industry: the farm supply sector, the farm sector, the food marketing system, and national economies. The totality of the farm input, farm production, and food marketing processes is sometimes referred to as *agribusiness*.

MARKETING IS PRODUCTIVE

Unfortunately, many people look upon those who are engaged in the many marketing jobs, such as grading, transporting, storing, arranging for the transfer of title, and advancing and collecting credit, as being parasitic on those who really "produce" the goods. Farmers often decry the "profits of middlemen" because they think that farmers alone produce the food that people eat. Of course, we realize that they produce only the raw materials from which the consumer's food is finally made. The farmer who produces a hog in Iowa has not produced pork for a housewife in New York. Many things must be done to the hog before it is pork in New York. These other activities are the contributions that the packers, railroads, truckers, livestock commission men, and retail butchers make to pork production.

Economists have defined *production* as the creation of utility—that is, the process of making useful goods and services. The utilities created in the productive processes are further classified into *form* utility, *place* utility, *time* utility, and *possession* utility.

The farmer who produces hogs adds form utility. The packer who slaughters the hogs and cuts them into pork carcasses also adds form utility. They change the form of raw materials and create something useful.

The railroad or trucker adds place utility by moving the hogs from Iowa to the packing plant, and then, after processing, moves the cuts of pork on to wholesalers, retailers, and finally to consumers. The product is more useful because of the activities of these agencies in getting the product to where it is most desired.

Furthermore, the packer may freeze some of the pork products for later use. The pork is more useful by being held from periods of relative plenty to periods of relative scarcity. Time utility is added to the product. Grain elevator and warehouse operators—and even the supermarket operator, through his inventory holdings—add time utility to products.

When the Iowa hogs are shipped to the terminal markets they are usually consigned to a commission man. This commission man seeks out a packer who needs the hogs and helps transfer the hogs from the farmer to the packer. A meat wholesaler facilitates the movement of meat to the retailer for distribution to the final consumers. These people, through their efforts to transfer the product to those who could better use it, add possession utility. Because of these actions the product is placed in the hands of others who can add still other utilities to it.

Most people accept the activities of the farmer and the manufacturer as being productive. They create visible changes in products. However, the other individuals who see that the product is moved through the various handlers, is sent to the needed place, and is available at the needed time are also productive. All of their activities are necessary to produce the final utility that the pork has for the New York housewife in feeding her family. So those engaged in the marketing process, too, are producers in the sense that they add usefulness or utility. To argue which group is more important is rather senseless. Both groups—the producers of raw products and the marketing agencies—are necessary to the creation of the final products for consump-

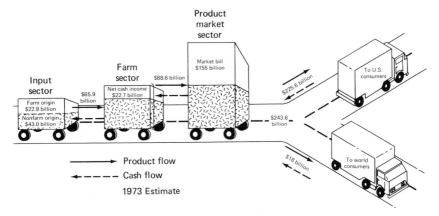

Figure 1-2. How products and cash flow through our food and fiber system. (U.S. Department of Agriculture)

tion. Both create something useful for which society will pay a price. Both groups are productive in the real sense of the word.

The value-adding productive processes in the food industry are illustrated in Figure 1-2. The food industry is divided into three components: (1) the input sector, which provides machinery, fertilizer, seeds, and other farm supplies; (2) the farm sector; and (3) the product-market sector. In 1973 farmers purchased $65.9 billion worth of farm supplies. They added $22.7 billion of value to these purchased supplies through their productive activities and sold farm products valued at $88.6 billion. Food marketing firms then added another $155 billion of value to farm commodities, bringing the total retail value to $243.6 billion. Thus, food "production" can be viewed as a sequential and value-adding process, having its origin in purchased and farm-supplied resources and ending with the meal on the table.

THE MARKETING PROCESS

If we take our definition of marketing as the business activities involved in the flow of goods and services from the point of initial production until they reach the ultimate consumer, two essential characteristics of the process become evident: (1) the marketing process is one of movements; it is a *series of actions and events* that take place in some *sequence;* and (2) some form of *coordination* of this series of events and activities is necessary if goods and services are to move in some orderly fashion from the hands of producers into the hands of consumers.

Figure 1-3 attempts to bring more clearly into focus some of the more pertinent aspects of this marketing process. It shows the agricultural marketing system starting with the farmer and his production. The nature and

11

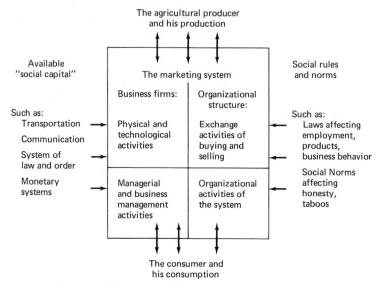

Figure 1-3. Dimensions of the agricultural marketing process.

way in which this production is initially offered to the marketing system has a major determining effect on the organization and operation of the system itself. At the same time, however, the dynamics of the marketing process itself may have a direct influence on agricultural production. A good example of this two-way flow of effects can be seen in the dairy industry. The extreme perishability and bulkiness of milk once required a costly assembly system of trucks picking up the milk in cans at the farm each day. However, the invention of large cooling tanks to provide storage for milk on the farms, combined with the development of bulk tank trucks, provided another possible assembly method. Because this method required large equipment investments, the small dairy farmer was at a disadvantage. Here, then, was a marketing technology that encouraged the reorganization of dairy farms into larger, more specialized units.

At the other end of the sequence of marketing activities is the consumer. Here again the path of influence is a two-way one. Certainly the consumers' wants and desires dictate to a major extent the activities of the marketing process. However, marketing firms expend a great deal of effort in trying to influence and change consumers' behavior and wants to the marketers' advantage.

Between these two forces—the agricultural producer and the consumer— is the marketing system. This complex system is partly composed of business firms engaged in physical and technological activities and run by managers who make the necessary decisions and direct people. A meat processing firm must assemble the animals, the proper slaughter equipment and people, and then organize and direct these into the finished product and move it to consumers. Another part of the system, however, is made up of those firms and organizations whose activities must evolve the mechanics of establishing the selling prices of the various ingredients and also establish the various arrangements, contacts, and organizations that will ensure an orderly and purposeful flow of goods and services. Here we see the complex operations of a large terminal market, the evolving of a trade association, or the instigation of an integration contract with farmers.

Finally, the whole system must operate within certain boundaries that are largely set by somewhat independent conditions. Certainly the type of marketing system that can be evolved is dictated to a large degree by what we might call *social capital*—that is, resources that are created by the society itself and are generally available to it. A large, specialized, and complex marketing system is not possible without a well-developed transport and communication system. Neither can a modern business system operate without an orderly society which can enforce and regulate such things as contractual agreements and a monetary system. Modern machinery and business can be properly operated only by a literate people who are the product of an educational system.

The behavior of the marketing system is also limited by the rules and norms that exist in a society. In the United States, firms cannot employ children regardless of how little they might cost. We do not advertise whiskey on television, though it is acceptable to advertise beer and wine. In our country the kickback, or collusion in business dealings, is not acceptable, although in certain other countries such practices are carried on without public censure. Though such rules may be changed by society, at any given time the marketing system must work out its activities within the currently existing framework.

This general pattern of the marketing process can be detailed for any one of the many agricultural products. The framework for each is the same. The many types of business firms and organizational activities are influenced by—and in turn influence to some degree—the agricultural producer and production, on the one hand, and the consumer and his consumption activities, on the other, and they operate within the area of the possible and the permitted as dictated by the extent of general social resources and the rules and customs of society.

Within this food marketing process there are many sorting and assorting decisions. *Sorting* refers to the concentration and accumulation of large lots of similar products for ease of handling and pricing. Every production process leads to decisions on sorting. The farmer, for example, starts the marketing process with a mixed lot of produce—some saleable and some not, some of high quality and some of low quality. Sorted commodities can be more effectively marketed than unsorted commodities. *Assorting* refers to the building of a complementary mixture of unlike products. For example, consumers require a wide assortment of foods to satisfy their wants. Sorting, then, is a concentrating process whereas assorting is a dispersing process. Sorting and assorting are fundamental to understanding such things as the purpose for food grades and standards, the reason for central food markets, and the role of wholesalers and retailers in the food economy.

GROWTH AND ROLE OF MARKETING

Marketing has developed in importance and complexity as economic development and specialization have increased our productive capacity and separated food producers from consumers. The early pioneers of our country did not have to concern themselves with marketing problems. Each family grew its own food and fiber and built its own shelter. Producers and consumers, if not actually the same individuals, lived next door to each other.

Very early in the development of any community, however, people realized that some were better adapted to certain kinds of activities than others. Thus, they specialized in their work. This specialization increased the output of goods but it also broke down the self-sufficiency of the family unit. As people specialized in different activities, they began to produce more than was needed for home consumption. Markets then developed to facilitate the exchange of this *marketable surplus* between rural and urban areas. Here, then, was the beginning of the marketing task and the group of people who specialized in its performance.

Another aspect of specialization is the growth of urban areas. With the disappearance of the necessity for a man to produce all of his own basic needs, he is able to leave the land and congregate in larger groups where his work may be carried on more efficiently. The people remaining on the farms can more efficiently produce his food and fiber. Of course this increasing urbanization further complicates the task of those engaged in the marketing process.

One of the limiting factors in the urbanization of our country has been the development of adequate transportation and communication facilities. Throughout most of our early history, one of the pressing agricultural marketing problems was that of providing adequate transportation facilities at a reasonable cost to move the increasing output from the farms to the consumers in our growing cities. Here we find an early interest of government in helping the marketing system function adequately. First turnpikes, then canals, and then railroads were subsidized through government help. This public concern has continued even to the present day as various governmental units have developed the interstate highways, subsidized the continued upgrading of our air terminals, and more recently showed concern over maintaining and improving our railroad services.

A complex and costly marketing machinery is not necessary in situations where the volume of production is limited. On the other hand, assembly-line mass production is not feasible until the marketing machinery opens the doors to the broad mass market. Many people have viewed with alarm the impersonal relationships of our huge factories, the growing proportion of our population living in cities, and the increasing numbers who are engaged in the marketing trades and services. Such developments, however, are usually the marks of the more productive countries with increasing standards of living.

This interrelationship between the increasing productivity of the agricultural production process and the development of an adequate marketing system is only belatedly being understood. Since the end of World War II there has been great interest in improving the economic lot of the underdeveloped countries of the world. At first, it was widely thought that if these countries would only apply the known improved production technologies, such as fertilizers, better seeds, and cultivating machinery, advancing output and progress would be forthcoming. In order for farmers to adopt such changes, however, they must be able to reap some benefits from the increased output—they must be able to sell their products profitably to someone else. Without marketing equipment such as communications, transportation, storage facilities, and financing arrangements, this is not possible. Once again it is demonstrated that agricultural production and food marketing must develop hand in hand. They are partners in a progressive system, not antagonists.

HISTORICAL BENCHMARKS IN FOOD MARKETING

The history of the growth and development of agricultural marketing is a rich and exciting one. Only a broad, sweeping picture of it can be presented here. But the study of marketing history serves a very useful purpose. Knowing the marketing problems confronted by our grandfathers and great-grandfathers will help prevent us from believing that our current problems are the only difficult ones that have ever begged solutions. The study of past developments also helps emphasize that changes are continually underway. New developments from many different sources have always challenged the existing marketing organization to adapt or die. The changing nature of the U.S. food system over the 1800–1960 period is illustrated in Figure 1-4.

Up to the end of the first half of the nineteenth century, the pattern was one of small industry with transportation and communication and other marketing problems of a largely local nature. Tobacco, as one of our first surplus crops, presented one of the earliest marketing problems. In seeking solutions, colonial governments and growers tried price controls, production regulations, and struggled with grading problems. Colonial flour milling also had problems of rate fixing, monopoly, and product adulteration.

However, immediately following the Civil War, a whole new set of problems

15

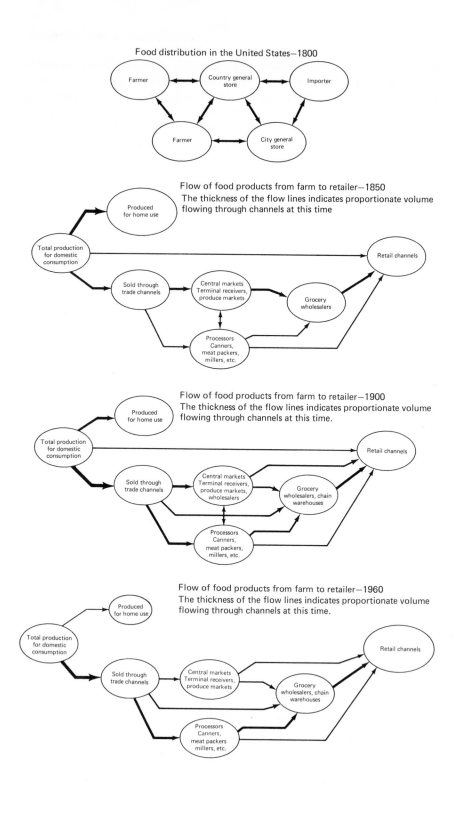

Food distribution in the United States—1800

Flow of food products from farm to retailer—1850
The thickness of the flow lines indicates proportionate volume flowing through channels at this time

Flow of food products from farm to retailer—1900
The thickness of the flow lines indicates proportionate volume flowing through channels at this time.

Flow of food products from farm to retailer—1960
The thickness of the flow lines indicates proportionate volume flowing through channels at this time.

developed as the foundations were laid for the modern nationwide commercial marketing system. Agricultural production grew tremendously with the opening of new western lands. Land in farms jumped from about 294 million acres in 1850 to 536 million acres in 1880. The number of farms increased from about 1.5 million to 4 million during the same period. Outlets for this potential production bonanza had to be found in both our own growing cities and in foreign countries.

About this time many of the large food industries were established. In 1865 the Union Stockyards at Chicago were formed and soon were the largest in the world. The Chicago Board of Trade was founded in 1848 and quickly developed into the nation's leading grain market. By 1870 ice was being used to preserve meat, and by 1880 the use of the refrigerated railroad car made the large national packers possible. In 1870 there were only a few flour mills at Minneapolis. By the late 1880's, Minneapolis was the milling center of the country, and the pattern of organization for the modern giant milling and grain corporations was established. With the introduction of tin cans and other canning equipment in 1880, large-scale canning of fruits and vegetables got underway.

While these changes were occurring, transportation also expanded tremendously. During the decade of the 1870's, the mileage of railroads almost doubled. The two coasts were joined and transcontinental shipments became possible. Telegraph communications were rapidly expanded. Extensive highway development, however, was to await the automobile.

This was a turbulent period. The extraordinary expansion of the farm production plant made suddenly available vast amounts of agricultural raw materials. The many technological developments made possible the rapid growth of a great number of processing firms. The marketing system was put under great pressures to move this productive capacity into the hands of consumers. The rapid growth of the food processing firms and their search for outlets led to cries of monopoly and unethical practices. To this situation was added a severe agricultural price depression during much of the latter part of the century.

Farmers organized to protest these situations. Railroads were bitterly attacked for charging exorbitant and unfair rates. In 1889 one of the farm organizations, the Farmer's Alliance, demanded government ownership of the means of communication and transportation in order to correct alleged abuses. Bitter attacks were made on the alleged evils of the middlemen. Congressional investigations of the practices of the meat packing and other companies were instigated. Demands were made for all kinds of corrective and regulative measures. The immediate result of this agitation was federal

---

Figure 1-4. Food distribution in the United States in 1800, 1850, 1900, and 1960. (from Edward C. Hampe and Merle Wittenberg: *The Lifeline of America.* Copyright © 1964, McGraw-Hill Book Company, New York. Used with permission of McGraw-Hill Book Company)

17

regulatory action. The Act to Regulate Commerce which, among other things, authorized the Interstate Commerce Commission and the surveillance of interstate freight rates, was passed in 1887. In 1890 the passage of the Sherman Act laid the basis for our antimonopoly policies and made private business activities a matter of public concern.

With an improvement in general economic conditions, the tension eased. And in the ensuing years until World War I, the marketing system was allowed time to grow up to its job. Agricultural production continued to expand, but there were no upheavals of the extent of the post-Civil War period. This period was one of changing emphasis in marketing. Previously, much of the effort of those working in agricultural marketing had been directed toward developing foreign markets for our exportable surplus. Now the emphasis was shifted toward developing the domestic outlets of our growing country. Recognition of this changing emphasis came in 1908, when the name of the Division of Foreign Markets in the United States Department of Agriculture was changed to the Division of Production and Distribution. In 1914 Congress officially set up the Office of Markets to collect and disseminate information concerning the marketing of farm products.

After World War I the attitude toward agricultural marketing took a still different perspective. It now appeared as if our production capacities had outrun our consumption capabilities. Throughout the 1920's many schemes were proposed to permit us to dump our excess production abroad. Domestically, however, improvement in the marketing machinery was to be the answer. Governmental blessings were given the cooperative movement as one way for more effective and orderly marketing. Such regulatory laws as the Packers and Stockyards Act and the Commodity Exchange Act were passed to prevent abusive practices by the marketing agencies. Increased marketing efficiency was the goal.

The depression decade of the 1930's further increased the troubles of moving the products of agriculture into consumption at satisfactory prices. Attention was now turned away from marketing to production. Developments in the marketing area could not solve the problem. We simply produced too much. Public attention was now directed toward perfecting various schemes that would reduce the amount of production.

With the demands of World War II, however, efforts were made to produce all that our resources would permit. After the wartime demands had receded, the marketing machinery again came in for increasing public attention and criticism. There was widespread belief that improvements in production had outdistanced improvements in marketing. Ways had been found to make two blades of grass grow where one did before, but no effective way had been found to market the extra blade. The feeling was that all that could be produced could be consumed at satisfactory prices if the marketing system was functioning well.

In 1946 Congress officially gave recognition to the renewed emphasis on marketing when it passed the Research and Marketing Act. Under this Act additional funds for expanding research into all phases of marketing were authorized. The post-World War II years were ones of far-reaching changes in almost every phase of marketing. The perfected quick-freezing of foods found rapid consumer acceptance. Our rising living standards led to demands for more services and more processing of food. More and more food preparation and processing was done by marketing firms, and less and less by the housewife in her kitchen. The retail food store experienced revolutionary changes as the mass, self-service merchandising techniques of the supermarket were perfected. With improved transportation and communication, most of the marketing activity became oriented to a national rather than a regional or local viewpoint. The great central market institutions established almost a hundred years earlier gradually have been replaced by a more decentralized activity. Increasing labor costs focused attention on ways to mechanize and standardize the operation of the marketing machinery. Great faith was placed in increased efficiency as a major solution for the problems of agriculture.

Now, as the last decades of the twentieth century approach, we are still faced with marketing problems and their conflicts. Beyond a doubt, the American food marketing system is a dynamic operation that is furnishing an ever-increasing variety of new and improved products at a high level of economic efficiency. Change is occurring at a very rapid rate. However, the domestic problem of how to obtain satisfactory prices for the steadily increasing potential of agricultural output still remains. Attention is focused, on the one hand, on how best to organize and control agricultural production, and, on the other, on how to expand the market potential for these products. In addition, there is concern about the growing potential power of giant firms in the food industry. Consumers are increasingly vocal about both the nutrition and health aspects of our proliferating food products. As the food sciences increasingly make a growing array of substitute and synthetic food possible, there is increasing concern of all affected groups—farmers, the public (both as consumers and the body politic), and the operators of the food marketing businesses.

SUMMARY

Food marketing encompasses all the business activities involved in the flow of food products and services from producers to consumers. The food marketing system is a complex and expensive network of channels, middlemen, and marketing activities which facilitates the production, distribution, and exchange of the nation's food supply. This system has increased in size and importance with the growth of specialized agriculture, urbanization, and other socioeconomic trends. Marketing is a productive process that adds form, place, time, and possession utility to farm commodities. The value-added in the food marketing process complements the productive processes in farming. The marketing process forms a vital bridge between food producers and consumers and is influenced by social resources, technology, and the laws and norms of society. The food marketing system has evolved in response to the changing needs of farmers and food consumers.

QUESTIONS FOR DISCUSSION

1. After reading Chapter 1, how would you explain "food marketing" to someone who is unfamiliar with the subject?

2. Some people associate food marketing with everything that happens on the other side of the farm gate. Critique this notion of marketing.

3. What does it mean when one says that farmers and food marketing firms are mutually interdependent?

4. How do laws and the technologies of transportation and communications influence the food marketing process?

5. What do you think the food production and marketing system will be like in the year 2000? What are you assuming about farming and consumers?

6. Can you think of any industry that has no specialized middlemen? Why is this so rare?

7. Why has the food marketing system become more complex and expensive with time?

8. Which of the four marketing utilities do farmers provide? Consumers? How are these provided?

9. Suppose you are hired as a consultant to a developing country that wishes to expand its food industry. How would you divide the available development resources between production agriculture and the food-marketing system?

SELECTED REFERENCES

BREIMYER, H. F. *Economics of the Product Markets of Agriculture.* Iowa State University Press, Ames, Iowa, 1976. Chap. 1.
———— "The Economics of Agricultural Marketing: A Survey." *Review of Marketing and Agricultural Economics* (1973), 115–65.
DAHL, D. C. and J. W. HAMMOND. *Market and Price Analysis, the Agricultural Industries.* McGraw-Hill Book Company, New York, 1977, Chap. 1,2.
DARRAH, L. B. *Food Marketing.* The Ronald Press Company, New York, 1971, Chap. 1,2.
DAVIS, J. H. and R. A. GOLDBERG. *A Concept of Agribusiness.* Graduate School of Business Administration, Harvard University, Boston, 1957, Chap. 1,2.
FARMER, R. N. "Would You Want Your Daughter to Marry a Marketing Man?" *Journal of Marketing,* (Jan. 1967), 1–3.
The Food and Fiber System—How It Works. U.S. Department of Agriculture. Agriculture Information Bulletin, No. 383, March 1975.

Marketing America's Food. U.S. Department of Agriculture. Economic Research Service Publication No. 446, Oct. 1970.

Marketing: the Yearbook of Agriculture, 1954. U.S. Government Printing Office, Washington, D.C., 1954.

PRITCHARD, N. T. "A Framework for Analysis of Agricultural Marketing Systems in Developing Countries." *Agricultural Economics Research,* (July 1969), 78–85.

SHEPHERD, G. S. and G. A. FUTRELL. *Marketing Farm Products,* 5th Ed. Iowa State University Press, Ames, Iowa, 1969. Chap. 1.

SOUTHWORTH, H. H. "Historical Evolution of Important Marketing Problems." *Journal of Farm Economics,* (Dec. 1963), 1243–53.

TAYLOR, H. C. and A. D. TAYLOR. *The Story of Agricultural Economics in the United States, 1840–1932.* Iowa State College Press, Ames, Iowa, 1953, Parts 1, 5.

Your Food: A Food Policy Basebook. National Public Policy Education Committee, Publication No. 5. Ohio State University, Columbus, Ohio, Nov. 1975.

CHAPTER 2

Analyzing Agricultural and Food Markets

"THE BIG STORY in agricultural markets is CHANGE . . . accelerating change . . . the concern is properly with the adjustments to change that will be necessary—adjustments by the farmer-producer, by the marketer, by the consumer."*

Preview

• This chapter provides some useful orientations and tools for studying and evaluating the food marketing system.

• Three major orientations to the study of food marketing are examined: the functional approach, the institutional approach, and the behavioral system approach.

• Discussed in this chapter are several key marketing functions which contribute to marketing utility and facilitate the marketing process.

• Numerous, often conflicting criteria for evaluating the performance of the food-marketing system are discussed.

• Marketing efficiency as a ratio of the benefits and costs of marketing activities is examined.

• Two kinds of marketing efficiency—operational efficiency and pricing efficiency—are developed.

• The economic rationale for food middlemen is reviewed.

• The doctrine of consumer sovereignty and the marketing concept are developed to show the important role of consumer decisions in the food industry.

• Several trends in the food industry are examined which raise important questions about food market performance.

---

* Kenneth E. Ogren, *Agricultural Markets in Change,* U.S. Department of Agriculture, Agricultural Economics Report No. 95, 1966.

- Key terms and concepts:

agent middleman	marketing function
behavioral system	marketing institution
commission man	middleman bias
consumer sovereignty	operational efficiency
division of labor	pricing efficiency
economies of scale	productivity crisis
giantism	risk-bearing
input-output system	search and transactions costs
market intelligence	specialization
market performance	speculative middleman
marketing concept	standardization

The difference between an orderly closet in which you can find what you want with a minimum of effort and a disorderly one in which nothing can be easily found can be traced to an adequate system of hooks, hangers, and shelves. The study of complex marketing systems and problems can be frustrating and confusing without a system of organization that organizes our observations, thoughts, and judgments. We now turn to building this organizational framework.

APPROACHES TO THE STUDY OF FOOD MARKETING

There are several ways to approach the study of food marketing, and each orientation provides a unique perspective on the nature and workings of the food marketing process. Some of the approaches are purely descriptive, whereas others attempt to evaluate the food marketing system and provide recommendations for improving it.

The Functional Approach

One method of classifying the activities that occur in the marketing processes is to break down the processes into *functions*. A marketing function may be defined as a major specialized activity performed in accomplishing the marketing process.

Any listing of functions must be recognized as an arbitrary one. Authors list from as few as eight to as many as three or four times that number. Each composer of a list, of course, believes his list best. Others disagree and propose lists of their own. We are looking for hooks and shelves on which to arrange our ideas. The exact terminology of the list is not of great importance so long as the scope of the individual functions is understood. We shall follow a fairly widely accepted classification of functions, as follows:

A. Exchange functions.
   1. Buying (assembling).
   2. Selling.
B. Physical functions.
   3. Storage.
   4. Transportation.
   5. Processing.
C. Facilitating functions.
   6. Standardization.
   7. Financing.
   8. Risk-bearing.
   9. Market intelligence.

The exchange functions are those activities involved in the transfer of title to goods. They represent the point at which the study of price determination enters into the study of marketing. These functions are never performed in our economy without a judgment of value, usually expressed at least partially as a price, being placed on the goods. Both the buying and selling functions have as their primary objective the negotiation of favorable terms of exchange.

The *buying* function is largely one of seeking out the sources of supply, assembling of products, and the activities associated with purchase. This function can be either the assembling of the raw products from the production areas or the assembling of finished products into the hands of other middlemen in order to meet the demands of the ultimate consumer.

The *selling* function must be broadly interpreted. It is more than merely passively accepting the price offered. In this function can be grouped all the various activities that sometimes are called merchandising. Most of the physical arrangements of display of goods are grouped here. Advertising and other promotional devices to influence or create demands are also part of the selling function. The decision as to the proper unit of sale, the proper packages, the best marketing channel, the proper time and place to approach potential buyers—all are decisions that can be included in the selling function.

The physical functions are those activities that involve handling, movement, and physical change of the actual commodity itself. They are involved in solving the problems of when, what, and where in marketing.

The *storage* function is primarily concerned with making goods available at the desired time. It may be the activities of elevators in holding large quantities of raw materials until they are needed for further processing. It may be the holding of supplies of finished goods as the inventories of processors, wholesalers, and retailers.

The *transportation* function is primarily concerned with making goods available at the proper place. Adequate performance of this function requires the weighing of alternatives of routes and types of transportation as they might affect transportation costs. It also includes the activities involved in preparation for shipment, such as crating and loading.

The *processing* function is often not included in a list of marketing functions because it is essentially a form-changing activity. However, in the broad view of agricultural marketing this activity cannot be omitted. The processing function would include all those essentially manufacturing activities that change the basic form of the product, such as converting live animals into meat, fresh peas into canned or frozen peas, or wheat into flour and finally into bread.

The *facilitating* functions are those that make possible the smooth performance of the exchange and physical functions. These activities are not directly involved in either the exchange of title or the physical handling of products. However, without them the modern marketing system would not be possible. They might aptly be called the grease that makes the wheels of the marketing machine go round.

The *standardization* function is the establishment and maintenance of uniform measurements. These may be measurements of both quality and quantity. This function simplifies buying and selling, because it makes the sale by sample and description possible. It, therefore, is one of the activities that makes possible mass selling, which is so important to a complex economy. Effective standardization is basic to an efficient pricing process. A consumer-directed system assumes that the consumer will make his wants known largely through price differentials. These differentials must then be passed back through the marketing channel so that marketing agencies and producers can know what is wanted. Only if a commodity is traded in well-defined units of quality and quantity can a price quotation do this job effectively. Standardization also simplifies the concentration process, because it permits the grouping of similar lots of commodities early in movement from the producing points. After their establishment, the use of standards must be policed. Such activities as quality control in processing plants and inspections to maintain the standards in the marketing channel can be considered part of this function. In addition, certain aspects of the packaging activity are a standardization procedure of units of sale as well as being part of the merchandising activity of the selling function.

The *financing* function is the advancing of money to carry on the various aspects of marketing. To the extent that there is a delay between the time of the first sale of raw products and the sale of finished goods to the ultimate consumer, capital is tied up in the operation. Anywhere that storage or delay takes place, someone must finance the holding of goods. The period may be for one year or more, as in the operations of the canning industries, or a relatively short time, as in the marketing of perishables. Financing may take the easily recognizable form of advances from various lending agencies or the more subtle form of tying up the owner's capital resources. In either instance, it is a necessary activity in modern marketing.

The *risk-bearing* function is the accepting of the possibility of loss in the marketing of a product. Most of these risks can be classified into two broad classifications—physical risks and market risks. The physical risks are those that occur from destruction or deterioration of the product itself by fire, accident, wind, earthquakes, cold, and heat. Market risks are those that occur because of the changes in value of a product as it is marketed. An unfavorable movement in prices might result in high inventory losses. A change in consumer taste might reduce the desirability of the product. A change in the operation of competitors might result in a loss of customers. All these risks in varying degrees must be borne in the marketing of a product. Risk-bearing may take a more conventional form, such as the use of insurance companies in the case of physical risks or the utilization of future exchanges in the case of price risks. Or, as is often true, the entrepreneur himself may bear the risk without the aid of any of these specialized agencies. The function of risk-bearing is often confused with the function of finance. Their differences can be kept clear, however, if it is remembered that the need for financing arises because of the time lag between the purchase and sale of products, whereas the need for risk-bearing arises because of the possibility of loss during the holding period.

The *market intelligence* function is the job of collecting, interpreting, and disseminating the large variety of data necessary to the smooth operation of the marketing processes. Efficient marketing cannot operate in an information vacuum. An effective pricing mechanism is dependent on well-informed buyers and sellers. Successful decisions on how much to pay for commodities or what kind of pricing policy to use in their sale require that a large amount of market knowledge be assembled for study. Adequate storage programs, an efficient transportation service, and an adequate standardization program all depend to a considerable extent on good information. Much of the market research that is carried on to evaluate the possible alternative marketing channels that may be used, the different ways of performing other functions, and the market potentialities for new products may be classified as part of the broad function of market intelligence. As with other functions, this function may be performed by those who specialize in its performance. On the other hand, everyone in the marketing structure who buys and sells products evaluates available market data and therefore performs this function to some degree.

USE OF THE FUNCTIONAL APPROACH

The functional approach considers the jobs that must be done; it is not concerned with the agency that performs them. Analyzing the functions of various middlemen is particularly helpful in evaluating marketing costs. Retailing is usually much more costly than wholesaling. The functional approach, however, points up the greater complexity of retailing by focusing attention on the increased extent to which the retailer must perform his various functions. The use of the functional concepts also aids in comparing the costs of two similar middlemen. Cost comparisons are meaningful only when they are related to the job done. Retailer A may operate at lower costs than retailer B, but does retailer A perform the same functions as B? Perhaps A is a cash-and-carry merchant whereas B extends credit and delivers. As such, A probably performs considerably less of the functions of financing, risk-bearing, and transportation than B.

The functional approach is also useful in understanding the difference in marketing costs of various commodities. For example, a perishable product is often more costly to market than one that is less perishable. Much of this difference may be because of the greater difficulty in the performance of the transportation, storage, and risk-bearing functions. The extent to which the processing function is involved also is a major determiner of difference in marketing costs.

But probably of greater importance, the breaking down of a complex marketing task into its component functions greatly aids in efforts to improve the performance of the marketing machinery. Again in reference to our retailer, perhaps retailer B is losing money even though other retailers having similar operations are not. A function-by-function study of B's business might show that the cost of its credit function is unduly high because of unpaid accounts. Or a careful analysis of his selling function may show he has not kept up with new methods in merchandising his products and thus is losing out to his competitors.

There are three important characteristics of these marketing functions. First, the functions affect not only the cost of marketing food but the value of food products to consumers. Processing, transportation, and storage provide form, space, and time utility for consumers. The exchange and facilitating market functions grease the wheels of the marketing machinery and perhaps provide services at costs lower than farmers and consumers can perform them. In evaluating marketing functions, consideration must be given to both the costs and benefits of the functions. The value-added by a marketing function may be greater or less than the cost of performing that function.

Second, although it is frequently possible to "eliminate the middleman," it is very difficult to eliminate marketing functions. Usually, eliminating the middleman involves the *transfer* of marketing functions—and costs—to someone else. For example, farmers may assume the storage, selling, and transportation functions, eliminating brokers and commission men. A neighborhood group of consumers can eliminate the food retailer by purchasing in large lots from wholesale food outlets, but in doing so they will assume some retailing functions—storage, standardization, and perhaps transportation. And the group often will settle for fewer services—such as check-cashing or price-marking. The cost of performing a marketing function, then, can be reduced, but the function cannot be eliminated from the marketing process.

The third characteristic of marketing functions is that they can be performed by anyone anywhere in the food system. Conceivably, all the functions could be performed by a single firm which had complete control of food, from farm to fork. On the other hand, there are specialized firms and industries, such as railroads, as well as grain brokers and speculators, who perform only one marketing function. Grain may be shipped direct from farm to storage in the city, or it may be stored on-farm and shipped to market later in the season. There are some traditional combinations, placements, and timing of food marketing functions. Food processors usually combine the storage, processing, and transportation functions; and many farmers view on-farm storage as an integral part of farming. But in general, a variety of firm combinations and timing of food marketing functions is observed. The functions may be indispensible, but they are quite fluid because they can be performed in various places within the food industry.

Two key issues concerning marketing functions are whether the necessary number of functions is being performed, and whether these functions are being performed in the most efficient manner. Because the functions add value as well as cost to food products, simply minimizing the functions is not an acceptable goal. The rule is that additional functions and services should be performed until the costs exceed the values of the functions—a difficult point to determine in practice. It is also important to determine when the shifting of a marketing function from one firm to another, or the combining of additional functions into one firm, is warranted. Some functions are most efficiently performed by specialized firms; others seem appropriately combined in multifunction firms.

Because of their traditional emphasis on the food production process, it is particularly important for farmers to consider whether they should perform more or fewer of the food marketing functions. There is no guarantee that profits will flow to those who assume additional marketing functions, even when the functions are known to be profitable. Some managers can perform the functions more efficiently than others. Food retailers would probably make poor farmers, just as farmers may lack the skills and interest to manage a modern supermarket or a complex railroad network. Then, too, the assumption of additional functions spreads each manager thinner, and some economies of specialization are lost. However, there is some trend in the food industry toward combining additional marketing functions within a single firm. There may be good reasons for this, especially when marketing functions are so complementary that profits can be made by performing them jointly. But this trend may also reflect a desire for additional market power on the part of farmers and food marketing firms.

The Institutional Approach

Another method of analysis is to study the various agencies and business structures that perform the marketing processes. Where the functional approach attempts to answer the "what" in the question of "who does what," the institutional approach to marketing problems focuses attention on the "who." Marketing institutions are the wide variety of business organizations that have developed to operate the marketing machinery. The institutional approach considers the nature and character of the various middlemen and related agencies and also the arrangement and organization of the marketing machinery. In this approach the human element receives primary emphasis.

MIDDLEMEN OF MARKETING

Middlemen are those individuals or business concerns who specialize in performing the various marketing functions involved in the purchase and sale of goods as they are moved from producers to consumers. Our concern here is with the place in the marketing processes which the middlemen occupy. There is no limitation as to the way in which they have organized for doing business. They may operate as individual proprietors, partnerships, or cooperative or noncooperative corporations. The middlemen of particular interest in food marketing can be classified as follows:

A. Merchant middlemen.
1. Retailers.
2. Wholesalers.
B. Agent middlemen.
1. Brokers.
2. Commission men.
C. Speculative middlemen.
D. Processors and manufacturers.
E. Facilitative organizations.

Merchant middlemen take title to, and therefore own, the products they handle. They buy and sell for their own gain. The *retailer* buys products for resale directly to the ultimate consumer of the goods. He is the producers' personal representative to the consumer. As such, his job is very complex. From the functional viewpoint, the retailer may perform all of the marketing functions. This group of middlemen is the most numerous of the marketing agencies.

The *wholesaler* sells to retailers, other wholesalers, and industrial users, but does not sell in significant amounts to ultimate consumers. Wholesalers make up a highly heterogeneous group of varying sizes and characteristics. One of the more numerous groups of wholesalers are the local buyers or country assemblers who buy goods in the producing area directly from farmers and ship the products to the larger cities where they are sold to other wholesalers and processors. In this group are such agencies as grain elevators, poultry and egg buyers, and local livestock buyers. Another group of wholesalers is located in the large urban centers. These may be "full-line" wholesalers who handle many different products or those who specialize in handling a limited number of products. They may be cash-and-carry wholesalers or service wholesalers who will extend credit and offer delivery and other services. Such terms as *jobbers* and *car-lot receivers* are often used synonymously with *wholesalers.*

Agent middlemen, as the name implies, act only as representatives of their clients. They do not take title to, and therefore do not own, the products they handle. Whereas merchant wholesalers and retailers secure their incomes from a margin between the buying and selling prices, agent middlemen receive their incomes in the form of fees and commissions. Agent middlemen in reality sell services to their principals, not physical goods to customers. In many instances, the principal stock-in-trade of the agent middlemen is market knowledge and know-how he uses in bringing the buyer and seller together. Their services are often retained by a buyer or seller of goods who feels that he does not have the knowledge or opportunity to bargain effectively for himself.

Though the names may differ somewhat, agent middlemen can be broken down into two major groups, commission men and brokers. The difference between these two types of agent middlemen is largely one of degree. The *commission man* is usually granted broad powers by those who consign goods to him. He normally takes over the physical handling of the product, arranges for the terms of sale, collects, deducts his fee, and remits the balance of his principal. The *broker,* on the other hand, usually does not have physical control of the product. He ordinarily follows the directions of his principal closely and has less discretionary power in price negotiations than commission men. In agriculture, livestock commission firms and grain brokers on the grain exchanges are good examples of these two classifications of agent middlemen.

Speculative middlemen are those who take title to products with the major purpose of profiting from price movements. All merchant middlemen, of course, speculate in the sense that they must face uncertain conditions. Usually, however, wholesalers and retailers attempt to secure their incomes through handling and merchandising their products and to hold the uncertain aspects to a minimum. Speculative middlemen seek out and specialize in taking these risks and usually do a minimum of handling and merchandising. Several names are given to these middlemen, such as "traders," "scalpers," and "spreaders." They often attempt to earn their profits from short-run fluctuations in prices. Purchases and sales are usually made at the same level in the marketing channel. For example, the livestock speculator may buy hogs today and sell them back either today or tomorrow in the same yards. The grain scalper may buy and sell grain futures several times within the trading day.

Speculative middlemen are often the result of the benefits of specialization. A merchant middleman may not wish to undertake added risks. A specialized risk-taker, called a speculator, may appear. He can usually perform this function more cheaply. In this case the speculator may perform a very important job in the market situation. However, in less desirable instances the existence of speculators may indicate that other merchant or agent middlemen are not effectively performing their tasks. In these situations speculators may represent unnecessary duplication of middlemen.

Processors and manufacturers primarily exist to undertake some action on products to change their form. Apart from their main processing activities, food processors take an active part in other institutional aspects of marketing. Some processors, such as meat packers, flour millers, and fruit and vegetable canners, often act as their own buying agents in the producing areas. And more and more, this group undertakes the wholesaling of their finished products to retailers. Many processors attempt to reach the ultimate consumer through advertising. So processing in itself is only a part of the activities of food manufacturers. Restaurants and other commercial food purveyors should be mentioned here. The restaurant most often is a retailing establishment in that it sells to final consumers. However, some of these businesses operate as wholesalers, preparing food in large quantities and selling to other retail outlets. And of course these businesses are, because of their preparation and cooking activities, processors.

Facilitative organizations aid the various middlemen in performing their tasks. Such organizations do not, as a general rule, directly participate in the marketing processes either as merchants, agents, processors, or speculators. One group of these organizations furnishes the physical facilities for the handling of products or for the bringing of buyers and sellers together. They establish the "rules of the game" which must be followed by the trading middlemen, such as hours of trading and terms of sale. They may also aid in grading, arranging and transmitting payment. They receive their incomes from fees and assessments from those who use their facilities. Examples of this group are the stockyard companies, grain exchanges and fruit auctions.

Another group of organizations falling in this general category are the trade associations. The primary purpose of a large majority of these organizations is to gather, evaluate, and disseminate information of value to a particular group or trade. They may carry on research of mutual interest. In many cases they also may act as unofficial policemen in preventing practices the trade considers unfair or unethical. Though not active in the buying and selling of goods, these organizations often have far-reaching influence on the nature of marketing.

USE OF THE INSTITUTIONAL APPROACH

The recognition of the various kinds of marketing organizations and the way in which they organize themselves furnishes another useful tool in analyzing marketing problems. Very often the "why" of certain marketing practices must be answered in terms of the characteristics of who performed them. Such analysis has the advantage of preventing the personal aspects of marketing from being ignored.

Attitudes toward change or improvement must often be examined in the light of the characteristics of the various marketing institutions. One of the greatest hazards to market improvement comes from institutions with large vested interests in the status quo. Marketing institutions give voice to the marketing machinery. From them develop "pressure" and "educational" groups attempting to mold public opinion. One of the cardinal rules to be followed in the analysis of any marketing controversy is first to ascertain which groups are vocal in the controversy and what they might stand to gain or lose.

The institutional approach can be helpful in understanding why there are specialized middlemen in the food industry. It is possible to imagine a food system without middlemen. Farmers can, and at times do, perform such middlemen activities as storage, transportation, selling, and even processing. By the same token, consumers can assume food middlemen functions. For example, a farm roadside market eliminates the food middleman by transferring his activities to farmers and consumers. Why, then, are there so many food middlemen if there are no practical reasons why farmers and consumers could not replace them? The rationale for the existence of food middlemen is that these specialized firms often can perform the food marketing functions more efficiently than either farmers or consumers.

The rise of middlemen specializing in such activities as storage, transportation, processing, retailing, and so forth is an example of division of labor and specialization. The middleman frees farmers for specializing in agricultural production, and frees consumers for nonfarm career specialization. Normally, there are gains from such specialization, and division of labor has become the hallmark of industrialized societies. Roadside farm markets, in contrast, may divert farmers' time from agricultural production and require the consumer to perform the transportation and processing functions. These gains from specialization mean that many of the food marketing functions are marked by economies of scale. That is, the average cost of performing the marketing functions falls as the volume of products handled rises. For example, the freight rate for a full carlot of grain is normally lower per bushel than for a less-than-carlot shipment. Typically, the average cost of processing and packing food declines with increasing plant volume. These marketing scale economies encourage the growth of specialized food middlemen. Middlemen also reduce market search and transactions costs. Markets are not costless. There are expenses associated with finding buyers and sellers and negotiating exchanges between them. By specializing in these functions, food middlemen relieve farmers and consumers of the considerable costs they would otherwise incur for search and transactions activity.

Without food middlemen, farmers and consumers would forfeit these economic gains from specialization and scale economies. This is illustrated in Figure 2-1. In Figure 2-1A, each farmer sells directly to each consumer; all of the marketing functions are performed on small lots of product by either farmers or consumers; and farmers and consumers bear the full costs of finding and consummating desirable exchanges. This represents the farm roadside market situation. In Figure 2-1B, specialized food middlemen perform the food marketing functions, allowing farmers and consumers to specialize in other activities and sparing them search and transaction expenses. Central markets facilitate middlemen specialization and scale economies by performing sorting and assorting activities.

Which is the better system? The general rule is that food middlemen will perform the food marketing functions when their costs for these functions are lower than those of farmers and consumers. The relevant comparison is the food middlemen's cost versus farmer or consumer costs for performing marketing functions, not middlemen's cost versus no costs. Judging by the

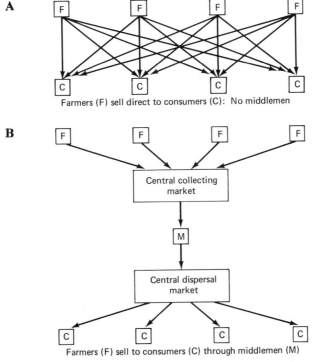

Figure 2-1. Alternative food marketing patterns.

number and variety of middlemen, this condition appears to be frequently met in the food industry. But this is not to say that all middlemen are efficient or necessary, nor that farmers and consumers should never perform their own marketing functions. There are undoubtedly situations where the farmer and consumer should play the middleman roles.

Figure 2-1 also illustrates that the need for food middlemen tends to make the food production-marketing-consumption system hourglass-shaped. There are many more farmers and consumers than middlemen, and middlemen will normally be larger in size than the farmers and consumers with whom they deal. This could provide food middlemen with an advantageous bargaining position in the food system, and this may work to the disadvantage of farmers and consumers.

Despite their demonstrated value, public distrust of middlemen continues. This is not unique to America; the "middleman bias" is even more pronounced in other countries. Throughout the world, middlemen are often scorned, sometimes outlawed, and usually merely tolerated. But because marketing is an activity practiced in some form in every country, those who take the time to understand it better usually come away with, if not a fondness for middlemen, at least a greater appreciation of their role in the economy.

The Behavioral Systems Approach

Both the functional and institutional approaches are useful in analyzing the existing marketing activities. However, the marketing process is continually changing in its organization and functional combinations. How to understand and predict change is a major problem.

Either a particular marketing firm or an organization of firms, such as the marketing channel, can be viewed as a system of behavior. Each is composed of people who are making decisions in an attempt to solve particular problems. If these problems and their behavioral systems for solving them can be classified, a greater understanding of changes that may be forthcoming can be obtained.

In either the firm or the organization of firms, four major types of problems, with their associated behavioral systems, can be identified. The first and perhaps most obvious is the *input–output system*. Each marketing firm or organization of firms is attempting to have an output of something. This is true whether it is a meat processor, a commission man, or a marketing channel consisting of many firms. Each is using as an input resources that are costly and scarce. Each hopes to find a satisfactory solution as to how to combine these input resources to secure a satisfactory output. Here we find the motives to develop and adopt new technology, new products, and different organization that may be cost-reducing or output-enhancing. It is in this system context that the discipline of economics and the various physical and engineering sciences make their major contributions to marketing understanding.

Another major concern is the *power system*. All firms and groups of firms have status and a vested interest in the present role they are playing. They may have developed a reputation for quality, being leaders, having a community conscience, being soundly conservative, or the fastest growing. No flippant decisions will be made that might deteriorate their particular niche of power, and means will actively be sought to enhance it. It is in this framework that we can understand the urge of many firms to grow and expand, to be innovators or followers, and so forth. Economic theory of monopoly and imperfect competition behavior, as well as the political scientists' concern with power behavior, give insights into this system of behavior.

Once a firm or organization develops beyond the simple unit of a unified manager-laborer, the problem of getting appropriate information to the manager and of transmitting his decisions into actions by other workers becomes of increasing importance. Each firm or organization of firms can therefore be viewed as a *communications system*. How to establish effective channels of information and direction is a major problem of large firms and complex organizations. Desirable actions may be frustrated by not receiving the right information or by the misinterpretation of the messages of action. It is in this area that the concern of psychology, sociology, and business management over the proper ways to organize and direct subordinate workers and units becomes of particular relevance.

Finally, if change is the essential characteristic of marketing, then one of the major problems of marketing firms and organizations is how to adapt to these changes. The behavioral *system for adapting to internal and external change* is then a major component of the firm or organization. As a rule, firms desire to survive and are prepared to pay some price to do so. How to operate in a manner that will assure that important changes are identified and adaptive solutions to these changes are effectively evolved is a major area of behavior.

Input-output, power, communications, and adaptive behavior are all components of the operation of the marketing system at any one time. Keeping this in mind may help explain actions which, when viewed only in the context of one of the systems, seem irrational or unintelligent. A firm may forego the ultimate in an input-output solution because its communications system has broken down or because of considerations of its power situation. For example, a firm may choose to acquire another related firm and integrate its activities in order to improve its internal communications problems or to enhance its power in the marketplace. Or in another instance it may acquire another firm because it thinks it foresees changes coming, and the purchase of the know-how and management of the acquired firm may present the most feasible method of adapting to the new conditions.

The analytical view of multiple behavior systems adds the important dimension of decision makers and their differing goals to the rather impersonal functional and institutional analyses. It points up sharply that market analysis is not the province of economics alone. Each of the social sciences, as well as the physical sciences, can contribute to the understanding of marketing problems.

ANALYZING MARKET PERFORMANCE IN THE FOOD INDUSTRY

It isn't possible to study the food marketing system for long without making some judgments about it. Is it competitive? Are prices fairly determined? How well does it serve farmers and consumers? Could it be improved? These are market performance questions. Market performance is defined as *how well the food marketing system performs what society and the market participants expect of it.* Questions of food marketing performance have become increasingly important in recent years.

Evaluating marketing performance raises the question, "What do we expect of the food marketing system?" Here we find that there are multiple and often conflicting goals for the marketing system. Compromises and tradeoffs are necessary to satisfy consumers,' farmers,' and society's goals for this system. What is more, the quality of market performance ranges on a scale from "good" to "bad," and there are more gray areas than easy judgments. There also appear to be rising standards for evaluating market performance in our society.

One way to begin the study of food marketing performance is to list some common concerns expressed about the industry. Consumers frequently complain about high and fluctuating food prices, expensive marketing practices, such as over-packaging and supermarket games, out-of-stock specials, slack filling of food containers, deceptive labels and advertising. Farmers voice other complaints: declining numbers of farm product buyers, reduced competition for supplies, large buyers with control over prices, the failure of retail and farm prices to move together, excessive marketing costs and prices, price speculation, and below-cost prices. Society in general might be more concerned with such issues as the food marketing sector's contributions to employment, investment, and economic growth; price stability; the standard of living and quality of life; resource use and conservation; and the overall health and prosperity of the rural economy.

The evaluation of market performance requires specific measures. Trends in retail food prices and consumer food costs are frequently used for this purpose, as are the level and stability of farm prices and income. The share of the consumers' income spent for food is also frequently taken as a measure of the food industry's contribution to the standard of living and quality of life. The farm-retail price spreads and the farmers' share of the consumers' food dollar are popular measures of market performance. Margins, profits, and trends in food marketing costs also indicate something of market performance. Parity farm prices and income could also be listed as food industry market performance measures.

Each of these have some value and limitations in the measurement of food marketing performance, but no single one tells the whole story. Care must be exercised in their use and interpretation. Market performance is a complex notion. It is dangerous to oversimplify it to a single market characteristic. The "bigness is bad" attitude is an example of this. Is bigness bad in and of itself, or is it the consequences of bigness that we object to? If the latter, is there a necessary identity between bigness and the undesirable consequences? There is room for debate here. Profit is another controversial market performance measure. We may take a different view of profits if we see them as rewards for superior performance rather than as the unearned booty of monopolistic firms.

The numerous conflicts between these performance criteria mean that compromises must be made in public policies that are designed to improve food marketing performance; a balance must be struck between the demands and dissatisfactions of each group concerned. It is unlikely that all dissatisfaction with the system will ever be eliminated, but this is not a reason to ignore critics or to cease searching for improved market performance. The balance of these criteria is frequently disturbed by a new technology, a new marketing procedure, a change in markets, or a change in political power. Thus, the analysis of food marketing performance is an ever-changing and dynamic area.

FOOD MARKETING EFFICIENCY

Efficiency in the food industry is the most frequently used measure of market performance. Improved efficiency is a common goal of farmers, food marketing firms, consumers, and society. Most of the changes proposed in food marketing are justified on the grounds of improved efficiency. It is a commonplace notion that higher efficiency means better performance whereas declining efficiency denotes poor performance.

Efficiency is measured as a ratio of output to input. Automotive efficiency, for example, is expressed as miles (output) per gallon of fuel (input). Student efficiency might be measured by grade level attained per hour of study. Efficiency ratios can be expressed in physical terms or in dollar terms. When dollars are used, the efficiency concept becomes a ratio of benefits to costs.

Food marketing can be viewed as an input-output system. Marketing input includes the resources (labor, packaging, machinery, energy, and so forth) necessary to perform the marketing functions. Marketing output includes time, form, place, and the possession utilities that provide satisfaction to consumers. Thus, resources are the costs and utilities are the benefits of the marketing efficiency ratio. Efficient marketing is the maximization of this input-output ratio.

The input cost of marketing is simply the sum of all the prices of resources used in the marketing process. However, it is less easy to measure the value of the marketing utilities to consumers. This makes it difficult to determine when the marketing efficiency ratio is rising and when it is falling. Probably the best measure of the satisfaction-output of the market process is the price that consumers will pay in the marketplace for foods with different levels of the marketing utilities. If consumers are willing to pay three cents more per orange for orange juice than for fresh oranges, we may infer that the processing of fresh oranges into juice adds three cents of form utility to fresh oranges.

The marketing efficiency ratio can be increased in two ways. Any marketing change that reduces the costs of performing the functions without altering the marketing utilities would clearly be an improvement in marketing efficiency. Or, enhancing the utility-output of the marketing process without increasing marketing costs would also increase efficiency.

Improved *operational efficiency* refers to the situation where the costs of marketing are reduced without necessarily affecting the output side of the efficiency ratio. An example would be a new labor-saving machine that reduces the cost of processing oranges into juice. Other examples of operational efficiency gains would be a new, less expensive method of handling and storing grain; a newly designed retail dairy case that reduces refrigeration energy costs; a lighter shipping carton for lettuce; or a new wrapping film that reduces the spoilage of prepackaged meat in the grocery store.

Operational efficiency is frequently measured by labor productivity or output per man-hour. Table 2-1 compares the trends in labor productivity of farming, food marketing, and the total private economy over the 1948–1972 period. As a result of rapid technological change, labor productivity in agricul-

Table 2-1. Labor Productivity in Agriculture and Food Marketing, 1948–1972.

	AVERAGE ANNUAL CHANGE IN OUTPUT PER MAN-HOUR	
	1948–1963	1957–1972
Total private economy	3.3%	3.0%
Farming	5.7	5.8
Food marketing:	2.7	2.1
Food processing	3.7	3.6
Food wholesaling, retailing	3.3	2.8

Source: U.S. Bureau of Labor Statistics.

ture has increased more rapidly than in other sectors of the economy. Operational efficiency in food wholesaling and retailing has lagged behind that of food processing and farming because of the greater difficulties in mechanizing and automating food wholesaling and retailing. The decline in recent years of operational efficiency in the food marketing sector has been called the "food marketing productivity crisis," and is one source of rising food marketing costs.

In practice, both the numerator and the denominator of the marketing efficiency ratio often change at the same time. Many changes in the costs of marketing influence consumers' satisfaction, and efforts to increase the marketing utilities normally affect marketing costs. Thus, a new marketing practice that reduces costs but that also reduces consumer satisfaction may increase *or* decrease the efficiency ratio. By the same token, higher marketing costs might *increase* marketing efficiency if they result in a more than proportionate rise in the marketing utilities. A true evaluation of any marketing change requires consideration of its effect on both the numerator and the denominator of the efficiency ratio; both costs and benefits must be compared.

The compromise that must be achieved between operational efficiency and consumer satisfaction explains the difficulty encountered in improving food marketing efficiency. For example, it is not difficult to lower food marketing costs by reducing the variety of food products and brands, eliminating prepackaging, or reducing the number of retail check-out lanes. The problem is that at some point these actions result in a greater loss of consumer satisfaction than is compensated for by the decline in marketing costs and consumer prices. A key task of the food marketing system, then, is to achieve the appropriate balance between marketing costs and consumer satisfaction.

Pricing efficiency is a second form of marketing efficiency. It is concerned with the ability of the market system to efficiently allocate resources and coordinate the entire food production and marketing process in accordance with consumer directives. Pricing efficiency is less than perfect when prices fail to (1) fully represent consumer preferences; (2) direct resources from lower to higher-valued uses; or (3) coordinate the buying and selling activities of farmers, marketing firms, and consumers. The goal of pricing efficiency is efficient resource allocation and maximum economic output.

Competition plays a key role in fostering marketing efficiency. Marketing firms compete for the consumer's favor by lowering marketing costs and increasing operational efficiency wherever possible. At the same time, there is competitive pressure on firms to add more utility to foods in order to gain an increased market share by catering to consumer preferences.

Frequently there are conflicts between these varieties of efficiency. For example, a new technological development may improve a firm's operational efficiency and permit it to grow very large. However, this growth may reduce the number of firms and competition in the industry, thereby lowering pricing efficiency. Or, a requirement of mandatory product grading to improve pricing efficiency might increase industry costs and thus lower operational efficiency. Similarly, the variety of products and brands developed to heighten consumer satisfaction may impose higher costs on the industry. Efficiency conflicts such as these contribute to the difficulties attending attempts to "improve" the food marketing system.

It is not the purpose of those concerned with improving the performance of marketing to dictate consumer choices. Rather, their task is to find ways in which the result desired by consumers can be accomplished at minimum cost. Suppose, for example, it is known that milk sold in grocery stores costs less than home delivery of milk, but that there are some consumers who want home delivery and will pay the extra cost. Should home delivery of milk be abolished under the pretense of "increased efficiency?" A preferable alternative is to recognize the convenience of home delivery as part of the value of milk and give consumers their choice of purchase alternatives. The dollar market vote will not be unanimous, but the consumers' freedom of choice will be preserved. The same line of reasoning can be applied to criticism of trading stamps, convenience foods, prepackaged produce, and other food industry problems.

Because of the profit opportunities involved, there is a constant market struggle in the food industry between more efficient and less efficient marketing strategies and techniques. The knowledge that more efficient marketing practices tend to replace less efficient practices is useful in predicting and understanding changes in the food system.

CONSUMERS AND FOOD MARKETING

The overall ruler and coordinator of marketing activity in our basically private enterprise economy is the consumer. The goal of the food system is to satisfy consumers. Food marketing firms serve as means to this ultimate goal. Failure to recognize the primacy of consumer preferences in the economic system has resulted in the downfall of many firms, and even entire industries.

The notion that all business and marketing activity is directed toward the satisfaction of consumers is called the *doctrine of consumer sovereignty.* The statement, "The consumer is king," illustrates this doctrine. Consumers exercise their sovereignty over the food industry by their dollar voting, rewarding firms and activities that please them and withholding approval from others.

Are food consumers really sovereign? The doctrine of consumer sovereignty is, simultaneously, a partial description and an economic prescription for the food industry. Consumer preferences and dollar votes are a powerful influence on food producers and marketing firms. Some areas of the food system are more sensitive and more responsive than others to changing consumer desires. But no firm or industry can completely ignore these desires for long without peril.

Food processors might prefer square tomatoes because they are easier to harvest, pack, and handle, but if consumers prefer round tomatoes, we will have round tomatoes. Nutritionists may prefer unrefined flour and sugar because of their nutritional value, but these will fail in the marketplace if consumers want "white" flour and sugar. Consumers may prefer white eggs to brown eggs despite the industry's insistence that they are nutritionally equivalent. Nevertheless, white eggs will be sold and brown eggs will be discounted—except of course in Boston, where brown eggs are preferred to white! Consumers may be irrational, ignorant, fickle, and capricious in their views and decisions, but, like kings, they are obeyed by successful firms.

This is not to say that all firms follow passively every consumer's whim. Through advertising, packaging, product design, merchandising, and other marketing strategies many firms attempt to educate, influence, and persuade consumers in their buying decisions. Costly advertising and sales promotion programs seek to persuade consumers to prefer one store, one product, or one brand over another. To the extent that these efforts are successful in altering preferences and changing consumer decisions, the consumer loses a degree of sovereignty. As a result, inefficient firms with low quality products and high prices might gain some freedom from the disciplinary nature of the consumer's dollar vote through persuasive advertising or merchandising programs. Many food industry laws and regulations attempt to restore the sovereignty of food consumers in the face of these increasingly sophisticated marketing techniques.

As the organizing principle of the food industry, the defense of consumer sovereignty does not rest entirely on the rationality and excellence of consumer judgments. Indeed, producing and marketing "what consumers want" may lead to a decline in the nutritional level of our diet, to consumption patterns that are associated with obesity, heart disease, and other diet-related problems. There is no guarantee that food consumers will behave in their own or in the public interest. The rationale for placing the consumer at the center of food industry decisions is that there is no other acceptable judge of these decisions. The phrase, *de gustibus non est disputandum* (what is pleasing is not disputable) applies here. Consumers are the *only* ones with insight into their own preferences and values. It is simply unacceptable for others—nutritionists, food scientists, farmers, or anyone else—to decide what is pleasing to consumers. Of course, we can hope that consumer food choices are rational and in the public interest. And we might even attempt to educate the consumer to make "wise" buying decisions. But, when all is said and done, the final success of food production and marketing decisions hinges on consumer choices, no matter how rational, ill-founded, or unfortunate.

The doctrine of consumer sovereignty is dependent on three basic conditions. First, the consumer must be provided with real alternatives from which

41

to choose. If all product choices are alike, or only trivially different, the consumer's freedom to choose is an illusion. Secondly, the consumer must have reliable and accurate information in order to accurately match available product choices with preferences. Deceptive or misleading advertising, packaging, or labeling subvert consumers' sovereignty. Lastly, prices of all foods must fully reflect all private and social costs of producing and marketing products. If consumers prefer foods that have an expensive environmental impact cost, or that impose high medical or productivity costs on the economy, their choices will not necessarily coordinate food production and marketing decisions in a satisfactory way. Generally, when these conditions limit the doctrine of consumer sovereignty, society intervenes through the instrument of government. However, there is substantial disagreement on the severity of these problems in the food industry and on the desirability of solving them through government intervention.

Consumer sovereignty is recognized in the marketplace through the implementation of a business philosophy called *the marketing concept.* This philosophy holds that the most important function of an industry or firm is to satisfy consumers at a profit, and that this goal directs all other company activities, including production, finance, packaging, distribution, and so on. The essence of the marketing concept is to identify consumer wants and to produce products that satisfy these wants at a profit.

The marketing concept is the third successive business philosophy of the Industrial Revolution. The first and earliest was the production-engineer orientation—"What can we make?" This was followed by the sales orientation—"How can we persuade consumers to buy more of our product?" In contrast, the marketing orientation is illustrated by the statement, "What do consumers want, and how can we satisfy these wants profitably?" In the food industry, this orientation involves a shift in emphasis from that of marketing what the farmer produces to that of finding out what the consumer wants, and then producing to fill that need.

This shift in business philosophy has been slow and subtle. One major result of the shift has been to give marketing—those activities of companies that are in closest contact with consumers—greater prominence within the firm. The business graveyard is filled with those who tried to sell a product that "couldn't miss," who failed to sense a change in consumer preferences, who produced a product so expensive or so cheap that it lacked a profitable market, or who first produced a product and then went looking for a market. Not all farmers and food marketing firms subscribe to the marketing concept. Some pork producers persisted in marketing fat-type hogs even though consumer preferences had shifted to lean-type pork, and the market for lard and animal fats declined. For years, the dairy industry refused to produce margarine, despite consumers increasing substitution of margarine for butter. And many food industry groups have spent millions of dollars advertising foods with declining consumer demand trends.

FOOD MARKETING TRENDS AND ISSUES

Change and adjustment are the hallmarks of the dynamic food industry. Some trends represent adjustments of food industry firms to changing market conditions and new technologies. Other trends can be traced to the attempts of firms to gain competitive and economic advantage in the marketplace. Still other trends result from public policies designed to foster better market performance in the food industry.

Whatever their source, these market trends affect farmers, food consumers, and the public interest. Typically, change creates both costs and benefits. There is increasing concern with the costs and benefits of the changing food marketing machinery. The major trends and issues are discussed in greater detail throughout this book. For this brief review, they can be grouped into four areas: (1) organization and competitive issues; (2) coordination and control issues; (3) farmer marketing problems; and (4) consumer and public interest issues.

Organization and Competitive Issues

Currently, there are declining numbers and increasing firm sizes in most segments of food marketing. This "giantism" and centralization of the food flow concerns farmers and consumers who are, by comparison, relatively small and unorganized. Americans have a distrust of bigness and concentrated economic power, even though they recognize that some efficiencies may result from large organizations.

Integration and diversification are two related trends in market organization. Multi-national and conglomerate food corporations add a new dimension to competition in food markets. There is also a trend toward mergers of similar food companies, and a combining of food marketing levels and functions within a single company. By and large, this has been a development of the post-World War II period, and the implications are not fully understood. Clearly, when food marketing firms assume control of some agricultural decisions, this threatens the farmers' freedom and independence.

The flow patterns of food within the marketing channels are also changing. Decentralized marketing has replaced the traditional central food markets which in the past played a key role in pricing, standardizing, and product exchange. As a result, farmers are selling more of their products directly to larger buyers who, in turn, are attempting to gain greater control of the flow, quantity, and quality of farm products. The meaning of this departure from traditional marketing patterns is not fully understood, but decentralization has vastly changed the way farmers market their products today.

How have these trends affected the nature of competition in food markets? Is competition among the few better or worse than competition among the many? Are decentralized contract markets as competitive as their predecessors? Is there sufficient competitive discipline in the new food marketing system to assure efficient and equitable results for all market parties? These are important questions to ask about the organizational trends in food marketing.

Coordination and Control Issues

There is concern that these organizational trends may have shifted the locus of control and balance of power in the food industry. This raises the issues of freedom, access to markets, and economic power. The questions "who will control agriculture?" and "who runs the food industry?" are continuing public policy concerns. The closure and domination of food markets by marketing firms is especially threatening to farmers.

Allegedly, there has been a decline in the coordinating role of prices in the food industry. This involves a separation of pricing from product exchange, a shift of the pricing process from the light of public markets to the secrecy of private negotiations, and a separation of prices from costs in large, multi-product firms. The capability of prices to perform their traditional market roles under these conditions is in question; and the economic impact of alternative coordinating devices is much debated.

The concern here is with the efficiency and equity of food markets. Without the traditional market price signals, can we be sure that efficient practices are winning over less efficient ones? Can we be confident that the consumer's food dollar is being fairly apportioned among farmers and food marketing firms?

Farmer Marketing Problems

There is a wide and growing gulf between farmers and the food marketing system. The relative numbers and sizes of these two sectors make them unlikely bedfellows, despite their mutual interdependence. There is reason to wonder whether the independent farmer can survive and prosper in this new food industry, regardless of the efficiency of agricultural production.

There is a growing concern regarding the farmer's place in the changing food industry. One school of thought believes that farmers must become as large, powerful, and market-oriented as the major food corporations. Others argue that food marketing firms should be broken up, or be made to behave like small-unit firms, in order to establish a parity of bargaining power between farmers and marketing firms. A third alternative is to foster farmer group action through cooperatives, bargaining associations, and other devices, in an attempt to preserve the present structure of agriculture and provide farmers with countervailing market power.

Food industry trends create other farmer marketing problems. Farmers need more and better market information in order to make production and marketing decisions. They also need periodic educational programs to learn about new market alternatives and choices. Farmers are also increasingly called upon to provide input into the public policy process which influences prices, markets, and regulations.

Consumer Issues

Consumers are the new factor in the food industry equation. The consumer movement has affected the food industry in many ways. Information programs, such as unit pricing, truth-in-packaging, nutritional labeling, open-code dating, and the like, illustrate the activist role consumers are assuming in the marketplace. Similar examples can be cited in the areas of food safety, nutrition, grades and standards, and wholesomeness. Consumers are also becoming involved in farm policies, such as import-export policy, price and income supports, and rural development. "Let the buyer beware" is clearly not an appropriate philosophy for the food industry today. But what is the appropriate role for consumers in the food industry decision-making processes?

Consumer sovereignty and efficiency-utility conflicts are at the heart of consumers' concerns with the modern food industry. The food marketing sector is increasingly merchandise-oriented, as can be seen in its emphasis on new products, packaging, advertising, and promotion. Its allies are food scientists and engineers, packaging experts, and advertising agencies. Consumers are searching for the appropriate environment for providing the necessary freedoms and incentives to develop new products and market programs, and for the regulatory climate necessary to insure that these efforts are in the public interest. It appears that the consumer increasingly will be involved in the food industry, not only as a final buyer but as a regulator and shaper of market decisions. In the future, food public policy issues will be hammered out on a broader anvil of public opinion than in the past.

SUMMARY

There are several approaches to the study of food marketing. Each provides a unique perspective of the food marketing system and process. The functional approach emphasizes the "what" of marketing; the institutional approach the "who"; and the behavioral systems approach analyzes the input-output processes, power relationships, communications, and techniques for adapting to changes in the marketing system. Three important characteristics of marketing functions are that they add value as well as costs to farm products; they are difficult to eliminate; and the arrangement of functions within the marketing system is somewhat flexible. A multidimensional approach to evaluating food industry performance is called for. Frequent compromises are necessary between the market performance criteria. Market efficiency is measured as a ratio of marketing utilities to marketing costs. Market performance can be measured by changes in operational and pricing efficiency. The doctrine of consumer sovereignty recognizes the primary role of consumer preferences in coordinating farm and food marketing decisions. Several organizational and competitive trends raise concerns about the performance of food markets.

QUESTIONS FOR DISCUSSION

1. Can you think of any other food marketing activities not included in the list of marketing functions provided in this chapter?

2. Comment on the meaning of the statement, "You cannot eliminate the middleman." Under what circumstances can middlemen be eliminated? Give an example.

3. How do farmers and consumers decide which of the marketing functions to perform for themselves?

4. Why are there so many different kinds of food marketing institutions?

5. Give familiar examples of changes in operational efficiency in the food industry.

6. What is your answer to the question, "Who should control agriculture?"

7. What are some reasons for the middleman bias in our society?

8. How sovereign are food consumers? Is their sovereignty increasing or decreasing?

SELECTED REFERENCES

ALDERSON, W. *Marketing Behavior and Executive Action.* Richard D. Irwin, Inc., Homewood, Ill., 1957.

BLOOM, G. F. *Productivity in the Food Industry.* MIT Press, Cambridge, Mass., 1972.

BRANDOW, G. E. *Appraising the Economic Performance of the Food Industry.* U.S. Department of Agriculture. Economic Research Service, Bicentennial Lecture Series, Sept. 1976.

COCHRANE, W. W. "The Market As a Unit of Inquiry in Agricultural Economics Research." *Journal of Farm Economics* (Feb. 1957), 21–40.

FARRELL, K. R. *Market Performance in the Food Sector.* U.S. Department of Agriculture. Economic Research Service, No. 653, Feb. 1977.

Food and Fiber for the Future. Report of the National Advisory Commission on Food and Fiber. U.S. Government Printing Office, Washington, D.C., July 1967.

Food from Farmer to Consumer. Report of the National Commission on Food Marketing. U.S. Government Printing Office, Washington, D.C., 1966, Chaps. 1, 2, 12.

FRENCH, B. C. "The Analysis of Productive Efficiency in Agricultural Marketing," in L. R. Martin, Ed. *A Survey of Agricultural Economics Literature,* Vol. 1. University of Minnesota Press, Minneapolis, 1977.

HANDY, C. R. and M. PFAFF, *Consumer Satisfaction with Food Products and Marketing Services.* U.S. Department of Agriculture. Agricultural Economics Report, No. 281, March 1975.

LERZA, C. and M. JACOBSON, Eds. *Food for People, Not for Profit.* Ballantine Books, New York, 1975.

MARION, B. W. and C. R. HANDY. *Market Performance: Concepts and Measures.* U.S. Department of Agriculture. Agricultural Economic Report No. 244, Sept. 1973.

Market Structure of the Food Industries. U.S. Department of Agriculture. Marketing Research Report No. 971, Sept. 1972.

MOORE, J. R. and R. G. WALSH. *Market Structure of the Agricultural Industries.* Iowa State University Press, Ames, Iowa, 1966.

SHEPHERD, G. S. and G. A. FUTRELL. *Marketing Farm Products,* 5th Ed. Iowa State University Press, Ames, Iowa, 1969, Chaps. 2, 31.

SOSNICK, S. H. "Operational Criteria for Evaluating Market Performance," in Farris, P. L., Ed., *Market Structure Research.* Iowa State University Press, Ames, Iowa, 1961, pp. 81–125.

CHAPTER 3

Agricultural Production and Marketing

"THE TRADITIONAL STRUCTURE of U.S. farm production and of farm markets can each be described in terms of a single identifying characteristic. In production that key feature is the holding of land in parcels small enough that the farmer combines two or more factors of production in his person. In farm markets, it is reliance on the process of exchange."*

Preview

- This chapter examines the nature of farming as it influences food marketing and also highlights several interrelationships of farming and food marketing.
- You will see that food products, the nature of farming, and the characteristics of agricultural output foster unique food marketing problems.
- It will be shown that the food marketing system has adjusted to changes in agriculture over time, just as farmers have adjusted to changes in food marketing.
- The basic elements of the "farm marketing problem" will be reviewed.
- The major farm marketing questions will be examined.
- You will be introduced to the farm marketing plan—the blueprint for farmer marketing decisions.
- Key terms and concepts:

  agricultural structure   cost-price squeeze
  corporate farming   enterprise specialization
  cost of production   family farm

---

* Harold F. Breimyer, *Individual Freedom and the Economic Organization of Agriculture,* University of Illinois Press, Urbana, Illinois, 1965.

farm inputs
farm marketing problem
farm productivity, efficiency
farm specialization
free-rider problem
marketing plan
price-taker

process specialization
product homogeneity
quality control
seasonality
strategies, tactics
supply control

Many of the operations of marketing firms and the marketing system's organizational arrangements can be explained only by considering the nature of the initial raw product and its production. It is at the farm that the concentration processes of marketing must start. It is this raw product which must be assembled by buyers, moved, and stored. Farmers need to better understand food marketing and the food consumer, whereas food consumers and those working in food marketing need to understand agriculture and the farmer's problems in the food industry.

THE AGRICULTURAL PLANT

Many people think of farms and land area as synonymous. The United States is a big country; hence it is commonly believed that there is a relatively unlimited amount of farmland upon which to produce food. This of course is not true. Nearly two fifths of the country's land area receives less than 20 inches of rainfall annually and therefore has very limited agricultural potential. Figure 3-1 shows the use of the country's land in 1974. Overall, about 45 per cent of the nation's land is farmed, but only 20 per cent of our land is in crops.

The marketing machinery links farmers to both the farm supply markets and the food product markets. As shown in Figure 3-2, U.S. agriculture's output per unit of input has increased steadily over the years as a result of new farming technologies and the substitution of machinery for labor on the farm. Crop yields increased 57 per cent from the 1946–1950 period to the 1971–1975 period.[1] This occurred during a period when man-hours worked in agriculture fell by 65 per cent, the use of agricultural chemicals rose by 140 per cent, and the farm use of machinery and mechanical power rose by 20 per cent. This has contributed to increased farm output. The

---

[1] *Changes in Farm Production and Efficiency, a Special Issue Featuring Historical Series,* U.S. Department of Agriculture, Statistical Bulletin No. 561, September 1976.

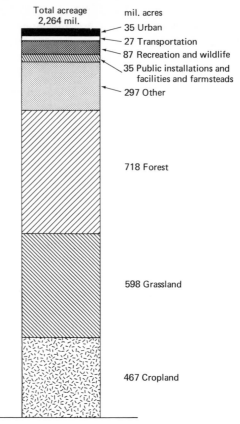

Figure 3-1. Major uses of land in the United States, 1974. (U.S. Department of Agriculture)

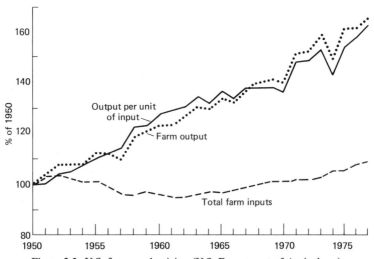

Figure 3-2. U.S. farm productivity. (U.S. Department of Agriculture)

food marketing system, of course, has grown apace with the supply of farm products.

Great improvements have been made in seed variety, livestock nutrition, fertilization, and a multitude of other areas, making agriculture more productive. Truly, technology has shown how to grow two plants where one grew before. But technology has also put greater pressures on the marketing machinery to move this added production into consumption. Not only has the volume of output from farms increased, but also an increasing portion of this output has moved into commercial marketing channels. With fewer people living on farms, less of the farm output is consumed at the place where it is grown and more must move to supply the increasing city population.

The United States' agricultural plant is changing in other ways that affect the food marketing system. Trends in the size, ownership, location, and specialization of farms are affecting how food is produced and marketed. There is also a trend toward closer ties between farmers and agricultural supply firms and marketing firms. At the same time, changes in the food marketing system are influencing farmers and the nature of farming. Table 3-1 illustrates some general trends in U.S. agriculture over the 1950–1975 period. Fewer farmers, representing a declining share of the population, are managing larger farms which, because of increased output and higher farm prices, are providing higher farm incomes, thus closing the historical gap between farm and nonfarm incomes.

THE STRUCTURE OF U.S. AGRICULTURE

The structure of U.S. agriculture refers to the number, size, ownership, and specialization of farms. Here we must use averages to generalize about farming, but we should avoid stereotypes and recognize the diversity of U.S. agriculture. There are very large and very small farms; there are family farms and there are giant corporate farms owned by nonagricultural firms; there are wealthy farmers and poor ones; there are full-time and part-time farmers; there are farmers who receive all of their income from farming and there are farmers who receive a good share of their income from nonfarm employment. This diversity of farming greatly complicates the food marketing process.

It is well known that the number of farms is declining and that the average farm size is increasing, as shown in Figure 3-3. These trends, however, do not show the great variation in farm sizes nor the dominance of larger farms. There is a tendency for a growing share of our agricultural output to come from a declining number of very large farms. According to Table 3-2, 4 per cent of the largest farms received 47 per cent of total cash farm receipts in 1975. In contrast, the very smallest farms, with cash receipts of less than

Table 3-1. United States Farming Trends, 1950–1975.

			AVERAGE FARM SIZE			FARM EFFICIENCY			REALIZED FARM INCOME (INCLUDING GOV'T. PAYMENTS)		
	MILLION FARMS	PER CENT OF POPULATION ON FARMS	ACRES	ASSETS ($000)	PRODUCE CONSUMED ON FARM ($MILLION)	PERSONS SUPPLIED PER FARM WORKER	OUTPUT PER INPUT (1967 = 100)	FARM PRICES (1967 = 100)	GROSS INCOME ($BILLION)	NET INCOME PER FARM	FARM INCOME AS A PER CENT OF NONFARM INCOME
1950	5.6	15%	213	$ 17.2	$2,063	16	73	102	$32.2	$2,400	53%
1960	4.0	9	297	42.6	1,250	26	93	94	38.5	2,900	55
1970	3.0	5	373	89.5	773	49	100	110	58.6	4,800	75
1975	2.8	4	387	162.3	1,186	—	113	186	98.2	9,100	90

Source: U.S. Department of Agriculture.

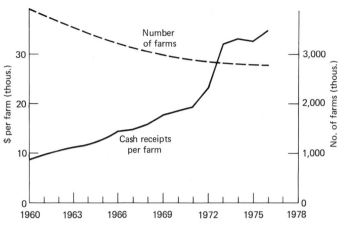

Figure 3-3. Trends in number and size of farms in the United States. (U.S. Department of Agriculture)

$2,500, accounted for 26 per cent of farms but less than 1 per cent of cash receipts. Thus, there are really two separate farm sectors: very large commercial farms, which are few in number but account for most of the total farm sales; and a large number of very small farms, which do not represent a large portion of total farm supplies or sales. Moreover, the large farm sector is expanding whereas the small farm sector is diminishing in importance. The importance of very large farms varies by commodities. As shown in

Table 3-2. Number of Farms and Farm Cash Receipts, By Sales Classes of Farms, 1960–1975.

ANNUAL SALES PER FARM	NUMBER OF FARMS		FARM CASH RECEIPTS (INCLUDING GOVERNMENT PAYMENTS)	
	1960	1975	1960	1975
$100,000 or more	1%	4%	17%	47%
40,000–100,000	2	12	15	24
20,000– 40,000	6	20	19	19
10,000– 20,000	12	12	21	5
5,000– 10,000	17	9	15	2
2,500– 5,000	16	17	7	2
less than 2,500	46	26	6	1
	100%	100%	100%	100%

Source: U.S. Department of Agriculture.

Table 3-3. Importance of Very Large Farms ($100,000 Annual Sales or More) in Agriculture, by Commodities, 1969.

| | PER CENT OF TOTAL | |
COMMODITY	ALL COMMERCIAL FARMS	ALL COMMERCIAL FARM SALES
Crops	—	29%
Vegetables	7%	68
Fruits	6	48
Cotton	4	33
Fieldseeds, forage, silage	2	21
Tobacco	1	9
Livestock		
Poultry and poultry products	5	54
Cattle, calves	3	51
Dairy cattle, calves	2	16
Hogs, sheep, goats	3	15
All agricultural products	3	34

Source: *Farming and Agribusiness Activities of Large Multiunit Firms,* U.S. Department of Agriculture, ERS-591, March 1975, p. 9.

Table 3-3, large farms with sales of $100,000 or more are more dominant for poultry, beef, and vegetables than for other commodities.

The family farm—defined as a farm in which the principle productive efforts and their rewards are vested in the family—dominates U.S. agriculture. In 1969, 95 per cent of farms operated with 1.5 man-equivalents of labor or less and were classified as family farms. These farms accounted for 62 per cent of farm product sales.[2] The importance of family farms in number and sales was stable over the 1949–1969 census years. Figure 3-4 shows the importance of family farms throughout the country.

Corporate farming worries many farmers and consumers. There are both family farm corporations as well as nonfarm corporations engaged in agricultural production. In 1968 there were an estimated 13,300 farm corporations representing 1 per cent of all commercial farms, 7 per cent of U.S. farmland, and 8 per cent of total farm product sales.[3] Two thirds of these were family corporations, and one third of the corporate farms were located in California and Florida.

Are farmers becoming more, or less, specialized? Specialization involves restricting the scope of economic activity. Farmers may specialize by enter-

---

[2] Nikolitch, R., *Family-Size Farms In U.S. Agriculture,* U.S. Department of Agriculture, Economic Research Service, ERS-499, February 1972.

[3] G. Coffman, *Corporations with Farming Operations,* U.S. Department of Agriculture, Agricultural Economic Report No. 209, June 1971.

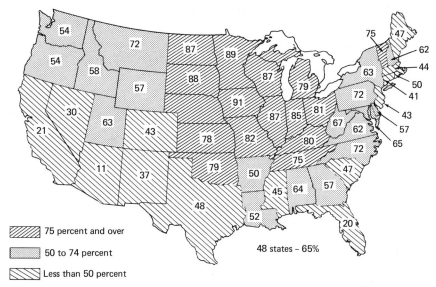

Figure 3-4. Sales of farm products by family farms as a percentage of total sales of farm products, 1964. (U.S. Department of Agriculture)

prise, by personnel, or by the number of processes performed. A farmer who discontinues livestock production to concentrate on crop production is specializing by enterprise. A farmer who elects to feed hogs but discontinues his sow farrowing operation is specializing in a process. A two-man farm, where one person is the crop manager and the other is the livestock manager, is considered to be specialized by personnel.

Farm enterprise specialization differs by commodities. Fruit, vegetable, and dairy farms tend to be highly specialized. However, many farms produce more than one commodity. The grain-livestock operation illustrates diversification by enterprises, even though grain and livestock are complementary products. Farmers also differ in process specialization. Many confine their activities to farming, but others increasingly are becoming involved in off-farm marketing activities.

These facts about the agricultural production plant add up to some very important marketing considerations. First, much of our production is made available to the marketing machinery in relatively small lots from a large number of relatively unspecialized individual units. A meat packer processing hogs must often assemble his supplies from a great many individual sellers scattered over a relatively large area. In addition, the hog marketing machinery cannot get all its hogs from farm group A, and the poultry marketing machinery cannot get all its poultry from farm group B. Some poultry must be assembled from A and some hogs from B. The marketing machinery must be set up to serve both groups for both products.

55

A second observation is that the farmer is by nature, and probably by necessity, a man primarily interested in production and only secondarily interested in marketing. Because he is the manager-laborer of his own highly diverse production unit, the complexities of modern agricultural production absorb a great deal of his time and energies. As a marketer, he either sells very small amounts at a time or very few times a year.

A third observation, and a very important one, is that changes are taking place. Larger, more specialized units are developing, and in some areas and products, they are developing very rapidly. With this change, the interest of the farmer in his selling arrangements is increasing. In addition, changes in the assembly and buying methods of marketing firms are possible. For example, a processor may find it feasible to buy more of his supplies directly from large, specialized producers instead of utilizing the services of country buyers who have specialized in assembly of products from many small producers.

A final observation is that the food marketing system must serve two very different agricultural groups: a few, large farm owners who sell the majority of farm products, and a large number of small farm owners who have much less to sell. Many feel that the marketing machinery serves the owners of large farms better than the owners of small farms.

CHARACTERISTICS OF THE PRODUCT

A Raw Material

The output of agriculture is largely a raw material that will be used for further processing. This processing may be limited, as in converting livestock into meat. It may be highly complex, as in converting wheat into Wheaties. Regardless of the complexity, however, the product sold by the farmer soon loses its identity as a farm product and becomes simply food.

Bulky and Perishable Products

Compared to most other products, agricultural products are both bulkier and more perishable. Bulk affects the marketing functions concerned with physical handling. Products that occupy a lot of space in relation to their value almost automatically raise unit transportation and storage costs. A truckload of drugs would be considerably more valuable than a truckload of wheat. In this sense, fruits, vegetables, grain, and meats are all quite bulky.

Perishability, too, can be measured only in relation to other products. All products ultimately deteriorate. Some agricultural products, like fresh strawberries or fresh peaches, must move into consumption very quickly or they completely lose their value. Such products as hogs or cattle continue to grow and change if "storage" in the form of withholding them from market is attempted. Wheat, on the other hand, can be stored for a considerable length of time without much deterioration. Even the most storable agricultural products, however, are usually more perishable than other industrial products.

These characteristics have their effect on the facilities necessary to market farm products. Bulkiness, plus varying production, requires large storage capacities. Perishable products require speedy handling and often special refrigeration. Quality control often becomes a real and costly problem. From the farmer's viewpoint, withholding from the market is extremely difficult; when products are ready, they must move.

Quality Variation

The general quality as well as the total production of agricultural commodities varies from year to year and from season to season. During some years the growing conditions are such that the crop in general is of high quality. In other years, unfavorable conditions prevail and the crop is of much lower quality.

Such variations in the quality of production make it very hard to apply uniform standards for grades from year to year. If the quality of the apple crop is uniformly high, the standards for top-grade apples may be strictly adhered to. On the other hand, if the quality of the apple crop is poor, grading standards may be relaxed somewhat to permit some apples to be marketed as top quality.

Variations in the quality may also change marketing patterns. For example, during a year in which corn does not mature properly, large amounts of "soft" corn are harvested. The corn will spoil if it is not used before the following spring. Farmers may then buy additional feeder stock in order to utilize this corn. The marketing pattern of these feeders, however, will be different from the usual pattern because the feeding period is adjusted to the condition of the corn.

Significant changes are occurring here also. Increasingly, the quality of a product may be controlled by following certain production practices. Some control over quality is possible through the control of the breeds and kinds of parent stock used. Spraying and other production practices can be used to affect quality. As such developments are perfected, the marketing machinery will have to contend with less variation in the quality of agricultural products. The possibility of quality control through different production practices is another dynamic factor that is encouraging closer relationships between marketing and production units.

Despite this quality variation, farm products in general are said to be homogeneous. This means that, overall, buyers have little reason to prefer one farmer's product over another. Consequently, each farmer receives about the same price for the same quality of product.

CHARACTERISTICS OF PRODUCTION

Total Output

The long-run trend in food production is upward. As shown in Figure 3-5, U.S. farm output rose faster than population growth over the 1950–1975 period. This rising food supply per capita has been a mixed blessing for U.S. farmers. On the one hand, it is dramatic proof of the efficiency of American agriculture and its contribution to the rising standard of living. On the other hand, this tremendous productive capacity of U.S. agriculture has frequently depressed farm prices and incomes. Maintaining an acceptable balance of rising food supplies and fair farm prices has been a difficult task for United States' food policy.

Annual Variability in Production

As is evident in Figure 3-5, there are years of increasing, decreasing, and stable farm output. These are caused by farmer responses to prices and other uncontrollable factors such as weather and disease. Such changes in farm output influence the food marketing process and the use of the food marketing system's capacity. Annual variations in farm output were more pronounced in the 1970's than in the 1950's and 1960's.

The annual output variability of individual farm commodities is even greater than that of total farm output. This variability is of critical importance to

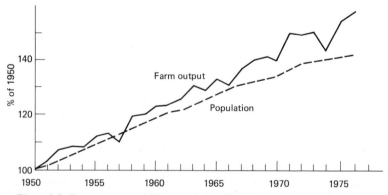

Figure 3-5. Farm output and U.S. population. (U.S. Department of Agriculture)

food marketing firms which, by and large, specialize in the handling of only a few agricultural commodities. A sharp reduction in the wheat crop will concern millers and bakers but is of little interest to meat packers. Year to year changes in farm supplies have a significant impact on the purchase prices, need for storage facilities, and plant utilization rates of food marketing firms. The desire to reduce the risks and uncertainties of fluctuating farm supplies is one of the forces creating closer contractual ties between marketing agencies and farmers.

Seasonal Variability in Production

In addition to the annual production variability, much of agricultural production is highly seasonal. Livestock receipts may vary substantially throughout the year. Egg and milk production is larger in the spring and early summer than in fall and early winter. The bulk of the nation's turkey crop moves to market during the last half of the year. And of course the harvest of such crops as wheat, cotton, soybeans, fruits, and vegetables is crowded into a relatively short period.

To the extent that the product is storable, storage facilities must be furnished to hold the product until it is consumed. This means that during part of the year, storage will be used at near capacity; at other times it will be almost empty. If the product cannot be stored it must either be processed or consumed immediately. This may result in processing plants running at capacity for some periods and well below capacity, or even shut down, for other periods. If the product must move directly into consumption, transportation and refrigeration facilities must be available immediately. All these situations affect the costs of the marketing process.

For many commodities considerable progress is being made toward reducing the seasonal variability of production. The seasonal production variation of such products as milk, eggs, and broilers, for example, is considerably less than years ago. Larger, more specialized farms often gear for evenly distributed production to fully utilize labor and facilities. New developments in management, breeding, and nutrition are making more uniform levels of production possible. Moreover, the widespread use of more rapid transportation and refrigeration has tended to reduce the seasonality of available supplies. Bananas today, for example, are plentiful all year, whereas a few years ago they were quite seasonable. The United States has a wide range of climatic conditions. By employing improved transportation methods, different geographic areas can be used to extend the season of availability for many commodities. For example, there is a relatively uniform supply of such vegetables as lettuce, fresh tomatoes, and green onions now available as area after area can be tapped in its appropriate season. Such operations, of course, mean that the marketing machinery must be a flexible one, geared to procurement and movement from a widespread and changing area.

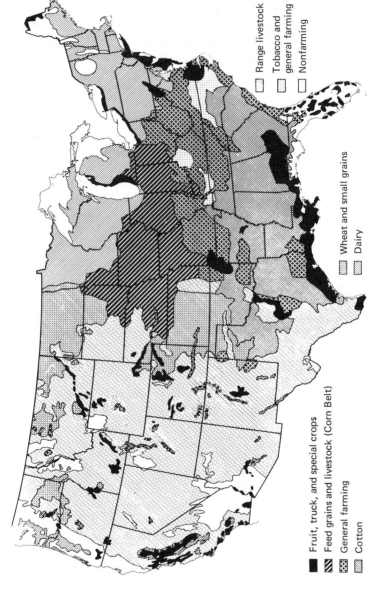

Fruit, truck, and special crops
Feed grains and livestock (Corn Belt)
General farming
Cotton

Wheat and small grains
Dairy

Range livestock
Tobacco and general farming
Nonfarming

Figure 3-6. Major types of farming in the United States. (U.S. Department of Agriculture)

Geographic Concentration of Production

Although a variety of farm products is produced in all states, there is increasing geographic specialization of farm production. Figure 3-6 shows the major types of farming throughout the United States. Each region tends to specialize in the production of commodities for which its resource base is best suited: oranges in California, Texas, and Florida, wheat in the Great Plains, poultry and eggs in the Southeast, and livestock in the corn belt. Geographic specialization changes from time to time, as illustrated by the slow drift of cotton production from the Southeast to the Southwest, and the marketing system, of course, must adjust to these changing geographic production patterns.

Varying Costs of Production

There is no single cost of production for all farmers. Farmers' costs of production are affected by climate, technology, farm size, and individual managerial skills. Consequently, the cost of producing a farm commodity varies widely by regions and among farmers. For example, it was estimated that the cost of producing a bushel of corn in 1976, excluding land costs, was $1.57 in the corn belt, $1.85 in the Northern Plain states, and $2.13 in the southeastern states.[4]

Are larger farmers more efficient, lower cost operators than small farmers? Most studies have found that the average cost of farm production falls as small farms grow larger, but there is a point at which average costs do *not* fall further as farm size increases.[5] There is also some indication that economies of size in marketing are more important than production economies of size for large farms. These marketing economies are associated with cost advantages in buying and selling large quantities of farm supplies and commodities.

This variability in farm costs of production is worth noting for two reasons. First, since farmers receive the same price for a commodity, even though their costs may differ, there are wide variations in farm profits and returns to farmers' management skills. Second, at any point in time and at any price there will be some farmers who are breaking even, some who are making money, and some who are losing money. Average profits can be deceptive. The fact that the price of cattle is above or below the average cost for the industry does not mean that all cattlemen are making, or losing, money.

---

[4] *Costs of Producing Selected Crops in the U.S.—1975, 1976, and Projections for 1977,* U.S. Senate Committee on Agriculture and Forestry, January 21, 1977, pp. 15–16.

[5] L. Tweeten, *Foundations of Farm Policy,* University of Nebraska Press, Lincoln, Nebraska, 1970; J. P. Madden, *Economies of Size in Farming,* U.S. Department of Agriculture, Agricultural Economic Report No. 107, February 1967.

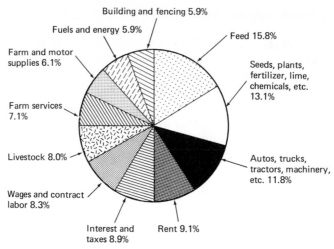

Figure 3-7. How the $81 billion dollars spent on farm production was divided, 1976. (U.S. Department of Agriculture)

The Farm Supply Industry

The farm supply industry provides such agricultural inputs as chemicals, seeds, machinery, feeds, capital, labor, land, and so on. These may be supplied by the farm or purchased from the industrial or farm supply sectors. In 1976 farmers spent almost 81 billion dollars for farm supplies (Figure 3-7). This was nearly 80 per cent of total gross farm income. The largest cash outlay went for feed (16 per cent), followed by seed, plant, and chemical expenses (13 per cent), and machinery costs (12 per cent). With increased farm size and enterprise specialization, farmers are purchasing more of their supplies from off-farm sources. In 1972 farmers purchased 62 per cent of their farm supplies from off-farm sources, a 20 per cent increase over 1950 levels.[6]

The growth and importance of the farm input sector affects farmers in several ways. It has added another market for the farmer to operate in. Farm income can be increased by skillful buying of supplies—just as in the skillful sale of farm commodities. The farm input markets have also been responsible for much of the dramatic gain in agricultural efficiency in recent years, especially the chemical and machinery markets. The farm capital or money markets, in turn, have financed mechanization and expansion of farming. Overall, the farmers' increasing dependence on off-farm inputs has reduced the self-sufficiency of farmers and tied their economic welfare more directly to the nonfarm economy.

---

[6] *The Food and Fiber System—How It Works,* U.S. Department of Agriculture, Agriculture Information Bulletin No. 383, March 1975, p. 5.

THE FARM MARKETING PROBLEM

The "farm problem" is usually associated with unstable and relatively low farm prices and incomes. A related set of farmers' problems can be termed "the farm marketing problem." There are several dimensions of this problem. First, farmers find it difficult to adjust precisely their production schedules to meet changing market conditions. Agricultural output comes from many small units operated independently. The production is to a great extent dependent on weather and biological patterns of reproduction. The farmer may wish to change his output and attempt to do so by planting more or fewer acres or by breeding more or fewer sows. However, the final output is considerably beyond his control, as weather, disease, and other relatively noncontrollable factors will affect yields per acre and the productivity of his animals. The fact must be faced that it is not possible quickly to shut off or turn on agricultural production. This means that marketing agencies in the short run must adjust to farm supplies rather than farmers adjusting to agencies.

A tomato canner must estimate how much of his product he can sell at a price estimated nearly a year in advance. From this estimate he can then contract suitable acreage with his producers. If his estimations of the market conditions and yields turn out correctly, he will pack and sell as planned. But his market estimates could be wrong. The weather could be unfavorable. Overestimates of yield will find him without enough tomatoes to meet his projected needs.

Aside from such short-run adjustment problems, it takes long periods to change materially the production of some commodities. Fruit groves are planted years in advance of their coming into production. The market situation may change during this period. The expansion of milk production is a slow process. Even significantly decreasing production is slow and difficult. Once an investment is made in buildings, equipment, and the herd, changes are very difficult and expensive to make.

This inability to adjust quickly to changing conditions creates a high-risk element in agriculture. The market for which a long-time production plan is made may be nonexistent when the production is finally available. Changes in consumer tastes may find large amounts of agricultural resources being devoted to the production of something that is no longer so greatly desired. High prices resulting from shortages of production may destroy the consumer market for that product when it finally arrives in quantity. This relative unpredictability and uncontrollability of production volume helps explain many of the actions that have been taken to strengthen the position of farmers.

A related component of the farm marketing problem is the difficulty farmers face in improving their prices through independent or group activities. Farmers are, for the most part, price-takers—they cannot, individually, influence the price of their products through their output decisions. In order to raise prices through the control of supplies or advertising programs, farmers must act as a group. However, the large numbers of farmers, and their differing economic circumstances frequently frustrate farmers in their attempts to organize and to act jointly.

The free-rider problem often plagues farmers when they do attempt to organize to influence farm prices. Free riders hamper any group effort that requires each member to sacrifice for the overall welfare of the group when the group benefits go to everyone regardless of their participation. For instance, farmers may try to raise their prices through voluntary supply-control programs, advertising efforts, or bargaining associations. If successful, the resulting price rise benefits all farmers, whether or not they have contributed to the program. Thus, it is difficult to achieve the group participation necessary for success.

The cost-price squeeze is another component of the farm marketing problem. The competitive conditions of agriculture tend to keep farm prices close to the cost of production. Falling farm prices would not be so critical if they were accompanied by falling farm costs, or if the farmer could adjust input costs as prices fell. However, the increased interdependence of farmers on off-farm produced supplies leaves farmers little leeway in order to adjust to falling farm prices. Rising farm prices, on the other hand, attract farmers to more profitable enterprises and tend to bid up the costs of production, especially land—another way that the farmer is caught in the cost-price squeeze.

To many, the superior bargaining power of the buyers of farm products as compared with that of farmers is the most serious farm marketing problem. Food marketing firms are usually larger and, because of their national and international activities, normally have better market information than the farmers from whom they buy. In addition, through contracts and other arrangements, food marketing firms are thought to gain some control over farm decisions and farm markets. "Who will control agriculture" has been a major controversial issue.

Changing food market pricing efficiency is still another element of the farm marketing problem. Perhaps at one time farmers did not need to be concerned with food marketing because competitive conditions assured all farmers a fair price. However, with today's direct negotiations and contractual arrangements, there is no longer any assurance of a high level of pricing efficiency in food markets.

Finally, there is growing concern about the increasing gulf between the farm sector and the food marketing sector. Farmers retain a commodity-orientation whereas food marketing firms stress a merchandise-orientation. Furthermore, farmers have chosen not to participate in many of the food marketing activities that appear to have the greatest growth potential. By not participating in the value-adding advertising, processing, and merchandising marketing functions, the farmer has accepted the status of raw material producer for the food industry. Food marketing firms have not shown the same restraint in crossing over the farm gate.

FARM MARKETING QUESTIONS

The farmer and those engaged in advising and helping him have a tremendous stake in an efficient marketing system. The income from the raw products that farmers sell is a function of the smooth operation of the marketing system. An effective and efficient marketing system from the farmers' viewpoint is one that will induce the production of those products and quantities which, when sold to consumers, will result in maximum returns after the deduction of marketing charges and farm production costs.

A knowledge of marketing and its problems will help a farmer make decisions that are important to him in the operation of his own farm, as a member of a particular group, or as an intelligent citizen of his country. These important decisions include:

1. *What to produce and how to prepare it for sale.* For example, some fruit varieties and hog types are more desired by consumers than others. Some harvesting practices may have an effect on the value of the product.

2. *When and where to buy or sell.* Different products have different high and low periods of prices throughout the year. Production and storage practices may be adjusted to take advantage of these. Many alternative outlets are usually available. Knowing how to appraise the advantages and disadvantages of each will help in selecting the one that will maximize returns.

3. *How much of the marketing job should be done by the farmer himself, either as an individual or as a member of a group.* In many instances transportation may be either hired or provided by the farmer himself. Similarly, someone may be hired to do the selling and other marketing tasks, or the farmer may perform these tasks himself. In addition, the choice is often available to farmers to own and operate part of the marketing system.

4. *What can be done to expand markets.* Many proposals and schemes for advertising and other techniques for influencing consumers are being offered. A knowledge of the factors that influence consumers and their behavior can help determine which of several proposals for action might be most effective.

5. *Which marketing arrangements are desirable.* Increasingly, farmers are being offered different methods of selling their products. Some proposals guarantee returns in exchange for the privilege of permitting a marketing firm to make certain operating decisions on the farm. Many other contractual possibilities exist. Knowing how to appraise different marketing arrangements is becoming increasingly important.

6. *How can changes necessary to correct undesirable practices be secured.* New laws are often proposed as a means of improving the marketing machinery's operation. Sometimes government intervention may be desirable; sometimes there are other and better means of accomplishing the desired end. Decisions in this area often have far-reaching implications.

These are just a few of the contributions that a knowledge of marketing can make toward more profitable farming. The objective of production, from the producer's standpoint, is profit. And profit is not realized until the product is sold. Coordination of activities that occur both within and outside the farm fence is necessary for maximum returns.

THE FARMER'S MARKETING PLAN

The farmer's marketing plan consists of a set of objectives, strategies, and tactics which assist the farmer in making production and marketing decisions. The marketplace presents the farmer with a wide variety of choices, decisions, and opportunities. The farmer's marketing plan is the farmers' blueprint for making these decisions and exploiting market opportunities.

The marketing plan begins with a statement of the farmer's goals and objectives. These will differ, depending upon the farmer's ambitions, talents, and resources. Usually a farmer will have several objectives, and it is necessary to rank these because conflicts sometimes arise when trying to achieve more than one goal at a time. When asked, "What is your goal?" many farmers will answer, "To make as much money as possible." This is not a very useful goal for guiding marketing efforts, however true it may be. Making money is more often the result of reaching a goal.

Farmers are motivated by a number of goals: farm growth; productive efficiency; preservation of the family farm; economic independence and market freedom; stability; the good life; and even the provision of a wholesome, reasonably priced food supply. Each farmer chooses from among these goals, or gives them different priorities, and this conditions all of his marketing decisions.

Objectives tell where you want to go. Strategies are the grand designs for getting there. There are a number of alternative strategies for achieving farmer goals: (1) rapid growth versus slow but steady growth; (2) top dollar for each sale versus a reasonable average price over the long haul; (3) high risk and high profit versus lower risk and lower profit; (4) profit improvement through cost reduction versus price enhancement; (5) maximizing returns from farm product sales versus maximizing the asset value of the farm.

Marketing tactics are the day-to-day decisions that implement farm marketing strategies. A farmer with a risk-minimizing strategy might prefer to contract-price his crop in the spring for fall delivery rather than take a chance on the harvest-time price. Another farmer with a high-profit, high-risk strategy might do just the opposite. A farmer with on-farm grain storage facilities will use different marketing strategies and tactics than the farmer who must sell at harvest time.

The market plan is a vital tool for making and evaluating farmer marketing programs. Strategies follow from goals and tactics follow from strategies, in a logical fashion. In this way the marketing plan organizes and coordinates the farmer's production and marketing decisions. The plan also provides a way to judge the success of a farmer's marketing effort. Success is achieved when the tactics and strategies lead to the chosen goals. The marketing plan must be flexible—to be altered at any time to fit new circumstances. However, it is important for the farmer to know when he is departing from his plan and when it is time to make a new plan.

SUMMARY

The nature of agriculture significantly influences the organization of the food marketing system and the complexity of the food marketing process. In general, fewer, larger and more specialized farms are producing the nation's food supply. The family farm continues to dominate United States agriculture, although there are also large, corporate farms owned and operated by food marketing firms and nonfood firms. The key farm product and output characteristics which influence the food marketing process are bulkiness, perishability, quality differences, output variations, and the geographic specialization of individual commodities. Farm input markets are increasing in importance as farmers purchase a growing share of their supplies from off-farm sources. The farm marketing problem has several dimensions, including the difficulty of adjusting farm output to rapidly changing market needs; the price-taking status of farmers; the farm cost-price squeeze; the imbalance of bargaining power between farmers and marketing firms; and declining pricing efficiency in agricultural markets. The farmer's marketing plan consists of objectives, strategies, and tactics that organize the farmer's production and marketing activities and help him in answering key marketing questions.

QUESTIONS FOR DISCUSSION

1. How is the economic position of the farmer in the food industry like the position of any other raw material producer (for example, the coal miner, the lumberjack)? How does it differ?

2. Suppose that scientists discover a way to produce the world's food supply from crude oil. How would this affect agriculture as we know it?

3. How would you expect the increasing geographic concentration of farm production to affect the cost of producing food? The cost of marketing food?

4. Debate the proposition: "All farm products are alike, and buyers have no preference for one farmer's product over another."

5. Why have farmers traditionally preferred to specialize in production agriculture to the neglect of involvement in food marketing activities? What are some consequences of this?

6. Farmer Brown says, "Farmers should get a fair price for their products and a fair income for their efforts." How would you define fair price and income?

7. In what sense has the agricultural productivity record been a problem for farmers?

8. Why are farmers purchasing a growing share of their production supplies from off-farm sources?

9. Give one solution to each of the farm marketing problems mentioned in this chapter.

10. Why do farmers need a marketing plan?

SELECTED REFERENCES

BAILEY, W. R. *The One-Man Farm.* U.S. Department of Agriculture. ERS-519, Aug. 1973.

BALL, A. G. and E. O. HEADY, Eds. *Size, Structure and Future of Farm.* Iowa State University Press, Ames, Iowa, 1972.

BREIMYER, H. F. *Individual Freedom and the Economic Organization of Agriculture.* University of Illinois Press, Urbana, Ill., 1965.

CARLIN, T. A. and W. F. WOODS. *Tax Loss Farming.* U.S. Department of Agriculture. ERS-546, April 1974.

Changes in Farm Production and Efficiency, A Special Issue Featuring Historical Series. U.S. Department of Agriculture. Statistical Bulletin No. 561, Sept. 1976.

Changes in Farm Production and Efficiency. U.S. Department of Agriculture. Statistical Bulletin No. 233, Annual.

COCHRANE, W. W. *The City Man's Guide to the Farm Problem.* University of Minnesota Press, Minneapolis, 1965.

COFFMAN, G. W. *Corporations with Farming Operations.* U.S. Department of Agriculture. Agricultural Economic Report No. 209, June 1971.

Farmers in the Market Economy. Iowa State University Press, Ames, Iowa, 1964.

Farming and Agribusiness Activities of Large Multiunit Firms. U.S. Department of Agriculture. ERS-591, March 1975.

Food and Fiber for the Future. Report of the National Advisory Commission on Food and Fiber. U.S. Government Printing Office, Washington, D.C., July 1967.

MADDEN, J. P. *Economies of Size in Farming.* U.S. Department of Agriculture. Agricultural Economic Report No. 107, Feb. 1967.

NELSON, P. E., JR. *The Farm Machinery and Equipment Industry: Changing Structure and Performance.* U.S. Department of Agriculture. Marketing Research Report No. 892, Aug. 1970.

NIKOLITCH, R. *Family-Size Farms in U.S. Agriculture.* U.S. Department of Agriculture. ERS-499, Feb. 1972.

_____. *The Expanding and the Contracting Sectors of American Agriculture.* U.S. Department of Agriculture. Agricultural Economic Report No. 74, May 1965.

Structure of Six Farm Input Industries. U.S. Department of Agriculture. ERS-357, Jan. 1968.

Who Will Control U.S. Agriculture? North Central Public Policy Education Committee. University of Illinois at Urbana-Champaign, Special Publication 27, Aug. 1972.

PART II

Food Markets and Institutions

CHAPTER 4

Food Consumption and Marketing

"THE SETTLERS who came to the New World were too busy with basic needs to bother about the niceties. In America, food initially was a matter of survival; later it was little more than a function. It wasn't until the end of World War II, says James Beard, the doyen of America's burgeoning food fraternity, 'that Americans begin to think of eating as a pleasurable thing, a sensual delight.' "*

Preview

- This chapter examines the role of consumers and their food preferences in the food marketing process.
- The major factors affecting consumer food preferences are studied: the physiological need for food, food nutrition, the socio-psychological values of foods, food prices, consumers' income, consumer information, and the availability of food substitutes.
- The concept of the food product bundle of form, time, place, and possession utilities is developed.
- The major socioeconomic trends influencing food consumption are reviewed.
- Trends in food prices, per capita food consumption, and the consumers' share of income going for food are discussed.
- The effects of the growth in convenience foods and the away-from-home food markets on the food production and marketing process are investigated.
- Key terms and concepts:

away-from-home food market	convenience food
consumer food preference	demographic trends

---

* Horace Sutton, *Saturday Review World,* November 20, 1973.

effective demand
Engel's law
foodways
income elasticity

product bundle of attributes
psychological satisfaction
superior and inferior foods

The ultimate task of the food marketing system is to deliver the food utilities that consumers desire. This involves much more than just matching the total food supply with the total food demand. It is the process of matching the right form of a product at the right place and time to a particular buyer. The facts that "we all have to eat" and "the stomach can only hold so much" do not tell us very much about food consumption. The interesting questions are *what* do people eat, *how much, when, where,* and *how often.* These food consumption patterns are influenced by physiological needs, tastes and preferences, habits, mores, social relationships, and economic factors.

THE ANATOMY OF FOOD PREFERENCES

Presumably, consumers choose their diet to satisfy their needs and wants. Because these choices condition all of the food industry's production and marketing decisions, it is important to understand the nature of consumer food preferences.

Man is omnivorous and can thrive on a wide variety of different foods. He is also choosy and no society defines all the potentially edible material in its environment as food. Man is also a social creature, and his food preferences and eating patterns are culturally bound and socially influenced.

It is not easy to understand the diverse food preferences of various societies. There seems to be no physiological reason why some societies cultivate certain crops for food and others shun these crops; why some people eat insects (an excellent protein source) and others do not; why some do and some do not eat animal flesh. The terms *culture, tastes and preferences,* and religion seem inadequate explanations for the food we eat, but they do suggest the complexity of food choices. Food idiosynchrosies are not limited to cross-cultural comparisons, either. There are substantial dietary variations within most societies, including America.

Each society develops common patterns of dealing with food, which we refer to as *foodways.* These govern how food is acquired, prepared, and eaten. Foodways are complex behavioral patterns which, from the standpoint of food marketing, have four important characteristics. First, no two societies have identical foodways. Second, standardized foodways result in somewhat similar and stable food preferences and eating patterns within a society. Third, foodways defining "how to eat" add social significance to the diet and are taught to each succeeding generation. And fourth, foodways adapt to socio-economic changes such as urbanization, education, income, technology, and changing lifestyles.

American foodways are the result of five influences: (1) the functional, physiological values of foods (their nutritional contributions to health and survival); (2) the socio-psychological values of foods (status, religion, aesthetics, and lifestyle); (3) the economic values of foods; (4) the availability of foods; and (5) consumers' knowledge and information about foods.

No one of these influences fully explains American food preferences. Consumers are concerned with nutrition, but it is doubtful that our diets maximize the nutritional value of each food dollar.[1] We are health-conscious, but overeating is as great a problem for many as insufficient food. There are some regional, ethnic and religious food preferences, although these appear to be breaking down in our mobile society. Food consumers are price conscious, but they do not always buy the least expensive foods. These examples caution against simple analyses of food preferences.

One thing seems clear. In a high-income, affluent, urbanized society food consumers buy much more than physical farm products; foods are purchased to satisfy more than mere physiological needs. The modern food consumer purchases a whole *bundle of attributes,* which includes, along with farm products, time, form, space, and possession utilities. Even the store where the food is purchased and the setting in which it is served contribute to consumers' satisfaction and must be considered part of the *product bundle.* Both the functional and the socio-psychological values of food are pleasing to consumers. Knowledge of this product bundle of satisfactions is necessary for understanding and predicting food preferences. The task of food marketing firms is to discover the product bundle of attributes that will appeal, profitably, to consumers. This search results in large expenditures for product innovation and design, packaging, merchandising, and advertising.

FOOD CONSUMPTION AND EXPENDITURE PATTERNS

Table 4-1 shows the trends in United States food consumption, prices, and expenditures from 1930 to 1975. Total spending and per capita food

---

[1] In 1945, the economist George Stigler studied the "rationality" of the American diet. He developed a subsistence diet which met recommended dietary allowances which cost only one third of the low-cost food budget developed by the U.S. Department of Agriculture. This nutritionally adequate diet included large quantities of flour, cabbage, and dried navy beans. He concluded that American food choices were influenced by sociopsychological factors in addition to nutrition. G. J. Stigler, "The Cost of Subsistence," *Journal of Farm Economics,* May 1945, pp. 303–14.

Table 4-1. Food Consumption Trends, 1930–1975.

| | CONSUMER FOOD EXPENDITURES | | FOOD SPENDING AS A PER CENT OF DISPOSABLE INCOME | FOOD PRICES (1967 = 100) | PER CAPITA FOOD CONSUMPTION (POUNDS) | CALORIES PER DAY |
| | DOLLAR EXPENDITURES | | | | | |
YEAR	$BILLION	PER CAPITA				
1930	$ 18	$146	24%	46	1,543	3,440
1940	17	127	22	35	1,550	3,340
1950	47	313	23	75	1,505	3,260
1960	71	390	20	88	1,427	3,130
1970	119	579	17	115	1,422	3,300
1975	185	866	17	175	1,402	3,210
1950–1975 Change	+294%	+177		+133	−7	−2

Sources: U.S. Departments of Commerce and Agriculture.

expenditures rose significantly over this period. However, because food spending rose less rapidly than consumers' income, the share of consumers' income spent for food declined from 24 per cent to 17 per cent.

What are consumers getting for their increased food dollar? Not more pounds of food nor additional calories, according to Table 4-1. These have fallen, over time, with changes in the way we live and work. Higher food prices account for part of the increase in food expenditures, but not all of it. The more rapid increase in food expenditures than in prices over the 1930–1975 period, coupled with a decline in the quantity of food eaten, suggests that consumers have substituted more expensive foods for staple items in their diet. Rising consumer incomes have facilitated this trend.

Food Expenditures

Food competes, of course, with other consumer goods and services for the consumers' dollar. As shown in Figure 4-1, there was a shift in consumers' budget dollars away from food, recreation, personal care, education, and health care toward transportation, clothing, and housing between 1960–1961 and 1972–1973. These expenditure shifts reflect changing prices and consumer preferences over this period.

While consumers are concerned with the size of the weekly food bill, food marketing firms are more concerned with the division of consumer food expenditures among different classes of foods. Table 4-2 shows that fresh meat, poultry, and fish accounted for 22 per cent of the average family's

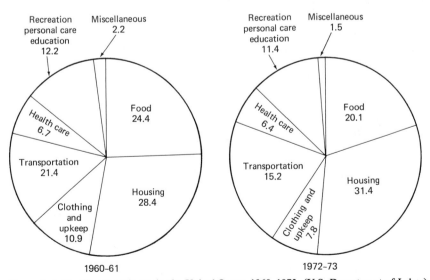

Figure 4–1. Family expenditures in the United States, 1960–1973. (U.S. Department of Labor)

Table 4-2. Composition of the $20 Grocery Bill, 1960–1975.

	CONTRIBUTION TO THE $20 GROCERY BILL		
ITEM	1960	1970	1975
Fresh meat, poultry and fish	$4.85	$4.53	$4.42
Produce	2.08	2.02	2.12
Dairy products, eggs, margarine	1.74	1.41	1.22
Canned foods	1.34	1.23	1.19
Baked goods, snacks	1.04	—	1.21
Frozen foods	.97	.97	1.00
Beer, wine, liquor	.88	.86	.99
Coffee, tea	.72	.56	.53
Soft drinks	.23	.44	.49
Pet food	—	—	.30
Non foods (paper, soap, etc.)	—	4.27	4.32

Source: *Supermarketing,* Gralla Publishing Co., New York. Reprinted by permission.

grocery bill in 1975; produce accounted for $2.12 of the $20 grocery bill; and canned foods accounted for $1.19 of this bill. These product shares of the consumers' food dollar are shifting with changing food preferences and marketing strategies of commodity groups. Consumers allocated almost 22 per cent of the grocery bill to nonfood items in 1975. This, of course, should not be counted as part of the food bill.

Food Consumption Trends

The American diet is in a state of flux. The broad changes in food consumption since 1910 are shown in Figure 4-2. In general, there has been a long-

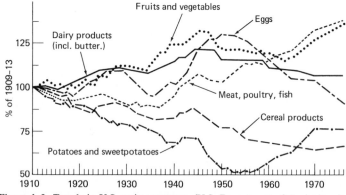

Figure 4-2. Trends in U.S. eating patterns. (U.S. Department of Agriculture)

Table 4-3. Consumption Trends of Selected Food Products, 1947–1976.

CONSUMPTION TREND	PRODUCT	PER CAPITA CONSUMPTION (POUNDS)			
		1947–1949	1957–1959	1969–1971	1974–1976
Decreasing					
	Lard	12	9	5	3
	Wheat flour	131	115	111	108
	Eggs	47	45	41	31
	Fresh citrus	52	32	29	28
	Butter	10	8	5	5
	Fluid milk	299	298	233	200
Little change					
	Ice cream	19	18	18	18
	Pork	64	59	68	55
	Sugar	92	92	101	91
	Fresh tomatoes	10	10	10	10
Increasing					
	Beef	52	63	83	90
	Chicken	19	28	41	42
	Margarine	6	9	11	11
	Fish	12	13	14	15
	Cheese	7	8	11	15
	Frozen potatoes	0	2	11	14

Source: U.S. Department of Agriculture.

term substitution of livestock products for staple items such as potatoes and cereals. More detailed changes in food consumption patterns are explored in Table 4-3. With the exceptions of pork and eggs, consumption of animal protein products increased most rapidly over the 1947–1976 period. Some direct substitutions can be observed in Table 4-3. For example, the increase in margarine consumption is exactly equal to the decline in butter consumption.

These food consumption trends are highly important to farmers and food marketing firms. They influence food sales, prices, and profits, and they require adjustments in food production, processing, and marketing.

THE DEMOGRAPHICS OF FOOD CONSUMPTION

Demography is the study of populations—how many people there are, where they live, and how they live. These trends influence food marketing by affecting the number of mouths to feed, where food is sold, and how people buy their food. A number of socio-economic and demographic trends influencing food consumption and the food industry are illustrated in Table 4-4.

Table 4-4. Socio-economic Trends Influencing Food Consumption and Marketing, 1950–1976.

TREND	1950	1960	1970	1976
U.S. population (million)	152	180	204	214
Population per square mile	51	60	58	60
Number of households (million)	40	48	63	73
One- and two-person households (per cent of total)	39%	41%	46%	50%
Life expectancy (male)	66	67	67	68
Number of marriages (million per year)	1.5	1.6	2.2	2.1
Number of births (million)	3.9	4.3	3.7	3.1
Average family size	3.5	3.7	3.6	3.4
Median age of first marriage (female)	20.3	20.3	20.8	21.3
Female-headed families (million)	3.7	4.5	5.6	7.2
Median age	30.2	29.5	27.6	29.0
Per cent of population:				
under age 18	34%	36%	34%	31%
over 64 years of age	8%	9%	10%	11%
Per cent of husband-wife families with wife in labor force	24%	31%	41%	44%
Per cent living in metropolitan areas	56%	63%	69%	73%
Per cent moving interstate	3%	3%	3%	3%
Median family income	$3,319	$5,620	$9,867	$13,719
Per cent below poverty level	—	22%	12%	12%
Median years of school completed	9.3	10.6	12.2	12.3
Per cent of homes with:				
home freezer	—	22%	30%	34%
air-conditioning	—	13%	43%	51%
food-waste disposal	—	10%	25%	—

Source: *U.S. Statistical Abstract,* Annual, U.S. Government Printing Office.

Population Trends

The geographic dispersion of food production in America is quite different from the concentration of population. Figure 4-3 shows the United States drawn in proportion to the 1975 distributions of population and food production. Although food is grown in every state, agricultural geographic specialization necessitates a complex marketing system to move the food from areas of production concentration to where the people are. The buying power of an area depends, of course, upon both its population and consumers' income. Within each state there are areas with substantial differences in income and in population density. The food marketing system faces a challenge in distributing a wide variety of economical foods to these different areas of the country.

The food market expands in proportion to the rate of population growth. The United States population grew from 152 million to 218 million people between 1950 and 1978. However, the rate of population growth has declined

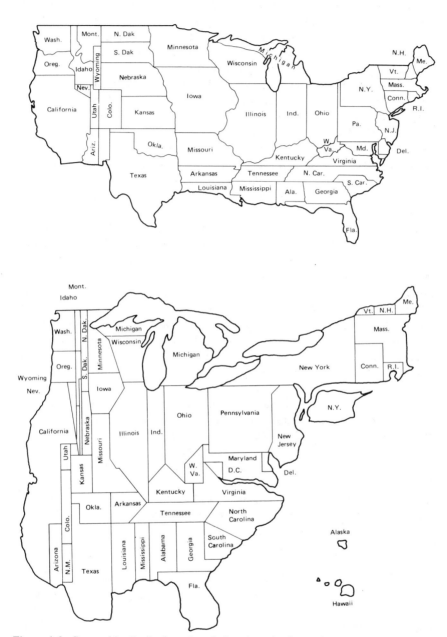

Figure 4–3. Geographic distribution of agricultural production and consumption. Sizes of states in top map show their relative contributions to food production. Bottom map shows the sizes of states in relation to their population (1975).

in recent years after climbing from record low levels in the 1930's: 1.8 per cent growth per year in 1950–1955; 1.5 per cent in 1960–1965; and 0.9 per cent in 1970–1975. The U.S. reached the zero population growth rate in the early 1970's. As a result of this slowdown in population growth, total food demand will not grow as rapidly in the future as it has in the past.

The mobility of the population also influences the food marketing machinery. About 20 per cent of Americans move each year, but only 3 per cent move to another state, thus potentially exposing themselves to new food consumption patterns. As a result of this migration, the population is growing most rapidly in the Sunbelt—the South, Southwest, and West coast states. Some predominately agricultural states have experienced declining populations. This alters the food distribution network. For example, an increasing amount of Western food production now finds a market nearer to home than heretofore.

There are differences in food consumption patterns between one region of the country and another that cannot be explained on the basis of income or other factors. Lamb consumption is very largely limited to the East and West coasts, with very little being consumed in the interior. Boston housewives prefer brown eggs, whereas New York housewives prefer white ones. Consumers in the South eat relatively more pork and less beef than consumers in other regions of the country. People in San Francisco are relatively heavy lamb and poultry consumers. Buffalo and Minneapolis consumers are heavy potato eaters, whereas Birmingham people consume more sweet potatoes.

Urbanization is another important demographic trend. In 1976, 73 per cent of the population lived in metropolitan areas compared to 56 per cent in 1950. The country-to-central city migration of earlier years was replaced by a migration out of central cities to the suburbs in the 1950's and 1960's. But the 1970's saw a back-to-the-country movement as rural areas and small towns grew more rapidly than cities and suburbs. These migrations shaped the modern food distribution network. The supermarket, for example, is a suburban product. The regional movement of population has required new investments in food marketing facilities and provided opportunities for some food marketing firms to gain a competitive advantage over others. The geographic distribution of the population influences the efficiency of food marketing because it is usually more economical to service highly concentrated populations than scattered consumers.

The age and education of the population also influence food consumption. Although the average age has not changed dramatically in recent years, there was a significant growth in the under-18 and over-64 age groups in the 1950's and, in the 1970's, the over-64 age group continued to grow. The elderly age group is expected to grow at twice the overall population growth rate during 1977–1987. Youthful and elderly consumers eat differently from other consumers. Recent declines in milk consumption and increases in red meat, cheese, and potatoes have been attributed to the changing age-distribution

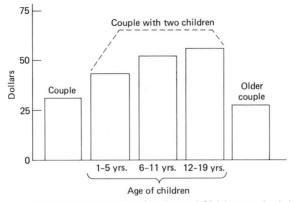

All meals at home or taken from home. USDA low–cost food plan.

Figure 4–4. Cost of a week's food over the family life cycle, 1977. (U.S. Department of Agriculture)

of the population. Figure 4-4 shows how food spending varies over the family life cycle. Figure 4-5 indicates the effects of age on dairy and meat product consumption.

Household Food Consumption

The household is the basic unit of food consumption. Household members typically pool their income, buy as a unit, and share somewhat similar food preferences. The number of households rose from 40 million to 73 million between 1950 and 1976. However, not all households are families. With the falling birth rate, the average family size reached 3.4 in 1976. At the same time, there was a rapid growth in the proportion of households with only one or two people, including young married and retired couples. These trends have resulted in increased demand for smaller food packages and more prepared foods. It is also possible that wastage of household food is greater for smaller households. Two important household trends are the increasing number of female-headed (no husband present) households and the prevalence of working wives in wife-husband households. These trends have probably contributed to the popularity of convenience foods and the growing away-from-home food market.

Household appliances also influence food consumption. Practically all families have some form of mechanical refrigeration, and, according to Table 4-4, 34 per cent of families had a food freezer in 1976. Air conditioning changes food patterns, and half of all U.S. homes were air conditioned in 1976. Undoubtedly, the rising number of two-car families, the exposure to television and other mass communications, and the growing market for outdoor grills and microwave ovens also affect food purchases and preferences.

83

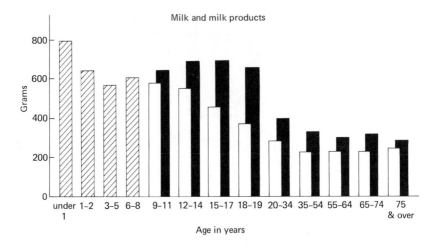

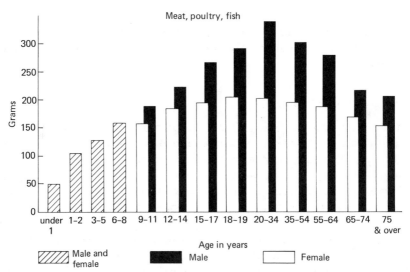

Figure 4–5. Amounts of milk and meat products consumed in the United States in one day by age, spring, 1965. (U.S. Department of Agriculture)

INCOME AND FOOD CONSUMPTION

Historically, population and income growth have been the two major sources of growth in food consumption. The number of people determine the total need for food whereas their income determines their ability to pay for it. *Effective food demand* consists of both needs and the ability and willingness to satisfy those needs with income. A need does not register in the marketplace unless it is backed up with purchasing power.[2] Many low-income countries and people have a great need for food but lack the income to register an effective demand in the marketplace. The high-income countries, such as the United States, are characterized by a strong effective demand for food.

Consumer incomes in the United States have been growing as a result of technological change, increased worker productivity, and general economic growth. Half of U.S. families had an income greater than $13,800 in 1976, compared to the median income of $5,620 in 1960. Income growth has to some extent moderated the effect of recent declining population growth on food demand.

The responsiveness of food consumption to an increase in income is called *income elasticity*. The more responsive consumption is to income changes, the greater the income elasticity. If the quantity of a food rises along with income, the product is termed a *normal good*. If quantity falls as income rises, the food is termed an *inferior good*. Livestock products generally are normal goods and have a higher income elasticity than crop products. There are few inferior foods; perhaps fresh potatoes, grits, and lard are in this category. In general, the income elasticity of food is lower than for other products consumers buy. Moreover, the income elasticity of raw farm products is lower than the income elasticity of the utilities added in the marketing process.

There are, of course, wide variations in consumers' incomes, and these influence food consumption. The poor do not eat or shop like the rich. In recent years there has been great emphasis on improving the diets of the poor. According to Table 4-4, about 12 per cent of the population was classified as poor in 1976. Studies suggest that the higher the income, the "better" the diet. However, other factors also influence diet adequacy, and high income itself does not assure a good diet. Figure 4-6 illustrates this.

Rising consumer incomes have affected U.S. food consumption patterns in several ways. First, consumers do not buy more pounds of food or calories as incomes rise. Instead, they "upgrade" their diet by substituting more expensive foods, usually meats, for staple items. This upgrading does not necessarily represent a nutritional improvement. As a result of decreased consumption of milk products, vegetables, and fruits, only 50 per cent of households were judged to have a good diet in 1965, compared to 60 per cent of households in 1955.[3]

---

[2] This is not to say that dollars alone determine who eats and who goes hungry in the world. The high-income countries provide food and economic development aid to the developing countries. However, the world food market is a commercial market, and effective food demand is important in the distribution of the world's food supply.

[3] *Dietary Levels of Households in the U.S., Spring 1965,* U.S. Department of Agriculture, ARS 62-17, January 1968.

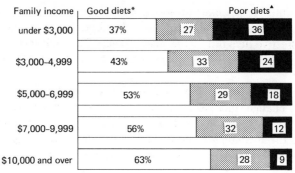

Family income	Good diets*		Poor diets▲
under $3,000	37%	27	36
$3,000–4,999	43%	33	24
$5,000–6,999	53%	29	18
$7,000–9,999	56%	32	12
$10,000 and over	63%	28	9

*Met recommended dietary allowances for 7 nutrients.
▲Had less than 2/3 allowance for 1 to 7 nutrients.

Figure 4–6. Income and quality of diets, 1965. (U.S. Department of Agriculture)

The second result of rising consumer incomes is to reduce the consumers' share of income going for food. Food expenditures do not normally increase as rapidly as income, so the ratio of food spending to income falls with rising income. This is Engel's law, named after a German statistician who first observed this tendency in Europe in 1857. Sometimes this falling food share of income is cited to imply that "food is a bargain," and it is true that a declining food share of income represents a growing share of income available for nonnecessities with which to increase the consumer's standard of living. However, as shown in Table 4-1, the food share of income can fall while food prices are rising. The universality of Engel's law is illustrated by Figure 4-7. The United States food share of income is an average, of

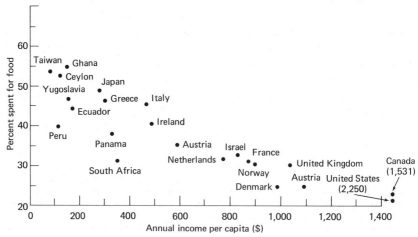

Figure 4–7. Percent of per capita income spent for food in various countries. (U.S. Department of Agriculture)

course. There are U.S. families that spend more than 40 per cent of their income for food and, probably, some who spend less than 1 per cent.

A third consequence of rising income is a broadening of the product bundle of attributes which are important to consumers. At low-income levels, price and perhaps nutrition are paramount concerns. As incomes rise, consumers add quality, variety, convenience, and service to the desired product-attribute bundle. Thus, in high-income societies and populations, the product bundle of attributes becomes more complex. These affluent attributes are added in the food marketing process, and they become equally as important, if not more important, than the farm-originating product attributes. Hence, the scope of food marketing activities is much greater in high-income than in low-income societies. The rapid rate of new product development, the growth in marketing services, and the rising sophistication with which the American food supply is marketed are evidence of the broadening of the consumer's preferred food product-attribute bundle.

Relatedly, rising consumer incomes increase the demand for convenience foods with built-in maid service. A convenience food is a product that reduces the amount of time, effort, or additional ingredients required of the consumer in preparing food. Higher income consumers can afford to buy preprocessed convenience foods, and the use of these products befits their lifestyles. However, there is conflicting evidence on the question of whether all convenience foods are more expensive than their home-prepared counterparts.[4] Of course, many people receive self-satisfaction from "cooking from scratch"; and others avoid highly processed foods for a number of reasons.

Highly processed foods do tend to cost more per unit than fresh foods. But because consumers purchase both fresh and processed foods, the increased form utility must offset the costs for some consumers. In effect, when they buy convenience foods, consumers are transferring processing functions from the kitchen to the food marketing system. Rising education levels, a desire for more leisure time, working wives, urbanization, and a number of other socio-economic trends favor this transfer of marketing functions. The growth in convenience foods should not be criticized without considering the rising value of the homemaker's time in the job market. Providing that they have alternatives, free choice from among these, and are aware of the consequences of their choices, consumers are probably the best judge of whether they should buy convenience or prepare-from-scratch foods.

How does the growth in convenience foods affect farmers? Because the

---

[4] A 1960 study showed that 116 of 158 convenience foods were more expensive than their home-prepared counterparts: H. H. Harp, et al., *Comparative Costs to Consumers of Convenience Foods and Home Prepared Foods,* U.S. Department of Agriculture, Marketing Research Report, No. 609, June 1963. A similar 1975 study showed that 104 of 162 convenience foods were cheaper than their corresponding "scratch" foods: L. G. Traub, "Convenience Foods—1975 Cost Update," *Family Economics Review,* Winter 1976, pp. 26–27. These studies have been criticized for failing to make nutritional value comparisons between convenience and "scratch" foods.

highly processed products, such as potato chips and snacks, probably do not reduce the amount of fresh potatoes eaten, there is no reason to believe that farmers will sell fewer potatoes as a result of increased use of "convenience" forms of potatoes. On the contrary, frozen potato products have expanded the total market for fresh potatoes. And there is no particular reason why farmers would receive a lower (or higher) price for potatoes that are to be processed rather than sold fresh.

There is evidence that the convenience food trend has slowed down considerably in recent years. Table 4-5 indicates growth in consumption of whole, fresh farm products, particularly meats, between 1952 and 1975 and relative stability in the share of food sold in highly processed forms. Nevertheless, the development of convenience foods has been one of the major forces shaping the modern food industry.

Rising incomes and educational levels intensify consumers' concern with the quality of food markets and the social impact of the food industry. Affluent consumers have been in the vanguard in supporting such consumer causes as unit pricing, nutritional labeling, and open-code dating. These informational

Table 4-5. Consumption of Processed and Convenience Foods, 1952–1971.

	PER CENT OF CONSUMER EXPENDITURES	
	1952	1975
Stage of processing:		
fresh farm products (meat, produce)	36%	40%
preserved whole farm products (canned, frozen, etc.)	30	27
transformed farm products (e.g., butter)	11	11
products combining several food ingredients (e.g., TV dinners)	23	22
All foods	100%	100%
Convenience stage:		
preparation required	5%	3%
ready to cook	48	50
ready to eat	47	47
All foods	100%	100%

Source: A. C. Manchester, "Total Consumer Buying of Fresh Versus Processed Foods Remains Stable," *The National Food Situation*, May 1973, pp. 35–36; "Are Highly Processed Products Taking Over the Market?" *The National Food Situation*, March 1977, pp. 34–35.

programs allegedly improve consumer food choices and contribute to competitive food markets. And increasingly, many consumers are concerned with food-related social problems: rural and urban poverty, farm labor, environmental issues, and so on. In their consumption decisions, affluent food consumers face difficult political and economic choices insofar as these also relate to energy use, environmental impact, packaging, and welfare programs.

THE AWAY-FROM-HOME FOOD MARKET

Increased consumer incomes, working wives, and changed lifestyles have contributed to a rapid growth in the away-from-home food market. As shown in Table 4-6, away-from-home expenditures accounted for 24 per cent of the total value of food consumed in 1975, up from 20 per cent in 1960. Because these meals have more "service" than home meals and are therefore generally more expensive, eating out accounted for one out of every three food dollars in 1975. Like convenience foods, this trend has increased the importance of the food marketing system relative to the farm sector. In 1975 there were an estimated 480,000 food services, including restaurants; school, factory, and hospital cafeterias; hotel and motel eating places; government food-service operations; and military feeding establishments. Many firms prepare ready-to-serve foods in central kitchens and transport meals 100 miles or so to restaurants and feeding establishments.

The fast-food industry has been the most rapidly growing segment of the food-service industry. During the early 1970's, one hamburger chain boasted of opening a new unit every 24 hours. Many food processors have entered this sector of the industry: Pillsbury (Burger King), General Foods (Red

Table 4-6. The Home and Away-From-Home Food Market, 1960–1975.

	FOOD EXPENDITURES ($BILLION)				
YEAR	FOOD FOR USE AT HOME	FOOD EATEN AWAY FROM HOME	FOOD FURNISHED COMMERCIAL & GOVERNMENT EMPLOYEES	FOOD PRODUCED AND CONSUMED ON-FARM	FOOD AWAY FROM HOME AS A PER CENT OF TOTAL
1960	$ 55.2	$13.0	$1.2	$1.1	20%
1970	91.1	24.7	2.1	0.7	23
1975	139.8	40.9	2.9	1.2	24
Percentage change, 1960–1975	+153%	215	141	9	

Sources: U.S. Departments of Commerce and Agriculture.

Lobster), Ralston-Purina (Jack-in-the-Box). There is also growing competition between grocery stores and fast-food chains. Many supermarkets have expanded their in-store delicatessens and even opened restaurants within the grocery store.

The trend toward eating out must be kept in perspective. Many people are required to eat out because of the distance they travel to work. It is also instructive to differentiate between "eating out" and "dining out." The fast-food restaurant sells a low-service, economy-oriented meal. Sit-down restaurants are selling service and atmosphere as much as food.

The away-from-home food market is quite different from the home food market. Prices tend to be more stable and there is a higher ratio of marketing-services-to-food in the food-service industry than in the home food industry. The eating-out trend has markedly affected sales of hamburgers, chicken, potatoes, and ketchup. Food-service managers are quite price-conscious and have somewhat different preferences for the product bundle of attributes than homemakers. These managers are interested in standardization, portion control, and labor-saving foods. Pre-cut butter, pre-pattied hamburger, bulk frozen french fries, and individual servings of jelly and syrup are examples of the types of services demanded by these food buyers.

SUMMARY

Food consumers' behavior and preferences condition, to a significant extent, all production and marketing decisions in the food industry. These preferences are complex attitudes relating to the physiological, socio-psychological, and economic values of food products. In high-income societies, the food product bundle consists of the raw farm product and an associated set of form, time, place, and possession utilities. Two key factors influencing the rate of change in the demand for food are population and income growth. Demographic trends such as urbanization, the changing nature of the family and household, working wives, educational levels, and the age distribution of the population are also influencing food consumption patterns. Rising consumer incomes result in a substitution of more expensive, animal protein foods for staples; a declining share of income going for food; a broadening of the food product bundle; a greater demand for convenience foods; more eating out; and a greater consumer concern for the quality of food markets.

QUESTIONS FOR DISCUSSION

1. Your friend argues, "Nutrition is the most important factor in buying food." Do you agree or disagree?

2. Do you think American food preferences are becoming more similar or less similar?

3. A famous psychologist stated that the economic factors, price and income, are not as important in explaining consumer behavior as culture, social influences, and psychological factors. Do you agree or disagree?

4. Debate the following resolution: "The United States should share its abundant food supply more generously with the low-income countries of the world."

5. A congressman has introduced a bill to prevent consumers from purchasing "convenience foods" with public assistance money and food stamps. Comment on this proposal.

6. What are the socio-demographic trends with the greatest potential for increasing farm product sales in the future?

7. What will the national diet be like in the year 2000?

8. Suppose a food company develops a pill that can be taken daily, supplying all nutritional needs. However, it has no taste and leaves one feeling hungry. At what price could such a pill be sold for (assume it costs one cent to make each pill)? How would eating patterns change? Should the pill be developed?

SELECTED REFERENCES

BAYTON, J. A. "Contributions of Psychology to the Microeconomic Analysis of Consumer Demand for Food." *Journal of Farm Economics* (Dec. 1963), 1430–35.

BENNET, M. K., AND R. H. PIERCE. "Change in the American National Diet." *Food Research Institute Studies,* Stanford University, May 1961, pp. 95–119.

BURK, M. C. *Influences of Economic and Social Factors on U.S. Food Consumption.* Burgess Publishing Company, Chicago, 1961.

"Consumption and Utilization of Agricultural Products," Vol. 5 of *Major Statistical Series of the U.S. Department of Agriculture.* U.S. Department of Agriculture. Agricultural Handbook, No. 365, April 1972.

EKLUND, H. M. *A Cross-Sectional View of U.S. Food Consumption.* U.S. Department of Agriculture. ERS-419, 1969.

Food Consumption, Prices, Expenditures. U.S. Department of Agriculture. Agricultural Economic Report, No. 138, July 1968, Annual Supplements, 1969–75.

GEORGE, P. S., AND G. A. KING. *Consumer Demand for Food Commodities in the U.S. with Projections for 1980.* Giannini Foundation Monograph No. 26. California Agricultural Experiment Station, Berkeley, California, March 1972, pp. 64–66.

HARP, N. H., AND D. F. DUNHAM. *Comparative Costs to Consumers of Convenience Foods and Home Prepared Foods.* U.S. Department of Agriculture. Marketing Research Report, No. 609, June 1963.

LEBOVIT, C. "The Impact of Some Demographic Changes on U.S. Food Consumption, 1975–90." *The National Food Situation* (May 1976), 25–29.

———— AND H. GALE. *Potential Effects of Fat-Controlled, Low Cholesteral Diet on U.S. Food Consumption.* U.S. Department of Agriculture. ERS-487, Aug. 1971.

MOORE, H. L., AND G. HUSSEY. "Economic Implications of Market Orientation." *Journal of Farm Economics* (May 1965), 21–40.

SHAFFER, J. D. "Contributions of Sociologists and Cultural Anthropologists to Analysis of U.S. Food Demand." *Journal of Farm Economics* (Dec. 1963), 1420–28.

Unconventional Foodstuffs for Human Consumption. Organization for Economic Cooperation and Development, Paris, 1975.

CHAPTER 5

Food Processing and Manufacturing

"THE ADVANTAGES of having processed food available are as obvious today as they were in 1400 B.C. when the migrating Hebrews found boiled quail superior to fresh manna. Many of the food processing innovations will be a long time coming—for example, deriving human food from algae on sewage water or in sea water. Tastes and preferences are slow to change. Other processing methods such as freeze-drying and freeze concentration are well past the development stage and in use. Some are concepts still in the laboratory. In the future we shall see other food preserving methods develop and probably more of these will revolve around foods being used as convenience items."*

Preview

- This chapter examines the role of food processors in the food marketing system.
- The food processing sector's contributions to form utility and new product development are emphasized.
- Food processors are compared with other kinds of manufacturers.
- The trends toward increasing size and market domination of the very large processors are traced.
- Special attention is given to the nature of competition and rivalry among food processors, including the "battle of the brands."
- Factors affecting the geographic location and sales territories of food processors are studied.
- The major marketing problems of food processors are reviewed.

---

* Kermit Bird, "An Appraisal of Some Food Processing Methods of the Future," VII International Congress of Nutrition, Hamburg, Germany, August 9, 1966.

- Key terms and concepts:
  battle of the brands
  brand
  competitive fringe
  consumer franchise
  dominant core
  law of market areas
  location decision

  market concentration
  plant capacity
  private label
  product innovation
  product life cycle
  quality control

Food manufacturers or processors are primarily engaged in adding form utility to raw farm products. Wheat is milled into flour, livestock is converted into meat products, fruits and vegetables are canned or frozen. These firms play a vital role in transforming bulky, raw, perishable farm products into storable, concentrated, and more appealing food products. In so doing, food processors become involved in several supportive marketing functions, such as transportation, storage, and financing. Thus, food processors occupy a strategic position in the food industry. Through the purchase of farm commodities, their activities are closely linked to farmers. As the source of many food product innovations and as the major brand advertisers in the food industry, they are also in close contact with consumer markets.

INNOVATION AND BRANDING IN FOOD MANUFACTURING

Innovation and change have become a way of life in the food industry. All sectors have been affected, from farm supply industries to farmers to food retailers. Most of the product innovation in the food industry has originated in the food processing sector. These firms employ market researchers, food scientists, and advertising agencies to monitor the demand for and acceptance of new products. Their success frequently hinges on scientific breakthroughs, such as freeze-dried coffee or soft margarine, minor changes in product composition or design, or even an advertising theme.

An innovation is the discovery and application of a new idea. Three types of innovations have been important for food manufacturers: (1) new marketing methods and techniques—which often increase operational efficiency; (2) new products or services—which add more consumer value to products; and (3) new business organizations—such as the cooperative food processor, joint ventures between firms, or new market channels (e.g., the fast-food outlet). Frozen concentrated orange juice illustrates all three forms of innovation.

This process was commercially developed in the 1940's and lowered marketing costs by concentrating the juice product. Many consumers preferred this product to fresh oranges or to single-strength juice, and a new food processing industry grew up in Florida.

New foods pass through a product life cycle. Early in their development they require substantial research and marketing costs. However, if the new product reaches the acceptance stage it is frequently quite profitable for the pioneering firm. As the product moves to the mass market stage, it begins to attract imitators and loses its initial uniqueness; profits begin to wane. Price cutting, low profit margins, and widespread imitation characterize the market saturation stage. At this point, the firm hopes to have the next product innovation ready to introduce. Only a few brands and products—Crisco, Jello, Campbell's Tomato Soup, and so on—have escaped this product life cycle.

Branding permits the food manufacturer to quality-certify his products, transfer the goodwill of the firm to new products, and otherwise differentiate his product from competitors' products. A well-known and trusted brand can earn the food processor brand loyalty (a "consumer franchise") from customers. This can be helpful in introducing new products, forestalling consumer substitutions of less expensive brands, and prolonging the product life cycle.

Food processors in recent years have emphasized the development of convenience foods and stressed their "built-in maid service" aspects: TV dinners, boil-in-the-bag foods, instant coffee, minute desserts, and brown-and-serve rolls. Processors have also led in the development of new processing techniques—dehydrating, irradiating, freeze-drying—and in the use of new packaging materials such as foil, cellophane, polyethylene, and so on. The search for new food products continually spawns new industries. Sometimes they compete directly with older established industries; sometimes they complement or supplement them. The output of the frozen food industry has grown rapidly. This in many ways competes directly with the canning industry. The technique of freeze-drying foods, which was practically nonexistent before 1960, may eventually offer the meat packing industry a method of solving the many processing and distribution problems that stem from its very perishable product. The new processed potato products, which have increased dramatically in recent years, represent another example of a new processing industry, as potatoes were previously sold largely in an unprocessed form.

THE STRUCTURE OF FOOD MANUFACTURING

Like most manufacturing sectors, the number of food processors and manufacturers has been declining while the average size of plants has been increasing. There were 22,000 food product manufacturing companies operating

28,184 plants in 1972. As shown in Table 5-1, food manufacturing plants have a higher volume in sales than the average U.S. manufacturing plant. Also, a greater number of food plants are associated with multiple-plant companies than is the case for all manufacturing plants. The ownership pattern of food processing plants is very similar to that of all U.S. manufacturing operations.

Food processing plants tend to specialize by product lines. Flour millers are primarily engaged in milling flour; dairy processing and poultry plants are seldom used for processing other products. There is frequently some combining of processing of related products within a plant, however. For example, several types of vegetables may be processed in the same plant, and complementary products, such as butter and cheese, may be processed jointly. Modern livestock packing plants, for the most part, specialize in either hogs, cattle, or sheep.

Despite plant specialization, food processors are becoming increasingly diversified in their product lines. Ralston Purina, for instance, was initially a livestock feed company but now produces breakfast cereals, pet food, and owns a chain of restaurants. National Dairy became so diverse that its name was changed to Kraftco. The names Consolidated Foods and Standard Brands describe aptly the broad range of products handled by these contemporary food processors.

Many food processors are also subsidiaries of conglomerate companies owning both food and nonfood firms. Swift and Co. is associated with Esmark; Armour is owned by Greyhound; and Sunshine Biscuit Co. is owned by

Table 5-1. Characteristics of Food Manufacturers and Other Manufacturers, 1972.

CHARACTERISTIC	FOOD MANUFACTURERS	ALL U.S. MANUFACTURERS
Number of plants	28,184	320,710
Average plant sales ($000)	$4,080	2,360
Number of plants	100%	100%
1–19 employees	56	64
20–99 employees	30	25
100 or more employees	14	11
Number of plants	100%	100%
Corporations	72	73
Individually owned	12	13
Partnerships	7	7
Other	9	7
Number of plants	100%	100%
Multi-plant companies	30	22
Single-plant companies	70	78

Source: *U.S. Census of Manufacturing, 1972;* U.S. Bureau of the Census, 1973.

American Tobacco Company. Food processors have not resisted this diversification trend. Hunt Foods owns, among other things, a steel company, a paint company and a woman's magazine; Beatrice Foods has purchased companies producing hospital equipment and sporting goods. General Mills owns Parker Brothers and produces the game of Monopoly!

Table 5-2 shows considerable variation in the number and average size of food processing operations. Fewer but larger plants are more typical for soybean oil mills, breakfast cereal plants, shortening and oil plants, and beet sugar processors. Milk, bread, and canning plants tend to be more numerous but smaller in size. These differences in industry size-structure are the result of (1) economies of size in food processing plants; (2) the perishability and cost of transporting the final product; and (3) the geographic concentration of raw farm products, which affects the ease and costs of assembling large quantities for processing at a central location.

The food processing industry can be divided into two sectors: (1) a dominant core, which consists of a few very large firms producing well-known brands, which accounts for a significant share of industry sales; and (2) a competitive fringe, which consists of a large number of smaller firms producing less well-known brands, and which accounts for a small share of industry sales. The nature of these sectors varies for different products, but the dominant core firms are well known to most people. Some of the larger food manufacturing companies are listed in Table 5-3.

Competition between the dominant core and the competitive fringe of food processors focuses on branding, advertising, and prices. Dominant core processors tend to emphasize product quality, nationally advertised brands, and product innovation in their competitive strategies. Competitive fringe pro-

Table 5-2. Number and Average Sales of Food Manufacturers, By Industry, 1972.

	NUMBER		AVERAGE SALES PER PLANT
INDUSTRY	COMPANIES	PLANTS	($000)
Soybean oil mills	54	94	$35,710
Cereal breakfast foods	34	47	23,960
Shortening, cooking oils	64	109	18,970
Beet sugar	16	61	14,430
Meat packing	2,291	2,474	9,300
Poultry, egg processing	110	130	4,520
Canned fruit, vegetables	765	1,038	3,900
Fluid milk	2,025	2,507	3,750
Bread, related products	2,801	3,318	1,850

Source: *U.S. Census of Manufacturing, 1972,* U.S. Bureau of the Census, 1973.

Table 5-3. Sales of the Largest Food Manufacturing
Companies, 1977.

COMPANY	1977 SALES ($MILLION)
Procter and Gamble	7,284
Beatrice Foods	5,289
Kraftco	5,239
General Foods	4,910
Ralston Purina	3,756
Borden	3,481
General Mills	2,909
Consolidated Foods	2,892
United Brands	2,422
Carnation	2,335
Nabisco	2,118
Iowa Beef Processors	2,024
H. J. Heinz	1,869
Campbell Soup	1,769
Quaker Oats	1,551
Kellogg	1,533
Del Monte	1,484
Pillsbury	1,461
Oscar Meyer	1,188
Nonfood companies:	
General Motors	54,961
Exxon	54,126
I. B. M.	18,133
I. T. & T.	13,146
U.S. Steel	9,610

Source: "The Fortune 500 Directory," *Fortune,* Time, Inc., May 8, 1978, p. 240–59. Reprinted by permission.

cessors frequently specialize in packing products under wholesaler and retailer private, or controlled, labels. These are not advertised as extensively, and usually retail at a lower price than the national brands. This competition is referred to as the "battle of the brands."

The size of the large food manufacturers is a concern to many. The dominance of firms in an industry is measured by market concentration—the share of total industry sales accounted for by a few of the largest companies. As shown in Figure 5-1, the four largest producers of breakfast cereals, wet corn millers, and processed seafoods accounted for more than 50 per cent of total industry sales in 1970. The four-firm market concentration of other food manufacturers varied from 24 per cent for meat packers to 47 per cent for malt liquor manufacturers. It is not true that market concentration is increasing in all food processing industries. For sixteen food industries, the four-firm market concentration of sales increased for four industries,

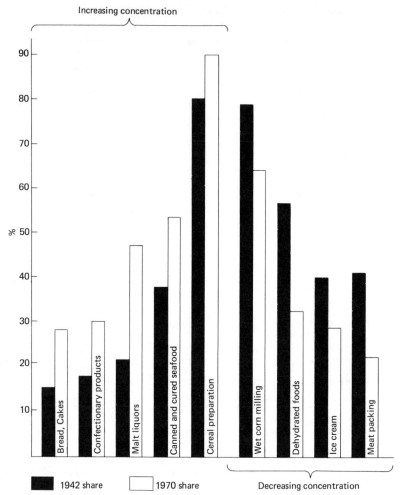

Figure 5–1. Market share of the four largest firms in selected food industries, 1942 and 1970. (U.S. Bureau of the Census)

decreased for six industries, and was stable for six other industries between 1963 and 1972.[1]

These changes in market share concentration of the dominant food processors reflect new processing technologies, changes in the location of food manufacturing, the success of fringe processors in competing with core firms, and other dynamic market conditions.

---

[1] *U.S. Census of Manufacturing, 1972;* "Concentration Ratios," U.S. Bureau of the Census, 1973.

THE LOCATION OF FOOD PROCESSING

The historical development of the United States has left its mark on the various food industries. As the country has expanded and agricultural production moved into new geographic areas, many of the processing industries have also moved. This has resulted in unused capacities and high costs in the firms that were left operating in old areas.

The grain milling industry is a good example of an industry that has undergone considerable movement. Milling first developed in the Atlantic coastal states. There it was near both wheat supplies and the water power to operate the mills. Then, as new wheat areas farther west were opened, Cincinnati and afterward St. Louis became important milling centers. With the growth of wheat production in the Northwest during the first years of the twentieth century, Minneapolis developed into the nation's leading milling center. Then as the wheatlands of the Southwest were opened, Kansas City rose in importance. Finally, a change in the freight-rate structure in 1920, plus the growing opportunity to mill Canadian wheat, led to the growth of the Buffalo, New York mills. As each of the gradual changes took place, much mill capacity was left in the declining area. Today it is the usual situation for the milling industry to operate at levels much below total capacity.

The East Coast packing industry is to some degree the vestigial remains of the earlier years before the development of the livestock industry in the Midwest. At first much livestock was shipped to the East alive, for slaughter. The end product, meat, was so perishable that processing had to be done near the center of consumption. However, with the development of refrigerator cars, Chicago and other midwestern cities became important packing centers. The packing industry in the past two decades has again followed production into the western part of the Corn Belt. Today there is excess and unused slaughter capacity in many of the major terminals of the eastern Corn Belt, such as Chicago.

The fact that the country is now settled will not protect industries against location change. New refrigeration, transportation, and other technological developments will continue to change existing patterns. For example, new developments in whole milk transportation are tearing down the past barriers which restricted milk collection and distribution to relatively limited areas. Milk plants are consolidating and getting larger. At the same time, the area in which they can effectively sell their products is increasing. Therefore, the number of effective competitors in a given town may not be decreasing even though the independent dairy in that town has been forced out of business.

Changes in the location of food-processing industries over the 1958–1972 period are shown in Table 5-4. Overall, there has been a movement of food

Table 5-4. Location of Food Manufacturing Plants, 1958 and 1972.

	NUMBER OF PLANTS				
PLANT TYPES	NORTHEAST STATES	NORTH CENTRAL STATES	SOUTHERN STATES	WESTERN STATES	U.S.
All food products					
1958	8,117	10,660	6,953	4,612	30,342
1972	6,309	8,632	8,024	5,219	28,184
Meat products					
1958	1,145	1,901	1,655	827	5,528
1972	813	1,471	1,474	679	4,437
Dairy products					
1958	2,700	4,618	1,470	1,091	9,879
1972	1,158	2,012	776	644	4,590
Canners and freezers					
1958	651	781	714	774	2,920
1972	534	685	565	773	2,557
Grain mill products					
1958	142	307	518	138	1,105
1972	352	1,171	1,052	505	3,080
Bakery products					
1958	28	107	276	71	482
1972	122	253	333	153	861

Source: *U.S. Census of Manufacturing, 1958 and 1972,* U.S. Bureau of the Census.

manufacturing from the Northeast and North Central states to the southern and western states. This trend resulted from population migration, changes in the geographic location of agriculture, and changes in the way foods are marketed. Many other factors affect plant location decisions, including taxes, labor supply, community facilities, and personal preferences of managers. History, too, has left its mark on the location of food processing. The breakfast cereal industry is centered in Michigan because both W. K. Kellogg and C. W. Post were patients at the same Michigan health sanitarium at the turn of the century.

Usually, the location of a particular food processing plant will depend upon the costs of transporting raw farm products to the plant and of shipping the processed product to consumers. Generally, if the farm product is quite bulky in comparison to the final product, and the unit value of the final product is higher than that of the farm product, the plant will probably be located near the source of farm products. This is the case for flour milling, meat packing, and butter and cheese manufacturing. On the other hand, if the final product is more perishable than the farm product, the plant will tend to be located nearer to consumers, as with baking, and milk and ice cream plants. The food processor will attempt to minimize the combined costs of raw product and finished product transportation. If raw products are cheaper to transport than final products, the plant location decision will be consumer-oriented. If raw products are more expensive to transport than final products, the location decision will be production-oriented. It should be clear that a change in either the cost of shipping farm products or final products might result in a shift to a lower-cost plant site.

THE LAW OF MARKET AREAS

Many food processors sell in only local or regional markets and others distribute foods nationwide. Usually, the national processors are multi-plant companies with processing and distribution facilities located throughout the country. This raises the question of how processors decide the size of market territory to service from each plant and distribution center. The law of market areas (LOMA) can help answer this question.[2]

The law of market areas states that the territorial boundary between two or more markets or plants is a locus of points such that the final selling prices, including transportation costs, are equal for sellers in each market. The law assumes that everything is equal between competing sellers, except the cost of transporting final products to buyers.

The LOMA is illustrated in Figure 5-2. Plant *A* has a factory price of $2.00/case and plant *B* has a higher cost and price of $3.00/case. The two plants will divide up the 500-mile market area between them in such a way

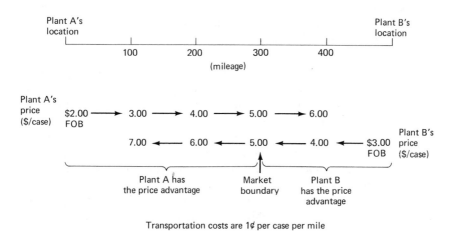

Transportation costs are 1¢ per case per mile

Figure 5–2. The law of market areas.

[2] This law is usually credited to F. A. Fetter's paper, "The Economic Law of Market Areas," *Quarterly Journal of Economics,* May 1924, pp. 520–29.

that plant *A* will service a 300-mile range and plant *B* will service a 200-mile range. At this point or market boundary, each plant is charging the same price of $5.00. At all other points, either plant *A* or plant *B* has a competitive advantage. Note that a change in plant costs or prices will shift the market boundary.

PROBLEMS OF FOOD PROCESSORS

Food processors experience problems and face challenges in three major areas.

Processing Problems

Food processing involves significant investments in plant and equipment. In order to operate efficiently, these facilities should be used to full capacity all year-round, every year. This is difficult to achieve when there are wide variations in farm product supplies from year to year and within seasons. Because of the short-term harvest season of many farm products, food processing plants operate at above-capacity rates for a few months of the year and at below-capacity rates for the rest of the year. These variations can influence significantly food processing costs. Some progress has been made in improving the full utilization of food processing plants. Expanded storage facilities, contracts that coordinate farm supplies with processor needs, and extension of the processing season by manufacturing nonseasonal food items have contributed to the solution of this problem.

Processors face a dilemma when deciding on the number and size of plants to build. The operational efficiency gains of large, central processing facilities can be nullified by the costs of assembling large quantities of raw farm products and transporting final products to consumers from centralized operations. Replacing a single, large plant with several smaller ones reduces some assembly and transport costs but may require sacrificing the operational efficiencies of large-scale, centralized plants.

A major thrust of food processors in recent years has been the replacement of human labor with machines and equipment. The continuous increase in labor costs has given added incentives for mechanizing and speeding up food processing operations. Labor costs accounted for 42 per cent of food processing costs in 1973, compared to 38 per cent in 1963.[3] Batch operations are giving way to continuous assembly-line techniques. New machines and processes are continually being experimented with. Technical changes in recent years have been so widespread and rapid in some fields that it often is more economical to shut down an old plant and build a new one than to remodel

---

[3] U.S. Department of Agriculture.

the old one. Since the end of World War II, the number of production workers employed by the food industry has tended to decline, but capital expenditures have increased sharply.

Buying Operations

All manufacturers are faced with supply problems. Any manufacturer desires to assure himself of an adequate amount of the desired kind and quality of raw material at the lowest possible cost. He may depend either upon other marketing agencies to do his purchasing for him or he may undertake to set up his own procurement machinery. One of two considerations may force the processor to become his own assembler. He may be dissatisfied with the operation of the existing agencies which are supposed to serve him. They may be slow in making improvements or otherwise operating inefficiently and at high cost, from the manufacturer's viewpoint. Or the processor may wish control over the machinery for his own competitive safety or to make his buying power a more effective price-affecting force.

Food processors utilize a wide variety of ways to procure their materials from farmers. Generally, meat and poultry processors use the existing independent agencies to secure their supplies. Many packing firms operate their own country buying points. However, the large majority of assembly agencies for livestock and poultry operate independently of slaughterers and packers. To a considerable extent the grain milling industries also depend upon the independent country elevator operators and terminal market merchants for procuring grain from the farmer. Nevertheless, some millers have become owners of elevators in the production areas. Also, some corn products manufacturers, who have developed a special variety of corn that best satisfies their needs, contract directly with farmers for its production.

Butter, cheese, and other milk product manufacturers, on the other hand, are their own country buying and assembly agencies. They often operate their own truck routes to pick up milk at the farms. Canners are also direct country buying agencies as well as processors. They often contract with the farmer for the products in advance of planting. In this way, both price and some indication of amount available for processing are established in advance.

Food processors have taken a more direct part in purchasing their raw supplies from farmers. Many processors use field men to work closely with producers. They also have been active in establishing pricing and contracting practices to encourage production in the desired volume and quality and have been active participants in contract integration activities with farmers.

Selling Strategies

As in procurement, processors are faced with the necessity of choosing between alternative methods of selling the finished product. They may either utilize the existing independent wholesale channels or set up their own sales organization to distribute products to retailers.

It is probably true that in the past food processors have been more interested in securing direct control over the selling phase of their operations than the buying phase. If the processor is large and has a relatively full line of products he will often operate his own warehouse and wholesaling system. If, on the other hand, his line of products is limited he will often have the sales work done for him by hiring a broker. Industries vary in the directions they have taken.

The meat packing industry, for example, has largely become its own wholesaler. It is handling a perishable commodity that has wide fluctuations in volume. In order to keep such a product moving effectively, many packers consider it imperative that they have control of the distribution channel to the retailer and operate their own wholesaling establishments.

The milling industry offers a good illustration of the way an industry adapts itself to changing conditions. Originally, flour millers shipped their flour on consignment to commission men in the consuming areas. These commission men sold and delivered the flour to retail stores who were their principal customers. However, abuse by some unscrupulous commission men gave rise to flour brokers. The broker acted as the miller's sales agent, but the miller himself kept control of the transportation and delivery arrangements. Then came the widespread movement away from home baking and the rise of large commercial bakeries. Bakers, not retail stores, became the principal flour consumers. This development of relatively large-volume customers caused the miller again to revamp his selling methods. Now large millers, like the packers, operate their own wholesaling organizations with direct salesmen and strategically located branch houses to facilitate delivery.

Though the processing units for butter and cheese are small, many have grown into large organizations with their own wholesaling setup. The large-scale canners also have developed their own wholesaling organization to sell directly to retailers. However, the small independent canner cannot afford his own selling organization. He must depend upon independent brokers and commission men to sell his products.

Although the competitive fringe food processors largely rely on price competition for their success, the national processors concentrate their selling efforts on innovation, quality, and other forms of non-price competition. Considerable resources are devoted to mass-media advertising, coupons, free samples, cents-off deals, promotional trade allowances, and point-of-purchase merchandising materials. These forms of competition have been criticized as cost and food price increasing. However, these promotional strategies can result in lower consumer prices. Also, consumers can choose between the highly promoted manufactured foods and their private-label, lower-priced counterparts. Both forms of competition appear to fill a need in the marketplace.

SUMMARY

The principle function of the food processing sector is to add form utility to farm products. This involves food processing operations, new product development, product changes and improvements, packaging, labeling, and branding. Competitive rivalry between food processors for the customer's favor centers on products, prices, and promotional programs. The battle of the brands is being waged between nationally advertised and lesser-known, unadvertised food product labels. The food processing industry is composed of large and small firms, corporate and individually owned companies, single- and multi-plant organizations, as well as specialized and diversified firms. Market concentration is increasing in some lines of food processing but decreasing in others. Food processors may locate in either production or consumption areas, depending upon transportation costs and product perishability. The chief marketing problems of food processors relate to the operational efficiency of their plants, their need to coordinate the flow of raw products from the farm, and their competitive selling strategies.

QUESTIONS FOR DISCUSSION

1. What would be the best marketing strategy for a small food processor just starting operations?

2. Give the reasons why many food companies are purchasing nonfood firms and nonfood firms are buying food processing operations?

3. Food engineers have suggested that the size, number, and location of food processing plants will depend on raw product transport costs, final transport costs, and the economies of plant size. How would these three factors affect those decisions.

4. Critics of the food industry sometimes allege that food processors manipulate consumer tastes and preferences through their advertising and merchandising programs. What does this mean, and do you agree or disagree?

5. Business theorists conclude that the law of market areas results in hexagonal, honeycomb market territories when there are several competing firms. Prove this. Why is it that actual selling territories do not follow this pattern?

6. Through cooperatives, such as the Sunkist Corp. or the Welch Grape Juice Company, farmers have become owners and operators of food processing facilities. Why have they done this? What are the pros and cons?

7. It has been suggested that food processors are too big and that the monopolies should be broken up. Do you agree? Why or why not?

SELECTED REFERENCES

APPLEBAUM, W., AND R. A. GOLDBERG. *Brand Stratagy in United States Food Marketing.* Harvard University Press, Cambridge, Mass., 1967.

ARNOLD, R. J. *Diversification and Profitability Among Large Food Processing Firms.* U.S. Department of Agriculture. Agricultural Economic Report No. 171, Jan. 1970.

BUZZELL, R. D., AND R. E. M. NOURSE. *Product Innovation in Food Processing.* Harvard University Graduate School of Business, Boston, 1967.

Economic Report on the Influence of Market Structure on the Profit Performance of Food Manufacturing Companies. Staff Report, Federal Trade Commission, Sept. 1969.

LANZILOTTI, R. F. "The Superior Market Position of Food Processing and Agricultural Supply Firms—Its Relation to the Farm Problem." *Journal of Farm Economics* (Dec. 1960), 1228–47.

MOORE, J. R., AND R. G. WALSH. *Market Structure of the Agricultural Industries.* Iowa State University Press, Ames, Iowa, 1966.

The Structure of Food Manufacturing. National Commission on Food Marketing. Technical Study No. 8, Washington D.C., July 1966.

Studies in Organization and Competition in Grocery Manufacturing. National Commission on Food Marketing. Technical Study No. 6, Washington D.C., July 1966.

WALDORF, W. H. *Demand for Manufactured Foods, Manufacturer's Services, and Farm Products in Food Manufacturing—A Statistical Analysis.* U.S. Department of Agriculture. Technical Bulletin No. 1317, Dec. 1964.

CHAPTER 6

Food Wholesaling and Retailing

"RETAILING IS and has always been an expensive economic function. The output of our economy which has been mass produced and mass handled must be broken up into small lots and sold, usually as individual items, to millions of individual consumers. This process requires the use of substantial amounts of human labor . . . an expensive economic resource. Despite significant efficiency gains through mass retailing systems and improved equipment, [food] retailing costs represent a large component of the cost of [food]."*

Preview

- This chapter examines the nature of food wholesaling and retailing and their roles in the food industry.
- Emphasis is given to the competitive adjustments food wholesalers and retailers have made over the years.
- The reasons for and effects of the supermarket and chainstore movements are studied.
- The belief that food wholesaling and retailing are simply "pass-through" activities in the food industry is evaluated.
- The nature of competition in food retail markets is explored.
- Food retail pricing tactics that reduce the dependence of retail prices on farm prices are reviewed.
- Key terms and concepts:

affiliated retail chainstore	cooperative groups
chainstore movement	food brokers
channel captain	gatekeeper

* D. I. Padberg, *Economics of Food Retailing,* Cornell University Food Distribution Program, Ithaca, New York, 1968.

gross margin

loss leader

mix pricing

private label

variable price merchandising

voluntary groups

wheel of retailing

Food wholesaling and retailing represent the final stages of the food marketing channel. In an earlier period, it was felt that these market agents simply passed along processed or fresh foods to the consumer, with little change or added value. It is now clear, however, that the wholesaling and retailing marketing functions and operations are quite complex, and that these firms are not simply pass-through agents. The efficiency with which the functions are performed at these levels, and the pricing-merchandising strategies of food retailers and wholesalers, substantially affect everyone else in the food industry.

PRINCIPAL CHANGES IN FOOD WHOLESALING AND RETAILING

Food wholesaling and retailing are prime examples of how marketing agencies change in response to competitive conditions. These market agencies have experienced continual change and adjustment in the twentieth century.

Contrast the turn-of-the-century "ma and pa" corner grocery store with the modern supermarket. Gone for the most part are the neighborhood markets, cracker barrels and other bulk-sales arrangements, personal service, credit, and home delivery. These were replaced with large supermarkets which handle a much wider variety of foods and nonfood items on a self-service, cash-and-carry basis. This trend reflected changing consumer preferences, competitive pressures, and changes in the relationships of food processors, wholesalers, and retailers.

The market agencies we are concerned with in this chapter are depicted in Figure 6-1. A complex network of relationships between processors, wholesalers, and retailers has evolved over time. For example, most food retailers are affiliated in some way with food wholesalers, and many food retail firms also own processing facilities. By the same token, many food processors operate their own wholesaling operations. Through sales offices and branch warehouses, they deal directly with retail buyers. Some food processing firms also compete indirectly with retail grocery stores through the ownership of restaurants. Thus, food processors and wholesalers are expanding their activities beyond their traditional range of marketing functions.

108

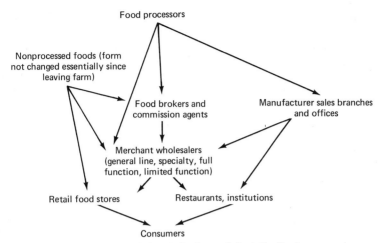

Figure 6–1. Structure of the wholesale–retail food distribution network.

FOOD WHOLESALING

Food wholesaling is a major step in the dispersion activities of marketing. Essentially, the food wholesaler operates between the food processor and the retailer. The food retailer stocks relatively small amounts of literally thousands of very different items. Retailers, who are primarily interested in the problems that arise from servicing their customers, could not possibly search out and deal with the producer and processor sources of all their products. On the other hand, processors cannot, in many circumstances, profitably service the small-unit needs of retailers. To assemble efficiently these various products in reasonable quantities from the relatively specialized processors and to sell them in smaller quantities is the job of the food whole-saler. Thus, the merchant wholesaler who actually buys and brings the needed products together is a focal point in the distribution scene.

Types of Wholesalers

Table 6-1 shows the number of establishments and sales volume for various food wholesaling operations in 1972. On the average, food wholesale opera-tions tend to be smaller than food processors or retailers. As shown in Table 6-1, the average sales of general-line grocery wholesaler firms were $7.7 million in 1972. However, there are many larger wholesale food operations of retailers not included in these figures.

Merchant wholesalers of various kinds are the most important type of wholesaler who sells to grocers. Generally speaking, commission agents and brokers do relatively little business directly with retailers. They operate more

Table 6-1. Numbers, Sizes, and Types of U.S. Food Wholesaling
Agencies, 1972.

TYPE OF ESTABLISHMENT	NUMBER OF ESTABLISHMENTS	AVERAGE SALES PER ESTABLISHMENT (MILLION DOLLARS)
Merchant wholesalers		
General-line grocery	2,818	$7.7
Dairy products	2,924	1.3
Poultry products	2,278	1.4
Meats, seafoods	6,411	0.9
Fresh fruits, vegetables	5,877	1.2
Grains	8,257	2.8
Livestock	2,035	2.7
Manufacturer sales branches and offices	4,043	5.4
Agents and brokers	7,413	5.3

Source: *U.S. Census of Business, 1972,* U.S. Bureau of the Census.

closely with other wholesalers. Merchant wholesalers may be classified on
the basis of the functions they perform. The service or full-function wholesaler
performs all the various marketing functions to some degree. He is an expert
in buying goods, and the retailer often looks to him for advice on what to
stock and how to merchandise individual items to the best advantage. He
extends a line of credit and delivers to his retailers. He often helps the retailer
set up his merchandising program, including suggested retail prices and advertisements for weekly "specials" in local newspapers. The full-function wholesaler may even provide bookkeeping services to retail stores. Because he
must be able to furnish retailers with small quantities at frequent intervals,
he stores large amounts of food in the form of inventory stocks.

In contrast, the limited-function wholesaler does not perform this complete
line of services. He may be a cash-and-carry merchant, extending no credit
or giving no delivery. He may set up order-size requirements for his customers,
thus requiring them to order larger amounts less frequently. Many of the
manufacturers' sales branches are limited-function wholesalers.

In addition to this functional basis, wholesalers may be classified as to
the kinds of goods they handle. The general-line grocery wholesaler will
stock a wide variety of goods so that a retailer can secure all his grocery
needs from one wholesaler. In the majority of cases he will also handle
frozen foods and dairy products. Relatively few wholesalers are completely
full-line to the extent that they handle meat, fresh produce, and bakery goods.
In contrast to the general-line wholesaler is the specialty wholesaler. He
handles only one line or a few closely related lines. For example, he may
specialize in fruits and vegetables, meat, flour, or breakfast cereals. A large

portion of the food wholesale business is done by the general-line wholesalers. The specialty wholesaler and food broker, however, have had a strong attraction for food processors. The processor can expect these specialized agencies to become expert salesmen for his particular product. He may also find them more likely to cooperate closely in processor-originating advertising and sales campaigns to push particular goods.

Manufacturers' sales branches, as would be expected, tend to be large in size. In addition, when a manufacturer is large enough to establish his own wholesale facilities he will generally have more than one unit.

Food brokers are rather small-unit operations. Many are highly specialized but some handle broad lines of goods. In a study of grocery brokers it was found the average broker represented twenty-two manufacturers. He had about eight salesmen and called on thirty-two wholesalers, eight chain buyers, and 550 retail food stores. From another viewpoint, the typical manufacturer sells through seventy broker firms.[1]

All three of these major types of wholesalers are growing in terms of the volume of business handled by individual firms. The trend is clearly toward fewer wholesalers doing larger volumes of business. This trend toward bigness emphasizes the importance of volume for efficient wholesaling.

Changes in the Wholesaler's Position

Historically, the independent wholesaler occupied a position of considerable influence in the food marketing channel. The small, independent retailer depended upon him for help in stocking his store and often for considerable amounts of credit. Processors also depended upon him to stock and sell their goods to retailers.

The power of the wholesaler began to decline with the advent of the food retailing chain. Very early in its development, the chain organization bypassed the independent wholesaler, set up warehousing facilities of its own, and began to buy directly from the processor. As a measure of self-preservation, independent wholesalers became active in forming closer arrangements with independent retailers who also were fighting a battle with the chain stores. The wholesaler-retailer affiliations are known as voluntary or cooperative groups, and they have become a very important part of the retailing picture. Sales of retailer-affiliated wholesalers have grown much faster than the sales of independent wholesalers. Affiliated wholesalers accounted for 51 per cent of wholesale food sales in 1954 and 75 per cent of these sales in 1972.[2] The growth of affiliated retail-wholesale operations put competitive pressures on the independent and specialty-line wholesalers. Many of these wholesalers responded by concentrating their sales efforts on the growing restaurant and institutional food-service operations.

---

[1] Special Food Broker Survey, *Progressive Grocer,* December 5, 1964.

[2] *U.S. Census of Business: Wholesale Trade, 1972,* U.S. Bureau of the Census.

All food wholesalers have searched for improved operating efficiencies. Labor costs account for about one half of food wholesaling costs. As a result of increased labor efficiency, larger operations, automation, and computerization, operating costs of general-line grocery wholesalers declined from 9.1 per cent of sales in 1929 to 7.1 per cent in 1972. This compares with a *rise* in operating costs over the same period, from 11.7 per cent to 13.9 per cent of sales, for all merchant wholesalers.[3]

These changes in food wholesaling are excellent illustrations of competitive responses to market trends. Each adjustment of wholesalers represents a successful meeting of a challenge. Firms that adjusted survived; those who failed to adjust are no longer operating.

FOOD RETAILING

The retailer is the food wholesaler's principal partner in the marketing process of dispersion. Here, products are placed before the individual consumer for acceptance or rejection. Like many wholesalers, the retailer will perform all the marketing functions to some degree. He must properly buy and arrange for sale literally thousands of different items that may be desired by his customers. A modern supermarket now offers over 11,000 items, and within the year some 1,000 new items will be offered and many old items withdrawn. Some of these items move rapidly in large volume, whereas others have a very slow turnover. The store manager must continually watch his inventory so that all these items are in available supply. Some items are highly perishable and require elaborate storage equipment and continual sorting and discarding of unsalable material. Display space must be properly allocated. The retailer carries on the wholesaler's breakdown job. For example, the wholesaler may purchase several bushels of apples or a carload lot of breakfast food. These items then are sold in smaller lots to the retailers, who then must package the apples for sale in 5-pound lots and display the individual boxes of cereal. Through advertising he furnishes information to his customers as to price and quality of goods that are available. Finally, he may carry the groceries to the buyer's car or perhaps even deliver them to the home.

Food retailing is big business. In 1975 consumers spent 17 per cent of their after-tax income for food; food purchases accounted for 19 per cent of total consumer expenditures; and, as shown in Table 6-2, food stores captured 23 per cent of all retail dollars spent by consumers. The modern grocery store, of course, sells more than food. It is estimated that about 22 per cent of grocery store sales are for nonfood items.[4]

---

[3] *U.S. Census of Business: Wholesale Trade, 1929, 1972,* U.S. Bureau of the Census.

[4] *Food Topics,* annual survey, 1975.

Table 6-2. U.S. Retail Sales, By Types of Stores, 1975.

RETAIL STORE	PER CENT OF RETAIL SALES
Food stores	23%
Automotive dealers	17
Department stores	11
Eating, drinking places	8
Gasoline service stations	8
Lumber, bldg. materials, hardware dealers	6
Furniture, home furnishings, equipment stores	4
Apparel, accessory stores	4
Drug stores, proprietary stores	3
Liquor stores	2
Variety stores	2
Mail order	1
Other retail stores	11
Total	100%

Source: Reprinted from *Progressive Grocer,* 1975, with permission.

Food retailing is one of the most expensive of the food marketing sectors. Retail marketing functions accounted for 29 per cent of the total cost of food marketing in 1974, compared to 23 percent in 1958.[5] Efforts are being made to improve the efficiency of food retailing operations. However, in recent years efficiency gains have been slower in retailing than in food wholesaling and processing. Consequently, the cost of food retailing has been rising.

Food retailing can be divided into two sectors: the home food market (grocery stores) and the food-for-off-premise consumption market (restaurants and institutional feeding operations). Although the away-from-home food market is growing rapidly, retail food stores still dominate the food retailing picture. In 1975, grocery store sales of food for home consumption totalled $140 billion, and sales of food eaten away from home amounted to $41 billion.[6] It is estimated that about one meal in five is eaten out today. Yet, because food prices are generally higher in restaurants, the away-from-home food market accounts for one of every three food dollars spent.

---

[5] U.S. Department of Agriculture.
[6] U.S. Department of Agriculture.

The Changing Structure of Food Retailing

Like food wholesaling, the food retailing sector has experienced considerable change over the years. The rise of the chainstore, the development of supermarkets, the introduction of food discounters and convenience stores, the continual growth in variety of food products, and the battle between national and private food labels have all left their mark on food retailing. These trends represent food retailer adjustments to changing consumer demands and to competitive pressures. As in food wholesaling, survival in food retailing has required continual adaptation.

Table 6-3 indicates the changing size and number of retail food stores. Between 1950 and 1975 the number of foodstores fell 50 per cent while average sales per store rose from $67,000 per year to $746,000. As a result of new product innovation and brand competition, the number of items stocked by food stores increased from 1,800 in 1940 to almost 12,000 in 1975.

A very large number of retail food stores are relatively small, independent units. In 1969 about 60 per cent of them did less than $100,000 annual business. Only 7 per cent of the units did a $1 million or more annual business. Most of these small stores have no employed help other than the owner and his family. These are the "ma and pa" stores. Though comprising a large share of the store population, these small stores do a relatively small share of the total food business. Stores in this large group are very often high-cost stores. Their volume is too small to make practical the utilization of much of the cost-saving technology of modern food merchandising. However, this group often sells service in addition to food. They are the convenient neighborhood stores, extending credit, offering delivery, and often staying

Table 6-3. Number and Sales of Retail Food Stores, 1920–1970.

Year	Number of Food Stores (000)	Retail Food Store Sales ($Billion)	Average Sales per Food Store	Number of Food Items Carried
1920	375	$ 11.5	$ 30,667	700
1930	436	9.1	20,872	1,000
1940	446	9.0	20,179	1,800
1950	401	27.1	67,581	3,750
1960	260	51.7	198,846	5,900
1970	208	88.4	425,000	7,800
1975	192	143.3	746,354	11,600

Note: Food stores include grocery stores, retail bakeries, meat markets, produce markets, and other stores selling food for home consumption.

Source: *U.S. Census of Business: Retail Trade,* U.S. Bureau of the Census; *Progressive Grocer.* Reprinted from *Progressive Grocer,* 1975, with permission.

open nights and Sundays. Therefore, one must use considerable caution in directly comparing the price of goods sold through these stores with prices in other types of grocery stores. However, over time the very large store units have been taking an increasing amount of the total retail food business. In 1939 about 112,000 of the largest stores accounted for 70 per cent of the total food store sales; in 1954 only about 50,000 stores accounted for the same volume. In 1968 the number accounting for this portion of business was estimated to be about 18,000 stores.

There are a variety of retail food operations, including the full-line supermarket, the small neighborhood convenience store, the specialty food store (meats, produce, bakeries, and so on), home food-delivery services, and farmer-direct sales to consumers. As shown in Table 6-4, the supermarket is increasingly dominating the home food market. The share of home food sales by supermarkets and convenience stores increased from 27 per cent of total sales in 1955 to 60 per cent in 1975. This growth came at the expense of food sales by smaller grocery stores, specialty food markets, home-delivery services, and farmer-direct sales.

Table 6-4. Sales of Food for Home Use, 1955–1975.

	PERCENT OF SALES				
MARKET	1955	1960	1965	1970	1975
Supermarkets	27%	37	44	50	56
Convenience stores	*	*	1	2	4
Other grocery stores	43	37	33	27	22
Other food stores	11	10	8	9	9
Other stores	6	5	5	5	5
Home-delivered	9	7	5	4	2
Farmers, processors, wholesalers, other	4	4	4	3	3
Total	100	100	100	100	100

* Less than 1 per cent.
Source: U.S. Department of Agriculture.

From these trends alone, many conclude that retail food marketing has become monopolistic and dominated by the national corporate chainstore operations. Although it is certainly true that large supermarkets have displaced the "ma and pa" corner grocery store and many of the specialty foodstores, this is not conclusive evidence of monopolistic food retailing. For this judgment, one must understand the two important twentieth-century revolutions in food retailing: the chainstore movement and the supermarket movement.

The Food Chainstore Movement

Although the terms *chainstores* and *supermarkets* appear synonymous today, these two forms of food retailing developed quite independently and for somewhat different reasons. A grocery store is usually classified as a supermarket if its annual sales are $1,000,000, or more than $20,000 per week. A chainstore operation is a group of 11 or more related grocery stores. Chainstores may or may not be supermarkets and supermarkets may or may not be part of a chainstore operation.

The contemporary food chainstore operation represents both a horizontal affiliation of retail stores and a vertical affiliation of food retailing, wholesaling, and, often, processing activities. The chainstore movement grew out of a search for operational efficiencies through large-scale buying and selling, and because of the drive for competitive market advantage among food retailers. The origin of chain retailing is usually traced back to the establishment of the Great Atlantic and Pacific Tea Company in 1858. However, it was not until after World War I and during the decade of the 1920's that real growth occurred. By 1929 it was estimated that chainstores were doing about 38 per cent of the total business of combination grocery and meat stores. At about this time many food chains also reached their peak in number of outlets. For example, the A & P chain reached a peak of 15,737 stores in 1929; the Kroger Company also reached its peak of 5,575 stores in that year.

Originally the chainstore organization collected several retail outlets under one management in order to secure the price advantage of large-volume buying from wholesalers and processors. At the retail level they adopted the policy of cash-and-carry. They aimed for low-cost, large-volume operations and competed with low prices instead of with service.

In time, however, the chains were not satisfied with horizontal expansion into more retail outlets. They began moving to integrate vertically. They became their own wholesalers, often buying directly from growers in the production areas. To broaden their control over the marketing channel, they acquired various processing facilities. Large chains have acquired canning companies, cheese and butter firms, bakeries, and other miscellaneous food processors. These firms operate under the brand label and standards set by the chain. Chains also take large portions of the output of independent processors who meet the chain's standards and use its brand label.

Chainstore expansion was temporarily brought to a halt in the 1930's and 1940's by the general economic conditions, World War II, and the development of more vigorous competition from the voluntary and independent retailers' cooperative chain organizations. The number of chainstore units was reduced as the small-service grocery gave way to the large supermarkets.

The growth of food chainstores after World War II is depicted in Figure 6-2. Chainstores' market share of grocery store sales rose from 35 per cent

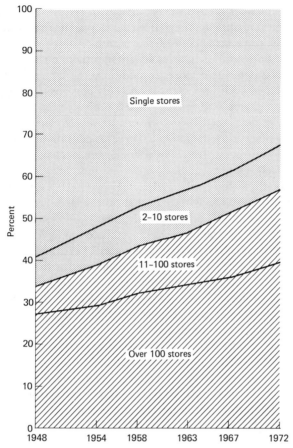

Figure 6–2. Distribution of grocery store sales by size of firm, 1948–1972. (U.S. Bureau of the Census)

in 1948 to 55 per cent in 1972. Nevertheless, even in 1972 single-store grocers still accounted for 33 per cent of food store sales. To be sure, the growth of food chains did displace the "ma and pa" corner grocery store, but this was not a complete market takeover by the large food chains. Many single stores remain and have survived by joining with wholesaling organizations.

The food chainstore movement triggered competitive reactions on the part of those threatened by it. Because both the independent retailer and the service wholesaler had much at stake, it was logical for these two groups to develop some kind of joint action. This joint action took the forms of retailer-owned cooperative wholesalers and the wholesaler-sponsored voluntary retail chains. In some instances independents organized to purchase and operate their own wholesale facilities cooperatively. In other instances a service wholesaler brought together several retailers into a voluntary chain

117

in which the wholesaler offered many services in return for the guaranteed business of the participating retailers. Both developments represented an effort to secure the low-price benefits of the corporate chain's mass buying power and at the same time retain whatever advantages there might be from owner operation of the independent store. In addition, the larger affiliated chains have made available such important services as advertising programs, store layout and design advice, and pricing guides. Similar to the corporate chains, these groups have developed their own private labels. They have also integrated into manufacturing operations. These organizations are an example of integration by contract instead of by a single management's outright ownership of all the facilities.

As a result of these competitive adjustments, food retailing is comprised of three segments today. The corporate chainstores (A & P, Kroger, Safeway, and so on) are the national and regional grocery wholesaling and retailing operations which are centrally managed. Affiliated independent chainstores (Super Value, Associated Grocers of Colorado, I.G.A. and so on) are independently owned grocery stores which have affiliated with food wholesaling operations in order to gain the economies of large-scale buying and to share the costs of retail services. There are also independent, unaffiliated chainstores not related in any formal way to a wholesaling operation. These grocers purchase from independent wholesalers.

Affiliated retail chainstores have been quite successful in competing with the corporate chainstores. Table 6-5 shows that between 1940 and 1964 the share of grocery sales made by affiliated independents rose from 30 to 50 per cent, whereas the market share of corporate chains rose from 36 to 41 per cent. Both chainstore types gained at the expense of the unaffiliated grocer.

Table 6-5. Market Shares of Food Chainstores, 1940–1975.

	INDEPENDENT CHAINSTORES			CORPORATE CHAIN-
YEAR	AFFILIATED	UNAFFILIATED	TOTAL	STORES
	Per Cent of Total Grocery Sales			
1940	30%	34	64	36
1945	32	37	69	31
1950	33	30	63	37
1958	45	16	61	39
1964	50	9	59	41
1969	46	8	54	46
1972	44	7	51	49
1975	NA	NA	50	50

Source: Reprinted from *Progressive Grocer*, 1975, with permission.

By 1975 there were few unaffiliated chainstores left, and grocery sales were about equally divided between the corporate chains and the affiliated independent chains. Thus, by imitating the corporate chains' movement into food wholesaling, the independent chainstores had gained a parity of competitive position.

The Supermarket Movement

The food chainstore movement was motivated by a competitive drive for greater retail operational efficiency. There is no doubt chainstores lowered the costs of food retailing as compared with the independent, single store "ma and pa" operations they displaced. The supermarket movement grew out of a competitive race to not only further lower food retailing costs but also to add greater utility to food shopping. The chainstore was economy-minded, the supermarket is merchandise-oriented.

The supermarket is best described as a full-line, departmentalized, cash-and-carry, self-service food store. This contrasts with its predecessors, the neighborhood, limited-line, full-service grocery store and the general store. Supermarkets can be thought of as food department stores. The supermarket gained operational economies over earlier food stores. Self-service reduced labor expense by transferring clerking jobs to consumers—another illustration of the principle that marketing functions can be transferred but not eliminated. The larger volume of supermarket sales, as well as specialized departmentalization of activities, also lowered retail costs.

Important to the evolution of the supermarket were the socio-economic changes taking place in consumer markets in the 1940's and 1950's. These included suburbanization, the development of shopping centers, rising consumer incomes, the greater shopping mobility provided by the automobile, the growth in home freezer facilities, the increased use of mass-media advertising, and the increased tempo of new food product development. The one-stop shopping environment provided by the supermarket was nurtured by the new American life style of the 1950's. Indeed, the supermarket became an American symbol of innovation, affluence, abundance, efficiency, and the good life.

Somewhat surprisingly, the supermarket was pioneered in the 1930's and 1940's by independent grocers, not by the corporate chainstores. The chainstores with established investments in smaller, neighborhood stores were slower to adapt to the supermarket form of food retailing. However, the superiority of supermarkets soon became evident, and virtually all retailers converted to them in the 1950's.

The 1970's brought further changes in food retailing. Supermarkets developed in a number of directions. Conventional supermarkets were joined by combination food-nonfood stores, food-drug stores, warehouse food outlets (where food is displayed in cases and consumers mark their own prices),

119

and discount supermarkets. Each of these retail store types found a competitive niche in the market and satisfied a unique set of consumer wants. Modern consumers face a wide variety of retail foodstore choices. There are neighborhood convenience stores, farm-roadside markets, mail-order food stores, consumer food buying clubs operating out of basements, and a host of other types of stores. From these, consumers can select their preferred product bundle of price, variety, service, frills, and conveniences.

COMPETITION AND PRICING IN FOOD RETAILING

The growing size of food chainstore organizations and their strategic position in the food industry raise many questions. Are food retailers too large and too powerful? Is there effective competition among food retailers? How do food retail pricing and merchandising strategies affect the sales and prices of others in the food industry?

Competition among food retailers today is certainly different from that of earlier periods, when neighborhood "ma and pa" grocery stores and general stores operated. The chainstore and supermarket movements have transformed food retailing in the direction of larger and more powerful firms. The small, independent grocers lost out in this process. Yet it does not automatically follow that competition in food retailing is less vigorous today than formerly. Independent affiliated retailers appear to have gained a parity of competitive position with the large corporate chains. There is no indication that the independent retailers are at a cost or merchandising disadvantage in competing with the national chains. On the contrary, in many local markets aggressive, independent retailers enjoy larger market shares than the national chains.

Consumer trends, such as increased mobility and income, have also added to the vigor of food retailing competition. Today's food shopper is no longer limited to the corner market which provides her with credit. Moreover, restaurants are an important factor in the food retailing environment today. It is difficult to judge the overall trend in food retailing competition, but it is by no means certain that competitive forces in retail food markets are less active today than in an earlier period.

The competitive flux in food retailing is illustrated by Table 6-6. The market share of the nation's largest corporate chainstore fell from 10.7 to 4.9 per cent between 1948 and 1975. Over the same period, the market share of the largest four chains fell from 20 per cent to 18 per cent. The evidence suggests that, over these years, the smaller chains grew more rapidly than the larger ones.

Market shares in local areas are frequently higher than the national figures implied by Table 6-6. None of the national chainstores operate in every city, and the large chainstores often do not meet head to head in every market.

Table 6-6. Market Shares of the 20 Largest Grocery Chains, 1948–1975.

RANK OF CHAINS	SHARE OF GROCERY STORE SALES						
	1948	1954	1958	1963	1967	1972	1975
A & P	10.7%	11.3	11.1	9.4	8.3	6.6	4.9
1st to 4th	20.1	20.9	21.7	20.0	19.0	18.1	17.9
5th to 8th	3.6	4.5	5.8	6.6	6.7	7.1	7.6
1st to 8th	23.7	25.4	27.5	26.6	25.7	25.2	25.5
9th to 20th	3.2	4.5	6.6	7.4	8.7	11.9	11.5
1st to 20th	26.9	29.9	34.1	34.0	34.4	37.1	37.0
Top 20 excluding A & P	16.2	18.7	23.0	24.6	26.1	30.5	32.1

Source: U.S. Census of Business; Federal Trade Commission, "Weekly Digest"; American Institute of Food Distribution.

A & P stores are concentrated in markets east of the Mississippi River; Safeway is primarily a western chainstore; Kroger stores are concentrated in the Midwest. In 1975, the four largest food retailers accounted for 31 per cent of grocery sales in the New York metropolitan area, and another four chains accounted for 57 per cent of Chicago area food sales.[7] Moreover, the average share of food sales made by the four largest grocery retailers in 194 metropolitan markets increased from 45 per cent in 1954 to 52 per cent in 1972.[8]

Just what the impact of this size and concentration has on the pricing efficiency of the food marketing system is one of the major current debates. That large retailing units struggle fiercely among themselves for the consumer's patronage seems to be true. However, it seems also true that the very large volumes that many retail firms handle and their great importance in selected areas give them great bargaining power with processors and other market agencies that wish to distribute their products in these areas.

The retail gross margin—the difference between what retailers pay for food and what they sell it for—is the "cost" of performing the food retail marketing functions. The gross margin includes all operating costs and net profits. Expressed as a percentage of sales, gross margin is widely regarded as a measure of trends in food retailing costs, efficiency, and profits. As shown in Figure 6-3, food retail gross margins generally fell from 1932 to 1950, reflecting operational efficiencies of the chainstore and supermarket movements. Food retail gross margins rose in the 1950's as a result of increased promotional and labor expenses and profit rates. Retail gross margins were relatively stable from 1963 to 1975, as the result of efficiency gains which

[7] *1976 Market Scope,* The Progressive Grocer Company, 1976.

[8] *The Profit and Price Performance of Leading Food Chains, 1970–74,* Joint Economic Committee of the Congress, U.S. Government Printing Office, April 12, 1977, p. 16.

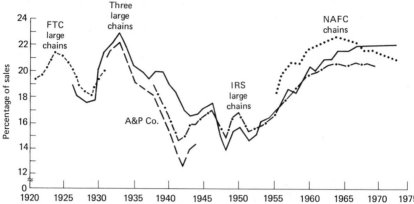

Figure 6–3. Retail gross margins of large food chains, 1921–1975. (Internal Revenue Service; Federal Trade Commission; National Association of Food Chains. Reprinted by permission)

offset, to some extent, rising labor costs, the growth of food discounters, and a price war touched off by the A & P Company in 1972.

This cyclical trend in food retail gross margins follows a familiar pattern called the wheel of retailing. Retailers tend to alternate between an emphasis on low service/low prices, and high service/high prices in attracting customers. The chainstore movement and the original supermarket movement of the 1930's represented the economy phase of the cycle. The high-service supermarket of the 1950's, with its trading stamps, games, and expensive facilities, represented the service phase of the cycle. The food discounting of the 1960's suggests another turn in the cycle.

Food retail pricing and merchandising practices are of special concern to farmers and consumers. Allegedly, through their pricing and promotional policies, food retailers influence consumer demand, farm prices, and the movement of farm products. Undoubtedly modern food retailing is more than just a conduit for passing through foods and farm prices to consumers. Pricing foods at retail is a complex process, for two reasons. First, food retailers are multi-product sellers, and second, they set prices to differentiate their stores from those of competitors. That is, retail food prices are a form of promotion. As a result, these prices are sometimes influenced more by consumer demand and competitive objectives of grocers than by farm prices.

Food retailers price each food product as a component of a total mix of foods (and nonfoods) offered by the store. *Mix pricing* provides the retailer considerable latitude in pricing any one food. Although total dollar sales must cover retail operating costs and the costs of purchased merchandise, there is no requirement that each retail food price must follow wholesale or farm prices. One store manager may elect to feature low-priced dry groceries and place a larger, compensating profit margin on meat or produce. Another store's competitive strategy may be to feature low meat prices and make up for low meat profits with higher canned goods profits. Consequently, within a community there are usually wide variations in retail prices for similar food products in different stores, even though the stores have comparable market basket prices and pay similar wholesale prices.

Variable-price merchandising is another retail pricing strategy that reduces the dependence of retail prices on farm or wholesale prices. Retailers use selective price cuts to differentiate their stores and attract consumers. The "loss leader" and weekend special are examples of these pricing strategies which are designed to build store traffic. Trade estimates indicate that about 20 per cent of grocery items are usually sold at or below cost. Chicken, coffee, bread, milk, and other popular items are frequently priced to attract the price-conscious shopper. This pricing strategy relies on the consumers' tendency toward one-stop shopping; therefore low profits or losses on the featured items can be made up by purchases of the higher-profit items.

Mix pricing and variable-price merchandising raise serious issues. Two criteria of pricing efficiency are that selling prices are related to purchase prices, and that farm and retail prices should move together in order to coordinate food supplies and demand. However, these retail pricing strategies break the link between retail and farm prices.

There is nothing illegal or conspiratorial in these retail food pricing practices. Indeed, they reflect competitive pressures in food retailing, and it is quite unintentional that these strategies might adversely affect farm prices. Before condemning retail food pricing strategies, it is well to remember that price features often have helped farmers move surplus food supplies, and loss leaders are a boon to consumers, who can stock up on specials and purchase only the items featured in several stores.

MARKETING IMPLICATIONS OF RETAILING DEVELOPMENTS

It is clear that the evolving food retail sector is having considerable impact on the rest of the food industry. Because of their size, power, and strategic position, food retailers are referred to as the "gatekeepers" and "channel captains" of the food industry. This means they are making many of the major market decisions for the entire food industry. They serve as consumer purchasing agents; and they control one of the most important food marketing resources—the shelf space which is vital to the success of farmers, food manufacturers, and food wholesalers. Therefore, retailers have considerable market power in the food industry.

More than any other sector of the food industry, food retailers orient the industry to consumer demand and to the marketing concept. Their pricing and merchandising decisions are directed toward either accommodating or influencing the consumer's purchasing behavior. Food chainstores are not indifferent to farm prices and agriculture, but they look *forward* to consumer markets for their profits, not backward in the marketing channel. They can adjust their merchandising strategies to assist farmers in selling seasonal gluts of production at reasonable prices. But increasingly, farmers and others are adjusting to the retailer's needs and strategies.

Food chainstores are reaching back in the marketing channel to control the timing, condition of delivery, and quality of foods—important variables in the retailer's merchandising strategy. Oftentimes this leads to retail ownership of food processing operations or to purchasing by quality specifications. Either way, food retailers have an increasingly greater voice in the production and delivery of food products.

The coordinating position that retailers now hold in the food industry was wrested from food manufacturers in the post-World War II period. Formerly, food processors were the focal point of the food industry. Food retailers gained this position through growth in size, the chainstore and supermarket movements, and the development of their own labels. These private or controlled labels weakened the dominance over the food industry which had been held by food processors through nationally advertised brands.

FOOD SHOPPERS' BEHAVIOR

How consumers buy food has shaped the modern food retailing picture. Consumers' willingness to shop around, compare values, and make store, product, and brand substitutions determines the competitive intensity of food markets. Table 6-7 illustrates some trends in food shopping behavior. As a result of increased shopper mobility, the growth of neighborhood convenience stores, and food retailers' efforts to even out sales over the week, the frequency of food shopping trips increased between 1954 and 1974. Fifty-six per cent of consumers shopped for food more than once a week in 1974, compared to 38 per cent in 1954. This probably did not directly affect total food spending or per capita food expenditures. However, the increased frequency of food shopping suggests some shifting of the inventory-storage function from consumers to food stores.

According to Table 6-7, there are indications of a trend toward more careful food shopping. Consumer readership of food ads and multiple-store patronage both increased between 1954 and 1974. Other food shopping trends, not shown on Table 6-7, include a greater willingness to try new food products, an increased acceptance of private, nonadvertised brands, and a greater influence of children and males on food shopping decisions.

When selecting food and foodstores, is today's consumer more or less price conscious than in the past? Most studies suggest that prices are a prime

Table 6-7. Trends in Consumer Food Shopping Patterns, 1954–1974.

| | PER CENT OF SHOPPERS | | |
	1954	1967–1969	1974
Food stores patronized			
one store exclusively	41%	17%	10%
more than one store	59	83	90
Food shopping trips per week			
one or less	62%	49%	44%
twice per week	18	26	28
three or more times	20	25	28
Average number of food			
ads read/week	1.7	2.6	2.7
Consumers receiving food			
trading stamps	90%	91%	65%

Source: *Study of Supermarket Shoppers, 1974,* Burgoyne, Inc., October 1974. Reprinted by permission.

consideration in shoppers' selection of grocery stores. Table 6-8 indicates that 42 per cent of consumers in 1974 rated prices the number one priority in store choice. However, these consumers also look at other attributes of the product bundle, such as quality, freshness, service, and variety. In short, value—as defined by the consumer—and not just price motivates the consumer's purchase decisions.

Table 6-8. Factors Affecting Food Store Choices, 1954–1974.

| | PER CENT OF CONSUMERS MENTIONING EACH FACTOR AS MOST IMPORTANT | | |
FACTORS	1954	1967	1974
Low grocery prices	13%	32%	42%
Quality, freshness of meats	18	23	19
Convenient location	19	15	13
Attractiveness and cleanliness			
of store	14	10	9
Variety and selection of gro-			
ceries	9	7	7
Quality, freshness of fruits,			
vegetables	8	3	4

Source: *Study of Supermarket Shoppers, 1974,* Burgoyne, Inc., October 1974. Reprinted by permission.

SUMMARY

Food wholesale and retail markets represent the final stages of the food marketing process. The chief activities at these market levels are dispersion, the addition of possession utility to food products, and facilitating the consumer's choice of a desired food product assortment. The modern forms of food wholesaling and retailing have evolved in response to competitive market pressures, changes in the consumer market, and attempts by firms to improve operational efficiency and to satisfy consumer wants. The food retail chainstore movement was fueled by a desire to lower the costs of retailing through large volume purchasing. The supermarket movement was motivated by a desire to improve retailer's competitive position by increasing consumers' satisfaction with the retail shopping experience. Both chainstores and supermarkets now dominate the food retailing picture, but many independent wholesalers and retailers survive in the form of cooperative and wholesale-sponsored affiliated chainstores. Food retailing operations other than supermarkets also appear to have a role in the food industry. Food retailing appears to follow alternating cycles: intense price competition between stores followed by periods of emphasis on cost-increasing, nonprice competitive tactics. The techniques of food retail pricing have weakened the link between farm, wholesale, and retail food prices. Retailers have assumed the role of channel captain in the food industry.

QUESTIONS FOR DISCUSSION

1. The Direct Farm Marketing Bill of 1976 attempts to facilitate direct farmer sales of food products to consumers. Comment on the probable reasons for this legislation.

2. Do you see any parallel in the evolution of food retailing with other industries—clothing, drugstores, and so on?

3. What is the significance of the fact that retailers do not price each food item based on its wholesale cost?

4. How did the chainstore and supermarket movements influence the market efficiency ratio?

5. Some food retailers are adding in-store restaurants and carry-outs to their facilities. What are the reasons for this?

6. State the reasons why food retailing passes through the stages known as the "wheel of retailing?" Where are we now in this cycle?

7. How do these consumer shopping patterns and characteristics affect food retail market strategies: (a) one-stop shopping; (b) brand loyalty; (c) service orientation; (d) working wives; (c) rising incomes.

SELECTED REFERENCES

BLOOM, G. F. *Productivity in the Food Industry: Problems and Potential.* MIT Press, Cambridge, Mass., 1972.

BUCKLIN, L. P. *Competition and Evolution in the Distributive Trades.* Prentice-Hall, Inc., Englewood Cliffs, N.J., 1972.

CASSADY, RALPH, JR. *Competition and Price Making in Food Retailing.* The Ronald Press Company, New York, 1962.

Economic Report on the Structure and Competitive Behavior of Food Retailing. Staff Report, Federal Trade Commission. U.S. Government Printing Office, Washington, D.C., Jan. 1966.

CROSS, J. *The Supermarket Trap.* Indiana University Press, Bloomington, Ind., 1970.

LEED, T. W., AND G. A. GERMAN. *Food Merchandising, Principles, and Practices.* Chain Store Age Books, New York, 1973.

MCLAUGHLIN, D. J., JR., AND C. A. MALLOWE, Ed. *Food Marketing and Distribution.* Chain Store Age Books, New York, 1971.

MUELLER, R. W. "Five Decades that Revolutionized the Food Industry." *Progressive Grocer* (June 1972), 19–38.

NELSON, P. E. "Price Competition Among Retail Food Stores—Theory, Practice and Policy Cues." *American Journal of Agricultural Economics* (Aug. 1966), 172–87.

PADBERG, D. I. *Economics of Food Retailing.* Cornell University, Ithaca, New York, 1968.

SOUTHARD, L., AND T. L. CRAWFORD. "Changes in Food Wholesaling." *The Marketing and Transportation Situation.* U.S. Department of Agriculture, May 1971, pp. 15–21.

CHAPTER 7

The International Market for Food

"NORTH AMERICAN AGRICULTURE has much to gain from freer trade in farm products and from freer trade generally. It is true that some sectors would be required to make significant resource adjustments and in some instances significant capital losses would result from reduction in protection. But the major sectors of North American agriculture—the sectors that employ most of the labor, land and capital—would gain from a significant expansion in demand."*

Preview

- This chapter examines the world market for food and international trade in argicultural products.
- The costs and benefits of trade for the U.S. economy are reviewed.
- The reasons for international trade in agricultural products are studied, and the principle of comparative advantage is introduced.
- The volume, importance, and recipients of U.S. farm exports are examined, as well as trends in U.S. food imports.
- The key issues in agricultural trade policy are discussed, especially the protectionism versus free-trade debate.
- The potential for expanding U.S. farm export sales is examined.
- Key terms and concepts:
  complementary imports
  export market expansion
  gains from trade

  nontariff trade barriers
  principle of comparative advantage

---

* D. Gale Johnson, "The Impact of Freer Trade on North American Agriculture," Meeting of the American Economic Association, Toronto, Canada, December 29, 1972.

protectionism
Public Law 480
resource endowment

state trading monopoly
supplementary imports
tariff

The United States is a trading nation and the world's largest exporter of agricultural commodities. In 1975 the production of three out of ten crop acres was exported; export sales supported one out of every eight farm jobs; and international sales contributed 20 per cent of gross farm income. U.S. agricultural exports accounted for 16 per cent of total world trade in farm products over the 1971–1975 period.

In recent years, our agricultural productive capacity and trade-orientation have made important contributions to worldwide economic development and to the world food problem. America is both a major food exporter and importer. These trading relationships have integrated U.S. agriculture with the world agricultural economy. Many U.S. farm prices are now set in world markets, and, through trade, the American consumer has access to a virtual worldwide smorgasbord of foods.

SIGNIFICANCE OF AGRICULTURAL TRADE

Imports and exports of food have several consequences for the U.S. economy. First, exports represent a source of market expansion for U.S. farmers. Increased exports can raise farm prices and incomes by providing a growing market for U.S. farm output. The contributions of farm exports to economic activity are illustrated in Figure 7-1.

Second, participation in world markets provides incentives for increasing productivity and output of U.S. agriculture. Competition in world markets stimulates American farmers to operate at or near full capacity and maximum efficiency. Indeed, the ability to compete in world markets is one test for whether America should be an exporter or an importer of a commodity. Trade and international competition provide guides for farmers' production decisions. Because of the beneficial effects of trade on resource efficiency, a potential exists for increasing total commodity output, and, consequently, the world's standard of living.

Trade also influences the size, variety, and price of the food supply for American consumers. Money earned from food exports can be used to purchase both food and nonfood imports desired by American consumers. At the same time, U.S. exports distribute the American food and industrial bounty to nations the world over. Trade-related commerce can also contribute

129

Table 7-1. The United States Balance of Trade, 1935–1976.

| | ANNUAL AVERAGE (BILLION DOLLARS) | | | | | | |
| | U.S. EXPORTS | | U.S. IMPORTS | | TRADE BALANCE | | |
YEARS	AGRICULTURAL	NONAGRICULTURAL	AGRICULTURAL	NONAGRICULTURAL	AGRICULTURAL	NONAGRICULTURAL	TOTAL
1935–42	$ .7	2.7	1.2	1.2	– .5	+ 1.5	+1.0
1942–49	2.8	9.3	2.2	2.6	+ .6	+ 6.7	+6.1
1950–59	3.5	12.2	4.1	7.0	– .6	+ 5.2	+4.6
1960–70	5.9	21.6	4.3	18.5	+ 1.6	+ 3.1	+4.7
1971	7.8	35.9	5.8	36.9	+ 1.9	– 1.0	+ .9
1972	8.0	36.8	6.0	44.0	+ 2.0	– 7.2	–5.2
1973	12.9	44.9	7.3	54.1	+ 5.6	– 9.2	–3.6
1974	21.3	63.6	9.5	73.0	+11.7	– 9.3	+2.4
1975	21.6	81.3	9.6	91.5	+12.0	–10.2	+1.8
1976	22.1	87.2	10.1	95.8	+12.0	– 8.5	+3.5

Source: U.S. Department of Agriculture.

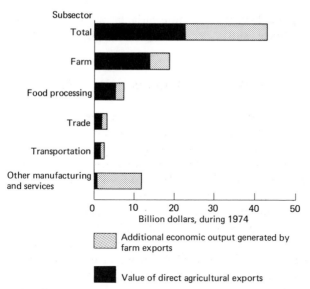

Figure 7–1. How farm exports stimulate added economic activity. (U.S. Department of Agriculture)

to the economic development of low-income countries by providing them with needed imports and with purchasing power in world markets.

Agricultural trade undoubtedly plays a role in international diplomacy and foreign relations. It is probably true that "two nations trading bushels are less likely to trade bullets." The improved political relationships and the opening of trade between America, the U.S.S.R., and the People's Republic of China in the early 1970's were not coincidental.

In recent years, agricultural trade has also made an important contribution to the U.S. balance of trade. The *balance of trade* is the difference between the value of U.S. exports and the value of our imports. A negative balance of trade (more imports than exports) tends to weaken the value of the dollar in world markets.

The U.S. balance of trade for the 1935–1976 period is shown in Table 7-1. Prior to 1942 and for much of the 1950's, the United States imported more agricultural products than it exported. A positive nonagricultural balance of trade, however, resulted in an overall favorable balance of trade during this period. In the 1960's, the balance of trade was positive for both agricultural and nonagricultural products. In the 1971–1976 period, a positive and growing agricultural trade balance more than offset the negative nonagricultural trade balance.

Finally, increased trade in agricultural commodities has made the nations of the world more interdependent. International trade exposes United States farmers to world economic conditions. As a result of increased trade, United

131

States farm prices have become more variable, affected as they are by climatic, economic, political, and societal changes throughout the world.

THE RATIONALE FOR TRADE

If we were to observe the planet from a satelite, we would see a vast armada of ships, planes, trucks, trains, and barges moving food and other products from country to country. Copra moves from Asia to America; the return trip carries corn or soybeans to India. Americans trade beef and pork for Japanese steel and TV sets. U.S. computers are shipped to Africa in exchange for cocoa and palm oil. In mid-ocean, ships carrying U.S. feedgrains for European poultry pass ships carrying European-made autos bound for New York. Nothing seems to be in the right place!

If we focus in more closely, we will see some puzzling aspects of this international bazaar. The United States imported sugar from 32 nations in 1975 despite a large domestic sugar producing industry. America produces considerable rice, but Americans eat little rice and most of it is shipped overseas. American consumers are eating Polish ham and Scandanavian cheese despite adequate supplies of domestic ham and cheese.

Specialization and the Gains from Trade

What is the reason for all this trade? Is it necessary? One explanation we can rule out is that countries only import products that they cannot produce themselves. There are very few agricultural products that cannot be produced almost anywhere in the world, though at some cost. America imports many food products that are also produced domestically.

A better explanation for trade is the profit incentive for countries to specialize in producing certain commodities and to trade these to countries specializing in other commodities. The United States might choose to trade wheat for bananas with a Central American country not because bananas cannot be produced in the United States but because both countries gain economically by this trading of product specialities. It is evident that there is a gain, for countries trade voluntarily.

The incentive for specialization and trade lies in the economies of producing commodities that are, relatively speaking, best suited to a country's resource endowment. These resources include land, labor, climate, management skills, and other factors affecting the costs of production. Central American nations are endowed with a labor force and climate relatively better suited to banana production than to wheat production. The United States has a land and climate base relatively more suitable for wheat production than for banana production. The fundamental bases for food trade are that productive resources are unevenly distributed throughout the world, each commodity requires a somewhat different resource base, and consumers desire a varied diet.

But would not the United States, with its diversified climate and resource base, be better off as a self-sufficient food producer rather than be dependent upon other countries? The answer is, not if the high cost of domestic production of bananas, coffee, tea, and so forth are considered. Moreover, even for commodities such as meat and dairy products, which are produced domestically, the market provides the best answer to the question. Consumers decide whether foods will be imported or not through their purchase decisions.

However, there is more than just freedom of choice and diet variety to support the case for international trade in food products. By their purchases, consumers indicate the appropriate products to be produced in each country. A consumer preference for Scandanavian dairy products rather than the American product is a consumer vote *for* the imports and *against* the domestic production. Through this competitive process, trade encourages farmers in each country to specialize in those products relatively best suited to their resource base. Put another way, competition in international markets discourages the production of high-cost products and encourages the production of low-cost products in each country. Trade therefore improves the efficiency of resource use throughout the world by encouraging the shift of resources to their most efficient uses. This resource efficiency gain can lead to greater output and/or reduced costs of production—both of which constitute an increased standard of living.

International price differences signal each country which products to produce, export and import. Each country will find its most competitive commodity to be that one which uses its resource base relatively most efficiently. For each commodity, food costs and prices will vary between surplus-producing regions and deficit-producing regions. This price differential will encourage exports from surplus areas to deficit areas. Of course, each country will be specializing in different commodities, so each will be exporting and importing at the same time.

Comparative Advantage

The *principle of comparative advantage* was formally stated by the English economist, David Ricardo, in 1817. This principle holds that there are economic gains when, under free trade, nations produce and export those commodities that they can produce relatively most efficiently by virtue of their resource endowment, and import those commodities that other nations can produce more efficiently.

The principle of comparative advantage goes counter to the common-sense notion that it is better to be self-sufficient than dependent upon others. It also suggests that trade is not just a one-for-one exchange between countries; that specialization and trade can increase the size of the economic pie as well as the standard of living of all trading nations. These ideas are widely accepted for specialization and trade within national boundaries; they are less widely accepted regarding international trade. But in fact, although there are some added political complexities involved in international trade not present in interstate trade, the principle of comparative advantage applies equally to both.

There is a controversy regarding which farm products the United States has a comparative advantage in. Table 7-2 illustrates one viewpoint; but it must be noted that comparative advantage is constantly changing as a result of new agricultural technologies, changes in the labor force, and other cost-affecting developments.

Table 7-2. U.S. Comparative Advantage and Disadvantage Farm Products.

CLEAR COMPARATIVE ADVANTAGE	UNCERTAIN	CLEAR COMPARATIVE DISADVANTAGE
corn	rice	Manufactured dairy products
barley	cotton	sugar
grain sorghums	flaxseed	wool
soybeans	pork	lamb, mutton
wheat	beef	peanuts
tobacco	oats	
poultry		

Source: D. Gale Johnson, "Where U.S. Agricultural Comparative Advantage Lies," in *U.S. Agriculture in a World Context,* Atlantic Council, 1974, pp. 27–61. Reprinted by permission.

The Costs and Benefits of Trade

Despite the economic gains from trade, there are some costs. The benefits of trade, for example, must be sufficient to offset the considerable costs of transportation involved in trade. The rising volume of world trade suggests this has been the case. Farmers sometimes feel they bear a trade cost when imports displace domestically produced products or lower their prices. And consumers sometimes feel they bear a cost of farm exports when exports raise domestic food prices. However, in trade analysis it is important to look at total costs and benefits for the nation as a whole rather than for any one group. The farmers' import cost can be balanced against farmer's export benefits, just as consumers' export costs can be balanced by their import benefits. The principle of comparative advantage demonstrates that the overall benefits from trade are greater than the costs for all groups.

Another cost of trade is that associated with the frequent resource adjustments imposed by competitive world markets and changing comparative advantages. Some adjustments impose considerable costs on owners of land, labor, and capital and may be particularly difficult in agriculture. For example, it may be difficult for farmers to adjust their production to rapidly changing world market conditions. Another cost of trade and specialization is the loss of self-sufficiency and increased dependency on others. This may be simply a psychological cost; or a very real cost, if other nations attempt to take advantage of this dependency by raising prices or threatening embargoes. For this reason, many nations choose to forego some gains from trade in strategic commodities, including agricultural products.

U.S. FARM PRODUCT EXPORTS

U.S. exports of farm products have fluctuated over the years because of changes in world economic conditions, American trade policies, war and peace, and the changing worldwide demand for food. Table 7-3 shows that U.S. farm product exports rose from 1900 to 1920; fell from 1920 to 1941; rose again in the 1940's; were relatively stable from 1951 to 1960; moved upward in the 1960's; and increased substantially in the 1973–1974 period. In the 1974–1976 period, farm exports averaged 24 per cent of farm commodity sales, compared to 20 per cent in the early 1920's; 17 per cent in the late 1920's; 11 per cent during the 1930's; 10 per cent in the 1940's; 12 per cent in the 1950's; and 15 per cent in the 1960's.

The 1973–1974 expansion in U.S. agricultural exports illustrates the importance of trade to U.S. farmers. Largely as a result of this increase in exports, American farm prices rose at an extraordinary 27 per cent annual rate during the 1972–1974 period; and in 1973, the average income of the farm population exceeded the average income of the nonfarm population for the first time in history.

Agricultural products made up about 22 per cent of U.S. exports during 1971–1975, as shown in Table 7-4. For the same period, the United States accounted for 16 per cent of world agricultural trade. The U.S. share of world agricultural exports has grown—from 12 percent in 1951–1955 to 16 per cent in 1971–1975.

The importance of foreign sales varies widely among commodities. Figure 7-2 shows that crop products (feedgrains, wheat, and oilseeds) dominate U.S. farm exports. Exports of meats and meat products are expanding but are still small compared with domestic sales. In the 1973–1976 crop years, 22 per cent of the corn crop was exported, as was 42 per cent of the soybean crop and 60 per cent of the wheat crop. Figure 7-3 illustrates the importance of exports for different commodities in 1977. Not all states share equally in

Table 7-3. U.S. Agricultural Exports, 1900–1976.

YEAR	MILLION DOLLARS	YEAR	MILLION DOLLARS
1900	$ 845	1940	738
1901	949	1941	350
1902	855	1942	1,032
1903	877	1943	1,497
1904	858	1944	2,305
1905	825	1945	2,191
1906	975	1946	2,857
1907	1,053	1947	3,610
1908	1,016	1948	3,505
1909	901	1949	3,830
1910	869	1950	2,986
1911	1,029	1951	3,411
1912	1,048	1952	4,053
1913	1,121	1953	2,819
1914	1,112	1954	2,936
1915	1,474	1955	3,144
1916	1,516	1956	3,496
1917	1,966	1957	4,728
1918	2,279	1958	4,003
1919	3,579	1959	3,719
1920	3,850	1960	4,519
1921	2,606	1961	4,946
1922	1,915	1962	5,142
1923	1,789	1963	5,078
1924	1,867	1964	6,068
1925	2,280	1965	6,097
1926	1,892	1966	6,676
1927	1,908	1967	6,771
1928	1,815	1968	6,311
1929	1,847	1969	5,741
1930	1,496	1970	6,719
1931	1,038	1971	7,758
1932	752	1972	8,047
1933	590	1973	12,894
1934	787	1974	21,300
1935	669	1975	21,578
1936	766	1976	22,147
1937	732		
1938	891		
1939	683		

Source: U.S. Department of Agriculture.

the agricultural export market. In the early 1970's, ten states accounted for 60 per cent of U.S. farm product exports: Illinois, Iowa, Texas, California, Kansas, Nebraska, Indiana, Minnesota, North Carolina, and Ohio.

Most U.S. farm product exports are shipped to the high-income countries,

Table 7-4. U.S. Market Shares of World Trade, 1951–1975.

YEARS	U.S. SHARE OF WORLD AGRICULTURAL EXPORTS	AGRICULTURE'S SHARE OF TOTAL TRADE	
		IN WORLD	IN U.S.
1951–1955	12%	32%	22%
1956–1960	13	28	22
1961–1965	15	25	24
1966–1970	14	19	19
1971–1975	16	16	22

Source: Food and Agriculture Organization, United Nations.

as shown in Figure 7-4. In 1976, 63 per cent of American farm exports went to the high-income, industrial countries of the world. Here we see the same marketing factor at work on a worldwide scale as is working domestically. Commercial export markets are composed of people with purchasing power. The fact that a great many of the poor and underdeveloped countries

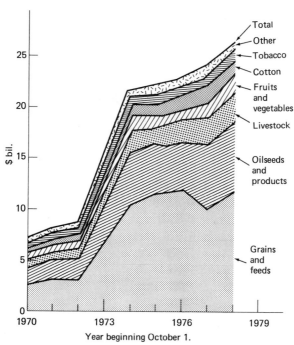

Figure 7–2. U.S. agricultural exports by principal commodity groups. (U.S. Department of Agriculture)

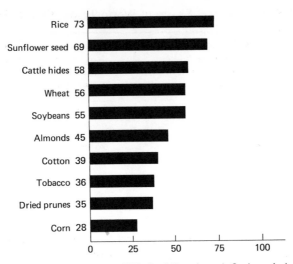

Year ending September 30, 1978. Partially estimated. Soybeans include bean equivalent of meal and oil.

Figure 7–3. U.S. agricultural exports as a percentage of farm production, 1978. (U.S. Department of Agriculture)

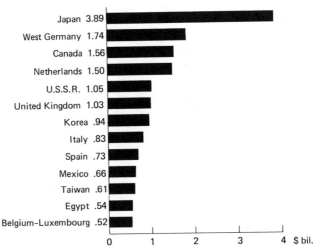

Figure 7–4. U.S. agricultural exports by country of destination, 1976; billions of dollars. (U.S. Department of Agriculture)

of the world have inadequate diets does not necessarily make them good trading customers. Effective demand, not just need, determines world food trading patterns.

U.S. FOOD IMPORTS

As a high-income country, the United States is also a major food importer. American consumers enjoy a cosmopolitan diet as a result of these imports. As shown in Table 7-1, U.S. food imports are increasing in dollar volume. Although agricultural imports have declined as a share of total U.S. imports, farmers are nevertheless concerned with food imports because they influence domestic food supplies and prices.

Not all agricultural imports are directly competitive with domestic production. In 1976 about 40 per cent of U.S. agricultural imports were *complementary* or noncompetitive, as indicated in Table 7-5. These products include bananas, cocoa beans, tea, coffee, spices, and so forth. Although these imports

Table 7-5. Competitive and Noncompetitive U.S. Agricultural Imports, 1975–1976.

	U.S. IMPORTS	
COMMODITY	MILLION DOLLARS	PER CENT
Competitive (supplementary) Imports:		
Sugar and related products	$ 1,457	
Meat and meat products	1,437	
Fruits, nuts, vegetables	877	
Oilseeds and products	539	
Wines, malt beverages	432	
Animal products	365	
Dairy, poultry products	299	
Unmanufactured tobacco	279	
Live animals	206	
Total, competitive products	6,307	60%
Noncompetitive (complementary) Imports:		
Coffee, cocoa, tea	3,027	
Rubber, allied gums	493	
Bananas, plantains	275	
Spices	95	
Total, noncompetitive products	4,208	40%
Total imports	10,515	100%

Source: U.S. Department of Agriculture.

139

do not directly displace U.S. farm products in the domestic market, they do compete indirectly with domestically produced substitutes. The major *supplementary* or competitive imports include meat products, sugar, fruits and vegetables, and oilseed products. These imports compete directly with domestically produced food products and are increasing relative to complementary agricultural imports. In 1950, supplementary farm products accounted for 50 per cent of U.S. imports, compared to 60 per cent in 1976. Many of the supplementary imports fill specialized market needs. For example, meat imports include specialty items such as Danish ham and also boneless beef, an inexpensive ground beef product used extensively in the away-from-home food market. Many of the fruit and vegetable products are imported during the winter months and do not compete directly with United States supplies.

Figure 7-5 shows the major exporters of food to the United States in 1976–1977. Latin America, Asia, and Western Europe were important suppli-

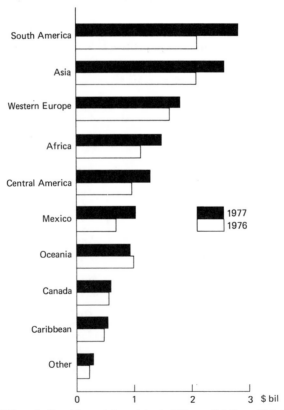

Figure 7–5. U.S. agricultural imports by origin, in billions of dollars. (U.S. Department of Agriculture)

ers. Brazil, Mexico, Australia, and the Philippines were the largest exporters of farm products to the United States.

AGRICULTURAL TRADE POLICY

All nations regulate trade in some fashion, and the United States is no exception. This is because trade is of great importance to national economies. Trade policy requires compromises in the political arena, and trade, of course, affects private economic interests. Why purchase from abroad when the products can be produced domestically? Why export American jobs and dollars to other countries? Is it in the national interest for America to become dependent on foreign food supplies? Should not American farmers be protected from the cheap labor and unfair competitive practices of other countries? How do we compromise between (1) the farmers' wishes to expand export sales and limit imports, and (2) the consumers' wishes to limit exports and increase food imports? These questions are major issues in a nation's trade policy.

Protectionism versus Free Trade

Government trade policies vary between the two extremes of protection from trade for domestic industry to free trade. The case for free trade rests on the belief that unrestricted trade among all nations will result in more efficient use of the world's resources and a higher standard of living for all. However, many nations choose to forego these benefits in favor of a protectionist trade policy. Throughout history there have been frequent shifts between these two policies. Since the 1930's, the world has been moving from a protectionist stance to a freer trading policy.

Trade protectionism refers to market policies and devices that prevent free trade among nations. Among these protectionist devices are tariffs (taxes on imports), quotas, licenses, restrictions on imports, and government subsidies to industries which could not otherwise compete in world markets. In agriculture, trade protectionism is often the result of a country's internal domestic policies, for instance, helping farmers via price supports and subsidies. These well-intentioned programs have two effects: (1) they shelter domestic farmers from the rigors of world competition, thereby delaying domestic resource adjustments; and (2) they make the domestic market more attractive to imports. In both cases, trade protection for the domestic industry is needed.

Since World War II, the United States and other nations have sought a freer trade policy in agriculture. There has been a worldwide lowering of tariff trade barriers. However, barriers to agricultural trade still exist. In many cases there has been a substitution of nontariff trade barriers (quotas, licenses, voluntary restrictions) for tariff barriers.

141

In recent years there have been many efforts around the world to bring groups of countries together into relatively free trade groups. The European Economic Community (common market countries) is a major example. Though such groupings permit freer trade among the members, there is no assurance that the same attitude will be taken with outsiders. There have been indications that such groupings will take additional measures to protect and subsidize their own agriculture in order to seek agricultural self-sufficiency.

The movement from a protectionist policy to a freer trade policy will be a slow one. Even though it can be shown that a nation or the world will gain from freer trade, some individuals, industries, and nations will be disadvantaged by a movement toward freer trade. It is always easier to grant protection than to withdraw it. The problem here is to distribute fairly the gains from trade among all parties—not an easy task. In addition, the benefits of protectionism to individuals and industries are quite significant in dollar value, whereas the costs of protectionism to consumers and the world's standard of living are diffused and not evident to most people.

Will American farmers benefit from a freer trade policy? Those farmers producing commodities in which the United States has a comparative advantage will benefit, but farmers producing products that cannot compete on world markets would need to make adjustments to other products. Overall, the United States probably has a greater comparative advantage in agricultural products than in industrial goods, and the United States will continue to be a major farm product exporter. To discontinue exporting would idle some 70 million acres of cropland and foreclose the U.S. farmers' opportunity to participate in the expanding world food market. The United States will also continue to be a major food importer, despite the farmer's concerns with competitive imports. It is unrealistic to expect other countries to buy our farm products if we do not buy something from them in return. As is frequently said, trade is a two-way street.

Export Expansion Programs

To many people viewing the world population explosion, the plight of the hungry and malnourished millions in the world, and the tremendous U.S. agricultural capacity, a simple solution would seem to be an expansion of our food exports. However, feeding the world with U.S. farm exports encounters the problem of effective demand; most U.S. agricultural exports go to the high-income countries. There are few untapped commercial markets that would allow rapid expansion of United States farm product exports. Until 1972, American farm exports grew slowly, along with increasing world population and economic development. An exceptional situation occurred in 1972 and 1973, when United States farmers gained access to the Russian and Chinese markets, which represent about a third of the world's population.

In 1975 these two countries purchased about 10 per cent of all U.S. farm exports.

Since the passage of the 1954 Agricultural Trade Development and Assistance Act (Public Law 480), the U.S. government has been actively engaged in encouraging the expansion of U.S. farm exports. This has been called the "food for peace" program. Under this program, the U.S. government finances farm product sales with long-term, low-interest credit; it also provides disaster relief and makes food donations to other nations. Food shipments under P.L. 480 are perhaps more aptly termed *aid* rather than *trade*. Between 1954 and 1976, the United States shipped 25 billion dollars worth of food under P.L. 480. The program was more important in the 1950's (when it accounted for 30 per cent of U.S. farm exports) than it has been in recent years (see Figure 7-6). P.L. 480 shipments represented only 5 per cent of U.S. farm product exports in 1976.

United States products do not "sell themselves" in the highly competitive, commercial foreign markets. It requires salesmanship, reliability as a source

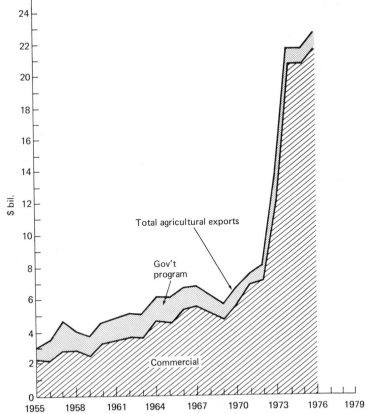

Figure 7–6. U.S. agricultural exports sold commercially and under government programs. (U.S. Department of Agriculture)

of supply, competitive pricing, and acceptable product quality to compete in world markets. Although the United States does not have a monopoly on these prerequisites for success, American farmers have a good performance record in world markets.

The potential for expanding foreign markets exists, but the expansion will not be dramatic or rapid. Increasing the incomes of the underdeveloped areas of the world, which would expand our markets, is not easily accomplished. In the major markets of the developed countries, competition from other potential sellers is severe. Food industries, if they wish to increase their foreign sales, will have to analyze carefully the potential customer and the market. Specialists in foreign marketing problems will be necessary for our domestic firms.

The U.S. Department of Agriculture is active in promoting foreign sales through joint efforts with American trade groups. These promotional efforts include market surveys, demonstrations, technical assistance to foreign users, advertising, test shipments, and many others. In some countries permanent trade centers for promotion of United States products are maintained, such as in London, Milan, and Tokyo. One promotion, "American Week," in April of 1968 in Tokyo featured U.S. products and resulted in sales of American foods of nearly $1 million.

Products must be actively sold to potential foreign customers. It has been observed that American processors and marketing people will spare no effort to exploit the domestic market successfully but pay very little attention to the problems of satisfying customers in other countries. The "bundle of attributes" concept that was developed for domestic consumers also applies to those that live in other countries. Each country may have its peculiar preferences, living conditions, holidays, and religious beliefs which help determine which products are acceptable.

State Trading Programs

For the most part, food trade is carried out by private firms operating within the framework of national trade policies. In some countries, however, international food trade is centralized in trading monopolies. These monopoly agencies may be government organizations or producer groups granted trade monopolies by the government. Such agencies frequently become involved in domestic marketing programs, including storage, transportation, and pricing activities. The Canadian Wheat Board, a producer-controlled organization, has a monopoly position in Canadian wheat exports. Australia has similar export monopolies for wheat and barley. The Japanese Food Agency regulates food imports into that country. The central plan countries of Eastern Europe and Asia also trade as state monopolies. There is some concern that these state trading monopolies have a competitive advantage over countries that organize trade through the private, free enterprise sector. The evidence for this is mixed. Nor is there concrete evidence that state trade monopolies can improve farm prices, or secure lower-priced imports, over the long run.

SUMMARY

The United States is a major trader of agricultural commodities, and foreign trade in food products has a significant impact on farmers, middlemen, consumers, and the American economy. The principle of comparative advantage underlies the rationale for trade in food products. Trade has the potential for improving the allocation of productive resources on a worldwide basis, increasing economic output, and enhancing the world's standard of living. U.S. farm product imports and exports have been increasing. In the 1972–1977 period, agriculture's positive balance of trade has been a key factor in maintaining an overall U.S. favorable balance of trade. Most U.S. farm product exports go to the higher-income countries of the world. Food imports that compete directly with domestically produced products are increasing more rapidly than noncompetitive imports such as coffee, tea, and bananas. Protectionist trade policies still exist in world agriculture, but some progress has been made in lowering trade barriers. The United States has a comparative advantage in producing several important agricultural commodities. The commercial export market for farm products is highly competitive.

QUESTIONS FOR DISCUSSION

1. Explain in your own words how a country can benefit from trade. How does the world benefit? U.S. farmers?

2. If trade has so many advantages, why are so many governments following protectionist policies?

3. A farmer argues: "The United States is the breadbasket of the world. U.S. agriculture is the most productive of all countries. We should strive to sell as much food as possible but limit imports so that we don't become dependent on others for our food supply." How would you respond to this?

4. Protectionist trade policies are frequently justified on the following grounds. Give your analysis of each:

   (a) United States producers should not have to compete with cheap foreign labor.

   (b) Taxes on imports are a good source of revenue for the U.S. Treasury.

   (c) "Buy American" and keep the money in the country.

   (d) Tariffs on imports increase the American standard of living by reducing imports that take American jobs.

5. Some countries have claimed that U.S. shipments under P.L. 480 were simply designed to dump U.S. food surpluses on foreign markets, and that these supplies retarded the development of these countries' own agriculture. Explain how this could

145

occur, and give your own recommendations for sharing, in a constructive manner, the U.S. food supply with developing nations.

SELECTED REFERENCES

AINSWORTH, R. G. "The Importance of Imports As a Source of Food." *The National Food Situation.* U.S. Department of Agriculture, May 1966, pp. 37–41.

DUYMOVIC, A., et al. *Effects of Alternative Beef Import Policies on the Beef and Pork Sectors.* U.S. Department of Agriculture. Agricultural Economic Report No. 233, Oct. 1972.

"Export Controls and U.S. Agriculture." *Business Conditions.* Federal Reserve Bank of Chicago, Dec. 1973, pp. 6–11.

How U.S. Farm Exports Have Grown. U.S. Department of Agriculture, Sept. 1974.

The Impact of Dairy Imports on the U.S. Dairy Industry. U.S. Department of Agriculture. Agricultural Economic Report No. 278, Jan. 1975.

International Food Policy Issues, a Proceedings. U.S. Department of Agriculture. Foreign Agricultural Economic Report No. 143, Jan. 1978.

JOHNSON, D. G. "The Impact of Freer Trade on North American Agriculture." *American Journal of Agricultural Economics* (May 1973), 294–300.

MACKIE, A. B. *Foreign Economic Growth and Market Potentials for U.S. Agricultural Products.* U.S. Department of Agriculture. Foreign Agricultural Economic Report No. 24, 1965.

TOLLEY, G. S., AND P. A. ZADROZRY, Eds. *Trade, Agriculture, and Development.* Ballinger Publishing Co., Cambridge, Mass., 1975.

TONTZ, R. L. *Foreign Agricultural Trade Policy of the U.S., 1776–1976.* U.S. Department of Agriculture. ERS-662, Jan. 1977.

VELLIANTIS-FIDAS, A., AND E. M. MANFREDI. *P.L. 480 Concessional Sales.* U.S. Department of Agriculture. Foreign Agricultural Economics Report No. 142, Dec. 1977.

VERMEER, J., et. al. "Effects of Trade Liberalization on U.S. Agriculture." *Agricultural Economics Research* (April 1975), 23–29.

What Makes U.S. Farm Trade Grow?. U.S. Department of Agriculture, Oct. 1974.

What Our Farm Exports Mean to the World. U.S. Department of Agriculture, Sept. 1974.

Who Buys Our Farm Products? U.S. Department of Agriculture, Oct. 1974.

The World Food Situation Prospects to 1985. U.S. Department of Agriculture. Foreign Agricultural Economic Report No. 98, rev. March 1975.

PART III

Prices and Marketing Costs

CHAPTER 8

Price Analysis and the Exchange Function

"THE CLASSIC FUNCTION of price is to coordinate the activities of independent firms so that resources are used to satisfy the demands of consumers as expressed in the market place. While this role is still important, it is being modified in many significant ways; and the problem of getting adequate information about market prices is increasing."*

Preview

- This chapter examines the role of prices and price-making forces in the food industry.
- The effects of changing relative prices on farmers', food marketing firms', and consumers' decisions are investigated.
- Differences between food and nonfood prices are evaluated.
- Supply and demand analysis is developed as a tool for understanding and predicting food prices. Applications of supply/demand analysis are given.
- The elasticity of demand for farm and food products is examined.
- The law of one price—a measure of pricing efficiency in farm markets—is explained.
- The price-discovery process is explained.
- Key terms and concepts:

administered prices	cost-price squeeze
bargained prices	cross elasticity
buyers', sellers' markets	derived demand
complementary products	equilibrium price

---

* *Food from Farmer to Consumer,* Report of the National Commission on Food Marketing, Washington, D.C., 1966.

formula prices	price system
law of demand, supply	relative price
price ceiling, floor	reservation demand
price discovery	short, long-run
price elasticity of demand	substitute products

The exchange functions of marketing, buying, and selling are the heart of marketing. As goods move through many hands before reaching the final user, title changes several times. Each time title changes, a price must be decided upon. This means that pricing is an integral part of marketing. Price analysts claim that marketing is an important branch of the study of prices. Marketing people claim that pricing is a major branch of the study of marketing. Regardless of viewpoints, the study of marketing and that of prices go hand in hand. One really cannot understand marketing adequately without some grasp of the fundamentals of pricing.

ROLE OF PRICES IN THE COMPETITIVE ECONOMY

The food marketing process is a system of communication, conflict resolution, and coordination. The system must transmit to buyers and sellers information that will be useful to them in their decisions; it must achieve compromises between producers' and consumers' goals; and it must provide incentives to encourage efficient decision-making. This is a tall order, not easily accomplished. There are three ways for the marketing system to achieve these objectives: (1) custom or tradition; (2) central, authoritarian control, or (3) decentralized coordination via prices determined by competition.

Although custom and tradition do influence food industry decisions, they appear to be a poor choice for guiding decisions in a dynamic economy. For example, it is unlikely that we would have the supermarket, convenience foods, farmer co-ops, and numerous other market innovations if tradition were shaping the food industry. Nor are centralized, authoritarian decisions palatable to our economic philosophy. The alternative is to coordinate food industry decisions with prices. This is a complex coordinating device. Basically, it requires that each firm and consumer make independent decisions, based on their own interests and guided by price signals. A key tenet of this market price system is that the firm's profit-seeking behavior will lead it to serve societys' interest by allocating resources to their highest-valued use. Most of the U.S. food system, and much of the world food economy, is coordinated by this competitive price system. This reflects our philosophical bias toward decentralizing economic and political power, maximizing personal freedom of choice, and encouraging flexibility in decisions in order to foster invention, innovation, and technological change.

If a competitively functioning price system is directing the market, it has the advantage of being impartial. The idea of "fair treatment" is left to the composite judgment of the marketplace rather than to the decisions of individuals in positions of political power. Such a system of direction also has the advantage of being in continuous operation—there is a continuous adjustment to changing conditions. This is in contrast to the sluggish "after-the-fact" type of direction which usually occurs when the direction job is delegated to various public agencies.

In a competitive economy the pricing machinery is expected to transmit orders and directions. To some firms, high and rising prices mean increased profits and more incentive to "go ahead." But to some consumers, they mean "slow down" or perhaps "do without." The opposite directions would result from low or falling prices. Briefly, then, fluctuating competitive prices have the following three major jobs to perform:

1. They guide and regulate production decisions.
2. They guide and regulate consumption decisions.
3. They guide and regulate marketing decisions over time, form, and space.

Prices are a form of communication signals that serve in various ways to coordinate market decisions. They serve as guides before decisions are made and as rewards for correct decisions. Pricing efficiency in food markets is determined by how well prices function in these roles.

RELATIVE PRICES AND FOOD MARKETING DECISIONS

Profitable marketing and production decisions require careful selection from among alternatives. Substitution possibilities abound at every stage of the food system. Farmers can use the same resources to produce corn, soybeans, or wheat. They may in turn elect to market these crops or to transform them through feeding them to animals. Likewise, food processors may substitute corn oil, soybean oil, cottonseed oil, or palm oil in the preparation of cooking oils. Dairy processors can sell milk in the fluid state or as cheese or yogurt. Consumers have the greatest range of alternatives. Beef, pork, chicken, and lamb are all substitute meat products, although consumers vary in the degree to which they view them as substitutes. Consumers also can obtain protein from vegetables rather than from livestock products. Peas can be substituted for carrots, national brands for private brands, A & P

151

for Kroger, giant economy sizes for small packages, and restaurant meals for home-cooked meals.

How do farmers, marketing firms, and consumers choose among these alternatives? Tradition, custom, and personal preference play some role in market choices. But these seem inadequate to explain the frequent changes in market choices which are evident to everyone. Farmers do substitute one crop for another, and over a longer period they expand and contract farm enterprises. Food processors frequently change their formulas, add new products, and drop others. And consumers are notoriously fickle in substituting one food, one brand, or one store for another.

Price signals and the profit motive are a better explanation of changing market choices. Farmers will plant more soybeans and less corn if prices and profit expectations favor soybeans rather than corn. Food processors also will respond to price and profit incentives, as when they substitute corn sugar for beet sugar in their processing formulas. And consumers can be encouraged to substitute ice milk for ice cream, if prices favor such a substitution.

It is the *relative price* of substitute products that influences what will be purchased, produced, and sold by farmers, marketing firms, and consumers. A relative price is simply a ratio stating the price of one substitute in terms of another. The relative price of soybeans to corn is 2:1 if the price of soybeans is $8.00 and the price of corn is $4.00. Put another way, this bushel of soybeans is twice as expensive as a bushel of corn. Producers and consumers will respond to changes in relative prices of subsitutes in such a way as to improve their economic position. For producers, this means the relative price adjustment will be toward increased profits. For consumers, it means cost-minimizing and value-maximizing decisions.

Relative prices, not the absolute prices of individual products, serve as the signals for market choices. Relative prices change, of course, when there is a change in the price of either the numerator or the denominator of the price ratio. However, the relative price ratio will remain constant if both of the substitute prices move together. An equally important point is that a product's relative price may change, even if its absolute price does not. For example, a $2.00 corn price and a $6.00 soybean price will make these two crops as equally attractive to farmers as a $3.00 corn price and a $9.00 soybean price. The relative price is the same (3:1). But, if the price of soybeans rises from $6.00 to $8.00 and corn prices remain at $2.00, some farmers will respond to this relative price change by producing more soybeans and less corn. Knowledge of relative prices is useful if one is to understand and predict the market choices of farmers, marketing firms, and food consumers.

Farmers respond to relative price signals. For example, farmers usually transfer acreage from corn to soybeans when the soybean/corn price ratio is 2.5:1 or better, everything else being equal. On the other hand, corn will be substituted for soybean acreage when this relative price falls below 2.5:1.

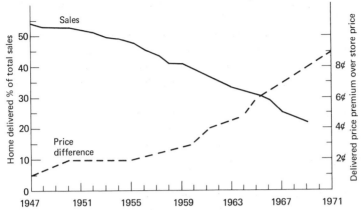

Figure 8–1. Relative price and sales trends of home-delivered and store milk, 1947–1971. (U.S. Department of Agriculture)

And, although wheat is normally used as a food grain, farmers frequently find it profitable to feed wheat to livestock when wheat prices are less than 40 cents above corn prices.

Consumers also are sensitive to changing relative food prices. One rule of thumb that many consumers follow is that medium-sized eggs are a better value than large eggs when the price differential between them is less than 7 cents per dozen. Another rule of thumb is that butter is a good buy when it is priced at less than twice the price of margerine. Figure 8-1 demonstrates how a rising price differential between grocery and home-delivered milk altered consumers' preferences for these two substitute products.

SUPPLY AND DEMAND ANALYSIS

The heart of price formation under competition is the supply and demand analysis. There is probably no more overworked and misunderstood phrase in economics than the "law of supply and demand." To some it is a form of magic or divine guidance invoked to explain away any major problem or dilemma. To others it is something that can be used or ignored, depending upon the desires of the moment. It is to these fundamental ideas of supply and demand that we shall now apply ourselves.

The Meaning of Demand

Demand is a schedule of different quantities of a commodity that buyers will purchase at different prices at a given time and place. The *law of demand* merely formalizes the logical relationship between quantities taken and prices.

153

The lower the price, the more will be purchased; and conversely, the higher the price, the less will be purchased.

The basis for such relationships between the prices charged and the amount sold at any given time and place stems from several facts about consumers and consumption. First, as a buyer has increasing amounts of an item, usually the usefulness and desirability of each succeeding additional amount decreases. Even though we highly desire steak at any meal, we certainly get much more satisfaction from the first steak than from the second. Therefore, if there are two steaks to be sold to each of us, we certainly will pay less than if there were only one. Second, we differ substantially as to our likes and dislikes. This we saw in our study of consumers and consumption. Most of us consider steak very desirable, but there is a considerably fewer number of us who feel the same way about lamb chops. Prices of lamb chops would certainly have to be lowered in order to sell them to the group that had this low preference. Also, for a great many of us, even though we like an item and would find it very useful, prices must be lower before we could buy it. Finally, it is an arithmetic necessity that we must buy less of a product as its price rises if our income does not change.

Table 8-1 gives a hypothetical demand schedule of prices and quantities that might exist for corn at any given time and place. Of course, for any one time period a definite amount of corn will be purchased at the stated price—say, 5,000 million bushels at $3.00. But the demand schedule shows what amounts would have been purchased *if* the price had been different. Figure 8-2 is the graphic presentation of the demand schedule given in Table 8-1. This is the *demand curve* for corn. If the law of demand is valid, the demand curve will always slope downward and to the right of a graph similar to Figure 8-2.

Table 8-1. Hypothetical Demand
Schedule for Corn.

PRICE PER BUSHEL	AMOUNT PURCHASED
$	(Millions of Bushels)
4.00	3,000
3.75	3,400
3.50	3,800
3.00	5,000
2.75	5,700
2.50	6,100
2.25	7,400

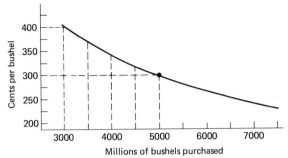

Figure 8–2. Hypothetical demand curve for corn.

The demand curve in Figure 8-2 and the demand schedule in Table 8-1 both illustrate the nature of the relationship between quantity and price as it is established by prospective buyers. *If* the price were $4.00, 3,000 million bushels would be purchased; *if* the price were $2.25, 7,400 million bushels would be purchased, and so on for any other possible prices assuming that all other things remained unchanged. The demand schedule and curve do not indicate what *the* price and quantity are; only what the effect different prices will have on the quantity purchased. *The* price that will exist has not yet been established, and demand alone cannot establish it.

Several important points must be kept in mind if the idea of demand is to be used correctly. First, it is a series, or schedule, of amount-price relationships. To forget this will often lead to the very common error of associating with demand a price change or a consumption change alone.

Second, demand indicates the differing amounts that will be purchased at differing prices, and not simply the amounts needed by purchasers. The demand that is important in marketing is *effective demand.* Effective demand is the desire of the consumer for the commodity backed up by purchasing power. The people of India both need and desire many things—more rice, better clothing, better homes, and so on. However, the Indians' demand for these things is very limited, because they do not have the purchasing power to make their needs and wants effective. The pertinent marketing question is always, "How much will be bought at a price?" and not, "How much will be needed or desired?"

We should add another important thought. In the example of the demand for corn, we have been concerned with the farm-level demand for this important product. However, consumers do not buy corn but rather the products made from corn, such as corn flakes and pork. Therefore, we say that the demand for corn is a *derived demand,* that is, its level is caused by the level of demand for the final products made from it. In Figure 8-3, the derived demands for retail pork chops are shown. There is a family of derived

155

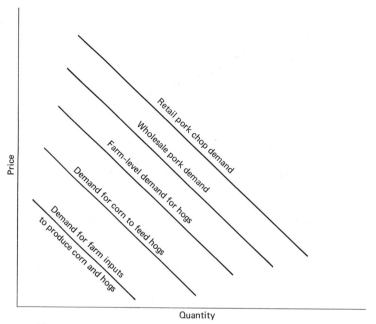

Figure 8–3. The family of derived demand curves for pork chops.

demand curves for each food product. The differences between the derived demand curves are the costs of adding time, form, space, and possession utility at each successive market level.

Reservation demand is another concept useful in understanding food prices. Sellers of products may reserve part of their supplies for their own use or for later sale. The rate of release of a stock of farm products to the market depends upon the farmer's desire to hold stocks, and his alternative, that of using farm products on-farm, for example, in livestock feeding. A farmer's reservation demand is influenced by present and expected market prices, product perishability and urgent need to sell, his on-farm uses of the product, and the availability of storage space.

Finally, we need to distinguish between the total market demand schedule—all purchases at each price—and the firm's or consumer's market demand schedule. Consumer demand schedules are added horizontally to obtain the firm's demand schedule, and all firms' demand schedules can be added horizontally to obtain the total market demand schedule.

The Meaning of Supply

Supply is a schedule of differing quantities that will be offered for sale at different prices at a given time and place. The *law of supply* is simply the

Table 8-2. Hypothetical Supply Schedule for Corn.

PRICE PER BUSHEL	AMOUNT OFFERED FOR SALE
$	*(Millions of Bushels)*
4.00	5,600
3.75	5,500
3.50	5,400
3.00	5,000
2.75	4,750
2.50	4,400
2.25	4,000

logical relationship that exists in these circumstances. The higher the price, the more will be offered for sale; the lower the price, the less will be offered for sale. Whereas demand indicates the relationship between quantity and price from the buyers' viewpoint, supply indicates a similar relationship from the sellers' viewpoint.

As we did for demand, we can make a *supply schedule* of quantities and prices and from this plot a *supply curve.* This is illustrated in Table 8-2. Here, too, it must be remembered that at any one time and place only one point on this curve represents the actual situation. But the curve presents what would be the effects of different prices on amounts offered. If the law of supply is valid, the supply curve will always slope upward and to the right on a graph like that shown in Figure 8-4.

Even more than in the case of demand, common usage has confused the meaning of supply. It is a commonly accepted practice to label changes in production as changes in supply. For example, the amount of hogs available today on the market is widely referred to as the supply available. To be

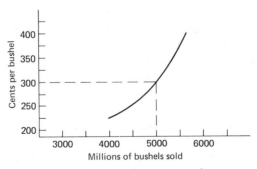

Figure 8-4. Hypothetical supply curve for corn.

realistic, we must accept this terminology confusion, but we should keep clearly in mind just what is meant. When supply is used in the economic sense, it always represents a series of price-quantity relationships.

Time is a very important consideration in supply analysis. One should remember that supply exists at a *given time*. These given time periods can be of different lengths, usually designated as the short run, the intermediate period, and the long run.

The major limitation on supply for the short run is the existing quantity of goods already produced and on hand. Because this stock of goods exists, costs that have been previously met in its production should not influence price. However, replacement costs and storage costs may influence the seller's judgment and therefore influence the supply schedule.

It is the interrelationship with future time that brings cost into the supply picture. When the given time period is future time, analysts usually consider two additional periods, the intermediate and the long run.

The intermediate period is that time during which goods can be produced only with the existing production facilities. The long run refers to that time during which the production facilities themselves may be expanded or contracted. It is in this problem of costs, output, and the time period involved where the differentiation between *fixed* and *variable* costs becomes useful. Fixed costs are those incurred in the investment in plants and equipment usable over several production periods. Once made, these are costs to the owner whether they are currently used or not. Variable costs represent those items used up in one full cycle of the production process and therefore vary with the amount of production. In hog production, feed-concentrate costs and vaccination charges are variable; the costs incurred from the already purchased hog feeders and houses are fixed. In fruit production the costs of spray chemicals are variable, whereas that of the spraying machinery once purchased is fixed. In the intermediate period the fixed cost of the existing facilities is not an element influencing the seller's decision with respect to supply. If prices cover his variable costs, he may decide to produce and sell. In the long run, however, the costs of all things used in production enter into the determination of supply. Though a grower may produce hogs at prices covering only his feed and other variable costs for a while, eventually his returns must cover the fixed costs of his equipment, for it too wears out in time and must be replaced.

Because the supply schedule of amounts to be produced refers to a period involving the passage of time, it must take into consideration the time necessary to initiate and complete the production process. For some commodities like broilers, this may be only a period of weeks; for others, like cattle, it may be a period of several years. Thus, the supply curve for the same commodity will be different for the different periods of time under consideration.

The time element greatly complicates the analysis of agricultural supply. Unwary observers who notice that large receipts on today's market move at lower prices, or that a large crop brings lower average prices, conclude that the law of supply is not valid. However, these situations point up the problem of determining the proper time lag between the price stimulus and the quantity response. High livestock prices on the market today will result in larger receipts one and two days later because of the time necessary to initiate the shipment from the farm. The proper supply schedule in this instance would probably be one that related today's prices with receipts two days later. The hog production coming to market during the fall months is in response to conditions that existed far enough in the past that hog producers changed their breeding plans. The supply schedule in this case would relate current prices with the level of production forthcoming at least twelve months later.

The Equilibrium Price

The forces at work on the buyers' side and the forces at work on the producers' side have often been referred to as the two blades of a scissors. Because it takes both blades to cut effectively, so must both demand and supply be considered in the determination of a price. Table 8-3 shows both the demand schedule of Table 8-1 and the supply schedule of Table 8-2. The question is, what will be the price of corn given these two sets of conditions? As we run down the list of prices we find that at $3.00 per bushel, buyers will take 5,000 million bushels. At this same price sellers will produce and offer for sale 5,000 million bushels. At $3.00, buyers will take all that sellers will offer. There will be no unsold corn; the market will be cleared. This, then, will be the price that will be established if the forces of competition are allowed to function. This is the *equilibrium price,* the point where demand and supply are equal. Figure 8-5 graphically presents the same picture. Where

Table 8-3. Hypothetical Demand and Supply Schedules for Corn.

AMOUNT PURCHASED	PRICE PER BUSHEL	AMOUNT OFFERED FOR SALE
(Millions of Bushels)	*$*	*(Millions of Bushels)*
3,000	4.00	5,600
3,400	3.75	5,500
3,800	3.50	5,400
5,000	3.00	5,000
5,700	2.75	4,750
6,100	2.50	4,400
7,400	2.25	4,000

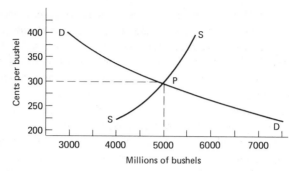

Figure 8–5. Hypothetical supply and demand curves for corn, illustrating the equilibrium price.

the demand *(DD)* and supply *(SS)* curves intersect, *(P)* is the equilibrium price.

Why, in Figure 8-5, must the price come to rest at $3.00? Suppose prices tried to come to rest at $3.50. At this price, sellers would be willing to sell more corn than buyers would purchase. The desire of these extra sellers to sell at some price above $3.00 would result in price concessions to attract buyers. Any price lower than $3.00 would find additional buyers but fewer sellers. In this situation the desire of eager buyers to secure corn at what they considered advantageous prices would result in the bidding up of prices. At $3.00, both the buyers and sellers who are willing to enter the market at all would be satisfied, and 5,000 million bushels would change hands. This price would be an equilibrium price.

The equilibrium price is a compromise between the desire of sellers for a higher price and the desire of buyers for a lower price. No other price is an acceptable compromise, although neither buyer nor seller is completely happy at the equilibrium price. Above the equilibrium price, it is a *buyers' market*—more is supplied than is demanded, and price cutting will occur. Below the equilibrium price, it is a *sellers' market,* and eager buyers will bid up the price to the equilibrium level.

The equilibrium price is not a point readily found or easily maintained. Rather, prices are always overshooting the mark in their search for the price that will clear the market. Changes may be small, but they occur frequently as buyers and sellers search for the market-clearing price. It is more correct to say that the equilibrium price is that price toward which actual prices will *tend to move.*

Changes in Demand and Supply Curves

The demand and supply curves show the responses of buyers and sellers to a change in price, everything else being equal. For example, when prices rise, producers are given a profit incentive to increase production and therefore the quantity supplied to the market. Consumers, on the other hand, receive a signal to reduce their consumption of that product. Thus, a change in price results in a change in the quantity supplied and demanded.

A shift in the supply or demand curve is quite different from a movement along the curves. If more of a commodity is produced or consumed at the same prices as previously, it is said that there has been a rightward shift in the supply or demand curve. If less is produced or consumed at the same prices as previously, it is said that there has been a leftward shift in the curves.

Many factors can cause shifts in consumer demand curves. Generally, such factors can be grouped as follows:

1. A change in number of buyers (providing per capita purchasing power and other factors remain unchanged). Such changes may occur from either population growth or the extension of the market served by the product.

2. A change in the incomes or purchasing power of people. We have seen from our previous discussion of consumers' buying patterns that income changes may be either positively or negatively related to demand changes, depending upon the particular product.

3. A change in the tastes and preferences for particular products. We have seen that these may be a result of many factors, such as religion, habit, or personal desires.

4. A change in the relative prices of products that are substitutes for each other. Most consumer goods have a substitute to some extent, and the price we will pay for a given amount of one product will depend to some extent upon what we would have to pay for the possible substitutes.

5. A change in the expectation of buyers as to the future levels of prices. In most instances there is some flexibility in the timing of purchases. Therefore, whether consumers will hurry into buying or wait a while will be affected by their evaluation of future price levels.

If we are concerned with demand at other levels of the marketing system, such as wholesale or farm levels, then still another factor that can cause change must be included. Marketing costs may change, which would mean that a change in the consumer level demand might not be fully reflected in the derived demand at the other marketing levels. For example, the precooking of potatoes might result in more consumer demand for this product than for uncooked potatoes. However, the additional processing costs might cancel out this change so that there would be no shift in the demand for potatoes at the farm level.

The most important factors influencing the longer-run demand for all agricultural products as a group are the changes in the general income levels of a country and the growth of the population. The other factors generally affect specific products and may be of a short-run nature.

The supply curve may also shift. If *more* of a product is offered for sale at the same or lower prices than before, supply will increase. Referring to the corn example, if 6,000 million bushels are offered at $4.00, 5,700 at $3.75, and so forth, supply has increased. If this new schedule were plotted on Figure 8-4, the increased supply curve would fall to the right of the original. When *less* of a commodity is offered for sale at the same or higher prices than before, supply will decrease. The curve for this decreased supply would fall to the left of the original curve.

As is the case for demand, many factors can combine to increase or decrease supply. Generally, they may be classified as follows:

1. In the short-run period there may be a change in the various factors that would induce sellers to offer their available stock of goods at a different schedule of prices. These would include such factors as costs of storage, the sellers' need for cash, and the general expectations as to the future situation.

2. In the intermediate and long-run periods, there may be a change in the costs of production of the commodity. This may be caused by changes in costs of needed inputs or in the technology of the production of the commodity itself. It may also be caused by changes in the costs of producing other commodities that compete for the same resources. For example, a technological change that increased the feed conversion rate for hogs and lowered their costs of production would increase the supply of hogs. At the same time, if there were no similar changes in cattle production, the supply of cattle would decrease, because hogs and cattle are farm enterprises that compete with each other for the same resources of production.

It is important to remember that although supply and demand curves frequently shift at the same time, the demand shifters are totally different from the supply shifters. This makes it possible to analyze the effects of most developments by shifting only one of the curves and moving along the other. Changes in demand and supply have their real importance in their effect on the equilibrium price. Figure 8-6 shows the effect on equilibrium price of four possible supply and demand shifts. The changed curve is always shown by the broken line and the new equilibrium price by P'. These examples can be expanded to show the results of all sorts of combinations of supply and demand changes.

Elasticity of Demand and Supply

We have yet to discuss one additional and very important concept relative to demand and supply analysis. Both demand and supply are schedule relationships of prices and quantities. The law of demand states that as prices go

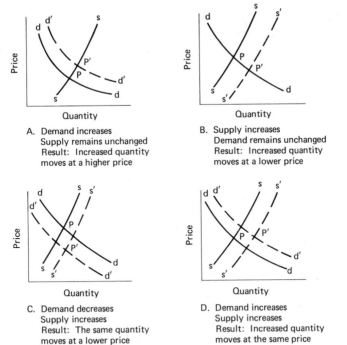

Figure 8–6. Situations illustrating some effects of changes in supply and demand.

down, the quantities purchased will increase. The law of supply states that as prices go down, the quantities offered for sale will decrease. But *how much* will the quantities respond to changes in price? The relationship of the changes in quantity to the changes in price is the concept of *price elasticity.*

Generally, demand curves are classified according to their elasticities into two broad groups. These broad groups represent demand that is elastic and demand that is inelastic. The dividing point between these two classifications is unit elasticity.

Demands with unit elasticity are those in which the changes in quantity taken are of the *same magnitude* as the changes in price. The elastic demands are those in which the changes in quantity taken are proportionately *greater* than the changes in price. The inelastic demands are those in which the changes in quantity taken are proportionately *less* than the changes in price. For example, let us assume that price has decreased by 10 per cent. The law of demand indicates that the quantity taken for commodities with demand curves of different elasticities would be as follows:[1]

---

[1] Elasticity can be mathematically calculated. When so presented, unit elasticity is −1; an elastic demand is something more than −1; and an inelastic demand is something less than −1.

1. With unit elasticity, amount taken would increase exactly 10 per cent.

2. With an elastic demand, amount taken would increase more than 10 per cent—perhaps 12 or 15 per cent.

3. With an inelastic demand, amount taken would increase less than 10 per cent—perhaps 5 or 7 per cent.

The necessity for the product and degree of *substitutability* of one product for another is the basic determinant of the elasticity of demand for a particular commodity. Substitutability may arise from any number of causes. There may be absolute physical need for a particular product and not another. Social, psychological, or religious factors may affect substitutability evaluations in individual minds. And of course the level of income itself will affect how substitutable one product is for another.

Commodities with inelastic demands are often those which fall into the classification of necessities and which have few substitutes. Consumers want them and are relatively insensitive to price changes. Commodities with elastic demands are often those whose use is not directed by necessity or habit and which have several close substitutes. Consumer response for such products is more sensitive to price changes.

On graphs of the same scale, the more inelastic the demand, the steeper is its plotted curve.[2] Figure 8-7 shows how food products generally increase in price elasticity as they move toward the consumer. This reflects the greater substitution possibilities for branded items at the local store than for commodity items at the farm level.

Cross-elasticity of demand refers to the effect of a price change in one commodity on the quantity demanded of another product. Economists classify related food products as complements or substitutes. Two foods are substitutes, for example beef and pork, if an increase in the price of one increases the consumption of the other. They are complements (such as ham and eggs) if an increase in the price of one decreases consumption of the other. Complementary products are eaten together, and they are often promoted together, as when the lettuce industry co-sponsors an advertisement with the salad dressing manufacturers. In contrast, producers of substitute foods are rivals for the consumers' dollar.

The most important implication of demand elasticity is its effect on consumer food expenditures and the amount of money received by food firms from selling different quantities at different prices. We can easily see this by studying the results of a 10 per cent cut in prices on three hypothetical commodities of different elasticities. For a commodity with a demand of unit elasticity, the quantity taken would increase 10 per cent and the total

---

[2] However, the slope of a demand curve is not the same as its elasticity, because slope is calculated in absolute units (the rise over the run) whereas elasticity is calculated in percentage terms. Therefore it is not possible to compare, visually, the elasticities of two different demand curves drawn on different scales.

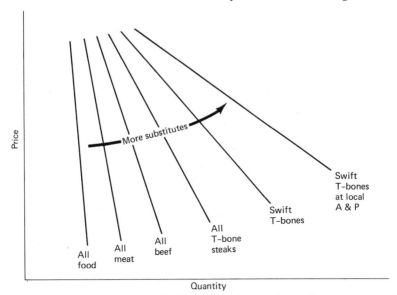

Figure 8–7. Demand elasticity at various market levels.

returns from sales under the new situation would be exactly the *same* as before the price cut. For a commodity with an elastic demand, the quantity taken would increase more than 10 per cent and the new total returns from sales would be *greater* than before. However, for a commodity with an inelastic demand, something less than 10 per cent more of the commodity would be taken and the total returns would be *less*. This is shown in Figure 8-8, where the total returns are indicated in parentheses.

Demand curves for the same product are often not of the same elasticity throughout the entire curve. Typically, elasticity is greater for small quantities of products, and the demand curve becomes less elastic at higher volumes. Elasticity may also change over a period of time. Thus, many things that were once luxuries with elastic demands may shift into the necessity category with inelastic demands.

Table 8-4 shows some price elasticities of demand for selected food products. Notice the wide range in elasticities, that farm level price elasticity of demand is always lower than retail price elasticity, and that most farm commodities have an inelastic demand.

Will a large crop return more money to growers than a small one, even though prices are lower? What will be the effect of restricting output on the total returns from sales? Should a store seek to lower its prices to sell more goods? Knowledge of demand elasticity and its relationship to total returns is the key to answering questions such as these.

The same elasticity framework also can be applied to supply. Commodities that are very responsive to price changes have elastic supply curves. Those

165

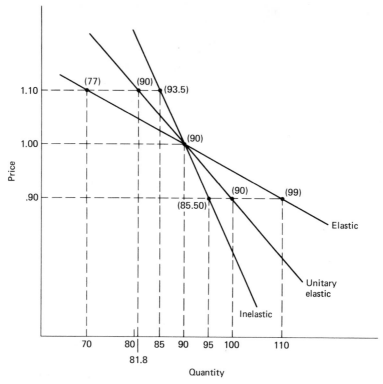

Price X Quantity = Total Returns
(Shown in parentheses)

Figure 8–8. Impact of a 10 percent price change on total returns: unitary, elastic, and inelastic demand curves.

that respond relatively little to price changes have inelastic supplies. As for the different elasticities of supply, on graphs of the same scale the more inelastic the supply the steeper the plotted curve.

Time is a very important factor in supply-elasticity analysis. Generally, as the time period under consideration lengthens, the supply curve tends to be more elastic. For example, the supply curve for hogs for the period September–December is nearly perfectly inelastic. Regardless of price changes, little can be done to change the number of hogs available for slaughter during this specific period. If an eighteen-month period is considered, farmers can change their breeding plans in response to price, and the curve will be somewhat more elastic. If a period of five or six years is considered, more hog houses can be built, more equipment can be obtained, and the supply curves will be more elastic. Such situations might be illustrated by the supply curves in Figure 8-9.

Within the intermediate and long-run periods, the degree of elasticity of

Table 8-4. Retail and Farm Price Elasticities for Selected Foods, 1946–1967.

| COMMODITY | EFFECT OF A 1 PER CENT CHANGE IN PRICE ON THE PERCENTAGE CHANGE IN QUANTITY CONSUMED | |
	FARM LEVEL	RETAIL LEVEL
Turkey	—	−1.56
Margarine	−.69	− .84
Chicken	−.60	− .78
Apples	−.68	− .72
Butter	−.46	− .65
Beef	−.42	− .64
Ice cream	—	− .52
Cheese	—	− .46
Pork	−.24	− .41
Fresh milk	−.32	− .34
Eggs	−.23	− .31
Potatoes	−.15	− .30
Bread, cereals	—	− .15

Source: P. S. George and G. A. King, *Consumer Demand for Food Commodities in the U.S. with Projections for 1980,* University of California, Giannini Foundation Monograph No. 26, March 1971. Reprinted by permission.

different products will depend largely upon the ease and costs of increasing or decreasing production. If it is difficult and costly to change the output of existing facilities or to get in or out of the production process itself, the supply will be relatively more inelastic. If such adjustments are easy and not too costly to make, the supply will be more elastic.

Within the short-run period, the elasticity of the supply curve of sellers'

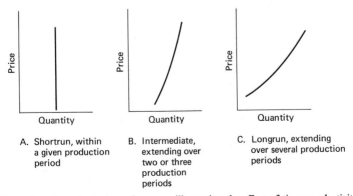

A. Shortrun, within a given production period

B. Intermediate, extending over two or three production periods

C. Longrun, extending over several production periods

Figure 8–9. Hypothetical supply curves illustrating the effect of time on elasticity.

167

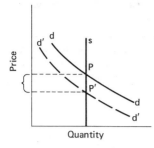 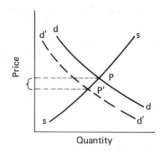

A. With inelastic supply
   price change is great

B. With more elastic supply
   price change is less

Figure 8–10. Hypothetical situations illustrating the effect of a demand change on situations with different supply elasticities.

offerings on the market will vary with the difference in storability of a product. An owner of a perishable product has little choice except to move the product at almost any price. The supply curve in this instance would be almost perfectly inelastic (similar to situation *A* in Figure 8-9). If the product is storable, however, owners have more control over the time when they may sell it and can respond more readily to price changes. The supply curve in this instance would be more elastic than for the perishable product (similar to situation *B* in Figure 8-9).

The probability that there will be highly inelastic supplies for many agricultural products in the short-run period and also relatively inelastic supply in both the intermediate and long-run periods has two major implications. First, it means that changes in demand are of tremendous importance in changing the equilibrium price. Second, it means that price fluctuations resulting from changes in demand are much more severe than when the supply curve is more elastic. Figure 8-10 illustrates the effect of an equal decrease in demand in two situations—one with a perfectly inelastic supply *(A)* and the other with a somewhat more elastic supply *(B)*. Notice the difference in the degree of price change (*P* and *P̂*) as the demand changes.

APPLICATIONS OF SUPPLY AND DEMAND ANALYSIS

It is not sufficient simply to be aware that supply and demand influence food prices. The student must understand the mechanics of supply and demand shifts in order to be able to analyze and predict food price changes. Some selected applications of supply and demand analysis will be helpful in building this skill.

The Instability of Farm Prices

We have seen that farm prices are more volatile than nonfood prices. The reason for this lies in the inelastic supply and demand curves for agriculture, and because of the unpredictable changes in food supplies as a result of weather conditions, disease, and other factors. Because of the inelastic curves, shifts in either demand or supply will result in proportionately larger price changes. The more elastic nonfood supply and demand curves serve to cushion price changes for those products. Instability of farm incomes is directly related to unstable farm prices. Because the demand for most farm products is inelastic, falling prices will reduce total returns and rising prices will increase these returns. The resultant income instability complicates the farmer's planning process.

Incentives to Restrict Farm Output

Inelastic demand provides farmers with a profit incentive to restrict output (shift supply leftward) and raise gross farm income, as shown in Figure 8-11. However, it has generally been difficult for farmers to achieve, independently, the levels of supply control necessary to raise total return. This is because farmers tend to increase output (which shifts supply rightward) in response to higher prices resulting from supply control programs. Conse-

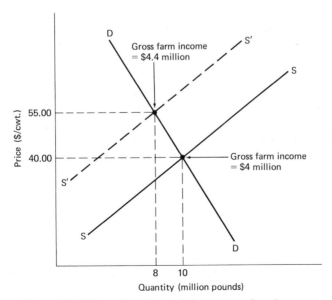

Figure 8–11. Effects of supply restriction on gross farm income.

quently, most successful agricultural supply control programs require government authority to prevent supply expansion from eroding higher prices. Consumers, of course, bear the costs of successful agricultural supply control programs.

Who Benefits from a Larger than Expected Crop?

The agricultural supply curve is drawn for normal, expected yields. An unexpected decrease in yields shifts the supply curve leftward; an unexpected yield increase shifts supply rightward. The leftward shift results in an increase in farm income because of the inelastic demand. The rightward supply shift lowers farm prices and, to add insult to injury, this movement along an inelastic demand curve reduces gross farm income. The farmer is penalized for an unexpectedly large crop!

Should farmers, then, hope or pray for poor yields to shift supply leftward in order to increase their income? No. A better solution is to provide farmers with good market information on which to base their planting decisions, so there will not be such surprises. A less-than-altruistic farmer might hope and pray that his neighbors suffer poor yields but that he himself reaps bumper crops! A large crop at high prices is the best of all possible worlds.

Who Benefits from Cost-Reducing Farm Technology?

New farming technologies shift the supply curve rightward. As prices fall along an inelastic demand curve, gross farm sales also fall. This means that the benefits of cost-reducing agricultural technology are passed on to the consumer in the form of lower relative food prices in the long run.

Does this mean that farmers should resist the development and adoption of new farm machinery and higher yielding crops? Not necessarily. Since many of these techniques are developed in the farm input sector or in universities, farmers do not control their development. In any case, there is good reason for each farmer to adopt new technologies and lower his costs in the short run, even though he simply moves to a new level of the cost-price squeeze in the long run. The ones who first adopt, of course, gain a profit advantage over those who adopt later.

How Do Exports Affect Food Prices?

There was an unexpected increase in U.S. farm product exports in 1972. In the short run, supplies could not be expanded, and this increased demand pushed prices up an inelastic supply curve, as shown in Figure 8-12. These high prices induced increased farm production in the following years, and prices fell as the supply curve became more elastic.

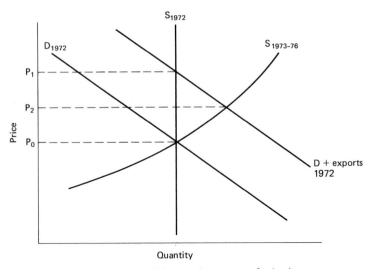

Figure 8–12. Effects of increased exports on food prices.

What Is the Effect of Food Price Ceilings and Floors?

A *price ceiling* is a legally set price below the equilibrium price; a *price floor* is a legally imposed price above the equilibrium level. Market prices are prohibited by law from falling below floors and from rising above ceilings. Price floors are sometimes used to "support" farm prices and incomes. Price ceilings are sometimes used to prevent inflation, although there is some question about their value in doing so.

Price floors and ceilings prevent buyers and sellers from reaching a market-clearing price. As shown in Figure 8-13, a price floor generates a surplus of supply over demand ($Q_0 - Q_1$). This may be stored, dumped, or sold in noncompeting markets. Price ceilings, on the other hand, result in black markets, rationing, and out-of-stock problems.

Almost all agricultural legislation has dealt with how to raise prices. During war periods, however, the problem has been how to keep prices from rising too fast or too high. The Office of Price Administration (OPA) during World War II and the Office of Price Stabilization (OPS) during the Korean War were direct attempts to control rising prices through price ceilings.

In initiating a control program, prices are "frozen" as of a given date by government order. From these freeze points, adjustments up or down are made as needed. The enforcement technique is simply to make it illegal to charge above the legal levels. The simplicity of the technique, however, belies the simplicity of the job. Effective price control is immeasurably complex. Agricultural prices are difficult to control. With wide annual and seasonal variations in production, differences in quality, and numerous and small pro-

171

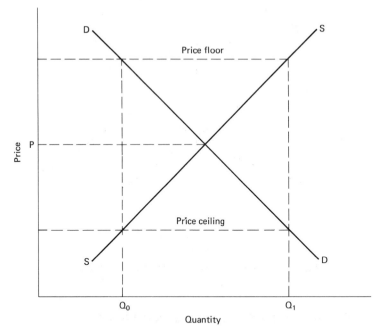

Figure 8–13. Food price floors and ceilings.

ducers, price ceilings always seem to be out of adjustment at some place or time. A rationing and subsidy system has to be devised. Though breakdowns and confusion occur, price control will probably remain a much-used technique in times of inflationary duress.

Relationship of Prices to Costs in Agriculture

The relationships of prices to costs under conditions of perfect competition are so frequently misunderstood, we should again review them. We have stated that the point where supply and demand are equal will be the equilibrium price situation for the short- as well as for the longer-run periods.

The relationship of this price in the short run to costs is quite clear. In the short-run period, goods have already been produced and are on hand. The level of demand may be such that sellers can dispose of their entire holdings at a profit. During this very short interval there can be no more goods produced and sold in order to capture part of the profits and as a consequence drive prices down. The supply is very inelastic, and for the individual sellers price may be very high. The same situation may exist in the opposite extreme. A low level of demand may mean that goods must sell at a loss. Therefore, in the short run there is no necessary relationship between costs and prices received in the market. In agriculture, the perishable and seasonal nature of production make these short-run profit and loss possibilities quite likely. Perfect competition does not guarantee the monetary success of any firm at any particular time.

The longer-run equilibrium price, however, is a result of the demand and the intermediate and long-run supply. In actuality, this then becomes the average of the many short-run prices over time. What about the relationship of the level of this longer-run average price level and costs?

In the intermediate period, it will be recalled, production can be altered within existing firms with existing technology. If demand is high, producers may expand production up to the point where rational conduct tells them to stop—that is, where the additional cost of another unit is equal to the price. At this output, profits will be maximized. If the level of demand is so low that prices will not cover the variable costs of production, such as seed and fertilizer, the producer may not produce at all. Or if the price will cover the direct or variable proportion of his costs but not his fixed costs, he may produce up to the point where his losses are minimized.

In the long run, however, new firms may enter an industry, or old ones leave it. Existing firms can change their size and seek the most efficient technology. Under such a long-run consideration, if demand and prices are high and high profits are being enjoyed, production will be increased as more firms enter the industry and existing firms expand. Thus, prices will be under pressure from the increased production. Similarly, if firms are operating at a loss, enough firms will eventually be forced out so that the remaining ones will share in the industry demand under conditions where there no longer are losses. Therefore, in the long run, production will adjust so that average prices will tend to equal average costs. That is, the returns to capital, land, labor, and management will be no more, or no less, than they could receive if they were used in other forms of production. This is the familiar cost-price squeeze in agriculture.

The problems facing an apple orchard operator offer a good illustration of these different time period relationships. Once fruit is harvested the operator has the alternative of either selling at the market price or not selling at all. The demand situation may be such that he may enjoy large profits or suffer substantial losses, but he cannot alter his previously made decisions to produce. And because there are so many other sellers, he cannot influence price by withholding part of his apples from the market.

In the intermediate period, as the harvest season approaches the orchard operator can take certain actions if the price appears too low. He may cut out part of his spraying activities. He may decide to pick and pack only the better fruit—or in an extreme case, none at all. Or if the prices are high he may exert every effort to handle his crop so that he can harvest as many high-quality apples as possible.

However, if over a period of several years the prices have been persistently very low, he may abandon his orchard completely or not replace his trees as they gradually die. Or if the prices have been very high, new orchards may be started for production, or the current one kept in a high state of productivity and expansion. From this it can be seen that, in the long run, adjustments will be made which will tend to lower prices if they have been above costs and raise prices if they have been below costs. A perfect equilibrium price in the long run would be that which would encourage neither an increase nor a decrease in production.

In the real world, with shifting supply and demand functions, the existence of such perfect long-run equilibrium situations is highly unlikely. In addition, the length of the long-run period varies, depending upon the nature of the costs and equipment involved. In some cases it may be only a few years, or as in the case of apple production it may be ten or more years.

THE SUPPLY-DEMAND BALANCE

Figure 8-14 summarizes the manner in which relative prices serve to coordinate food supply and demand. When supply and demand are in balance, a "normal" relative price is established. An increase or decrease in either the supply or demand factors tips the scale to change per capita availability and relative prices. Prices move opposite to per capita food supplies.

The indicator needle in Figure 8-14 portrays the inelastic demand for food. By placing the fulcrum near the bottom of the diagram, a small change in per capita supplies produces a larger change in food prices.

This figure illustrates the communicating role of prices in food markets and the built-in stabilizing features of price-coordinated markets. For example, an increase in the relative price of a commodity signals producers to expand output and consumers to reduce consumption. As this happens, per capita supplies swing back to a normal level and the price indicator swings back to the center.

MARKETING AND THE LAW OF ONE PRICE

A market has been defined as an arena for organizing business activity. We have also seen that the business of the food marketing system is to add time, form, place, and possession utilities to basic farm commodities. In our economic system, prices and the profit motive play a key role in coordinating this marketing activity. The way in which this occurs bears closer examination.

In economic analysis, the term *market* has a special significance—that of an arena wherein all buyers and sellers are highly sensitive to each others' transactions. What one does affects the other. In this market, all buyers and sellers must be able to communicate with one another, must be capable of exchanging products with each other, and must be exposed to similar price signals.

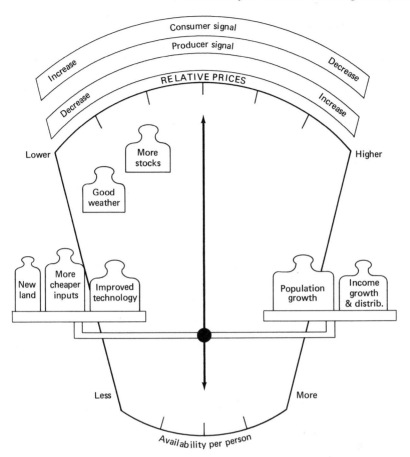

Figure 8–14. The food supply–demand balance. (Adapted from James P. Houck and Wallace Barr, *Your Food: A Food Policy Basebook,* Ohio State University Press, revised 1977, p. 6. Reprinted by permission)

We normally think of markets as geographic areas. But in the context of market analysis, there are three other types of markets: (1) geographic (place utility markets), (2) product (form utility) markets, and (3) seasonal (time utility) markets. If the price of corn in Chicago varies with the world price of corn (which it does), we may infer that the Chicago market is a part of the world corn market. Or if the price of beef is sensitive to changes in the price of pork, we would suspect that both are in a single market, the red meat market. Or, if the June 1978 price of soybeans fluctuates with the October 1977 price of soybeans, we would say that both months are in the same market, namely the 1977–1978 soybean market. Market boundaries, then, are defined by the degree of interdependence of buyers and sellers over time, form, and space, and this interdependence is measured by price

175

sensitivity. These boundaries are not fixed. They could be compared to the ripples caused by dropping a pebble into a pond. We may find it useful, at one time, to identify a "beef market"; at another time we might refer to beef as being in the "red meat market"; at still other times, beef might be considered a part of the "all-food market." A market is a flexible tool of analysis.

Geographic markets may be local, regional, national, or international in scope. Bulky products such as hay have a small geographic market area because high transportation costs prevent distant buyers and sellers from trading with each other. Milk and livestock can be transported more economically so they tend to have regional or national markets. Wheat and cotton are easily transported and have international markets. With improved communications and transportation facilities, market areas usually increase in size.

There is a special relationship among prices in space, time, and form markets. It is known as the *law of one price* (LOOP). This law states that under certain conditions all prices within a market are uniform, after taking into account the costs of adding place, time, and form utility to products within the market. The law can be very useful in determining the size of a market, predicting price changes within a market, and evaluating the pricing efficiency of a market.

Figure 8-15 illustrates the law of one price in the international corn market. This map shows the prices and transportation costs for four shipping points (Farnhamville, Seneca, Champaign, and Columbus), three export ports, (Chicago, New Orleans, and Norfolk), and the major port of entry into the European Economic Community, Rotterdam. Grain tends to flow from the surplus-producing shipping-point areas, through the U.S. ports, and on to the deficit-producing European countries. The prices in Figure 8-15 are aligned according to the law of one price. They differ only in the cost of transportation—the cost of adding place utility to the corn. Put another way, each price can be divided into two parts: (1) a uniform price of corn throughout the market, and (2) the cost of adding place utility to the corn.

Under competitive market conditions, there is a tendency for prices within a market to remain aligned according to the law of one price. To illustrate: If the price European consumers are willing to pay for corn were to increase by 10 cents per bushel, there also would be an increase in the price of corn at the three U.S. ports and, ultimately, at the farm level. Within the market area, these prices are tied together and will move together.

The law of one price results from the profit-seeking behavior of food marketing firms and traders. If the Rotterdam corn price increases by 10 cents per bushel, grain traders will see that extra profits can be made by increasing the flow of corn from the United States to Europe, because the price difference exceeds the transportation cost. As traders respond to this profit incentive, they will bid up the United States price of corn and reduce the Rotterdam price. After all adjustments are made, the United States-Rotterdam price

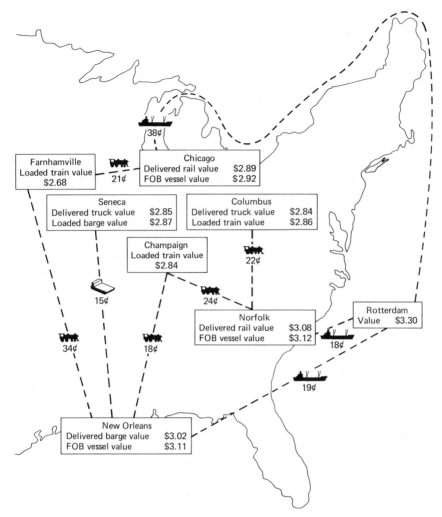

Figure 8–15. Prices per bushel in the international corn market, 1976.

difference will return to the level of the cost of transportation. And the U.S. farm price and the Rotterdam price will be higher than originally. Interestingly, the traders' behavior will serve to reduce the extra profits promised to them, because price differences within the market will return to the alignment that is consistent with the law of one price. In the meantime, however, the traders will have performed the very useful function of shifting the corn from the lower-valued to the higher-valued market.

The law of one price also can be applied to the addition of form and time utility to the product markets and the seasonal markets. For example, a dairy processor can change the form of raw farm milk into fluid milk, cheese, butter, ice cream, or yogurt. Processors will allocate their supply of raw milk to these alternative products in such a way that their final retail prices, less the costs of processing each product, will equal a uniform raw-milk price. For seasonal commodities, storage costs are the clue to price changes. Farmers, for example, would be expected to store enough grain at harvest so that the following spring's price would be equal to the fall harvest price, plus the cost of storage from fall to spring.

The law of one price is helpful in evaluating pricing efficiency within a market. Pricing efficiency is maximized when there is a tendency for prices to maintain the relationship suggested by the law of one price. Under these conditions, resources will be allocated correctly between their alternative uses; prices will serve as accurate guides for food industry decisions; and total industry output will be maximized. Conversely, with less than maximum pricing efficiency, resources will not be efficiently allocated, prices will not serve as good guides to marketing decisions, and there will be some loss in output. Poor pricing efficiency is usually associated with the presence of large, dominant firms, trade restraints, price manipulation, poor market information, or other barriers to trade.

PRICE DISCOVERY

It is useful to distinguish between *price determination*—the process by which the broad forces of supply and demand establish a general, market-clearing, equilibrium price for a commodity, and *price discovery*—the process by which buyers and sellers arrive at a specific price for a given lot of produce in a given location. The supply and demand price target must be "discovered" and applied to each transaction in the marketplace.

Price discovery is a human process, beset by errors in judgment and fact, and subject to the relative bargaining power of buyers and sellers. There is no guarantee that buyers and sellers will always immediately discover the equilibrium price. Only in perfect competition will discovered prices always equal the market-clearing price. In real life, variations in the price-discovery process make it profitable for buyers and sellers to shop around among alternatives and to bargain on prices and other terms of trade.

This distinction gives us a two-stage price-discovery process for farm products. Stage one consists of evaluating the supply and demand forces and estimating the market-clearing price. Stage two is the application of this estimated price to a specific trade, taking into consideration grade premiums, quality, discounts, buyer and seller services, and bargaining power. Pricing errors can arise at both stages of the pricing process, but these errors can be minimized, and price-discovery improved, by high quality market information and grading programs.

Five systems of price discovery for farm products have been identified:

(1) individual, decentralized negotiation; (2) organized, central market trading; (3) formula pricing; (4) bargained prices; and (5) administered prices. These alternative pricing systems vary in pricing efficiency, in the amount of price information they generate, in the freedom allowed buyers and sellers in arriving at prices, and in the relative bargaining strength conferred on buyers and sellers.

In *individual, decentralized negotiations,* each farmer bargains individually with buyers of farm products until a price is established. "Private treaty" negotiations are quite common in agriculture. The resulting fairness of prices depends upon the information, trading skills, and relative bargaining power of buyers and sellers. Consequently, prices discovered in this way tend to vary widely for different transactions. Moreover, the time and energy costs of this form of price discovery are rather high compared with the alternatives.

Organized, central markets shift the locus of price discovery from the farm gate to a central marketplace. All buyers and sellers and their supplies and demands are represented in the central market. Terminal markets and auctions are examples. These markets generate considerably more information than private-treaty markets and probably also reduce some costs of price discovery. Also, prices for individual transactions are likely to be more uniform.

Formula pricing systems evolved in attempts to secure the benefits of central-market price discovery without physically routing all produce through central markets. Egg producers, for example, frequently are paid a formula price, which is related to the "market price" reported by the U.S. Department of Agriculture Market News Service or the Urner-Barry report (a private market newsletter). These prices are adjusted, again by formula, for transport costs and quality differences. Meat frequently is purchased in advance to be priced "at the yellow sheet," a private price newsletter. Formula pricing can reduce transaction and bargaining costs. However, formulas can become obsolete; moreover, they require at least one "correct" price on which to base other prices.

Bargained prices are common for fruits, vegetables, nuts, and milk. Bargaining implies collective pricing on the part of farmers. The collective bargaining process used in labor is frequently cited as the process model for farmers to follow in order to discover farm prices. However, there are differences in labor and farm products. Bargained price discovery probably works best for commodities (1) with relatively few producers; (2) produced in a concentrated geographic area; and (3) which can be stored or withheld from the market.

Administered pricing systems are those in which the government becomes a third party in the price discovery process. Price supports, price ceilings, and supply control programs are the techniques of administered pricing. These are used for milk and, periodically, for feedgrains and food grains.

A number of price discovery systems are used in agricultural markets, as is shown in Table 8-5 (pp. 180–181). For each commodity, a unique pricing

179

Table 8-5. Pricing Systems for Selected Agricultural Products.

COMMODITY	GENERAL TYPE OF PRICING SYSTEM	BASIC PRICE-LEVEL DETERMINATION	METHODS OF DETERMINING OTHER PRICES
Eggs	Free market	Daily base-price quotations in a few wholesale markets. In New York and Chicago supported by cash-exchange trading	Premiums, discounts to other trading levels, grades and sizes, quantities, and geographical locations. Some producer-returns under contracts not related to short-run price changes
Broilers	Free market	Prices paid by large retailers for ready-to-cook broilers, selected cities, for future deliveries	Premiums, discounts to other trading levels, quantities, and geographical locations. Periodic specialing at retail. Most producer-returns under contracts related to performance standards
Fluid milk	Authoritarian, to determine minimum levels	Formula or negotiation under Federal-State orders, generally a pooled price to producers based on classified pricing for various end uses	Some negotiation on differentials but many wholesale and retail prices specified under orders
Butter	Free market, with government price supports providing a floor	Quotations based on cash-exchange trading at Chicago and New York by primary receivers and central market wholesalers	Averaged differentials for location and grade at country plants and also to cover margins for services in selling to wholesalers and retailers
Natural cheese	Free market, with government price supports providing a floor	Prices established on Wisconsin Cheese Exchange in Friday trading by plants and processors the primary indicator	Assembly-point prices tend to follow the exchange. Processed cheese prices become administered type
Live meat animals	Free market	Decentralized negotiations at auctions, country plants, or terminal market values	Reflections to and from dressed meat prices

Cotton	Free market, with government price supports providing a floor	Series of central market committees, under specific legislative authority, issue price quotations at central market level	Application of differentials for location, grade, etc. Become manufactured products in use; original identity largely lost in pricing consumer items
Tobacco	Free market	Warehouse auctions held for several weeks or months after harvest and curing where producer's tobacco is sold to tobacco companies	Become manufactured products in use original identity largely lost in pricing consumer items
Many fresh fruits and vegetables	Free market	Auction shipping-point, or terminal market sales to receivers or retailers	Differentials from shipping-point price or pool price to grower, from terminal market values to shipping firms. Distributor and retail margins likely to vary seasonally, etc.
Many vegetables for canning or freezing	Free market	Mainly contract prices between producer and packer, determined in advance of planting or harvest. These have fairly close relationship to selling prices of packers	Contract prices may be affected before and during harvest seasons by fresh market prices. Canned and frozen food prices are administered and/or determined by broker or direct sales to distributors, institutions, and retailers
Wheat	Free market, with government price supports providing a floor	Terminal market price quotations supported by cash and futures trading by country elevators and terminal market firms	Application of differentials for geographical location, trading level, etc. Become manufactured products in use, with identity largely lost in pricing consumer items but somewhat reflected in animal feeds

Source: G. B. Rogers, "Pricing Systems and Agricultural Marketing Research," *Agricultural Economics Research*, January 1970, pp. 1–11.

system has evolved to accommodate the needs of buyers and sellers and, through government action, the public interest. These systems are still evolving and should not be viewed as permanent.

SUMMARY

Prices are the signals that direct and coordinate the decisions of producers, consumers, and food marketing firms. These prices are the result of supply and demand forces operating within the framework of an open exchange, freely competitive marketplace. There is a tendency for farm prices to return to the supply and demand equilibrium point when disturbed. Shifts in the supply and demand curves result in new equilibrium prices. In the short run, farm and food products tend to have an inelastic demand in addition to an inelastic supply. As a consequence, farm prices and incomes tend to be highly variable, farmers can increase their gross incomes if they can restrict production and supplies, and the benefits of cost-reducing agricultural technology are passed on to consumers in the long-run. The almost perfectly competitive nature of agriculture results in a perpetual cost-price squeeze for farmers. Discovering market-clearing farm and food prices is a difficult task for farmers and food marketing firms.

QUESTIONS FOR DISCUSSION

1. You wish to help a businessman determine the elasticity of demand for his product. He indicates that sales behave as follows:

Price change	Sales change	Elasticity
$4.00 to $3.00	Increase	_____
$3.00 to $2.00	No change	_____
$2.00 to $1.00	Decrease	_____

Fill in the elasticity of demand for each price range.

2. Explain in your own words why some foods are more price-elastic than others, and the meaning of this for farmers.

3. What is the effect on farmers' prices and incomes when there are inelastic demands for most farm products?

4. How would the pricing conflict be resolved if a product had an inelastic demand at farm level and an elastic demand at retail level?

5. Suppose beef is selling at $40/cwt at the farm level, and the farm-price elasticity of demand is $-.40$. What would be the market-clearing price of beef if there was suddenly a 2 per cent increase in beef supply (hint: assume supply is perfectly inelastic and shifts rightward by 2 per cent).

6. Test your knowledge of the relationship between total sales, the direction of price change, and the elasticity of demand, by filling in the blanks:

	Change in total sales (gross income)	
	Price increase	*Price decrease*
Unit elasticity	No change	_____
Inelastic	_____	____↓____
Elastic	_____	_____

7. What impact would the following have on the equilibrium of prices:
   a. A successful consumer boycott of meat.
   b. Increased unemployment.
   c. A disease that reduces the hog crop by 10 per cent.
   d. A new combine that reduces harvest costs by 5 per cent.
   e. Consumer complaints that food prices are too high.
   f. An increase in wages of food marketing workers.

8. How does price discovery differ from price determination? Why are there so many variations in agricultural price discovery systems?

9. What is meant by this statement: Prices coordinate resource allocation in agricultural production and marketing.

10. Apply the law of one price to the seasonal increase in feedgrain price from fall harvest to the following spring.

SELECTED REFERENCES

A Handbook on the Elasticity of Demand for Agricultural Products in the U.S. Western Extension Marketing Committee. WEMC Publication No. 4, July 1967.

BREIMYER, H. F. "On Price Determination and Aggregate Price Theory." *Journal of Farm Economics* (Aug. 1957), 676–94.

LEFTWICH, R. H. *The Price System and Resource Allocation.* Holt, Rinehart & Winston, Inc., New York, Rev. Ed., July 1961, Chap. 3, 6, 7.

ROGERS, G. B. "Pricing Systems and Agricultural Marketing Research," *Agricultural Economics Research* (Jan. 1970) 1–11.

———— *Price Control Programs, 1917–71: Origins, Techniques, Effects on Food Prices.* U.S. Department of Agriculture. Agricultural Economic Report No. 223, April 1972.

WAUGH, F. V. *Demand and Price Analysis: Some Examples from Agriculture.* U.S. Department of Agriculture. Technical Bulletin No. 1316, 1964.

———— *Graphic Analysis.* U.S. Department of Agriculture. Agricultural Handbook, No. 326, Nov. 1966.

CHAPTER 9

Competition in Food Markets

"COMPETITION is an indispensible mainstay of a system in which the character of products and their development, the amount and evolving efficiency of production, and the prices and profit margins charged are left to the operation of private enterprise. . . . [Competition] . . . is the form of discipline that business units exercise over one another, under pressure of the discipline customers can exercise over the business units by virtue of their power of choosing between the offerings of rival suppliers."*

Preview

• This chapter examines the role, nature, and implications of competition in food markets.

• Four important types of competition, found in varying degrees in the food industry, are examined: perfect competition, oligopoly, monopolistic competition, and monopoly.

• The perfectly competitive nature of farm markets is described.

• The sources of competitive imperfections in food marketing are examined.

• The criteria for evaluating the competitive performance of food markets are reviewed.

• Key terms and concepts:

cartel	oligopoly/oligopsony
market concentration	perfect competition
monopolistic competition	price takers/price makers
monopoly	price war

---

* J. M. Clark, *Competition As a Dynamic Process,* The Brookings Institution, Washington, D.C., 1961.

product differentiation
residual-income claimant

weak seller
workable competition

Adam Smith, one of the founders of economics, pointed out that competition is the mechanism that harnesses individual profit-seeking for the public good. Competitive rivalry between firms, industries, products, and regions is constantly changing the nature of the food industry. We will examine here the nature of competition in the food industry and its impact on farm and food prices, efficiency, and the nature of the food marketing system.

Freedom is at the heart of our concern for competitive food markets: (1) freedom of consumers to choose what they wish to eat; (2) freedom of firms to develop new products and market them as they see fit; (3) freedom of new firms to enter the food industry; (4) freedom of farmers to make decisions about what to produce, how to produce it, and where and when to sell it; and (5) freedom of buyers and sellers to bargain together and arrive at mutually advantageous exchanges. These freedoms are vital to our decentralized, private enterprise economy. When they are threatened, competition breaks down and there is no longer assurance that private profit-seeking behavior is serving the public good. Some form of market intervention is often the result.

Competition in the food industry takes several forms. *Product competition* refers to rivalry between two alternative or substitute products, such as beef and pork, for the consumers' dollar. *Firm competition* concerns the rivalry between sellers of similar products. Firm rivalry frequently focuses on *brand competition*—rivalry between competing brands within a product class, e.g., Del Monte versus Green Giant canned peas. *Interregional competition* is illustrated by the rivalry between California and Florida oranges, or Maine and Idaho potatoes. *Institutional competition* relates to the rivalry between competing market institutions, for example grocery stores, fast-food restaurants, and vending machines. *Functional competition* arises when two or more firms vie to determine who will perform a particular marketing function, such as storage, financing, or transportation.

There are other ways to view market competition. *Horizontal competition* involves rivalry between firms at the same market level—processors or wholesalers or retailers. *Vertical competition* is concerned with the bargaining relationships between buyers and sellers of food and how the consumers' food dollar is divided. It is also frequently useful to distinguish between *price* and *nonprice competition*. The emphasis here will be on the competitive relationships of similar firms at the same market level.

185

PERFECT COMPETITION

Perfect competition requires certain conditions:

1. There are a great number of both buyers and sellers, no one of which is large enough to influence price through his actions alone.
2. Both buyers and sellers have perfect and equal knowledge of all the factors that affect market conditions. In addition, they will utilize this information in an economically rational manner so as to maximize their own individual gain.
3. There are no collusive or restrictive agreements among either buyers or sellers. In fact, there are so many buyers and sellers that coalition by a relatively large group of them would be administratively infeasible.
4. There is no product differentiation. This does not mean there are no differences in quality. However, products of like quality will not be differentiated by brand name, advertising, extra services, and so on.
5. The factors of production are perfectly mobile and free to leave one industry to enter another in which they could secure greater returns. No barrier to the flow of capital, labor, and management exists.

In perfect competition, the individual business firm can sell all of its production at the market price. If its price is slightly above the market price, it can sell nothing. If it is slightly below, it will be swamped with buyers. Its individual output is such a small part of the total that it can have no effect on price. In addition, because its product is exactly the same as the product of every other firm, it cannot establish any particular specialized demand for its output. Under conditions of perfect competition, then, the individual firm has no price and selling policy considerations to worry about.

With the selling side of operations thus simplified, the firm devotes its time to adjusting its production. Because there is perfect knowledge and freedom of entry and exit from business, the firm will adjust its output to that point at which total profits are maximized. It would be forced to adopt improvements and pass on their benefits. At any given time some firms may be making more money than others. However, this situation would be a production-adjustment phenomenon, and would be temporary in nature. In other words, under conditions of perfect competition, the place of the individual business is to accept the prevailing market conditions and adapt itself to them.

A situation where farmers are in perfect competition is illustrated in Figure 9-1. Each farmer produces such a small portion of the total farm supply that he "sees" only a point on the downward-sloping market demand curve. To the individual farmer, it may appear that he can produce and sell as much as he wants at the $3 price determined by the market supply and demand curves. That is, the farmer's demand curve *(dd)* is perfectly horizontal

186

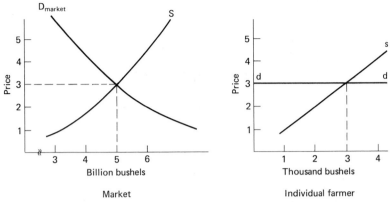

Figure 9–1. Supply and demand curves for the market and the farmer under perfect competition.

at the $3 price established by all farmers' supply and the total market demand curves.

This is a key feature of farm markets. The individual farmer feels he can produce and sell as much as he likes at the going market price without influencing that price. However, if all farmers increase, or reduce, output, the market supply curve will shift and the market price will change. Because of perfect competition, farmers may, as individuals, make rational, profitable decisions which are not necessarily in the best interests of farmers as a class.

To summarize the consequences of farmers being in a nearly perfect competitive situation:

1. Individual farmers are price-takers. They receive whatever price is dictated by the total market demand and supply curves. And they have no way of influencing market demand and supply. Consequently, they do not "price" their products in the same way as other firms.

2. Because individual farmers cannot affect their prices, there is a strong incentive for them to increase their profits by lowering their costs and by improving technological efficiency in agriculture.

3. Farmers are subject to a perpetual cost-price squeeze so long as they remain perfectly competitive. Any short-term increase in profits will stimulate a long-term increase in production, which then forces market prices back to "normal" profit levels.

These statements should be qualified: Farm markets are not *absolutely* perfectly competitive, but they are more nearly perfect than any other type of market. Moreover, some farmers *are* large enough to influence market prices; information is *never* 100 per cent perfect; there is *some* product differentiation, even in farm markets; and productive factors are *not* perfectly mobile in agriculture. Nevertheless, the actual state of the farm market is quite close to that predicted by the perfectly competitive model.

MONOPOLY/MONOPSONY

The extreme opposites of perfect competition are a monopoly and a monopsony. A monopoly is a single-seller market; a monopsony is a single-buyer market. Monopolists are said to be price-makers because the individual firm's demand curve *is* the market demand curve. Hence, monopolists have some protection from rivals and enjoy some freedom in pricing their products.

In most situations, if the monopolist is seeking profit maximization his output will be somewhat less and his prices somewhat higher than if the industry were operating under conditions of perfect competition. In addition, it is thought that monopolists in time tend to be less interested in seeking out new methods to lower costs or improve their products than would be the case under perfect competition.

However, we must not assume that a monopolist has complete freedom to alter his production and price policies. On the demand side, if the price is pushed too high consumers may seek out a substitute product. On the production side, if profits are too high, outside firms may enter into production. His freedom to extract monopoly profits is therefore limited by the closeness of substitute products and the kind of barriers to entry that face potential producers.

Monopolies can come into being through the control of the sole source of an important raw material, a patent control of a very important process, through the effects of drastic economies of scale and developing financial power, or through the actions of government. They are similar to perfect competition in that examples of perfect monopoly are rare. Where they have existed for any length of time, it is likely that they have been established or protected by the power of government.

There are monopolies involved in food marketing: trains, telephones, energy companies, and other public utilities. However, these monopolies are regulated by government, and their profit-seeking, in most cases, is limited also by the availability of alternatives. For example, natural gas, electricity, propane, and even solar energy are capable of drying grain. Trucks and barges are, of course, alternatives to trains.

OLIGOPOLY/OLIGOPSONY

In an oligopoly (few sellers) or an oligopsony (few buyers), the control of sales is in the hands of a few large firms. This market concentration is so great that the leading firms can influence the market price by changing their production. Each firm, in making production and price decisions, must consider the effect of its actions on the market price and how the rival firms will react. In such a situation of interdependence of firms, the oligopolist must always consider the potential retaliation of his business rivals.

In a true oligopolistic situation, the real business challenge to the individual firm is how to live with its competitors and not openly fight them. A fight among giants may end by crippling all concerned, with none of them benefiting. Price wars sometimes occur among oligopolists. Such a situation results in a stability of prices and production which may not represent profit maximizing for any one firm but rather a profit situation in which all can find tolerable existence.

Prices charged by individual firms in an oligopolistic industry, similar to that of perfect competition, will be practically the same. The industry is likely to develop a hierarchy of leaders and followers. When the leader changes his price, the followers do likewise almost immediately. Such a price situation does not mean there will be no rivalry among firms. Such rivalry, however, will take the form of nonprice efforts, such as product differentiation and innovation, added services, and advertising and merchandising efforts. Such industries may be very dynamic and progressive in their search for new cost-reducing methods of production and improved products that are more acceptable to consumers.

Because of their interdependence, oligopolistic firms sometimes attempt to form associations—*cartels*—to agree on prices, level of output, and division of profits. Cartels reduce competition and make life easier for oligopolists. Many farm products are traded in international markets by government-sponsored cartels. In the United States, the price of milk is set by government regulated cartels of milk producers and processors.

MONOPOLISTIC COMPETITION

Monopolistic competition lies between perfect competition and oligopoly. There are several firms in the market—not enough to meet the "no effect on others" criteria of perfect competition, but more than would make them as interdependent of one another's actions as are the very few firms of oligopoly. Each firm, however, seeks to make its product or service unique or different from that of every other firm. In a sense, then, each firm is a "little monopoly." But the monopoly is of very limited power because in the consumer's eyes, the products of competitors are very close, but not perfect substitutes.

The demand facing each firm is no longer the horizontal, perfectly elastic one that faces the firm under perfect competition. Because of the product differentiation it has some downward slope, but it is still very elastic because of the closeness of substitutes. Prices under such conditions will also be

189

nearly alike among firms, not because of fear of retaliation of rival firms, but because of the easy loss of consumer markets if prices are out of line.

In the monopolistic competition situation, prices are not likely to be as "sticky" as in the oligopoly situation. As in oligopoly, however, the emphasis will be on product change, packaging, branding, advertising, credit and discount policies, fieldmen service, and a host of other nonprice weapons to secure business. The successful differentiator must continually persuade the consuming public that his products are a better buy than ever before. The market acceptance of a differentiated product or service is likely to be quite dynamic, and for a firm to lag behind its competitors is to die.

COMPETITIVE CONDITIONS IN FOOD MARKETS

Agricultural producers have long been used as examples of firms operating nearest to the concept of perfect competition. They meet the requirements of numbers and undifferentiated products very well. But to assume near-perfect competition of the agencies and firms engaged in buying, processing, and selling agricultural products is to assume away many of the real problems of marketing.

Food marketing firms have a price policy and attempt to follow some market strategy. Many firms realize that the demand curve for their output does not consist of a horizontal line, but rather has a downward slope. They cannot sell all they could produce at the same price but must take a lower price for larger outputs. The questions of elasticity of their demand curve and what output will maximize profits become the important ones to be answered. They may be price leaders in their industry, or may follow the leadership of other firms. They may decide not to compete on the basis of price, but rather on nonprice items, such as delivery, advisory services for their customers, and the like. Large advertising expenditures may be used to attract and influence customers. Through their trade organizations they may attempt to police and control the form that competition will take.

Certainly it is true that major processors or food retailers cannot make price and output decisions without considering what the impact of their actions will have on market prices and the reactions of rival firms. It is also true that product differentiation, extra services, and other nonprice competitive activities are major undertakings of these firms. Moreover, agricultural marketing and processing firms have not been immune from suspicion of illegal acts in restraint of trade. The antitrust dockets have had a liberal sprinkling of cases involving meat packers, millers, canners, bakers, milk distributors, retail chains, and others. Some have resulted in convictions and some have not.

It is not necessary to go to the processing giants for evidence of trade-restraining actions. Many of the regulations affecting food marketing are the outgrowth of practices that were believed not to be conducive to vigorous competition. There is no reason to believe that price fixing, market sharing, following the leader, economic coercion by some members of an industry, and other actions attributed to industry in general are not practiced at least to some degree by firms engaged in marketing agricultural products. In fact, it has been estimated that about half of the government prosecutions for violations have been against firms in the food processing and distribution, building materials, and the service trades.[1]

Sources of Competitive Imperfections

Trade barriers have often laid the groundwork for competitive imperfection. Whether by intent or not, many regulatory actions by states or local units have the result of restricting freedom of entry and the free flow of goods. In this way some degree of monopoly power is obtained by the favored firms. City milk ordinances, state grading regulations, and truck-size regulations, which vary widely from state to state, are examples of these artificial barriers.

However, probably the greatest amount of competitive imperfection stems from product differentiation, either real or assumed; from various kinds of services offered with the product; from locational advantages; and from the power of habit and ignorance. These are neither illegal nor spectacular and are often ignored.

Product differentiation in agricultural marketing has on occasion been neglected because effective branding of farm products is very difficult. However, we have seen that farm products are raw material for the food marketing machinery. The great majority of our food, by the time it reaches the consumer, has been differentiated by brands and packaging. Even meat and fresh fruits and vegetables are not overlooked. Packers work hard to build acceptance for their particular brands of ham and bacon. The Sunkist label is stamped on oranges. Canners attempt to make their various labels synonymous with different kinds of packs and qualities. Even farm groups are attempting special labeling. Several states have passed legislation permitting the special branding of "home-grown" products.

Of equal if not more importance than product differentiation as a weapon of competition is the differentiation of the particular firm itself. One of the most obvious examples of this is a supermarket. Here, with the products and prices of one store very similar to those of another, additional differentiation must be sought. The larger parking lot, brighter store interiors, music-while-you-shop, more friendly clerks, and the use of trading stamps are all ways used to make one store uniquely different and more acceptable than

---

[1] R., Caves, *American Industry: Structure, Conduct, Performance.* Prentice-Hall, Inc., Englewood Cliffs, N.J. 1964, p. 65.

another. These differentiation techniques also are becoming of increasing importance among firms buying from and selling to farmers. The use of service fieldmen, discounts, premiums, and tie-in arrangements with other activities has become increasingly prevalent.

The objective of most differentiation is to remove the emphasis from price. The purpose of much advertising is to associate the name of a product or firm with the buying urge and to reduce association with the price. We are urged to buy from a particular store because the clerks are friendly, because it is sparkling clean, or because it stays open all night. We are told to buy bread X because it is made by a company that bakes only "quality goods."

Locational advantage also furnishes the foundation for many departures from competition. Spatial monopoly need not be regional or nationwide to be effective. Many country buyers of farm products can pay lower prices because of their location. Many retail outlets can charge higher prices because of their location. Some locational advantage arises because customers are willing to pay extra for convenience. Other locational advantages arise because of the limited area over which products can be transported. But some of the competitive power of location arises because of the lack of nearby competitors. Such firms have limited monopoly power in exploiting their limited territory. A baker in a very small town or an isolated livestock buyer in the country may have more effective monopoly power than a huge baking concern or the agencies in a large central market.

Habit can also contribute to imperfect competition. The pricing of eggs is an example. Originally a large amount of the nation's eggs was marketed through the Chicago and New York exchanges. The quotations of these exchanges were widely accepted as correct indicators upon which to base egg prices throughout the country. The marketing structure of eggs has changed, and now only a very small amount is sold through these exchanges. Trade pricing habits have not changed in step, however, and some country buyers still rely heavily on the old quotation patterns.

Margins taken by various marketing agencies often become habitual. In time, a given margin receives trade acceptance as being "fair." This margin often tends to exist long after the marketing activities and structure that gave rise to it have changed. It was partly the resistance to changing margins in line with changed practices that led processors and retail-chain organizations to bypass the service wholesaler and set up their own wholesaling agencies.

Habitual buying or selling is something a firm attempts to cultivate on the part of its patrons and customers. A strong brand allegiance may hold long after the conditions that initially helped establish it have changed. The selling of products to a given buyer may become habitual and be done simply because the farmer has always sold to that buyer. Such actions, therefore, contribute to the "little monopoly" that each firm strives to cultivate.

Many of the rapid developments that have occurred in the fields of communication, sociology, psychology, education, and general research methodology may act either to enhance the forces of competition or to thwart or manipulate them. Much has been learned in recent years about how people learn and what causes individuals and groups to behave and react as they do. To these advances in knowledge must be added the nearly universal access to the communication devices of television, radio, and the printed word.

Consumer research in this country is big business. For many firms this activity is their sole business. Most large manufacturing and distribution firms also will have their own scientists to probe consumer behavior and market test products. Certainly this knowledge and communication improvement can be used to improve the rapid dissemination of factual market and product information and to reduce ignorance and apathy. Consumer and market research can be used to uncover what consumers think is wrong with present products and services or what they would desire in new ones. From this information companies discover how to improve their products and what potentially successful new ones might be devised. This of course would greatly strengthen the competitive concept of consumer direction of productive activity. However, from the same type of information, new packaging design, new merchandising gimmickery, and new advertising approaches can be formulated in an attempt to manipulate the consumer into increased ignorance and habit-reaction to the firm's product in the marketplace.

Farm and Food Marketing Competition

These conditions of imperfect competition in food markets are a concern to many because they influence the efficiency of operations throughout the food industry. However, some observers are even more concerned with the divergence of competitive conditions found in agriculture versus those found in the food marketing system.

What happens when an almost perfectly competitive farm sector meets an imperfectly competitive food marketing sector at the farm gate? The concern is that the influence on market prices and on supply and demand of marketing firms leads to an imbalance of bargaining power between the farmers and the buyers of farm products. The outcome of bargaining between price takers and price makers seems quite predictable.

Because he lacks a voice in pricing, yet holds a perishable, undifferentiated product, the farmer is sometimes said to be a weak seller when compared with the powerful farm product buyers. Furthermore, because price makers are likely to price in such a way as to cover costs—passing whatever is left of the consumers' dollar back to farmers—farmers are sometimes referred to as the *residual-income claimants* in the food industry. There are two alternatives to correct this imbalance of market power between farmers and food

193

marketing firms: (1) make farmers less perfectly competitive, or (2) make food marketing firms more perfectly competitive. There are government programs and policies directed toward both of these goals.

Market Concentration

There are many ways of measuring the state of competition in the food industry. Trends in numbers of firms, sizes of firms, the extent of product differentiation, and the level of entry barriers are indications of the level of market competition. Price and promotion policies, product quality levels, and coercive or predatory behavior are market conduct manifestations of competition. Finally, profits and efficiency reflect the competitive status of food markets.

Considerable attention has been focused on market concentration as a measure of competition in food marketing. Concentration refers to the proportion of industry sales made by its largest firms. In general, the more concentrated the industry sales, the more likelihood that the market will be imperfectly competitive. Table 9-1 suggests a wide range of market concentration in food manufacturing industries. In 1972, the four largest companies selling blended and prepared flour accounted for 68 per cent of total product sales, whereas the four largest meat packing plants accounted for only 22 per cent of industry sales. Moreover, four-firm market concentration fell over the 1963–1972 period in meat packing, fluid milk, and canned fruits and vegetables, while concentration rose in creamery butter and soybean oil mills. A rule of thumb is that strongly oligopolistic industries have a four-firm concentration ratio of at least 50 per cent; a 33–50 per cent ratio denotes a weak oligopoly; and unconcentrated industries have ratios of 33 per cent or less.[2] By these criteria, all competitive varieties are represented in the food industry.

USEFULNESS OF THE COMPETITIVE MODEL

As one becomes more familiar with the agricultural marketing machinery, it is evident that departures from the models of competition are the rule rather than the exception. Prices made automatically under the workings of a competitive market are not the sole factor differentiating one firm from another firm. Firms do attempt to differentiate their products and services. Firms do attempt to have a price policy which may or may not have a direct relationship to costs. Firms do attempt to manipulate consumer demand for their products. Firms do attempt to keep their rivals under control.

However, it is not a case of perfect competition or none at all. With the

---

[2] F. M., Scherer, *Industrial Market Structure and Economic Performance,* Rand McNally & Co., Chicago, 1970, p. 61.

possible exception of some government-made or sanctioned monopolies, little if any business is transacted under either perfect competition or monopoly. The great bulk of business activity is carried on between these extremes where there is some degree of competition and rivalry between firms in their struggle for customers and profit.

How useful, then, are the ideas of how prices are formed and how business operates under perfect competition? Its principal use is as a model or measuring stick against which to compare the actual situations. The analysis of equilibrium prices, the one-price nature of a market area, and the nature of the relationships between cost and prices are useful tools in studying price behavior. By isolating the nature of the departures from the model, we may be better able to see the cause and to prescribe a correction if one is really desired.

There is usefulness, too, in the knowledge that the agricultural marketing machinery does not operate perfectly. Why are new techniques not accepted eagerly by marketing firms? Why do consumers not share rapidly in improvements? Why do tremendous inequalities exist year after year? Questions such as these find many of their answers in the imperfect competition which exists. Such knowledge also prevents us from thinking of the marketing machine as an impersonal mechanism that will react in a precisely predictable fashion to given economic forces. It also should prevent us from believing blindly that a "hands-off" policy is always best. Marketing is carried out by individuals who take economic forces as something to struggle with and to mold to their advantage and not as something to obey without question.

WORKABLE COMPETITION

Competition exists and is a force, even though it is not perfect. The perfect competition of the textbook is not a realistic goal for a modern society. However, we must have some criteria for judging when competition is effective and when situations have developed which are not desirable. How can we decide when competition is "adequate" or "effective?" The following are guideposts for judging an effectively competitive system:

1. There must be an appreciable number of buyers and sellers. They do not need to be so numerous as to have no individual market influence, but the number must be great enough to provide alternative possibilities.

2. No trader must be so powerful as to be able to coerce effectively his rivals.

3. Traders must be responsive to incentives of profits and loss—they must not be so huge that they can ignore commercial incentives over long periods of time.

4. There must be no agreements on commercial policy among rivals.

195

Table 9-1. Share of Value of Shipments Accounted for by the Largest Companies in Food Manufacturing Industries, 1963–1972.

INDUSTRY	YEAR	COMPANIES (NUMBER)	TOTAL (MILLION DOLLARS)	PER CENT OF INDUSTRY VALUE OF SHIPMENTS ACCOUNTED FOR BY			
				4 LARGEST COMPANIES	8 LARGEST COMPANIES	20 LARGEST COMPANIES	50 LARGEST COMPANIES
Meat packing plants	1972	2,293	2,968.1	22	37	51	66
	1967	2,529	2,220.5	26	38	50	62
	1963	2,833	1,908.3	31	42	54	64
Poultry dressing plants	1972	406	3,254.1	17	26	42	62
Poultry and egg processing	1972	110	588.1	23	36	65	91
Creamery butter	1972	201	808.3	45	58	78	92
	1967	510	958.8	15	22	36	60
	1963	725	988.8	11	19	31	48
Fluid milk	1972	2,024	9,395.7	18	26	42	56
	1967	2,988	7,826.0	22	30	42	51
	1963	4,030	7,025.9	23	30	40	48
Canned fruits and vegetables	1972	766	4,043.8	20	31	53	71
	1967	930	3,467.8	22	34	52	70
	1963	1,135	2,742.8	24	34	50	68
Flour and other grain mill products	1972	340	2,380.0	33	53	75	91
	1967	438	2,457.4	30	46	70	89
	1963	510	2,176.5	35	50	71	88

Industry	Year						
Rice milling	1972	48	680.6	43	68	92	100
	1967	54	548.4	46	68	89	99+
	1963	62	423.0	44	66	86	99+
Blended and prepared flour	1972	115	704.6	68	81	92	98
	1967	125	547.5	68	82	93	98
	1963	140	434.0	70	82	92	98
Frozen fruits and vegetables	1972	136	1,848.8	29	43	69	91
	1967	495	2,081.6	24	36	55	74
	1963	566	1,548.7	24	37	54	70
Raw cane sugar	1972	60	406.5	44	62	84	99+
	1967	61	368.5	43	65	82	99+
	1963	50	378.7	47	65	82	100
Cane sugar refining	1972	22	1,742.7	59	85	99+	100
	1967	22	1,375.7	59	82	99+	100
	1963	16	1,271.2	63	83	100	(x)
Beet sugar	1972	16	880.2	66	96	100	(x)
	1967	15	560.7	66	96	100	(x)
	1963	11	564.1	66	97	100	(x)
Cottonseed oil mills	1972	74	458.7	43	61	80	99
	1967	91	405.9	42	60	80	96
	1963	115	555.2	41	56	72	91
Soybean oil mills	1972	54	3,357.2	54	69	92	99+
	1967	60	2,148.3	55	76	94	100
	1963	68	1,473.4	50	70	88	99+

Source: U.S. Bureau of the Census, Department of Commerce.

5. Entry must be free from handicap, except that which is automatically created by the existence of already established firms.

6. There must be free access of buyers with sellers. There must be no substantial preferential treatment of any particular trader or group.[3]

The idea of competition represented by the preceding criteria accepts the real-life propositions that wide differentiation in products does exist, that both price and nonprice competition are used, and that large firms will develop as they exploit the economies of scale which are the result of modern technology. These criteria then furnish us with a measuring stick for the extent of economic efficiency that exists in the marketing system.

Society, through its government, in the United States has gone on record as being generally against monopoly and for effective competition. Actions have therefore to be taken to help assure the maintenance of effective competition. Our various antitrust laws have been enacted to make certain types of business behavior illegal. Other laws deal with the regulation of businesses, such as public utilities, in which monopolistic tendencies are recognized. Certain laws, such as those dealing with farmer cooperatives and marketing orders, attempt to strengthen the weaker participants in the market bargaining process. Society has also sanctioned the actions of its government which attempt to create the general conditions for more effective competition. Government participates in providing accurate market news and improved product standardization and in preventing faulty and misleading advertising.

SUMMARY

Competition plays a key role in harnessing the rivalry and the profit-seeking of the marketplace in order that it may serve the public interest. The competitive state of food markets disciplines firms' behavior and practices, encourages new technologies and products, and regulates prices and profit levels. Farm markets tend to be nearly perfect competitive, and farmers are price takers. Competition in food marketing firms is closer to the oligopolistic and monopolistic types of competition, and these firms can influence prices by output and marketing decisions. Product and firm differentiation, consumer habits, and locational advantages are important reasons for competitive imperfections in food marketing. The standards of workable competition represent a compromise between unattainable perfectly competitive market conditions and the real world of imperfect competition. Public policies can influence the state of competition in food markets.

---

[3] C. D. Edwards, *Maintaining Competition,* McGraw-Hill Book Company, New York, 1949, pp. 9–10.

QUESTIONS FOR DISCUSSION

1. Explain in your own words what this means: Farmers are price-takers and food marketing firms are price-makers.

2. What is the difference between a true monopolist and monopolistic competition?

3. Suppose that the U.S. Attorney General, who enforces the antitrust and monopoly laws, is given the following market concentration ratios. Which industries should he investigate first for anticompetitive practices?

	1963 four-firm concentration ratio
Passenger cars	99%
primary aluminum	96
electric lamps	92
chewing gum	90
cigarettes	80
soap, detergents	72
farm machinery, equipment	43
flour mills	35
cement	29
bread	23
fluid milk	23
brick, tile	12
screw-machine products	5

4. Discuss the government programs and policies that attempt to improve the farmers' bargaining position in the food system. How do these affect competition?

5. Your senator charges that monopolistic food companies are cheating consumers out of millions of dollars through advertising, merchandising, cents-off campaigns, and other nonprice competition gimmicks. How do you respond?

6. What are the differences between how businessmen view competition and the economic view of competition presented in this chapter.

7. Discuss the following statement: "We wouldn't need competition in food markets if businessmen were honest."

8. Given their choice, do you think farmers would choose perfect competition over imperfect competition in their markets? What is the relationship between farmers' and society's preference for family farms and the nearly perfect competitive nature of farm markets?

SELECTED REFERENCES

BUCKLIN, L. P. *Competition and Evolution in the Distributive Trades.* Prentice-Hall, Inc., Englewood Cliffs, N.J., 1972.

CAVES, R. *American Industry: Structure, Conduct, Performance.* Prentice-Hall, Inc., Englewood Cliffs, N.J., 2nd Ed., 1967.

CLARK, J. M. *Competition As a Dynamic Process.* The Brookings Institution, Washington, D.C., 1961.

Farmers in the Market Economy. Iowa State University Press, Ames, Iowa, 1964.

FARRIS, P. L., Ed. *Market Structure Research.* Iowa State University Press, Ames, Iowa, 1964.

Food from Farmer to Consumer. Report of the National Commission on Food Marketing, "Overview and Appraisal," U.S. Government Printing Office, June 1966, Chap. 12.

FOX, K. A. "Monopolistic Competition in the Food and Agriculture Sectors," in R. E. Kuenne, Ed., *Monopolistic Competition Theory: Studies in Impact.* John Wiley & Sons, Inc., New York, 1967, pp. 329–56.

HAMMOND, L. H., Ed. *Competition in Food Marketing.* North Carolina State Agricultural Policy Institute, 1967.

HARRIS, E. S. *Price Wars in City Milk Markets.* U.S. Department of Agriculture. Agricultural Economics Report No. 100, Oct. 1966.

HEIMSTRA, S. "Concentration and Competition in the Food Industries," *American Journal of Agricultural Economics* (Aug. 1966), 137–47.

LANZILLOTTI, R. "The Superior Market Power of Food Processing and Agricultural Supply Firms—Its Relation to the Farm Problem." *Journal of Farm Economics* (Dec. 1960), 1240–50.

Market Structure of the Food Industries. U.S. Department of Agriculture. Marketing Research Report No. 971, Sept. 1972.

MIKLIUS, W., AND D. B. DeLOACH. "Do Lettuce Buyers Exert Oligopsony Power?" *Agricultural Economics Research* (Oct. 1965), 101–108.

NICHOLS, W. H. *Imperfect Competition within Agricultural Industries.* Iowa State University Press, Ames, Iowa, 1941.

SCANLON, P. D. "Oligopoly and Deceptive Advertising: The Cereal Industry Affair." *Antitrust Law and Economic Review* (Spring 1970), 99–110.

CHAPTER 10

The Behavior of Farm Prices

"AGRICULTURE AND INDUSTRY are of different temperaments in committing resources to production; one is slow and gradual in its movements and the other sensitive and erratic . . . Many of the more serious economic difficulties that confront agriculture are born out of this difference in the pace of agriculture and industry . . . Farmers, in the main, stay in 'full production' regardless of the effects of business fluctuations upon the demand for farm products . . . this behavior on the part of farmers assures consumers products, but it also has meant great instability in farm prices and farm incomes."*

Preview

- This chapter examines the behavior of farm prices and factors influencing these prices.
- Three sources of farm price variations are investigated: the business cycle, agricultural production cycles, and seasonal production and pricing factors.
- The effects of the business cycle on farm prices and net incomes are evaluated.
- The reasons for livestock price cycles are discussed.
- The nature of seasonal farm price variations is examined.
- The effects of changing farm prices, volume, and production costs on net farm income are discussed.
- Key terms and concepts:

biological, psychological lag	gross and net farm income
business cycle	real prices
depression, recession	seasonal prices

---

* T. W. Schultz, *The Economic Organization of Agriculture*, McGraw-Hill Book Company, New York, 1953.

Prices and incomes play key roles in farm and food marketing decisions. In the long run, prices, incomes, and profits are expected to allocate farm and marketing resources efficiently. In the short run, these economic signals and incentives motivate food producers to shift food products from low-valued to high-valued markets, according to the law of one price. Farm income, price and marketing problems result when prices and incomes fail to perform these functions efficiently.

FORCES INFLUENCING FARM PRICES

The forces influencing farm prices can be grouped into four broad categories. Supply conditions affecting farm and food prices include farm production decisions, weather, disease, harvested acreage, and food imports. The demand conditions include income, prices, tastes and preferences, population, and exports. The food marketing sector influences farm prices through its value-adding activities, price and cost behavior, and procurement strategies. Finally, government may influence farm prices through price supports, supply controls, trade policies, or policies influencing domestic demand for food.

There is sometimes a debate over whether farm prices are determined at the farm level, in the marketing system, or by consumers at the retail level. Often it appears that farm prices are "set" first—related in some way to costs of production—and then marketing costs are added to arrive at the retail prices. This impression is reinforced when a change in retail prices follows on the heels of a change in farm prices.

To others, it appears that the buyers of farm products—food processors, wholesalers, or retailers—"set" the price of food and that this "determines" farm prices. This impression is created when price-taking farmers sell to less than perfectly competitive buyers of farm products. The fact that prices are more easily *discovered* at points of product concentration in the marketing system also leads many to conclude that prices are *determined* at those points.

Actually, prices are determined jointly—by consumer demand, farm supply, and the food marketing system. And no one of these is any more important than the other in the determination of farm prices. A change in any one usually results in adjustments of the other two; therefore it is rather pointless to argue about precisely where farm prices are determined.

Land prices present an excellent illustration of the joint interdependancy of costs and prices. Land prices are price-determining in that land is a cost of production that must be paid for out of farm prices. However, the co-movement of farm and land prices supports the view that land costs are determined by farm prices. If farm prices rise, farmers can afford to pay higher prices for land and will bid the higher prices into the cost of land. Both views of land costs and prices are correct.

FARM AND FOOD PRICE TRENDS

Food prices are one of the most controversial aspects of food marketing. Are food prices too high or too low? Do food prices cause, or moderate, inflationary trends? How well do farm and retail food prices move together? Examining trends and relationships in food prices can provide a better understanding of the food marketing process.

Figure 10-1 illustrates the trends in wholesale food and nonfood prices between 1890 and 1976. Although food and nonfood wholesale prices moved together broadly over the long run, there were significant short-run differences in these prices. First, food prices fluctuated much more than nonfood prices. Second, food prices were flexible both upward and downward, whereas nonfood prices tended to rise steadily except for the 1929–1932 period, and there were occasional declines at other times. A major reason for this difference in year-to-year price movements is the greater control over output that is possible for nonfood products. Annual variability in food prices reflects the difficulty of tailoring supply to demand when the product is susceptible to weather, disease, and other unpredictable elements. Factory production of nonfood goods is much more stable.

Over the long run, there is a tendency for retail food and nonfood prices to move in the same direction, but at different rates. Table 10-1 shows that retail food price changes are sometimes greater and sometimes less than nonfood price changes. There are three reasons for these prices moving to-

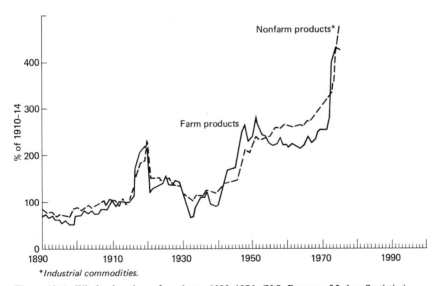

Industrial commodities.

Figure 10–1. Wholesale prices of products, 1890–1976. (U.S. Bureau of Labor Statistics)

Table 10-1. Trends in Food and Nonfood Prices, 1913–1977.

	AVERAGE ANNUAL PERCENTAGE CHANGE	
PERIOD	FOOD AT HOME RETAIL PRICES	ALL OTHER RETAIL PRICES
1913–1920	11.1%*	9.8
1920–1930	− 3.5*	− 1.2
1930–1940	− 2.4*	− 1.2
1940–1950	11.2	5.0
1950–1960	1.6	2.5
1960–1970	2.7	3.1
1970–1971	2.4	4.6
1971–1972	4.5*	3.0
1972–1973	16.3*	3.9
1973–1974	14.9*	10.0
1974–1975	8.3	9.3
1975–1976	2.1	6.6
1976–1977	6.0	6.5

* Period when food price changes exceeded nonfood price changes.

Source: U.S. Bureau of Labor Statistics.

gether over the long run: (1) 60 per cent of retail food prices is determined by food marketing costs, such as energy, labor, packaging, and freight, which affect, equally, both food and nonfood prices; (2) farmers' purchases of supplies from the industrial sector tend to build these costs into food prices; and (3) over the long run, the same economic forces affect both food and nonfood prices.

How closely do farm, wholesale, and retail food prices move together? How long does it take a change in price at the farm level to reach the consumer? These are questions of pricing efficiency. There are several reasons why farm and retail food prices might not, on a day-to-day basis, move together. First, there are lags in the time necessary to move the product from the farm to the grocery shelf. Fresh foods move through the marketing channel more rapidly than highly processed foods, but all products spend some time in transit and in inventory. Therefore, a snapshot of today's farm and retail prices would not record exactly the same commodity at each market level. Changes in marketing costs and profits also will reduce the relationship between farm and retail food prices. In addition, many consumer products often are made from an individual farm commodity. For example, a steer is used for meat, hide, tallow, and other by-products. Soybeans produce oil and meal. Because each of these products is subject to different economic conditions, the farm price of the commodity may not correlate precisely with any one of the retail prices. Merchandising strategies, such as weekend specials and loss leaders, may also alter the day-to-day relationship between farm and retail food prices.

Figure 10-2 indicates that farm, wholesale, and retail food prices have generally moved together over the long run. Farm prices are more closely related to wholesale prices than to retail prices, suggesting that the market price relationships decline as foods move closer to the retail level and more marketing services are added. The correlation of farm and retail prices is greater for fresh foods than for highly processed foods.

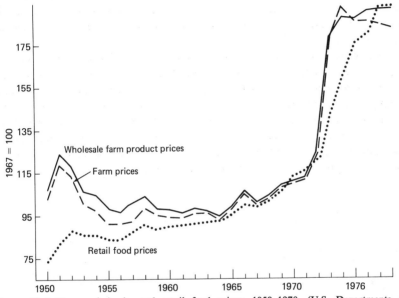

Figure 10–2. Farm, wholesale, and retail food prices, 1950–1978. (U.S. Departments of Agriculture and Labor)

There is continuing concern about short-term pricing efficiency in food markets. In particular, many farmers feel that farm price reductions are not fully and quickly transmitted to consumers. If true, this would be a deficiency in pricing efficiency. The evidence is somewhat contradictory on this aspect of food pricing efficiency. However, a 1976 study concluded:

1. Farm and retail food prices do move together, although the degree of association varies widely by the amount of processing involved.

2. The greatest impact of a change in farm prices on retail prices occurs in the first month of the change, with the full impact spread out over a number of months.

205

3. Retail and wholesale food prices respond equally to both rising and falling farm prices.[1]

COMMODITY PRICE FLUCTUATIONS

Wide and frequent commodity price variations are the rule; stable prices of individual commodities are the exception. Figure 10-3 shows the quarterly variations in livestock and crop prices between 1950 and 1976. These are averages of even greater hour-to-hour, day-to-day, and month-to-month price variations. As shown, quarterly crop prices tend to be somewhat more stable than livestock prices, and both often move counter to each other, suggesting relative stability in "all farm prices."

Numerous conditions contribute to agricultural price instability. On the supply side, variations in producer output decisions, weather, disease, and other unpredictable events affect acreage, yields, output, and prices. Some supply factors can be controlled by farmers and some cannot, but even a farmer's efforts to tailor supply to demand can be frustrated by uncontrollable events or the elements. He may respond to price predictions or expectations by changing acreage, but the yield may be lower than average. The results of these supply changes are illustrated in Figure 10-4.

Figure 10–3. Prices received by farmers, 1950–1976. (U.S. Department of Agriculture)

---

[1] *The Responsiveness of Wholesale and Retail Food Prices to Changes in the Costs of Food Production and Distribution,* U.S. Council on Wage and Price Stability, Staff Report, Washington, D.C., November 1976.

206

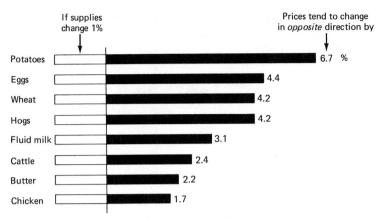

Figure 10–4. How change in supply affects price received by farmers.

In most cases, farmer responses to changing prices will reduce price fluctuation, just as when high prices encourage increased supply, which in turn reduces prices. There is, of course, a biological lag in this process which prevents immediate supply responses to high or low farm prices. At other times, it appears that the aggregate behavior of large numbers of farmers can contribute to the instability of farm prices.

Demand factors also contribute to price variations in agriculture. International trade links U.S. farm markets with consumers throughout the world, adding world demand variations to the U.S. farm price picture. Particularly destabilizing is the practice of some large countries, which make substantial purchases of U.S. farm products one year but not the next. Some countries view the United States as the world's residual or stand-by food supplier.

Domestic changes in consumer incomes, employment, and business conditions influence the demand for food and its price. Like the supply shifts, in the short run the food demand curve shifts up and down a relatively inelastic supply curve, making most of the adjustment in prices.

Table 10-2 shows the level and variation of selected "real" farm prices over the 1929–1975 period. These prices have been adjusted to eliminate the effects of inflation on the level and stability of prices. These price variations make it difficult for farmers to make production, marketing, and investment decisions. They result in rather wide swings in net farm income and profits; they require frequent and sudden farm resource adjustments, and these are difficult to make without significant farmer losses or change in farm resource prices. Farm price and income variations also have affected farm marketing practices such as storage, contracting, and timing of sale.

Food marketing firms must adjust to agricultural price variations. Many processors operate their own farming operations to supply needs when prices are high, and most have become involved in farm contracts to assure both

207

Table 10-2. Average Annual Real Prices Received by

YEAR	WHEAT	CORN	HAY	RICE	COTTON
	$/bu.	*$/bu.*	*$/ton*	*$/100 lb.*	*¢/lb.*
1929	2.34	1.72	32.02	5.03	38.0
1935	2.32	1.78	30.20	4.53	31.4
1940	1.86	1.66	27.09	4.99	27.4
1945	3.22	2.66	42.01	8.60	48.6
1950	3.23	2.45	34.77	8.21	64.6
1955	2.87	1.96	30.40	6.81	46.9
1960	2.28	1.31	26.70	5.97	39.6
1965	1.66	1.43	28.80	6.06	34.6
1970	1.33	1.33	24.20	5.17	22.0
1975	3.00	2.14	44.63	7.52	42.0

Sources: *Agricultural Prices,* U.S. Department of Agriculture, Annual. Actual prices divided by the Consumer Price Index, 1970 = 100.

quality and prices. These firms also can use the commodity futures market to protect themselves and to profit from changing farm prices.

FARM PRICES AND COSTS OVER THE BUSINESS CYCLE

Farm prices change with shifts in the aggregate supply and demand curves for farm products, as shown in Table 10-3. If demand shifts rightward faster than supply—as in 1914–1920, 1941–1951, and 1967–1974—farm prices will rise. If supply shifts rightward faster than demand, or demand shifts leftward—as in 1929–1932 or 1951–1964—farm prices will fall. What causes these shifts in farm supply and demand?

Over the years, the American economy has traced a cyclical pattern of boom and bust—prosperity, then depression or recession, inflation, then deflation. These changes in real growth of economic output and price levels are referred to as the *business cycle*. There have been seventeen U.S. business cycles (trough-to-trough) in the twentieth century. The cycles are caused by wars, the psychology of consumers and investors, and a host of other factors.

Business cycles affect farm prices, costs, and incomes. Agricultural prices have tended to move up and down with the general rate of price inflation and deflation over the years. During prosperous periods, rising employment and incomes contribute to a strong demand for food and to rising farm prices. Similarly, during depressions or recessions, declining consumer demand weakens farm prices.

U.S. Farmers for Major Commodities in 1970 Dollars.

Soybeans	Peanuts	Beef	Poultry	Sugar beets
$/bu.	*$/100 lb.*	*$/100 lb.*	*$/lb.*	*$/ton*
4.22	8.46	21.47	—	16.05
2.01	8.90	17.11	.57	19.72
2.49	9.22	20.94	.47	19.39
4.49	17.86	26.13	.65	27.69
3.98	17.58	37.48	.44	22.10
3.22	16.98	22.64	.36	19.61
2.80	13.12	26.77	.22	18.33
3.12	14.02	24.48	.18	17.48
2.85	12.80	27.10	.14	17.06
3.98	16.85	27.77	.22	23.56

Table 10-3. Changes in Aggregate Demand, Supply and Farm Prices, 1914–1976.

Period	Aggregate demand and supply trends	Farm price trend
1914–1920	World War I demand shifts rightward faster than food supply	Farm prices rise 120%
1929–1932	Demand falls with income and employment, little change in supply	Farm prices fall 47%, returning to 1900 levels in 1932
1941–1951	War-related demand expands faster than food supply	Farm prices rise 222%
1951–1964	Technological change in agriculture shifts the supply curve rightward faster than rising income shifts the demand curve	Farm prices fall 20%
1967–1974	Rising incomes and exports shift demand rightward faster than supply	Farm prices rise 92%
1974–1976	Increased supply follows the 1972–74 high prices, demand stabilizes	Farm prices fall 3% in 1975, hold constant in 1976

Sources: U.S. Department of Agriculture; W. W. Cochrane, *Farm Prices, Myth and Reality,* University of Minnesota Press, Minneapolis, Chap. 3, 1958. Reprinted by permission.

These rises and falls in farm prices would not necessarily affect net farm incomes if the costs of farm production also rose and fell with the business cycle. A decline in the price of cattle from $40/cwt. to $30/cwt. would not be disastrous for farmers if all costs of producing beef fell proportionally. However, the prices of farm inputs purchased from the nonfarm sector—which accounted for 62 per cent of all farm costs in 1972—do not respond to the business cycle in the same way as farm prices.

Machinery, hardware, and chemicals purchased by farmers are produced by firms that adjust production in response to changes in the business cycle. These firms shift their supply curve leftward in response to declining demand by reducing plant capacity, cutting back on output and laying off workers. This moderates the downward pressure on industrial prices during contracting phases of the business cycle.

Farmers react differently to the business cycle. They maintain, or even increase, output regardless of the business cycle. For example, agricultural output increased 15 per cent during the 1930's, a period when the total output of the U.S. economy declined. Agriculture, then, takes the impact of depressions and recessions in its prices without making price-moderating output adjustments. Consequently, as shown in Figure 10-5, farm prices fluctuate more than the prices of farm inputs purchased from industry. In turn, net farm income falls in depression or recessionary periods and rises in prosperous and inflationary periods.

The differences in the supply response of agriculture and industry to the business cycle are the result of the competitive nature and cost structure of these two sectors. In the industrial sector, there are few enough firms of

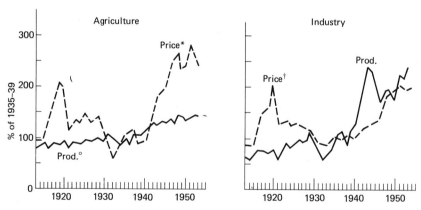

* Prices received by farmers
° Farm output
† Wholesale prices of manufactured products

Figure 10–5. U.S. production and prices for agriculture and nonfarm industry. (U.S. Department of Agriculture)

210

sufficient size that each can affect price through output decisions. These monopolistic competitors and oligopolists reduce production during business contractions in order to cushion price and profit impacts. Nearly perfectly competitive farmers cannot, individually, prevent falling prices by reducing production. In addition, new technologies may actually shift the farm supply curve *rightward* during a business contraction, because these technologies originate outside of agriculture. Moreover, farmers have a larger part of their costs in the fixed category than do manufacturers; this means that prices must fall further in order to trigger output responses.

The relationship between farm prices, costs, and net income over the business cycle changed after 1945, as shown in Table 10-4. Prior to that time, farm prices followed the general trend in prices and fluctuated more than farm costs, so that net farm income rose with inflation and fell with deflation. After 1945, the costs of farm inputs generally rose more rapidly than farm prices, and farm prices were more influenced by government price policies and supply conditions than by the business cycle.

Table 10-4. Farm Prices and Costs Over the Business Cycles, 1914–1976.

PERIOD	CONSUMER PRICE INDEX	ANNUAL PERCENTAGE CHANGE	
		INDEX OF FARM PRICES RECEIVED	INDEX OF FARM PRICES PAID FOR PRODUCTION ITEMS
Pre-1945:			
1914–1920	16.5%	18.0	15.0
1920–1932	− 2.7	− 6.0	− 4.2
1932–1945	2.5	16.2	6.0
Post-1945:			
1945–1951	7.3	7.8	9.3
1952–1965	1.5	1.0	0.0
1965–1976	7.4	8.9	10.3

Source: U.S. Bureau of Labor Statistics and Department of Agriculture.

AGRICULTURAL PRICE CYCLES

The business cycle affects farm prices through periodic shifts in the aggregate supply and demand of food. Agricultural price cycles, in contrast, are regular fluctuations in prices owing to periodic expansions and contractions in the supply of individual agricultural products. These price variations are supply-based; they reflect producer output decisions.

Some agricultural price cycles are illustrated in Figure 10-6. The price cycles run counter to production cycles. When supplies increase, prices fall,

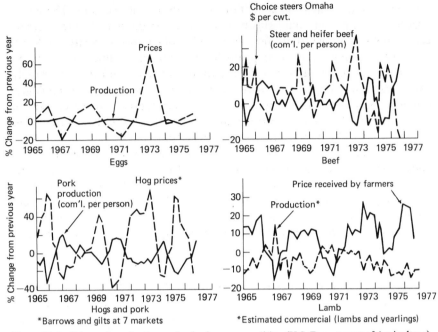

Figure 10–6. Price and production cycles for four commodities. (U.S. Department of Agriculture)

and when supplies decrease, prices rise. The price swings are much greater in magnitude than the production swings because of the inelasticity of farm demand.

Agricultural price cycles are caused by the tendency of farmers to base future production plans on current prices and profits, rather than on future prices. For example, let us suppose that hog production is relatively low and hog prices high. People in the hog business look at their favorable earnings of the past year and decide to expand their hog enterprise. Others who previously had left the business decide to re-enter. But to expand hog production means that more gilts must be withheld from market and bred. Time must elapse before pigs can be born, fattened, and sent to the market. All in all, some two to three years will elapse before the full, intended expansion may result in additional hog supplies on the market. By that time increasing supplies will be driving prices down. Producers will be appraising the situation as unprofitable and decide to raise fewer hogs. The faint of heart may liquidate their hog enterprises altogether. The cycle will then reverse itself; production will decline and prices will increase.

The length of agricultural price cycles (peak to peak) depends upon the psychological and biological lags involved in producing the commodity. The *biological lag* is the time period between when farmers decide to expand or contract production and when market supplies actually change. There is a

212

longer biological lag for cattle than for chicken because it takes longer to expand the cattle herd than it does to increase chicken production. Most agricultural price cycles are longer than the biological lag, however. The hog cycle, for example, is three to four years, whereas the cattle cycle runs eight to twelve years. The psychological lag accounts for the remainder of the cycle. This is the period of time when prices must be high or low in order to convince farmers that production plans should be changed.

Several conditions are necessary for the development of identifiable price cycles. First, there must be a time lapse between a change in price and producers' response to that change. Second, producers must gear production decisions to current prices rather than to expected future prices. Third, producers must have reasonably good control over output. There are no well-defined price cycles in crops, as there are in livestock, because producer decisions are only partially responsible for crop size. Finally, price cycles are more likely to develop in almost perfectly competitive industries, where each producer believes that his output decision will not influence prices.

Knowledge of agricultural price cycles can be helpful in decision-making for farmers, marketing firms, and consumers. Price analysts and forecasters can also benefit from a knowledge of price cycles. However, it should be noted that the cycles do not follow perfectly predictable patterns. The magnitude and length of the cycles vary over time. Extraordinary conditions, such as a sharp change in food supplies, a sudden burst of export demand, or yield-affecting weather, may prolong the expansionary phase of a cycle or cut short a contracting phase. At best, the cycles are tendencies. In many cases, turning points are evident only after they have passed. The cattle production cycle shown in Table 10-5 illustrates the regularity yet variation in cycles.

Table 10-5. The U.S. Cattle Production Cycle, 1867–1976.

CONTRACTING PHASE OF CYCLE			EXPANDING PHASE OF CYCLE		
LOW YEAR	THOUSAND HEAD	NUMBER OF DECLINING YEARS	HIGH YEAR	THOUSAND HEAD	NUMBER OF EXPANDING YEARS
1867	28,636		1890	57,649	23
1996	49,205	6	1904	66,442	8
1912	55,675	8	1918	73,040	6
1928	57,322	10	1934	74,369	6
1938	65,249	4	1945	82,654	7
1949	76,830	4	1955	96,592	6
1958	91,176	3	1965	109,000	7
1967	108,783	2	1975	132,000	8

Source: *Livestock and Meat Statistics,* U.S. Department of Agriculture. Annual.

Farmers adjust to agricultural price cycles in three ways. Most farmers contribute to cycles by expanding during periods of high prices and contracting during periods of low prices. Other farmers opt to produce at a steady rate over the long haul, regardless of the cycle, averaging the high prices with the low prices. Still others attempt to gear their production counter to the cycle—expand when others are contracting and contract when others are expanding.

Why is it that farmers do not stop the livestock production and price cycles? This is easier said than done. The cycle is caused by rational producers' adjustments to changing farm prices. The cyclical problem reflects the near-perfectly competitive nature of farming and the biological and psychological lags in agriculture. These are difficult to change.

SEASONAL PRICE VARIATIONS

Seasonal price variations are more or less regular patterns of price changes occuring within a crop or marketing year. These variations are the result of seasonality of demand, production, and marketing patterns. Fall turkey prices are a classic example of a demand-induced seasonal price variation. The seasonal rise of grain prices from harvest to harvest illustrates a supply-induced seasonal price change.

Retail food prices follow a seasonal pattern, as illustrated in Figure 10-7, with little deviation from year to year. This trend primarily reflects meat prices, which are lowest in the spring and fall and rise to a summer peak. Crop prices tend to be more stable over the year, with rising prices of some commodities matched by falling prices of others.

The seasonal change in livestock prices is largely the result of traditional production practices and seasonal eating habits. Chicks purchased in the

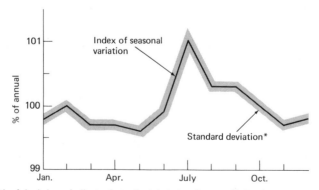

*Width of shaded area indicates 1 standard deviation above and below index of seasonal variation.

Figure 10–7. Retail food price seasonality. (U.S. Department of Agriculture)

spring will start laying eggs late in the year, and reach their peak production the following spring. Pigs farrowed in the spring and fall are ready for slaughter about six months later. The resulting pork and egg seasonal prices are shown in Figure 10-8.

The seasonality of crop prices depends upon the suddenness of the harvest, the potential for storing the crop over the year, and the cost of storage. For most crops, prices reach their low point during harvest when the supply available for sale greatly exceeds the day-to-day demand. For example, July is normally the low wheat price, November for corn, and December for cotton.

The seasonal crop price rise from harvest to harvest is influenced by the cost of storage. The market must pay the storage costs of firms who defer selling at harvest. Thus, the seasonal price rise will tend to be greater for commodities with more expensive storage costs.

Changes in seasonal production practices, demand patterns, storage capacity, or storage costs would be expected to change the seasonal price variations of farm products. For example, year-round egg production and hog feeding appear to have reduced the seasonal price variation for eggs and pork. Food storage and processing technologies have altered the seasonal price patterns of highly perishable commodities. Development of new products has to some extent reduced seasonal turkey prices.

As with price cycles, knowledge of seasonal food price movements can be valuable to farmers, marketing firms, and consumers. Again, however,

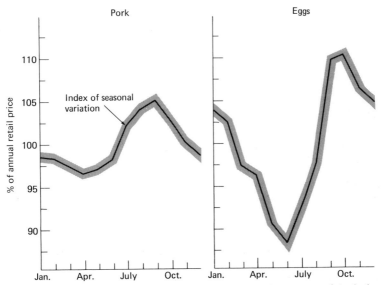

Figure 10–8. Retail price seasonality of pork and eggs. (U.S. Department of Agriculture)

215

seasonal price variations are not perfectly predictable in any year, nor wholly reliable from year to year. The high and low price periods shift unpredictably, and there are years when the seasonal price rise will be much greater or much less than the cost of storage.

FARM INCOME AND PRICES

Net farm income is influenced by three factors: (1) the volume of farm products sold; (2) the price of farm products; and (3) farm costs of producing and marketing these products. A change in any one of these will change net farm income. Moreover, these components do not move independently. A change in farm prices affects the quantity of farm products produced, just as the price of farm products influences the costs of farm inputs.

The price, quantity, and cost contributions to net farm income can be examined in Table 10-6. Gross farm income increased from $86.8 billion in 1973 to $100.5 billion in 1974 as a result of a 16 per cent increase in farm prices and a slight increase in the quantity of farm products marketed. Farm costs increased less rapidly than gross income, so net farm income increased from $28.8 billion to $30.2 billion from 1973 to 1974.

Farm prices fell in 1975, along with the volume of farm products sold. However, farm expenses continued to rise, so net farm income fell more

Table 10-6. Farm Income, Marketings, and Prices, 1973–1976.

	1973	1974	1975	1976
	1967 = 100			
Volume of farm marketings	113	114	112	120
Prices received by farmers	165	191	187	189
	$ Bil			
Cash receipts from farming	78.2	92.7	90.3	94.5
Livestock	43.0	43.9	40.9	47.5
Crops	35.2	48.1	49.4	47.0
Nonmoney and other farm income*	8.6	7.8	8.4	9.0
Realized gross farm income	86.8	100.5	98.7	103.5
Farm production expenses	60.2	71.1	75.3	79.0
Realized net farm income	26.6	29.4	23.4	24.5
Net change in farm inventories	2.2	.8	.9	1.2
Total net farm income	28.8	30.2	24.3	25.7

* Includes government payments to farmers, value of farm products consumed in farm households, rental value of farm dwellings, and income from recreation, machine hire, and custom work.

Source: *Agricultural Outlook,* U.S. Department of Agriculture, September 1976.

than gross farm income. Farm costs continued to rise in 1976, but increased prices and volume of sales pushed up both gross and net farm income.

Examination of Table 10-6 will reveal that farm supplies, prices, and net income are quite variable from year to year, whereas farm costs are less variable, and tend to rise regardless of the trend in farm prices. This is shown in Figure 10-9. Net farm income was relatively stable from 1967 to 1971 as gross farm income rose at about the same rate as production expenses. Net farm income jumped significantly in 1972 and 1973 as farm prices outpaced rising production expenses. These rising costs of production exceeded rising farm prices in 1974, 1975, and 1976, and net farm income fell.

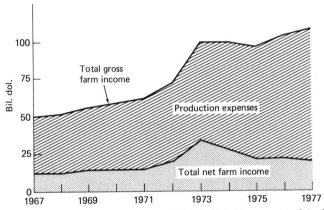

Figure 10–9. Gross and net farm income, 1967–1977. (U.S. Department of Agriculture)

How have these farm income trends affected farmers? Wide fluctuations in income affect different farmers in different ways. Young farmers, who usually have large debts, may be more adversely affected than older, more well-established farmers with considerable equity; the latter can average the highs and lows of farm income over longer periods of time.

Farm income trends narrowed the urban-rural income gap during the 1960–1976 period. Average farm income even exceeded average nonfarm income in 1973. Income, of course, is not synonymous with wealth, and on the average it is likely that farmer's average *net worth* exceeds the net worth of the nonfarm population.

Farmers also have adjusted to the level and variability of farm incomes by increasing their nonfarm income. This includes income from off-farm jobs and investments. The nonfarm income of the farm population exceeded their farming income in the 1969–1976 period, with the notable exceptions of 1973 and 1974. Nonfarm income is more important to smaller farmers than larger farmers.

217

SUMMARY

Farm prices and incomes play a key role in allocating resources in agriculture and in rewarding efficient producers. Whereas commodity prices often appear to be set in central markets by food marketing firms, they are in reality jointly determined by farm supply, consumer demand, and the food marketing agencies. There are wider variations in farm prices and incomes than in nonfarm prices and incomes because of the greater inelasticity of demand for food, farmers' failure to adjust output to prices when aggregate demand falls, and the greater difficulty in controlling the output of a biological commodity. Three important sources of farm price variations are the business cycle, agricultural production cycles, and seasonal changes in production and supplies. The livestock price and production cycles are caused by a biological and psychological lag in farmers' response to changing prices and profit opportunities. Net farm income is influenced by farm prices, the quantity of farm products sold, and farm costs of production.

QUESTIONS FOR DISCUSSION

1. How does the inelasticity of demand for farm products contribute to agricultural price and income variations?

2. It is sometimes said that farmers, by nature, prefer variable prices to stable prices. Do you agree or disagree?

3. Why doesn't agriculture respond to changes in prices in the same manner as the industrial sector of the economy? How does this result in a farm cost-price squeeze?

4. What steps could be taken to stop the cattle or hog cycle?

5. Some observers have argued that price instability presents no problem for farmers so long as prices are predictable. Is this true?

6. Comment on the statement, "Inflation is good for farmers."

7. How can consumers benefit from knowledge of cyclical and seasonal farm price variations?

SELECTED REFERENCES

DAHL, D. C., AND J. W. HAMMOND. *Market and Price Analysis, the Agricultural Industries,* Chap. 6. McGraw-Hill Book Company, New York, 1977.

"Gross and Net Farm Income." *Major Statistical Series of the U.S. Department of Agriculture,* Vol. 3. Agricultural Handbook No. 365, Sept. 1969.

SHEPERD, G. S. *Agricultural Price Analysis,* 6th Ed. Chap. 10, 11. Iowa State University, Ames, Iowa, 1963.

TOMEK, W. G., AND K. L. ROBINSON. *Agricultural Product Prices,* Chap. 9, 10. Cornell University Press, Ithaca, New York, 1972.

WAUGH, F. V. *Demand and Price Analysis, Some Examples from Agriculture.* U.S. Department of Agriculture. Technical Bulletin No. 1316, Nov. 1964.

———— *Graphic Analysis: Applications in Agricultural Economics.* U.S. Department of Agriculture. Agriculture Handbook No. 326, Nov. 1966.

CHAPTER 11

Food Marketing Costs

"WITH RISING INCOMES, consumers will continue to expand their purchases of food marketing services much more than their purchases of food products. Food processors and distributors have made marked gains in efficiency, especially in recent years, but increases in labor and other costs have more than offset these gains. Some further cost increases are likely. There are more rigidities built into the marketing-cost structure—on the downward side—than at any previous time."*

Preview

- This chapter examines the size, composition, and behavior of the food marketing margin—the difference between retail and farm prices.
- Several questions are addressed: Does food marketing cost too much? Too little? Are there excess profits and unnecessary costs in food marketing? How do changes in marketing costs affect farm and retail food prices?
- Two measures of the food marketing margin—the marketing bill and the farm-retail price spread—are discussed.
- The factors contributing to rising food marketing costs are evaluated.
- The farmer's share of the consumer's food dollar is investigated.
- The sticky marketing margin is discussed.
- Key terms and concepts:

cost components	marketing margin
farm-retail spread	marketing profits
farmer's share	profit rates
market basket	sticky margin
marketing bill	

Agricultural Markets in Change, U.S. Department of Agriculture, Agricultural Economic Report No. 95, July 1966.

Excessive profits, inefficiency, unnecessary services, and high marketing costs are often cited as responsible for high retail food prices and low farm prices. As a result, few areas have been studied as intensively as the costs of food marketing. The U.S. Department of Agriculture has a long history of research into marketing costs. Scarcely a Congressional session passes that does not see legislation requiring investigation of food marketing costs. In 1921 the Congress directed a Joint Commission of Agricultural Inquiry to investigate ". . . the cause of the difference between the prices of agriculture products paid to the producer and the ultimate cost to the consumers." In 1935 the Congress gave the Federal Trade Commission the responsibility of analyzing ". . . the distribution of the consumer's dollar paid for farm products between the farmer, processor, and distributor." In 1966, the National Commission on Food Marketing was established to study, among other things, the reasons for the difference between farm and retail prices and the reasons why these differences were widening. Each of these studies has added to our knowledge of food marketing costs and their impact on farm and retail food prices.

The central questions relating to food marketing costs are: Does food marketing cost too much? Why are marketing costs rising? How do changes in marketing costs affect farm and retail food prices? How could food marketing costs be reduced? And, are food marketing profits excessive? In our study of food marketing costs, it is important not to over-generalize. As we shall see, the costs and profits of food marketing vary considerably over time and for different products. In addition, as in all lines of business there are profitable and unprofitable firms in food marketing, though this is frequently hidden by industry averages.

THE FOOD MARKETING MARGIN

Consumer food expenditures can be broken down into their constituent marketing and farm components. Changes in these marketing and farm "shares" are watched carefully because they are indicators of trends in costs, profits, and services provided by farmers and food marketing firms. The portion of the consumer's food dollars that goes to food marketing firms is referred to as the *marketing margin*. This is the difference between what the consumer pays for food and what the farmer receives. In a sense, the marketing margin is the price of all utility-adding activities and functions performed by food marketing firms. This price includes the expenses of performing marketing functions and also the food marketing firms' profits.

The allocation of the consumer's food dollars between farmers and food marketing firms is one of the most controversial aspects of food marketing. Consumers do not earmark part of their expenditures for farm production and another part for marketing services. This division of the consumer's dollar is determined by competition and bargaining between these two sectors of the food industry. In effect, consumers face two prices for food: the farm price and the marketing "price" or margin. These prices reflect the cost of producing farm products, the cost of marketing services, as well as the consumers' desires for these two "products." Consumers influence farm prices by substituting one food for another, just as they influence the marketing margin by substituting high-service foods (for example, TV dinners) for low-service foods (such as fresh produce at a roadside market).

There are some widely held misconceptions about the food marketing margin. Many believe that a small margin denotes greater marketing efficiency, and that this is more desirable than a large margin. If this were true, farm roadside markets—where the marketing margin is zero and the farmer receives all of the consumer's food dollar—would represent the most efficient method of food marketing. In fact, although roadside marketing is becoming more prevalent, it is difficult to envision marketing our entire food supply in this direct-from-farmer-to-consumer way. Food marketing functions may or may not be performed efficiently, but efficiency cannot be judged solely by the size of the marketing margin.

Another widely held belief is that the large marketing margin reflects "too many" middlemen, and that the margin could be reduced by eliminating middlemen. The rule that middlemen may be eliminated but not their marketing functions and costs applies here. It is more correct to say that the size of the marketing margin depends upon the number and costs of marketing functions performed rather than the *number* of middlemen. The division of labor resulting from the addition of more and highly specialized middlemen might well increase rather than decrease marketing efficiency.

Another misconception is that a large marketing margin "causes" low farm prices, and that an increase in the margin must necessarily lower the farmer's price. Here it is important to remember that marketing functions add both value and costs to raw farm products. Thus, an increased marketing margin also increases the retail value and price of food. So it is quite possible that the farm price and the marketing margin will rise together as retail food prices rise. We should also remember that some of the marketing activities, such as advertising and merchandising, are designed to increase the demand for food, and this can lead to higher farm prices.

Finally, the size of the food marketing margin is sometimes taken as a measure of the profits to be gained by farmers and consumers as a result of performing additional marketing functions. Both farm and consumer cooperatives have been justified as a means of lowering the food marketing margin and of capturing marketing profits for their patrons. However, the marketing margin is composed of both *costs* and profits. There is no guarantee that farmers or consumers will perform marketing functions as efficiently as middlemen and thus capture food marketing profits.

THE FOOD MARKETING BILL

The food marketing bill is the difference between total consumer expenditures for all domestically produced food products and what farmers receive for equivalent farm products. The marketing bill is calculated annually and serves as one measure of the food marketing margin. In 1976, consumers spent $164 billion for food at retail, including away-from-home purchases. About two thirds ($110 billion) of this went to food marketing agencies and the other third ($54 billion) represented the farm value of food marketed. By this measure, then, consumers were paying twice as high a "price" for food marketing services as for basic farm products. That is to say, farmers received 34 per cent of consumer food expenditures, whereas food marketing firms received 66 per cent.

It is difficult for most people to view with detachment this 66:34 division of consumer food expenditures. To many, these shares seem both unfair and an underestimation of the contribution that agriculture makes to society. However, we should be careful in making this value judgment. The marketing bill tells us nothing about the *level* of farm prices or of the marketing margin. Nor is it an indicator of costs or efficiency in either sector. Much more information is needed to evaluate the marketing bill in order to determine whether it is "fair."

Figure 11-1 shows the food marketing bill increasing steadily and more rapidly than the farm value of food over the 1958–1977 period. Three factors are responsible for this rising food marketing bill. First, as a result of population growth, the physical quantity of food that is marketed has increased, raising the total expenses of marketing food. Second, the costs of most food marketing inputs, especially labor and energy, have added to the rising cost

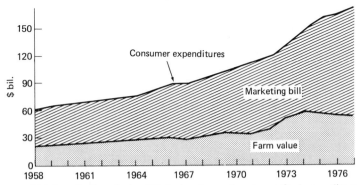

Figure 11–1. U.S. farm food marketing bill, farm value, and consumer food expenditures, 1958–1977. Includes farm products consumed at home and away from home. (U.S. Department of Agriculture)

223

of marketing food. Finally, consumer desires for additional food marketing services, such as represented by convenience foods, have further increased the food marketing bill.

These are the only factors that can increase the food marketing bill. Although each contributed to the rise in the bill, as shown in Figure 11-1, their importance has varied over the years. In the 1950's and 1960's, the trend toward more convenience foods had a greater impact on the bill than it had in the 1970's, when increased costs of marketing services accounted for most of the rise in the bill.

The fact that the food marketing bill is rising more rapidly than the farm value of food should not be surprising. Food marketing services are more income-responsive than are raw farm products. Hence, as consumer incomes rise, we would expect the growth in demand for marketing services to outpace the rise in demand for farm foods.

The contributions of the various marketing agencies to the food marketing bill have changed over time, as shown in Figure 11-2. The share of the bill contributed by food processors has declined, while the retail share has risen. This reflects operational efficiency gains in the two sectors. Between 1967 and 1974, processors reduced their labor per unit of food output by 17 per cent, whereas food stores increased labor use per unit of food marketed by 3 per cent. Food processors have been more successful than food retailers in reducing labor costs via mechanization and automation.

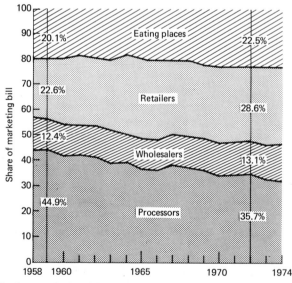

Figure 11-2. The food marketing bill by agencies, 1958–1974. (U.S. Department of Agriculture)

COST COMPONENTS OF THE MARKETING BILL

Food marketing firms incur a number of costs when performing marketing functions. Thus it is helpful to look at the composition of the marketing bill when evaluating the costs of food marketing. The cost components of the food marketing bill for 1976 are shown in Figure 11-3. Labor is the most important food marketing expense. Other significant components are packaging materials, transportation, and profits.

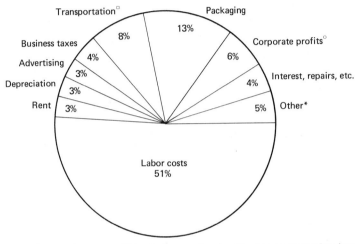

*Residual includes such costs as utilities, fuel, promotion, local for-hire transportation, insurance.
○Before taxes.
□Intercity rail and truck.

Figure 11–3. Components of the bill for marketing farm foods, 1976. (U.S. Department of Agriculture)

Labor Costs

Labor costs accounted for 51 per cent of the food marketing bill in 1976, compared to 44 per cent in 1960. As in all phases of American life, wage rates in marketing have tended to increase steadily. Unionization of the working force, which first entered through the manufacturing arena, has gradually spilled over to where it is a growing factor in the distribution fields. Minimum wage provisions, which at first did not affect the relatively small businesses of marketing, have gradually extended their coverage. Developments of the past several years have tended to result in higher wage rates and increased inflexibility in both labor force use and costs.

The predominance of labor costs in the food marketing bill has three impor-

225

tant consequences. First, the marketing bill has closely followed the rate of increase in wages. Between 1960 and 1975 the food marketing bill rose 131 per cent while average hourly earnings of food marketing workers rose 127 per cent. Second, rising labor costs have given food marketing firms a powerful incentive to increase operational efficiency through the substitution of machinery for labor. This has occurred more rapidly for food processors than for food distributors. However, all food marketing activities are constantly being scrutinized for potential labor-saving improvements. Third, the dominance of labor costs in the food marketing bill introduces a downward rigidity in the marketing margin. Wages do not adjust to downward food price pressures.

Are wage rates too high in food marketing? Table 11-1 provides a comparison of wage rates in food marketing with wages paid in related fields. Average 1970–1974 wages in food processing and wholesaling were lower than in comparable nonfood businesses. The average wage rate in retail food stores was somewhat higher than in other retail establishments, while wages in eating and drinking places were lower than in other retail places. Thus, wage rates in food marketing do not appear to be out of line with wages elsewhere in the economy.

Rising wage rates need not automatically result in higher food marketing costs. If labor productivity increased at the same rate as hourly wages, there would be no increase in unit labor costs and thus no inflationary labor cost pressures. However, wages have been rising more rapidly than labor productivity in much of the food marketing system as wage gains have followed wages elsewhere in the economy; but food marketing labor productivity has lagged behind productivity gains in other sectors. The result has been a steady rise in per unit labor costs in food marketing.

Table 11-1. Average Hourly Earnings In the Food Industry, 1970–1974.

SECTOR	AVERAGE HOURLY EARNINGS 1970–1974
Manufacturing	
Food processing	$3.62
All manufacturing	3.85
Wholesaling	
Food wholesalers	3.71
All wholesalers	3.92
Retailing	
Retail food stores	3.11
Eating and drinking places	1.99
All retailers	2.73

Sources: U.S. Departments of Labor and Agriculture.

Profits in Food Marketing

Profits are easily the most controversial component of the food marketing bill. There are several conceptions of "profit" which make more complex the appraisal of its role in the marketing bill. To the accountant, profit is what is "left over" after all expenses are paid. On this basis, some conclude that profits are an unnecessary residual that can be reduced or eliminated without serious consequences. To the businessman, profits are a reward for efficient behavior, and profit-seeking is a vital force which encourages lower costs and improved products. To eliminate these profits would destroy the free enterprise system which has contributed so much to the American standard of living. The economist views profits as another *cost* of doing business. Profits are the cost of attracting capital for investing in the growth and efficiency of the food marketing system. This is not to say that all profits are justified and therefore immune from criticism. Where profits result from anticompetitive behavior or market conditions, corrective action is necessary. Although profits per se are not evil, then, there is room for argument as to whether a particular level of profit is justified.

Comparing profit rates between firms and industries is hazardous. Differences in accounting methods and reporting techniques are one reason for this. In addition, there is no logical basis for arguing that profit rates should be equal in all firms or industries. Profits will vary depending upon the riskiness of the business, the competitive nature of its markets, and a host of other factors. Nevertheless, direct comparisons of profit rates between firms and industries frequently are made.

Profits are usually reported in two ways. Net profits as a per cent of sales are calculated by dividing dollar net profits by total sales. This profit measure is useful to show the share of the consumer's dollar going for profits. However, it is difficult to use this profit measure to compare profits among firms and industries because of their different turnover rates and sales volumes. Many financial analysts prefer to calculate dollar profits as a per cent of the investment in the firm—usually measured by stockholders' equity. This facilitates comparing firm's returns to invested dollars with other investment alternatives. For both of these measures, profits may be taken before or after taxes.

Table 11-2 shows the after-tax profit rates of food retailers and manufacturers from 1963 to 1975. These are average profit rates and reflect some very profitable firms and some firms that suffered losses. The information in Table 11-2 suggests that the profit rates for this period in food retailing and food manufacturing were about equal to each other and equal to the rates in all manufacturing industry, based on the percentage return on stockholder's equity. When profits are viewed as a percentage return on sales, food retailer profits are considerably lower than food manufacturing profits, which in turn are lower than the profits of all manufacturing. However, these "low" food

Table 11-2. Profits After Federal Income Taxes of Food Chains
and Manufacturers, Annual 1963–1975.

Year	15 LEADING FOOD CHAINS[1]	FOOD MANUFACTURERS[2]	ALL MANUFACTURING INDUSTRIES[2]
	Per cent return on stockholder equity		
1963	11.4	9.0	10.3
1964	11.5	10.1	11.7
1965	11.3	10.7	13.1
1966	11.4	11.3	13.6
1967	10.3	10.9	11.8
1968	10.3	10.8	12.2
1969	10.4	10.9	11.5
1970	10.6	10.8	9.3
1971	9.6	11.0	9.7
1972	5.1	11.2	10.6
1973	8.2	12.8	12.8
1974	4.8	13.9	14.9
1975	11.0	14.4	11.6
	Per cent return on sales		
1963	1.2	2.4	4.7
1964	1.3	2.7	5.2
1965	1.2	2.7	5.6
1966	1.2	2.7	5.6
1967	1.1	2.6	5.0
1968	1.1	2.6	5.1
1969	1.1	2.6	4.8
1970	1.0	2.5	4.0
1971	.9	2.6	4.1
1972	.5	2.6	4.3
1973	.7	2.6	4.7
1974	.4	2.9	5.5
1975	.8	3.2	4.6

[1] Compiled from "Moody's Industrial Manual." [2] Compiled from "Quarterly Financial Reports" published by the Federal Trade Commission. Data for 1974 and 1975 are imperfectly comparable with prior data because of changes in accounting methods. Reprinted by permission.

industry profits are more a result of high sales volume and turnover than actual low dollar profits.

Although profit levels do not appear to be excessive in food marketing, we should not conclude from this that these firms are necessarily competitive or efficient. Monopolistic conditions frequently lead to higher costs and prices rather than to abnormal profits. In addition, operational inefficiencies are often disguised by higher price levels and do not necessarily lead to lower profit levels.

The profit rates of food retailers, as shown in Table 11-2, show remarkable stability. Food retailer profits were depressed in 1972–1974. This was a period of price controls and an intensive price discounting program by the A & P Company. However, food retailers' profits returned to their average 11 per cent level in 1975, and there is no indication of a trend in these profit levels. Food manufacturers' profits, on the other hand, rose steadily from 1970 to 1975, after a stable period in the 1960's.

Profits, of course, vary widely for different lines of business. Figure 11-4 compares the 1963–1973 profit rates of dairy processors, bakeries, and meat-packing plants. These profits vary as a result of marketing conditions, management skills, and other factors affecting costs and prices.

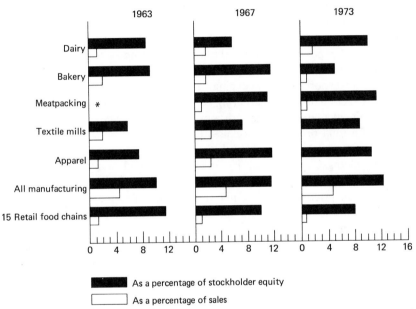

Figure 11–4. Profit ratios of manufacturers and food chains, 1963–1973. *Not available. (U.S. Department of Agriculture)

Are food marketing profits excessive? And are they responsible for high marketing costs? Several conclusions can be drawn. First, profits account for 6 per cent of the marketing bill, a significant but not dominant share of the bill. A 17 per cent increase in food marketing profits would be necessary to raise the food marketing bill by 1 per cent. Profits rarely jump this much on a year to year basis. Food marketing profits appear to be about comparable with profits elsewhere in the economy—neither higher nor lower when viewed as a return on a stockholder's investment. Profit rates on the order of a 10 to 15 per cent return on investment are considered satisfactory but not spectacular by financial analysts. Food marketing profits are certainly not unduly low, except when measured by return on sales. Considering the relatively low risk of the food industry in general, profits appear to be adequate to attract capital to the industry and to reward investors sufficiently.

FARM-RETAIL PRICE SPREADS

The marketing bill provides an aggregate view of the division of consumer food expenditures between farmers and food marketing firms. Farm-retail price spreads allow a more detailed view of this division for individual food products. The marketing bill is concerned with expenditure margins, whereas the farm-retail spreads are concerned with price margins.

The *farm-retail spread* is another measure of the marketing margin. It is the gross return per retail unit to the food marketing system for its activities and functions. As a margin, it includes profits as well as costs of labor, overhead, transportation, packaging, and the like. Changes in farm-retail spreads reflect changes in marketing costs, profits, or both. Farm-retail price spreads are calculated each month and each year for a specific quantity and quality of a food product. Consequently, changes in spreads can result only from a change in the costs of marketing services. The spreads are not influenced by changes in the quantity of food marketed or by the substitution of convenience foods for fresh foods.

Farm-retail price spreads are not simply the difference between farm and retail food prices. Instead, the spread is the difference between the retail price per unit and the farm value of an *equivalent amount* of food sold by farmers. For example, a 1,000 pound steer usually cuts out to 440 pounds of retail beef cuts. Thus, it requires 2.28 pounds of live steer to "produce" a pound of retail beef. Consequently, in 1976 the farm-retail price spread for beef was 61 cents per pound—or the difference between a pound of choice beef at retail ($1.39 average all cuts) and 2.28 pounds of live steer (78 cents = $34/cwt. × 2.28).

Figure 11-5 shows how farm-retail spreads can be utilized to trace changes in marketing costs over time. The retail price of bread is composed of four margins: the retail margin, the baker-wholesaler margin, the farm value or "farmer's margin", and other margins of commission men and transportation agencies involved in marketing wheat and bread. The figure suggests that up to 1972, the increasing retail price was the result of growing spreads at the retail and baker-wholesaler levels. From 1972 to 1974, a rising value of farm products (principally wheat) was primarily responsible for rising retail prices. After 1974, widening retail and baker-wholesaler margins offset declining farm value to push retail prices up further.

Farm-retail spreads also can be helpful in understanding the breakdown of the consumer's food dollar among marketing agencies and functions. Figure

11-6 shows this for several foods. It is clear that the division of the retail price among agencies and functions varies considerably by products, but some generalizations are possible. The assembly market functions typically account for a small portion of the spread. The farm values are usually large relative to the marketing margin for fresh marketed products and small relative to the marketing margin for highly processed products. Also, transportation and wholesaling costs tend to be larger for highly perishable items.

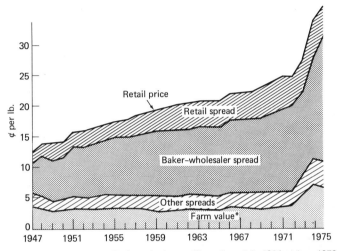

*All ingredients including miller's marketing certificate from July 1964 to June 1973.

Figure 11–5. The consumer's bread price and where it goes, 1947–1975. (U.S. Department of Agriculture)

Farm-retail price spreads also can be helpful in analyzing the cost components of the marketing margin for different products. The shares of the marketing margin allocated to various expense categories are shown in Table 11-3. The portion of the marketing margin accounted for by labor, for example, varies from 21 per cent for canned orange juice to 46 per cent for white bread. Percentage profit levels also vary by commodities.

Because of the rising costs of marketing, the post-World War II period has been one of steadily increasing farm-retail spreads. However, farm-retail spreads for individual foods have not all increased at the same rate. Table 11-4 shows the changes in a number of food spreads between 1960 and 1975. The spreads for sugar, shortening, and salad and cooking oil increased much more rapidly than the spreads of other foods. These differences reflect changing farm and retail price relationships over the 1960–1975 period as well as the varying marketing cost conditions for these products.

231

Table 11-3. Distribution of Consumer's Dollar According to Cost Items, 10 Leading Farm Food Products, 1973.

Item	Beef, Choice (pound)	Pork (pound)	Broiler (pound)	Eggs, Grade A or AA Large (dozen)	Fresh Milk Sold in Stores (½ gallon)	Apples (3-pound bag)	Frozen conc. Orange Juice Florida (6-ounce can)	Canned Orange Juice Florida (46-ounces)	Fresh Potatoes (10-pound bag)	White Bread (1-pound loaf)
					Cents					
Retail price	135.5	109.8	59.6	78.1	65.4	87.3	25.1	49.3	122.5	27.6
Farm value	89.9	71.5	35.3	54.4	33.2	30.4	8.2	13.0	49.8	4.1[1]
					Per cent					
Share of marketing margin:										
Labor	39%	42	43	32	44	39	27	21	38	46
Packaging	7	4	6	16	10	10	14	30	9	5
Transportation	4	5	10	9	11	11	9	21	18	1
Business taxes	2	2	2	3	4	2	1	1	2	2
Depreciation	2	3	2	2	4	2	2	2	2	2
Rent	2	3	2	1	2	2	2	4	1	2
Repairs	1	2	2	1	4	1	2	2	1	1
Advertising	5	5	4	5	5	2	5	4	3	5
Interest	1	1	1	1	1	1	1	1	1	1
Energy	2	4	3	2	2	2	2	1	3	
Other	7	12	7	9	6	7	5	7	6	28[2]
Profit	5	6	6	7	7	6	11	6	5	6
Unallocated[3]	23	11	12	12	—	15	19	—	10	—
Total	100	100	100	100	100	100	100	100	100	100

[1] Cost of wheat only.
[2] Includes cost of non-flour ingredients to the baker of 2.5 cents.
[3] Consists mainly of assembly, storage, and wholesaling charges which could not be allocated to cost components because of lack of data.

Source: U.S. Department of Agriculture.

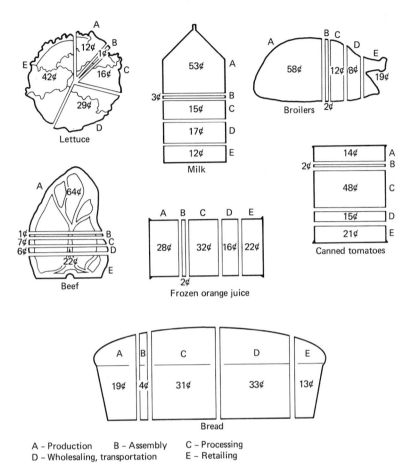

Figure 11–6. What the food dollar pays for, 1975. (U.S. Department of Agriculture)

A - Production   B - Assembly   C - Processing
D - Wholesaling, transportation   E - Retailing

THE FARMER'S SHARE

The farmer's share is computed from farm-retail price spreads and is the farm value expressed as a percentage of the retail price of food. The farmer's share is widely regarded as a measure of the fairness of farm prices and the efficiency of food marketing. In fact, it measures neither of these very well.

A composite farmer's share for 65 farm products is computed annually by the U.S. Department of Agriculture, and it is widely publicized. The results for the 1915–1976 period are shown in Table 11-5. In 1976, the farmer's share of the consumer's food dollar was 40 per cent, so the marketing share was 60 per cent. The farmer's share calculated from farm-retail spreads is generally higher than the share calculated from the marketing bill, but the

233

Table 11-4. Changes in Farm-Retail Price Spreads, Selected Foods, 1960–1975.

| | FARM-RETAIL PRICE SPREAD (¢) | | |
PRODUCT	1960	1975	DIFFERENCE 1960–1975
Choice beef	28.1	53.1	25.0
Pork	27.2	48.1	20.9
Broilers	17.8	26.2	8.4
Grade A eggs	19.8	26.2	6.4
Grade A whole milk	25.2	37.3	12.1
Butter	20.5	35.2	14.7
Apples	10.6	22.2	11.6
Fresh oranges	48.4	90.3	41.9
Frozen orange juice	14.0	19.6	5.6
Fresh tomatoes	20.2	34.0	13.8
Canned tomatoes	14.0	30.4	16.4
Lettuce	13.2	27.7	14.5
Fresh potatoes	45.1	89.0	43.9
Frozen french fried potatoes	12.0	20.8	8.8
Long grain rice	13.6	32.7	19.1
White pan bread	17.0	29.2	12.2
Salad and cooking oil	33.8	82.8	49.0
Margarine	18.9	41.9	23.0
Vegetable shortening	55.9	117.0	61.1
Sugar	36.8	105.4	68.6

Source: U.S. Department of Agriculture.

two series have moved together. This "spread" share of 40 per cent is the more widely used of the two series.

Table 11-5 shows a tendency for the farmer's share to fluctuate around a long-term average of 40 per cent. The share rises during periods of rapidly rising retail food prices (1915–1919, 1940–1944, 1972–1973) and falls during periods of declining food prices (for example, the 1930's). The fact that the farmer's share has hovered around the 40 per cent level for so long does not mean this is necessarily the "correct" distribution of the consumer's dollar between farmers and marketing firms. There is no guarantee that market forces will result in an equitable farmer's share. Nevertheless, the stability of the farmer's share is remarkable and disputes the often-held belief that farmer's are receiving a decreasingly smaller portion of the consumer's food dollar over time.

The Farmer's Share by Commodities

The farmer's share varies widely for different commodities. There are many farm products with a greater than 40 per cent farm share and many with a

Table 11-5. The Market Basket of Farm Foods and the Farmer's Share of the Food Dollar, 1915–1976.

YEARS	MARKET BASKET RETAIL COST[1]	MARKETING CHARGES	FARM VALUE	FARMER'S SHARE OF CONSUMER'S DOLLAR
	$	$	$	%
1915–19	399	210	189	47
1920–24	444	263	181	41
1925–29	439	256	183	42
1930–34	327	211	116	35
1935–39	341	204	137	40
1940–44	397	208	189	47
1945–49	762	381	384	51
1950–54	940	509	431	46
1955–59	957	576	381	40
1960–64	1,004	625	379	38
1965–69	1,101	666	435	39
1970	1,229	750	478	39
1971	1,250	771	479	38
1972	1,311	787	524	40
1973	1,538	837	701	46
1974	1,750	1,002	747	43
1975	1,876	1,092	784	42
1976	1,895	1,146	749	40

[1] The market basket contains the average quantities of 65 domestic farm-originated food products purchased in 1960–1961 by wage earners and clerical worker families and workers living alone. The composition and weighting of the market basket were revised several times from 1915 to 1976.

Source: U.S. Department of Agriculture.

smaller share. Several commodities are classified in Figure 11-7 by their farm share. There are numerous reasons for these variations in farmer's shares. The marketing job for some products is more complex than for others. By and large, the differences in farm shares shown in Figure 11-7 reflect product characteristics which affect the complexity of marketing different farm products. These product characteristics can be classified as follows:

1. Processing and marketing services. The more work that must be done in changing the form of the product and providing the service to satisfy the consumer, the greater the marketing charges will be.

2. Perishability. Marketing perishables is usually more costly than marketing nonperishables. Spoilage is greater; expensive refrigeration may have to be used both in transportation and in the marketing channel's various stages.

3. Bulkiness in relation to value. Some products will require more space in both transportation and storage. This would tend to increase cost.

4. Extreme seasonality of production. Commodities that must come to

235

Under 25 percent	25 to 50 percent	Over 50 percent
Canned corn	Frozen orange juice	Beef
Canned tomatoes	Peanut butter	Pork
Canned spaghetti	Fresh apples	Butter
Corn flakes	Lettuce	Eggs
Sandwich cookies	Ice cream	Milk
Bread	Flour	Frying chickens
French fried potatoes	Potatoes	Turkey

Figure 11–7. The farmer's share of retail price for selected items, 1976. (U.S. Department of Agriculture)

market within a very short time require facilities that may be only partially used during the rest of the year. If such commodities are also perishable, increased spoilage costs will result.

Figure 11-8 illustrates the effects of these product characteristics. The farmer's share tends to be larger for bulky, perishable, or fresh marketed commodities and lower for highly processed, concentrated foods.

In generalizing about the farmer's share for different commodities over time, care must be exercised. These shares do not rise and fall uniformly. As shown in Figure 11-8, the farmer's share for bakery and cereal products

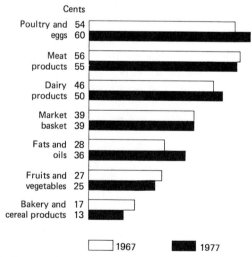

Figure 11–8. The farmer's share of the consumer's food dollar by food group, 1967–1977. (U.S. Department of Agriculture)

fell three cents between 1966 and 1976, a period when the share for poultry and eggs rose two cents; the share for meat products fell four cents, and the share for dairy products rose four cents. These differences reflect changing farm and retail price relationships and marketing cost trends for the various commodities.

The Meaning of the Farmer's Share

Caution is advised in interpreting and evaluating the size of the food marketing margin and changes in the farmer's share. A large marketing margin or a declining farm share are not necessarily indicative of the level of farm prices, farm income, marketing efficiency or profits, or the value of food to consumers.

An example will point out the hazards of making judgments about farm prices and income from the farm share. Table 11-6 illustrates the prices, costs, and shares of alternative sources and varieties of potatoes. Notice that producers of New York potatoes received a 46 per cent share of the consumer's dollar although farmers producing potatoes sold as frozen french fries received only 16 per cent of the consumer's dollar. Yet, because of the difference in retail prices, the dollar grower return was about the same ($2.02–2.06) in both instances. A small share of a large number can easily exceed a large share of a small number. Notice that the Maine potato growers received a larger share but a smaller grower return than the Idaho potato growers. The farmer banks dollars, not percentages. This example suggests that a falling farm share does not necessarily indicate falling farm prices or returns. Suppose that more and more potatoes were consumed in their processed and frozen forms. The total aggregate marketing costs for potatoes would increase and the farmer's share of the consumer's potato dollar would de-

Table 11-6. Retail Price, Marketing Margin, Grower Return and Farm Share For Potatoes and Potato Products, Washington D.C., 1960.

	FRESH			FROZEN FRENCH FRIES
	IDAHO	MAINE	LONG ISLAND NEW YORK	
Retail price (100 pounds fresh equivalent)	$9.82	$6.52	$4.51	$12.94
Marketing margin	6.63	3.75	2.45	10.92
Grower return	3.19	2.77	2.06	2.02
Farmer's share	32%	43%	46%	16%

Source: H. T. Badger, *The Impact of Technological Change on Marketing Costs and Grower's Returns,* U.S. Department of Agriculture, Marketing Research Report No. 573, December 1962, p. 8.

crease. But if through this change, consumers could be encouraged to buy more potatoes at higher prices reflecting the increased processing costs, the net dollar returns to potato producers might actually be increased. This could represent a situation in which higher marketing costs were desirable from both the consumer's and producer's point of view.

It should also be evident that changes in the farmer's share over a period of time are not an adequate indicator of changes in marketing efficiency. In fact, there is reason to believe that in very prosperous times when the share is relatively large, marketing may be less efficient than in depressed times when the share is small. Prosperous periods often encourage poor management and organization, because large profits come easily. Hard times furnish the impetus to operate as efficiently as possible. The difference in the size of share among the various commodities is not an indicator of relative efficiency. Rather, in most cases it merely reflects the complexity of the job that must be done in marketing the product.

It is doubtful that the statistics of the farmer's share merit the attention they receive. The important thing is not the size of the share, but the total return received by agricultural producers from the sale of their products. Higher marketing costs and a more prosperous agriculture are compatible ideas. It is very probable that as the standard of living rises, increased demands for more processing and marketing services will increase marketing costs. In some instances, maybe enough is not being spent to market the product to its best advantage. This situation could be true regardless of the size of the farmer's share. Businessmen in all fields are continually attempting to discover new ways of attracting and influencing the consumer. In a sense, they are always asking the question, "Does marketing cost enough?" It is not a matter of low dollar costs alone but rather of getting the marketing job done with the best combination of resources. And the end product of the marketing job is the movement of goods into consumption with top priority given to consumer satisfaction.

INTERRELATIONSHIPS OF THE MARKETING MARGIN AND FOOD PRICES

Farmers often feel that rising marketing costs depress farm prices; consumers frequently complain that falling farm prices are not readily transmitted to them in the form of reduced retail prices. Both criticisms are relevant to the relationships between the marketing margin and farm and retail food prices. Mathematically, the marketing margin is always equal to the difference between the retail price and the farm price. If one of these changes, the others must adjust in order to maintain the equality. However, this does not tell us which determines which, nor how changes in one specifically influence the others.

There are two views of the price-margin relationship. The "cost-plus" theory is that the retail price of food is "built-up" by adding the marketing margin to the farm price. Thus, changes in farm prices or marketing costs are simply passed through to consumers in the form of higher retail food prices. It follows that the consumer—not the farmer—would bear the cost of a rising food marketing bill or higher farm prices. The "derived demand" theory of prices and margins is that the farm price is what is left over from the retail price after all marketing costs are paid. According to this view, an increase in marketing costs would reduce farm prices, unless retail prices also increased.

The cost-plus theory appears to be the correct one over the long run when the consumer's food dollar must cover all farm and marketing costs. However, in the shorter run, the derived demand theory of farm prices appears to be a more accurate view of the real world. Frequently there are periods when farm prices are below costs of production, but rarely does the marketing margin fail to cover marketing costs.

We have seen that the food marketing bill has been increasing steadily as a result of rising marketing costs. Yet, over the long run, the farmer's share has fluctuated around the 40 per cent level. This supports the cost-plus theory of marketing margins.

Figure 11-9 illustrates the impact on farm and retail food prices of a rising-dollar marketing margin and a constant farmer's share. It is evident, according to Figure 11-9, that a rising marketing bill is not inconsistent with rising farm prices. In the long run, rising farm prices and marketing costs will be passed along to consumers. Consumers of course may or may not elect to pay these higher prices, which they can avoid by reducing food purchases or by substituting low-priced foods for high-priced foods.

Although the evidence suggests that there is a stable *percentage* marketing margin and farm share for the longer run, on a day-to-day, month-to-month, or year-to-year basis the marketing margin is more likely to be a constant *dollar* amount. This has important consequences for pricing efficiency, the stability of farm prices, and the farmer's share. The tendency for the marketing margin to remain constant in dollars, with short-term variations in farm and retail prices, is referred to as the "sticky" or *inflexible marketing margin*. Table 11-5 shows that the farm value and farmer's share rise during periods of rising food prices (for instance, 1972–1973) and fall during periods of falling food prices (for instance, 1975–1976); the sticky marketing margin is responsible for this behavior of farm and retail food prices.

Figure 11-10 illustrates the effects of an inflexible dollar marketing margin on changing retail and farm prices. With a sticky marketing margin, any change in the retail price is immediately transmitted to the farm level, and changing farm prices are immediately reflected at the retail level. This results in farm price instability and rather wide swings of the farmer's share in the short run. If, on the other hand, the dollar marketing margin adjusted

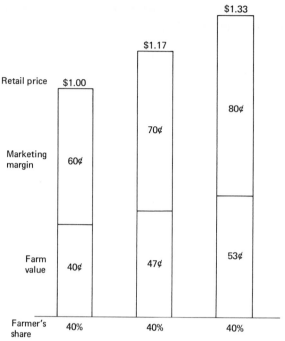

Figure 11–9. Effects of a rising marketing margin on farm and retail prices when the farmer's share is constant.

Figure 11–10. Effects of a fixed dollar marketing margin on farm and retail prices.

simultaneously with a changing retail or farm price, farm prices and the farmer's share would be more stable.

Several reasons are given for the stickiness of the dollar marketing margin in the short-run period. First, most of the costs of performing marketing functions are related to the physical volume of food marketed rather than to the price of food. It costs the same to grade, store, transport, and process a bushel of wheat regardless of its price. There is no reason why such marketing costs should adjust to food prices. The dominance of labor costs in the food marketing bill also contributes to the sticky marketing margin. Wages simply do not adjust to price changes in the short run. Increased unionization of food marketing workers further adds to the inflexibility of the marketing margin. Finally, imperfect competition in the food marketing industries contributes to margin inflexibility.

The inflexible food marketing margin is frequently criticized by farmers and consumers who feel that food marketing firms should "share" with farmers and consumers retail and farm price changes. It is true that the sticky marketing margin results in a greater farm price and farmers' share variability than would be the case if the dollar margin adjusted at the same time as farm and retail prices. However, although the farmer is disadvantaged by the sticky marketing margin when prices are falling, he benefits from it in rising markets.

THE FUTURE OF FOOD MARKETING COSTS

Are there any unexploited opportunities to reduce food marketing costs, increase farm prices, or reduce retail food prices? What can we reasonably expect the future trend to be in marketing costs and in the food marketing margin?

Continued Large Marketing Margin

Even with a highly efficient marketing system that functions perfectly, the costs of marketing food will continue to be high and to increase. The food marketing task grows more complex and more expensive with urbanization, geographic specialization of agriculture, the affluence of consumers, and an increase in population.

Cost inflation and consumer demand for marketing services hold the key to the rate of future increases in the marketing margin. Most marketing costs are influenced by general economic forces outside of the food economy, especially labor, transportation, packaging, and energy costs. These rising costs will maintain their pressures on the rising food marketing bill, and government regulations, affecting such areas as occupational safety, plant sanitation, energy sources and uses, and environmental protection, also will add costs. Consumer demand trends will further contribute to the rising food marketing bill in coming years. The demand for more processing and convenience services has already contributed to the rising marketing bill. This demand is closely linked to trends in consumer incomes, which are expected to continue to rise.

Opportunities for Reducing Costs

In 1966, the National Commission on Food Marketing made a comprehensive evaluation of food marketing costs. The conclusions of this study were that the rising cost of labor was chiefly responsible for the growth in the farm-retail spread between 1960 and 1966; that few unnecessary or wholly wasteful marketing functions were performed in the food industry, but that some selling activities, especially advertising, could be reduced without loss of consumer value; and that most food marketing functions were performed efficiently but that there were places where efficiency could be improved.[1]

As we have seen, profits are not abnormally high or distressingly low *on the average* in food marketing, and in any event profits do not account for a very large share of the food marketing bill. Therefore, to reduce profits is probably not a very good approach to lowering food marketing costs.

Labor is the most obvious area in which to cut costs, but food marketing wages could not be reduced to any great extent without affecting the ability of the industry to attract and hold qualified labor. Therefore, the logical approach to reducing labor costs is through improved productivity resulting from the substitution of machinery for labor. Progress will be slow, however, because productivity gains in food marketing have lagged behind labor efficiency gains elsewhere in the economy.

Some observers have suggested the elimination of certain marketing functions as a cost-reducing measure. The rule that it is difficult to eliminate marketing functions without changing the value of food products to consumers applies here. Integration of marketing functions into a single firm promises some economies, as has occurred in food retailing and wholesaling, but in general, those who seek to eliminate the middleman usually wind up simply changing his identity.

Attempts to reduce other food marketing costs or functions in order to improve operational efficiency often reduce consumer satisfaction, pricing efficiency, or consumer freedom of choice. Some food industry critics have argued, for example, that many food industry advertising, packaging, and promotional practices could be eliminated without loss. This viewpoint, however, presumes to judge what is a necessary and an unnecessary cost—a judgment that many feel should be left to the consumer and to the competitive market processes.

---

[1] *Food from Farmer to Consumer,* Report of the National Commission on Food Marketing, Washington, D.C., June 1966, Chap. 3.

The National Commission on Food Marketing cited the shift of the food industry from a commodity orientation to a marketing/merchandising orientation as a major reason for the increasing farm-retail spread.[2] This shift probably sacrificed some operational efficiency for nonprice competitive advantages. Food manufacturers' and retailers' success increasingly hinges on the differentiating value of cost-increasing services such as advertising, trading stamps, coupons, games, and elaborate merchandising. These activities may or may not represent "true" consumer desires, but there is no doubt that they have added significantly to the cost of food marketing.

Market researchers often report that the costs of food marketing could be reduced if the large number of firms were reduced to an "optimal" number, or if all firms would distribute their products optimally among geographic markets. These studies often neglect the competitive impact of improvements in operational efficiency. Should we reduce the number of food marketing companies to gain economies of size, even at the expense of weakening competition in the marketplace?

Thus, the goal of "lowering food marketing costs" must always be reconciled with the consumer's freedom of choice, the firm's freedom of behavior, pricing efficiency, and consumer satisfaction. The result is a compromise, which is easy to improve upon only if one goal is viewed independently of the others.

SUMMARY

The food marketing margin is the price of all the utilities added in the marketing process. The size, composition, and behavior of this marketing margin are controversial aspects of food marketing. The bill for marketing food continues to rise each year because of the increased volume of food marketed, higher costs of marketing services, and consumer demands for more marketing services. Marketing utilities are more income-responsive than the demand for farm commodities, so the marketing bill is about twice the value of farm foods. Labor costs account for one half of the food marketing bill whereas profits account for about 6 per cent of the bill. Food marketing labor costs and profits do not appear to be excessive, but neither are profits abnormally low in the industry. The farmer's share varies widely for different food products. The market basket share has fluctuated around the 40 per cent level over the long term. The dollar marketing margin tends to be sticky or inflexible in the short run, and this contributes to instability in farm prices and in the farmer's share. Although some progress is being made in improving operational efficiency and lowering unit costs of food marketing, rising marketing costs are contributing to an increasing marketing margin. There does

---

[2] Ibid, p. 91.

not appear to be any potential for dramatically reducing food marketing costs in the near future. Considering the contribution that marketing activities can make to increased consumer satisfaction and demand, farmers and consumers might well ask, "Is enough being spent to market the nation's food supply?"

QUESTIONS FOR DISCUSSION

1. You have been asked to explain to a group of laymen why the farmer's share for beef was 50 per cent in 1977 although the share for bread was only 7 per cent. Outline the major points you would make in your presentation.

2. Compare the percentage cost components of the food marketing margin with the components of farm production costs published by the U.S. Department of Agriculture. What are the differences and similarities?

3. In 1970, the farmer's share of the consumer's food dollar was 33 per cent, according to the marketing bill data, and 39 per cent, according to the price spread data. Why do these estimates differ?

4. What are the principal efficiency conflicts preventing rapid reductions in food marketing costs?

5. Using your own figures, demonstrate that farm prices can rise even when the farmer's share is falling. What are you assuming about the dollar and the percentage marketing margin?

6. Prove the following: If the marketing margin is a constant percentage, percentage changes in retail prices will exactly equal percentage changes in farm prices. Whereas, if the margin is a constant dollar amount, percentage changes in farm prices will exceed percentage changes in retail prices.

7. Criticize the statement, "Food marketing costs too much."

SELECTED REFERENCES

"Agricultural Marketing Costs and Charges." *Major Statistical Series of the U.S. Department of Agriculture.* Agricultural Handbook No. 365, Vol. No. 4, 1970.

BADGER, H. T. *The Impact of Technological Change on Marketing Costs and Grower's Returns.* U.S. Department of Agriculture, Marketing Research Report No. 573, Dec. 1962.

Cost Components of Farm-Retail Price Spreads for Foods. National Commission on Food Marketing. Technical Study No. 9, U.S. Government Printing Office, June 1966.

Cost Components of Farm-Retail Price Spreads for Selected Foods. U.S. Department of Agriculture. Agricultural Economics Report No. 343, July 1976.

CRAWFORD, T. L. "The Bill for Marketing Farm-Food Products." *The Marketing and Transportation Situation.* U.S. Department of Agriculture, Aug. 1974, pp. 15–30.

Developments in Marketing Spreads for Agricultural Products in 1976. U.S. Department of Agriculture. Agricultural Economic Report No. 367, March 1977, issued annually.

"Distribution of the Food Dollar by Marketing Function and Expense Item." *The Marketing and Transportation Situation.* U.S. Department of Agriculture, Nov. 1974, pp. 23–45.

DUEWER, L. A. *Price Spreads for Beef and Pork: Revised Series, 1949–69.* U.S. Department of Agriculture. Miscellaneous Publication No. 1174, May 1970.

GOLDBERG, R. "Marketing Costs and Margins: Current Use in Agribusiness Market-Structure Analysis." *American Journal of Agricultural Economics* (Dec. 1965), 1352–65.

HAMMOND, J. W., W. E. ANTHONY, AND M. K. CHRISTIANSEN. "A Look at the Farm-Retail Price Spread." *Journal of Marketing,* **32** (July 1968), 62–70.

Marketing Spreads for Food Products. Council on Wage and Price Stability, Staff Report, May 1975.

"Output Per Unit of Labor Input in the Retail Food Store Industry." *Monthly Labor Review,* U.S. Department of Labor, Jan. 1977.

Price Spreads for Farm Foods. Monthly report of the Economic Research Service, U.S. Department of Agriculture.

The Profit and Price Performance of Leading Food Chains, 1970–74. Joint Economic Committee of Congress. U.S. Government Printing Office, April 12, 1977.

The Responsiveness of Wholesale and Retail Food Prices to Changes in the Costs of Food Production and Distribution. Council on Wage and Price Stability, Staff Report, Nov. 1976.

PART IV

Functional and Organizational Issues

CHAPTER 12

The Changing Organization of Food Markets

"THE NEW U.S. FOOD SYSTEM cannot develop under conditions of high uncertainty regarding price, quality, and supply of raw products. Coordination of farm production, processing, food preparing, marketing, and service is essential. This requirement is stimulating contracting for future delivery rather than buying at time of harvest or time of slaughter . . . the major decisions regarding what to produce and how much are moving away from the farmer to the food firms."*

Preview

- This chapter discusses several important trends influencing the organization of food markets.
- The task of vertically coordinating the successive stages of food production and marketing is described.
- The reasons for specialization and diversification of food marketing firms are examined.
- The trend toward market decentralization and direct buying is explained.
- The process of market integration is examined, and several types of food market integration are defined.
- The effects of decentralization and integration on operational and pricing efficiency and the complexity of the farmers' marketing task are evaluated.

---

* Eric Thor, "The Impact of Changing Marketing Practices Upon the Structural Organization of Agriculture," National Colloquium on Marketing Horticultural Crops, August 29, 1972.

- Key terms and concepts:

conglomerates	horizontal integration
contract integration	mergers
cross-subsidization	specification buying
decentralization	terminal market
direct buying	thin markets
diversification	vertical coordination
farm-factory	vertical integration

The food industry is a dynamic one. It is in a constant state of flux. The food marketing machinery continues to make adjustments to changes in agricultural production patterns, new marketing technologies, and trends in food consumption. These adjustments alter the market organization of the food industry—the kinds of firms involved, the relationships of firms within the industry, the allocation of marketing functions among firms, and the nature of food product flows. Three important market organization trends in the food industry are (1) specialization and diversification; (2) decentralization; and (3) integration.

VERTICAL COORDINATION IN FOOD MARKETS

The food industry might be thought of as an orchestra. Each level of the market contributes its utility to the final product. The numerous decisions about what to produce, how much to produce, where, how, and when to sell must somehow be coordinated. *Vertical market coordination* refers to the process of directing and harmonizing the several interrelated and sequential decisions involved in efficiently producing and marketing the nation's food supply.

Simple economies do not have vertical coordination problems because there are limited marketing activities, and often, many production and marketing functions are performed by the same firm. In advanced economies, more marketing functions are performed, the marketing channels are longer, and firms specialize in performing separate but related marketing functions. This presents coordination problems.

Vertical market coordination is particularly critical in the food industry because of the length of the marketing channel, the large number of specialized firms involved, the inherent uncertainty of prices, supplies, and qualities of farm products, and the urgency of marketing perishable products. For these reasons, errors in food production and marketing decisions are quite costly to both the firms in the industry and to the efficiency of the system.

250

There are two ways to vertically coordinate food industry decisions. Prices can serve to communicate the needs of each firm to others in the marketing channel. Or, other coordinating devices, such as contracts, can be used to communicate information between firms, such as price, quality, timing, and other market considerations. The search for improved vertical market coordination has resulted in a change in food market organization in recent years. Two important changes in vertical market coordination are, first, that the major decisions—what to produce and how much to produce—have in large part passed from the farmer to the food marketing firms. The buyers of farm products (the food marketing firms) are directing and coordinating the food economy today, including farm decisions. Agricultural production takes place on order from food marketing firms. Second, there is a trend toward replacing price coordination with administered coordination techniques, such as contracts, bargaining associations, and the like. Both trends are affecting the farmer's position in the food industry.

Evolving Market Organization

In the colonial period of our history, the food marketing channel was a simple one. Much of the food was consumed on the farm, and surpluses were marketed directly to nearby consumers. As population centers developed, country storekeepers came on the scene to assemble farm products for local sale or shipment to distant markets.

During the nineteenth century, food marketing channels continued to lengthen as the distance between farmers and consumers increased. Direct farmer sales to consumers declined as specialized assemblers of farm products and wholesalers developed to bridge the gap between farmers and consumers. Large, central terminal markets were established in the major population centers where grain and livestock products were collected and sold to processors, exporters, and retailers. The Chicago Union Stockyard, established in 1865, was an important livestock terminal market. Wholesale terminal markets for fresh fruits and vegetables, eggs, butter, and other products developed near railroad yards and port facilities in the larger cities. Food processors were often located adjacent to these terminal markets.

Each level of the food marketing channel was made up of substantially independent firms. Country buyers, such as cream stations, elevators, and poultry and egg buyers were independent businesses buying from farmers and selling to the processors and wholesalers in the cities. Most processors were engaged only in processing activities. Wholesalers performed a few specialized marketing functions, as did retailers.

All of this trading was coordinated by prices determined in open market competition among buyers and sellers. There were few contractural arrangements and little in the way of formal bargaining relationships. Prices were discovered in the central terminal markets where all buyers and sellers met and could physically examine the produce. This market was rather close to the perfectly competitive condition.

If the nineteenth century was a period of open, lengthening food marketing channels and increased specialization of marketing functions, the twentieth century has been a period of shortening and closing of these channels, diversification of marketing functions by firms, and a substitution of administrative coordination for price coordination.

SPECIALIZATION AND DIVERSIFICATION IN FOOD MARKETS

Specialization and diversification are two pervasive characteristics of food markets. Farmers usually specialize in a few, or in one, commodity or enterprise. Food processors operate specialized plants or company divisions yet provide a wide variety of brands and products. The supermarket can be thought of as a collection of specialized departments (dry groceries, meat, produce, nonfood, and so on) selling a diversified assortment of products. Which is more efficient, specialization or diversification? And why are they occurring together in the food industry?

Specialization in the Food Industry

Specialization and division of labor are two of the universal characteristics of markets, primitive or advanced. In the food industry we observe product, functional, and institutional specialization. Battle Creek, Michigan is the breakfast cereal capital; citrus is a southern crop; food processors specialize in adding form utility to farm products; and livestock production takes place in and around the corn belt. Specialization is so common in the food industry that it is taken for granted. Farmers and food marketing firms usually find it profitable to specialize because it can improve operational efficiency and increase profits.

Specialization and division of labor have three important consequences for the food marketing system because they: (1) increase the interdependency of food producers, marketing firms, and consumers; (2) increase the volume of exchange and thereby the importance of marketing activity; and (3) tend to lead to larger firms. The latter needs further explanation.

Typically, food marketing plants' costs of production decline with rising output. Table 12-1 provides some examples. These economies of size result from the specialization of labor, machinery, and management which is possible in large plants. Not all costs rise with volume, and average costs of firms fall as these fixed costs are spread over more volume of output. Thus, there is a profit incentive for food marketing firms to increase in size. However,

Table 12-1. Illustrations of Economies of Size in Food Processing.

INDUSTRY		PLANT SIZE	AVERAGE COSTS
Dairy processing	(1962–1969)		
		6,000 qts. per day	6.7¢/qt.
		100,000 qts. per day	3.4
		800,000 qts. per day	2.4
Bread baking	(1965)		
		250,000 lbs. per week	3.87¢/lb.
		500,000 lbs. per week	3.59
Canned tomatoes	(1969)		
		100 cases per hour	$3.60/case
		800 cases per hour	3.03
		1,500 cases per hour	2.85
Soybean processing	(1952)		
		25 tons per day	63.5¢/ton
		300 tons per day	37.9
		1,000 tons per day	35.1

Sources: *Market Structure of the Food Industry,* U.S. Department of Agriculture Marketing Research Report No. 971, September 1972, p. 23; *Organization and Competition in the Milling and Baking Industries,* National Commission on Food Marketing, June 1966, pp. 132–35; G. A. Mathia, et.al., *An Economic Analysis of Whole Tomato Canning Opportunities in the South,* North Carolina State University, Economic Information Report No. 17, May 1970; *Size of Soybean Oil Mills and Returns to Growers,* U.S. Department of Agriculture Marketing Research Report No. 121, 1953, p. 24.

there are limits to this profitability. Beyond a particular volume, the average costs of food marketing firms stabilize and eventually may even rise as the plant grows in size and as transportation costs to and from the plant increase. A typical food firm's average costs are shown in Figure 12-1. There is a range of output *(AB)* where costs fall with size of plant as operational efficiency

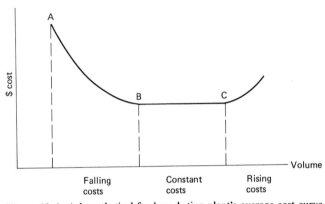

Figure 12–1. A hypothetical food marketing plant's average cost curve.

is improved. The output range, *BC,* is a level of stable average costs, and beyond *C,* plant costs rise with further growth.

Knowledge of food marketing firms' average costs can be helpful in evaluating the trend toward larger food marketing firms. The cost savings of firm growth from *A* to *B* in Figure 12-1 represent potential food price reductions for consumers and increases for farmers. However, as these operational efficiencies are gained by the firm, pricing efficiency may be reduced, so there is no guarantee that the cost savings will be passed on to farmers or to consumers. This is the *pricing-operational efficiency dilemma.*

Other uses can be made of these cost relations. The falling average cost is usually steeper for food processors than for wholesalers and retailers as a result of their mix of fixed and variable costs. Thus, there may be more justification for firm growth in processing than in the distributive trades. The constant cost-volume range presents a problem. Is there any reason to tolerate firms of size *C* when they are no more operationally efficient than firms of size *B?*

Numerous studies have been made of these economies of size in food marketing. One observer of these studies concluded: (1) larger plants always have lower costs than smaller plants, and no firms operate in the rising cost range; (2) the economies of size are greater for highly capitalized food industries (such as dairy processing, flour milling) than for lower-capital industries (egg or fruit and vegetable packing); and (3) many food processing plants are much larger than is justified by economies of size.[1] The National Commission on Food Marketing found that the smallest firms in the food industry suffered handicaps because of inefficient size; medium-sized plants were operationally as efficient as larger plants; and the larger firms experienced economies of size in advertising and sales promotion.[2] A Federal Trade Commission report concluded that economies of size are insignificant in food manufacturing, and that maximum operational efficiency can be achieved by relatively small plants.[3]

Diversification in the Food Industry

In view of these economies of specialization and size it may seem contradictory that most food marketing firms are diversifying their product offerings, their range of marketing functions, and the institutional levels of the market in which they participate. Farmers perform storage and transportation func-

---

[1] B. C. French, "The Analysis of Productive Efficiency in Agricultural Marketing," in L. R. Martin, Ed., *A Survey of Agricultural Economics Literature,* Vol. 1, University of Minnesota Press, Minneapolis, 1977.

[2] *Food From Farmer to Consumer,* Report of the National Commission on Food Marketing, U.S. Government Printing Office, Washington, D.C., June 1966, p. 93.

[3] *The Structure of Food Manufacturing,* Staff Report of the Federal Trade Commission, Technical Study No. 8, National Commission on Food Marketing, U.S. Government Printing Office, Washington, D.C., June 1966, p. 104.

tions, and farmer cooperatives operate food processing plants. Food processors have farming operations and are merging with nonfood firms. Many retail chain organizations operate food processing plants and are diversifying their product offerings into nonfood areas. Are these trends consistent with specialization? Do they require a sacrifice in specialization economies?

There are a number of explanations for this diversification. For one thing, specialization is not inconsistent with diversification. Food manufacturers can operate multiple plants, each specializing in separate products and lines. Another reason for diversified growth is that many large food companies have exhausted the specialization economies or are prevented from further growth by antitrust regulations. Growth by diversification is their only alternative.

There also appear to be considerable economies to market and product diversification in advertising, promotion, and merchandising. A broad product line can be an asset in the battle for retail shelf space. Diversification also can protect the firm from the risks of price changes and market losses for a single product.

Functional diversification in the food industry is motivated principally by market coordination economies. Food chains and processors reach back into the food marketing system to influence the quality and timing of products consistent with their scheduling and merchandising programs. For example, a food processor may be able to lower his costs by assuring a certain quality or delivery schedule for products. These coordination economies reflect the mutual interdependency of all firms in the food industry.

DECENTRALIZATION OF FOOD MARKETS

A major structural change that has occurred in food marketing since the 1920's has been in the direction of decentralization. Fundamentally, decentralization means that farm products move from farms and into the hands of processors and wholesalers without utilizing the services of the older, established terminal facilities. Buying agents of processors, wholesalers, and the retail firms contact producers and take title to the products in the production area.

In a centralized marketing process, products are collected into centralized locations for the operation of exchange, standardization, and market information functions by a physical concentration of buyers and sellers and other market agencies. In decentralized marketing, buyers and sellers move into the production area to operate at widely separated locations. Instead of products coming to the processor-wholesaler-retailer buyers, these buyers go to the products. Thus, decentralization constitutes a rearrangement of the marketing functions among firms—not an elimination of these functions—and

255

Table 12-2. Decentralization In The Purchase of Livestock and Eggs, 1923–1976.

PER CENT OF PACKER OR PROCESSOR PURCHASES, BY MARKET OUTLET

YEAR	CATTLE			HOGS			EGGS	
	TERMINAL MARKETS	AUCTIONS	DIRECT PURCHASES	TERMINAL MARKETS	AUCTIONS	DIRECT PURCHASES	TERMINAL MARKETS	AUCTIONS, DIRECT PURCHASES
1923	90%	—	10	76	—	24	77	23
1940	76	—	24	47	—	53	NA	NA
1950	75	16	25	40	—	60	40	60
1960	46	16	38	30	9	61	30	40
1970	18	16	66	17	14	69	17	83
1975	14	20	66	16	12	72	NA	NA
1976	13	21	66	17	11	72	NA	NA

Source: Packers and Stockyards Administration, U.S. Department of Agriculture, P & SA Research Report No. 2, May 1973; P & SA *Resume,* December 24, 1976, December 23, 1977.

a displacement of the wholesale terminal market by direct sales from shipping-point markets to wholesalers, retailers, and processors.

Decentralization involves more than just by-passing the terminal market and rearranging marketing functions. The trend has altered significantly the nature of farm marketing patterns. The farmer often acts as his own salesman in decentralized markets, whereas in centralized marketing, he was more likely to employ the services of a wholesaler or broker as a sales agent. This means that in decentralized markets the farmer not only is more involved with marketing his products, but also he is dealing directly with large buyers of his products. Moreover, there is no "perfect" market buffer between the farmer and farm product buyers. The price discovery process shifts to shipping-point markets. Finally, buyers of farm products exert greater control and coordination over farm decisions in decentralized markets than is possible in central markets.

Extent of Decentralization

Decentralization has proceeded somewhat more rapidly for livestock products than for crops, although fresh fruit and vegetable markets are highly decentralized today. The trend in livestock decentralization is evident, as shown in Table 12-2. Cattle purchases by meat packers from terminal markets declined from 90 per cent of total purchases in 1923 to 13 per cent in 1976. Hog purchases by packers followed a similar trend over this period. Direct marketing of shell eggs, broilers, and turkeys from packer/processors to retail stores also increased.

The decentralization of food marketing channels occurred in two steps. First, the buyers of farm products bypassed the central terminal markets and began purchasing directly from shipping-point markets or from farmers. The following step was the transfer of processing facilities from the urban terminal markets to the producing areas. For example, in 1950, 24 per cent of the livestock slaughter plants were located in the urbanized North Atlantic states, and 10 per cent were located in the West North Central states—the corn belt. By 1970, 23 per cent of livestock slaughter plants were located in the West North Central region and only 11 per cent were located in the North Atlantic states. This movement of physical facilities permitted some new firms to enter the packing industry, and the new facilities resulted in an increase in packing plant efficiency.

Reasons for Decentralization

Perhaps the best way to understand the reasons for this decentralization movement is to outline the reasons for the initial development of the centralized market channel and then look at the changes that have occurred in these factors.

Basic Factors Favoring Development of Centralized Channel	*Changes in These Factors Over Time That Encourage Decentralization*
1. Limited transportation facilities with major dependence upon the railroad. This resulted in the limitation of advantageous points for product concentration.	1. Development of the truck and highway system. This has vastly increased the flexibility of assembling products.
2. Poor communication facilities. This meant that buyers and sellers had to physically assemble, establish price, and transfer title.	2. Continuous improvement in the speed and flexibility of communications. A seller in California and a buyer in New York can now talk quickly and cheaply without coming face to face.
3. High perishability and poor standardization of products. Physical inspections were necessary in order to ascertain just what was being purchased.	3. Improved techniques of refrigeration and storage along with much improved grading procedures. The feasibility of the transfer of products by sample or description has increased.
4. Production units small and unspecialized. The cost to buyers purchasing small lots from production points was high.	4. Rapid development of fewer but larger and more specialized production units. The output of individual farms now a feasible purchase unit.
5. Great variation in consumer preferences from area to area and the multitudinous, small retail units. This prohibited mass, uniform servicing by large-scale distributors.	5. Development of large-scale retailing with mass-standardized products. New potentialities of mass production and economies of scale are possible.
6. Commodity-oriented food industry with need to efficiently sell what is produced.	6. Merchandise-oriented food industry with need to coordinate farm production with needs of farm-product buyers.

It is not possible to state categorically which of the preceding changes were the most important in fostering decentralization. No doubt it was the developments in transportation and communication that first started the process. However, in recent years, decentralization has received its impetus from the product, farm production, and consumer developments. Decentralized markets permit food marketing firms to better control and coordinate the flow and quality of farm products than was possible under centralized marketing. Quality control is improved through *specification buying*—the process of stating market requirements and securing product offers from alternative suppliers.

258

Implications of Decentralization

The principal concerns with decentralization relate to its effects on pricing and operational efficiency as compared with central markets. Pricing efficiency considerations seem to favor centralized markets whereas operational efficiency is perhaps better served by decentralized markets.

Decentralized markets seem to be economical to operate. For example, shipping farm products directly to buyers, without routing them through terminal markets, could result in transport and shrinkage savings. Freight savings are particularly evident where slaughter and processing facilities have moved out to the production areas. Many of the older terminal market facilities were also congested and inefficient, contributing to the cost savings of decentralized markets by comparison. On the other hand, there were significant operational economies of scale as the result of marketing large volumes of produce through a relatively few terminal markets, and these may be sacrificed in the more numerous and smaller-volume decentralized markets.

The greater concern is with the effect of decentralization on pricing efficiency in food markets. Terminal markets were close to perfectly competitive in the large numbers of buyers and sellers involved, in the great amount of public market information they generated, and in the homogeneous nature of graded farm products. Consequently, price discovery was considered quite good in these markets, and terminal market prices were believed to represent fairly market conditions and product values. By contrast, in decentralized markets there are fewer buyers and sellers at each shipping-point market; it is more difficult to collect adequate market information from the widely scattered, private transactions; and specification buying makes it more difficult to compare market prices. In short, price discovery is more complex in decentralized markets, and decentralized markets *appear* to be less perfectly competitive than central markets. Farmers face large-volume buyers in these markets, and price discovery is a more subjective process—open to the relative bargaining power of buyers and sellers. Consequently, there is less assurance that the law of one price will align all market prices competitively.

Do farmers receive less when they market direct than they would if they sold through terminal markets? A single answer cannot be given. Some farmers prefer decentralized marketing, others prefer terminal markets. Obviously their experiences with the two markets, and their attitudes toward them, influence preferences. The farmer is likely to become more involved with marketing his product in decentralized markets than in centralized markets, where commission men and brokers perform more of the marketing functions. Some farmers feel, too, that they have more bargaining power in decentralized markets because they are pricing the product before releasing it to the market. In terminal market sales, the commodity is shipped to market prior to pricing it, and the farmer has no alternatives except to sell it at the going market price.

259

Another concern is the continuing practice of using terminal market price quotations to price direct, decentralized sales. With decentralization, many terminal markets have become *thin markets;* that is, they handle a small and declining volume of product. Many feel that the prices discovered in these thin markets do not represent true market conditions and should not be used as guides in pricing direct sales.

Experimental programs are underway to retain the pricing efficiency of central markets and to secure the operational efficiency gains of direct markets. These usually involve separating the price discovery process from the physical product flows. With advanced communication and computer technologies, it would seem unnecessary that all buyers and sellers and commodities be *physically* present in order to insure their *competitive* presence. In the future, computerized price discovery programs will probably be used to assist in the price discovery process for decentralized marketing.

INTEGRATION OF FOOD MARKETS

Another market organization development in the food industry has been the tendency toward mergers and *integration.* This process refers to expansion of firms by consolidating additional marketing functions and activities under a single management. Examples are food retailers who establish wholesaling facilities, one milk processor purchasing another's plant and routes, or the joining together of a meat packer with a bus company. In each case, there is a centralization of decision-making into the hands of a single management.

Varieties of Integration

There are three basic kinds of integration. *Vertical integration* occurs when a firm combines activities unlike those it currently performs but which are related to them in the sequence of marketing activities. Such integration is illustrated by the meat packer who decides to reach both backward toward the producer and operate his own livestock buying points in the countryside and forward toward the consumer and operate his own meat wholesaling establishment.

Horizontal integration occurs when a firm gains control over other firms performing similar activities at the same level in the marketing sequence. The development of line elevators, in which many individual elevators are brought under one management, is one example; the many retail chains provide another.

Firms often expand both vertically and horizontally. The modern retail grocery chain is a good example of this type of growth. They have grown horizontally by adding additional retail food stores; and they have grown vertically by operating their own wholesale establishments, sometimes owning their own canning factories or operating their own country buying points for eggs and other commodities.

There is still another type of organizational expansion, sometimes called *conglomeration.* Here other agencies or activities that do not have any direct relation to the activity of the individual firm are brought under a unified management. Examples of this are the operation of butter and cheese plants by meat packers, or the addition of nonfood lines by the food retailer.

Another way to view integration in the food industry is by studying the extent of the transfer of decisions among integrated firms. *Ownership integration* or merger occurs when all the decisions and assets of one firm are completely assumed by another, as for example when a food processor buys a food wholesale firm or sets up its own wholesaling facilities. In contrast, *contract integration* involves an agreement between two firms on certain decisions, but each firm retains its separate identity. For example, a vegetable producer may sign a contract with a canner specifying variety, delivery date, or price.

All of these integration efforts are attempts to organize or coordinate the marketing process to obtain increased operating efficiency or more power over the selling and/or buying process. In recent years this process of integration has reached down to include the farm firm itself through various contractual arrangements between the farm and nonfarm firms. Like decentralization, integration of the marketing channel may have both advantageous and disadvantageous effects.

Integration has the effect of shortening and closing the marketing chain. Integrated supplies do not enter the open market for changes in ownership and pricing. Commodities flow between integrated firms on an administered basis rather than on an open market, competitive basis. Integration and decentralization have proceeded hand in hand in the food industry. Both contribute to closer coordination of product flows and quality control.

Reasons for Integration

The motives for integration in the food industry vary widely among firms and products. A number of reasons for vertical integration of food firms and functions have been suggested, including the profit potential from assuming additional functions; risk reduction through improved market coordination; improved bargaining power and the prospect of influencing prices; and lower costs through gaining operational efficiencies. Fundamentally, vertical integration represents a substitution of an administered coordinating system for price coordination of markets. To the extent that prices fail adequately to coordinate these markets, firms find the market a poor guide for their decisions and so substitute integrated arrangements.

261

Other motives stimulate horizontal integration in the food industry. Buying out a competitor is a time-honored way to reduce competition, gain a larger share of the market, and perhaps improve profits. Gaining economies of size and specialization is perhaps a more noble motive for horizontal integration. Because of its potential impact on competition, the antitrust laws limit horizontal competition in the food industry.

The motives underlying conglomerate integration in the food industry are little understood, but they appear to be related to risk-reduction through diversification; the acquisition of financial leverage; and the empire-building urge. And the conglomerates may have been blocked in attempts to grow horizontally. Food conglomerates have allegedly been guilty of cross-subsidization—the use of nonfood profits to support aggressive price competition in food markets.

INTEGRATION INTO FARMING

Integration is not new to agriculture. In recent years, the declining number of farms, and their increasing size, reflect horizontal integration of farmers. Through cooperatives, many farmers are vertically integrated into the food marketing channel. And, to the extent that farmers invest in nonfarm securities (stocks, bonds, and so on) and exercise their ownership rights, farmers are conglomerate integrators.

There is increasing concern with vertical and conglomerate integration, which crosses over the farm gate and provides nonfarm firms some influence on farm management decisions. Does "corporate agriculture" (excluding the family farm corporation) threaten the independence of farmers? How will a fully integrated food industry perform? Will agribusiness corporations use their control over farming to lower farm prices, raise retail food prices, and improve their profits? Integration into agriculture has become a key public policy issue.

Extent of Agricultural Integration

The importance of nonfarm corporations engaged in agricultural production was discussed in Chapter 3. There we noted that the family farm dominates U.S. agriculture, and that most "corporate farms" are family owned. This, however, is not an adequate measure of agricultural integration nor a measure of the influence of off-farm firms on farm management decisions. Contract integration of agriculture is more common than ownership integration.

Table 12-3 shows the importance of contractual and ownership vertical integration into agriculture in 1960 and 1970. The remainder of sales are assumed to be made in open markets. There was a gradual increase in agricul-

Table 12-3. Agricultural Output Produced Under Production Contracts and Vertical Integration, United States, 1960 and 1970.

PRODUCT	PRODUCTION CONTRACTS 1960	1970	OWNERSHIP VERTICAL INTEGRATION 1960	1970	OPEN MARKET 1960	1970
Crop			*Per cent*			
Feed grains	0.1	0.1	0.4	0.5	99.5	99.4
Hay and forage	.3	.3	—	—	99.7	99.7
Food grains	1.0	2.0	.3	.5	98.7	97.5
Vegetables for fresh market	20.0	21.0	25.0	30.0	55.0	49.0
Vegetables for processing	67.0	85.0	8.0	10.0	25.0	5.0
Dry beans and peas	35.0	1.0	1.0	1.0	64.0	98.0
Potatoes	40.0	45.0	30.0	25.0	30.0	30.0
Citrus fruits	60.0	55.0	20.0	30.0	20.0	15.0
Other fruits and nuts	20.0	20.0	15.0	20.0	65.0	60.0
Sugar beets	98.0	98.0	2.0	2.0	0	0
Sugar cane	40.0	40.0	60.0	60.0	0	0
Other sugar crops	5.0	5.0	2.0	2.0	93	93
Cotton	5.0	11.0	3.0	1.0	92	88
Tobacco	2.0	2.0	2.0	2.0	96	96
Oil bearing crops	1.0	1.0	.4	.5	98.6	98.5
Seed crops	80.0	80.0	.3	.5	19.7	19.5
Miscellaneous crops	5.0	5.0	1.0	1.0	94.0	94.0
Total crops	8.6	9.5	4.3	4.8	87.1	85.7
Livestock or Livestock Products						
Fed cattle	10.0	18.0	3.0	4.0	87.0	78.0
Sheep and lambs	2.0	7.0	2.0	3.0	96.0	90.0
Hogs	.7	1.0	.7	1.0	88.6	88.0
Fluid-grade milk	95.0	95.0	3.0	3.0	2.0	2.0
Manufacturing-grade milk	25.0	25.0	2.0	1.0	73.0	74.0
Eggs	5.0	20.0	10.0	20.0	85.0	60.0
Broilers	93.0	90.0	5.0	7.0	2.0	3.0
Turkeys	30.0	42.0	4.0	12.0	66.0	46.0
Miscellaneous	3.0	3.0	1.0	1.0	96.0	96.0
Total livestock items	27.2	31.4	3.2	4.8	69.5	63.8
Total crop & livestock	15.1	17.2	3.9	4.8	81.0	88.0

Source: The estimates for individual items are based on the informed judgments of a number of production and marketing specialists in the U.S. Department of Agriculture. The totals were obtained by weighting the individual items by the relative weights used in computing the ERS index of total farm output.

tural integration over the 1960–1970 decade and a corresponding decline in open-market sales. Integration is generally more advanced for livestock products than for crops—particularly for fluid milk and for broilers—but open-market sales are limited for processing vegetables, citrus fruits, sugar beets and cane, and seed crops.

The sectors of the food industry that have integrated into agriculture have varied for different commodities. Input suppliers in the feed business have integrated the broiler and egg industries, food processors and manufacturers have integrated the processed fruit and vegetable industry. Farmers integrated the sugar beet, citrus, and milk industries through cooperatives and bargaining associations. Food retailers and wholesalers have not integrated into agriculture to any great extent, although they have integrated various stages of the marketing system.

Varieties of Farm Contracts

Several types of contracts are used in vertically integrating farmers with their input suppliers and buyers of farm products. These differ in the number of decisions influenced by the contract, the sharing of costs and risks, and the specificity of contract terms.

Market-specification contracts simply specify some of the product characteristics that will be acceptable to the integrator and usually establish some of the basis of payment to the producer. Little or none of the producer's management decisions are transferred. The producer receives little or no financial or technical help. Little or none of the producer's price or income risk is assumed by the integrator, as returns are still fundamentally tied to the open market. These contracts are an effort on the part of the integrator to improve the effectiveness of grades and standards and market information. From the viewpoint of the producer, they guarantee a buyer if the specifications are met. Such contracts obtain very little integration of the two parties in the sense of any centralized management control.

Resource-providing contracts often specify certain production resources to be used and the place of their purchase. The integrator usually provides the producer with financing, ranging from operational to fixed investment financing, and a degree of managerial help and supervision. Product prices are usually based upon the open market, and income guarantees to the producer are minimal. In such contracts the integrator influences the technology and size of operations of the producer in order to increase and stabilize the market for his own products.

Management- and income-guaranteeing contracts often include the marketing and production stipulations of the aforementioned two types of contracts. In addition, they provide for the transferring of part or all of the market-oriented price and income risks from the producer to the integrator. This is usually done by paying the producer a prearranged return per unit of product or by guaranteeing against market-oriented financial loss. In these contracts the integrator assumes a substantial part of the managerial responsibility of the producer. These contracts come closest to obtaining the managerial and financial control and risk which occurs when the integration is effected through complete ownership.

Reasons for Farm Production Integration

There are substantial reasons why marketing firms may want to have some control over the farm source of their raw materials, or in the case of those selling to farms, such as feed companies, control over their market. One of the big costs to processors and handlers is the great fluctuation—yearly, seasonal, and day to day—of both the amount and quality of their raw products. In recent years this problem has taken on added significance as the development of large-scale, self-service retailing has increased the demand for an orderly flow of a large volume of uniform products.

Until recently the difficulties of effectively managing any large-scale agricultural production by nonresident managers were so great that the costs of such efforts were greater than the potential gain. This barrier, however, has been increasingly reduced as scientific management practices have been developed in agricultural production. More and more, if certain practices are followed under adequate supervision, farm products can be produced in a specified form and on a predetermined schedule of output. The term *farm-factory* has increasing validity for many agricultural enterprises and, as in a factory, management and supervision can be separated successfully from the actual production activities.

In addition, this move toward scientific management is often accompanied by increased needs on the part of farmers for the capital necessary to put the new technology into practice. Also, the larger and more specialized farming becomes, the greater is the vulnerability to unpredictable prices. The advent of "predictable production" has made farm and off-farm integration feasible. The farmer's need for financing and price insurance have furnished the avenue by which integrators could secure the farmer's cooperation.

The Future of Farm Production Integration

Neither of the early extreme predictions made concerning farm integration have come to pass. The use of contract integration has not developed with forest-fire speed in all commodities. On the other hand, neither has it collapsed as a wild-hair experiment.

Farm leaders early expressed dismay and gloom concerning a development that would make a "hired hand" of the once proudly independent farmer. This idea was apparently a fear more of farm leaders than farmers themselves. Many farmers do not see a conflict between their independence and their position as contract growers. The fact that many farmers voluntarily sign contracts when they have market alternatives suggests that contracts can be beneficial to both farmers and integrators. They prefer the income protection the contract gives them and feel they have enough to say about the management of their operations.

On the other side, all integrated arrangements are not highly profitable for the integrators. Analysis of different types of livestock and poultry contracts finds both profitable and unprofitable ventures. The importance of the integrator's ability underscores the obvious point that if management is to be "lifted" from the farmer to the integrator, the integrator must be able to supply the necessary managerial skills for the larger and more complex operation.

The major limiting factor to the use of contract integration between farm and nonfarm firms rests in the production processes of the enterprise itself. Only if the production activities have become standardized and the technology quite scientific can important management direction be done in absentia by the integrator. If successful operation still takes close, personal supervision and skill, such management cannot successfully be lifted to the integrator. This development of scientific agriculture has progressed much farther in some enterprises than others.

If the production process permits feasible integration, will integration take place? Answers to this rest upon the mutual gains that seem possible to farmers and potential integrators. Does the producer need the extra production know-how and financing that the integrator might provide? Is the present market mechanism operating poorly in providing the integrator the appropriate kind of product in adequate amounts at the needed time? Will the market absorb the additional production, which integration usually encourages in its initial stages, at satisfactory prices?

Some farm enterprises meet many of the preceding criteria for integrated operations, and production under contract is expanding rapidly. Other farm enterprises do not, and the extent of contract operation is only minimal and exploratory.

Implications of Producer Integration

There seems to be little doubt that integrated production and marketing complexes can result in improved operational efficiencies. However, as with decentralization, there is considerable debate over its effect on pricing efficiency. In one sense, integration tends to hasten the further decentralization of the market channel, in that it effectively contracts for the output of each individual producer. As integration progresses, less and less of the production moves through the "open market" for pricing purposes. In the middle 1960's, for example, the reporting of live broiler prices by the federal market news service was discontinued in several southern states. With most of the broilers being produced and sold under contract, there were not enough being sold alive to establish a realistic live price. As the use of contract arrangements becomes a major part of the market structure of a commodity in a given area, it becomes increasingly difficult to maintain the business firms necessary to operate an effective open-market channel for those who do not wish to accept contracts. Also, price discovery becomes more and more difficult with the integration of food markets.

The operation of an integrated channel theoretically need not reduce effective competition so long as there are many firms competing for the contracts of capable, informed producers. In fact, in situations where the existing market news, grading procedure, and pricing facilities operate poorly, the use of integration arrangements can improve the operating situation. However, in practice, the growth of integration has sharpened the debate concerning the relative bargaining power of farm producers and marketing agencies. Contract details are complex and often are not public information. As with labor contracts, the negotiation of the contractual terms becomes the basic "pricing" activity between the parties to the contract. How to police this process has become a growing issue.

FUTURE ORGANIZATION OF FOOD MARKETS

The organization of food markets is being shaped by various trends: (1) the industrialization of agriculture; (2) specialization and diversification of firms; (3) technological change in food marketing; (4) decentralization; (5) integration; and (6) the shift from a commodity-oriented to a merchandising-oriented food industry. These trends will continue to shape and mold the industry.

Efforts to more closely vertically coordinate the several market levels of the food industry will continue, and the results will determine who controls the food industry and its market performance. Farmers in particular are expected to press their efforts to be more than just a raw-material supplier, residual-income claimant, and price-taker in the food system.

The direct-marketing and integration trends will proceed at different rates for various commodities. Some parts of agriculture will follow the broiler and sugar beet industries and will achieve full integration of most production and marketing stages. The remainder of agriculture will follow the traditional concept of independent farming, limited integration, and open-market sales. Both sectors will require new price discovery techniques to substitute for the terminal markets.

When will the Henry Ford of the food industry integrate all sectors of the food production-marketing chain? There are companies with plans to fully integrate from farm to fork. This may be the next step in the organization of food markets. However, there are also companies withdrawing from unprofitable integrated arrangements in the food industry.

SUMMARY

Specialization, diversification, decentralization, and integration are the key trends shaping the modern organization of food markets. Powerful economic incentives are propelling these trends, and they raise several public policy issues. These changes in market organization also affect the status and behavior of farmers in the food industry. Specialization and diversification in food marketing are leading to larger, more complex firms. Efforts to vertically coordinate farm production and food marketing decisions have fostered both ownership and contractual integration of food marketing firms into agriculture. Horizontal and conglomerate integration of food marketing firms is also a pronounced trend. Decentralization and integration of food markets affect the operational and pricing efficiency of these markets.

QUESTIONS FOR DISCUSSION

1. Explain the problem of vertical coordination in the food industry. Why can't price be relied upon to serve this coordinating role?

2. What are some reasons for the variations in contract and ownership integration among the commodities shown in Table 12-3?

3. Compare the farmer's marketing task for a highly integrated commodity, such as broilers, to that for a less integrated commodity, such as corn.

4. What kinds of competitive regulations should the United States have toward the following kinds of integration:
   a. Foreign nationals purchase U.S. farms.
   b. A steel firm purchases and operates U.S. farmland.
   c. A vegetable canner owns company farms.
   d. A vegetable canner signs contracts with farmers for their supplies.
   e. Farmers own a vegetable cannery.
   f. Farmers purchase more farmland.

5. What do you think is the possibility, or feasibility, of one company's fully integrating the food industry, from the farm-supply sector all the way to food retailing?

6. A farm leader states, "Farmers should resist integration into agriculture, and there should be laws to prevent it." How do you respond?

7. Many observers feel that food marketing firms are taking the initiative in vertically coordinating the food industry. What have farmers done and what more can they do to participate more actively in the vertical coordination process?

8. The Egg Clearinghouse, Inc., of Durham, New Hampshire, the Virginia Tel-O-Auction, the Ontario (Canada) Hog Producers Marketing Board, and the Plains Cotton Cooperative Association's TELCOT system are examples of electronic price discovery mechanisms. Describe how these operate after reading about them in trade publications.

9. How is a contract sale of farm products different from an open-market sale?

10. How do you think consumers have been affected by the organizational trends discussed in this chapter?

SELECTED REFERENCES

Agricultural Markets in Change. U.S. Department of Agriculture. Agricultural Economic Report No. 95, July 1966.

Agricultural Organization in the Modern Industrial Economy. North Central Regional Report No. 20, Ohio State University, April 1968.

ARNOULD, R. J. *Diversification and Profitability among Large Food Processing Firms.* U.S. Department of Agriculture. Agricultural Economic Report No. 171, Jan. 1970.

BREIMYER, H. F. "Future Organization and Control of U.S. Agricultural Production and Marketing." *Journal of Farm Economics* (Dec. 1964), 930–40.

GARORIAN, L., Ed. *Economics of Conglomerate Growth.* Agricultural Research Foundation, Oregon State University, Corvallis Nov. 1969.

GODWIN, M. R., AND L. L. JONES. "The Emerging Food and Fiber System: Implications for Agriculture." *American Journal of Agricultural Economics* (Dec. 1971), 806–19.

HARRIS, M., AND D. T. MASSEY. *Vertical Coordination via Contract Farming.* U.S. Department of Agriculture. Miscellaneous Publication No. 1973, March 1968.

MARION, B., Ed., *Coordination and Exchange in Agricultural Subsectors.* North Central Regional Research Publication No. 228, Jan. 1976.

Marketing Alternatives for Agriculture: Is There a Better Way? U.S. Department of Agriculture. Public Policy Education Committee. Leaflets 7–3 and 7–7, 1976.

MIGHELL, R. L., AND W. S. HOOFNAGLE. *Contract Production and Vertical Integration in Farming, 1960 and 1970.* U.S. Department of Agriculture. ERS-479, April 1972.

———— AND L. A. JONES. *Vertical Coordination in Agriculture.* U.S. Department of Agriculture. Agricultural Economic Report No. 19, Feb. 1963.

NELSON, P. E., AND L. BRITT. "Diversification in Five Food Processing Industries and the Farm Machinery and Equipment Industry." *The Marketing and Transportation Situation* (Aug. 1973), 27–32.

REIMUND, D. A. *Farming and Agribusiness Activities of Large, Multi-unit Firms.* U.S. Department of Agriculture. ERS-591, March 1975.

ROY, E. P. *Contract Farming and Economic Integration,* 2nd Ed. Interstate Printers and Publishers, Inc., Danville, Ill., 1972.

CHAPTER 13

Cooperatives in the Food Industry

"AMERICAN FAMILY FARMS fall in the category of small business firms, and face the problems of such firms in a national economy in which there is a definite trend toward more and more concentration of economic power. The farmer is in a weak competitive position in dealing with individual control. He has sought and continues to seek means of overcoming his isolation and improving his position by joining with other farmers to gain mutual advantages and protection through self-help. From such efforts have come the many and diverse forms of cooperatives found in rural America today."*

Preview

• This chapter explores the roles, activities, and problems of cooperatives in the food industry.

• The various kinds of farm cooperatives are examined and the differences between cooperatives and other forms of business organizations are discussed.

• A history of the agricultural cooperative movement is provided.

• The importance of farm cooperatives in farm supply markets and in the marketing of various commodities is examined.

• The principal factors affecting farm cooperatives' success and the problems of cooperatives are enumerated.

• The retail food cooperative is compared with the farm cooperative.

• Key terms and concepts:
Capper-Volstead Act
cooperative
cooperative patron

* *American Cooperation—1961,* American Institute of Cooperation, Washington, D.C., 1961.

Farmer Cooperative Service
independent, federated, and centralized cooperative associations
marketing, processing, service, and supply cooperatives
patronage refund

Agricultural history is full of examples of the continuing battle of the farmer against the abuses, either real or imaginary, of the marketing middleman. The farmer has continually complained about having to sell cheap as a producer and buy high as a consumer. He is also very concerned about his relative bargaining power. Cooperative organization has been proposed by farmers as one possible solution to these problems.

Mutual action by farmers to help solve large tasks has long been a part of agricultural life. Barn raisings, husking bees, and threshing rings all required that many act together with a common purpose. Cooperative enterprises of today are similar in nature but have been established as formal business organizations.

Most cooperatives in the United States are among farmers. They are sometimes called the off-farm arm of farmers. They have been organized to provide a wide variety of services, to help sell the farmers' products, and to help farmers purchase their needed goods. Many cooperative leaders look upon cooperation as a way by which the multitudinous, independent, small farm units can effectively compete in a business world composed of larger, more powerful units.

WHAT IS A COOPERATIVE?

Almost all cooperative leaders of the past and present have had their pet concept of what constitutes a good definition of a cooperative. H. E. Babcock, an eastern cooperative leader, phrased it well when he said that cooperatives are a legal, practical means by which a group of self-selected, selfish capitalists seek to improve their individual economic position in a competitive society. Another leader in cooperative thought defined a cooperative as "a business voluntarily owned and controlled by its member-patrons and operated for them on a nonprofit or cost basis." [1] Two aspects of these definitions deserve attention. First, a cooperative is a legal, institutionalized device which permits group action that can compete within the framework of other types of business organization. Second, cooperatives are voluntarily organizations set up to serve and benefit those who are going to use them.

---

[1] Marvin A. Schaars, "Farmer Cooperatives—What They Are and What They Are Not," *News for Farmer Cooperatives,* U.S. Department of Agriculture, March 1963.

Much of the intent of these definitions has been incorporated into the body of law which sanctions American cooperation. The legal definition of what constitutes a cooperative has gradually evolved through the passage of laws by the different states. The passage of the Capper–Volstead Act by Congress in 1922 helped codify this legal concept of agricultural cooperation, though even today the details of laws vary among the several states. Even though differing in detail, there are three fundamental concepts that help differentiate a cooperative from other forms of business enterprises. These concepts must be incorporated in the organizational and operating pattern of an enterprise in order for it to qualify as a cooperative.

The first of these distinctive concepts is that the *ownership and control of the enterprise must be by those who utilize its services.* The control is exercised by the owners as the patrons of the business rather than by the owners as investors in the business. In no other form of business enterprise is there a comparable patron-owner relationship. Such a relationship means that the primary objective of the cooperative enterprise is to do the job assigned to it at a minimum of cost and with maximum satisfaction for its owner-patrons. In contrast, the primary objective of nonpatron firms is to maximize returns over costs for the benefit of the owner-investors. In order to assure the effectiveness of this concept, some provision is often made in the bylaws of cooperatives to limit the amount of business that can be transacted with nonmembers. In addition, the voting control of the business is restricted in various ways to help ensure that the user is dominant over the investor orientation. Traditionally, control has been on a one-man, one-vote basis regardless of the amount any individual has invested. Several states now permit some variation from this view and permit restricted accumulation of voting rights according to the extent of either ownership or patronage.

The second distinctive cooperative concept is that the *business operations shall be concluded so as to approach a cost basis* and any returns above cost shall be returned to patrons on an equitable basis. From this concept arises the common practice of referring to cooperatives as nonprofit business concerns. The patronage refund of cooperatives is the device used to return to the owner-patrons the overcharges or underpayments that have resulted in earnings above cost. In noncooperative businesses, earnings or profits belong to the business for distribution or use as the business sees fit. In cooperatives such earnings are a liability owed to the patron-owners.

The third distinctive cooperative concept is that the *return on the owner's invested capital shall be limited.* The capital requirements of a cooperative may be no different from those of any other type of business organization engaged in similar activities. However, the relationship of the investor to the business is quite different. In a cooperative the patron-owner invests his money primarily so that the organization may provide desired services for him. His decision to enter or remain as a patron-owner of the cooperative is made largely on the basis of his opportunity to benefit as a patron-user.

Table 13-1. Similarities and Differences of Three Types of Business Organizations.

CONDITION	INDIVIDUAL OR PARTNERSHIP	NONCOOPERATIVE CORPORATION	COOPERATIVE CORPORATION
Operated for profit motive?	Yes	Yes	Yes
How are earnings distributed?	To owners or partners	To owners on basis of shareholdings	Largely to patrons on patronage basis
Who controls the firm, selects manager, etc.	Individuals or partners	Board of Directors elected by stockholders	Board of Directors elected by patron-owners
How is voting done?	None or by agreement	Usually 1 vote for each share of stock	Usually 1 member, 1 vote
What is owners' liability?	All property of owners	Assets of corporation	Assets of cooperative
With whom is the business conducted?	Public	Public	Chiefly members but often others also

In noncooperative forms of business, investors offer their money in expectation of a profitable return on it. The need for capital may be as urgent for a cooperative as for any other kind of business, but the methods of capital accumulation must acknowledge the fact that returns on the capital are limited.

These distinctive differences give rise to the principal unique quality of a cooperative. The *point of view* which guides its activities is that of the owners of the business who are *also* its customers and users. It seeks to undertake profitable ventures like any other business. However, these profits accrue to the owners through their own use of the organization instead of to owners as investors. These distinctive differences also give rise to several operational differences between cooperative corporations and noncooperative corporations. These differences are summarized in Table 13-1.

KINDS OF COOPERATIVE BUSINESS

Cooperative associations, like other business organizations, are established to perform certain tasks. When classified according to the tasks performed, cooperatives fall into four broad categories—marketing, purchasing, service, and processing associations. However, strict classification for any particular cooperative is difficult, because many operate in more than one category. Many farmers belong to one or more of these cooperative associations.

Marketing Cooperatives

Marketing cooperatives are those through which farmers sell the products of their farms. These cooperatives may collect members' products for sale, grade, package, and perform other functions. Cooperative livestock commission organizations, producers' milk associations, and cooperative elevators are examples of cooperatives acting as marketing agents. The objective of such organizations is to secure the greatest possible amount for the products of their farmer-owners. Some associations act solely as commission agents. Some associations act as bargaining agents and do not actually handle the products. Others will actually buy the commodity from the farmer for resale.

Marketing cooperatives of various types handle approximately 30 per cent of all farm commodities sold. The proportion of commodities marketed cooperatively varies from commodity to commodity, as can be seen in Table 13-2. Some of the marketing cooperatives are large and powerful organizations and carry out marketing orders and agreements as part of their responsibilities. Many of the common branded products such as Sunkist oranges, Sun-Maid raisins, SunSweet prunes, and Diamond Brand walnuts are products of cooperative associations.

Purchasing Cooperatives

Purchasing cooperatives are those through which members buy the supplies they need. In these cooperatives the farmer reaches back toward the raw-material source for his supply. Purchasing cooperatives often engage only in retailing and wholesaling. In other instances they manufacture the products they sell and acquire the sources of raw materials. Most states have large statewide associations that are examples of this type of cooperative. The objective of such organizations is to effect savings for the farmer on the things he buys. The principal source of such savings will usually come from lower prices or from higher-quality and better-adapted supplies and equipment.

The sale of various farm supplies accounts for most of the business volume of these cooperatives, although increasing amounts of items for farm household use are being handled. Table 13-2 shows the relative importance of these cooperative activities.

Service Cooperatives

Service cooperatives are organized to provide their members with improved services or with services they could not otherwise obtain. The services under-

Table 13-2. Number and Share of Market, Farmer Marketing and Supply Cooperatives, 1950–1975.

FUNCTIONAL GROUP AND COMMODITY	1950–1951		1960–1961		1964–1965		1969–1970		1974–1975	
	Number of cooperatives handling and per cent of cash farm receipts									
	No.	*Pct.*	*No.*	*Pct.*	*No.*	*Pct.*	*No.*	*Pct.*	*No.*	*Pct.*
Product marketed										
Cotton & cotton products	550	12	561	22	581	25	554	26	494	26
Dairy products	2,072	53	1,609	61	1,346	65	971	73	631	75
Fruits & vegetables	951	20	697	21	592	25	499	27	436	25
Grain & soybeans	2,740	29	2,661	38	2,596	40	2,539	32	2,540	40
Livestock & livestock products	753	16	532	14	479	13	546	11	572	10
Poultry products	760	7	567	10	410	9	295	9	167	9
Other	405	15	284	22	224	25	189	27	164	35
Total	7,276	20	6,548	23	6,009	25	5,415	26	4,817	30
	Number of cooperatives handling and per cent of farm supply expenditures									
Farm supplies purchased										
Feed	4,406	19	4,412	18	4,363	18	4,214	17	3,744	18
Seed	3,636	17	3,912	19	3,962	21	4,007	16	3,553	16
Fertilizer & lime	3,352	15	4,276	24	4,409	30	4,294	28	3,865	30
Petroleum	2,677	19	2,798	24	2,773	26	2,774	29	2,624	35
Farm chemicals	na	11	3,014	18	3,329	16	3,721	18	3,328	29
Other supplies & equipment	5,937	5	4,558	7	4,858	7	4,856	7	4,224	10
Total	7,409	12	7,016	15	6,763	15	6,209	15	5,554	18

Source: *News for Farmer Cooperatives,* U.S. Department of Agriculture, February 1977.

taken may include credit, insurance, electric power, telephone, irrigation and drainage, hospitals, and mortuaries. Membership may be of rural or urban people or a combination of the two. Farmers obtain substantial amounts of their farm credit from the Production Credit Associations and Federal Land Bank Associations. Rural Electric Associations furnish electricity to a large majority of rural people. Over half of farmers' fire insurance is carried by their mutual insurance companies. The principal source of savings from membership in such associations occurs largely because they are able to meet the specialized needs of the farmer-members better than other kinds of organizations.

Processing Cooperatives

The processing cooperative is organized to engage in the packing or processing of the farmer's products. Cheese and butter manufacturing, fruit packing, and vegetable canning associations are examples of this type of cooperative. In a great many instances the processing activities are part of the overall

275

activities of marketing cooperatives. It is common, for example, for cooperative cheese manufacturing associations to undertake the marketing service of wholesaling the finished product. This is another way in which farmers, through the integration of processing and marketing made possible by their cooperative associations, attempt to extend control over their products as they move into consumption. The number and membership of these kinds of associations are shown in Table 13-3.

Table 13-3. Number and Membership of Farmer Cooperatives, 1973–1974.

TYPE OF COOPERATIVE	NUMBER OF ASSOCIATIONS	ESTIMATED MEMBERSHIP (000)
Marketing and processing cooperatives[1]	4,800	3,111
Grain	2,012	1,301
Livestock	818	698
Tobacco	28	318
Dairy	659	278
Cotton	493	128
Poultry	38	111
Fruits and vegetables	436	95
Farm supply cooperatives	2,778	2,972
Service cooperatives		
Federal Land Bank Associations	533	431
Production Credit Associations	433	521
Banks for Cooperatives	13	3
Rural credit unions	351	478
Rural electric co-ops	980	7,800
Rural telephone co-ops	235	782
Dairy herd improvement co-ops	1,105	32
Trucking, storage, misc. services	155	21

[1] Classified by major business activity.

Source: *Statistics of Farmer Cooperatives, 1974–75,* U.S. Department of Agriculture, Farmer Cooperative Service, Research Report No. 39, April 1977.

TYPES OF COOPERATIVE ORGANIZATION

Cooperatives can also be classified on the basis of membership affiliation and control. From this viewpoint, cooperatives are usually grouped as independent local associations, federated associations, centralized associations, or a combination of these types of organizations.

Independent Local Associations

The simplest type of cooperative is the independent local association in which people hold direct membership and are able to participate in the affairs of the cooperative. The relatively small area of coverage and number of people involved mean that the opinion and action of each member can have influence. Because of the size limitation, however, such cooperatives are often limited in what they can do. These local cooperatives often join to form larger organizations to conduct mass marketing, purchasing, or manufacturing operations.

Federated Associations

The federated association is a cooperative composed of several local associations which operate together as an integrated unit. Farmers are members of the local association, and the local is a member of the overall association. Usually the motive for banding together is to secure greater business power and efficiency. In such an association the basic channel of control is from the local up to the overall organization. The local associations have a considerable degree of autonomy, and any powers that are not expressly granted to the central organization are retained by the locals. Savings made from the operations of the overall association are allocated back to the member local associations. The local then adds them to whatever savings have accrued from its own operations, and this total amount is then distributed to the patron-member.

Centralized Cooperative Associations

Centralized cooperatives are those in which the patron is a direct member of the central organization and exercises control through delegates sent from the different areas to the annual meeting of the central organization. The central organization in turn controls the local branch cooperatives which serve the members. This plan has the advantages of centralized control which makes possible prompt and uniform action by all the local outlets. But it lacks the direct membership participation possible in federated cooperatives. The central association itself is dominant and delegates certain powers to the local branches. In such an association the local units have a very limited amount of autonomy. Savings are distributed directly from the central association to the members.

Mixed Associations

Many large cooperative organizations today are neither totally centralized nor totally federated but are a mixture of the two kinds. Associations that are basically federated in nature often undertake new operations that are organized on a centralized basis. Through stronger bargaining power or other methods, the overall association may essentially gain control of the member local cooperatives. On the other hand, cooperatives that were originally organized on a centralized basis sometimes find it practicable to establish at the local level a committee of farmers to suggest operating procedures for the local units. Theoretically, these committees do not have any absolute authority, but often in practice they control the policies of the local units.

Most states have statewide organizations combining both the marketing and purchasing operations. These state associations often, in turn, combine into regional and national associations. This may be done in order either to operate manufacturing enterprises or to enhance bargaining power with noncooperative manufacturing concerns. In some instances, the regional or national associations may acquire raw materials for their manufacturing enterprises. Savings made from the operations of these regional and national associations are apportioned among their member state associations. The way in which the state associations handle these savings depends on their individual type of organization.

HISTORY AND STATUS OF AMERICAN COOPERATION

Looking at cooperation in a broader social sense, it is possible to say that cooperation has existed ever since the first two men discovered that by working together they could accomplish their work more efficiently. This type of approach contributes little to the understanding of the development of cooperation as a method of doing business.

Cooperative enterprises have been undertaken in a disorganized fashion in this country since the early colonial days. Throughout the nineteenth century, organized cooperative businesses in most commodity lines were attempted. Cooperation among farm groups as a method of presenting their opinions to the public and the government developed largely in the period of agricultural distress following the Civil War.

The Active Period, 1910–1930

Starting after the turn of the century, more serious attention was given to the organization of all kinds of cooperative business. The movement gained momentum during World War I and reached its peak in the postwar depression of the 1920's. The number of marketing and purchasing cooperatives doubled in the fifteen-year period 1915–1930, as shown in Table 13-4.

Several factors favored the expansion of cooperation in this period. First, rapidly falling prices in the period immediately following World War I led many cooperatives to be organized in order to stabilize or raise prices.

In addition, there were loud complaints that private suppliers of necessary farm supplies, such as fertilizer and feeds, were taking exorbitant margins. Farmers further complained bitterly that the middlemen of the market were

Table 13-4. Trends In the Number, Membership and Sales Volume of Farm Marketing and Supply Cooperatives, 1915–1974.

		MEMBERSHIP		SALES VOLUME	
YEAR	NUMBER OF COOPERATIVES	TOTAL (000)	PER COOPERATIVE	$ MILLION	PER COOPERATIVE ($ 000)
1915	5,424	651	118	$ 635	$ 117
1920	7,374	NA	NA	1,256	170
1930	11,950	3,000	251	2,400	201
1940	10,600	3,400	320	2,280	215
1950	10,035	6,584	705	8,726	810
1960	9,345	7,273	797	12,036	1,354
1970	7,790	6,355	816	19,080	2,449
1974	7,755	6,106	787	35,899	4,629

Source: *Statistics of Farmer Cooperatives,* Annual, U.S. Department of Agriculture, Farmer Cooperative Service.

not interested in improving either quality or service. There was just enough truth in many of these complaints that Congress, through the passage of the Capper-Volstead Act in 1922, gave official sanction to cooperatives as a way of "self-help" and as a way of restoring and maintaining reasonable competition in the marketing and purchasing of agricultural products and supplies.[2]

The Consolidation Period, 1930–1950

In the flush of early enthusiasm it was inevitable that many cooperatives would be started which were unsound in their business structure. Also, it was soon evident that cooperation could not be depended upon to stabilize general price fluctuations and automatically cure the many ills of the general economic situation. These things, plus the depression of the 1930's, contributed to the short life of many cooperatives.

In order to gain economic strength, many small independent cooperatives consolidated into the large federated associations. Twelve of the twenty-two major regional supply cooperatives were organized between 1925 and 1935. The number of cooperatives tended to decline throughout most of this period. However, this decrease was caused largely by the decline in numbers of

---

[2] Many stories of the early problems and efforts of cooperatives to solve them are available in the histories of many cooperative associations. Illustrative of these are K. D. Ruble, *Men to Remember,* R. R. Donnelley, Chicago, 1947; O. M. Kyle, *The Farm Bureau Through Three Decades,* Waverly Press, Baltimore, 1948.

marketing cooperatives. Purchasing cooperatives continued to grow both in numbers and membership.

The Period of Economic Growth, 1950–?

Though the total number of cooperative marketing and purchasing associations has continued to decline since 1950, membership has remained relatively stable. When put into the framework of the rapidly declining farm population, this means that cooperative membership is more widespread among farmers than previously. The total dollar business of these cooperatives has also continued to increase. Much of this increase, of course, has been the result of increasing farm production and its increased dependence on purchased inputs. Though the total numbers of cooperatives have tended to decline, new cooperatives continue to be formed. During the period 1960–1968 some 1,600 associations closed their doors as active businesses for various reasons. Another 869 associations lost their identity through mergers and consolidations with other associations. During this same period, however, 1,051 new marketing, purchasing, or service cooperatives were formed.[3] Added interest in cooperatives as a development tool has also occurred as part of the national concern over the continuing problem of poverty of sizable groups of people.

Throughout this period the size of the average association has grown both in membership and dollar volume of business. The larger cooperatives have taken their place among the nation's largest businesses. The largest ten U.S. agricultural cooperatives in 1975 are shown in Table 13-5.

Cooperation has expanded into many new fields during the last twenty

Table 13-5. The Ten Largest U.S. Farm Cooperatives, 1975.

Cooperative name	1975 sales ($ million)
Farmland Industries	$1,529
Associated Milk Producers	1,478
Agway	1,329
Grain Terminal Assn.	1,261
Land O' Lakes	1,124
Far-Mar-Co	1,007
Gold Kist	828
Illinois Grain	806
Indiana Farm Bureau Cooperative	697
Farmers Grain Dealers Association of Iowa	652

Source: "The Fortune 500," *Fortune,* April 1976.

---

[3] Richard M. Ackley, "117 New Farm Coops Started Each Year," *News for Farmer Cooperatives,* U.S. Department of Agriculture, July 1970.

years. The depression years of the 1930's gave impetus to governmental sponsorship of both credit and electrification cooperatives. The Production Credit Associations, the National Farm Loan Associations, and the Rural Electric Associations were originally established during this period. In recent years the government has also extended aid to the formation of rural telephone associations. There has also been an expansion in insurance cooperatives, irrigation cooperatives, and other miscellaneous associations to perform special services for rural areas.

Since the late 1950's there has been increased interest in the potential role of cooperative organization in bargaining for price and contract terms with processors and handlers. The increased use of state and federal marketing orders usually fosters the cooperative organization of growers. But much interest in bargaining associations has developed outside this legal structure. The basic goals of the National Farmers' Organization are to establish advance contractual arrangements with processors. The American Farm Bureau has established as an affiliated organization the American Agricultural Marketing Association, whose purpose is to help establish and coordinate the activities of various bargaining associations across the country. In addition, there has been growing involvement of marketing cooperatives in owning and operating processing facilities.

COOPERATION BY REGIONS AND COMMODITIES

The prerequisite for successful cooperative business ventures is large production volume. Chiefly for this reason the principal area of commercial

Table 13-6. Farmer Cooperative Sales Volume, by Regions, 1973–1974.

REGION	PER CENT OF COOPERATIVE MARKETING, SUPPLY, AND SERVICE SALES
New England	2%
Middle Atlantic	7
East North Central	20
West North Central	31
South Atlantic	8
East South Central	5
West South Central	10
Mountain	4
Pacific	12
Alaska-Hawaii	1
Total Sales	100%

Source: *Statistics of Farmer Cooperatives, 1974–75,* U.S. Department of Agriculture, Farmer Cooperative Service, Research Report No. 39, April 1977.

agriculture, the North Central states, is the region which accounts for over half of the cooperative business of the country, as shown in Table 13-6. Extensive cooperation is very difficult in low-producing, noncommercial agricultural areas.

Similarly, successful commodity cooperation also rests to a considerable extent on the nature of production. Continuous, large-volume production by specialized farm units favors large-scale cooperation much more than scattered production by nonspecialized farm units. The relative importance of cooperative business done in various farm products and supplies is shown in Figure 13-1.

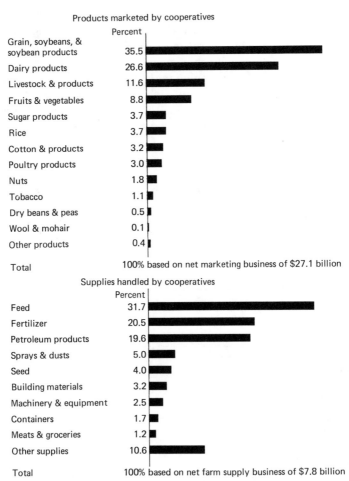

Products marketed by cooperatives

	Percent
Grain, soybeans, & soybean products	35.5
Dairy products	26.6
Livestock & products	11.6
Fruits & vegetables	8.8
Sugar products	3.7
Rice	3.7
Cotton & products	3.2
Poultry products	3.0
Nuts	1.8
Tobacco	1.1
Dry beans & peas	0.5
Wool & mohair	0.1
Other products	0.4
Total	100% based on net marketing business of $27.1 billion

Supplies handled by cooperatives

	Percent
Feed	31.7
Fertilizer	20.5
Petroleum products	19.6
Sprays & dusts	5.0
Seed	4.0
Building materials	3.2
Machinery & equipment	2.5
Containers	1.7
Meats & groceries	1.2
Other supplies	10.6
Total	100% based on net farm supply business of $7.8 billion

Figure 13-1. Relative importance of food products marketed by cooperatives and farm supplies handled by cooperatives, 1973–1974. (U.S. Department of Agriculture)

282

WHAT MAKES A SUCCESSFUL COOPERATIVE ASSOCIATION?

In a broad sense, a cooperative, if it is to be more than a passing fancy, must accomplish one, two, or all of the following three things:

1. Increase the returns from sales of products of its members, and/or

2. Reduce the price or improve the quality of the purchase of its members, and/or

3. Render new or improved service or give more equitable treatment to its members.

All these goals add up to the improvement of the economic well-being of the individual members. Many studies have shown that, whatever other benefits there may be from cooperation, the economic one is of the foremost importance. It is not enough for a cooperative to do a job as well as it is done by other agencies. The cooperative must do it better from the viewpoint of its patron-owner. A good cooperative should be the pacesetter for the industry with which it is associated. Only under these circumstances is the creation of an additional market agency justified.

There are things even a successful cooperative cannot do for its members. A clear understanding of these limitations is necessary for successful operation. The cooperative should recognize that it cannot set prices unless it has control of the supply.[4] This means that it cannot guarantee cost of production to its members. Cooperative associations cannot eliminate the marketing functions performed by other middlemen, nor can they successfully, for any period of time, coerce their members against their will into trading with the association. Cooperatives are circumscribed by the same set of economic restrictions as any other form of business organization. Their success depends not upon their uniqueness, but rather upon their business ability to operate profitably and satisfy their patron-owners.

The fundamental premise guiding the establishment of a successful cooperative association is that there be an economic need for the venture. There must be the opportunity to do a job better than it is being done. This can take the form of more advantageous prices or better quality products and service. To establish whether there is such a need that can be met by a cooperative must be determined by an assembly and objective study of the existing facts. Far too many cooperatives have been wished into existence

---

[4] An extreme example of the attempt and failure of a cooperative to control price monopolistically by controlling production was the Burley Tobacco Society in the early 1900's. Physical force by night riders was used to coerce growers into reducing production. Within a short time, however, the attraction of higher prices soon caused the control scheme to fail. See E. F. Dummeier and R. B. Heflebower, *Economics with Application to Agriculture,* 2d Ed., McGraw-Hill Book Company, New York, 1940, pp. 264–66.

only to fail when it was discovered there was no real additional service they could perform.

After the need has been established, it must be ascertained whether the factors necessary for a successful business operation are available. These factors are fundamentally the same as for any other business undertaking:

1. Can an adequate volume of business be secured and maintained? The economies of large-scale operation are just as important to cooperatives as to private corporations.

2. Can adequate and reasonable financing be secured? To build an efficient plant takes capital—to build less than an efficient plant invites failure.

3. Is efficient management available and will the association pay its price? In management, as in other things, high quality demands a high price. Successful cooperatives need as high a level of managerial ability as other businesses.

4. Is the membership prepared to meet competitive trouble? Especially in the initial stages, competitive conditions usually get worse rather than better. A new cooperative can usually expect that the rest of the business community will unite against it during the early period of its existence.

The reasons that cooperatives fail point up the importance of these factors. Difficulties in the field of management and membership relations account for many failures. Insufficient business volume and financing troubles account for other failures. An analysis of the failure of cooperative meat-packing plants is instructive. Of seventeen cooperative plants organized between 1914 and 1920, all failed; of the thirteen started between 1930 and 1950, five were still operating in 1957. Reasons for failure were given as (1) lack of sufficient capital and credit; (2) inadequate membership support; and (3) inefficient management.[5]

PROBLEMS OF MODERN COOPERATIVES

Cooperative business units have been increasing in size and complexity. Merger activity has been great among cooperative businesses as well as among noncooperative corporations. There is also a tendency toward more vertical integration in both marketing and supply organizations. This growth in size of cooperatives has been necessary both to take advantage of modern management and technology and to compete effectively in the marketplace.

Such growth, however, has sharply focused on a developing weakness of one of the cooperative operating principles. Close control of the membership so as to obtain a business operation oriented to user rather than investor needs was one of the important premises of early cooperation. This was

---

[5] Nelda Griffin and Roger Wissman, *Financial Structure of Farmer Cooperatives*, Research Report 10, Farmer Cooperative Service, U.S. Department of Agriculture, 1970.

assumed to be obtained by the one-man, one-vote provision in most cooperative bylaws.

Size and complexity has resulted in the breakdown of the membership into districts or units. The elected board which sets the cooperative policy has become further removed from membership control. Students of the modern corporation are concerned with the growing ability of corporate management to perpetuate itself. In large cooperatives the same problem exists.

Producers themselves are often dissatisfied with the one-man, one-vote principle. There is a tendency for the production units to become fewer, larger, and more specialized. This means that a given cooperative may depend upon relatively few large patrons for most of its business volume and that a much larger number of smaller patrons actually furnish very little volume. These few large patrons are not satisfied to be out-voted by the more numerous, smaller patrons. In many instances the one-man, one-vote idea has been set aside in favor of cumulative voting on the basis of business volume.

Modern cooperatives must solve the problem of maintaining user control and orientation in the current world of complexity and bigness of business organization. This will probably have to take some form other than the dependence upon the one-man, one-vote principle to elect the controlling board from among the patrons. Somehow, cooperatives must find a solution that will keep the larger patrons loyal and satisfied, obtain the services of a knowledgeable board of directors, and still retain the user-benefit orientation of operation.

Financing

Cooperatives require the same amount of capital as noncooperatives to perform similar functions. But with limitations placed on voting rights, share transferability, and the returns paid on invested capital, cooperatives cannot utilize the noncooperative method of selling additional shares to the investing public in order to secure additional funds.

When cooperative enterprises were relatively simple, only limited amounts of capital were needed. However, the desire of cooperatives to expand has focused attention on the techniques of securing growth capital. In general, cooperatives have relied on members to provide much of the financing needed, although other sources also have been used occasionally.

How does the cooperative obtain its equity capital for operations, growth, and expansion? The sale of common or preferred stock provides capital for some cooperatives. The market for such stock must be limited mainly to cooperative members. Common stock has voting rights, usually one vote per member, but no guaranteed income. If nonmembers hold common stock, they usually are not permitted to vote. Preferred stock usually carries a fixed dividend and no voting rights. These sometimes can attract investors other than cooperative members.

In the early years all earnings of the cooperatives were returned to patrons in the form of cash refunds. Most cooperatives have discontinued this practice in favor of retaining some part of the earnings in the association for capital purposes. Of the equity capital of cooperatives, about half is carried in the form of these retained earnings that are either covered by being allocated to the patron in the company books or by certificates of equity issued to the patron. This procedure has the advantage of spreading the financial burden among the users of a cooperative. Because the earning allocations are based on the amount of business done with a cooperative, ownership is divided in direct proportion to the use each patron makes of the association. The methods under which a member may withdraw his investment from a cooperative will vary from one association to another. Generally, when a member ceases to be a farmer or moves out of the trade area, his investment is returned. If a member dies, his investment is usually returned to his estate. Usually the member may also sell his stock or earning certificates to any buyer, subject to approval of the cooperative directors, or hold them until redeemed by the cooperative. Some cooperatives have a fixed time for redeeming these investments; others do not. If the cooperative regularly redeems its certificates after a fixed time, such practice is generally referred to as the use of a revolving fund. These funds may receive interest, but usually they do not.

In the present setting of increasing size and complexity of modern manufacturing and distribution, huge amounts of capital are necessary to make effective and competitive entry into new fields. How to secure these large amounts of needed capital is a major problem of the modern cooperative. The past process of obtaining capital either internally from the business itself or from traditional borrowing is not likely to be adequate. Some innovational way of obtaining capital that will not change the patron-user orientation of the cooperative over to the owner-financier orientation of the regular corporation needs to be found.

Management

Three groups of people are involved in the management of a cooperative—the members, the board of directors, and the hired manager. The members exercise their control through their elected directors. The directors have the responsibility of formulating general operating policies and of obtaining a manager to carry out these policies and report the results to the members. The manager is charged with the operating responsibility of the cooperative enterprise. He puts into actual practice the policies laid down by the board.

The problem of securing adequate hired management for a cooperative is essentially no different from that of any other business. To obtain excellent management, cooperatives must be willing to pay a price competitive with other businesses. They must also be willing to finance a staff that will furnish them with needed research and information.

286

The problem of the board of directors is quite different. Corporations staff their boards with whatever talent they need and can find from the business and financial world. Cooperatives, however, usually require that their boards be selected from the patron-members. Excellent farmers do not necessarily make excellent managers and advisers to a large and complex manufacturing or distributing enterprise. How to secure such talent and yet retain the patron-user viewpoint is another of the major current cooperative problems.

Membership Relations

The nature of cooperative business makes it imperative that good relationships be maintained between the members and their association. In many ways this is more important to cooperatives than stockholder relations are to noncooperative corporations. A stockholder's relationship to the corporation is that of an investor, and when he is dissatisfied with the returns he may dispose of his stock through sales to anyone who will buy it. Members of a cooperative, however, are at the same time both owner-investors and owner-users of the business itself. They cannot as readily divorce themselves from the responsibility of the business by selling their holdings.

Many of the problems of membership relations are fundamentally by-products of the increased size and complexity of the associations. In large associations members often feel it is *"the* co-op" instead of *"my* co-op." In a great many instances only a very small minority of the member-owners take an active interest in the problems and management of their association.

Other problems of members, however, stem from the changing structure of farming itself. Cooperatives, historically, have prided themselves on their free and voluntary membership and that each member is treated equally both in matters of voting control and rates of patronage refunds. This system was adequate when farming was largely made up of small general farmers and the cooperative enterprise was rather simple. However, today's farm structure is increasingly made up of a relatively few very large specialized producers, on the one hand, and a large number of very small producers, on the other. These two diverse groups do not have equal interests in the cooperative organization and they are not of equal importance from the viewpoint of the success of the cooperative. Many cooperatives are having to face the issue of treating some members differently from others if they wish to retain their patronage. Some cooperatives have established cumulative voting, differential rates of payment, a limitation on eligibility for membership, and a contractual obligation between acceptable members and the cooperative.

A good member is an informed member. Farmers who support cooperatives are those who know what cooperatives have done and what they can and cannot do. The really successful cooperatives rank this task of keeping an informed and participating membership high on their list of problems.

287

Relations with the General Public

In the early years, with few exceptions, the general public was disposed favorably toward cooperation. This attitude took concrete form in the passage of legislation favorable to cooperatives by both the state and federal governments. The Capper–Volstead Act, although not exempting cooperatives from antitrust prosecution, for all practical purposes made prosecution improbable. The federal government provided public funds for the Farm Credit Administration to aid cooperation with research and other services. It has actively participated in the formation of some cooperatives. In the U.S. Department of Agriculture there is a special division, Farmer Cooperative Service, which provides research services for cooperatives.

In recent years—probably as a result of the growing size and success of some cooperatives—the public image of the cooperative has been a mixed one. As a matter of official agricultural policy, the cooperative is still encouraged as a major tool for helping farmers secure equitable treatment in the marketplace. On the other hand, income-tax procedures have been changed to remove some of the automatic advantages for cooperatives that they previously enjoyed. In addition, courts appear more willing to find cooperatives in violation of antitrust laws. It is not at all clear how present laws will affect some of the bargaining activity that cooperatives wish to pursue.

One of the principal contributions of a good cooperative is as a pacesetter and competitive prod to other businesses. Large cooperatives, however, like other businesses, often concern themselves with maintaining the status quo. Several examples can be found of cooperatives fighting changes instead of welcoming them. Such situations cannot long receive the public blessing.

CONSUMER FOOD COOPERATIVES

Just as farmers frequently view cooperatives as a way to improve their market position, consumers also have formed food-buying cooperatives to lower food costs and participate more fully in food retail decisions. These buying cooperatives range from informal groups of neighbors who purchase in large volume to full-fledged, integrated wholesale and retail food operations owned and managed by consumer-patrons.

Consumer food co-ops are a growing but still small part of the retail food industry. They accounted for an estimated one-half of one per cent of retail grocery store sales in 1968, and as a group they would represent the thirtieth largest national grocery chain.[6] Food co-ops are more important in other

---

[6] L. L. Mather, "Consumer Cooperatives and Consumer Protection", in L. L. Mather, Ed., *Economics of Consumer Protection,* Interstate Printers and Publishers, Danville, Illinois, 1971, p. 126.

countries, such as Great Britain, where they account for 18 per cent of grocery store sales, and Sweden, where they represent 27 per cent of food store sales.

Food co-ops are most prevalent in the Midwestern States of Ohio, Michigan, Wisconsin, Minnesota, and the Dakotas. The largest co-ops are found in the major cities: Berkeley Consumers' Cooperative of California, Greenbelt Consumers' Cooperative of Washington, D.C., the Common Market Food Coop of Madison, Wisconsin, and Chicago's Hyde Park Coop.

Consumer food co-ops face many of the same problems as farm cooperatives—the need to provide unique services, the difficulties of hiring and keeping good managers, and the difficulties of securing adequate capital. Their cooperative nature does not guarantee them automatic success. Properly financed and managed, they provide a viable alternative to the traditional retail food store. However, it is unlikely that food co-ops will ever completely replace corporate chainstores.

THE CHANGING ROLE OF COOPERATIVES

In the coming years, one of the major problems of cooperatives will be to adjust to the rapidly changing agricultural scene and decide upon what are their most needed functions. We have already seen how the marketing organization is changing—often to more closely coordinated and integrated aggregates. Where does the farmers' cooperative fit in this developing picture? Some believe that cooperatives must expand still further into the ownership and operating of marketing and supply facilities. Others see a growing emphasis on bargaining activities. An extreme view holds that the future role of the cooperative will be more similar to the contemporary labor union than to today's association. One thing is certain. Change will be necessary if cooperatives are to continue to serve a useful and constructive role in the future. Such change will mean many debates, experimentation, failures, and successes in cooperative board rooms across the country.

SUMMARY

Cooperatives are a unique and increasingly important marketing tool for farmers. They are owned by and managed for the benefit of their farmer-patrons. They provide farmers an alternative to private or publicly owned marketing channels. Agricultural cooperatives are important in the areas of farm supplies, farm services (credit, electricity, telephones, and the like), farm marketing, and food processing. Agricultural cooperatives may be independent local associations, members of federated associations, or members of centralized cooperative associations. Although the number of agricultural cooperatives is declining, membership has been stable and the dollar volume of farm cooperative business is growing rapidly. To be successful, farm cooperatives must either increase member returns, decrease costs, or render a service not provided by the noncooperative sector. Cooperatives face challenges in the areas of member relations, control of decisions, financing, management, and public relations. To date, consumers' retail food cooperatives have not been as successful as farmer cooperatives.

QUESTIONS FOR DISCUSSION

1. Most cooperatives follow the Rochdale Principles, named for a pioneering cooperative in Rochdale, England. What are these principles and how faithfully do modern cooperatives adhere to them?

2. It is sometimes said that to successfully compete with established firms, co-ops must copy their management and operating procedures. Does this conflict with the uniqueness which is so important to the purpose of co-ops?

3. Why are cooperatives so much more important in the marketing of dairy products than in livestock marketing?

4. What are the differences between federated and centralized cooperative associations?

5. Why haven't consumer food buying cooperatives been as successful as farmer cooperatives?

6. The Capper-Volstead Act exempts farmer cooperatives from antitrust legislation. Yet recent court cases have found some cooperatives in violation of antitrust laws. How is this possible?

7. Discuss the most important factors affecting the success of an agricultural cooperative.

8. Discuss the pros and cons of the present financing arrangements for farmer cooperatives.

9. It has been observed that farmer cooperatives have had their greatest success in performing marketing activities closely associated with farming. Why haven't farm cooperatives moved to other levels of food marketing—processing, wholesaling, and retailing?

SELECTED REFERENCES

ABRAHAMSEN, M. A. *Cooperative Business Enterprise.* McGraw-Hill Book Company, New York, 1976.
——— AND J. W. MATHER. *Approaches and Problems in Merging Cooperatives.* U.S. Department of Agriculture. Farmer Cooperative Service, Information Bulletin No. 54, July 1966.
A Supply Cooperative As Farmers See It. U.S. Department of Agriculture. Farmer Cooperative Service, Research Report No. 12, March 1970.
"The Billion-Dollar Farm Co-ops Nobody Knows." *Business Week* (Feb. 7), 1977.
Cooperative Facts. U.S. Department of Agriculture. Farmer Cooperative Service, Information Bulletin No. 108, June 1977.

DAVIDSON, D. R. *How Farm Marketing Cooperatives Return Savings to Patrons.* U.S. Department of Agriculture. Farmer Cooperative Service, Research Report No. 7, Dec. 1969.

Farmer Cooperatives. U.S. Department of Agriculture. Farmer Cooperative Service, Bulletin No. 1, rev. 1965.

GOLDBERG, R. A. "Co-ops in a Changing Agribusiness." *News For Farmer Cooperatives* (June 1971), 3–10+.

——— "Profitable Partnerships: Industry and Farmer Co-ops." *Harvard Business Review* (March–April 1972), 108–121.

KNAPP, J. G. *Capper-Volstead Impact on Cooperative Structure.* U.S. Department of Agriculture. Farmer Cooperatives Service, Information Bulletin No. 97, Feb. 1975.

KOHLS, R. L. "Cooperatives As a Part of the Private Enterprise System." *American Cooperative* (1955), 693–701.

Legal Phases of Farmer Cooperatives. U.S. Department of Agriculture. Farmer Cooperative Service, Information Bulletin No. 100, May 1976.

ROY, E. P., *Cooperatives, Development, Principles, and Management.* Interstate Printers and Publishers, Danville, Ill. 1976.

SCHEARS, M. A. "Farmer Cooperatives—What They Are and What They Are Not." *News for Farmers Cooperatives* (March 1963).

Statistics of Farmer Cooperatives. U.S. Department of Agriculture. Farmer Cooperative Service, Annual.

THURSTON, S. K., et al. *Improving the Export Capability of Grain Cooperatives.* U.S. Department of Agriculture. Farmer Cooperative Service, Research Report No. 34, June 1976.

VOLKIN, D. "Any Corporation Can Achieve a Tax Status Comparable to Cooperatives." *News for Farmer Cooperatives,* Oct. 1966.

YOUDE, J. G., AND P. G. HELMBERGER. "Marketing Cooperatives in the U.S.: Membership Policies, Market Power and Antitrust Policy." *Journal of Farm Economics* (Aug. 1966), 23–36.

CHAPTER 14

Market Development and Demand Expansion

"THE HIGH PRODUCTION AND INCOME which are the fruits of advanced technology and expansive organization remove a very large part of the population from the compulsions and pressures of physical want. In consequence their economic behavior becomes in some measure malleable. No hungry man who is also sober can be persuaded to use his last dollar for anything but food. But a well-fed, well-sheltered and otherwise well-tended person can be persuaded as between an electric razor and an electric toothbrush. Along with prices and costs, consumer demand becomes subject to management."*

Preview

- This chapter introduces the concept of market development—those activities designed to influence the demand for food products.
- Discussed are the food market development activities, including consumer advertising, consumer education, product development, trade promotion, merchandising, packaging, couponing, games, and so on.
- The roles and social criticisms of market development activities are reviewed.
- Various demand states for food are examined, including negative, latent, full, and unwholesome demand.
- Food processors are shown to be the principal advertisers in the food industry. Food retailers are second. Farmers do comparatively little product advertising.
- The reasons for, potentials, and limitations of farmer advertising are reviewed. Criteria for the advisability of farmer advertising are discussed.

* John K. Galbraith, *The New Industrial State.* Copyright © 1967, 1971 by John Kenneth Galbraith. Houghton Mifflin Company, Boston, Massachussets.

- The impacts on food demand of nonfood uses of agricultural commodities, agricultural substitutes and synthetics, and public food programs are examined.
- Key terms and concepts:

agricultural substitutes and synthetics	market segmentation
demand states	marketing mix
food analog and extender	parasitic advertising
free rider	product differentiation
generic advertising	public food programs
market development	the 4 P's

Advertising and promotion are important elements of the food marketing picture. At its best, advertising contributes to possession utility by encouraging the flow of products from low- to high-value markets; and in this way advertising and promotion also contribute to the exchange and facilitating marketing functions.

Total U.S. advertising expenditures amounted to $28.3 billion in 1975—about 2 per cent of the Gross National Product, or $135 for each man, woman, and child. The food industry spent an estimated $4–5 billion on advertising in 1975—16 per cent of all advertising expenditures, 2.4 per cent of consumer food expenditures, and $19 per capita. These food advertising dollars accounted for 3 per cent of the total cost of marketing food.

Advertising and promotion are among the more controversial aspects of food marketing. Do these activities contribute to or interfere with consumer sovereignty and freedom of choice? What value do consumers get for their advertising dollar? What affect does advertising have on competition in the food industry? And, should farmers advertise and promote food products?

MARKET DEVELOPMENT IN THE FOOD INDUSTRY

Food market development refers to a wide range of marketing activities designed to enhance the value of food products for consumers. Advertising, quality control, packaging, new-product development, personal sales, merchandising, trading stamps, coupons, cents-off, and a host of other activities are instruments of market development. The goal of market development is to increase consumer satisfaction and, in the process, increase firm or industry profits. Advertising is one of the more visable market development tools. In the modern food industry, millions of dollars may hinge on market development tactics: a slight variation in the taste of a product, a new package design, a penny-off, or even a catchy advertising jingle can spell the difference between profit and loss or the success or failure of a business. Many criticize this aspect of food marketing as trivial or wasteful, but such market-making activities are inevitable in a high-income, free enterprise economy.

These activities are particularly important in the competitive battles waged between individual food firms and brands. However, market development is also becoming increasingly important in competition between food products (beef versus pork, margarine versus butter), food concepts (fresh versus frozen foods), and food distribution channels (retail foodstores versus restaurants). As a result, farmers have also become concerned with market development as a marketing tool.

Market development activities are used either to shift food demand curves rightward or to alter their slope. This is more than just "selling" or "increasing consumption"; consumers can be encouraged to buy more food at lower prices. Market development activities seek to expand consumption without sacrificing prices and profits. This is done by developing and marketing more pleasing products, providing better or more persuasive information for consumers, or building consumer loyalty for the product.

Market development activities are frequently classified by the *4 P's:* product, price, promotion, and place. These are the four variables which the firm can control to accomplish its sales and profit goals. Each firm or industry puts together a unique combination of the 4 P's, termed its *marketing mix.* Supermarkets have a mix different from that of convenience food stores, and the mix of grocery stores differs from that of restaurants, farmer markets, and vending machines. One mix cannot be judged, overall, to be better than another; each satisfies different consumer tastes and preferences.

As consumer incomes rise and consumers shift their efforts from satisfying survival needs to satisfying socio-psychological needs, such as status, esteem, affiliation, and distinction, market development activities gain in importance. These needs require a wide variety of differentiated products, services, and marketing channels. Few factors have been more important in shaping the modern food industry than the contemporary emphasis on market development.

VARIETIES OF FOOD DEMAND

Although it is convenient to speak of the general demand for a food product, actually there are several states of demand. These are important to the firm's market development strategies.[1]

A *negative demand* represents a situation where most potential consumers

---

[1] The following classification of demand states is adopted from P. Kotler, *Marketing Management,* 3rd Ed., Prentice-Hall, Inc., Englewood Cliffs, New Jersey, pp. 8–11.

dislike the product and would not buy it. This is the condition for many edible materials that are not defined as food: seaweed, eels, fish worms, insects, and so on. These would be of little interest except that negative demand states can become positive. The tomato was considered poisonous in colonial America, and liver was once fed only to pets. Frequently, new information can convert a product from a negative to a positive state.

A *no-demand state* exists when consumers are unaware of their needs for a product. There was no recognizable consumer demand, for example, for soft margerine, instant coffee, or presweetened cereals prior to their development and market introduction. Most new food products and concepts go through an extensive period of trial, acceptance, or rejection. Advertising, couponing, and samples may be helpful in converting a no-demand state into a profitable demand.

Latent demand refers to a general need for which there is no present product. Examples: a calorie-free potato, a low-cholesterol egg, or a safer cigarette. The marketing task here is to develop new or revised products to meet latent needs.

Faltering demand occurs when consumption of a product is declining or failing to grow at an acceptable rate. This may be because of deteriorating quality, the availability of preferred substitutes, high price, or a change in consumer preferences. Lamb appears to be in this category. Faltering products can sometimes be revitalized with new advertising themes or quality improvements. Medical reports on the dubious healthfulness of certain foods sometimes cause faltering demand.

Full demand is the ideal state of demand. Here, the current levels of consumption and prices are satisfactory. The task is to maintain demand at this level in the face of changing consumer preferences and competition from alternatives.

Irregular demand is a fluctuating demand situation, such as for turkey, cider, or cranberries. The task is to level out the peaks for a more stable year-round level of demand. For seasonal food products, this may require considerable cost and effort as well as substantial production adjustments on the part of farmers.

Over-full demand is rare in the food industry but can occur when a product is so popular or in such short supply that it is difficult to maintain adequate stocks without having prices rise to levels that adversely affect future product sales. The solutions lie in better coordination of supplies with demand.

Unwholesome or excessive demand represents a situation where high levels of consumption may prove detrimental to the long-run acceptability of the product. Clearly, there are value judgments involved in labeling the consumption of a product unwholesome. The classic examples are tobacco and alcoholic beverages. However, statements declaring that certain foods and consumption patterns are detrimental to the public interest will continue to be made. Counter-marketing efforts to cope with these situations include sponsorship of research and development, reformulation of products, consumer education programs, and label indentification.

These states of demand indicate that there is no one universal food demand problem, but from time to time all states are represented in the food industry. Successful marketing development programs require tailoring marketing tactics to specific demand states.

ROLES AND CRITICISMS OF ADVERTISING

Advertising contributes to the market intelligence and information dissemination functions. Traders and consumers must be informed about the availability of products, their attributes and uses, and their prices. Supplying this information can contribute to a smoothly operating market system, increased consumer satisfaction, and lower overall transaction costs of buyers and sellers. As advertising proponents would say, if advertising "sells", it is creating utility and must be considered a productive and valuable marketing activity.

In practice, however, advertising is much more controversial than the aforementioned statements suggest. The supplier and controller of information has power, and information can be manipulated to serve private interests. Advertising is frequently divided into classes: informative and persuasive (manipulative), but in practice, often it is difficult to distinguish one from another. Good information is frequently persuasive, and persuasive messages usually contain some information. A concern of many is that advertising is simply a huge economic waste, or a marketing function whose cost greatly exceeds its value.

It is easy to criticize advertising as being biased, often tasteless, intrusive, deceptive, or trivial—it is the most visible and vulnerable of all marketing activities. However, as with most institutions that survive and even prosper, advertising does perform some useful functions.

A major debate concerns the effect of advertising on consumer prices. Those who argue that eliminating the cost of advertising would lower consumer prices are focusing only on the cost side of a marketing function, ignoring the benefits advertising can provide in the way of information. The question is whether the benefit or value of advertising to consumers exceeds its cost. Such difficult judgments are probably best left to the market testing of consumers. Also to be considered is the cost of whatever is to replace advertising. For instance, personal selling is usually more expensive than mass-media advertising.

There are also questions concerning the impacts of advertising on competition in the food industry. National advertising has gone hand in hand with the decline in numbers and the increasing size of firms in many industries. This presents an operational-pricing efficiency dilemma; advertising may permit the growth of firms and markets, thus contributing to economies of scale, but in doing so the number of competing firms may decline, adversely affecting pricing efficiency.

Still another criticism of advertising is that it distorts consumer choices and interferes with consumer sovereignty. Producers and marketing firms are charged with not only creating products but with creating the demand for their products. Proponents of advertising, on the other hand, argue that advertising simply helps consumers to identify their needs and to match them with available products; and that advertising reinforces rather than creates or manipulates consumer preferences. Consumer preferences are so complex that it is doubtful that this question ever will be answered to everyone's satisfaction. It does seem naïve to believe that firms would spend $28 billion to sell products if they were not influencing consumers; however, there are sufficient product and advertising failures to suggest that advertisers do not exercise as much control over consumer preferences and choices as is sometimes believed.

Advertising also is frequently credited by its supporters with stimulating new product development and marketing innovations and generally contributing to the American mass-consumption society and to our high standard of living. Advertising probably does foster a favorable innovative climate by encouraging the search for product advantage and by facilitating the exposure of new products to consumers. However, there are other countries with high standards of living that devote considerably fewer resources to advertising than does the United States.

Overall, advertising is neither black nor white but a gray area with many unanswered questions. Even if it could be proved that it is a wasteful marketing activity, it probably would not be eliminated or outlawed. Businessmen presumably have a right to spend their money in wasteful, if not destructive, ways, and advertising is a freedom which is protected by the first amendment to the Constitution. But this is not to say that there will not be increasing regulation of the content of food advertising.

ADVERTISING BY FOOD MARKETING FIRMS

Food marketing firms spent $3.8 billion to advertise their food and nonfood products in 1972. Over the 1950–1972 period, their advertising expenditures increased at an average rate of 22 per cent each year. Food processors accounted for 66 per cent of total food advertising expenditures in 1972. However, food processors' and wholesalers' shares of these advertising expenditures fell between 1950 and 1972, whereas the shares of retail food stores and eating places increased.[2]

Marketing agencies use different forms of advertising. Food processors

---

[2] *Source Book of Statistics of Income,* U.S. Internal Revenue Service, 1973.

Table 14-1. The Largest Food Advertisers, 1975–76.

COMPANY	ADVERTISING EXPENDITURES ($000)	ADVERTISING EXPENSES AS A PERCENT OF SALES
General Foods	$300,000	5.6
General Mills	160,500	4.9
Norton Simon Inc.	127,000	7.2
Beatrice Foods Co.	123,000	1.9
McDonald's Corp.	122,000	3.8
Kraft Inc.	99,000	1.9
Nabisco Inc.	96,400	4.6
Pillsbury Co.	86,000	5.0
Ralston Purina Co.	81,000	2.1
Nestle Enterprises	71,000	5.7

Source: *Advertising Age,* Crain Communications Inc., August 28, 1978, p. 30. Reprinted by permission.

tend to use themes of quality and nonprice and advertise in national consumer media. Wholesalers and processors lacking strong brand identification are likely to emphasize price and service themes in trade media. Food retailers spend much of their advertising budget on local, price-oriented advertising— the weekly newspaper ads. Thus, there is a variety of price and nonprice, national and local advertising in the food industry. Overall, in the food industry there is probably as much price-oriented, informative advertising—as well as persuasive/emotional advertising—as in most other consumer product markets.

The 1975 and 1976 advertising expenses of several large food manufacturers are shown in Table 14-1. The larger advertisers are those with highly branded and differentiated products. Breakfast cereal manufacturers, for example, tend to spend more on advertising than do meat packers.

Advertising expenditure expressed as a percentage of sales is an indication of a firm's reliance on advertising as a market development tool. This advertising-to-sales ratio is usually higher for firms and industries with more intensive brand competition. Over the 1950–1966 period, the ratio averaged 3 per cent for confectionary manufacturers, 2.7 per cent for canners and freezers, 2.5 per cent for grain mill product processors, 1.5 per cent for dairy processors, and 0.5 per cent for meat packers.[3]

Food processors' and grocery manufacturers' advertising receive the most criticism in the food industry. These firms face a highly elastic demand, one which can be shifted rightward with a successful advertising program or shifted leftward by a competitor's advertising. The resulting advertising

---

[3] *Ibid.*

battle for the consumer's favor produces some valuable information, a great deal of entertainment, some competitive waste, and many headaches for the advertising and marketing managers of these firms. Food processors engage in two broad types of advertising. Product-line or institutional advertising attempts to promote a favorable image for the company or for its general brand. Brand or item advertising emphasizes the merits of a particular product or brand. Illustrated in Table 14-2 are the consequences of brand advertising for the breakfast cereal industry, where brand advertising is intense. The small changes in cereal product market shares, shown in the table, are worth millions of dollars to these firms.

Advertising is a natural complement to the process of developing new food products. Considering that the consumer is already faced with a bewildering array of various brands, any new product must be introduced into the

Table 14-2. Company and Brand Market Shares in the Breakfast Cereal Industry, 1972–1976.

		PERCENTAGE OF CONSUMER CEREAL EXPENDITURES	
COMPANY	BRAND	1972	1976
Kellogg	all brands	43.3%	42.5%
	Sugar Frosted Flakes	5.5	5.4
	Corn Flakes	5.1	5.0
	Rice Krispies	6.9	5.0
	Product 19	2.0	1.2
General Mills	all brands	22.2	21.4
	Cheerios	6.9	6.4
	Wheaties	3.1	2.5
	Trix	1.4	2.0
General Foods	all brands	15.7	16.8
	Raisin Bran	3.0	3.6
	Grape Nuts	2.0	2.4
Quaker Oats	all brands	4.9	8.9
	Cap'N Crunch	4.0	3.4
	Life	2.1	2.1
Nabisco	all brands	4.9	4.2
	Shredded Wheat	—	3.0
Ralston Purina	all brands	2.3	3.4
	Chex	—	2.3
Others		1.9	2.8
All breakfast cereals		100.0%	100.0%

Source: *Advertising Age* and John C. Maxwell, Jr., March 24, 1975, p. 52; August 1, 1977. Reprinted by permission.

consumer's mind. Advertising and other forms of promotion are effective ways of accomplishing this.

Advertising expenditures are also stimulated by the struggle for relative power between large processors and large retailing units. More and more, retailers wish to produce products under their own label in order to secure additional customer allegiance. Processors, understandably, want to retain the connection to customers through their own brands. Therefore, both groups find themselves spending more money to favorably influence the consumer.

Food marketing firms often build their brand marketing programs around two strategies: product differentiation and market segmentation. *Product differentiation* seeks to find a product's unique features that set it apart from its competitors. The objective is to build brand loyalty in order to achieve a less elastic demand curve. *Market segmentation* is a complementary strategy concerned with developing unique product variations that will appeal to different consumer classes or segments of the market. Both these strategies are apparent in food firms' advertising.

FARMERS AND MARKET DEVELOPMENT

Considering its success elsewhere in the economy, it is not surprising that farmers have frequently viewed advertising and promotion as a solution to their price and income problems. Farmers have made numerous efforts to "expand the demand" for farm products, using advertising, consumer education, foreign market promotions, support for research and development of new foods and uses of agricultural commodities, and encouragement of public food programs, such as school lunches and food stamps.

These programs and promotions have been particularly attractive to farmers during periods of surplus food production, but the results appear to be mixed. California orange growers seem to have had more success in promoting the Sunkist label than Iowa farmers have had in promoting Iowa beef. Cotton promotion has not stopped the incursion of synthetic fibers into its market, but may have slowed it. There are reports that dairy industry advertising has influenced milk sales and prices on occasion, yet consumption of fluid milk has continued to decline.

Can farmers advertise their way out of their problems? Should they? What results can farmers reasonably expect from commodity promotions? How could these efforts be made more successful?

The Rationale for Farmer Promotion

The goal in expanding the demand for farm products is not simply to increase consumption but to improve prices and the producers' incomes. Consumption and sales always can be increased by lowering prices and profits.

What the farmer means by "expanding demand" is to shift the demand curve rightward so that the same product volume can be sold at higher prices, or so that increased volume can be sold without lowering prices. Also, farmers sometimes attempt to make the demand for their products less elastic by convincing consumers not to make substitutions when prices rise. But simply shifting demand is not sufficient for a farmer advertising program. Like any other marketing activity, advertising has a cost. The farmer wants to influence demand in such a way that profits will be higher even after the advertising costs are paid.

Extent of Farmer Advertising

As price-takers, most individual farmers do not find it worthwhile to advertise their own products or brands to consumers. Farmers usually form groups to promote generic or branded products. *Generic advertising* refers to attempts to alter the demand curve for an entire class of food, such as beef, milk, or almonds. Sometimes this involves a generic brand, for example, the Woolmark. Frequently, farmers in one area will engage in regional-generic promotions: Maine potatoes, Georgia peaches, Florida oranges.

Several commodity research and promotion programs are authorized by special federal laws: The National Wool Act of 1954, the Cotton Research and Promotion Act of 1966, the Wheat Research and Promotion Act of 1970, the Potato Research and Promotion Act of 1971, and the Egg Research and Consumer Information Act of 1974. These laws authorize the collection of funds for farmer-sponsored research and market development activities.

Cooperatives, voluntary groups of farmers, legal boards, and State Departments of Agriculture are all involved in farm product promotions. Table 14-3 indicates that 917 of these groups spent $138 million to promote farm products in 1972—less than the advertising budget of the largest food processor. About one half of this money was spent for paid media advertising, with the remainder going for public relations, consumer education, and point-of-purchase merchandising aids. The dairy and fruit industries accounted for more than one half of all farm commodity promotional dollars in 1972. Perhaps 50 per cent of these dollars were contributed directly by producers, with the rest paid for by cooperatives, marketing agencies, and government.

Effectiveness of Farmer Advertising

The goal of farmer promotional programs is to influence the demand for farm products and improve prices and profits. Some promotional programs have been quite successful, some have produced mix successes, and others must be judged unsuccessful. It is difficult to generalize and say that all farmers should, or should not, promote their products; each product and farm group must be considered individually.

Table 14-3. Organizations Promoting Agricultural Products, 1958–1972.

PROMOTIONAL ORGANIZATIONS	NUMBER		ADVERTISING EXPENDITURES ($000)	
	1958	1972	1958	1972
Farm cooperatives	574	283	$25,149	$ 38,900
Voluntary producer-processor groups	345	412	25,508	33,700
Commissions, councils, boards established by law	120	146	13,961	61,800
State departments of agriculture	20	43	1,385	3,400
Other	73	33	596	905
Total	1,132	917	$66,599	$138,705

Source: U.S. Department of Agriculture, Marketing Research Reports, 380, 742, 911, 1960–1970.

To assist farmers in deciding whether to promote their products, several criteria have been suggested. Generally, promotional efforts have been more successful for specific, highly differentiated products than for generic classes of homogeneous products. Some brand or regional indentification is important in differentiating farm products. Also, the more substitutes there are for a product, the more effective the advertising, even though one goal of advertising is to convince consumers that a product *has* no good substitutes. For example, advertising "beef" would be more effective than advertising "all meat"; and peaches are more promotable than "all fruit."

A second criterion is that production and marketing of the product should be in the hands of an organized group of farmers. This is necessary in order to obtain financial support of the promotional program and to prevent supplies from expanding too rapidly in response to higher prices and profits. These events can prove troublesome for a commodity produced by a large number of geographically dispersed producers. For this reason, walnuts and avocados, presumably, can be promoted somewhat more easily than apples and peaches. The need for supply control is critical to the success of advertising. Higher prices, sales, and profits will encourage expansion and entry into the market, and in the long run, this supply response could nullify the economic effects of the advertising. The need for farmer organization is also evident. Unless all farmers in a position to reap the benefits of the promotion share in its costs, free-rider problems will undermine the program.

The advertising program must be closely coordinated with other marketing activities. Advertising is only one component of the marketing mix and is seldom successful without reinforcement from the other components. It must be coordinated with quality control, flow of supplies, prices, product development, and point-of-purchase materials.

It is frequently observed that farm product advertising is most successful for commodities that move to the consumer in fresh form, with little change in identity. These products, of course, are easier to brand than products that lose their identity. They also tend to have a higher farmer's share, so that a shift in retail demand has a considerable impact on farm prices.

A final criterion is that a substantial sum of money be available if mass-media promotions are to have an impact. The effectiveness of advertising is not directly proportional to the dollars spent, and a critical mass of promotional exposure must be achieved in order to penetrate the mass market.

Another concern in farmer promotional efforts is that because most foods are more or less substitutes for one another, an advertising program that shifts demand rightward for one product may shift the demand leftward for another. This *parasitic advertising* may benefit one group of farmers at the expense of another. Farmers need to consider the group impact of farm product advertising in evaluating the success of their separate programs. The felt need to launch a defensive promotional program to combat parasitic advertising may result in forcing farmers to engage in commodity advertising when it would not otherwise be advisable.

Should There Be Compulsory Farmer Advertising?

The entry of farm groups into advertising ventures and the belief or assumption that such efforts are successful have brought two major reactions. First, there is the attitude that because advertising is successful, it is unfair to support it by voluntary efforts. Under these circumstances the noncooperators benefit equally from the expenditures of the cooperators. Second, there is the attitude that if promotion is successful for one commodity, it should be expanded to all agricultural commodities. Thus, the total demand for agricultural products could be increased.

The first attitude has led to pressures for legislation to make fund collections compulsory on all producers. Various laws, ranging from those authorizing compulsory check-offs to those that merely authorize group activity in promotion, have been passed by nearly all the states. The California program is probably the most varied and covers many separate products. Most of these state programs are administered by special advisory boards, often with some state appropriations being used.

The next logical step is to obtain national legislation for this purpose. The precedent for this already has been established in the National Wool Act, which provides for the collection of wool promotional funds. Other proposals that have been put into the legislative hopper would set up systems of compulsory national collection of promotional funds.

303

Promotional activities by farm groups, therefore, have entered into the policy picture at the national level. Here is where the second attitude mentioned becomes pertinent. Can the success of an individual commodity campaign be generalized to the total output picture? Can all groups promoting all products persuade consumers to allocate more money for the raw products of agriculture than they would have allocated without the promotion expenditure?

Concerning the issue of potential success on the total level, there is much more agreement among economists than was true for the individual promotional programs. The extra money must come from the consumer's decision to transfer some funds from nonfood expenditure or to purchase "food" items manufactured from nonagricultural materials. At the present time, with only a few notable exceptions (butter, sugar) food in the aggregate does not have close substitutes.

All available evidence points to the conclusion that most Americans are well fed. The people in this group are not good candidates for spending more on food. There is a group of consumers who might prefer more or different foods and who are not adequately nourished. However, most of these consumers are not in this condition by choice but because of the lack of income. Persuasion is a poor tool when lack of income is concerned. At present the potentialities of increasing the demand for all agricultural products through a massive, across-the-board advertising campaign appear meager except in areas where close substitutes are available. As synthetic foods become more important, defensive promotional programs can be expected to take on added importance as producer groups struggle to maintain their position. It appears likely that more and more general commodity advertising will be done by farm groups. Individual groups are concerned only with the sales of their particular commodities. As in individual companies, competitive pressures from other companies that advertise force them to increasingly greater efforts in order to maintain their share of the market. Trade groups threatened by synthetics will develop more aggressive promotional programs. Because most products are sold in a market that is national in scope and will require sizable amounts of money to exploit successfully, more pressures will develop to find ways to collect resources to spend on advertising on a broad, continuing basis.

EXPANDING NONFOOD USES FOR AGRICULTURAL PRODUCTS

The demand for food products cannot be expanded rapidly, but what are the possibilities for making nonfood products from agricultural commodities? This idea has always excited the imagination of those who wish to expand the demand for farm products. However, in many instances the high cost of agricultural products rather than lack of knowledge stands in the way of additional utilization. For example, a very satisfactory fiberboard for use in the building trades has been developed from cornstalks. However, the cost of collecting the cornstalks from the field makes the present product uncompetitive. It has been estimated that the incorporation of 2 to 5 per cent starch in pulp and paper products would provide outlets for 40 to 100 million bushels of grain. However, such a procedure is not now considered economical by the paper trade. We can make alcohol for automobile fuel from corn, but it is estimated that corn would have to be quite cheap to compete in the gasoline market.

It is true, however, that compared to the chemical-process industries and others, a relatively small amount of research is being done in the potential industrial utilization of farm products. Agricultural chemists point out that we know much less about the basic chemistry of farm products than we do about coal and petroleum. An improvement in such basic knowledge is a necessary first step to any major breakthrough in increased economically feasible nonfood utilization.

Most analysts in this area conclude that additional expenditures on utilization research and development are necessary not only if we are to expand this demand, but also if we are to retain the outlets that now utilize agricultural products. However, any major increases in demand from this effort will be unpredictable. It is like drilling for oil. Many dry holes may have to be explored in order to bring in one producer.

SYNTHETICS AND AGRICULTURAL SUBSTITUTES

The history of the food industry is one of constant substitution. In the nineteenth century, cane sugar, coffee, and European rapeseed encountered competition from beet sugar, chicory, and whale oil. The twentieth century saw the appearance of cereal sugars, tropical oils, soya, and fish oils. Recent developments include the production of yeasts, fungi, bacteria, amino acids obtained by fermentation, synthetic sweeteners, and petroleum-based fatty acids.

At least part of the expected moderate increase in the demand for agricultural products may be offset by the growth of synthetic foods and food substitutes. *Synthetic products* are manufactured from nonagricultural raw materials, principally petrochemicals. Synthetic sweeteners, shoe "leather," fabrics, and livestock feeds are good examples. *Agricultural substitutes* are manufactured from agricultural raw materials but replace traditional agricultural products. Examples of agricultural substitutes are bacon bits and other meat substitutes made from soybean proteins, as well as "artificial" milk products. In the case of substitutes, the effect is really a transfer of the demand from one agricultural sector to another. The use of margarines, for example, increases the demand for soybeans as the demand for dairy products is reduced. These trends will have varying effects on farm producers and agricultural industries and may cause shifts of agricultural resources between them.

To date, losses to synthetics and substitutes have been most extensive among the nonfood agricultural products. Some of the more significant of these are shown in Table 14-4. Cotton and wool lost about one third of their share of the textile market over the 1957-1968 period. During this same period cotton prices declined by 30 per cent and wool prices declined 44 per cent; synthetic prices, however, fell only 23 per cent.

Synthetics and substitutes have made gains on some agricultural products for several reasons. Manufacturers and consumers can usually be guaranteed a more stable supply of these than agricultural products because they do not have to depend on weather conditions. It is easier to maintain constant quality of man-made goods. Additionally, manufactured goods are usually easier to differentiate and are often cheaper to produce.

Meats provide interesting examples of agricultural substitutes. A meat *analog* is a vegetable soy protein product that is fabricated to resemble meats in texture, color, and flavor. Sometimes even a plastic bone is added to the

Table 14-4. Changes in Agriculture's Market Share of The Food and Fiber Market, 1957–1968.

AGRICULTURAL PRODUCT OR MARKET	MARKET SHARE HELD BY AGRICULTURAL PRODUCT		MARKET GROWTH RATE	
	1957–1959	1968	AGRICULTURAL PRODUCT	TOTAL MARKET
Cotton	56%	34%	1.8%	7.4%
Wool	4	2	−1.5	7.4
Cane and beet sugar	86	80	2.0	3.0
Oilseed meal	90	84	5.4	6.3
Fats and oils for soap	20	12	−1.9	2.5
Drying oils for paints	39	28	−2.8	3.6
Glycerine	55	42	1.7	4.6
Starch and dextrin for adhesives	16[1]	14	5.3	6.9
Soya meal and casein for adhesives	10[1]	8	2.7	6.9
Leather for shoe uppers	85	78	−3.2	1.7
Citrus	32[2]	34[2]	5.6	4.4
Fluid milk	100	100[3]	0.5	0.5

[1] For 1962.

[2] Share of retail fruit beverage market for 1965.

[3] Synthetic and imitation milk was less than $\frac{1}{10}$ of 1 per cent of the market.

Source: *Synthetics and Substitutes for Agricultural Products, A Compendium,* U.S. Department of Agriculture, Miscellaneous Publication No. 1141, April 1969.

"soy-steak." A *food extender* is a vegetable protein product that can be added to traditional meat products (hamburgers, meat loaf) to increase their volume. Certain meat analogs and extenders are competitive with red meats in cost per serving (after cooking). This cost factor has encouraged their use in the hotel, restaurant, and institutional market. The growth of meat analogs and extenders for home food consumption has been slower because of labeling regulations, nutritional requirements, and flavor and texture preferences.

PUBLIC FOOD PROGRAMS

Most societies accept some responsibility to provide food assistance for the disadvantaged. However, there is considerable debate about how to do this and how much assistance is desirable. Publicly subsidized food programs are predicated on humanitarian, moral, and economic bases. A well-fed society may be happier and more productive than a hungry one.

During the 1930's, there were emergency distributions of surplus foods, but domestic food-aid programs expanded rapidly in the 1960's and 1970's. These programs now include: (1) the food stamp program; (2) the school lunch and breakfast program; (3) the special milk program; (4) the food-service program for camps, day care centers, and nursery schools; (5) programs providing needy mothers, infants, and children with nutritionally rich supplemental foods; and (6) the commodity distribution program which serves disaster victims, Native Americans, schools, hospitals, and institutions. There are also food and nutrition education programs designed to help people buy and prepare food for more nutritional diets.

The volume of participation in some of these programs is shown in Figure 14-1. The federal budget contribution to the food assistance programs amounted to 3 per cent of U.S. food expenditures in 1974. Public food-aid programs are important to farmers, food marketing firms, and consumers. They probably increase the total demand for food, although it is not clear how much. They also probably change *what* people eat. However, a commodity-specific aid program, such as the school milk program, probably has a greater impact on the composition of the diet then the food stamp program, which allows the purchase of a variety of foods.

As shown in Figure 14-1, the food stamp program is replacing the food-to-the-needy program. The number of people receiving food stamps increased from 3 million in 1965 to over 20 million in 1975, almost 10 per cent of the population. In general, purchasing-power aid programs, such as food stamps, give consumers greater latitude in diet choice but have less impact on total food demand and on food consumption patterns than in-kind programs such as food-to-the-needy.

307

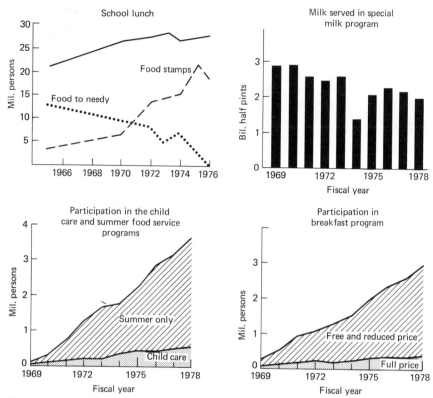

Figure 14–1. Participation in U.S. food assistance programs. (U.S. Department of Agriculture)

SUMMARY

Market development activities—advertising, public relations, product research and development, quality control, and merchandising—are extremely important elements of food marketing. These demand-influencing activities can alter consumer demand states, affect the intensity of competition in food markets, and influence farm and food prices. Advertising is the most visible and controversial food marketing development activity. Food industry advertising is a blend of persuasive and informative messages conveying both price and nonprice aspects of the marketplace. Food processors dominate the food advertising picture. By comparison, farm groups and related organizations engage in a small amount of generic, and sometimes brand, advertising. The success of farm product advertising has been mixed, depending upon the ability to brand the product, the number of substitutes for the product, the organization of farmers and their ability to control supplies, and the amount of money available for farm product advertising. The rate of farm commodity demand expansion is influenced by the development of nonfood uses of farm products, the development of agricultural substitutes and synthetic foods, and the growth of public food programs.

QUESTIONS FOR DISCUSSION

1. Why does market development become a more important aspect of marketing as consumer incomes rise?

2. Identify a food product in each of the demand states discussed.

3. Your friend states, "Advertising is a waste of money." How do you respond?

4. How do you distinguish between informative and persuasive food advertising? Give examples.

5. Why do food processors and grocery manufacturers account for the largest amount of food industry advertising?

6. You are asked by a group of wheat farmers to advise them on whether they should advertise and promote their product. What is your advice?

7. The Beef Research and Information Act was a program to improve beef sales and prices in 1977. Based on your research of this program, why was it defeated by cattlemen in a national referendum?

8. How would you evaluate the "effectiveness" of a nationwide program to promote increased consumption of milk?

9. How does branding of farm products alleviate the free-rider problem in farmer advertising programs?

10. Do you think farmers will do more or less commodity advertising in the future?

11. What are some current nonfood uses of agricultural commodities?

12. Do farmers support such government programs as food stamps, the school lunch program, or the special milk program? Do consumers?

SELECTED REFERENCES

BACKMAN, J. "Is Advertising Wasteful." *Journal of Marketing* (Jan. 1968), 2–8.

CLEMENTS, W. E., AND P. L. HENDERSON. *Consumer Response to Various Levels of Advertising for Fluid Milk.* U.S. Department of Agriculture. Marketing Research Report No. 805, Oct. 1967.

———— *Promotional Activities of Agriculture Groups.* U.S. Department of Agriculture. Marketing Research Report No. 742, Dec. 1965.

DEGRAFF, H. "The Place of Food Promotion and Advertising in Expanding Demand for Farm Products," in *Policy for Commercial Agriculture,* Joint Economic Committee, 85th Congress, 1st Session, 1957.

ENGLE, J. F., H. G. WALES, AND M. R. WARSHOW. "The Economic and Social Role for Promotion," *Promotional Strategy.* Richard D. Irwin, Inc., Homewood, Ill., 1971.

GALLIMORE, W. W. *Synthetics and Substitutes for Agricultural Products: Projections for 1980.* U.S. Department of Agriculture. Marketing Research Report No. 947, March 1972.

HENDERSON, P. L. *Butter and Cheese: Sales Changes Associated with Three Levels of Promotion.* U.S. Department of Agriculture. Agricultural Economic Report No. 322, Jan. 1976.

———S. E. BROWN, AND J. F. HIND. *Special Promotional Programs For Apples, Their Effects on Sales of Apples and Other Fruits.* U.S. Department of Agriculture. Marketing Research Report No. 446, Jan. 1961.

——— AND R. PARLETT. *Agricultural Commodity Promotions: Features Encouraging Participation of Retailers and Wholesalers.* U.S. Department of Agriculture. Marketing Research Report No. 911, Oct. 1970.

——— AND M. E. Thigpen, *Evaluation of a Special Promotional Campaign for Frozen Concentrated Orange Juice.* U.S. Department of Agriculture. Marketing Research Report No. 693, Feb. 1965.

HOOFNAGLE, W. W. "The Effectiveness of Advertising Farm Products." *Journal of Advertising Research* (Dec. 1963), 2–6.

HOOS, S. "The Advertising and Promotion of Farm Products—Some Theoretical Issues." *Journal of Farm Economics* (May 1959), 349–63.

KAITZ, E. F. *Household Consumers' Acceptance of an Experimental Dry Whole Milk.* U.S. Department of Agriculture. Marketing Research Report No. 880, May 1970.

NERLONE, M., AND F. V. WAUGH. "Advertising without Supply Control: Some Implications of Study of the Advertising of Oranges." *Journal of Farm Economics* (Nov. 1961), 813–37.

SEROW, W. J. "The Implications of Zero Growth for Agricultural Commodity Demand." *American Journal of Agricultural Economics* (Dec. 1972), 955–63.

SHAFFER, J. D. "Advertising in Social Perspective." *Journal of Farm Economics* (May 1964), 387–97.

SOUTHWORTH, H. M. "The Economics of Public Measures to Subsidize Food Consumption." *Journal of Farm Economics* (Feb. 1945), 38–66.

TWEDT, D. W. "How Much Value Can Be Added Through Packaging?" *Journal of Marketing* (Jan. 1968), 58–61.

TWINING, C. R., AND P. L. HENDERSON. *Promotional Activities of Agricultural Groups.* U.S. Department of Agriculture. Marketing Research Report No. 742, Dec. 1965.

CHAPTER 15

Market and Bargaining Power

"UNORGANIZED FARMERS have no positive market power at all and depend upon competition among buyers to obtain the full value that market conditions justify for their products. Especially when products must be sold to buyers in a local market and the local buyers are few, competition may not be fully effective in achieving this result."*

Preview

- This chapter explores the nature and balance of market power in the food industry.
- The relationship of market power and bargaining power is examined and the types, sources, and indicators of market power are explored.
- Special attention is given to farmers' market power and the tools available for enhancing this power: marketing orders and agreements and bargaining associations.
- The legislative history and current status of agricultural bargaining laws are discussed.
- Potentials and limitations of farmer market power tools are enumerated.
- Key terms and concepts:

Agricultural Fair Practices Act of 1968.
bargaining association
bargaining power
collective bargaining
countervailing power

economic price discrimination
exclusive agency bargaining
flow-to-market
market allotment
market order and agreement
market power

---

* *Food from Farmer to Consumer,* Report of the National Commission on Food Marketing, Washington, D.C., 1966.

311

Key terms and concepts (continued):
marketing board
National Agricultural
Bargaining Acts

opponent-pain, opponent-gain
power
orderly marketing

Market power is a perennial area of concern in the food industry. Most firms complain about their lack of power. Food processors maintain they are at the mercy of giant retailers. Food retailers argue that the large food processors have "undue market power." Consumers complain that they are being exploited and are powerless to do anything about it. Farmers, feeling they are the smaller and most unorganized element of the food industry, have historically complained of their lack of bargaining power. Many food industry laws seek to restore bargaining power or to strike a better balance of power among market parties.

What is market and bargaining power? Who has it and who lacks it in the food industry? How is market power achieved and maintained? And, most importantly, what are the consequences of market power in the food industry? These are vital questions in the design of agricultural and food marketing policies.

MARKET POWER IN THE FOOD INDUSTRY

Market power is an intangible characteristic of markets. Unlike the physical marketing activities, it cannot be observed directly, nor can it be measured precisely. It is largely known through its effects on the marketing processes—through prices, contract terms, firm behavior, and other features of markets. None have seen it, but many have felt it.

Market and Bargaining Power

Market power is the ability to advantageously influence markets, market behavior, or market results. While market power is typically associated with influence over prices, it also can take the form of influence over demand, product flows, quality, marketing functions, and other firms' market behavior. Firms seek and use market power in order to achieve their economic goals.

A large retailer or processor with influence over prices and profits through consumer advertising has market power. A dominant food wholesaler who is a price leader for other wholesalers has a degree of market power. A nonfood company that finances discount prices of its food subsidiary is employing market power. A food processor who controls the quality and timing of product flows in a profitable manner through farm contracts is exerting market power. Farmers who succeed in raising prices through supply control programs have gained market power. A consumer boycott of a food product is an attempt to exercise consumer market power. In each of these cases, one marketing agency or group of marketing participants is influencing, in an advantageous manner, either the market or the market behavior of others. Market power involves shaping and influencing the market process, rather than simply reacting to the market environment.

Bargaining power is a related term, and refers to the relative strength of buyers and sellers in influencing the terms of exchange in a transaction. Bargaining power requires market power, but market power is a broader concept, not limited to the buyer-seller situation. Food retailers, for example, may influence farm prices and sales through their merchandising and pricing practices without ever directly negotiating with farmers.

A firm's market and bargaining power can be defined only relative to the lack of market power of others. If all market agencies possess equal market power, none of them has an undue influence on the market; they nullify each other's power. Market power becomes a problem when it is unequally distributed—when one marketing agency can take advantage of its superior influence. Accordingly, there are two approaches to solving market power problems in the food industry: (1) reduce the influence of the more powerful to the level of the weaker; or (2) increase the influence of the weaker to the level of the more powerful. Regulatory and legal measures to maintain competitive conditions at all levels of the food industry illustrate the first approach. Attempts to build "countervailing power," or equal influence, illustrate the second approach.

Market power is frequently associated with the perfectly competitive market. Imperfectly competitive firms have market power, but perfectly competitive firms have no power. The association of market power and imperfect competition is correct. However, imperfect competition is not synonymous with market power. Two imperfectly competitive firms may have no market power over one another, if their power is roughly comparable and countervailing; yet both may have superior market power over a third, perfectly competitive firm. Under the conditions of perfect competition there is no market power problem because market influence is equally lacking for all. However, the real world is made up of shades of imperfect competition, and there is opportunity and room for maneuvering and strategies in the attempt of one market party to gain and exercise more market power than another.

It is useful to distinguish between short-term and long-term market power. Marketing agencies may not always take full advantage of their market power. Using short-term market power may conflict with the firm's long-term position, as, for example, when a buyer does not bargain prices to their lowest level because he wishes to build long-term goodwill among suppliers. Similarly, a marketing agency may resist using its full market influence if it feels that

313

to do so would invite more competitors into the industry or might trigger unwanted government intervention.

It is also useful to distinguish between horizontal, vertical, and conglomerate market power. *Horizontal power* refers to the influence that similar marketing agencies have over one another. For example, large retailers and food processors may be able to influence the pricing and output decisions of smaller firms. *Vertical power* relates to the influence that vertically related firms in the marketing channel have over one another. *Conglomerate market power* refers to the influence that a firm might have in the food industry by virtue of its ties to nonfood companies.

Types of Bargaining Power

Three types of bargaining power have been identified in the food industry. *Opponent-pain* bargaining power is concerned with the influence of a buyer or seller in a negotiation gained through the ability to threaten or make opponents worse off. Most people associate bargaining power with this form. The influence stems from coercion and the power to inflict damage on others. "Either sell to me or you will have no market," "that's my price, take it or leave it," and "give us our terms or we will destroy the product," are illustrations of opponent-pain bargaining. In practice, however, these threats are usually more subtle.

Opponent-gain bargaining power represents an alternative to opponent-pain tactics. This power stems from the advantages that one market party can offer to the other in exchange for accepting terms. For example, farm marketing associations may be able to perform certain market activities that increase the efficiency of food processors. Quality control, full-supply contracts, delivery services, and improved scheduling of production are examples of such activities. In this case, neither party to the negotiation needs to be made worse off; cooperation, rather than threats, dominates the negotiations. How to allocate between participants the benefits of the gain is also a subject of the negotiations.

In practice, both opponent-pain and opponent-gain power stances are evident in most negotiations. A food processor may agree to higher wages if the union will permit the use of new labor-saving technologies (opponent-gain). If the union refuses this offer, the company may threaten to move its plant, and the union may threaten to strike (opponent-pain).

In another type of bargaining power, a buyer and seller may agree to terms which secure a gain from third parties—either consumers, other market agencies, farmers, or the government. In this situation, the two parties to the negotiation cooperate to secure gains (higher prices, government subsidies, protection from imports, and the like) from other sources.

314

Sources of Market Power

A number of interrelated factors or market conditions have been identified with market power in the food industry:

1. *Size, number, and market concentration of firms.* Ordinarily, large firms are believed to have superior market power in dealing with small firms. The key here is the number of alternatives for the weaker market party. Large firms in concentrated markets draw their power from the lack of alternatives that others have in dealing with them. The relationships of firm numbers and sizes to market power are complex in the food industry, where superior vertical power relations might be nullified by countervailing horizontal power relations.

For farmers, organization is a more important influence on market power than simple numbers and sizes of sellers. The greater the organization and cohesion of farm groups, the greater their market power.

2. *Supply control.* The most important source of market power stems from the ability to effectively control the amount of product produced and offered to the market. Normally those who have inferior market power are sellers of products that are difficult to regulate production of, that need to be marketed because of perishability or lack of storage space, and that are subject to frequent price fluctuations.

3. *Unequal information.* Information is power that can be used to take advantage of market situations. Typically, firms with the greatest amount of market information have superior market power.

4. *Diversification.* Buyers and sellers who are diversified by products, geography, and marketing functions appear to have more market power than specialized agencies. Diversification contributes to flexibility in market decisions and reduces market risks.

5. *Product differentiation.* Firms with highly differentiated products are in a better position to "manage demand" profitably than firms with homogeneous products.

6. *Control of strategic resources and decisions.* "Gatekeeper" firms control strategic market variables such as brands, consumer loyalty, retail shelf space, or retail prices. Control of these appears to give firms some power.

7. *Financial resources.* Firms with large financial resources often can withstand competitive battles and inflict greater opponent-pain power than weaker firms. This is believed to be an important source of market power of the conglomerate food company.

8. *Ratio of fixed-to-variable costs.* Firms with relatively high fixed costs tend to suffer chronic excess capacity and do not respond quickly to changing prices. Because of this inflexibility, these firms are frequently considered to have low market power.

315

Indicators of Market Power

Market power is difficult to isolate and study in the marketplace. Firms do not proclaim that they have market power! And almost everyone in the food industry complains of a lack of market power, or claims to be the victim of someone else's market power. Unfortunately, there is no litmus test to identify market power. Several market conditions seem to be identified with the presence or absence of market power. "Low," below-cost, or fluctuating prices are not conclusive evidence of superior or inferior market power. In the case of agriculture, these conditions may simply reflect the inelastic demand and supply conditions. Neither is the level or trend in the farmer's share of the consumer's food dollar a useful test of market power. This share can be explained by consumers' low income elasticity of demand for farm products and high elasticity for food marketing services.

Many feel that higher-than-normal profits are an indication of superior market power. In addition to the difficulties of determining "normal" profits and of adjusting these profits according to the levels of associated risks, to use this as an indication of power discounts the role of management skills in profits. Some firms may have higher profits not because they are powerful but because they are better managed. Moreover, firms with market power may show low profits as a result of poor management.

Sometimes market power is attributed to those firms or market levels which quote prices. However, these firms may simply be the point of price discovery as a result of industry tradition or convenience. The firm which quotes prices may be a good price-discoverer but may have no power to influence prices or other market results.

Evaluation of Market Power in the Food Industry

Despite the difficulty of identifying and measuring market power in the food industry, some judgments have been made.

Generally there is a concensus that, compared with food marketing firms, farmers have inferior market and bargaining power. The reasons for this are farmers' numbers, relative sizes, low levels of organization, high fixed costs, geographic and product specialization, and homogeneous products. There is also a concern that decentralization and integration have reinforced this prevailing imbalance of power between farmers and food marketing firms. This imbalance could contribute to relatively low farm prices and incomes, frequent below-cost or fluctuating farm prices, and the shifting of the cost of some marketing functions and risks to farmers. However, other farm market conditions, such as elasticities of supply and demand, also contribute to these conditions and are not necessarily related to the market power of food firms.

Throughout history farmers have used various means to improve their

316

bargaining power—some formal and some informal, some coercive and some voluntary. Some were partially effective and others were completely ineffective. In the nineteenth century, night riders in the tobacco belt burned the barns of farmers who refused to cooperate in withholding the crop from the market. During the 1920's, Aaron Shapiro preached the message of "cooperative bargaining power." In the 1930's, the Farmer's Holiday Movement used coercion to gain farm market power. Each period of low farm prices sees a new wave of farmer strikes, witholding threats, and dumping actions by farmers.

The National Commission on Food Marketing identified two other market power positions in the food industry.[1] Food retailers, it found, possessed market power by virtue of their size, control of private labels and shelf space, direct contact with consumers, and geographic and product diversity. The same study also indicated that food manufacturers with strong brands also have superior market power. In addition, the Commission felt that brand loyalty, large, diversified product lines, a heavy investment in new-product development, and conglomerate affiliations were the sources of this power.

Market power is a dynamic feature of food markets. Large, dominant firms are supplanted by smaller, more vigorous competitors. Food retailers' power may be eroded by vending machines and the fast-food industry. Farmers may gain countervailing power against large buyers through their cooperatives and other marketing efforts. Few power positions have persisted for long in the industry. Even so, transitory power is a public policy concern. New laws and regulations will continue to be developed to regulate market power in the food industry.

In this book we are principally concerned with marketing policies and tools which influence food producers' market power. These range from the government farm price and income programs, discussed in Chapter 21, to the marketing cooperatives discussed in Chapter 13. In this chapter we will explore two other producer market power tools: marketing orders and agreements and cooperative bargaining associations.

MARKETING ORDERS AND AGREEMENTS

Marketing orders and agreements are unique self-help marketing tools intended to improve agricultural producers' prices, incomes, and market power. These marketing tools had their origin in the Agricultural Adjustment Act of 1933 and the 1937 Agricultural Marketing Agreement Act. Through these

---

[1] *Food from Farmer to Consumer,* Report of the National Commission on Food Marketing, Washington, D.C., June 1966, pp. 95–97.

instruments, farm product producers and handlers are authorized by law to engage in collective marketing activities, the objectives being to enhance the level and stability of producer returns. Marketing orders and agreements strive for more *orderly marketing*—a term that means profitable farmer management of commodities over time, form, and space.

Technically, marketing orders are different from marketing agreements, but both have the same goals and are normally used together. The principal difference is that agreements are purely voluntary arrangements between producers, handlers of farm products, and the Secretary of Agriculture on how a particular product will be marketed. In contrast, a marketing order is established by a majority vote of producers—whether or not handlers or buyers approve—and is legally binding on all producers and handlers of the commodity within the market order area. Because voluntary agreements often break down, and farm product buyers' interests do not always coincide with producer interests, today virtually all marketing agreements are reinforced by marketing orders.

Market orders and agreements may be authorized by either or both state or federal laws. Though not every state has such a law, state orders usually have the same objectives and work in the same fashion as federal orders. Marketing orders are authorized for a limited set of commodities, the most important of which are milk, fresh fruits and vegetables, tobacco, hops, peanuts, navel stores, turkeys, and apples for processing. Marketing orders are prohibited by law for many important commodities, including the major food grains and feedgrains: soybeans, livestock, poultry (except turkeys), and eggs. Milk, fruits, vegetables, and nuts account for the majority of market orders today.

In 1975 there were 30 federal fruit marketing orders in effect, 12 vegetable and potato orders, 3 nut orders, 1 peanut, and 1 hop order. These orders involved 144,000 producers and some $3.7 billion of farm products. California was involved in 14 of these orders, Washington in 9, and Florida in 8. There were 55 federal milk marketing orders in 1975, rather evenly scattered throughout the country.

Marketing order legislation is *enabling,* not *mandatory.* Agricultural producers petition for orders, and orders must be approved by two thirds of the producers or by producers accounting for two thirds of production. Separate orders are written for each commodity; and orders usually cover a limited geographic area. Many orders operate in conjunction with marketing cooperatives. The Secretary of Agriculture authorizes and supervises orders and is responsible for insuring that orders operate in the public interest. Administration of the terms of nonmilk marketing orders is in the hands of a board of directors composed of producers and handlers. Milk marketing orders are supervised by a market administrator appointed by the Secretary of Agriculture.

318

Marketing Order Provisions

The authority granted under market orders is broad and varies to accommodate a wide range of problems and producer objectives. Table 15-1 illustrates the variety of provisions contained in fruit, vegetable, and nut marketing orders. No two orders are alike. The most important provisions and uses of marketing orders are as follows:

1. To classify milk according to its use, set minimum producer prices, and to average (pool) returns to milk producers.
2. To manage the flow of commodities to market—either in total or by grade, size, or timing.
3. To establish producer or handler marketing allotments.
4. To control and equalize the burden of "surplus" production.
5. To regulate the size, capacity, weight, and other dimensions of pack or containers.
6. To set up market information, product inspection and standardization, and market research and development programs.
7. To establish systems for pooling or averaging returns to producers and handlers for different time, form, and spatial markets.
8. To prohibit unfair trading practices.
9. To engage in commodity advertising programs.
10. To regulate the grade, size, quality, and maturity of imported commodities.

Milk marketing orders provide for setting minimum producer prices, and even allow a limited form of production controls. However, other marketing orders do not give producers authority to set prices directly nor to control agricultural output. Instead, these orders provide producers a vehicle for indirectly influencing farm prices and returns—and, in turn, production—through control of product flows to market. In this sense, market orders complement government farm price and income programs, which have directly influenced farm production, prices, and incomes.

Orders As Monopolistic Devices

By providing the machinery for control over marketed supplies, marketing orders confer monopolistic power on agricultural producers which they would not have as individual sellers. Orders transform the farm marketing process from one of independent decisions on the part of many small firms to an imperfectly competitive process. The potential monopolistic gains from this market power result from control over total marketed supplies and control over the flow of supplies to time, form, and space markets.

Table 15-1. Fruit, Vegetable, and Nut Federal Marketing Agreements and Orders, May 1, 1974.

Area and Commodity	Grade	Size	Pack & Container	Flow to Market	Market Allocation	Reserve Pool	Producer Allotments	Research & Development	Advertising	Committee Headquarters
Fruits										
Florida citrus fruit	X	X		X						Lakeland, Florida
Texas oranges & grapefruit	X	X	X					X	X	Pharr, Texas
Calif.-Ariz. navel oranges		X		X				X		Los Angeles, Calif.
Calif.-Ariz. valencia oranges		X		X				X		Los Angeles, Calif.
Calif.-Arizona grapefruit	X	X		X				X		Phoenix, Arizona
Calif.-Arizona lemons		X		X				X		Los Angeles, Calif.
Florida limes	X	X	X	X				X	X	Homestead, Florida
Indian River grapefruit				X						Lakeland, Florida
Florida interior grapefruit	X			X						Lakeland, Florida
Florida interior oranges	X			X						Lakeland, Florida
Florida avocados	X	X	X					X	X	Homestead, Florida
California nectarines	X	X	X					X	X	Sacramento, Calif.
Calif. pears, plums & peaches	X	X	X					X	X	Sacramento, Calif.
Georgia peaches	X	X								Macon, Georgia
Colorado peaches	X	X						X		Palisade, Colorado
Washington peaches	X	X	X					X		Yakima, Washington
Washington apricots	X	X	X					X		Yakima, Washington
Washington cherries	X	X	X					X		Yakima, Washington
Wash.-Oreg. fresh prunes	X	X	X					X		Yakima, Washington
Idaho-Oreg. fresh prunes	X	X	X					X		Parma, Idaho
California Tokay grapes	X	X	X	X				X	X	Lodi, California

Commodity	1	2	3	4	5	6	7	Location
Oreg.-Wash.-Calif. winter pears	X	X	X				X	Portland, Oregon
Hawaii papayas	X	X				X	X	Hilo, Hawaii
10 States-cranberries	X	X				X	X	Wareham, Massachusetts
Mich.-N.Y.-Wisc.-Pa.-Ohio-Va.-W.Va.-Md.-cherries	X	X	X			X	X	Hartford, Michigan
Wash.-Oreg. bartlett pears	X	X	X				X	Portland, Oregon
California olives	X	X	X				X	Fresno, California
Vegetables								
Idaho-E. Oregon potatoes	X	X	X					Pocatello, Idaho
Washington potatoes	X	X	Pack					Moses Lake, Wash.
Oregon-Calif. potatoes	X	X	Pack			X	X	Redmond, Oregon
Colorado potatoes	X	X	X			X	X	Monte Vista and Greeley, Colorado
Maine potatoes	X	X	X					Inactive
Va.-North Carolina potatoes	X	X	X	X			X	Eastville, Virginia
Idaho-Oregon onions	X	X	X	X			X	Parma, Idaho
South Texas onions	X	X	X	X	X		X	Mercedes, Texas
Texas Valley tomatoes	X	X	X	X	X		X	Pharr, Texas
Florida tomatoes	X	X	X	X			X	Orlando, Florida
Florida celery	X	X	X	X	X	X	X	Orlando, Florida
South Texas lettuce	X	X	X	X	X		X	Mercedes, Texas
Dried Fruits and Nuts								
California almonds	X	X			X		X	Sacramento, Calif.
Oregon-Wash. filberts	X	X	Pack		X		X	Tigard, Oregon
Calif.-Oreg.-Wash. walnuts	X	X	Pack		X	X	X	San Mateo, Calif.
California dates	X	X	Cont.		X		X	Indio, California
California raisins	X	X		X	X		X	Fresno, California
Wash.-Idaho-Oreg.-Calif. hops	X	X		X		X	X	Portland, Oregon
California prunes	X	X	Pack	X		X	X	San Francisco, Calif.
146 peanuts (16 States Virginia to California)	X	X						Atlanta, Georgia

Source: U.S. Department of Agriculture, Agricultural Marketing Service.

Market order restrictions on quality, size, imports, and other market elements constitute a form of supply control for producers. This power can be used to raise farm prices above what they would be without supply controls. The advertising programs authorized by orders, if successful, have a similar effect on prices.

The control over flow of products to time, form, and space markets presents still another opportunity to enhance farm prices and returns through what is known as *economic price discrimination*. This practice, which is not illegal, rests on the notion that there is not one demand curve of a given elasticity for a commodity but several curves of differing elasticity. There may be a variety of elasticities of demand—according to cities, income levels of consumers, qualities of product, or seasons of the year. By wisely managing the flow of total supplies into these markets, differing prices may be established, which will result in greater total returns than if the same price is charged in all markets. The marketing strategy of price discrimination involves restricting supplies in the less demand-elastic markets and increasing supplies in the more elastic markets. Remember that total revenue rises when prices *increase* in an inelastic market and when prices *decrease* in elastic markets.

Three conditions are necessary for successful price discrimination. First, there must be more than one identifiable market in time, form, and space, with each market having a different elasticity of demand. This is a common situation for agricultural commodities. Second, a tool, or system, must permit a controlled allocation of the total supplies to each of these markets. The marketing order is tailor-made for this. Third, buyers in each of the markets must be persuaded to pay different prices for the product, and must be prevented from all purchasing in the lowest-priced market. The advertising, grading, sorting, and control of market flows provided by orders can help to accomplish this.

Price discrimination is a valuable marketing tool for farmers. It is also practiced by other food marketing agencies. A food processor who packs both a nationally advertised label and a nonadvertised label is practicing price discrimination. A food retail chain, operating full-service supermarkets, warehouse economy-food stores, and neighborhood convenience stores, also has the opportunity to practice economic price discrimination. Marketing orders, then, do not give producers extraordinary monopolistic power, but they do allow producers to do what others are doing in the food industry.

Evaluation of Marketing Orders

Marketing orders and agreements are intended to improve farm prices, returns, and incomes. Their record in doing so is mixed. Many orders have been judged successful on these criteria and have enjoyed a long life. Other orders have been discontinued after a short trial period or after several years.

Many proposed orders have failed to obtain the majority producer support necessary to put them into operation.

Each order must be evaluated separately and continuously, as must proposals for new orders on additional commodities. The principal results and achievements of successful market orders might be listed as follows:

1. More orderly marketing of farm products, with somewhat greater stability in farm returns.

2. Modest to inconsequential increases in farm prices.

3. Some transfer of market power and decision-making from marketing firms to producers and greater producer participation in the marketing process. Perhaps a psychological and morale-building gain for producers, who lose their price-taking status.

4. Some increase in farm product differentiation and increased farmer-controlled advertising of commodities.

5. The generating of considerable market information and research, contributing to improved market understanding.

Clearly, marketing orders do not solve all farm market power and price problems, but used with other marketing tools, they can be a valuable marketing device. However, their limitations and problems are evident.

For one thing, orders are not permitted on all products. Even if they were allowed for many of the excluded commodities, they would probably continue to find their widest use among the specialty crops, which are produced in geographically concentrated areas. Marketing orders have been least successful for commodities produced by large numbers of geographically scattered producers.

Nor do orders, except for milk, guarantee producers a price or income. They influence, but are not the only determinant of, prices. Also, orders involve a measure of coercion of the majority over the minority, and this is distasteful to many. Their compulsory nature results from the free-rider problem in agriculture.

The most important limitation, however, is their lack of control over agricultural production. Marketing orders cannot "cure" overproduction or surplus production. Indeed, to the extent that orders are successful in improving farm prices and incomes, they encourage entry into agriculture and supply expansion. Other farm and marketing programs directed at supply control are thus necessary to insure the effectiveness of orders and agreements.

Food marketing firms are also influenced by market orders. Farm product buyers lose a degree of market freedom because orders shift some marketing decisions to farmers, and marketing firms are thus obliged to follow the provisions of an order. In addition, food marketing firms' costs, sales, and prices are influenced by supply-restricting order provisions.

There is some debate about the extent to which market orders and agreements have affected consumers. Without production controls and price-setting authority, it is unlikely that nonmilk orders could significantly raise consumer prices over the long run. Price and supply stability would appear to be of some benefit to consumers so long as it was not accompanied by higher food prices. The severity of the impact of price discrimination upon consumers depends upon their willingness and ability to make product substitutions over time, form, and spatial markets. In each of these respects, milk marketing orders appear to have had a greater impact on consumer prices and supplies than nonmilk orders. (Milk marketing orders are discussed further in Chapter 24.)

COOPERATIVE BARGAINING ASSOCIATIONS

Agricultural producers may attempt to improve their market and bargaining power through the formation of bargaining associations. These cooperatives constitute a horizontal integration of producers and are organized to act as bargaining agents for farmers. Their principal purpose is to influence producer terms of trade through contractual negotiations with the buyers of farm products. Farmer bargaining associations are often compared to collective bargaining between labor unions and management; but there are important differences between wage bargaining and farm product price bargaining. The tendency toward decentralization, integration, and increasing size of food marketing firms has resulted in growing interest in both formal and informal farmer bargaining efforts.

Bargaining associations frequently operate in conjunction with farm marketing cooperatives and marketing orders. The major difference between the cooperative bargaining association and other marketing cooperatives is that the associations normally confine their activities to contract negotiations, whereas marketing cooperatives usually perform a wider range of services and functions for their patrons. And the difference between cooperative bargaining associations and the market order approach is that the former is of a voluntary nature and therefore not subject to government policing or enforcement.

Formal bargaining associations are not common in agriculture, but they are relatively important for a few commodities, notably milk and fruits and vegetables for processing. In 1973 there were approximately 300 agricultural bargaining associations in the United States. Some 11,000 fruit and vegetable producers marketed $200 million of produce through these associations; 5 sugar beet bargaining associations represented 28,000 growers; and 21 American Agricultural Marketing Associations—affiliates of the American Farm Bureau Federation—marketed some $5 million of fruits, vegetables, and livestock. The National Farmers Organization (NFO) is also essentially a bargaining association. Producer bargaining associations are probably most highly developed in milk markets, where bargaining is closely integrated with marketing cooperatives and federal and state marketing orders. Using both opponent-gain and opponent-pain bargaining tactics with processors of milk, producer milk cooperative/bargaining associations often have been successful in securing prices above the minimum levels specified in milk marketing orders.

Producer Bargaining Legislation

Agricultural producer bargaining associations are organized under the 1922 Capper-Volstead Act, which permits farmers to market collectively through a single agent without violating the antitrust laws. This law has an important stipulation—that cooperative membership be voluntary, a requirement that many feel limits the effectiveness of cooperative bargaining associations.

The agricultural marketing order and agreement legislation of the 1930's has reinforced the concept of farmer bargaining associations. Public support for farmer bargaining was further demonstrated in the Agricultural Fair Practices Act of 1968. This act prohibits food marketing firms from discriminating against producers who participate in bargaining activities or stopping producers from joining bargaining associations.

Many observers feel that additional laws and public support are necessary in order for agricultural bargaining associations to achieve their full potential. Several such bills were introduced into Congress in the early 1970's, collectively known as the "National Agricultural Bargaining Acts." Their provisions varied but in general they called for a National Agricultural Bargaining Board to oversee, facilitate, and mediate producer-buyer bargaining relations; some form of farm production controls; a broadening of the list of commodities eligible for marketing orders; producer authority to set minimum prices for commodities other than milk; and exclusive farmer bargaining agencies, with complete bargaining rights for all production, as well as power to require all producers to sell through the agency. There is much debate on the need for and the wisdom of these additional producer market power tools.

Problems and Potentials of Agricultural Bargaining ·

Agricultural cooperative bargaining associations can influence food markets in many ways. Clearly they have increased the role of farmers in the marketing and pricing processes. Although bargaining associations are not free to set any price they wish, the bargaining association does remove farmers from a pure price-taking status. These associations have also provided members with considerable market intelligence and understanding.

Through opponent-gain tactics, bargaining associations may well have increased operational efficiency in the food industry by encouraging cost-reducing and mutually advantageous terms of trade. Through opponent-pain and third-party-gain bargaining tactics, these associations also may have altered the distribution of the consumers' food dollar between producers and food marketing firms and, possibly, increased consumer food prices in the short run.

There are several limitations to the market and bargaining power that bargaining associations can provide farmers. These associations do not control agricultural supply. Most associations bargain for terms of trade and leave production decisions to members and to the buyers of farm products. Thus, if the association is successful in improving member prices and returns, it will also encourage increased production—which, over time, will build downward price pressures. Processor integration into agricultural production also complicates the bargaining association's supply-control problem.

The effectiveness of a bargaining association depends upon its having control over a substantial volume of the product to be marketed. This is particularly important where witholding threats or strikes are part of the bargaining strategy. The voluntary nature of cooperatives may prevent the co-op from gaining control over a sufficient volume of product to bargain effectively. Some producers will choose not to join the bargaining effort, because they object to giving up pricing decisions to the group, or perhaps because they are motivated by free-rider incentives. These considerations have favored the formation of bargaining associations for commodities which are produced by a relatively small number of geographically concentrated farmers.

Bargaining associations also need alternative marketing outlets to facilitate control of product flows to market. Some associations have vertically integrated into processing activities in order to provide alternative markets if the desired terms of trade are not achieved. Storage facilities serve the same purpose. Marketing order provisions also can assist associations in controlling market flows to achieve the association's goals.

Finally, the self-discipline of members and the skill of the bargaining association leaders are important to the bargaining effort. Bargaining frequently requires some sacrifice on the part of members. Leadership, group cohesion, and the financial ability to make short-term sacrifices for long-term gains are necessary. And the members as well as the leaders should have realistic goals for the bargaining process. Bargaining is a useful marketing tool, not a panacea for all price problems. In particular, bargaining association members and leaders must understand and appreciate both opponent-gain and opponent-pain bargaining power.

MARKETING BOARDS

Marketing boards are potent marketing agencies with the combined powers of cooperatives, marketing orders, and bargaining associations. They are quite common in Canada (over 120 boards in 1971) and are also operating in Australia, France, England, and Africa.

Marketing boards are essentially producer-controlled organizations with government monopoly power over a broad range of farm production and marketing activities. The chief functions of operating boards are:

1. Collective bargaining and price negotiation, acting as a single agent for all producers of the commodity.
2. Sole marketing agent for the commodity, with broad controls over all aspects of marketing, including the ownership of storage facilities.
3. Sponsorship of market-intelligence activities and market research.
4. Producer pooling arrangements to divide receipts among farmers.
5. Setting production and marketing controls and quotas.

Although there are not yet any operating marketing boards in the United States, and farmers have shown mixed interest in them, in 1966 the National Commission of Food Marketing recommended legislation to authorize food marketing boards as a useful tool for improving farmer bargaining power.[2]

SUMMARY

Market power is the ability to advantageously influence market outcomes in one's own favor. Bargaining power is concerned with influence over the terms of trade in negotiations. The balance of market power in the food industry is a subject of continuing concern. Producers, food marketing firms, and consumers all have a stake in the distribution and impacts of food marketing power. Three sources of gains from bargaining power are the opponent's loss, the opponent's gain, and third parties to the transaction. Several market conditions are associated with market power positions, including sizes and number of firms, supply control, access to information, product differentiation, and financial resources. Agricultural cooperatives, marketing orders and agreements, and bargaining associations are three complementary farmer market power tools. Each can contribute to solving the farm market power problem through orderly marketing and greater involvement of farmers in the marketing and pricing processes. The success of these marketing tools depends upon the organizational strength of farmers, the control over supply which they provide, and the skill with which farmers use these tools.

QUESTIONS FOR DISCUSSION

1. Explain why control of agricultural output is so important to the long-run success of a bargaining association whereas control of flow-to-market is so crucial to associations' short-term success.

---

[2] *Food from Farmer to Consumer,* Report of the National Commission on Food Marketing, Washington, D.C., June 1966, p. 110.

2. Give an example of opponent-gain and opponent-pain bargaining tactics with which you are familiar.

3. Is the present legislation adequate to achieve equality of bargaining power between producers and buyers of farm products? If not, what additional authority is needed?

4. In what ways is agricultural bargaining different from, and similar to, the collective bargaining of labor unions?

5. Which approach do you favor to solve the "farm market power problem": (1) reduce the power of farm product buyers; (2) increase the power of farmers? What difference does it make which approach is taken? Which approach is being used today?

6. How would you identify and measure market power in the food industry?

7. How is the consumer interest affected by each of the market power tools discussed in this chapter?

8. Should farmers be required to bargain and market their commodities through a central farmer-controlled agency? What percentage of farmers should agree to this approach in order to make it mandatory for all?

9. Why haven't marketing orders and bargaining associations been more widely used for livestock and grain products?

10. The price of farm products is determined by supply and demand conditions so farmer bargaining power can have no influence on prices." Comment.

SELECTED REFERENCES

ABEL, M. E., AND M. M. VEEMAN. "Marketing Boards." *Marketing Alternatives for Agriculture: Is There a Better Way?* U.S. Department of Agriculture. Public Policy Education Committee, Leaflet 7–10, 1976.

ARMBRUSTER, W. J. "Farm Bargaining Boards As an Agricultural Policy Tool." *Marketing and Transportation Situation.* U.S. Department of Agriculture. MTS-185, May 1972, pp. 22–25.

———— et al. "Marketing Orders." *Marketing Alternatives for Agriculture: Is There a Better Way?* U.S. Department of Agriculture. Public Policy Education Committee, Leaflet 7–9, 1976.

Bargaining in Agriculture: Potentials and Pitfalls in Collective Action. North Central Regional Extension Publication No. 30, University of Missouri, Columbia, C-911, June 1971.

BRANDOW, G. "Market Power and Its Sources in the Food Industry." *American Journal of Agricultural Economics* (Feb. 1969), 1–12.

BREIMYER, H. F. *Individual Freedom and the Economic Organization of Agriculture.* University of Illinois Press, Urbana, Ill., 1965.

DUBOV, I. "Market Power Problems of Agricultural Producers." *Journal of Marketing* (April 1962), 48–53.

Farmers in the Market Economy. Iowa State University Press, Ames, Iowa, 1964.

FOURAKER, L., AND S. SEIGEL. *Bargaining Behavior.* McGraw-Hill Book Company, New York, 1963.

FULLER, VARDEN. "Bargaining in Agriculture and Industry: Comparisons and Contrasts." *Journal of Farm Economics* (Dec. 1963), 1283–90.

GALBRAITH, J. K. *American Capitalism: The Concept of Countervailing Power.* Houghton-Mifflin, Boston, 1956.

HELMBERGER, P., et al. "Bargaining in Agriculture," *Journal of Farm Economics* (Dec. 1964), 1270–80.

—— AND S. HOOS. "Economic Theory of Bargaining in Agriculture," *Journal of Farm Economics* (Dec. 1963), 1273–80.

JAMISON, J. A., AND K. BRANDT. *Marketing Orders: Performance, Potential and Limitations,* Stanford University Food Research Institute, Stanford, Calif., July 1965.

KNUTSON, R. D. "Alternative Legislative Frameworks for Collective Bargaining in Agriculture." *Agricultural Organization in the Modern Industrial Economy,* NCR-20. Ohio State University, Columbus, 1968.

LADD, G. W. *Agricultural Bargaining Power.* Iowa State University Press, Ames, Iowa, 1964.

LANZILLOTTI, R. F. "The Superior Market Power of Food Processing and Agricultural Supply Firms—Its Relation to the Farm Problem." *Journal of Farm Economics* (Dec. 1960), 1228–47.

MOORE, J. R. "Bargaining Power Potential in Agriculture." *American Journal of Agricultural Economics* (Nov. 1968), 1051–58.

MORRISON, D. E. "Farm Bargaining Problems and Prospects." *Journal of Cooperative Extension* (Fall 1968), 80–87.

Price Impacts of Federal Market Order Programs. U.S. Department of Agriculture. Farmer Cooperative Service, Special Report No. 12, Jan. 7, 1975.

Proceedings of the National Conference of Bargaining Cooperatives, Annual, 1953–77. U.S. Department of Agriculture, Farmer Cooperative Service.

ROY, E. P. *Collective Bargaining in Agriculture.* Interstate Printers and Press, Danville, Ill., 1970.

SHAFFER, J. D., AND R. E. TORGERSON. "Exclusive Agency Bargaining." *Marketing Alternatives for Agriculture: Is There a Better Way?* U.S. Department of Agriculture. Public Policy Education Committee, Leaflet 7–6, 1976.

TORGERSON, R. E. *Producer Power at the Bargaining Table: A Case Study of S.109.* University of Missouri Press, Columbia, Mo., 1970.

CHAPTER 16

Market Information

"WE IN THE UNITED STATES probably have the best agricultural statistics in the world. Moreover, these statistics are constantly improving; they are becoming more accurate and more comprehensive. Farmers, businessmen, administrators, and legislators have come to rely more and more on statistics—to tell them what's happening, to show where their economic problems are, and to assist in finding answers or serving as a guideline both for current activities and planning ahead."*

Preview

- This chapter explores the several forms of market intelligence in the food industry—market information and news, market research and analysis, and situation and outlook reports.
- The roles of market information in decision-making, the competitive market processes, and how information contributes to the public interest are examined.
- A set of criteria which good market information should satisfy is given: comprehensiveness, accuracy, trustworthiness, confidentiality, timeliness, and equal access.
- The major public and private sources of food marketing information are explored, with emphasis on U.S. Department of Agriculture information services.
- Major problems and criticisms of market news and information are examined.
- An annotated bibliography of food marketing references is provided.
- Key concepts and terms:

bid and offer prices	market information
demand and supply conditions	market intelligence

---

* O. V. Wells, *Major Statistical Series of the U.S. Department of Agriculture,* U.S. Department of Agriculture, Agricultural Handbook No. 118, 1957.

market news

market research

market situation reports

market tone

outlook

spot and futures prices

Market information is a facilitating marketing function, and market intelligence is essential to a smooth, efficiently operating marketing system. Accurate and timely market information facilitates marketing decisions, regulates the competitive market processes, and lubricates the marketing machinery.

Market news, information, and research are the *lifeblood* of markets. Market information agencies take the pulse of the market (are sales active or sluggish?), measure the temperature of markets (are prices rising or falling?), and monitor the market's pressure (are supplies adequate, short, or in glut?). The market's history is recorded in statistical data series, and agencies offer a prognosis or estimate of the market's future health.

Everyone who produces, buys, and sells agricultural products is continuously amassing, revising, and using market information on prices, supplies, demand, and other market conditions. In addition, there are public and private agencies specializing in food marketing information and research.

ROLES OF MARKET INFORMATION

One important function of market information is to improve decision-making. Farmers use market information when selecting enterprises, changing production plans, making long-term investments, and deciding the when, where, and how of their marketing strategies. Food marketing firms, farmer cooperatives, farm organizations, and legislators also depend upon market information for good decision-making.

The role of market information is also important in the competitive market processes which regulate prices in the food industry. Although the perfectly competitive requirement of perfect information is unattainable, in the competitive process more information is better than less. Information is, accordingly, critical to the law of one price and to the price discovery process.

Although it is not widely recognized, market information also contributes to operational efficiency in the food industry. Without the widespread availability of market information, buyers and sellers would need to devote considerably more time and money to market search activities than they currently do. The value of information is evident in markets where firms will pay a high price to specialized agencies for profitable information.

PUBLIC AND PRIVATE FOOD MARKET INFORMATION

There are both publicly and privately sponsored sources of market information in the food industry. Much information is collected by businesses from their own market activities or is purchased from private market news and research companies. Large food companies maintain their own market analysis and research staffs to provide constant market intelligence. This information is usually not published, nor is it available to those outside the firm.

Some private market research companies in the food industry do publish their findings in addition to selling information to clients. The *Leslie Report,* for example, is a monthly crop estimate which is released just before the monthly U.S. Department of Agriculture crop estimates are made. The "Yellow Sheet," published by the *National Provisioner,* is a daily livestock price reporting service which is sold by subscription and also is widely distributed throughout the meat industry. The "Urner-Barry Report" is a similar daily price report for agricultural products, notably eggs.

Trade associations also compile and frequently publish market information about the food industry. Typically, these associations secure information from individual members on a confidential basis and then release summary averages. Organizations such as the American Meat Institute, the National Canners Association, the National Grocery Manufacturers of America, and the American Dairy Association carry on these informational activities.[1]

Other proprietary firms specialize in market research for a fee but do not publish their findings. They may evaluate the market potential for a new product, study how an older product may be revitalized, investigate overseas trade opportunities, design packaging, merchandising, and promotional programs, or perform a number of other services.

Public agencies play a major role in collecting, analyzing, and disseminating U.S. agricultural and food marketing information. The U.S. Department of Agriculture is the most important but not the only one of these agencies. A substantial public subsidy is involved in these federal, state, and local market information and news programs. Why should the public support a market information program for farmers and food marketing firms? There are two principal justifications for this public support. First, although farmers and food marketing firms are the direct beneficiaries of the programs, ultimately there are benefits to the consumer as a result of increased market efficiency and enhanced competition. Second, information has been considered a market *equalizer,* which strengthens the farmers' bargaining power when dealing with food marketing firms.

The appendix to this chapter provides an annotated bibliography of private and public food market information and news references.

---

[1] For a complete list of farm and food marketing trade associations see, M. Fisk, Ed., *Encyclopedia of Associations,* Gale Research Co., Detroit, Michigan, 1976.

CRITERIA FOR EVALUATING MARKET INFORMATION

To be of maximum benefit, market news and information must meet a number of criteria. First, information must be complete and comprehensive. This is a difficult task in a large country with a geographically dispersed agricultural plant producing over 200 different farm products and a food marketing system handling over 11,000 different supermarket items. Food market conditions also change frequently, further adding to the difficulty of providing complete market information.

A reasonably complete description of a food market includes prices, price trends, production, supply movements, stocks, and demand conditions at each level of the market. Food industry decision-makers benefit from market outlook assessments and forecasts of future market conditions, and farmers frequently find it helpful to learn of other farmers' production intentions. Providing such a mass of information, especially under the constantly changing conditions of food markets, is a formidable and expensive task. As a consequence, there are many gaps in food market news and information.

Accuracy and trustworthiness are also necessary criteria for market information. The credibility of the U.S. Department of Agriculture's market information reports and news services are highly protected assets. By its nature, market information can never be 100 per cent accurate, but it must be an honest market appraisal in order to earn the trust of information users. Considerable, and constant, efforts are made to improve the accuracy of market information and news services.

Information also must be relevant and in usable form. It is not enough to simply collect a mass of numbers and report them. Information must be collected, packaged, and disseminated with the user's interests in mind. Much market information goes unused because it is not in usable, easily accessible form.

Confidentiality is important to the U.S. Department of Agriculture market information and news services. Market prices and supply reports of individual firms are amassed to provide a general picture of the market without revealing information about any one firm. This has proven essential to programs which rely on voluntary reporting of market conditions.

Market information also must be timely, in the sense of being relevant to current decisions, and must be speedily transmitted to users. Much market information is highly perishable. Orbiting earth satellites, computers, and rapid telecommunications contribute to market information timeliness. The immediacy of information needs varies throughout the food system: futures market traders require minute-to-minute information, daily reports suffice for other traders, and monthly or annual reports are sufficient in other cases.

Finally, it is desirable to have a balance of market information at all levels of the food industry. Each marketing agency should have equal access to all the information relevant to the bargaining and marketing processes.

U.S. DEPARTMENT OF AGRICULTURE
INFORMATION PROGRAMS

Although the Departments of Commerce and Labor issue some reports of interest to farmers and food firms, in this book we emphasize the U.S. Department of Agriculture market information services. The large number and variety of these programs is illustrated in the appendix to this chapter. The USDA information programs can be divided into several categories: market news reports, market situation reports, outlook and forecasting services, statistical reports, and research reports.

The Federal-State Market News Service

Market news consists of descriptive information on current market conditions, such as prices, supplies, stocks, demand, and so on. This information can be used directly in market decisions. Market news quickly becomes obsolete and requires frequent updating—often hourly.

Prior to the establishment of the USDA market news service, rumor and hearsay were important factors in agricultural markets. Allegedly, farm prices could be "talked down" by an appropriate and well-placed rumor. There was no third-party check against these rumors. The more affluent could afford more information and therefore could take advantage of the less knowledgeable.

The first USDA market news report covered the movement and prices of strawberries at Hammond, Louisiana in 1915. USDA market news services were begun for meat in 1917, for livestock, dairy products, poultry, hay, grain, seeds, and feeds in 1918, for cotton in 1919, and for tobacco in 1931.

Today, nearly 1,000 USDA market news reports are issued daily. There is a separate USDA market news division for each of the major products—livestock, dairy products, poultry, grain, fruits and vegetables, cotton, and tobacco. In 1977, 43 of the 50 states cooperated with the USDA in collecting, disseminating, and sharing the costs of the public market news service.

Market news reporters stationed at the various important markets and production areas of the country collect much of the data for the market news reports. These men are specialists in their individual fields. The market information must be collected from the various individuals and agencies actively marketing the product. The information that agencies give might be incorrect or biased. The news reporter must be thoroughly acquainted with the market and the product so as to appraise the accuracy of the information obtained. For example, a livestock news reporter must be able to grade livestock and be thoroughly acquainted with the methods of the livestock trade. The same is true for the news reporter for each of the other commodities.

The 200 market news offices are tied together by leased wire and telephone services, as shown in Figure 16-1. With this communication system, information can be exchanged almost instantaneously with all other points in the country. Messages placed on the wire at any one point reach all other points on the circuit and, when desired, can be relayed to offices on other circuits. Daily, weekly, and monthly market news reports are available from selected markets. These may be received by mail, telephone, broadcast, or print media. Direct teletype connection to the market news service, through leased telephone wires, is available for a fee. In 1977 there were also 234 toll-free telephone market news message services in operation. A 24-hour "Washington farm report" toll-free message service is also available (800–424–7964). Table 16-1 shows the importance of the USDA market news reports to country elevator managers.

Market news reports have a special vocabulary for describing market conditions. *Market tone* refers to the general attitude of buyers and sellers toward prevailing prices; *market supplies* means all stocks currently in trading positions; and *demand* refers to the immediate desire, ability, and willingness of buyers to purchase at current prices. *Bid prices* are buyer offers, and *offer prices* are sellers' asking prices. *Spot prices* are current cash prices, and *futures prices* are the current prices at which commodities are traded for future delivery.

USDA Statistical Reporting Service[2]

The Statistical Reporting Service (SRS) is the chief fact-gathering arm of the USDA. Its mission is to report the basic statistical facts of the nation's food industry. It releases some 650 reports each year and covers 150 crops and 50 livestock items, as well as farm labor, fertilizers, seeds, prices paid and received by farmers, and other information. In addition to the Washington, D.C. headquarters, there are 44 state SRS offices.

The SRS is perhaps best known for its surveys of farmer production intentions and for periodic crop and livestock estimates during the year. The SRS Crop Reporting Board is responsible for these information programs.

A whole series of Crop Reporting Board reports covers the development of a particular crop. Prior to planting time there are reports of farmers' intentions to plant, which are followed later by reports on the number of acres actually planted. Then, throughout the growing season, there are prog-

---

[2] On January 1, 1978, three U.S. Department of Agriculture agencies—the Statistical Reporting Service, the Economic Research Service, and the Farmer Cooperative Service—were merged into a single agency: Economic, Statistics and Cooperative Service (ESCS).

Figure 16–1. Location of market news offices, 1970. (U.S. Department of Agriculture)

Table 16-1. Market Information Sources Used By Country Elevators, 1974.

SOURCE	FREQUENCY OF USE RANK	IMPORTANCE OF INFORMATION RANK
Telephone: merchants	1	1
Radio	2	4
Telephone: terminal and subterminal elevators	3	2
USDA: published reports	4	5
Newspaper	4	8
Telephone: processors	6	6
Face-to-face contact	7	10
Television	7	14
Telephone: head offices	9	3
Grain Instant News	10	7
Telephone: country elevators	11	11
USDA: telephone contact with price reporters	12	9
Bid cards	13	12
Reuters	14	16
USDA: recorded telephone reports	14	17
USDA: teletype	16	13
AP	17	18
Telephone: foreign buyers	18	15
UPI	18	19
Telex with buyers or sellers	20	20

Source: R. Heifner, et al., *The U.S. Cash Grain Trade In 1974,* U.S. Department of Agriculture, Agricultural Economic Report No. 386, September 1977.

ress reports and estimates made of the potential size of the crop. In this manner, long before the harvest is ready for market, various marketing agencies are well aware of what production volume to expect and can make the necessary plans and arrangements for handling it.

The procedures followed in securing, preparing, and releasing data are elaborate. The questionnaire, which has been designed to secure the needed information, is sent out from the various states to their list of cooperating reporters. When the questionnaires are returned to the state offices, they are checked, edited, and tabulated. The state statistician may even do some spot-checking in the field to verify the information. The final forms are then sent by special delivery to the Crop Reporting Board in Washington, D.C. Here the opening, tabulation, and releasing of the compiled data are done with the greatest of care to prevent information leaks. The following description of the final stages of this procedure will illustrate the great care used:

On the morning of the release of a report, the chairman of the board, the secretary of the board (who has the key for one lock), one other board member, and a representa-

337

tive of the Secretary of Agriculture (who has the key for the other lock), go to the locked room accompanied by an armed guard. There they unlock the mailbox and take the state reports to another room. The night before, the venetian blinds on all windows within this corridor have been lowered, closed, and sealed. No one may open or even adjust these blinds while the board is in session. All telephones in the wing have been disconnected, the door at the other end of the corridor is locked, and a guard is on duty outside. These are called the lock-up quarters.

When forecasts or estimates have been adopted for all states for a given crop, they are handed to the computing unit. The tables and stencils are prepared. Mimeograph machines are brought into the quarters the night before so that the report can be processed inside the locked corridor.

After approval by the Secretary of Agriculture, two or three minutes before the release time the chairman and secretary of the board leave the lock-up quarters and proceed under guard to the release room, looking neither to right nor left and speaking to no one nor acknowledging any greeting, according to regulations. In the release room telephone and telegraph instruments are already connected, and the operators are assembled in a prescribed space, out of reach of the instruments.

The chairman places one report face down beside each telephone and telegraph instrument. At the precise time, a representative of the Secretary of Agriculture says "go" and the various reporters rush to their instruments and begin sending out the reports.

Also at this time the information is sent to the various state offices for their release.[3]

This elaborate procedure is testimony to the value of the information. Estimates of the size of crops and other important information are immediately used in the buying and selling of products. An early information leak might be used by an individual for his personal advantage. To illustrate, suppose the last estimate of the wheat crop had been for a crop of 900 million bushels. The new estimate to be released, however, will reestimate the production figure to be 825 million bushels. Such a predicted reduction in the crop would no doubt at least temporarily strengthen prices. Someone with advance knowledge could have purchased wheat and profited by the short-run fluctuation.

USDA Economic Research Service

The Economic Research Service (ERS) is the analytical and interpretive arm of the USDA. Its market situation reports attempt to interpret and appraise the meaning of market conditions and developments for farmers, food marketing firms, and consumers. ERS outlook reports forecast future prices and market developments. ERS research reports present economic research findings and relationships or trends that will foster a better understanding of food markets.

---

[3] *The Agricultural Estimating and Reporting Services of the USDA,* U.S. Department of Agriculture, Miscellaneous Publication No. 703, December 1949, p. 13.

338

PROBLEMS OF MARKET NEWS AND INFORMATION

There are several problems regarding the collection, compilation, and dissemination of food market information that should be taken into account by users of the information.

Price Specification

The statement that cattle are selling for $40 per hundredweight is not very useful until other, more specific information is provided, for example: Where? When? What grade? What weight? How? These specifications are necessary to make a price quotation meaningful for decision-makers. Price has meaning only with reference to a particular time, form, and spatial market.

The wide range of qualities and uses of agricultural products adds to the food market information problem. The usefulness of price quotations depends upon uniform acceptance and application of grades and standards. For example, fresh fruit price quotations cannot be mixed with processed fruit prices. Feeder livestock conditions need to be reported separately from slaughter livestock conditions. Market information programs must be continuously revised to reflect buyer and seller needs as well as changing trade practices.

Net Versus Gross Price

Another complicating factor in market information programs is that publicly quoted figures are frequently not the actual price at which commodities are traded. Premium and discount schedules vary from place to place and from buyer to buyer. Some farm prices include allowances for marketing costs such as hauling, packaging, and other marketing activities. But because industry practices vary, making accurate price comparisons is very difficult.

Studies that report significantly higher (or lower) prices in one market as compared with another sometimes neglect the fact that buyer and seller responsibilities differ. Frequently, when all marketing and other costs are considered, net prices among competing markets are more similar than they at first appear to be.

The price comparability problem also arises at the retail level of food markets. Food prices at a cash-and-carry, low-service grocery store should not be compared, superficially, to prices at a full-service supermarket. The product bundles differ at these stores, and a simple gross price comparison fails to take these differences into account.

Information Costs

The cost of gathering and disseminating market information to the public requires that some choices be made. The value of more complete and more accurate information must be weighed against its costs.

Market information is not available for all commodities and is somewhat incomplete for all products. Thus there are continuing requests for more information. One group would like to see a market information program for riding horses or timber prices. Such requests led to the establishment of a USDA mink market news service in 1970. As new programs are added, old ones are dropped. USDA buckwheat reports were discontinued in 1964 because of the small amount of acreage involved. Should the USDA continue its molasses, hops, and navel stores (timber product chemicals) market reports?

The same amount of information is not available for all levels of the food industry. In general, much more is known about supplies, demand, and marketing at the farm level than at the retail level. Also, more complete information is available for products that are marketed principally through organized, central markets than for those moving through decentralized channels.

Some sacrifice in accuracy and timeliness probably results from a broadening of the range of commodities covered by USDA market news. For example, as their markets become more geographically dispersed and their commodity responsibilities broadened, market reporters rely more on telephone conversations with buyers and sellers than on personal market observation.

Changing Market Organization

Trends in farming and marketing have also complicated the food market information task. Because of decentralized, direct sales, products now bypass the central terminal markets, where at one time price reporters could fairly easily take the pulse of markets. Market reporters in these days must obtain information from more numerous and more geographically dispersed shipping-point markets, and the cost of obtaining accurate and complete information has risen accordingly.

Changing transportation patterns also alter the market information picture. At one time, railroad freight movement data adequately represented the supply flow of most farm products. Over time, the proportion of products moving by truck, barge, and even air has increased, and market information programs have had to adjust to these trends.

Contractual and ownership integration in farm and food markets present still another problem. Farmers who sign contracts specifying prices and other terms of trade in advance of product delivery need market information different from that needed by farmers who sell on the cash markets at harvest time. In addition, vertical integration of markets tends to "close-up" the marketing process and reduce cash price trading. Commodities change hands on the basis of prearranged agreements without being priced in open, organized markets. This adds to the difficulty of assessing market conditions, because much less of the commodity is moving through the channels monitored by the public market information programs.

340

Voluntary Cooperation

The USDA and the private market news and information programs depend upon the voluntary cooperation of buyers and sellers to report prices, supplies, and other market conditions. But because there is no mandatory requirement that they provide this information, many farmers and food marketing firms do not participate in the programs. Statistical techniques can compensate somewhat for the missing information and the resultant statistical bias. However, many observers feel that the voluntary nature of market information programs continues to be one of their principal limitations.

Voluntary reporting presents many problems. For instance, buyers and sellers may quote only those prices and conditions favorable to themselves; they may choose to quote "asking" or "bid" prices rather than actual selling prices. Because the public market information system is run on a voluntary basis does not mean that it is easily manipulated or that there is fraud, but it does complicate the food marketing information task. Of course, attempts to correct this situation through mandatory market reporting would pose different, but equally difficult, problems—those having to do with buyers' and sellers' freedom.

CRITICISMS OF MARKET INFORMATION PROGRAMS

Despite the value of food marketing information programs, these services have been severely criticized from time to time, especially by farmers. Typical criticisms are (1) the forecasts are usually inaccurate; (2) market reports inevitably depress farm prices; (3) market information is of greater value to buyers of farm products than to farmers; and (4) market reports are manipulated.

Many farmers have stated that the USDA crop and livestock intentions reports (intentions to plant crops, farrow pigs, or feed cattle) are of little value because they frequently prove to be wrong. There have been cases where predicted production varied considerably from actual production, because of inaccurate field reporting, sampling errors, and other factors. Such situations make a persuasive case for improving the methods of collecting market information and estimating future market conditions.

However, even if these sources of error were eliminated, intentions reports would never forecast with perfect accuracy the future of farm markets. In fact, intentions reports are not intended to be forecasts. (It is obvious that farmers may change their intentions after learning what other farmers intend to produce.) Although this makes the intentions reports "wrong" when measured against actual production, the reports nevertheless contribute to farmers' decisions. Weather and other unexpected events occurring between intentions to plant and harvest time may also make intentions reports "wrong."

Farmers also have frequently charged that farm supply reports usually depress farm prices. In evaluating this criticism it must be remembered that the purpose of market information is to inform traders and farmers, not to drive prices either up or down. Prices, of course, would be expected to move opposite to changes in reported supplies. In a series of reports in 1976 and 1977, researchers found that, immediately following USDA market reports, crop and hog prices rose just as frequently as they fell, and that prices *after* the reports were issued often continued in the same direction they had been moving prior to the reports.[4]

Farmers have also expressed the belief that USDA market news and information benefits the buyers of farm products more than it benefits farmers. There is some truth to this, because food marketing firms are generally more flexible, and can more easily adjust to market conditions than can farmers. However, this does not build a persuasive case against farmers' participation in and support for USDA information services. Farmers *can* use this information in their decisions, and without a public market information program food marketing firms would have much more market information—and probably even greater bargaining power—than farmers.

Finally, there are persistent charges of bias, misrepresentation, and manipulation of market news and information reports. These allegations are leveled against both private and public market information sources. Again, such charges probably make a stronger case for improving market information services than for discontinuing them.

INFORMATION USERS' RESPONSIBILITIES

The finest information system in the world will contribute little to the efficient working of the marketing system unless it is wisely used by those wishing to buy or sell products. Farmers, for example, must seek out and compare the information available for different outlets if they are to sell to the best advantage. The same is true of homemakers in their buying activities. It is probably an unfortunate truth that our informational system is only haphazardly used. Study after study has indicated that opportunities exist to make money by becoming better informed.

There are many indications that in the future individuals will have to assume more responsibility in collecting and evaluating their own market information. As marketing becomes more decentralized and integrated and nonprice competition increases, centralized market news agencies will furnish less meaningful information. Selling agricultural products becomes more like buying a household appliance. The only way to find out about the market may be to shop around, compare, and then choose!

---

[4]*Agricultural Situation,* U.S. Department of Agriculture, August 1976, pp. 2–5; April 1977, pp. 2–6; August 1977, pp. 2–4.

An educational program for the users of the information is also needed. Only in this way will data be used for the purposes for which they were intended and nothing more. The use of price ranges instead of single specific prices is an example of the misunderstanding of information. In many markets, because of the number and variation of the transactions, the reporting of a specific meaningful price is not possible. Only a price range represents the true picture. However, some of the users of the information desire a single quotation and criticize the use of price ranges. This demonstrates the misunderstanding of the mechanics of the marketing and price-making process. All things considered, securing adequate dissemination and wise use of information present problems no less difficult than those involved in collection.

SUMMARY

Information and market intelligence are critically important to the efficient functioning of farm and food markets. As a facilitating marketing function, market information improves the decision-making of firms and enhances the competitive processes in food markets. Market information must be comprehensive, accurate, trustworthy, confidential, timely, understandable, and fairly distributed throughout the marketplace. The U.S. food industry has an elaborate network of public and private market information services. The U.S. Department of Agriculture provides food market news, market outlook and forecast reports, market situation and analysis reports, and market research and statistical reports. These services have their limitations and are the subject of frequent criticism. Nevertheless, the USDA information programs contribute to market efficiency and a better balance of information between farmers and the buyers of farm products. Market information programs must continually adjust to market trends and user needs.

QUESTIONS FOR DISCUSSION

1. Discuss the rationales given for public support of food marketing information programs. Do you see any trends that might alter this public support?

2. Contrast advertising (as a form of market information for consumers) with the market information available to farmers and food marketing firms.

3. It is frequently observed that farm prices change very little after the release of a USDA estimate which greatly differs from previous estimates. Can this be explained by the growth in private market news services? How?

4. "Farmer planting intentions reports in the spring always turn out to be wrong at harvest time, so they shouldn't be published." Comment.

5. What revisions in the procedures of market news collecting and reporting are made necessary by decentralization and integration of food markets?

6. If you were a market reporter and observed the following prices and sales of apples, what price would you say apples sold for today:

Time	Per cent of daily sales	Price per bushel Standard grade	Fancy grade
8:00 AM	10%	2.00	2.50
10:00 AM	20	1.80	3.00
11:00 AM	5	2.25	2.50
1:00 PM	50	2.35	3.00
2:00 PM	20	2.16	2.90
3:00 PM	5	4.00	5.00
	100%		

7. From *Crop Production* (USDA), record the intended acreage, indicated yield, expected production, final acreage, yield, and production for a crop over a season. How much did these change? Why?

8. If you were a farmer, what would determine your willingness to supply accurate information to government reporters? Is there a free-rider problem in a voluntary market news system?

9. How could a consumer make use of the USDA food market information programs?

SELECTED REFERENCES

"Crop and Livestock Estimates." *Major Statistical Series of the U.S. Department of Agriculture, How They Are Constructed and Used,* Vol. 8. U.S. Department of Agriculture. Agricultural Handbook No. 365, May 1971.

"Market News." *Major Statistical Series of the U.S. Department of Agriculture, How They Are Constructed and Used,* Vol. 10. U.S. Department of Agriculture. Agricultural Handbook No. 365, 1972.

MOULTON, K., AND D. I. PADBERG. "Mandatory Public Reporting of Market Information." *Marketing Alternatives for Farmers: Is There a Better Way?* Leaflet No. 7-5, National Public Policy Education Committee, Cornell University, Ithaca, New York, 1976.

Statistical Reporting Services of the U.S.D.A. U.S. Department of Agriculture. Miscellaneous Report No. 967, 1964.

The Story of U.S. Agricultural Estimates. U.S. Department of Agriculture. Miscellaneous Publication No. 1088, April 1969.

Appendix

Annotated Bibliography: Food Marketing Research, Information, and News

The literature of food marketing research, information, and news is vast. No one can read it all. Nevertheless, the student of food marketing must be acquainted with available reference sources. These include industry studies and reports, government publications, books, and periodicals. The references range from the specific to the general, from the highly technical to those written for lay readers, and from highly perishable market news to enduring, classic studies of food marketing. The following references are organized along the general outline of this text.

1. General Marketing and Economic References

A. BIBLIOGRAPHIES

These references contain a wealth of information on food and food marketing. Articles and studies may be classified by general subjects (e.g., food, food regulations, cooperatives, etc.) or by commodities (e.g., beef, grains, cotton, etc.).

Bibliography of Agriculture. Monthly. National Agricultural Library, Ornyx Press.

Business Periodicals Index. Monthly. H. M. Wilson Co.

Marketing Information Guide. Monthly. Trade Marketing Association.

Monthly Catalog of U.S. Government Publications, U.S. Government Printing Office.

Readers Guide to Periodical Literature. Monthly. H. M. Wilson Co.

B. PERIODICALS AND REPORTS

These references provide economic and marketing information of general interest to the food industry. They frequently contain specific articles on food industry products, trends, problems, and firms.

Advertising Age. Weekly newspaper. General marketing information, merchandising, advertising, regulations.

Barrons. Weekly newspaper. Commercial news, industry and company reports and trends.

Business Week. Weekly magazine. Economic news, market analysis, firm and industry reports.

Economic Indicators. Monthly report of the U.S. Council of Economic Advisors. Summary of major U.S. economic statistics, prices, output, employment, etc.

Forbes. Monthly magazine. Investment news, firm and industry studies.

Fortune. Bimonthly magazine. General economic trends, industry and firm reports.

Journal of Commerce. Daily newspaper. Economic and commerce news, international markets.

Journal of Marketing. Quarterly journal. General marketing studies, abstracts of the marketing literature, review of market regulations, book reviews.

Statistical Abstract of the U.S. Annual; *Historical Statistics of the U.S., Colonial Times to 1970.* U.S. Government Printing Office. Summary of all government statistical series relating to economics and food markets.

Survey of Current Business. Monthly. U.S. Department of Commerce. Current economic statistics and trends, food industry sales statistics.

Wall Street Journal. Daily newspaper. General economic and market news, farm prices, analysis of farm and futures prices.

2. General Food Marketing References

A. MAJOR STUDIES OF THE FOOD INDUSTRY

Large-Scale Organization in the Food Industries. Temporary National Economic Committee, Monograph No. 35, Washington, D.C., 1940.

Food from Farmer to Consumer. Report of the National Commission on Food Marketing. U.S. Government Printing Office, June 1966. General Report plus ten industry technical studies.

Agricultural Markets in Change. USDA, Agricultural Economic Report No. 95, July 1966. Separate chapters on each commodity and market functions.

Food and Fiber for the Future. Report of the National Advisory Commission on Food and Fiber. U.S. Government Printing Office, July 1967. Broad study of food industry, including food policy and food marketing system.

Market Structure of the Food Industries. USDA, Marketing Research Report No. 971, Sept. 1972.

B. FOOD MARKETING BOOKS

Breimyer, H. F. *Economics of the Product Markets in Agriculture.* Iowa State University Press, Ames, Iowa, 1976.

Dahl, D. C., and J. W. Hammond. *Market and Price Analysis, The Agricultural Industries.* McGraw-Hill Book Company, 1977.

Darrah, L. B., *Food Marketing.* The Ronald Press Company, New York, 1971.

Hampe, E. C., Jr., and M. Wittenberg. *Food Distribution: The Development of the Food Industry.* McGraw-Hill Book Company, New York, 1964.

McLaughlin, D. J., Jr., and C. A. Mallowe, *Food Marketing and Distribution Selected Readings,* Chain Store Age Publishing Co., New York, 1971.

Moore, J. R., and R. G. Walsh. *Market Structure of the Agricultural Industries.* Iowa State University Press, Ames, Iowa, 1966.

Shepherd, G. S., and G. A. Futrell. *Marketing Farm Products.* Iowa State University Press, 5th Ed., Ames, Iowa, 1970.

Waugh, F. V. *Readings on Agricultural Marketing.* Iowa State College Press, Ames, Iowa, 1954.

C. JOURNALS AND TECHNICAL REPORTS

Agriculture and the Third Century. Issued several times a year. USDA, Economic Research Service. Summary of ERS economic projections of U.S. food and fiber production, use, and trade for the future for several major commodities.

Agricultural Economics Research. Quarterly journal. USDA, Economic Research Service. Technical articles on agricultural economics research, frequent marketing topics.

American Journal of Agricultural Economics. Quarterly journal. American Agricultural Economics Association. Technical articles on agricultural economics subjects, with occasional marketing topics.

Food Policy. Quarterly journal. Food policy analysis, international food policies.

Mergers and Acquisitions. Quarterly journal. Information on mergers in the food industry.

USDA Technical Bulletins. Issued periodically. USDA. Occasional reports of interest in food marketing, demand, and price analysis.

D. STATISTICAL REFERENCES

Agricultural Statistics. Annual. U.S. Government Printing Office. Comprehensive statistics on all important trends in agriculture.

Census of the U.S. U.S. Bureau of Census. U.S. Government Printing Office:
- *Agriculture Census.* 1925–35–45–54–59–64–69–73.
- *Business Census.* 1948–54–58–63–67–72.
- *Manufacturing Census.* 1935–54–58–67–72.
- *Population Census.* Every 10 years.

Commodity Year Book. Annual. Commodity Research Bureau. Statistical data on raw commodity prices.

Handbook of Agricultural Charts. Annual. USDA, Agricultural Handbook series. Charts and tables of key agricultural and economic trends.

USDA Statistical Bulletins. Issued periodically. USDA. Summary agricultural market statistics.

E. SEMI-TECHNICAL, POPULAR REPORTS

Agricultural Economic Reports. Issued periodically. USDA, Economic Research Service. Food industry studies, food industry trends.

Agricultural Outlook. Monthly. USDA, Economic Research Service. Outlook for food supplies and prices, commodity analysis, food marketing trends, food consumption, world agriculture, farm income, general economics. This publication replaces the *Marketing and Transportation Situation,* the *Demand and Price Situation,* the *Farm Income Situation,* and *Agricultural Outlook Digest.*

Agricultural Handbook Series. Issued periodically. USDA. Studies of food grades and standards, food transportation, food inspection, and other marketing topics.

Agricultural Information Bulletins. Issued periodically. USDA. Occasional bulletins on food marketing topics.

Agricultural Situation. Monthly. USDA, Statistical Reporting Service. Popular reports of USDA market research studies, farm developments, agricultural trends; summary of key agricultural statistics; review of agricultural research.

Economic Research Service Reports. Issued periodically. USDA, Economic Research Service. Economic trends and food industry studies.

Farm Index. Monthly. USDA, Economic Research Service. Economic research findings, digest of agricultural outlook, leading economic indicators, agricultural trends.

Feedstuffs. Weekly newspaper. The weekly newspaper of agribusiness; industry trends, problems, and developments.

National Food Situation. Quarterly. USDA. Price and market outlook; food prices, expenditures, and consumption; USDA food programs; Comparative living costs; population trends; food demand.

USDA Marketing Bulletins. Issued periodically. USDA. Information on government market services, market news.

USDA Marketing Research Reports. Issued periodically. USDA. Many studies of food marketing trends, consumer preferences, market developments, and industry studies.

3. Farming and Farm Market References

A. GENERAL AGRICULTURE

Changes in Farm Production and Efficiency. Annual. USDA, Economic Research Service. Farm production, production inputs, and efficiency trends.

Crop Production, by States. Monthly. USDA, Crop Reporting Board. Prospective plantings, planted acreage, indicated yield, and expected production of major farm commodities over the production and marketing seasons. Annual summary in January.

Farm Futures. Monthly magazine. Farm market developments and outlook; farm marketing strategies.

Farm Numbers. Annual in May. USDA. Number of farms in operation and land in farms.

Farm Population Estimates. Annual. USDA. Estimates of current farm population, geographic location of farmers.

Farm Production Expenditures. Annual in May. USDA. Farm costs and expenses.

Progressive Farmer. Monthly magazine. Frequent articles on farm marketing topics.

Successful Farming. Monthly magazine. Emphasis on farm management, including farm marketing.

Weekly Weather and Crop Bulletin. Weekly. National Oceanography and Atmospheric Administration. Summarizes weather and its effects on crops for previous weeks, by states. Weekly summaries of world weather conditions.

B. FARM INPUTS AND SUPPLIES

Agri Finance. Monthly magazine. Topics on farm management and farm finance.

Agricultural Finance Outlook. Quarterly. USDA. Prospects for future farm finance.

Agricultural Finance Review. Annual. USDA. Developments and research in farm finance; farm and rural credit; financial management; agribusiness financial institutions.

Balance Sheet of the Farming Sector. Biennial. USDA. Farm assets, liabilities, and net worth.

Farmer Credit Association Research Journal. Biennial. USDA. Research on farm credit associations.

Agri-Marketing. Monthly magazine. Articles of interest to those selling to the farm market; agricultural trends; sales management.

Commercial Fertilizer. Monthly. USDA. Consumption of fertilizers, by class.

Fertilizer Situation. Annual in December. USDA. U.S. fertilizer use in past year; potential demand and supplies in coming year; foreign trade in fertilizer.

Farm Labor. Quarterly. USDA. Family and hired employment on farms; wage rates.

Hired Farm Working Force. Annual. USDA. Ethnic groups, sex, age, wages, duration of time in farm employment, education, and other characteristics of the hired farm labor force.

Farm Real Estate Market Developments. Midsummer. USDA. Trends in farmland values; land costs per state; financing.

Implement and Tractor. Bimonthly magazine. Farm equipment news and market analysis.

4. Food Consumption References

Current Population Reports. Issued periodically. U.S. Bureau of the Census. Trends in consumer income, sociodemographic characteristics of population, family trends, population growth and projections.

Family Economics Review. Quarterly. USDA. Family food consumption, food prices, retail price outlook, occasional reports on food-consumption trends.

Food Consumption, Prices, and Expenditures. Annual. USDA, Statistical Bulletin No. 364, June 1965; Agricultural Economic Report No. 138, July, 1968, plus annual supplements. Comprehensive sources of food consumption and price statistics, 1909 to present.

Food Consumption Statistics, 1955–1973. Organization for Economic Co-operation and Development. Paris, 1975. Per capita food consumption of 44 countries over the 1955–72 period.

Food Market Alert. Issued periodically. USDA. Periodic reports of food supplies in abundance.

Survey of Buying Power. Annual in June. *Sales Management* Magazine. Population characteristics of major markets.

5. Food Processing References

Canner/Packer. Monthly magazine. Analysis of processed food markets, particularly canned foods.

Food Product Development. Monthly magazine. Market research and development of new foods.

Food Processing. Monthly magazine. Developments in food processing techniques and equipment.

6. Food Wholesaling and Retailing References

Chain Store Age: Supermarkets. Monthly magazine. Analysis of supermarket trends, merchandising, consumer buying patterns.

Cold Storage Report. Monthly. USDA. Report of cold storage food stocks for meats, fruits, vegetables, and dairy and poultry products.

Nation's Restaurant News. Monthly magazine. Trends in restaurant and fast-food industry.

Progressive Grocer. Monthly magazine. Food retail developments; market analysis; merchandising; annual survey of food retailing in spring.

Selected Research Abstracts of Reports Pertaining to the Food Service Industry. USDA, Dec. 1969. Review of food-service literature; restauranting, institutional food market.

Supermarket News. Weekly newspaper. Developments in food wholesaling and retailing; government regulations; industry reports.

7. Agricultural Trade References

Export Outlook. Quarterly. USDA, Economic Research. Prospects for trade, market analysis; February issue gives a forecast for next fiscal year.

Food Marketing in Developing Countries: An Annotated Bibliography. U.S. Agency for International Development. Bibliography Series No. 6, Dec. 1971.

Foreign Agricultural Economic Report. USDA, Economic Research Service. Foreign market analysis.

Foreign Agricultural Trade of the U.S. Monthly. USDA, Economic Research Service. Current status and outlook for U.S. agricultural trade; government trade programs; price developments; ocean freight rates; export shares by states and countries; annual export statistics.

Trade Yearbook. Annual. U.N. Food and Agricultural Organization. Trade statistics of the world.

World Agricultural Production and Trade. USDA, Foreign Agricultural Service. World trade conditions and analysis.

World Agricultural Situation. Three times per year. USDA, Economic Research Service. Appraises world agriculture for current year—output, use, trade; trends and policy developments by regions.

World Agricultural Conditions in Relation to Agricultural Trade. Biennial. USDA, Economic Research Service. Review of economic growth conditions in developed and developing countries; trends in international finance and trade; implications for the U.S.; contribution of agriculture to the U.S. balance of payments.

8. Supply, Demand, and Price References

Agricultural Prices. Monthly. Annual June summary. USDA, Statistical Reporting Service. Monthly prices of major commodities; prices paid by farmers; feed-price ratios; farm energy costs.

Consensus. Weekly newspaper. Reproduces commodity brokerage house reports, government reports, and futures market charts.

Agricultural Supply and Demand Estimates. Monthly. USDA, Economic Research Service. USDA forecast of supply/demand balance for major commodities.

Consumer Price Index. Monthly. U.S. Department of Labor. Prices of all goods and services, by months, including food.

Estimated Retail Food Prices by City. Monthly. U.S. Department of Labor. Monthly retail prices of 100 food items in 24 major metropolitan markets.

Wholesale Price Index. Monthly. U.S. Department of Labor. Wholesale prices of food and nonfood products.

9. Marketing Cost References

Developments in Marketing Spreads for Agricultural Products. Annual. USDA. Interpretation and analysis of market margins and costs.

Price Spreads for Farm Foods. Monthly. USDA. Farm-to-retail price spreads for a market basket of farm foods and for selected foods—beef, milk, pork, bread, etc.

Quarterly Financial Report for Manufacturing, Mining, and Trade Corporations. Quarterly. Federal Trade Commission. Financial data for food firms, including profits.

Statistics of Income. Annual. U.S. Internal Revenue Service. Profit-and-loss statements and balance sheets for food processors, wholesalers, and retailers.

Weekly Estimates of Prices and Price Spreads for Beef and Pork. Weekly. USDA. Weekly marketing margin trends for beef and pork.

10. Agricultural Cooperative References

Farmer Cooperative Service Reports. Issued periodically. USDA. Studies of farm cooperative trends and problems.

News for Farmer Cooperatives. Monthly. USDA, Farmer Cooperative Service. Popular articles on cooperative developments, laws, and trends.

Statistics of Farmer Cooperatives. Annual. USDA Farmer Cooperative Service. Statistical trends in cooperative numbers, sizes, services, and other factors.

11. Government and Agriculture References

FDA Papers. Monthly magazine of the U.S. Food and Drug Administration. FDA regulations and activities.

Agriculture-Food Policy Review. Issued periodically. USDA, Economic Research Service. Analysis of farm policy programs and implications. Recommendations for policy improvements.

12. Livestock and Meat References

Feedlot Management. Monthly magazine.

National Livestock Producer. Monthly magazine.

National Provisioner. Weekly magazine. Developments in processed meats.

Calf Crop. Biennial. USDA, Statistical Reporting Service. Number of calves born during previous year by states, and number of calves expected to be born during current year.

Cattle and Calves on Feed. Monthly and quarterly. USDA, Statistical Reporting Service. Number of cattle on feed, by states, classes, and weight groups; cattle sold for slaughter at selected markets.

Commercial Livestock Slaughter and Meat Production. Monthly plus annual summary in April. USDA, Statistical Reporting Service. Number of head and live weight of cattle, calves, hogs, sheep, and lamb; commercial slaughter by states; meat production by species.

Hog and Pigs. Quarterly. USDA, Statistical Reporting Service. Inventory of animal numbers; farrowings for past quarter, farrowing intentions for future quarter; pig crop.

Livestock and Meat Market News. USDA, Agricultural Marketing Service:
- *Livestock and Meat Statistics.* Annual.
- *Livestock, Meat and Wool Market News, Weekly Summary.* Weekly.
- *Federally Inspected Slaughter Report.* Daily.

Livestock and Meat Situation. Monthly. USDA, Economic Research Service. Market outlook for cattle, hogs, sheep, lambs; livestock on farms; foreign trade in meat.

Livestock, Meat, Wool Market News. Weekly. USDA, Consumer and Marketing Service. Livestock market receipts, feeder cattle, slaughter, Chicago futures prices, wholesale meat prices, imports.

Meat Animals, Farm Production, Disposition, and Income. Annual, in April. USDA, Statistical Reporting Service.

Sheep and Lambs. Three times per year. USDA, Statistical Reporting Service. Number of sheep and lambs on feed.

13. Dairy Market References

Dairyman's Digest. Monthly magazine. Dairy industry trends and developments.

Dairy Record. Monthly magazine. General dairy industry news.

Hoard's Dairyman. Monthly magazine. Dairy production, marketing, and public policy.

Dairy Market News Service. USDA, Agricultural Marketing Service:
- *Cheese Reports.* Daily.
- *Fluid Milk and Cream Reports.* Daily.
- *Processed Milk Products.* Daily.
- *Wholesale Butter Reports.* Daily.

Dairy Products. Monthly, plus June summary. USDA, Statistical Reporting Service. Production and prices of butter, cheese, dry milk, whey.

Dairy Situation. Quarterly. USDA, Economic Research Service. Dairy industry trends, statistics, developments; interpretations of industry trends.

14. Poultry Market References

Eggs, Chickens, and Turkeys. Monthly. USDA, Statistical Reporting Service. Number and value of chickens and turkeys on farms; eggs per 100 layers; potential layers; intentions to breed turkeys.

Egg Industry. Monthly magazine. Egg market developments.

Poultry and Egg Situation. Quarterly. USDA, Economic Research Service. Poultry and poultry market developments, trends, and problems. Analysis of poultry market prices, supplies, and demand.

Poultry Market News Service. USDA, Agricultural Marketing Service:
- *Commercial Egg Movement Report.* Weekly.
- *Egg Inventory Report.* Weekly.
- *National Market-At-a-Glance.* Daily.
- *Poultry Slaughter Report.* Weekly.
- *Weekly Chick and Egg Placement Report.* Weekly.

15. Grain and Feed Market References

Feed Situation. Quarterly. USDA, Economic Research Service. Supply, demand, price, and outlook for feedgrains, wheat, soybeans, and related products.

Grain and Feed Market News. USDA, Agricultural Marketing Service:
- *Cash Grain Price Reports.* Daily.
- *Dry Edible Bean Reports.* Weekly.
- *Feedstuffs Price Reports.* Weekly.
- *Hay Reports.* Daily and weekly.
- *Hops Reports.* Weekly.
- *Molasses Reports.* Weekly.
- *Rice Reports.* Daily and weekly.

Rice Situation. Quarterly. USDA, Economic Research Service. Economic and market developments in rice industry.

Stocks Reports. USDA, Statistical Reporting Service:
- *Grain Stock.* Quarterly.
- *Hops Stocks.* Biannual.
- *Onion Stocks.* Annual.
- *Peanut Stocks.* Monthly.
- *Potato Stocks.* Issued periodically.
- *Rice Stocks.* Quarterly.

Wheat (and Rye) Situation. Quarterly. USDA, Economic Research Service. Wheat production, stocks, consumption, prices, and trade.

16. Fruit and Vegetable Market References

Fruit and Vegetable Market News. USDA, Agricultural Marketing Service. Reports for 100 fruits and vegetables, 40 ornamentals, peanuts, pecans, honey, Christmas trees, and beeswax:
- *Air Shipments.* Daily.
- *Carlot Shipments, by Commodities, States and Markets.* Annual.
- *Fresh Fruit and Vegetable Prices, Chicago, New York and Leading Shipping Areas.* Annual.
- *Honey Report.* Issued periodically.
- *Market Arrivals and Unloads.* Daily.
- *National Shipping Point Trends.* Weekly.
- *Peanut Report.* Weekly.
- *Pecan Report.* Issued periodically.
- *Rail and Boat Shipments.* Daily.
- *Shipping Point Market Reports.* Daily.
- *Terminal Market Reports, 41 cities, 23 terminals.* Daily.
- *Truck Shipments.* Daily.
- *Wine Reports.* Issued periodically.

Fruit Situation. Quarterly. USDA, Economic Research Service. Market and production developments in fruit.

Packer. Weekly newspaper. Fresh fruit and vegetable industry news.

Vegetable Situation. Quarterly. USDA, Economic Research Service. Market developments and trends in vegetables.

17. Oilseed, Fats, and Oils Market References

Fats and Oils Situation. Quarterly. USDA, Economic Research Service. Production, consumption, stocks, prices, and trade in oilseeds and fats and oils.

Soybean Digest. Blue Book Issue, annual in March. American Soybean Association. Summary of industry statistics.

Soybean Stocks. Annual in September. USDA, Statistical Research Service.

U.S. Fats and Oils Statistics, 1961–76. USDA, Statistical Bulletin No. 574, June 1977. Summary statistics.

18. Cotton and Wool Market References

Cotton Market News. USDA, Agricultural Marketing Service:
- *Area Weekly Cotton Market Review.* Weekly.
- *Area Weekly Cottonseed Review.* Weekly.
- *Cotton Price Statistics.* Monthly and annual.
- *Cotton Varieties Planted, U.S.* Annual.
- *Mills Margins Reports.* Monthly and annual.
- *Monthly Long Staple Cotton Review.* Monthly.
- *Spot Cotton Quotations.* Daily.
- *Weekly Cotton Market Review.* Weekly.
- *Weekly Quality of Cotton Classed Reports.* Weekly.

Cotton Situation. Quarterly. USDA, Economic Research Service. Cotton market developments.

Wool Situation. Quarterly. USDA, Economic Research Service. Domestic wool situation, outlook, prices, production, consumption, imports, world production, textile imports.

19. Tobacco Market References

Tobacco Market News. USDA, Agricultural Marketing Service:
- *Annual Market Reviews.* Annual.
- *Annual Report on Tobacco Statistics.* Annual.
- *Daily Press Release.* Daily.
- *Daily Price Report.* Daily.
- *Daily Sales Report.* Daily.
- *Season News Report.* Seasonal.
- *Tobacco Stocks Report.* Annual.
- *Weekly News Report.* Weekly.

Tobacco Situation. Quarterly. USDA, Economic Research Service. Tobacco market developments, industry trends.

20. Other Commodities

Naval Stores Market News. USDA, Agricultural Marketing Service:
- *Crude Pine Gum*
- *Dispetene*
- *Distilled Wood Turpentine*

357

- *Gum Spirits of Turpentine*
- *Pine Oil*
- *Rosin Oil*
- *Tall Oil*

International Sugar Journal. Monthly magazine. Sugar market developments.

Sugar and Sweetner Situation. Quarterly. USDA, Economic Research Service. Analysis of sugar market production, prices, consumption.

CHAPTER 17

Standardization and Grading

"GRADING HAS BEEN PROMOTED by producers and traders, and largely because they stood to gain by it; but grades must rest solidly on consumers' preferences or on basic utility to consumers if they are to be effective . . . the fundamental economic justification of grades . . . is that they afford a means for consumers to register their preferences more accurately . . . so that . . . consumers are better able to encourage the production of the grades they prefer and to discourage production of the less desirable grades."*

Preview

- This chapter investigates the nature of food quality grades and standards and their applications in the food industry.
- The market impacts of food quality grades are highlighted in relation to operational and pricing efficiency, enhanced possession utility and consumer satisfaction, and potentially higher farmer returns.
- The difficulties of determining food quality standards, designing food grades, and implementing these grades are examined.
- The complementary and conflicting relationships of government and private food grading systems are explored.
- Farmer, marketing agency, and consumer uses of food quality grades are discussed.
- Several criticisms of current food grades and the food grading system are evaluated.

---

* Special Report to the Secretary of Agriculture, 1939.

Key terms and concepts:

grade labeling	standardization/standards
grading	standards of identity
quality	

The sorting of farm and food products into standardized grades is a facilitating marketing function. *Grades and standards* constitute an agreed-upon market language which can greatly simplify the marketing processes and reduce marketing costs. Product grades and standards also furnish an ethical basis for buying and selling. Without some market standards, the rule of *caveat emptor* ("let the buyer beware") prevails, along with confusion and unfairness. Indeed, the standardization of market weights, qualities, and practices is so widespread that it is taken for granted, and the role of standardization in the marketing processes is sometimes unappreciated.

Market standardization has potential benefits for everyone in the food industry. Producers of high-quality farm products can obtain price premiums over lower-quality products when they are differentiated by grades. Food marketing firms can better communicate their needs to farmers, lower their search and transaction costs, and better inform consumers of their market offerings when there are grades and standards. And consumers benefit when grades and standards assist in matching their needs and budgets with the heterogenous supply of products available in the marketplace.

Farm commodities are standardized and government-graded to a greater extent than any other consumer products. Nevertheless, government grades and standards have not been developed for all food products, and those grades and standards which are available are not universally used. In this chapter we will investigate the nature and prevalence of food grades and standards, their roles in the marketing processes, and the problems of food grading.

STANDARDIZATION IN THE FOOD INDUSTRY

Standards are commonly agreed upon yardsticks of measurement. There are a number of standards affecting the food marketing process.

The U.S. Bureau of Weights and Measures supervises the standardization of weights and other measures. The Public Health Service enforces food sanitation standards. The Food and Drug Administration (FDA) sets food processing standards for "good manufacturing practice," regulates food additive levels, and supervises the nutritional labeling of food. FDA food standards of identity also require that products sold under a common name (for example, mayonnaise) meet certain ingredient specifications. The Environmental Protection Agency enforces pesticide residue standards for food, and the Fair Packaging and Labeling Act sets food package and label standards.

The U.S. Department of Agriculture supervises a broad range of food standardization programs. Its food inspection services certify the safety and wholesomeness of farm products. This department also is authorized by the Standard Container Acts of 1916 and 1928 to establish packaging standards for fruits and vegetables. In this chapter emphasis is given to perhaps the best-known U.S. Department of Agriculture standard program—food quality grades.

FOOD QUALITY GRADES AND STANDARDS

Quality is a subjective property referring to the usefulness, desirability, and value of a food product. Buyers must constantly judge the qualities of foods in their purchase decisions. Consumers may prefer larger strawberries to smaller ones; steaks with a moderate degree of marbling may be preferred to leaner or fatter steak. A corn processor may prefer one corn variety to another for his particular wet-milling purposes. The fact that buyers are willing to back up their preferences for certain products over others with purchasing power is evidence that product qualities differ.

Because of the biological nature of production, agricultural commodities are produced in a wide range of qualities. There are almost an infinite number of combinations of such food properties as taste, aroma, color, tenderness, texture, size, age, shape, and moisture for each food product. The unique way that these and other food properties are combined into a product determines its quality.

Although we often associate quality with an objective scale ranging from inferior to superior, in reality quality is a highly subjective property of foods which is measured in the minds of consumers. Two products may differ in sensory qualities but be equally attractive to consumers, for example, California and Florida oranges, or brown- and white-shelled eggs. These are known as horizontal quality differences. Even when there is general agreement on inferior and superior product forms—that is, when there are vertical quality differences—consumers may not always choose the highest quality. For example, a consumer may purchase a different quality of meat for preparing steak than for preparing stew, but both qualities fulfill a need. The purpose of quality standards is not to assure the marketing of only top-quality products but to facilitate the matching of consumer needs with the different qualities of products available.

Food quality standards are commonly accepted properties that differentiate food products in terms of their value to buyers. Food standards may be physiological—for example, the nutritional value of a commodity—but most

361

Table 17-1. Selected USDA Food Grades.

FOOD CATEGORY	FOOD PRODUCT	TOP GRADE	2ND GRADE	3RD GRADE	4TH GRADE
			NOMENCLATURE FOR		
Dairy	Butter	U.S. Grade AA	U.S. Grade A	U.S. Grade B	
	Cheddar cheese	U.S. Grade AA	U.S. Grade A		
	Instant nonfat dry milk	U.S. Extra Grade			
Fruits and vegetables Fresh:	Cantalopes	U.S. Fancy	U.S. No. 1	U.S. Commercial	U.S. No. 2
	Cucumbers	U.S. Fancy	U.S. Extra No. 1	U.S. No. 1	
	Peas	U.S. Fancy	U.S. No. 1		
	Potatoes	U.S. Extra No. 1	U.S. No. 1	U.S. Commercial	U.S. No. 2
	Watermelons	U.S. No. 1	U.S. Commercial	U.S. No. 2	
Processed:	Fruits	Grade A or Fancy	Grade B or Choice	Grade C or Standard	Substandard or cull
	Vegetables	Grade A or Fancy	Grade B or Extra Standard	Grade C or Standard	Substandard or cull
Poultry	Poultry	U.S. Grade A	U.S. Grade B	U.S. Grade B	
	Eggs	U.S. Grade AA or Extra Fancy	U.S. Grade A		
Livestock	Beef	USDA Prime	USDA Choice	USDA Good	USDA Standard

Source: U.S. Government, *Code of Federal Regulations,* 7CFR 46–57, Washington, D.C., 1976.

food standards are sensory (taste, smell, and so on). The standards vary for individual foods. The properties that differentiate high-valued from low-valued steak are quite different from those differentiating potato quality.

Grading refers to the sorting of unlike lots of products into uniform categories, according to quality standards. The appropriateness and accuracy of the grading process depend upon the correspondence between the quality standards and consumer preferences, the range of qualities to be sorted, and the relevance of the sorting to consumer choices. Some selected USDA food grades are illustrated in Table 17-1.

It is in the area of quality sorting that some of the greatest standardization problems of agriculture arise. What should be the criteria for various grades of quality? How many grades should there be? How uniformly interpreted and widely accepted are the standards for grading from one area to another or from one grader to another? What terminology should be used? Should the standards be compulsory or permissive?

MARKET IMPACTS OF STANDARDIZATION

If widely used, uniform food quality grades and standards can, potentially, contribute to both operational and pricing efficiency in the food industry.

By making possible the sale of farm products by sample or description, thus generating more accurate market information, the use of uniform food quality grades lowers search and transactions costs and fosters a more efficient price discovery process. Large quantities of farm commodities, for example, are traded in the futures markets on the basis of standardized grades and contracts without the need for buyer and seller personal meetings or inspection of products. How much more expensive the food marketing processes would be without the trust of traders, which results, in part, from the use of standardized grades!

Grading also can lower other marketing costs. For example, transportation costs may be reduced by distinguishing between the higher-valued products, to be shipped forward, and the lower-valued products, which can be sold nearer to home. Grading may also reduce market spoilage, separating poorer-quality products from higher-quality ones.

Food grading also can contribute to market competition and pricing efficiency. The product homogeneity resulting from grading can move the market closer to perfect competition, encourage price competition between sellers, and reduce extraordinary profits.

Standardization of quality grades can improve pricing efficiency in two ways. First, the use of grades gives consumers specific information with which to signal their preferences to producers, thus increasing the consumers' sovereignty over the production process. Figure 17-1 shows, for instance, how

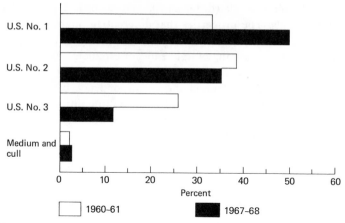

Figure 17–1. Grade distribution of hogs marketed, 1960–61 and 1967–68. (U.S. Department of Agriculture)

changes in consumer preferences for a leaner pork product altered the grade distribution of hogs produced and marketed in the 1960's.

Second, the use of uniform quality grades provides incentives for producers to adjust to changing consumer preferences. Grade-price differentials reward farmers and marketing firms for shifting their production efforts from lower- to higher-valued products. If each producer received the average price of all grades of products, there would be little individual incentive to produce the higher grades. Thus, the use of grades not only provides a standard code which consumers can use to get their message to producers, but also guarantees the desired producer response.

Classification by grades also facilitates the cost-reducing concentration processes in food marketing. For instance, without grades some sort of identifying mark would have to be affixed to Farmer Brown's wheat throughout the market channel in order that the wheat's exact, ultimate value be paid to him. By using the grading system, farm products can be pooled according to grades, making possible lower-cost marketing, without interfering with the communication role of the pricing system.

Uniform grades and standards also can contribute to market development in the form of greater consumer satisfaction and increased producer returns. For example, if by the use of grading there is greater consumer confidence in the product's quality, and a better matching of supplies with consumer wants, the demand curve will shift rightward. At the same time, different prices for each grade of a product can result in a total producer return which would exceed the average price of an ungraded lot of products. This form of price discrimination was discussed in Chapter 15.

GOVERNMENT AND FOOD QUALITY STANDARDS

Many food marketing firms have their own grading, standardization, and quality control programs. However, the U.S. Department of Agriculture grades are the only universal quality standards for U.S. food products. These grades evolved hand in hand with the commercialization of agriculture and the growth of the food marketing system. Some USDA grades grew out of early trading practices; others were developed by trade groups and then formalized by federal and state agencies; and others were developed from research efforts to solve market problems associated with nonstandard grades.

Early History of Standards

In the early days, each grain market had its own grades and grading methods. Different standards for No. 2 corn required that the corn "be dry," "reasonably dry," "have not more than 16 per cent moisture," or "have not more than 15.5 per cent moisture." Study of the terminology used in grading grain in 1906 disclosed 338 names or grade titles being used. There were 133 designations for wheat alone.

The early cotton trade was also plagued by grade confusion. The term "middling" apparently was adopted from its use in England. Such terms as "good," "fair," and "ordinary" were in general use about 1825. In 1847, efforts were made to adopt a standard classification system, but it failed within a few years.

Livestock was once sold on the basis of the girth of the belly. In the literature of the 1850's hogs were sometimes classified as "fat distillery-fed" hogs and "fat corn-fed" hogs. In most of the early market reports the point of origin was indicated as one method of classifying the animals. Such terms as "prime," "choice," and "good" were not uniformly used either within an individual market or between two different markets.

The lack of accepted standards for fruits and vegetables resulted in especially chaotic trade conditions. These perishable products were shipped long distances, and there was no intelligible basis for price comparison or the settlement of damage claims. Some growers attempted to secure recognition by placing their names on all shipments. In this way they hoped to establish a reputation that would give them market premiums.

The lack of generally accepted standards resulted in many unfair practices and abuses. Not only did producers suffer, but also the middlemen of the trade were often defrauded. In most instances, pressure developed for reform of the grading system from within the trade itself. Trade groups and organizations attempted to systematize nomenclature and grades. Generally, however, substantial permanent progress was not made until the federal government stepped in to coordinate the efforts to improve the grading system. In 1907

365

Congress appropriated funds to study federal food standardization. The passage of the Cotton Futures Act in 1914 and the Grain Standards Act in 1916 initiated a series of laws that have gradually broadened the area of federal responsibility in promulgating uniform standards. The importance of establishing standards was also recognized in the Agricultural Marketing Act of 1946, in which the Secretary of Agriculture was given both broad powers and funds to further the development and administration of standards. From 1953 to 1977, the federal grade and standard program was supervised by the U.S. Department of Agriculture's Agricultural Marketing Service. In 1977 this program was transferred to USDA's Food Safety and Quality Service.

The Present Situation

Federal standards for farm products fall into three classifications—mandatory, permissive, and tentative. *Mandatory standards* are those whose use is compulsory under certain conditions. *Permissive standards* are those officially recommended but whose use is not compulsory. *Tentative standards* are those offered for use but still subject to further study before becoming permissive or mandatory. It is mandatory that grains and cotton that move into interstate commerce, and also those traded on the futures exchanges, be graded according to federal standards. Apples and pears sold in the export trade, tobacco, and naval stores also have mandatory standards.

In 1977 there were federal food grades for 13 dairy products; 85 fresh fruits and vegetables; over 225 canned, dried, and frozen products; 18 grains and beans; 18 livestock and livestock products; and 13 tobacco products. The proportion of selected foods graded is shown in Figure 17-2.

Many states cooperate in food grading programs using standards adopted from the federal program. In some cases, however, state grading standards differ from the federal standards, and these grade variations can prevent interstate food shipments, thus increasing marketing costs and food prices. Local grading variations are gradually decreasing through the cooperation of federal and state agencies.

Changes in federal standards, or the development of new ones, come about slowly. Initial suggestions for changes generally come from the trade or from research findings. If a suggestion is considered to be reasonable, the appropriate government agency will confer with interested industry groups to explore the suggestion. Out of the research and suggestions the agency develops tentative grades, which are then tried out. Eventually, if it appears that the proposed standards meet as many of the criteria for good standards as possible in the light of current knowledge, and are usable by the trade, they are issued as the federal standard. This process may extend over a period of several years. The changing of standards, however, is often a difficult and time-consuming process. Many persons have a vested interest in maintaining the

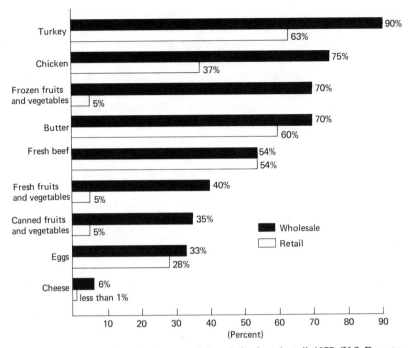

Figure 17–2. Proportion of food products graded at wholesale and retail, 1977. (U.S. Department of Agriculture)

existing standard. Others think of the existing standard as being right because it exists. But as long as consumer preferences, manufacturing processes, and production patterns change, so must standards change if they are to achieve maximum usefulness.

Mandatory Versus Optional Grades

With few exceptions, the use of USDA food quality grades is optional for food marketing firms. This is the reason for the variations in food grading among products shown in Figure 17-2. Some firms and food industries have used the USDA grades more than others. Periodically, there have been proposals to require quality grading of all food products. Proponents of this change argue that mandatory grading is necessary to realize the potential contributions which quality grades can make to consumer choices and marketing efficiency. If grades can improve food market performance, they reason, why should they be optional and only partially used?

The following are reasons given in favor of continuing a voluntary food quality grading program: (1) there is no historical precedent for a compulsory, federal grading system for any product; (2) the cost of food grading might increase significantly if it were mandatory because the present voluntary system is financed primarily by user-firms; (3) USDA quality grades would be redundant with existing brand quality standards; and (4) grades and standards might inhibit product innovation and differentiation of food products.

The latter two arguments raise an important point about the relationship of product standardization and product differentiation: the branding that accompanies food product advertising and differentiation can be viewed either as an alternative form of food quality standardization or as the opposite of product standardization, product differentiation.

From the viewpoint of an individual marketing agency, the production process for a differentiated and branded product represents a high degree of standardization. Building consumer loyalty to a branded product requires strict quality control in order that consumers will eventually rely on the brand as a guarantee of quality. However, if every firm develops its own standards and grades, the result will be a lack of standardization among food products, making comparisons more difficult for consumers.

The voluntary food grading system allows marketing agencies to decide between standardized U.S. grades and private brand grades. The effect of this upon consumers depends upon the nature of consumer preferences for food products. If quality criteria vary widely among consumers, brand differentiation may well be the best method of matching products to consumer wants. But if consumers use quite similar quality criteria in purchasing a product, brand differentiation probably confuses consumer choices, and mandatory grades might be judged desirable.

OBJECTIVES AND PROBLEMS OF FOOD QUALITY GRADING

Food quality grading involves compromises between ideal grades and workable grades; between the needs of consumers for grades and trade needs; and between the costs and benefits of grades.

Criteria for Grades and Standards

The food grading system sets up a channel of communication between food producers and consumers. Ideally, grades will result in a perfect match between the diverse wants of consumers (according to their incomes and preferences) and the heterogeneous qualities of commodities produced and marketed. This sorting and matching process has the potential of increasing both consumer satisfaction and farm profits. Whether these potentials are achieved depends upon the choice of quality standards, the design of grades, and the implementation of the food grading system.

The development of a system of perfect and ideal standards is highly unlikely. Each agricultural product presents different problems. Realizing that it is very improbable that any standard will meet them all, the following may be used as criteria upon which to judge the adequacy of standards:

1. Standards should be built on characteristics the users consider important, and these characteristics should be easily recognizable. Grades must be oriented to user opinion of value and not that of a few technical experts.

2. Standards should be built on those factors that can be accurately and uniformly measured and interpreted. If the major part of a standard consists of subjective measurements, uniform application by different graders, or at different points, will be very difficult. Excessive quality variation within a grade reduces the usefulness of the grade itself.

3. Standards should use those factors and that terminology that will make the grades meaningful to as many users of the product as possible. The ideal situation would be that in which the same grade terminology is used at all levels of the marketing channel, from the consumer to the producer. This is complicated by the fact that many products have several different uses.

4. Standards should be such that each grade classification includes enough of the average production to be a meaningful category on the market. Though grading standards should be consumer-oriented, they cannot ignore the real facts of production. Consideration must be given to the quality of the product produced. It is of little value to have a standard for the top quality set up in such a fashion that very little of the actual production can meet it.

5. The cost of operating the grading system must be reasonable. Absolute uniformity at any price is not a feasible goal.

Probably the best practical test of the adequacy of standards is their acceptance and use by the various marketing agencies. If the grading standard is widely used, it is probably true that the standards are fairly adequate and economically meaningful. However, if large segments of the trade do not use the standards, it usually can be assumed that some of the criteria have not been adequately met.

Problems of Food Grades and Standards

Several practical problems arise in the development of a food grading system and in its implementation in the field:

DETERMINING QUALITY STANDARDS

The subjective nature of "quality" makes it difficult to get agreement on universal food quality standards. Which food properties are most important in consumer preferences? Most standards have been determined by food scientists and the trade. As a result, food grades tend to be based on easily measured sensory characteristics: color, size, shape, tenderness, and so forth. No doubt these are important quality criteria or quality surrogates. But some critics have suggested that the present quality standards are not complete and accurate representations of all the food properties influencing consumer preferences. It has been suggested, for example, that nutritional value ought to be added to the list of food quality standards. Obviously, the cost and complexity of food grading increases with additional standards.

There is evidence that the current food grades do not correspond well to consumer preferences. Blind taste studies have shown that some consumers cannot, or do not, discriminate between different grades of foods. Market studies also have shown that consumers are not always willing to pay premium prices for the higher grades of food. Indeed, some consumers seem to prefer the lower grades to the higher grades. Considering the wide range of consumer tastes within the population, perhaps these results are not surprising.

Another criticism of present food grades is that they are convenient for traders but are not consumer-oriented. This is a serious charge, because consumer sovereignty over the food system requires that grades correspond closely to consumer quality preferences. It is true (as shown in Figure 17-2) that food grades are used more extensively at the wholesale than at the retail level, and that brands are often substituted for USDA grades at the retail level. However, it is unlikely that the grades would be used at the wholesale level if they did not correspond in some way to consumer preferences and final product values. Therefore, some might consider it unfortunate that the USDA grades are not more widely used at the retail level; but the motive for this is probably product differentiation, rather than because of defects in the grading system. It may also be true that farmers and food marketing agencies have a vested interest in the current grading standards and are hesitant to change these standards, even though consumer preferences change.

DESIGNING FOOD GRADES

Even if accurate and meaningful quality standards are agreed upon, numerous problems remain in developing a grading system. Measuring product quality against standards, for example, can be troublesome. Physical and chemical properties can be measured fairly accurately and consistently by trained graders. But measurement of sensory qualities is more difficult. These depend upon the grader's sense of sight, taste, and smell. The standards for dairy products, for example, depend heavily on the sense of taste, and in such cases variability and error is possible.

Generally speaking, the more mechanical and objective the methods used in grading, the more accepted are the standards by the trade. One of the scientific advancements of recent years has been the replacement of some of the sensory tests with chemical tests and mechanical devices. Photoelectric colorimeters, reflectometers, and other devices have been developed to replace the old color chart comparison method. Tenderometers are now used in measuring texture and consistency of peas and lima beans and a few other vegetables. The succulometer is a device used for measuring the juice content of sweet corn. Researchers are even experimenting with a mechanical thumb that will give more uniform results in checking for ripeness in fruit.

When the total supply cannot possibly be graded, or where grading damages the product, sampling variation is a problem. The size and height of egg yolk may be important to consumers, but is difficult to determine by observation of the shell. Similarly, sweetness is desirable in a cantaloupe, but the grader cannot taste every melon.

Other problems are in determining the number and limits of food grades. Presently, there are eight beef grades and only three chicken grades. How many grades should there be? This is an extremely important question because it can influence the total amount of dollars received from the sale of the total production. Within the limits of the consumer's willingness to pay premiums for certain qualities, the amount that will fall in each grade can be changed. However, agricultural products do not fall into classifications with definite breaks between them. Instead, the quality of agricultural products varies over a wide range. It has been suggested that most products have a quality distribution very similar to the normal frequency distribution curve, as shown in Figure 17-3.

One of the criteria for good grades is that there be enough of the normal production falling in each grade to make it a meaningful market category. How many grades should there be and where should the boundaries of the grades occur for the commodity illustrated in Figure 17-3? There are some products of very low, and some of very high quality. Most, however, fall somewhere between these two extremes.

It is evident from this illustration that the grade boundaries will be "zones" rather than clear-cut lines. The more the grade factors are measured subjectively, the wider will be the zone of indecision. This has led to a system of

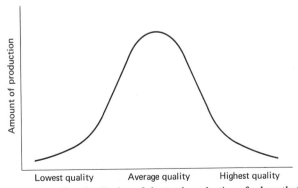

Figure 17-3. Average quality distribution of the total production of a hypothetical product.

tolerance in standards. For example, grades of fruits and vegetables usually provide for 5 to 10 per cent of off-grade specimens.

The quality of the production of a commodity also changes from year to year. The curve in Figure 17-3 might shift either to the right or to the left. One year might find a larger amount of higher-quality products and a smaller amount of lower-quality products. Or the situation might be reversed. Such conditions make it extremely difficult to maintain consistent standards. Again, this is particularly true when grade factors depend upon subjective measurement. For example, if the apple crop is very poor in quality, very few apples would meet the top-grade requirements if the standards were rigidly adhered to. Under these circumstances, the pressure is strong to "reach a little farther down" for the top-grade apples.

This tendency to "upgrade" or "downgrade" means that the composition of particular grades will vary from year to year. Under such circumstances, the consumer is faced with a product of a given grade that will not be the same product, even though the grade is the same one time as compared with another. It has been suggested that preference studies concluding that consumers are not discriminating as to grades do not necessarily mean that the standards are incorrectly measuring consumer quality preferences. On the contrary, they may indicate that consumers have found the stated grades an unreliable measure of actual product quality and therefore ignore them.

Grade nomenclature is another problem. In the trade, there is a reluctance to use grade names that suggest inferior quality. Consequently, fruit and vegetable grades may range from U.S. Fancy, to U.S. Extra No. 1, to U.S. No. 1, while the third-lowest meat grade is "Good." These names may prevent consumers from undue discrimination against perfectly good products, but they probably also cause some consumer confusion.

Finally, there are practical problems in designing a single set of grades that are appropriate for trading at all market levels. This is especially true where the farm product undergoes substantial processing. For example, are the carcass grades for beef at the wholesale level also appropriate for grading retail beef cuts? How can consumer preferences for different qualities of bread be communicated to wheat farmers?

IMPLEMENTING FOOD GRADING SYSTEMS

Still other problems arise in implementing the use of food grades in the marketplace. Because grades are initiated at the request of the trade and are voluntary, not all food products have grades, and not all products which could be graded are. There are no quality grades, for example, for bacon.

Another difficulty is that products may change grade in the marketing process. Many agricultural products are perishable. The fact that a commodity was a given quality at one point in the marketing channel does not mean that it will be of the same quality when it reaches consumers.

The problem of quality loss during marketing brings up the question of where in the marketing channel grading should be done. If grades are to fulfill their objective of telling producers what consumers consider desirable, grading must first be done when the farmer sells his commodities. Only then will he know what the quality and actual worth of his product is. However, if quality deteriorates during the marketing process, this grade will not remain accurate. Therefore, grading must be done as often as needed throughout the marketing process to assure accurate grade when the product reaches the final user.

Sometimes there is also confusion between the requirements for sanitation and edibility and those for quality. For example, meat entering into interstate commerce must be federally inspected to make sure it is fit for human consumption. The packing plants themselves must also meet certain sanitary requirements. But such inspection has nothing to do with the grading of meat for quality.

On the other hand, sanitary requirements are sometimes written into the grading standards. Milk quality standards are a case in point. Though the grade standards consider bacteria count, they also may prescribe the conditions under which the cows must be housed and milked, the way the milk is cooled, and so forth. Regardless of bacteria count, milk cannot meet the grade requirements unless it has been produced and handled under the designated conditions. Such practices confuse the issue. Often, instead of facilitating marketing processes, such standards turn into practical trade barriers and techniques to control production.

FARMERS AND UNIFORM GRADING

Only if the farmer sells on the basis of grades will the fullest benefits of the grading system as a method of consumer-producer communication be realized. The wider the practice of selling on a graded basis, the less is the possibility of fraud and deceit in the selling of goods by farmers. However, it is probably also true that not all farmers stand to gain from selling on a graded basis. The farmers who produce the higher-quality products would gain at the expense of those producing the lower-quality products.

Producing high-quality products is seldom costless. More careful and often more expensive handling of the product is usually required. In some instances the extra cost would probably outweigh the extra returns. In these situations farm selling on a graded basis has little attraction.

Generally the larger specialized producers to whom the product is financially important are more receptive to the idea of graded selling. Those producers who are farthest from the consumption centers also are usually more interested in such a program. If the product is accurately graded, the best of the lot can be shipped to distant markets and the poorer portions sold nearer home. This system enhances the competitive position of the producer

373

in the distant markets. It also reduces transportation costs, because it generally costs the same amount to ship high-quality, high-valued products as it does the lower-quality, lower-valued products.

There is evidence that a program of graded selling raises the quality of the goods sold. This improvement usually comes about as the producer realizes the things he can do to produce a crop of higher quality. Many of these things consist of changes in his present practices, not the adoption of new or additional ones. For example, picking fruit and vegetables at the proper degree of ripeness can reduce spoilage. Such practices might become more widespread if the producers know what constitutes higher-quality and higher-valued products.

It is in the area of standardization of quality that one of the substantial differences between agricultural and industrial production has existed. Much of industry produces a product *to* the quality specification. If the product does not meet the quality standards, it is either rejected or sent back for correction.

In agriculture, however, only a limited amount of such production quality control has been possible. The role of standardization, as we have seen, has been to establish grade limits and sort the available production into lots that are as uniform as possible. It now appears that in the future agricultural producers may also be able to produce *to* grade specifications.

With improved technology and knowledge in production, it often is possible to follow certain procedures and practices and thereby closely control the quality of the output. After extensive research in plant breeding, one concern developed a new strain of corn which uniformly gave the starch content needed in its manufacturing. Vegetable processors, through the control of the strains of plants and planting and harvesting procedures, can come much closer to securing the quality of product desired. The "fresh-fancy" program in eggs, through controlled production and marketing processes, produces a given quality of eggs. Under these conditions it is possible to certify the flock as a grade A flock and only a sample grading of the eggs is required. Likewise, hog producers, through controlled breeding and husbandry practices, are able to produce a much more uniform-quality product.

To the extent that quality control in production is feasible, many of the practices and problems associated with heterogeneous and fluctuating qualities will be substantially changed in the future.

MARKETING AGENCIES AND FOOD GRADING

It is in the marketing area that many of the conflicting goals of different firms come into focus. A firm may have one view if it is procuring supplies for its own operation and a different one if it is selling its product to its buyers. It may be in favor of the simplification of procurement that uniform grading permits, but strongly desire to differentiate its product to its own customers in order to secure some competitive advantage.

The use of federal grades for meat is a good example of these conflicting interests. Large chain retailers like federal grading because it simplifies their problem of obtaining large quantities of uniform products. Smaller packers also like the system of federal grades because it permits them to act as partial suppliers to large chain organizations. Large packers, however, may be opposed to the use of federal grades because the federal grades compete directly with their own grades and brands that they wish to use in their sales. In many other areas, moreover, large retail organizations are not in favor of uniform grade designations of their products because they would prefer to merchandise under their own brand to their customers.

There is some evidence that food grades and standards have affected market concentration and competition. One study found that federal meat grades contributed to declining meat packer market concentration following World War II, because new firms found it relatively easy to compete with the larger, established packers.[1] It is interesting, too, that eggs and butter are highly graded commodities with relatively low market concentration levels.

Certainly the increasing size and complexity of food processing and merchandising operations will require larger volumes of more uniform lots of commodities; this will probably increase marketing agencies' use of standardized food grades, at least in their procurement activities. However, food marketing firms can achieve a comparable result with integrated purchasing contracts and with greater use of specification-buying based on private grades. Therefore there is no guarantee that marketing agencies will increase their voluntary use of USDA food quality grades in the future.

CONSUMERS AND FOOD GRADES

Generally speaking, consumers' goods are not sold on the basis of uniform standards of grade terminology. One of the problems in the complex society of today is that the consumer knows relatively little about the quality of the goods among which she makes her choice. In purchasing foods, for example, the consumer is faced with a confusing array of brands and quality terminology. The terms designating top quality vary widely. In canned goods, companies use different brand names to designate different qualities. There is little to guide the shopper who is not familiar with the brands themselves. In a marketing system theoretically based largely upon consumer direction, the average consumer is faced with the problem of how to make her wants known.

---

[1] *Food from Farmer to Consumer,* Report of the National Commission on Food Marketing, Washington, D.C., June 1966, p.25.

Even with the more widely accepted USDA grades that are used on some commodities, many consumers are confused and show a general lack of knowledge. One study revealed that over half of the consumers interviewed could not correctly identify any of the common USDA grades for meat, potatoes, apples, or turkey.[2] Less than 30 per cent were aware of what the U.S. Department of Agriculture inspection mark was. Nonetheless, most respondents rated government grades as "very helpful." Many consumers believed that there were bacon grades, but there are none; that "Grade A" milk was a quality grade, when in fact it is a local and state sanitation certification.

There have been proposals to adopt a single set of grades for all food products, for example, grade A, B, or C, or grade #1, #2, #3. Such grade-labeling proposals have the benefit of simplicity and would greatly facilitate the consumer's quality evaluation process. However, some people question whether such a system could represent the wide variations in qualities of individual foods. Occasional proposals are made that would require grade-labeling of all foods.

Improvement in the area of consumer grading will be slow. There is widespread acknowledgment that the average consumer needs help. There is not much agreement as to how to help her. Large concerns that have built up preferences for their brands are very reluctant to sanction a uniform labeling system. Much of the emphasis on brands and advertising is based on the fact that the consumer is faced with a bewildering selection of goods and can be persuaded into simple brand dependence. This does not necessarily mean that inferior products can dominate the market. Even brand shopping cannot prevent consumers from turning away from unsatisfactory products. It does mean, however, that new products and new concerns may have difficulty in securing consumer acceptance even if their product is of good quality.

SUMMARY

Quality standards are measurable properties of foods which differentiate them for consumers. Grading is the sorting of unlike lots of products into heterogenous categories according to accepted quality standards. Foods are the most extensively government-graded consumer products, but not all are graded. Because government food grades are voluntary and of little value in differentiating the firm's offerings, brands are frequently substituted for USDA food quality grades. Standardized food grades can contribute to operational and pricing efficiency as well as to increased consumer satisfaction and producer returns. There are several problems in translating ideal food quality standards into practical grades for use in food marketing. U.S. food

---

[2] T. Q. Hutchinson, *Consumers' Knowledge and Use of Government Grades for Selected Food Items,* U.S. Department of Agriculture, Marketing Research Report 876, April 1970.

quality grades have been criticized as being inadequate reflectors of consumer preferences, trade rather than consumer-oriented, and confusing for consumers. The food grading system has adjusted and will continue to adjust to changing market needs.

QUESTIONS FOR DISCUSSION

1. What are the roles of quality grades and standards in the food industry? How well are these capabilities being achieved? Why is food more extensively graded than other consumer products?

2. Do you favor more or less U.S. Government grading of foods? Should grading be optional or mandatory?

3. Explain how grading can both increase consumer satisfaction and the total dollars that consumers pay farmers for food.

4. Investigate the reasons for, and effects of, the 1976 change in USDA beef grades.

5. What are the pros and cons of a mandatory, uniform grade-labeling program for foods? How would you react to this as president of a large food processing firm? As director of a consumer's lobby? As a farmer?

6. Should nutrition be added as a food quality standard?

7. How would you estimate that decentralization and integration have affected food marketing agencies' voluntary use of government food grades in their procurement activities? Their selling activities?

8. How would you change food grades?

SELECTED REFERENCES

CAMPION, D. R., AND V. L. HARRISON. "The New Beef Carcass Quality Grade Standards: What the Changes Mean." *Livestock and Meat Situation.* U.S. Department of Agriculture, April 1976, pp. 41–46.

ERDMAN, H. E. "Problems in Establishing Grades for Farm Products." *Journal of Farm Economics* (Feb. 1950), 15–29.

FARRIS, P. L. "Uniform Grades and Standards, Product Differentiation and Product Development." *Journal of Farm Economics* (Nov. 1960), 854–63.

FERRIS, E. "USDA Grades Can Help Out Food Shoppers." *1974 Yearbook of Agriculture.* U.S. Government Printing Office, 1974.

Food Labeling: Goals, Shortcomings, and Proposed Changes. U.S. General Accounting Office, Jan. 29, 1975.

FRENUP, D. F. "Economic Effects of Recent Changes in Lamb Standards." *Journal of Farm Economics* (Dec. 1961), 1388–98.

HUTCHINSON, T. Q. *Consumers' Knowledge and Use of Government Grades for Selected Food Items.* U.S. Department of Agriculture. Marketing Research Report No. 876, April 1970.

LENNARTSON, R. W. "Grading Over the Years." *Agricultural Marketing.* U.S. Department of Agriculture, Oct. 1966, 3–4.

NELSON, K. E. *Economic Effects of the 1976 Beef Grade Changes.* U.S. Department of Agriculture. Technical Bulletin No. 1570, June 1977.

Perspectives on Federal Retail Food Grading. U.S. Congress, Office of Technology Assessment, June 1977.

SHAW, S. T. "A Merchandiser's View of the Function of Grades." *Journal of Farm Economics* (Dec. 1961), 1399–1404.

USDA Grade Standards for Food—How They Are Developed and Used. U.S. Department of Agriculture, PA-1027, Jan. 1973.

USDA Standards for Food and Farm Products. U.S. Department of Agriculture. Agricultural Handbook No. 341, rev. Feb. 1977.

CHAPTER 18

Transportation

"THE SPECIAL CHARACTERISTICS which make agricultural producers uniquely dependent on an adequate and flexible transportation system may be grouped in two categories. One is the extent to which agricultural products depend on geographic movement to acquire their market value. Frequently, these movements are over long distances, and perishable commodities have very short time tolerances. The other, even more critical, is the extent to which climate or weather determines where, when and in what quantities transportation services will be needed."*

Preview

• This chapter examines the food transportation marketing function—the creator of place utility.

• The unique transportation needs of the food industry are discussed, with special attention to the agricultural commodity trucking exemption from regulation.

• Alternative food transport modes are examined, their advantages and disadvantages are reviewed, and special attention is given to the competitive battle between trucks and railroads.

• Regulation of transportation rates, routes, and schedules is discussed, and the regulatory versus de-regulation argument is highlighted.

• Ways to improve the operational efficiency of the food transportation system are reviewed.

• Key terms and concepts:

agricultural exemption	common carrier
alternative transportation modes	demurrage
class, commodity rates	diversion privilege

---

* I. W. Ulrey, *The Economics of Farm Products Transportation,* U.S. Department of Agriculture, Marketing Research Report No. 843, March 1969.

Key terms and concepts (continued):
freight forwarder   transit privilege
Interstate Commerce Commission   unit train

The American food industry is critically dependent on physical distribution. U.S. consumers may enjoy a meal of Hawaiian pineapple, California fruits and vegetables, Texas beef, Brazilian coffee, Wisconsin cheese, and Florida oranges. This wide variety of food would not be available without the complex transportation system which serves the food industry. Indeed, adequate and efficient transportation is a cornerstone of the modern food marketing system.

Like all other marketing functions, transportation influences both the numerator and denominator of the marketing efficiency ratio. The movement of farm products from where they are produced to consumption centers creates place utility. The fact that consumers are willing to pay for this utility suggests that it often exceeds the costs of transportation.

Transportation also plays an important role in market development, expansion, and competition. The size of the market area depends upon whether products can be moved. Improved transportation has expanded the market area for farm products from a local to a national to a worldwide level. In this sense, improved transportation, or lower transport costs, can be a rightward demand shifter for farmers and marketing firms. At the same time, the ability to ship great distances increases competition between firms and areas. Changes in freight rates usually alter the competitive advantage of sellers throughout the market.

Transportation also influences other marketing functions and decisions. The speed and flexibility of the transporation system can affect inventory and other storage costs throughout the food system. Transportation costs also affect the location of food processing plants and food distribution warehouses. Finally, transportation expenses contribute to the size of the food marketing margin and thus influence farm and consumer food prices.

TRANSPORTATION FOR THE FOOD INDUSTRY

Intercity truck and rail transportation expenses are the third largest component of the food marketing bill, after labor and packaging costs. In the 1950–1976 period, these transport costs accounted for about 8 per cent of all food marketing costs. The addition of air, water, and local trucking costs would probably raise the food transportation bill to about 11 per cent of total marketing costs.

Farm products depend upon transportation for the creation and preservation of their value. Food transportation costs—a measure of place utility—usually constitute a higher share of the retail price than is the case for nonfoods. This varies, however, even for foods. As shown in Table 18-1, the contribution of transportation to a food's final monetary value varies by the distance it is shipped, its perishability, and its bulkiness.

The food industry presents a number of special transportation needs. Food production is geographically dispersed, and the task of linking the several food production centers with the consumption centers is no simple one. However, a flexible transportation network can compensate for the inflexibility of geographically specialized agriculture.

The variability of agricultural production also complicates the food transportation picture. Food transport needs vary widely—annually and by seasons—and are as unpredictable as farm supplies. A large crop puts severe strains on the capacity of the transportation system, just as a small crop results in excess capacity of transportation equipment.

The biological and bulky nature of farm products make special demands on the transportation system: food and feedgrains require high-capacity equipment, live animals need special equipment, and perishable products require rapid transportation. Few other industries have such diverse transportation needs.

Because of these conditions, farmers have always been concerned with the adequacy and costs of the farm product transportation system. Pioneer agriculture developed hand in hand with the national transportation network. The first laws regulating transportation rates in the nineteenth century were promulgated by farmers' complaints that they were the victims of monopolistic railroads. In 1935, farmers sought and gained special regulatory treatment

Table 18-1. Contributions of Intercity Transportation
Costs to Retail Food Prices, 1975.

Product	Intercity transportation costs as a per cent of retail price
California oranges	10.7%
California tomatoes	8.2
California catsup	8.0
Frozen orange juice	5.3
Broilers	2.2
Eggs	1.9
Margerine	1.9
Butter	1.8
Pork	1.6
Beef	1.4
Bread	1.1

Source: U.S. Department of Agriculture.

of trucks hauling agricultural commodities. More recently, dock strikes, freight rate increases, and shortages of railroad cars have again focused the attention of farmers on the transportation system.

ALTERNATIVE MODES OF TRANSPORTATION

Agricultural and food products are transported by virtually every sort of carrier except pipelines, as shown in Figure 18-1. However, rail and truck transportation are the dominant modes of transportation for farm products, with water and air carriers playing a small but important role for certain commodities. In the 1970's, farm and food commodities accounted for perhaps 15 per cent of all railroad freight, 10 per cent of all truck freight, and 5 per cent of all barge freight.

Rail Versus Truck Transportation

A major trend in transportation has been the diversion of freight from railroads to trucks. Between 1946 and 1974, the railroads' share of *all* freight

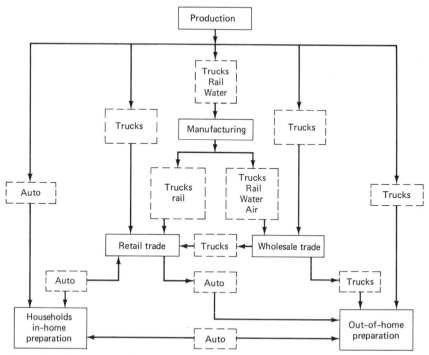

Figure 18–1. The farm and food transportation system. (*Energy Use in the Food System,* U.S. Federal Energy Administration, May 1976)

ton-miles fell from 68 per cent to 38 per cent, whereas trucks' share rose from 9 to 22 per cent. The transportation of farm and food products has followed a similar pattern. In 1929, trucks accounted for 24 per cent of the food transport bill, but this had grown to 70 per cent by the 1970's.

Railroads, nevertheless, continue to be important shippers of farm and food products, especially for long-distance shipments of grain, fresh and frozen fruits and vegetables, and fresh meats. However, trucks now dominate in the short-haul movement of food products and are also important in long-haul shipments. This trucking trend is related to a number of developments, the most important of which have been lower trucking freight rates compared with rail rates, and the greater speed and flexibility of trucks as a result of the development of the interstate highway system. About one out of every three trucks hauls farm-related items. Many farmer-owned trucks are used for short hauls. (It has been estimated that farmers own almost 30 per cent of all trucks in the United States.)

Water Transportation

When compared to that hauled by truck and rail, the volume of agricultural commodities carried on the country's inland and coastal waterways is small. However, where speed is not important and the commodity has great bulk and weight, water transportation is often the cheapest method.

The Great Lakes and the Mississippi River system are the most important water commerce arteries in the United States. In 1975, grains and soybeans accounted for 8 per cent of domestic barge traffic, and the Mississippi River system accounted for three-fifths of the soybeans, wheat, and corn moved by barge. The Snake River, flowing through Oregon, Washington, and Idaho, has also become an important waterway for wheat.

Domestic farm product exports move primarily by ocean vessels. Houston, San Francisco, Baltimore, and New Orleans are important grain ports. The 1959 opening of the St. Lawrence Seaway provided an alternative route for Midwest grains flowing to Europe. The volume of this trade greatly expanded in the 1970's.

Air Transportation

Though agricultural air freight has increased rapidly, the quantities of agricultural commodities moved by air freight are very small indeed. Cut flowers, nursery products, and fresh fruits and vegetables are the biggest single agricultural users of air freight.

The future of air transportation cannot be evaluated on the basis of current freight rates alone. Substantial economies may be forthcoming in other ways. Lighter containers may be used. Some packing and other marketing costs may be largely eliminated. For example, the usual method of handling off-

383

season tomatoes is to pick them green and ripen them after they reach the consumption centers. If tomatoes were picked when vine-ripened and shipped by air overnight to the markets, the ripening costs might be reduced. Similarly, the air shipment of lettuce from California might substantially reduce the icing costs.

In addition to these savings in marketing costs, there is the unknown factor of the effect upon demand. Many believe that consumers supplied with tree-ripened fruit buy more at the same or higher prices. Perhaps it is in this area of increased consumer acceptance that the real net gain from air transportation may develop.

The potential for air transportation of selected high-value, perishable, and seasonal products appears considerable. The new jumbo jets are capable of transporting large amounts at a cost per ton-mile that is quite competitive with other forms of transportation. However, additional costs of handling food products in and out of airports may offset any advantage, except where time is critical. Currently, experiments are being performed with quick-freezing of foods using the cold upper atmosphere—a unique combination of transportation and food processing technology.

Advantages of Different Types of Transportation

Farmers and other handlers of agricultural products have a choice among several types of transportation. A major decision is between the use of the railroad or truck, and increasingly the truck is being chosen. Among the types of truck transportation, common carriers, exempt carriers, or self-owned trucks are available. The majority choose the exempt carrier.

However, some movement of agricultural products is provided by all kinds of transport, which indicates that each has its advantages and disadvantages in doing a particular job. In Table 18-2 these advantages and disadvantages are summarized. A close study of this summary will show that costs, flexibility of service, and dependability of equipment are major areas of difference. Selection is based upon which of these factors are of prime importance. A study of the frozen orange juice concentrate industry concluded, for example, that trucks were widely used in the expansion period, when markets were being developed and speed and flexibility of service were important. However, the use of rail transportation increased later, when large-volume shipments were essential and speed was not so important.

TRANSPORTATION REGULATION AND FREIGHT RATES

The Interstate Commerce Commission, created in 1887, supervises the transportation industry. This agency has broad authority to regulate freight

Table 18-2. Advantages and Disadvantages of Alternative Food
Transportation Modes.

TRANSPORT MODE	MAJOR ADVANTAGES	MAJOR DISADVANTAGES
Railroad	1. Lowest cost for long haul 2. Can handle large volumes 3. Transit privileges available	1. Inflexible route 2. High cost for short hauls 3. Service problems 4. May be car shortages when needed
Regulated motor carrier	1. Flexibility of roads 2. Government regulated	1. Rates lower than rail but higher than exempt carriers 2. Prefer truckload lots.
Exempt motor carriers (nonregulated)	1. Low rates 2. Highly flexible routes 3. Will handle small lots	1. No government supervision of financial responsibility or reliability
Motor carriers owned by shipper	1. Flexible routes 2. Good control by shipper	1. Large investment 2. Difficult to attain full utilization
Air freight	1. High speed	1. High cost 2. Inflexible routes 3. Airport waiting time
Water	1. Low cost 2. Can handle large volumes	1. Inflexible, limited routes

rates, competition, and transportation routes. This regulatory authority is based on the notion that transportation is vital to the national interest, that there are natural monopolistic tendencies in transportation, and that there would be destructive competition among competing carriers in the absence of government regulation. There is considerable debate today over these assumptions, and whether they justify governmental regulation of transportation rates and routes. There are also differences in regulations for the various transportation modes.

Railroad Freight Rates

The railroad freight rate structure of the United States is very complex. Freight rates are not always directly proportional to distances traveled. It is sometimes cheaper to ship a carload of grain a long distance over one route than a shorter distance over another route. Also, separate rail rates have been established for different commodities. For example, grain rates per ton-mile differ substantially from canned goods rates per ton-mile.

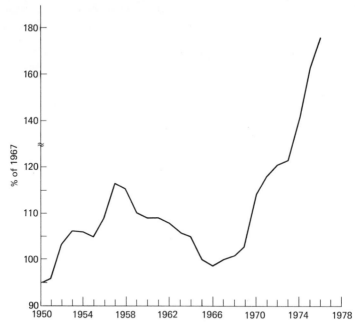

Figure 18–2. Railroad freight rate index for agricultural commodities, 1950–1976. (U.S. Department of Agriculture)

In general there are two basic types of rates, the class rates and the commodity rates. *Class rates* are those established for a limited number of broad categories into which thousands of different products can be placed. This eliminates the necessity of establishing individual rates for each different product. *Commodity rates* are those established specifically for an individual commodity, considering the needs and problems of shippers. Such rates are established for large-volume, low-valued items, such as coal, ore, and grain. Most agricultural products move under commodity rates. Over four-fifths of the total carloads of all products is moved under commodity rates. Commodity rates are generally lower than class rates.

There are also rate differences depending upon whether the shipment is in carlot (c.l.) or less than carlot (l.c.l.) amounts. The rate is generally lower on the carlot than the less-than-carlot shipment. This preferential rate for carlots was one of the reasons for the development of early cooperative livestock shipping associations. As the railroad was the only method of moving livestock to major markets, the association assembled small lots from individual farmers so they could ship to the terminal markets at carlot rates. Lower rates for *unit trains* (whole trains of one commodity) have also favored farm cooperatives.

Rates are also differentiated on the basis of whether they are local or through rates. Because of the terminal expense involved, longer hauls usually are moved at a lower rate per mile. The through rate is less than the sum of several local rates covering the same distance.

There also are several special services available to rail shippers. Two such services of special importance to agriculture are the transit privilege and the diversion and reconsignment privilege. The *transit privilege* permits a shipper to stop a shipment en route to permit some processing or operation to be performed and then to reship it to the original destination, still at the original through rate. This privilege is widely used by the grain trade. Wheat en route from a western point to the East can be stopped for cleaning, grading, and milling. The flour can then continue onward at the original through rate from the initiating point to its eastern destination.

The *diversion and reconsignment privilege* allows a shipper to change the destination of his product either while en route or after arrival at the originally desired destination. Within limits, reconsignment and diversion can take place and the through rates apply to the new destination. This service is one of the major reasons why shippers choose rail over truck transport. Often produce is sold after it is en route so that the exact destination cannot be known at the time it is shipped. Then too, the original market for which the shipment was intended becomes glutted and prices break so that it would be more profitable to reship to another market. The use of diversion and reconsignment aids better allocation of supplies of perishables and reduces the spoilage and waste which accompany market gluts.

The ICC attempts to regulate rail freight rates in a manner that promotes the free movement of agricultural products at reasonable freight rates, provides railroads a reasonable return on investment, keeps railroads competitive with other transportation modes, and fosters a railroad network which serves the public interest. In practice, these have been difficult objectives to reconcile, and the "railroad problem" is today almost as well known as the "farm problem." Although much of the nation's rail passenger service was incorporated into the public utility, Amtrak, in the early 1970's, the rail freight business is still a private-enterprise operation. Rail rates thus reflect the private pricing decisions of the railroads that are regulated by the ICC.

The trend in rail freight rates for agricultural commodities over the 1950–1976 period is shown in Figure 18-2. The 1950–1957 rise in rates reflected the railroads' and the ICC's resistance to competitive pricing. As a result of these rises, much of the agricultural commodity freight was shifted to trucks and barges. The Transportation Act of 1958 gave railroads wide authority to reduce rates to levels competitive with alternative transportation modes. Consequently, rail freight rates fell substantially from 1957 to 1966, as shown in Figure 18-2. However, rising wages, fuel prices, and other costs resulted in an 80 per cent increase in agricultural rail rates between 1966 and 1976. In recent years, railroads have also increased the cost of transit and diversion privileges as well as *demurrage,* the charge for extra loading or unloading time. Overall, these developments have continued to encourage the diversion of agriculture commodities from rail to truck transport. The Railroad Revitalization and Regulatory Reform Act of 1977 resulted in selective rail freight rate reductions for some agricultural commodities.

Trucking Freight Rates

There are three varieties of trucks hauling agricultural commodities. Trucks operating on regulated schedules and routes, and which are available for hire, are classified as *common carriers*. These firms are regulated by the ICC in a manner similar to the railroads. Agricultural products make up less than 2 per cent of the business of these common carriers, much of which is fresh meats and meat products.

Another classification of motor carriers consists of trucks privately owned by manufacturing or marketing firms for their own use. Generally, so long as these trucks are used by their owners in trucking their own products, they do not fall under the regulatory power of the Commission.

Of greatest importance in agricultural marketing, however, is the group of trucks operating for hire which are exempt from federal rate supervision. The "agricultural commodities exemption" clause of the Interstate Commerce Act provides that motor carriers which transport fish, livestock, and all agricultural commodities do not fall under federal regulation. The exemption does not apply to the movement of manufactured products. The purpose of Congress in establishing the exemption privilege was to assure farmers of as low-cost and flexible transportation as possible. For exempt carriers, rates are usually established by direct negotiation between the truck owner and the one who wishes to hire the service.

Exempt trucking firms are usually small operators with one to five over-the-road units. Because their rates and routes are not regulated, they are quite flexible in responding to changing agricultural transportation needs. The truck broker is a special type of agent middleman, his function being to help match available trucks with available cargoes. He also helps establish rates in the negotiation between the exempt carriers and shippers for a percentage fee of the gross freight costs. The freight forwarder is another specialized middleman; he aggregates small lots of commodities into larger shipments, for more favorable transport rates.

FOOD PRICES AND TRANSPORTATION COSTS

As a marketing cost, transportation expenses influence farm and retail food prices. Increases in the cost of transportation fall primarily on farmers in the short run; an increase in freight rates reduces the price that food marketing firms can offer farmers for their products, or it increases the farmer's cost of getting his products to market. However, in the longer run, as farmers adjust production to prices and profits, the increased transport costs are partially passed on to consumers. The sharing of a freight rate increase between farmers and consumers depends upon the elasticity of the supply and demand curves.

Freight rates react to changing farm prices in much the same way as other marketing costs. These rates are relatively stable during the initial stages of rising agricultural prices. However, freight rates eventually accelerate with farm prices, and may even continue to rise after farm prices begin to fall. The failure of freight rates to adjust simultaneously to changing farm prices contributes to agricultural price variability.

This freight-price relationship becomes particularly critical for those shippers located long distances from markets. The inflexibility of the rates often explains why a sharp market price decline for perishables, for example, will result in California growers either destroying their crops or leaving them unharvested. After freight and harvesting costs are met, the result may be an actual net dollar loss to the grower. He, quite logically, attempts to minimize his losses by not incurring the expenses of harvesting his crop.

The severity of these problems for farmers depends upon their access to alternative transportation carriers. Although it is true that today's farmer has more transportation alternatives than in the past, and, in addition, has a special transport alternative which is exempt from ICC regulation, many farmers have limited transportation alternatives. In these cases, farmers' prices are critically influenced by transportation rates.

REDUCING THE FOOD TRANSPORTATION BILL

The American transportation system is good by most standards, but it is by no means perfectly efficient. Railroad cars stand idle 90 per cent of the time; perhaps 40 per cent of all trucks are running empty at any given time; railroad cars and trucks are lost, delayed, or arrive with damaged cargo; and trucks and rail cars stand idle for hours waiting to be unloaded. It has been said that in 1973, it took longer to move certain food commodities by rail from the West Coast to New York City than it did in 1953.

As in all efforts to reduce marketing costs, attention must be paid to both the numerator and the denominator of the marketing efficiency ratio. It would be an easy task to reduce food transportation costs if consumers were willing to drive 100 miles to pick up their groceries from central food depots, or if consumers would forego a wide variety of year-round fresh food products. But these economies would also reduce consumer satisfaction and, probably, overall marketing efficiency. A number of areas show promise as possible ways to improve the operational efficiency of the food transportation system, and reduce transportation costs, without sacrificing consumer satisfaction.

Technological and Other Improvements

In recent years there have been several innovations in farm and food product transportation. The increased availability and reliability of mechanically re-frigerated rail cars and trucks, the increased number of covered hopper cars, the double-bottom (two-unit) truck, and larger-sized rail cars are examples of cost-reducing transportation technology. The interstate highway system, the St. Lawrence Seaway, and inland waterway improvements also have con-tributed to transportation operational efficiency. At the consumer level, free-ways and the increasing number of two-car families have increased the mobil-ity of food shoppers.

Another improvement is palletized shipping. Many products may be placed on pallets at the manufacturing point and moved all the way to the retail outlet on the same pallet, thus reducing labor requirements and reducing the chance for damage of products. Containerization is a further refinement of palletization. This consists of packing many smaller packages into one large container, such as a semitruck trailer without wheels. Sometimes special equipment is installed to preserve a particular environment, particularly for fresh fruit or vegetables.

The unit train concept, that of an entire train carrying a single product, has reduced transportation costs for grain products. Unit trains can be handled directly and efficiently but require exceptionally large shipments. Computers are now being used extensively to route and schedule complex shipments.

Regulation and Competition

Competition between alternative forms of transportation has played a role in holding down food industry freight costs and in improving services. The rivalry between the rails and trucks, for example, resulted in downward pres-sures on freight rates as well as the development of new services. Railroads have attempted to improve their speed and services to regain lost traffic. The "piggy-back" combination rail-truck-and-water service is an example of this. There are also "fishyback" and "birdyback" services which combine alternative transportation modes.

Despite this competition, the transportation industry remains one of the most highly regulated of all industries. With the notable exception of exempt agricultural carriers, the rates, routes, and schedules are not set by free, competitive market forces but by regulatory agency. It is unlikely, therefore, that rates are as low as they would be in the absence of regulation. Hence, eliminating rate regulations would probably reduce transportation costs.

In the 1970's, the purposes and effects of transportation regulations were being reconsidered. Those favoring de-regulation argued for allowing free market forces to determine transportation rates and service levels. Those arguing for continued regulation emphasized the need to prevent excessive competition among carriers and to preserve alternative transportation modes for shippers.

Part of the cost of truck transportation arises from the barriers that individual states have erected in the form of varying regulations on weight and dimensions. Such regulations make it impossible for trucks to pass freely from state to state. Loads must often be changed or rerouted if the truck passes over state borders. There is a movement among states to work out these differences and establish more uniform regulations. Greater uniformity in these regulations should increase both the speed and efficiency of truck movements.

Increased Capacity Use

There appear to be several ways to improve the capacity utilization of existing transportation equipment. This would include the elimination of excessive duplication of some transportation facilities and the better arrangement of routes so as to assemble a full load more efficiently. The pickup of two or more commodities might be combined to secure a larger load with less travel. Careful planning in many instances might eliminate an empty return trip, which often occurs when commodities are hauled to market.

The local assembly of products from farm to initial market offers one area in which more effective use of transportation equipment could be obtained. This has been illustrated by several studies of milk assembly. These studies found that trucks were traveling long distances to pick up small amounts of milk. Many times two or more truck routes would be traveling down the same road, each carrying less than capacity. Consolidation and better planning were offered as ways to reduce hauling costs substantially. However, the new technique of bulk handling of milk has tended to solve this problem by permitting farmers to store up larger quantities of milk which then can be transferred to tank trucks on an every-other-day basis. Hauling costs to farmers are then often reduced. This is a good example of a new technological development opening up new solutions to an old problem.

Farm assembly of products is not the only area where poorly planned and under-utilized transportation facilities exist. The pressures to economize have exposed many other areas in the marketing system where the same type of savings could be made. Every-other-day delivery of bottled milk to consumers can be substituted for daily delivery. A change from the practice of single-layer to double-layer packing of cauliflower by closer field trimmings was estimated to reduce the California-to-New York freight charges by three cents per head. Refrigeration and container costs were also reduced. The loading of every other basket of perishable produce upside down in the rail car results in hauling more baskets per car. Better planning found return loads of fertilizer and other needed supplies for the trucks which transported

391

livestock to central markets. Often many of these trucks previously had made the return trip empty.

Reduced Spoilage and Damage

This is an area that offers considerable opportunity to reduce transportation costs. Many of the remedies to reduce spoilage and breakage are remarkably simple. Three factors account for much of the wide variation in damage claims presented to railroads. These are differences in the value of the carload because of the density and bulk of the product, types and suitability of the containers, and the degree and efficiency of loading and bracing methods used to prepare the car for shipment.

Many of the damage claims for fruits and vegetables occur because of unsuitable and faulty containers and poor loading practices. These are factors subject to control and improvement. For example, it was found that cantaloupe crates loaded on end had only about one third the breakage of crates loaded on their sides and lengthwise of the car. The tying of a single wire around lettuce crates was found to reduce crates damaged in shipment. Experimentation is now going on with new containers and new packing methods for many commodities. Many of the methods and containers used have not changed from the early days of railroad transportation. Imagination coupled with a lack of reverence for the status quo can produce cost-saving results.

Changing the Product

In this area are probably some of the greatest potentialities for attacking the transportation cost problem. High damage claims to a substantial extent hinge on the nature of the product itself. The product should not be accepted as a given, unchangeable fact. It too can be changed.

High perishability is one of the basic reasons for expensive transportation. But poor quality products are more perishable than top quality products. An expanded program of farm selling on grades might result in products being more closely graded before shipment. Then, only those products best able to stand up during movement would move long distances. Those that might deteriorate more quickly would be sold in the nearby markets.

Bulky, low-valued shipments can also be changed. The shipment of frozen concentrated orange juice in place of the whole fruit is an example of one kind of possible change. The production area slaughter of livestock and the shipment of carcasses rather than live animals is another example of a possible change that can be made. In general, production area processing will result in less bulky, higher-value, and often less perishable products for shipment to consumption areas.

Continued High Food Transportation Bill

Though a fresh and imaginative approach can perhaps lower costs, the total transportation bill will remain high. The inherent nature of agricultural production and products makes for an expensive transportation situation. The great distances between production and consumption areas will still exist in a large country. The job of assembling the production from scattered small production units will remain an expensive operation. Many commodities will still be perishable, resulting in high spoilage and extensive use of refrigeration. The seasonal nature of agricultural production will continue to create peak transportation demands at some seasons. Costs of the transportation agency will not suddenly become flexible so that rates can respond quickly to price level changes. Finally, the rising costs of labor, energy, and other inputs into the transportation function will keep upward pressures on freight rates. The reduction in the speed limit to 55 mph in the early 1970's offset many of the operational economies of the trucking industry.

SUMMARY

Transportation is the key link in the food systems' marketing chain, connecting geographically specialized farmers and an urbanized consumer population. This marketing function constitutes 8 per cent of the food marketing bill and contributes significantly to the creation and preservation of place utility for consumers. Owing to special product and production characteristics, agriculture has unique transportation needs. These are recognized in the agricultural exemption which permits food freight rates, routes, and schedules to adjust freely to changing transportation needs. Most farm and food products move by rail and truck; but the trend continues to be a shift from rail to truck. For a few commodities, water and air carriers are important. Transportation costs influence both farm and consumer food prices as well as the costs of storage and inventory. Although there have been some improvements in transportation efficiency, they have not been sufficient to prevent rising freight rates. Consequently, the food industry transport bill will continue to rise.

QUESTIONS FOR DISCUSSION

1. What are the principal features of the alternative transportation modes which would affect a food marketing firm's choice of transportation? A farmer's choice?

2. Critically examine the rationale and justification for exempting the transportation of unprocessed agricultural commodities from ICC regulation. Are there other prod-

ucts for which a similar case for exemption might be made? Why aren't processed foods exempt?

3. Why do you think railroads have been anti-ICC regulation, whereas the trucking industry has been pro-regulation in recent years?

4. Railroads have sometimes cited public subsidies for water, air, and motor carriers as the reasons for their competitive disadvantage in attracting freight. What are these subsidies? Are the railroads correct?

5. Although pipelines are very efficient at moving some products (oil, gas) long distances, they are not used to transport farm products. Do you see any potential for pipeline transportation of farm commodities? How about blimps?

6. Improvements in transportation efficiency are sometimes said to lower inventory costs. Explain how this occurs.

7. Debate the proposition: "Rate regulations should be removed from all transportation carriers so that the free market sets rates."

8. How could a change in freight rates change the comparative advantage of a country? Of a U.S. region?

SELECTED REFERENCES

BLOOM, G. F. "Transportation." *Productivity in the Food Industry.* MIT Press, Cambridge, Mass., 1972.

BOLES, P. P. *Cost of Operating Trucks for Livestock Transportation.* U.S. Department of Agriculture. Marketing Research Report No. 982, Jan. 1973.

—— *Operations of For-Hire Livestock Trucking Firms.* U.S. Department of Agriculture. Agricultural Economic Report No. 343, July 1976.

—— *The Freight Car Supply Problem and Car Rental Policies.* U.S. Department of Agriculture. Marketing Research Report No. 953, April 1972.

—— "The Role of Railroads in Hauling Farm Products." *The Marketing and Transportation Situation,* U.S. Department of Agriculture, Nov. 1973.

GAIBLER, F. D. *Water Carriers and Inland Waterways in Agricultural Transportation.* U.S. Department of Agriculture. Agricultural Economic Report No. 379, Aug. 1977.

Highballing to Market in Unit Trains: A Report on Food Unit Train Feasibility. National Association of Food Chains, Washington, D.C., 1968.

HOFFMAN, L. A., P. P. BOLES, AND T. Q. HUTCHINSON. *Livestock Trucking Services: Quality, Adequacy, and Shipment Patterns.* U.S. Department of Agriculture. Agricultural Economic Report No. 312, Oct. 1975.

HUNTER, J. H. *The Role of Truck Brokers in the Movement of Exempt Agricultural Commodities.* U.S. Department of Agriculture. Marketing Research Report No. 525, 1962.

LIMMER, E. *Chief Factors Underlying General Changes in Rail Freight Rates, with Special Reference to Farm Products, 1910–51.* U.S. Department of Agriculture. Bureau of Economics, May 1951.

MIKLIUS, W. *Economic Performance of Motor Carriers Operating Under the Agricultural Exemption in Interstate Trucking.* U.S. Department of Agriculture. Marketing Research Report No. 838, Jan. 1969.

MILLER, E. B. *Transportation Activities of Selected Farmer Cooperatives.* U.S. Department of Agriculture. Farmer Cooperative Service Information Bulletin No. 96, Aug. 1974.

PEGRUM, D. F. *Transportation Economics and Public Policy,* rev. Richard D. Irwin, Homewood, Ill., 1968.

"Transportation." *Marketing Structure of the Food Industries.* U.S. Department of Agriculture. Marketing Research Report No. 971, Sept. 1972, pp. 109–118.

ULREY, I. W. *The Economics of Farm Product Transportation.* U.S. Department of Agriculture. Marketing Research Report No. 843, March 1969.

CHAPTER 19

Storage

"DESPITE IMPROVEMENTS in mechanical handling equipment and construction of new facilities . . . the available evidence suggests that there has been little increase in productivity in retail food chains or wholesaler-operated warehouses during [1967–72] . . . If we look at the entire distribution process in the food industry, it seems evident that during the decade of the seventies, major improvements in productivity will be felt primarily at the [retail] store level, but these changes may be bought at the expense of a slower rate of improvement and perhaps even a decline in productivity at the warehouse level."*

Preview

- This chapter explores the nature and roles of storage and warehousing in the food industry.
- Distinctions are drawn between working inventory stocks, seasonal stocks, carryover, and food reserves. Food stocks are also classified as voluntary-intentional and involuntary-accidental.
- The pervasiveness of the storage operation throughout the food industry—including that of the household and government—is shown.
- The interrelationships of food production and storage patterns and food prices are discussed.
- The varieties of storage costs and the potentials for reducing these costs are examined.
- Key terms and concepts:
  carryover   food reserve
  Commodity Credit Corporation   free stocks

---

* Gordon F. Bloom, *Productivity in the Food Industry,* The MIT Press, Cambridge, Massachusetts, 1972.

price stability   voluntary stocks
U.S. Warehouse Act   working inventory stocks

Storage operations are carried on at every level of the food industry. All food marketing firms perform some storage and warehousing. Farmers are assuming increased responsibility for commodity storage. Consumers also store considerable quantities of food in refrigerators, freezers, and pantries. The storage marketing function is associated with the creation of time utility. This is an important source of value in the food industry, where supply and demand are seldom in immediate balance. Storage operations are necessary to bridge the time gap between periodic harvests and marketings and relatively stable consumption of food on a year-round basis.

Storage is interrelated with other marketing functions, such as transportation, processing, financing, and risk-bearing. In a sense, farm products are being "stored" at the time they are in transit or are in the processing operation. The relationship of storage and transportation is particularly critical at harvest time. A shortage of transportation facilities during a harvest glut backs up grain at the farm and at the local elevator, resulting in falling cash prices. Processing fresh products by canning or freezing them is another form of storage. And because storage operations delay sales and subject the firm to inventory risks, financing and risk-bearing are considered part of the storage function.

A number of issues concern the food storage function. How large should U.S. food stocks be? World food stocks? Who should own these stocks? How should food stocks be managed and financed? These are important public policy questions. For the firm, there are other problems. How can storage and inventory costs be reduced? What level of stocks is necessary for efficient plant operation? Should storage capacity be increased?

FOOD STOCKS, CARRYOVER, AND RESERVES

There are several kinds of food storage, serving various purposes. A certain level of supply, or *working inventory,* is necessary for an efficient marketing process. These stocks keep the marketing pipeline full, contributing to full-capacity operations and preventing supply disruption. Both consumers and food marketing firms maintain these working inventories for convenience and efficiency.

Seasonal food stocks are a related form of food storage. Over the marketing year, these are held to balance out supplies with demand. Seasonal stocks are usually larger for products that are harvested in a short time but that are consumed throughout the year. Both farmers and food marketing firms hold seasonal food stocks. Consumers may also build these stocks by increasing purchases of in-season commodities for later consumption.

Carryover stocks refer to the amount of commodity left over from one marketing year to the next. Annual production and consumption seldom balance precisely, and there may be carryovers ("old crops") or shortfalls, going into the next harvest period. These carryovers then become an addition to the supply available for consumption in the following year. The 1968–1976 carryover of grains is shown in Figure 19-1.

Food reserves are intended to balance food supplies with demand over the long-run and between countries. The objective is food security—storing in "fat" years as protection against "lean" years. As an example, the 1977 farm bill contained provisions to encourage an international system of farmer-held food grain reserves for the world.

A fourth form of food storage might be termed *speculative stocks.* Farmers, food marketing firms, and consumers may at times hold larger than normal food stocks when they expect prices to rise. These speculative stocks would then increase in value and result in an inventory profit.

A distinction should be made between voluntary and involuntary storage of food stocks. The farmer or marketing firm may voluntarily increase stock levels for efficiency or speculative reasons. However, at other times stocks may rise as a consequence of an unanticipated harvest glut or a slow demand.

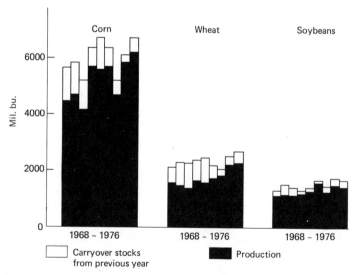

Figure 19–1. Production and carryover stocks of commodities. (U.S. Department of Agriculture)

These stock level changes are involuntary. During the 1950's, for example, the United States unintentionally built up a grain reserve as a result of farm price and income policies. The difference between voluntary and involuntary stocks is that the former is a purposeful, intentional change in food stocks, and the latter is accidental and unanticipated.

STORAGE OPERATIONS

Farm and food commodities can be stored at several places in the food system. Over time, changes in food production and in storage technology have altered food storage patterns.

Storage Locations and Capacities

It is extremely difficult to estimate the amount of food in storage at any time, or even to measure the total food storage capacity available. A considerable proportion of the total food storage takes place within the channels of trade in the form of inventories. Civil defense studies in 1963 estimated that on a minimum 2,000-calorie basis there was 15.1 days' supply of foodstuffs on hand in retail food stores, 1.9 days' supply in restaurants and other eating places, and 16.1 days' supply in public warehouses, private processors, and wholesalers. If we adjust these figures to the approximately 3,000-calorie level of consumption that exists in the United States, they indicate about a three weeks' supply of food in the wholesale and retail marketing channels. As would be expected, over 80 per cent of this food was in cans, bottles, and packages; the remainder was in fresh and frozen products.

Processing plants are also an important part of the storage structure, either by holding substantial amounts of the raw material before it is processed or the finished product after processing. For example, a large cereal manufacturer stores large amounts of grain but generally does not keep a large inventory of finished cereals on hand. On the other hand, a large tomato canner must can his entire year's supply at tomato harvest time and carry his holdings in the form of the canned product.

Perishable commodities, of course, require more specialized and expensive storage facilities than nonperishables. As shown in Table 19-1, refrigerated warehouse space more than doubled between 1953 and 1975. This includes public warehouses, private warehouses, and freezer-locker plants that rent space to consumers. Frozen food storage capacity has also increased rapidly in retail food stores. In addition, almost all homes have mechanical refrigeration, and 34 per cent of families had a home freezer in 1976.

The storage capacity of farms is particularly difficult to estimate because general-purpose farm structures are frequently used to store grain. Farm storage capacity has undoubtedly increased in recent years because govern-

399

Table 19-1. Refrigerated Warehouse Space. 1953–1975.

YEAR	PUBLIC COLD STORAGE ONLY	PRIVATE AND SEMIPRIVATE COLD STORAGE	MEAT PACKING ESTABLISH- MENTS	TOTAL ALL TYPES
	1,000 Cu. Ft.	*1,000 Cu. Ft.*	*1,000 Cu. Ft.*	*1,000 Cu. Ft.*
1953	466,470	202,491	79,089	748,050
1955	498,599	245,850	68,568	813,017
1957	545,061	294,174	62,162	901,397
1959	569,199	325,313	50,872	945,384
1961	595,463	379,355	51,985	1,026,803
1963	633,447	428,250	50,372	1,112,069
1965	683,972	473,515	45,903	1,203,390
1967	734,804	517,468	41,833	1,294,105
1969	762,203	554,611	35,932	1,352,746
1971	774,265	624,442	28,272	1,426,979
1973	828,691	686,477		1,515,168
1975	876,292	754,565		1,630,857

Source: U.S. Department of Agriculture.

ment grain storage operations declined and more on-farm storage facilities were built. It has been estimated that there was on-farm grain storage capacity of 6.2 billion bushels in 1977 and an equivalent off-farm grain storage capacity. Perhaps three-fourths of this grain storage capacity was concentrated in Washington, Kansas, Texas, Oklahoma, Nebraska, Illinois, Iowa, Ohio, Missouri, North Dakota, Montana, Colorado, Minnesota, Kentucky, and Tennessee.[1]

Commodities, of course, change storage locations as they flow from farmer to consumer. Table 19-2 shows how stocks of corn and barley change location during the marketing season.

Changing Seasonal Storage Patterns

Changes in production and utilization patterns may also change storage practices. For example, seasonal variation in egg production has decreased, with the consequence that the storage holdings of eggs have been getting smaller and smaller. On the other hand, though livestock production also has less seasonal variation with passing time, seasonal variability in meat storage is increasing. The growth of processed meats has tended to increase the usefulness of frozen holdings.

Technological developments may also change the places and methods of storage. Prior to the perfection of quick-freezing techniques, for example, the fruit preserve industry could operate only at the time of harvest. Now,

---

[1] "Storage and Transportation," *Agricultural Outlook,* U.S. Department of Agriculture, August 1977, p.13.

400

Table 19-2. Changes in the Location of Corn and Barley Storage During the Season, 1965–1969 Average.

QUARTER AND COMMODITY	ON-FARM	TERMINAL MARKETS, INTERIOR MILLS, ELEVATORS, WAREHOUSES	GOVERNMENT-OWNED STOCKS		TOTAL STORAGE
					Million Bushels
		Percent of total bushels			
Corn					
January 1	77%	18	5	100%	4,010
April 1	73	20	7	100	2,919
July 1	73	18	9	100	1,929
October	62	22	16	100	993
Barley					
October 1	64	35	1	100	400
January 1	62	36	2	100	312
April 1	57	41	2	100	218
July 1	50	46	4	100	132

Source: U.S. Department of Agriculture.

however, it can operate on a year-round basis by securing most of its supplies in the frozen form. Before refrigeration equipment was developed, the basic unit of storage was the canned finished product. Now food is stored in the frozen raw form.

Public Warehouse Supervision

The United States Warehouse Act gives the Secretary of Agriculture authority to supervise warehouses operating under its provisions. Agitation for some type of public supervision of commodity storage arose when farmers were unable to secure adequate loans on crops they wished to store. Such a situation often forced the farmer to sell his crop immediately upon harvest in order to secure needed money.

Whether a warehouse wishes to operate under the provisions of the Warehouse Act is optional. However, if it desires to so operate, then the operator and his business must meet certain requirements. The warehouse must pass an inspection of its condition and facilities and the operator must post a bond and furnish a guarantee of his financial responsibility.

All commodities stored in a supervised warehouse are inspected for quantity, condition, quality, and insurance coverage. The owner is then given a warehouse receipt showing the exact nature of the commodity in storage. Because the commodity has been verified by a third party, these receipts are usually accepted by banks as collateral for loans ranging up to 90 per cent of the receipt value. In this way the person who does not wish to sell his product immediately has a source of reasonable credit through which he can secure needed cash. Here, then, is another illustration of the close interrelationship of various marketing functions. The public warehouse system is a very important factor in financing the marketing processes. The negotiable nature of the warehouse receipts also greatly facilitates the transfer of title and reduces the amount of physical handling.

WHO SHOULD STORE?

Like the other functions of the marketing system, storage is a necessary function, but it is not always clear who should do it. Obviously, the storage within the trade channels, in the form of inventories, is the responsibility of the various businessmen of the system. But the storage throughout the season may be provided by several agencies—the farmer, the commercial storage operator, the food processor, the speculator, and others.

Costs of storage are not necessarily the same in all positions in the marketing channel. Though the theoretically perfect seasonal price fluctuation covers the cost of storage, it does not necessarily cover the operations of highest cost. Even though storage is necessary, it is not equally profitable for all individuals at all levels of the marketing channel to store.

Normally each level of the marketing system tries to push much of the storage function to another middleman in the system. Retailers struggle to hold inventories at the lowest level consistent with serving their customers. Processors attempt to schedule production in order to avoid tying up their capital in costly storage stocks.

Whether or not the farmer should store his own products is a debated point. No generalized rule can be made, but the case of each commodity must be decided on its cost-return conditions. In some circumstances it may pay the farmer to build his own facilities and provide his own storage; in others, it may be best to rent commercial storage. In still other circumstances, it may be best to sell at harvest and let some other agency of the marketing system undertake the storage operation. Nor can the profitability of farm storage be generalized for all years. The outlook for general business conditions may make storage desirable for one year and not for another. The 1977 farm bill encouraged expansion of on-farm storage facilities by providing easier credit terms for building these facilities.

The Commodity Credit Corporation (CCC) is the government agency that buys, stores, and sells farm commodities in connection with federal price- and income-support programs. These are carryover, seasonal, and reserve food stocks, some of which are voluntary and some involuntary. As shown in Table 19-3, CCC food stocks generally fell over the 1963–1975 period. This was the result of expanded U.S. agricultural exports, and of changes in farm policies from purchase and storage programs to greater emphasis on supply control programs. As a result, most of the food stocks in the mid-1970's were "free stocks"—that is, in the hands of the trade rather than government-held stocks.

FOOD STORAGE AND PRICES

Having food in various kinds of storage generally serves to stabilize prices over time and in various countries. Inventory, seasonal, carryover, and reserve food stocks each shift the supply of farm commodities from lower-valued to higher-valued time periods. This raises the price in the low-valued market and reduces it in the high-valued market.

The stabilizing effect of storage on farm and consumer prices is sometimes considered a mixed blessing by farmers and consumers. To be sure, stable prices do facilitate farmers' investment and enterprise decisions; they also simplify consumers' purchase decisions. Nevertheless, many farmers appear to prefer the ups and downs (especially the ups!) of a market free from the depressing effects of government stocks. And consumers appear to be less concerned with variable prices than they are with stable, but high, food prices.

REDUCING FOOD STORAGE COSTS

The storage function will always be a complex and expensive one in the food marketing industry. Like other marketing functions, storage cannot be eliminated, but the costs of storage can be reduced by a decrease in storage activities and increased operational efficiency. It is extremely difficult to isolate realistically the cost of the storage function from the costs of the functions of financing and risk-bearing. When goods are stored, the owner either foregoes possible money income or borrows money against the goods. With the holding of goods, the owner also incurs various kinds of risk. In determining the total costs of holding commodities, five possible categories of costs must be considered:

1. *The costs necessary to provide and maintain the physical facilities for storage.* These costs would include such items as repairs, depreciation, and insurance against loss.

2. *The interest on the financial investment in the product while it is in storage.* Whether the money is actually borrowed or not, this is a cost that should be assessed at the rate of interest that would have to be paid if money were borrowed during the storage period.

Table 19-3. Food Stocks Owned by the U.S. Commodity Credit Corporation, 1963–1975.

YEAR	BARLEY	BUTTER AND BUTTER OIL	CHEESE	CORN	COTTON	DRY BEANS	FLAXSEED	SORGHUM GRAIN	NONFAT DRY MILK
	Million Bushels	Million Pounds	Million Pounds	Million Bushels	1,000 Bales	Million Cwt.	Million Bushels	Million Bushels	Million Pounds
1963	41	290	40	849	5,955	0.2	3.2	585	554
1964	23	61	33	835	7,793	.7	2.9	587	151
1965	18	32	*	530	10,155	.1	5.2	493	131
1966	7			156	8,389	*	9.1	332	*
1967	6	153	80	138	1,247	.3	2.1	193	191
1968	6	124	65	261	135	*	2.9	192	268
1969	49	72	*	296	2,221	*	7.7	188	212
1970	28	108	4	215	2,077	.1	19.1	163	119
1971	36	104	7	144	*	*	24.0	58	80
1972	9	108	0	140	*	0	7.7	37	26
1973	1	18	0	70	*	0	.1	8	2
1974	*	17	2	6	*			1	172
1975	*	3	5	*	*				442

YEAR	OATS	PEANUTS	RICE	RYE	SOYBEANS	TUNG OIL	WHEAT	VALUE OF ALL COMMODITIES OWNED
	Million Bushels	*Million Pounds*	*Million Cwt.*	*Million Bushels*	*Million Bushels*	*Million Pounds*	*Million Bushels*	*Million Dollars*
1963	19	84	1.5	0.9	*		982	5,023
1964	33	40	1.1	.5	*	15	712	4,611
1965	41	37	.8	5.7	*	15	572	4,110
1966	47	78	.4	8.2		15	216	2,340
1967	45	35	.1	6.7	7	9	109	1,005
1968	46	6	*	9.0	53	12	100	1,064
1969	76	6	6.4	11.7	178	28	168	1,784
1970	146	2	6.9	17.6	80	42	283	1,594
1971	199	10	4.9	24.0	*	38	372	1,118
1972	172	8	.6	29.8	0	27	267	830
1973	121	*	*	15.7	0	19	139	394
1974	69			2.6		1	15	188
1975	36	365	*	*			*	402

* Less than 50,000 units.

Source: U.S. Department of Agriculture, Agricultural Soil and Conservation Service.

3. *The cost of quality deterioration and shrinkage during storage.* Many commodities either deteriorate in quality or shrink in volume—or both—while in storage. In a few cases, some commodities, such as corn, may increase in quality while shrinking in volume. In such cases, storage may result in a net gain instead of a net loss for this particular factor.

4. *The loss that may result from poor consumer acceptance of the stored as against the fresh product.* Packing companies maintain that frozen meat will be accepted by consumers only at a price discount, even though its quality as measured by the grading system has not deteriorated. There is consumer resistance to storage eggs as opposed to fresh eggs, though the quality as measured by the grading system may be the same. This is not a problem in all commodities. Nor do such consumer preference patterns remain unchanged. For example, there is evidence that the widespread acceptance of food lockers and home freezers is overcoming the resistance to frozen meats.

5. *The risk that the price of the product might unexpectedly decline.* Under these circumstances the product might have to be sold at less than its value at the time it was placed in storage. The possibility of a favorable movement in prices, on the other hand, is a major factor in encouraging speculative storage.

Increasing the Productivity of Storage Facilities

There are indications that the operational efficiency of grocery warehouses began to fall in the mid-1960's and continued to decline in the 1970's. The probable reasons for this were an increase in the number and variety of food products stored, the shifting of some marketing functions from retailers to wholesalers, and a slackening in the rate of technological innovations in food warehousing. Nevertheless, there are ways to improve food storage efficiency in the future.

The most promising might be that of increasing labor efficiency by reorganization of handling methods and by additional mechanization. Often, a by-product of increased efficiency is an increase in the storage capacity of a given area.

The concept that storage is not static but is an integral part of the movement of goods has directed increasing attention toward problems of handling. Much of the work (and costs) of warehousing occurs during the unloading and loading operations. Attention to this area has led to the construction of one-story warehouses with ample loading facilities in contrast to the old multiple-story buildings. The use of pallet storage, along with the fork-lift truck, conveyor systems, automatic dumping devices, and other mechanical devices is giving some storage operations a long-needed face-lifting. One multiple-story warehouse originally handled a maximum of five trucks a day and

40,000 cases a month, with a work force of fourteen. After redesigning and installing new equipment, it could handle ten trucks a day and 50,000 cases a month, with a work force of seven.

Developments in ventilation and insulation are making both cold and general nonrefrigerated storage possible in the same space. New advances in the science of refrigeration are reducing the cost and increasing the dependability of refrigerated storage. Study is underway on the problem of odor contamination of one product by another. If odor controls can be worked out, commodities which now must be kept in different facilities may be stored together. This would greatly increase the flexibility of storage space. A system of mechanized aeration of stored grain has removed much of the necessity of moving grain from bin to bin in order to maintain its quality. This has increased the useful capacity of elevators because some bins no longer need to be held empty for this process. Because part of the storage problem lies in the interrelationship between production and consumption patterns, some of the cost-reduction practices must be initiated on the farm, in the factory, or in the store.

In some commodities, such as eggs and hogs, production has gradually shifted to a more uniform year-round pattern. Such changes reduce the amount of storage needed. In other cases, product developments have changed the nature of the storage operation. The rapid development of frozen orange juice concentrate has shifted the emphasis from that of maintaining fresh fruit to that of properly maintaining the frozen product. The trend toward more processed, table-ready meats has changed some of the meat storage requirements. The development of frozen and dried eggs in addition to shell eggs has increased the flexibility of egg storage operations. Some varieties of crops have been found to be better for storage than others.

Basic seasonal price patterns can be affected by changes in storage costs. Any changes that will reduce the costs of holding a commodity will tend to reduce the amount of seasonal price variation. This helps explain why a relatively new crop often has a greater amount of seasonal variation, which declines as the years pass. In a new situation, storage facilities may not be well organized. The costs of storage are therefore quite high. Then, as the situation improves, storage costs may decline. The seasonal price pattern then tends to become less pronounced. Such developments and their effects on the amount of seasonal price variation are, of course, not limited to new commodities. The price pattern of any commodity may be changed by changes in the storage situation.

Many of the improved business management techniques have contributed to improved inventory and production control techniques. This means that fewer goods per dollar of sale need to be kept on hand at retail and wholesale levels. Processors, through improved scheduling of activities, can produce more to order. These developments speed up the flow of goods and thereby reduce the amount of needed storage. For example, inventory on hand in a supermarket has always been an expensive proposition. Although the cost of "stocking out" of products is costly, so is the money tied up in inventory. Modern management techniques now allow computerized inventory and ordering systems that provide daily ordering and store deliveries. Even more efficient systems are being experimented with. Optical scanning devices at the check-out counter "sense" what products have been purchased and automatically reorder appropriate products from the warehouse to restock the shelves. These techniques reduce the need for large investments in inventory and facilities and help reduce the cost of marketing.

Reducing Product Deterioration

Wine and cheese may improve with storage and age, but most food products deteriorate in quality and decline in volume while in storage. Arresting these quality and quantity changes also has potential for reducing storage costs. Great advances have been made in discovering the best storage conditions for individual products. It is now recognized that different commodities have different temperature and humidity requirements for optimum maintenance of quality. Many examples could be noted. Temperatures of 30° to 32°F. are usually recommended for apple storage, but it has been found that Grimes Golden apples hold up best at 34° to 36°. For most fresh products the recommended relative humidity is 80 to 90 per cent, but 70 per cent is better for onions and nuts. Temperature and humidity conditions are now known to be important even for storage of canned goods, to control deterioration and rusting.

Chemistry is making increasing contributions to quality control. One example is the potato sprout inhibitor. Potatoes sprayed with this chemical when placed in storage will not sprout readily. Another example is the use of "modified atmosphere" wherein proportions of various gases are controlled in gas-tight rooms to retard deterioration.

Practices followed in preparing products for storage have an important effect on their storability. The deterioration rate of many products can be reduced if the temperature is reduced as soon after harvest as possible. The discovery that cuts and bruises received during harvesting reduce storage life has led to redesigning of machinery to reduce sharp edges and dropping distances. The use of polyethylene liners in boxes has been found to cut quality losses of such products as pears, sweet cherries, and apples.

The proper farm use of insecticides and fungicides has reduced storage rotting caused by insect injury. Experimentation with the use of antibiotic chemicals and irradiation has uncovered some potentialities in retarding the spoilage of various commodities. Some antibiotics have already been approved for use in the preservation of poultry. And new ways may be found to retard the spoilage of red meats. The degree of ripeness at harvest has also been related to length of storage life. In grains this knowledge has led to experimentation on various methods of quick-drying immediately after harvest.

Storage Financing and Risk-Bearing

The futures market can assist in managing the financing and risk-bearing operations associated with food storage. Whether or not money is borrowed on a stored product, the interest lost on the value of the stored commodity is a cost to the farmer or the food marketing firm. Frequently, it is easier to borrow working capital on a hedged commodity. Moreover, the storage hedge can be used to transfer the price risk from the hedger to the speculator. This, too, can result in decreased food industry storage costs.

SUMMARY

Because of imperfect coordination between supplies and demand, the need to maintain pipeline-level stocks, and the perishable nature of the product, food storage and warehousing is an important marketing function. Food stocks can be classified into working inventory stocks, seasonal stocks, carryover stocks, and food reserves. These stocks are held at all levels of the food industry and also by the household and by government. Although changes in seasonal food production have in some cases reduced food storage needs, food storage capacity is increasing overall, both on-farm and off-farm. Storage operations play an important role in stabilizing prices. Costs of physical facilities, interest costs, quality deterioration, and risk costs all affect food storage expenses. These costs may be reduced through increased warehousing productivity and improved storage management.

QUESTIONS FOR DISCUSSION

1. Explain how food storage operations contribute to time utility, and show how the law of one price operates over the storage season.

2. It is sometimes said that food processing is an alternative to storage. Explain why this is so.

3. How could improved coordination of food supplies and demand reduce the costs of food storage?

4. What are the principal differences between inventory stocks, seasonal stocks, carryover stocks, and food reserves?

5. Specify the alternatives farmers have to selling or storing their grain at harvest. What factors influence the storage decision?

6. Examine the most recent farm bill for provisions relating to on-farm storage and food reserves.

7. "The United States government should not be involved in food storage operations." Comment.

SELECTED REFERENCES

BLOOM, G. F. "Warehousing." *Productivity in the Food Industry: Problems and Potentials.* MIT Press, Cambridge, Mass., 1972.

CHANDLER, W. M., JR., and GHETTI, J. L. *Cost of Storing and Handling Cotton at Public Storage Facilities, 1972–73.* U.S. Department of Agriculture. ERS-554, June 1974.

DARRAH, L. B. "Storage." *Food Marketing.* The Ronald Press, New York, 1971.

A New U.S. Farm Policy for Changing World Food Needs. Committee for Economic Development, New York, 1974.

SCHIENBEIN, A. G., and C. A. VOSLOH, JR. *Cost of Storing and Handling Grain and Controlling Dust in Commercial Elevators, 1971–72.* U.S. Department of Agriculture. ERS-513, March 1973.

SHEPHERD, G. S., and G. A. FUTRELL. "Grain Prices and Costs of Storage." *Marketing Farm Products.* Iowa State University Press, Ames, Iowa, 5th Ed., 1969.

WYNN, N. A., JR., and J. PEARROW. *Costs of Storage and Selected Services for Farmers' Stock Peanuts in Commercial Facilities, 1971/72.* U.S. Department of Agriculture. ERS-517, Aug. 1973.

CHAPTER 20

Risk Management and the Futures Market

"FUTURES TRADING is little known and less understood. Only a small percentage of people know what futures markets are or have seen one in operation. More people have heard of the futures markets. But people who have seen markets are even more mystified, if this is possible, than the people who have not even heard of the markets. There is a mystery about these markets that seems difficult to penetrate."*

Preview

• This chapter describes the fundamentals of the commodity futures markets and illustrates how these markets can be used by farmers and food marketing firms.

• A distinction is drawn between physical product risk and price risks in food marketing.

• The operations of the commodity futures markets are described.

• The relationships between cash and futures prices are examined.

• The process by which hedging transfers price risks and facilitates forward pricing is described.

• The perfect hedge, the storage hedge, and the pre-harvest hedge are discussed.

• Criticisms of the futures markets are reviewed.

• Key terms and concepts:

basis	Commodity Futures Trading
bears, bulls	Commission
carrying charge	corner

---

* Thomas A. Hieronymus, *Economics of Futures Trading,* Commodity Research Bureau, Inc., New York, 1971.

Key terms and concepts (continued):

delivery month, contract maturity	market corner
economic (price) risk	perfect hedge
futures contract	pre-harvest hedge
futures market exchange	round turn
hedging, hedgers	speculators
leverage	spot price
long, short	storage hedge
margin	Texas hedge

We have seen that storage, financing, risk-bearing, and market intelligence are important marketing functions. Commodity futures markets are marketing tools for farmers and food marketing firms that can aid in the performance of these functions.

TYPES OF MARKET RISK

Risk is inherent with the ownership of goods. And as with the other functions of marketing, risks must be borne by someone. They cannot be eliminated. Kinds of risk may be classified as follows:

1. *Production destruction* from natural hazards, such as fire, wind, and so on.
2. *Product deterioration* in value resulting from (a) quality deterioration; or (b) price change largely because of change in consumer preference or acceptance, change in the supply situation, or change in general business conditions.

Product Destruction

Those engaged in marketing must face the possibility that fire or other forces may suddenly damage or destroy the products they have on hand. A marketing firm, especially if it is a large one, may build up its own fund to cover such a possibility. However, as in the case of many individuals, firms may transfer this risk to an insurance company for a fee.

Insurance companies are specialized risk bearers which spread the risk over a wide area and groups of people or businesses. Most marketing firms find buying insurance more economical than attempting to provide for their own protection. In the marketing of agricultural products, insurance companies of varying types are of considerable importance. They range from those insuring products in transit from farm to market to those insuring the inventory of the retail store.

Product Deterioration in Value

Every marketer runs the risk of physical deterioration of a product while he owns it. Aside from using the best technical equipment and knowledge available, there can be little transference of this risk from the owner of the products. A rapid change in temperature, a breakdown in equipment, and the like are all possibilities which cannot be ignored. This is one of the factors that increase the marketing costs of perishables.

Value deterioration that stems from price changes may originate from many sources. Risks from changes in consumers' preference or acceptance is greatest in the style-goods lines. For example, women's dresses which may be high-priced one year will bring much less the next because they are out of style. Of course, most food products do not face such rapid preference shifts. Food preferences usually change much more slowly over a longer period of time. However, price changes that occur because of large annual shifts in production and in the general price situation are common for agricultural products. A handler who purchased large amounts of eggs for storage in the spring at what he considered "safe prices" may find himself facing a highly unfavorable fall egg market because of an unforeseen deterioration in general business conditions. An untimely frost may greatly increase the value of current apple storage holdings by sharply reducing the crop. A series of rains may make or break the wheat crop, and thereby greatly affect the fortunes of those who are holding large inventories of wheat in storage.

Wide and unpredictable fluctuations in both the volume and amounts of available products cause food processors, handlers, and retailers additional costly uncertainties. Successful advertising and merchandising require a reliable flow of uniform products. Equipment and personnel must be geared to an optimum volume of flow. Because the volume of products available to agricultural marketing agencies is predetermined by the level of farm production, uncertain production levels mean uncertain cost levels to many marketing firms.

It is in this area of price and cost change that agricultural marketing agencies probably face their greatest risk. Many devices are used either to minimize this risk or to shift it from one person or firm to another.

Because much of the risk may stem from lack of knowledge or inaccurate knowledge, efforts that improve the gathering and dissemination of market news and statistics and the standardization of products may reduce this risk. Much of the government price-supporting activity is a mechanism for transferring price risks from producers and handlers to the tax roles of society. The government storage activities, which often accompany such supports, help reduce the other risks inherent in wide variations of available market volume.

The efforts toward vertical integration of the marketing channel also attempt to reduce or transfer risk. Many of the integration contracts with farmers arrange for a fixed return, and thereby transfer the risks from changing prices to the integrator. The integrator in many instances attempts to obtain some effective control over the kind and amount of production available to him and thereby help reduce the risks involved in his activities.

Also, products are often sold "in advance"; that is, the price is fixed in the present for delivery at a specified future date. Elevators may sell grain f.o.b. their elevator, and once the grain is loaded in cars on the railroad siding, their responsibility ceases. Vegetable canners often sell their packs immediately to other middlemen who then must assume the price risk on inventories. Fresh produce dealers may obtain their supplies from growers with whom they share returns and thereby share market risks.

Some of these devices help reduce the risk that accrues and which people must bear. Others are devices for shifting the risk from one agency to another within the market channel. There are also ways by which the risk of price change may be shifted to those outside the market channel proper. The principal mechanism for contacting outside risk-bearers and financing is the futures market.

THE FUTURES MARKET

The cash price for agricultural commodities—often called the *spot price*—is today's price for products delivered today. The *futures price* is today's price for products to be delivered in the future. Pricing and product delivery usually occur simultaneously in the cash markets, but these two events take place separately in the futures market. Futures contracts are not limited to agricultural commodities. Magazine subscriptions, pick-of-the-litter stud service, and even college tuition are forms of futures contracts in which prepayment is made for goods or a service to be delivered in the future at a guaranteed price.

The futures market is a mechanism for trading promises of future commodity deliveries among traders. As such, it is a unique risk-management and profit tool for farmers and food marketing firms.

Futures Market Exchanges

Commodity exchanges are marketplaces designed to facilitate trading in futures contracts. In 1975 there were ten organized commodity exchanges in operation in the United States. The Chicago Board of Trade and the Chicago Mercantile Exchange were the largest, accounting for perhaps 75 per cent of all commodity futures trading.

The commodity exchanges are somewhat like the stock market. They are

414

composed of member-traders who are authorized to buy and sell futures contracts for the public. There is a trading floor, where buyers and sellers meet; a governing board, which sets and enforces the rules for orderly trading; and a clearinghouse, which facilitates trading and delivery of commodities. Most commodity exchanges are found in cities which are major transportation centers and through which a substantial portion of the product moves (Chicago, New York, Kansas City, Minneapolis, and Winnipeg, Canada).

The most visible aspects of the exchanges are the exchange floor and the trading "pits," where the actual trades are made. Less visible but equally important is the communication network which links brokers throughout the world to the traders in these pits. The commodity trading floor is a physical place, but it represents a worldwide market. Some fifty different commodities are traded on futures markets. Some of these are shown in Table 20-1. Futures market daily price quotations can be found in the principal sections of most newspapers, and up-to-the-minute reports of exchange prices are available in the offices of most commodity brokers.

Commodity exchanges are quite close to the perfectly competitive market. At any moment there are thousands of buyers and sellers of futures contracts participating in the market, and there are an even greater number of potential participants. Prices are established through open trading on the floor of the exchange, where all buyers and sellers are represented either personally or via electronic communication through their brokers. Anyone can trade on the exchanges. Most information on developments affecting futures prices is public, and the prices themselves are communicated worldwide. It would be extremely difficult to fix or manipulate futures prices.

The futures market has grown rapidly in recent years. As shown in Figure 20-1, the number of contracts traded increased from 6 million in 1961 to 33 million in 1975. This market is expected to continue to grow as more traders are attracted to it and as more farmers and food marketing firms become better acquainted with the market and its role as a marketing tool.

The Futures Contract

The futures contracts that are traded on commodity exchanges are promises to deliver or accept delivery of a specific commodity at a specified time in the future. No physical commodity changes hands when the contract is traded and priced. Deliveries are made against the contract when it matures (or becomes due) in the month for which it is named. Payment for delivery of the commodity is at the price determined when the original trade was made, often several months prior to delivery. Thus, a seller of a futures contract guarantees delivery of the commodity at the price agreed upon when the contract is traded, and the buyer is assured of receiving the commodity in the specified month at this price. Futures contracts allow *forward pricing* of commodity deliveries.

Table 20-1. Selected Agricultural Commodities Traded on Futures Markets, 1975.

COMMODITY	CONTRACT SIZE	PRIMARY EXCHANGES	TOTAL CONTRACTS TRADED, 1975 (MILLION)	REGULAR ROUND TURN COMMISSION RATE[1]	INITIAL MARGIN REQUIREMENT[2]
Soybeans	5,000 bu.	Chicago Board of Trade Mid America Commodity	4.6	$30.00	$3,000
Corn	5,000 bu.	Chicago Board of Trade Mid America Commodity	5.6	30.00	1,000
Wheat	5,000 bu.	Chicago Board of Trade Kansas City, Mid America Commodity, Minneapolis	3.4	30.00	1,250
Live cattle	40,000 lbs.	Chicago Mercantile	2.5	40.00	900
Cotton #2	50,000 lbs.	New York Cotton	0.5	62.00	2,500
Frozen pork bellies	36,000 lbs.	Chicago Mercantile	1.4	45.00	1,200
Sugar #11	5,000 lbs.	New York Coffee & Sugar	4.6	30.00	3,000

[1] A *round turn* is a complete buy and sell transaction. This brokerage fee is levied on each contract traded, regardless of profits or losses incurred. Brokerage fees vary from time to time, and there are special rates for trades completed within one day.
[2] Margin is the amount of money which must be posted with the broker when the initial buy or sell of a contract is made. It is used to cover losses or is returned to the trader if a profit is made. Margin requirements vary over time.

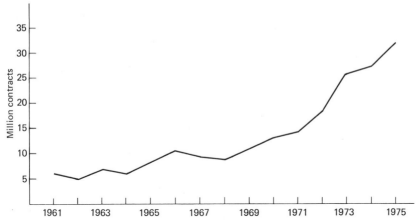

Figure 20–1. Volume of futures trading on all U.S. markets combined, 1961–1975. (T. A. Hieronymus, *Economics of Futures Trading,* 2nd ed. Commodity Research Bureau, Inc., New York, 1971, p. 28. Reprinted by permission)

These contracts represent standardized quantities and qualities of commodities, as indicated in Table 20-1. For example, a Chicago May corn futures contract could be traded at $2.50 on January 5. This means that a seller agreed to deliver 5,000 bushels of No. 2 yellow corn (not more than 15% moisture) to a Chicago warehouse in May. Upon delivery of the warehouse receipt for the product, the buyer who bought the contract in January will pay the seller $2.50/bushel. The exchange clearinghouse finances and guarantees the delivery of the product against the contract.

Each commodity has different delivery (maturity) months. For instance, wheat can be contracted for delivery in July, September, December, March, or May. Other commodities have other delivery months.

Where do futures market contracts come from? Here the futures market differs from the stock market. Anyone may legally "create" a futures contract to buy or sell commodities at any time by simply calling a brokerage house and doing so. That farmers and merchants can make a promise to deliver 5,000 bushels of corn in the future seems reasonable. However, it is surprising to many that doctors, lawyers, and even students may also legally create and trade these contracts.

Trading and Pricing of Futures Contracts

The futures market may be described as a place where sellers make promises to deliver something they do not have to buyers who promise to accept delivery of something they do not want—and both legally break their promises. A strange market indeed!

There are two kinds of futures market traders: *speculators* and *hedgers.*

417

Speculators are traders who attempt to anticipate and profit from futures price movements. Speculators generally have neither the capability nor interest in fulfilling their futures contracts by taking or making delivery at contract maturity. Hedgers also attempt to profit from anticipated price changes, but they usually can take or make delivery of the commodity at contract maturity. However, like speculators, hedgers seldom allow futures contracts to mature. There are always many more speculators than hedgers in the futures market.

Futures contract promises can be fulfilled in either of two ways. The commodity can be delivered or accepted at contract maturity, or the promise can be nullified by an offsetting futures market transaction prior to contract maturity. Sellers can buy back their promise, or buyers can sell out their promise. Most futures contracts are nullified prior to contract maturity, and relatively few contracts result in product delivery. This is evident from Table 20-1, which shows that 28 billion bushels of corn (5.6 million contracts $\times$ 5,000 bushels per contract) were traded in futures markets in 1975, a year when only 4.6 billion bushels of corn were produced!

The profit motive is the reason why so many contracts are nullified before delivery. A trader who sells a May futures contract for $2.50 on January 5 would make a ten-cent profit (ignoring brokerage fees) per bushel if the contract could be bought back later at $2.40. Similarly, a trader who bought a November futures contract in June at $4.00 and later sold it at $4.20 would also make a profit. Of course, the traders on the other sides of these transactions would have lost equivalent sums of money.

The attraction of futures market speculative trading lies in its potential for frequent, and somewhat unpredictable, commodity price swings. The uncertainty of futures commodity prices assures that there will be a large number of both buyers and sellers of futures commodities at all times. Buyers will always be able to find sellers, and vice versa.

Some specialized terms and names have evolved in futures trading. A seller of a contract is said to be in a *short* position—he owes the commodity. A buyer of a contract is said to be *long*—he is committed to take delivery of the product. *Bulls* are traders who feel prices will rise, so they "go long" (buy). *Bears* feel prices will fall, so they "go short" (sell). It takes a bull and a bear to make a transaction.

In the futures market, speculative profits can be made from either rising or falling prices. A bull makes money by buying today, watching the price rise, and then selling out at the higher price. The price rise is the profit. A bear does the opposite, selling today and buying back the contract later at a lower price. Speculative profits depend upon the traders' correct anticipation of price movements. Clearly, for every futures contract traded, there must be a bull and a bear, a long and a short trader, and a winner and a loser (unless price stays constant).

What determines the price of a futures contract? Like any other commodity that can be traded, a futures contract price is determined by how much

418

buyers are willing to buy it for, and how much sellers are willing to sell it for. In turn, these attitudes toward buying and selling futures contracts reflect the value of the actual product represented in the contract at maturity. Why would anyone pay $2.50 for a contract calling for November delivery of soybeans if they thought the cash price of soybeans would be less than $2.50 in November? Conversely, why would anyone sell a promise to deliver soybeans next November if they thought soybeans might sell for more than $2.50 next November? Because there is the possibility of delivery, or accepting delivery, of a futures promise, today's price of a futures contract can be viewed as an estimate of what buyers and seller feel the cash price will be when the contract matures.

Hence, a futures price is somewhat more complex than a cash price. A cash price reflects "what is" today. A futures price reflects the market as traders think it will be. Because of the time lag between pricing and delivery of a futures commodity, and the uncertainties of agricultural prices, there is always a wide difference of opinion as to the "correct" futures price. As commodity conditions and attitudes toward buying and selling futures contracts change, the futures price will also change. These differences of opinion and unpredictable price changes insure that there will always be plenty of bulls and bears in the market at the same time. In fact, because it takes two to make a trade (a bull and a bear), there is usually an equal number of buyers and sellers in the market at all times. If there is an unequal number of sellers and buyers, the price of the futures contract will adjust to bring these numbers back to equality. More buyers than sellers will raise prices, transforming some buyers into sellers, and more sellers than buyers will lower prices, changing some bears into bulls.

Futures trading involves two costs. As shown in Table 20-1, there is a brokerage fee for executing orders. There is also a *margin* requirement, which is a form of earnest money. For example, a trader must post a $1,000 margin when making an initial buy or sell of a corn futures contract. This can be used by the broker to cover losses and brokerage fees, or it is returned to the trader in the event of profitable trades. This margin "downpayment" amounts to only a small portion of the value of the corn represented by the contract, say one-tenth if corn is selling for $2.00/bushel. This ability to trade a large value of product (say, $10,000 of corn) with limited capital is known as *financial leverage.* Futures markets are highly leveraged, meaning that there are opportunities for large profits on investments—or large losses.

RELATIONSHIPS BETWEEN CASH AND FUTURES PRICES

The difference between a cash and a futures price is called the *basis.* The basis is very important to an understanding of the futures market. In fact,

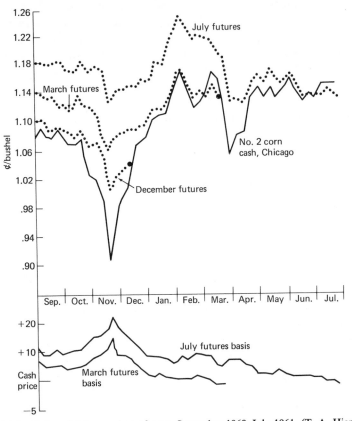

Figure 20–2. Cash and futures prices of corn, September 1960–July 1961. (T. A. Hieronymus, *Uses of Grain Futures Markets in the Farm Business,* Illinois Agricultural Experiment Station Bulletin No. 696, 1963, p. 2. Reprinted by permission)

agricultural commodity prices are often described by their basis. For example, a local elevator owner may quote a spot grain price of "30 cents under." This means that today's cash price is 30 cents under the nearby futures price. Commodity traders often are more interested in the level or change in basis than in actual cash prices.

There are three normal relationships between cash and futures prices for a storable commodity. First, because actual commodities can be delivered against futures contracts at contract maturity, the cash price of a commodity will be almost the same as the futures price at that time. That is, the basis will approach zero at contract maturity, when "the future becomes the present."

Second, prior to contract maturity, futures prices are normally above cash prices by the cost of holding the commodity until contract maturity. This storage cost declines as contract maturity approaches, therefore the basis is

420

said to "narrow" as the contract matures. This also follows from the fact that cash and futures prices must approach each other at maturity.

Third, cash and futures prices tend to move up and down together because both are affected in the same way by changes in supply and demand. A change in market conditions that increases the cash price will also tend to raise the futures price. The two markets do not move together perfectly because of errors in price discovery, expectations, and other random variations. Nevertheless, the tendency toward similar cash and futures price movements means that there are periods when the basis will be constant despite changing cash and futures prices.

These relationships are illustrated in Figure 20-2, showing the cash and futures prices for corn in 1960–1961, along with the March and July bases. The cash and futures prices do come together at contract maturity; the futures price is generally above the cash price; the basis narrows as contract maturity approaches; and there are short-term periods when the basis is relatively constant.

One other important point is that the basis level and the basis changes tend to follow predictable patterns from year to year. In fact, basis is more predictable than cash prices. For example, the July corn basis might average 10 cents in November at harvest, then narrow to 2 cents in June. Or, a farmer might know from experience that, at harvest time, local elevators normally offer a cash price for soybeans of "35 cents under the November futures." Knowledge of these historical basis patterns is vital to the use of the futures market in risk management.

HEDGING AND RISK MANAGEMENT

Price risk is inherent in the ownership and handling of agricultural commodities. By the nature of their activities, farmers and food marketing firms are exposed to unpredictable price swings. A food processing company that holds commodities for a few days, weeks, or months during the manufacturing and marketing processes is subject to an inventory price risk. An elevator owner buying cash grain for later sale assumes a price risk between the time of purchase and sale. A farmer who plants in the spring with uncertain knowledge of fall harvest prices is in a sense speculating on cash prices and is facing a risk.

Farmers and food marketing firms can make profits by speculating in cash prices or by performing utility-adding marketing functions. However, speculating in cash prices involves the risk that prices might fall rather than rise. Because agricultural prices are highly volatile, many firms cannot afford to speculate on cash price changes—or choose not to do so—preferring instead to profit only from their conventional marketing functions. For these firms, the futures market provides an opportunity to limit their exposure to price risks.

A hedge implies a protective mechanism. A futures market hedge is such a risk-management device. It involves the temporary substitution of a futures market transaction for a cash transaction. The mechanics of a hedge consist of making opposite transactions on the cash and futures markets in order to protect the firm against adverse cash price movements.

The Hypothetical Perfect Hedge

The process of hedging can be explained by the operations of the owner of a grain elevator. The owner buys cash grain from farmers and ships it to a terminal market for cash sale one week later. (Owners of grain elevators normally operate on a small profit margin per bushel, and attempt to make their profits from handling charges rather than from speculative market positions.)

The elevator owner is long in the cash market when he originally purchases the grain from farmers. Until this grain is sold, the owner is exposed to a cash price risk because the price of grain could fall by the time it is sold one week later. To protect against this possibility, the owner could hedge as follows:

Date	Cash market	Futures market	Basis
March 19	Buy 100,000 bu. @ $2.00 (LONG)	Sell 100,000 bu. @ $2.50 (SHORT)	$ .50
March 25	Sell 100,000 bu. @ $1.90 (SHORT)	Buy 100,000 bu. @ $2.40 (LONG)	$ .50
Gain or Loss	$−.10	$+.10	

$$
\begin{aligned}
\text{March 25 cash price} &= \$1.90 \\
+ \text{Futures gain} &= \underline{\quad.10} \\
\text{Net value} &= 2.00 \\
- \text{Original cash cost} &= \underline{2.00} \\
\text{Profit or loss} &= -0-
\end{aligned}
$$

When cash grain was purchased, futures were sold to "set" the hedge. When the cash grain was sold, the futures contracts were purchased back. The cash market declined, as the owner of the elevator feared it would, and he lost 10 cents per bushel on the cash transaction. However, the futures market also declined, and the opposite position there resulted in a 10 cents per bushel gain. On balance, the futures gain offsets the cash loss, and the owner of the elevator nets $2.00/bushel from the combined transactions.

This illustrates the *perfect hedge,* where the gain in one market exactly offsets the loss in the other. Thus, the futures hedge "protected" the owner from the 10-cent decline in the cash market. Notice that the owner did not deliver against the contract, even though delivery could have been made; he had no intention of making this delivery and knew the grain would be sold in one week. Most hedgers do not deliver against their contracts but turn their hedges in the same manner as speculators, buying back a previously sold position. The futures position is simply a temporary substitute for a planned cash sale.

There are two reasons why this hedge was effective. First, the cash and futures prices both declined, therefore the opposite positions provided compensating gains and losses. The second reason for the success of this perfect hedge was that the basis remained constant at 50 cents on both days. A constant basis, as indicated previously, is common for short-run periods such as this, but is by no means guaranteed. If the basis changes during the hedge, it will not be a perfect hedge but it can still provide some protection against falling cash prices. For example, if the basis were to rise from 50 to 55 cents, so that on March 25 the futures contracts were purchased at $2.45, the futures transaction would offset 5 cents of the 10-cent cash market loss— a useful, but not perfect, hedge.

Basis changes, then, are an important influence on the success of hedges. Hedgers are more concerned with basis than with actual cash prices. Cash prices could have fallen from $20.00/bushel to $2.00/bushel and the hedge would still have been perfect if futures prices fell from $20.50 to $2.50, keeping the basis constant at 50 cents. Because basis is not perfectly predictable, it is often said that hedging involves speculation in basis rather than in cash prices. However, because basis is somewhat more predictable than cash prices, this can represent a risk reduction for the hedger.

What if cash and futures prices had risen instead of falling? In that case the cash market gain would have been exactly offset by the futures market loss, if the basis had remained constant at fifty cents. And the elevator owner still would have received a net value of $2.00/bushel on the two transactions. Of course, the elevator would have been better off without the hedge when prices rise, but this is hindsight. Without the hedge, the owner would run the risk of the price falling. This illustrates an important point about hedging: a hedge not only protects the hedger against falling prices, but also prevents him from benefitting from rising prices. The hedger's cost of protection against falling prices is that he must sacrifice speculative profits if the cash markets should rise.

Where does the hedger's price protection come from? The answer is that another hedger or, more probably, a speculator bought from the elevator owner the 100,000 bushels of corn contracts on March 19 for $2.50/bushel; and still another futures trader sold corn contracts back to the elevator at $2.40 on March 25. The futures market provides the hedger with price protection when prices fall. In turn, the hedger pays the cash price rise to the futures market when prices increase.

The example just mentioned illustrates a *short hedge,* when a sale of futures is made as a temporary substitute for the cash sale of a commodity. A *long hedge* is used when the firm makes a promise today to deliver commodities, not yet owned, to the cash market at a specified future time. For example, an exporter might agree today to deliver 100,000 bushels of grain to a foreign port next month at a price of $4.50/bushel. For this hedge, the firm is initially short in the cash market, and a long position is taken in futures to set the hedge. The cash transaction is completed one month later when the firm purchases the 100,000 bushels at the going price and delivers them to the port. The hedge is "turned" by selling the original long position in the futures market.

Both of these hedges highlight the importance of equal and opposite positions on the two markets. They also illustrate the "no-profit" nature of the perfect hedge. The purpose of these hedges is to gain risk protection, not to increase profits. Unhedged cash market positions offer a greater opportunity for profit (and for loss) than hedges. For people who like price risks and can afford the accompanying potential losses, the futures market also offers the *Texas hedge*—one which doubles the firm's risk position by taking similar positions (long or short) in both cash and futures markets.

The Storage Hedge

Although the perfect hedge provides valuable insights into the hedging process, it is not an accurate picture of how hedging is practiced by firms. The perfect hedge is a no-profit situation and would be unattractive to most firms. Nor could farmers use these short-term perfect hedges. In the real business world, hedging is both a risk-management and a profit-making tool. Businesses normally use the storage hedge when commodities are to be held for a period of time during which the basis is expected to narrow. This hedge has two purposes: (1) to protect the firm against adverse cash price movements, and (2) to assist the firm in earning *carrying charges* (storage costs, interest, and insurance) during the storage period. The storage hedge can be used by farmers and food marketing firms. Storage facilities are expensive to maintain, and to get the most from these investments the facilities should be used each year. However, there is no guarantee that the seasonal price rise over the storage period will be sufficient to cover these carrying charges. The storage hedge provides the firm with an opportunity not only to protect itself from a cash price decline but also from the possibility that cash prices at the end of the storage period may not compensate the firm for its storage expenses.

The storage hedge is based on the expectation that the basis will narrow for a storable commodity as the futures contract matures. For example, suppose our elevator owner has storage costs of 35 cents per bushel from November to June, and fears that the seasonable cash price rise may be less than this. The elevator owner could refuse to store corn this year, but this would inconvenience his customers. An alternative is to set a storage hedge as follows:

Date	Cash market	Futures market	Basis
November 1	Buy corn @ $2.00/bu and store for spring sale	Sell July corn contract @ $2.50	$ .50
June 1	Sell corn @ $2.30/bu	Buy July corn contract @ $2.40	$ .10
Gain/loss	+.30	+.10	$ +.40

$$
\begin{aligned}
\text{June 1 cash price} &= \$2.30 \\
+\text{ Futures gain} &= \underline{.10} \\
\text{Net value} &= \$2.40 \\
-\text{ Original cash cost} &= \underline{2.00} \\
\text{Return to storage} &= \$\ .40
\end{aligned}
$$

Without this storage hedge, the elevator would receive $2.30/bushel for grain in June—a 5-cent loss on storage operations. The hedge allows the elevator owner to realize a 40-cent gain from storage. This price gain is composed of a 30-cent cash price gain and a 10-cent futures gain. Where did the 40-cent storage return come from? It was paid to the elevator owner by futures market traders who bought the contracts in November and sold them in June. An important point about the storage hedge is that it extracts storage charges from the longs in the futures market. The change in basis (40 cents, in this case) will always be equal to the carrying charge return from the storage hedge.

In actual practice, a firm would decide whether, and when, to set a storage hedge based on its knowledge of the historical spring basis. Because the firm's return to storage is always equal to the basis change, a firm that expected basis to narrow to 10 cents at its lowest point next spring would set the hedge in the fall at the point of widest basis. The elevator owner would not set the hedge until the November basis was at least 45 cents, insuring a 35-cent basis change to just cover storage costs. The firm can "lock-in" any profit above a November basis of 45 cents by using the storage hedge. Thus, storage hedges are motivated by profit seeking as well as risk protection.

To illustrate, suppose that the elevator owner observes a 48-cent basis for July futures when he purchases and stores the corn in November. The 10-cent expected June basis is then promising the elevator owner a 3-cent profit above storage costs ($.48 − .10 − .35). The owner can lock-in this profit with a storage hedge, or wait to see if the November basis will widen more and provide a greater storage profit. If three days later, the November basis has widened to 50 cents, the futures market is promising the firm a 5-cent profit for storage ($.50 − .10 − .35). If the elevator owner feels this

425

is as high as the November basis will go, he can set the storage hedge and lock-in the 5-cent profit. Thus, hedging is a form of speculating on basis; and it does not eliminate the need for intelligent market decisions. And even after the storage hedge is set, there is no guarantee that the basis will follow historical patterns precisely.

The Pre-Harvest Hedge

This hedge is appropriate for farmers during the period between planting and harvesting a crop. It allows farmers to lock-in a profitable selling price before or after the crop is planted and prior to harvest. The pre-harvest hedge requires that the farmer be knowledgeable regarding the *local harvest basis*—the normal difference between local cash prices and the nearby futures price at harvest time. This basis differs widely and therefore must be studied for each area of the country. The basis is more stable for some areas than others.

Suppose that on March 1 the farmer has to decide how much corn to plant. March cash prices are of little help in estimating the following November cash price. But the December futures market is an estimate of what traders believe will be the cash price of corn in December. However, the futures price is a Chicago price, and the farmer will be selling to local elevators. The farmer can subtract the historical harvest basis from the December futures price to estimate the harvest cash price that his local elevator will offer him. This is the "target price" to which he will gear his production to. In order to lock-in this estimated harvest cash price, the farmer can use a pre-harvest hedge as follows:

Date	*Cash market*	*Futures market*	*Expected Nov. basis*
March 1	Plant at estimated Nov. cash price of $2.60 ($3.00 − .40)	Sell Dec. futures @ $3.00/bu	$ .40
November 1	Harvest and sell locally @ $2.40	Buy Dec. futures @ $2.80	$ .40
Loss/Gain		+.20	

Nov. 1 cash price = $2.40
+ Futures gain = .20
Net value = $2.60
Estimated cash price = $2.60

A 40-cent historical basis provides the farmer with a spring estimate harvest cash price of $2.60. If the farmer fears that cash prices might be lower than this at harvest, he can sell December futures in March and buy them back in November when he sells the crop locally. The futures market gain can be added to the $2.40 cash price in November to bring the two transactions back to $2.60—the price the market was promising and the farmer locked-in in March.

The success of the pre-harvest hedge hinges on an accurate prediction of the harvest basis. To the extent that this basis follows its historical pattern, the hedge allows farmers to lock-in desirable harvest prices. It does *not* provide the farmer with any influence on cash prices. Nor can it be helpful to the farmer if the difference between the December futures and the historical harvest basis is an unsatisfactory cash price. The farmer is still a price-taker.

FUTURES MARKET PARTICIPANTS

It should be clear now that there are several different kinds of traders in futures markets, and that these markets perform a number of roles. There are speculators in futures prices and speculators in basis (hedgers). There are traders who wish to assume risks, and others who wish to avoid risks. There are hedgers who fulfill their contracts by delivery of the commodity, and hedgers who nullify their contract positions in the same manner as speculators. There is no typical hedger. One firm may use hedges to protect the value of inventories, another to reduce the risk of an increase in raw material costs, and still another to establish the price of its products in advance.

The futures market serves a variety of purposes. It is a speculative medium, a price-discovery mechanism, and a risk-transfer device. It can also serve to lock-in profitable prices and to facilitate the financing of stored commodities. Despite this versatility, or perhaps because of it, the futures market is not universally understood. And many firms do not use the futures market. Most hedging is done by grain dealers, livestock buyers, and others to whom farmers sell, but not all buyers of farm products hedge.

Only a small portion of farmers trade futures contracts, and many of these do so for speculative reasons rather than for hedging. A national survey in 1977 indicated that about 6 per cent of United States farmers with gross sales of $10,000 or more traded futures contracts in 1976; that large farmers are more likely to trade than smaller ones; and that many farmers trade speculatively but do not hedge.[1] However, the survey indicated that about one third of all farmers keep track of futures prices even though they do not trade. Among the reasons farmers gave for not using the futures market were (1) lack of familiarity with trading, (2) farm too small, (3) trading too risky, and (4) lack of capital for trading.

A special study of the corn futures market was made on January 27,

---

[1] Commodity Futures Trading Commission Report, January 1977.

1967, in order to better understand the nature of traders.[2] As expected, on that day, the number of speculators exceeded the number of hedgers by eight to one, farmers and food marketing firms were among the most active speculators, and more than one third of the long speculative positions were held by farmers. However, virtually every occupation was represented among the traders; architects, physicists, doctors, plumbers, barbers, and secretaries. There were 16 housewives with positions of over 100,000 bushels! One large trader in Liechtenstein was short 200,000 bushels, and a South Vietnamese trader was long 10,000 bushels.

THE FUTURES MARKET CONTROVERSIES

Controversy has surrounded organized futures trading since it began in this country at the Chicago Board of Trade in 1865. The speculative activity of these markets, the close relationship of cash and futures prices, the fact that more commodities are traded than are produced, and the occasional stories of futures market manipulation have resulted in continuing concern with these markets on the part of the trade, the farmer, and the public.

Criticism of the futures market has often led to regulation and sometimes prohibition of these markets. In the 1800's, many states passed laws limiting futures trading. In 1958, after considerable debate, Congress passed a law against onion futures trading on the grounds that excessive speculation resulted in extreme and unwarranted price fluctuations. Over the years, the critics of futures markets have been successful in securing increased federal regulation of the commodity futures markets.

Attitudes toward these markets range from violent opposition to what their detractors call "organized gambling" to staunch defenders of the futures markets as the best example of a perfectly competitive market and the last outpost of a free economy. Many of the criticisms are unfounded, but there are serious questions about these markets. Are they necessary? Do they perform a useful function? How do they affect cash prices, marketing costs, and farm prices? What would be the result of laws prohibiting futures trading?

Most serious observers agree that the futures markets play a valuable role in risk-transfer, equity financing, and forward pricing. But there are other ways to organize these functions and activities in the food industry; moreover, many commodities appear to be marketed efficiently without the benefit of futures trading. The legitimacy of these markets must rest on their positive contributions outweighing whatever drawbacks they have. We shall examine some of the alleged criticisms and contributions of these markets.

---

[2] *Trading in Corn Futures, September 1966-March, 1967,* Commodity Exchange Authority, U.S. Department of Agriculture, August 1967.

Are Speculators Necessary?

Some critics concede the importance of the hedging and risk-transfer roles of these markets but advocate eliminating speculation in futures trading. Speculators, they argue, know nothing of agriculture or farm prices, so their judgments should not be permitted to enter into the futures pricing machinery. They might somehow "misprice" commodities, or the psychology of the speculators might result in exaggerated price swings detrimental to the efficient marketing of commodities.

This line of reasoning suggests that hedgers and speculators are somehow different, and that one is more legitimate than the other. We have seen that both are speculators—one in prices, one in basis. The criticism also neglects the symbiotic relationship of hedgers and speculators. Speculators make active markets for hedgers, and assume the hedgers' risk. Hedging may be the rationale for futures markets, but to be effective for hedging, a futures market needs large numbers of speculators.

Do speculators trade in futures commodities without regard to cash prices, and could they somehow "misprice" commodities? We have seen that cash and futures prices move together in somewhat predictable fashion, and become one at contract maturity. Speculators cannot ignore these price relationships. Speculators do make wrong decisions about prices. However, for every "wrong" decision which loses money there is a corresponding "right" decision on the part of the other speculators who make money.

A related concern is that more contracts are traded than there is product to deliver. However, we have seen that hedgers as well as speculators nullify contracts before they mature. This is necessary if hedging is to be useful to traders who buy and sell other than at contract maturity. The many broken promises in the futures market make it an unusual—but not illegal—market.

Finally, critics sometimes argue that speculators follow mob psychology— everyone buying and selling at once—which exaggerates price swings. Again, every "buy" position is matched with a "sell" position; for every bull there must be a bear; and for every price increasing action (buy) there must be a price decreasing action (sell). The market is symmetrical. Whatever "psychology" is used on one side of the market, an equal psychological force usually exists on the other side.

Do Futures Prices Determine Cash Prices?

The contention that futures prices fluctuate wildly, without regard to fundamental market conditions, is usually linked with a statement that futures prices "determine" cash prices. Undoubtedly, the practice of basing cash prices on futures prices is widespread. Most traders reinforce the suspicion that futures prices determine cash prices when they quote a spot price of "10 cents under the futures price." Nevertheless, the aforementioned statement is not true. Because cash and futures prices are systematically related by the basis, to say that cash determines futures makes as much sense as to say that futures determine cash. Both prices are jointly determined by the same market forces. Another reason for the illusion that futures prices determine cash prices is that the future price *anticipates* events which later affect cash prices. If this occurs accurately, an event will affect first the futures price and then the cash price.

This is not to say that futures trading has no influence on cash prices. One of the most important contributions of futures exchanges is that of establishing a sensitive price-registration machinery. All kinds of news and statistics are focused on the trading floor and are then incorporated into prices. Futures markets are close to perfect competition and thereby contribute to an accurate price-discovery process. By comparison, many imperfectly competitive cash markets are relatively sluggish in responding to market developments.

Studies of the effect of speculators on short-run futures price variability provide mixed results. Some research shows that speculators increase price variations, whereas others suggest that speculators moderate price variability. However, there is general agreement that futures trading does diminish seasonal price fluctuations of storable commodities, and does reduce the magnitude of price changes from one season to another.

Effects on Marketing Costs

Because risk-bearing has a cost, the shifting of risk through futures trading can potentially lower hedgers' marketing costs. In turn, lower marketing costs hold the promise of higher farm prices or lower retail prices. Whether the shifting of risk from food industry hedgers to speculators outside the industry actually lowers hedgers' marketing costs depends upon what speculators can extract from hedgers in the way of risk-handling charges. Most observers have concluded that speculators willingly assume and finance hedgers' price risks at *no cost* whatsoever to the food industry. Therefore marketing costs are reduced by the costs of risk for a net increase in operational efficiency for the food industry. In effect, the speculators are subsidizing the hedgers' price risks.

Is Speculation a Fair Game?

Above all, the futures markets are speculative vehicles. Most speculators are not even aware of their role in the hedging and risk-transfer operations. Their only interest is in profits and losses.

As an almost perfectly competitive market, the futures markets are "fair." No one is barred from trading, and all who trade do so willingly. Each trader recognizes—or should be aware of—the opportunities for gains and the possibility of losses.

As a group, speculators do not break even. Total speculative gains are equal to total speculative losses—a break-even proposition—but brokers are paid regardless of profits or losses. Despite stories of enormous speculative gains, the brokers are probably the only participants in the futures market who consistently make a profit. Among speculators, the consensus is that the great majority of speculative trades result in losses. The speculative gains are concentrated among a few, large traders. Even for professional speculators, trading success requires a few highly successful trades to offset the small losses of numerous losing trades.

Does Hedging Work?

The perfect hedge is rare. And most hedges are motivated by a desire to earn profits rather than to avoid losses. But, clearly, hedging can transfer risks and thus be a profitable marketing tool. Basis *is* more predictable than cash prices. And hedging is widely— if not universally—practiced by the trade. The reason that more firms do not hedge is probably the result of a lack of understanding of the process rather than because of deficiencies in hedging per se.

The role of hedges in financial management is also important. Firms can usually borrow working capital on the value of hedged inventories. Farmers also can secure equity financing by fixing the selling price of commodities in advance through storage or pre-harvest hedges.

Can Futures Prices Be Manipulated?

The history of futures trading is sprinkled with reports of price fixing, rigging, corners, power plays, and market manipulation. These allegations continue today. The markets attract big spenders, and the profits to be won by the successful manipulation of "wheeler-dealers" are enormous. The market is fueled by greed, which is only kept in check by competitive forces and by regulated trading rules.

There were several famous market "corners" in the late nineteenth century. A *corner* results when a single individual holds a large portion of the outstanding long positions and also controls most of the commodity that could be delivered by the short sellers at contract maturity. As maturity approaches, the shorts can either buy back their speculative positions or purchase grain and deliver it against the contracts. However, they face the same seller in both cases, and must pay his price—which is steep!

Today, the manipulation of futures markets is a difficult and hazardous venture. Recent regulations on the quantity of contracts that can be held by one individual, increases in the number of delivery points, and more careful

431

scrutiny of these markets for anti-competitive behavior limit the opportunities for manipulation of the markets. Overall, the futures markets are probably no more subject to manipulation than are cash markets.

FORWARD CONTRACTS AND FUTURES CONTRACTS

A distinction should be made between a *forward contract* and a *futures contract.* In the spring, farmers can sign contracts with local elevator owners for the delivery of grain at harvest time, at a prearranged price. This is a forward contract, and works somewhat like the pre-harvest hedge: the farmer can lock-in a favorable price for his crop in the spring when planting decisions are being made.

However, the forward contract has two disadvantages as compared with the pre-harvest hedge. The reason why the buyer can offer a guaranteed price to the farmer in the spring is because once the spring contract is signed, the elevator owner sets a pre-harvest hedge. So the first disadvantage of the forward contract is that the farmer is, in effect, asking the elevator owner to do his hedging for him. And the charge for this service is reflected in the contract price. The second disadvantage is that farmers have less flexibility with forward contracts than with hedges. A farmer can remove his hedge if it becomes certain that cash prices at harvest will be higher than the estimated hedge price. On the other hand, farmers must deliver against their forward contracts, regardless of the cash price.

PUBLIC REGULATION OF FUTURES TRADING

Public concern with futures markets—and especially alleged "excessive" speculation—has resulted in state and federal regulation of these markets. The regulations complement the very extensive self-regulating efforts of the commodity exchanges.

The Grain Futures Act of 1922 was the initial federal regulation of futures markets. In 1936, this law was amended to the Commodity Exchange Act. These laws granted authority to the federal government to prevent market abuses, price manipulation, cheating, and fraud in futures markets.

From 1936 until 1975, futures trading was regulated by the Commodity Exchange Authority (CEA), a division of the U.S. Department of Agriculture. Regulatory authority over these markets was shifted to the Commodity Futures Trading Commission (CFTC) by the Commodity Futures Act of 1974.

SUMMARY

There is inherent price risk in producing, handling, and processing agricultural commodities. The futures market exchanges are highly developed markets, resembling the perfectly competitive markets, where speculators and hedgers transfer price risks and compete for profits. A hedge is a risk-management and profit-seeking marketing tool that involves the temporary substitution of a futures market transaction for a cash market transaction. The predictability of the difference between cash and futures prices—termed the basis—is essential to effective hedging. Both farmers and food marketing firms may use storage hedges. Farmers, in addition, may use pre-harvest hedges or contract sales to forward price their commodities during the production process. The commodity futures markets are much criticized, but they play necessary and important roles in risk management, financing, market intelligence, and the price discovery process.

QUESTIONS FOR DISCUSSION

1. Discuss the following markets as futures markets: (a) a college education; (b) a lay-away purchase from a department store; (c) a newspaper subscription. What are the price risks in each case?

2. Discuss the wisdom of setting hedges in inflationary periods versus deflationary periods.

3. What are some possible reasons why there are no organized futures markets for automobiles, homes, and other consumer items?

4. Show that a rising basis for a storage hedge provides less than full price risk protection when prices fall.

5. On October 5, 1947, the President of the United States criticized the commodity futures markets by saying, "the cost of living in this country must not be a football to be kicked about by gamblers in grain." Comment on this statement.

6. It is frequently felt that amateur commodity speculators lose so often because they "cut their profits short and let their losses run," whereas the professionals "cut their losses short and let their profits run." How do you account for these differences in trading behavior?

7. On a chart, plot the basis of a grain commodity and a livestock commodity for three months. What are the differences in basis patterns for these?

SELECTED REFERENCES

ARTHUR, H. B. *Commodity Futures As a Business Management Tool.* Harvard University Press, Cambridge, Mass. 1971.

Commodity Futures Trading, Annual Bibliography, 1967–1976, Chicago Board of Trade, Annual.

GOLD, G. *Modern Commodity Futures Trading.* Commodity Research Bureau, Inc., New York, 1971.

HAMMONDS, T. M. *The Commodity Futures Market from an Agricultural Producer's Point of View.* MSS Information Corp., New York, 1972.

Hedging Potential in Grain Storage and Livestock Feeding. U.S. Department of Agriculture. Agricultural Economic Report No. 238, Jan. 1973

433

HIERONYMUS, T. A. *Economics of Futures Trading,* 2nd Ed., Commodity Research Bureau, Inc., New York, 1977.

PAUL, A. B., R. G. HEIFNER, AND J. W. HELMUTH. *Farmers' Use of Forward Contracts and Futures Markets.* U.S. Department of Agriculture. Agricultural Economics Report No. 320, March 1976.

POWERS, M. J. *Getting Started in Commodity Futures Trading.* Investor Publications, Inc., Columbia, Md., 1973.

SWARTZ, A., et al. *Trading in Commodity Futures Contracts on the Chicago Board of Trade.* U.S. Department of Agriculture. Marketing Research Report No. 999, July 1973.

PART V

Government and Food Marketing

CHAPTER 21

Government Price, Income, and Marketing Programs

"ALTHOUGH IT IS WIDELY AGREED, and has long been held, that the fundamen-
.al goal of farm policy is to maintain a prosperous, productive farm sector
with a family-farm type of organization, differences arise—important differences—with regard to the means for achieving that broad policy goal. Should
equitable farm incomes and the family-farm structure be obtained solely through
the marketplace or through direct governmental assistance? This question is
at the heart of most farm policy debates and influences the selection and evaluation of particular policy proposals."*

Preview

- This chapter introduces the fundamentals of government farm price and
income policies and discusses their impacts on food marketing.
- A rationale for government intervention in farm markets is developed
and discussed.
- The history of U.S. farm price and income policies from 1920 to 1977
is reviewed.
- The calculation and role of parity prices in farm policy are discussed.
- The nature and costs of three farm policy techniques—storage loans,
government purchases, and target price deficiency payments are examined.
- Discussed in this chapter are the key issues in the debate over the effects
of farm policy on farm prices and incomes, agricultural output and stability,
food marketing costs, and consumer prices.

* W. W. Cochrane and Mary E. Ryan, *American Farm Policy, 1948–73,* University of Minnesota Press, Minneapolis, 1976.

437

- Key terms and concepts:
  agricultural treadmill   parity
  deficiency payment   set-aside
  loan rate or price   support price
  nonrecourse loan   target price

Farm policies are attempts to achieve broadly held social goals through the instruments and powers of government. Because the state of the rural economy is considered so important, some form of government involvement in farm and food markets is found in most societies. In the United States government farm policies have been shaped by the American "farm problem"—unstable farm prices and incomes, periodically declining farm prices, and low farm incomes relative to nonfarm incomes.

Government intervention in prices, incomes, and markets is always controversial. There are philosophic conflicts, as well as differences in opinion, as to what the problems are, how government could contribute to the solutions, and the precise form the policy should take. Two polar views are (1) that the government should play *no direct role* in influencing farm markets or farm incomes (the free market approach), and (2) that the food industry should be *regulated like a public utility,* with strong government controls. Actual farm policies are somewhere between these two views. Government involvement in farm prices and incomes in the United States appears to alternate between increasing and decreasing intervention. These cycles are triggered by changes in the level of farm prices, shifts in the balance of political power, and changing attitudes toward government intervention.

Although farm policies usually are directly addressed to farmers' problems and production agriculture, they invariably influence the marketing of food in important ways. Price-support programs, land-retirement or set-aside policies, and government surplus-purchase programs not only affect farm production and prices, they also influence all the other actors in the food industry. At the same time, many farm policies require direct intervention in food marketing activities: trade policy; demand-expansion programs; processing taxes, and the like. Thus it is practically impossible to isolate "farm policy" from "food and marketing policy" today.

RATIONALE FOR GOVERNMENT MARKET INTERVENTION

Throughout this book, a number of the dimensions of the "farm problem" and the "farmer's marketing problem" have been discussed. Because these are frequently cited as justifications for government involvement in agriculture, they are reviewed here.

Many farm price and income problems stem from the nearly perfect competitive nature of agriculture and the inelastic demand for most farm products. As price-takers, farmers attempt to improve profits by expanding production. This shifts the agricultural supply curve rightward along an inelastic demand. Farmers do not adjust output to falling prices, and they face a cost-price squeeze because the prices of purchased inputs do not adjust downward as much as farm prices. Although the inelastic demand gives farmers an incentive to restrict supply and raise prices, their large numbers, geographic dispersion, and widely varying economic levels make organization of farmers difficult. And it is difficult for farmers to influence the demand for food as other firms do with advertising, promotion, and other market development tools.

In contrast to these conditions, the farmer sells his products to an imperfectly competitive food marketing system which adds some 60 per cent of the total value of food products, readily adjusts quantity and prices to changes in consumer demand, engages in extensive market development activities, and has varying degrees of control over the final selling price of food products. The balance of power at farm gate markets is quite predictable.

In addition to these farmer marketing problems, the uniqueness of food as a product has fostered government involvement in its production, marketing and consumption. The availability of an adequate and reasonably priced food supply influences social stability and international power relations. As a strategic commodity, nations may elect to trade off some economic efficiency for self-sufficiency in food production. Society may also elect to interfere with "free markets" where it is judged that these will lead to unacceptable income or product distribution. Should the rich man's cat get the milk needed by the poor man's child? Should food prices be permitted to rise when the effects will be more damaging to the poor than to the rich? Should consumers be permitted to choose poor diets if this influences national health, worker productivity, and unemployment? Do farmers have a right to a guaranteed price above costs of production? Obviously, value judgments are involved, and these will color society's attitudes toward free markets for food.

THE EVOLUTION OF UNITED STATES FARM PRICE AND INCOME POLICY

Although farm policies change, the basic instruments of farm policy—price-fixing, income supplements, supply control, government purchases, and storage and demand expansion programs—have been used throughout history. They were part of the farm programs of the early Egyptians, Romans, and Greeks.[1] And they are found in the 1977 farm bill. Twentieth-century U.S.

---

[1] See Mary G. Lacy, "Food Control During Forty-Six Centuries," *Scientific Monthly,* June 1923.

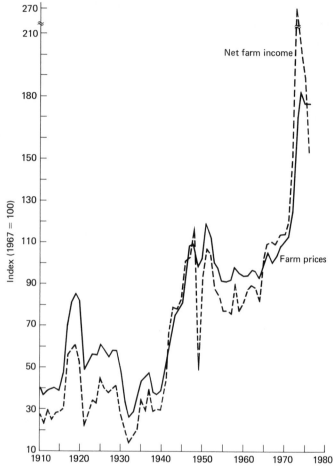

Figure 21–1. Farm prices and net farm income, 1910–1976. (U.S. Department of Agriculture)

farm policy can be best understood when viewed in the context of the trends in farm prices and income as shown in Figure 21-1.

The 1920's

Attempts to influence farm prices can be traced to colonial days, when there were restrictions on tobacco supplies. However, modern U.S. farm policy began in the 1920's against the setting of the great farmer movements of the late 1800's, the Populist political movement of the early 1900's, and the post-World War I depression.

Within two and a half years after World War I, prices farmers received had fallen 52 per cent from their postwar peaks. Prices paid by farmers had declined only 18 per cent. Net farm income in 1921 was only 39 per cent of its 1919 peak. Though prices received recovered somewhat, the relationship between prices received and prices paid remained about 15 per cent below the prewar relationship throughout the 1920's.

The cry for agricultural relief arose out of this difficult price and income situation. Several bills aimed at relieving the situation were poured into the legislative hoppers by farm-sensitive Congressmen. However, the one principal plan, which was debated throughout the decade of the 1920's, was based upon separating the domestic and foreign markets. Domestic prices were to be pegged at a "fair" level. All that could not be sold domestically at that level was to be purchased by the government. This excess amount would then be sold on the world market for what it would bring. High tariffs were to protect the domestic markets from foreign imports. The government loss between the domestic support prices and the world prices was to be shared equally, through various methods, among agricultural producers. The net price to farmers would then be the domestic support prices minus the losses suffered in the world market. This basic idea was introduced into Congress as the McNary-Haugen Bill. The bill was approved twice by Congress, in 1927 and in 1928, but was vetoed both times by President Coolidge.

Though the McNary-Haugen plans never became law, they merit attention because they represented the opening guns of the battle to guarantee a "fair" price for agriculture. The assumption was that domestic demand was inelastic whereas the world demand was elastic, or at least less inelastic than domestic demand. By restricting amounts and raising prices, the total returns from the domestic market could be maximized. If the world market demand for U.S. farm products was more elastic, selling more in the world market would increase the total returns. Because the domestic price level would be substantially above the world price level, the total dollars for the wheat crop would be increased. In addition, such a system still permitted products to sell at the world price levels in the export trade even though domestic prices were protected at much higher levels.

In 1929, with the passage of the Agricultural Marketing Act, emphasis changed from the two-price approach of the McNary-Haugen plans to one of "orderly marketing." The basic philosophy of this law was that agricultural problems resulted from disorganized distribution methods. If products could be stored by farmers and released in an orderly fashion throughout the year, higher price and income levels could be secured. To attain this goal, farm cooperatives were to be encouraged vigorously.

The Federal Farm Board, established to put the program into effect, was given an initial appropriation of $500 million to undertake loan-storage programs to stabilize farm prices. However, the newly established board was just taking its first tottering steps when the depression struck. By 1933 it had spent all its funds, acquired large stocks of commodities, and prices had still fallen drastically. The Board died when Congress did not grant it additional funds.

The 1930's

Starting in 1930, prices began to slide again. By early 1933, prices received by farmers were 62 per cent below 1929. Prices paid, again lagging behind, were only 32 per cent lower. Net farm income in 1932 was 70 per cent below 1929. For those whose memories are only of the recent price levels, a look at the depression prices of several commodities will help in gauging the seriousness of the situation.

The United States average farm prices for several commodities in 1932 were as follows:

Corn	$0.32	Milk	1.28
Oats	0.16	Hogs	3.34
Wheat	0.38	Cattle	4.25
Cotton	0.07		

Though we are here concerned with agricultural developments, we must not overlook that the whole country was on its economic knees. Businesses failed; banks shut their doors; one out of every four workers was without a job. The agricultural program that developed was only a part of a broad program that included social security and unemployment insurance for workers, special legislation for banks, and the National Industrial Recovery Act for other businesses.

The legislative developments of the 1930's signaled a change in the basic approach to the problems of a depressed agriculture. During the 1920's the two-price system was offered as a device by which our agricultural production could have a protected domestic market and yet secure what it could get from the world market. The Federal Farm Board proposed to solve the problem by helping farmers to level out the peaks and valleys of their marketings and thereby stabilize the prices of agricultural products. The basic approach now to be followed was to reduce production. In this manner, demand and supply were to be brought into balance at prices that were "fair" to farmers. Though many camouflaging terms were used, the basic concept of curtailing production prevailed.

The Agricultural Adjustment Act of 1933 and 1938, along with the 1936 Soil Conservation and Domestic Allotment Act and the 1937 Agricultural Marketing Agreement Act, were the forerunners of modern farm programs. The 1977 Agricultural Act, detailing the federal farm program for 1978 and 1979, was an amendment to the 1938 Agricultural Adjustment Act. These depression-born farm policies attempted to help farmers through supply control and "orderly marketing" measures. The Commodity Credit Corporation

(CCC) was founded to make storage loans to farmers and to support farm prices at above equilibrium levels through government purchase and storage activities. Acreage controls, import quotas, and soil conservation programs were authorized to limit food supplies, and income supplements were granted to farmers for compliance with these programs. Marketing orders and agreements permitted farmers to control the quantity and quality of farm products marketed and, in the case of milk, set minimum prices. Surplus food distribution, the school lunch program, and food stamps were instituted in the 1930's to attack the demand side of the farm problem.

1940–1952

Farm prices and incomes rose dramatically from 1940 to 1952. Food production and supplies were curtailed by the diversion of resources and output to defense needs. Food demand was fueled by World War II, the inflation following this war, the Marshall Plan, and the Korean conflict. These were prosperous years for agriculture, and only minor adjustments were made in the 1933–1938 farm programs. Consumers experienced food rationing and food price controls.

The 1950's and 1960's

During this period, the scientific and technological revolution in agriculture resulted in greatly expanded food production capacity. These increased supplies pressed against an inelastic and more slowly growing demand for food. The result was a downward pressure on farm prices which, combined with persistently rising farm input costs, intensified the cost-price squeeze in agriculture. Farmers reacted predictably to this situation by readily adopting the newest output-increasing and cost-reducing technologies and by further expanding output. This was called the *agricultural treadmill* because farmers had to run fast just to stay in one place. By and large, consumers received the benefits of this situation through declining relative prices of food. Farm prices fell drastically in 1953 and 1954 and then stabilized from 1954 to 1957, propped up by acreage controls, subsidized exports, price supports, and government purchase programs.

A number of farm policies were developed in the 1954–1967 period to improve farm prices and incomes. The Agricultural Trade Development and Assistance Act of 1954 (P.L. 480), also known at the "food for peace program," attempted to bolster farm prices by exporting surplus commodities to needy countries. The 1956 soil bank program authorized the government to rent cropland from farmers, thus withdrawing this land from production.

By the end of the 1950's, the efficient agricultural machine had reduced farm prices 21 per cent from 1951 levels; annual net farm income had fallen from $15 billion in 1950–1953 to $12 billion in 1957–1959; P.L. 480 food

443

exports (some would call them giveaways) were running at more than $1 billion per year; and the federal treasury costs of the farm surplus program were estimated at $9 billion in 1960. The value of government-owned food stocks rose from $1.3 billion in 1952 to $7.7 billion in 1959, and by 1961 the cost of storing a bushel of grain purchased by the government exceeded the original farm value of the grain.

The 1960's saw a movement toward stronger farm supply control programs and the payment of direct income supplements to farmers. Some supply control programs were mandatory, others were voluntary. Under voluntary programs farmers were offered incentive payments to comply with supply controls to avoid surplus production at the support price levels. The acreage diversions and set-asides, particularly for feedgrains, wheat, and cotton, resulted in a slow rise in farm income and the gradual working down of stocks in the 1960's. Diverted acreage rose from 29 million acres in 1960 to a peak of 63 million acres in 1966, as shown in Figure 21–2. Government payments to farmers for this diversion rose from $177 million in 1960 to $1.3 billion in 1969.

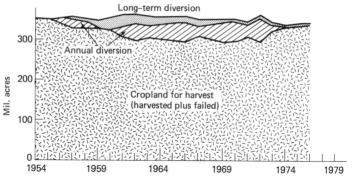

Figure 21–2. U.S. cropland intended for harvest and diverted acreage. (U.S. Department of Agriculture)

The 1970's

Farm policy in the 1970's reflected rising farm prices and income in the first half of the decade and falling prices and incomes in the second half. Farm prices rose at an annual rate of 5 per cent from 1967 to 1972, increased 43 per cent in 1973 (largely on the strength of greatly expanded exports), and 7 per cent in 1974, then fell in 1975, 1976, and 1977. Net farm income (including government payments) rose from $14 billion in 1970 to a peak of $30 billion in 1973. Farm prices were lifted from support levels in the 1970–1974 period, and then worked back down to support levels in the 1975–1977 period.

THE DEVELOPMENT OF PARITY

Throughout the 1920's, farmers sought an economic *parity,* or equality, with other sectors of the economy. The Agricultural Adjustment Act of 1933 established the criterion for a fair price for agriculture. Parity, or fair price, was that price which would give agricultural commodities the equivalent purchasing power over articles which farmers bought that they had in a base period. The base period for the great majority of products was established as the five-year period from August 1909 to July 1914. This period was chosen because it was believed that farm and nonfarm prices were in reasonable and fair balance during those years.

To find the parity ratio for agriculture as a whole was then a simple process as follows:

$$\frac{\text{Current index of prices received (1910–1914 base)}}{\text{Current index of prices paid \quad (1910–1914 base)}} \times 100 = \text{Parity ratio.}$$

Obviously the parity ratio for 1910–1914 would be 100. Whenever prices received by farmers did not rise as much—or fell more—than prices paid, the ratio would fall. Conversely, when prices received rose more—or fell less—than prices paid, the ratio would rise.

The parity price for an individual commodity also could be calculated as follows:

$$\frac{\begin{array}{l}\text{Average price} \\ \text{received for} \\ \text{the commodity} \\ \text{during 1910–1914}\end{array} \times \begin{array}{l}\text{Current} \\ \text{index of} \\ \text{prices} \\ \text{paid}\end{array}}{100} = \text{Current parity price.}$$

When the actual current price was below the price obtained from the preceding calculation, the commodity was below parity. The market price was not one that would give the commodity the same purchasing power as it had in 1910–1914.

As time passed, it became obvious that such a formula had a great shortcoming. There was no provision for taking into account any changes that had taken place since 1910–1914 in either the demand or the supply of the commodity. For example, the present parity or fair price of horses under the preceding formula would still be the price comparable to the purchasing power horse prices represented in 1910–1914. But with modern mechanized farming and the reduced demand for horses this was a ridiculous goal for a fair price. The example is an extreme one, but it shows the problem of handling change when only a fixed period in the past is used.

In 1948 the parity formula for individual commodities was changed. Though the desired purchasing power was still tied to the 1910–1914 base, the base period for prices of a commodity was to be calculated for the most recent ten years. Therefore, the formula for calculating the current parity price of a commodity would be as follows:

$$\frac{\text{Average price of commodity, most recent ten years}}{\text{Average index of all prices received, most recent ten years}} \times \frac{\text{Current index of prices paid}} = \text{Current parity price.}$$

A little experimentation with this formula will demonstrate how changes that have occurred in the supply-demand pattern of a commodity are incorporated into the parity price. For the parity ratio for all agricultural prices,

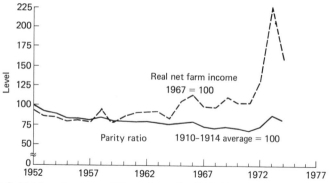

Figure 21–3. Net farm income and the parity ratio, 1952–1974. (F. Holland, "The Concept and Use of Parity in Agricultural Price and Income Policy," *Agricultural Food Policy Review,* U.S. Department of Agriculture, 1977, pp. 54–60. Reprinted by permission)

calculations remain unchanged, because 1910–1914 is still the benchmark for over-all purchasing power.

The parity ratio does not measure the cost of farm production nor farmers' standard of living. As a ratio of price, it indicates the purchasing power of farm commodities but does not reflect returns to labor, management, or farm assets. As shown in Figure 21-3, real net farm income can rise (as in 1959–1962) even when the parity ratio is falling.

The parity ratio reached its highest point—120—in 1918 and its lowest point of 58 in 1932. Farm prices were at or above parity for the 1942–1952 period, but were below parity for the 1953–1978 period.

Although parity prices remain a feature of current farm bills, the role of parity in setting support prices has changed. Since 1948, Secretaries of Agriculture have had the authority to vary support price levels from 60 to 90 per cent of parity. Only milk prices were linked to the parity ratio—at the 80 per cent level—in the 1977 farm bill.

ANALYSIS OF FARM PRICE AND INCOME SUPPORT PROGRAMS

Contemporary farm programs have employed three techniques to directly influence farm prices and incomes: (1) storage loans; (2) government purchase and disposal programs; and (3) direct farm income supplements. These alternative approaches to the farm price and income problems vary in method of operation, government costs, and other details. They are illustrated in Figure 21-4, using the supply and demand analysis.

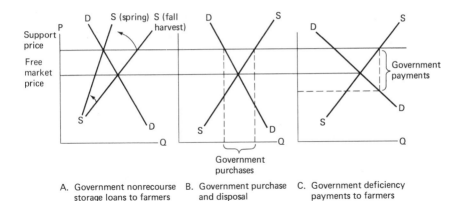

A. Government nonrecourse storage loans to farmers
B. Government purchase and disposal
C. Government deficiency payments to farmers

Figure 21–4. Analysis of government farm price and income programs.

Nonrecourse Storage Loans

Under the terms of a *nonrecourse loan,* the farmer obtains a government loan on his crop at harvest, when he stores. The *loan price,* or rate, is the price level at which the government supports the commodity. By taking the loan, the farmer is assured of this minimum price for his crop.

The nonrecourse loan assists the farmer to pay for storing his crop and prevents his having to sell for cash at the harvest-time low prices. If, later in the season, the cash market price rises above the loan rate, the farmer may reclaim his crop, sell it at the going market price, repay the loan and interest, and thus take advantage of seasonal price rises. If the seasonal market price never reaches the loan rate, the farmer delivers the crop to the government's Commodity Credit Corporation as payment for the loan.

The cost to government of storage loan programs depends upon the loan rate, the interest rate charged on the loans, the seasonal price rise, and the amount of the crop that is delivered to the CCC against the loans. These programs have been important forms of farm price supports for most grains, tobacco, and cotton.

Government Purchase and Storage Programs

The government can also support farm prices through direct purchase, storage, and disposal programs. For these programs, the government purchases that quantity of the commodity necessary to make the price rise to the desired support level. This is shown in Figure 21-4. These government stocks can be sold later (in periods of higher prices), disposed of through noncompeting outlets, or, as a last resort, destroyed.

This type of farm program led to the high stock levels of the 1950's. As a result, in the 1960's government purchase programs were tied to supply control provisions, such as acreage allotments and marketing quotas. There was also, in the 1960's, an expansion of government food programs—such as school lunches—to which these stocks could be channeled.

The costs of these programs obviously depend upon the elasticity of supply and demand for farm products. As supply and demand become less elastic, the government cost of supporting prices at any level declines. Government purchase, storage, and disposal programs are the chief way of supporting U.S. milk prices.

Direct Farm Payments

The 1973 and 1977 farm bills represented a movement away from stock-building government purchase programs and toward direct government price supplements. *Deficiency payments* are made to farmers when prices are below the target or support levels. This approach is illustrated in Figure 21-4. Farm supplies are permitted to clear markets at equilibrium levels, and the deficiency payment goes to the farmer directly from the government, rather than through the medium of higher market prices. Eligibility for these deficiency payments may or may not require participation in the allied supply control programs.

The government cost of direct farm payments depends upon the level of the support price relative to the free market clearing price and upon the elasticity of the supply and demand curves. In the late 1970's, direct payment and loan programs were the principal forms of government farm price supports for grains, tobacco, cotton, and dairy products. These programs have never been used to support livestock prices.

IMPACTS OF FARM PROGRAMS ON MARKETING

Each of these agricultural price and income programs have affected food marketing firms, the costs of performing several food marketing functions, and the retail cost of food to consumers.

The programs are intended to raise farm prices and income—or at least prevent them from falling. To the extent that this goal is accomplished, food marketing firms and consumers pay either higher food prices or higher taxes in order to support these farm programs. In this sense, the programs represent a transfer of income from the nonfarm to the farm sector. What do consumers, marketing firms, and society get for this? Here there is considerable difference of opinion. Although many of the farm programs have price and income enhancement and supply control as objectives, agricultural output has continued to grow in the fertile economic environment of higher and more stable farm prices. Some might say that the programs are a reasonable price to pay for an abundant, relatively inexpensive food supply and an agricultural sector where incomes are brought closer to nonfarm incomes. Others might point out that the almost perfectly competitive nature of agriculture would guarantee an abundant and even cheaper food supply even if there were no such programs. The debate quickly comes down to, what is a "reasonable" price for consumers to pay for food? and what is a "fair" return for the farmers' productive effort?

The precise level of farm prices and incomes are probably not of great concern to food marketing firms. These firms can adjust their selling prices to farm prices within a broad range. However, food marketing firms' costs are influenced by the quantity of farm products produced. Thus, these firms would have reason to support output-increasing farm policies.

Food marketing firms also benefit from the price-and quantity-stabilizing effects of farm price support and stock programs. Stability in farm markets assists these firms in accurately forecasting product costs and in making future investments in plants and equipment. Government subsidy and storage programs also probably reduce the costs of storage and risk-bearing functions for food marketing firms. The sales of these firms benefit too when the government supports prices by purchasing food products, such as milk and canned goods, or attempts to expand the demand for food through food stamps. Some food processors also benefit from school lunch and milk programs.

Do consumers benefit from the stabilization of food markets by government programs? The answer appears to be yes, in the case of programs that increase and stabilize food supplies. However, most consumers do not carry large food stocks and are somewhat flexible in their purchases. Fluctuating food

449

prices pose no great burden for consumers so long as some prices are falling while others are rising, because acceptable substitutions can be made.

SUMMARY

Throughout history and in most societies, governments have intervened in farm production, prices, and incomes. The United States has been no exception. Contemporary farm policies date from the 1920's, and have been shaped over the years by farm price and income trends, changing attitudes toward government's role in farm and food policy, and the changing political constituency. The parity ratio—the ratio of farm prices received to prices paid—does not directly measure farm income but indicates the purchasing power of farm commodities. Government loan, purchase, and direct payment programs are the chief techniques by which government has influenced farm prices and incomes in the post-World War II period. The trend is toward direct government or deficiency payments to farmers when prices fall below support levels. These farm price and income programs can benefit food marketing firms and consumers through increasing output and stabilization of food prices. However, there is debate about whether their benefits justify the costs of these programs.

QUESTIONS FOR DISCUSSION

1. Discuss the pros and cons of government farm price and income policies.

2. In Figure 21-1, trace the impacts of farm price and income levels, wars, and the urbanization of the American people on farm policy.

3. What problems arise as the result of basing a parity price for agriculture on the 1910–1914 years?

4. How would knowledge of the costs of storing grain from harvest to the following spring be helpful in setting the nonrecourse loan rate?

5. Demonstrate that government purchase programs are less costly to the government than deficiency payments when the demand and supply curves are highly inelastic.

6. Farmers frequently complain that government storage programs depress farm prices. Do you agree or disagree?

7. How do the buyers of farm products benefit from government programs that increase the supply of agricultural products and stabilize farm prices?

SELECTED REFERENCES

Agricultural Prices and Parity. Major Statistical Series of the USDA. Agricultural Handbook No. 365, Vol. 1, Oct. 1970.

BENEDICT, M. R. *Farm Policies of the United States, 1790–1950.* Twentieth Century Fund, New York, 1953.

BRANDOW, G. E. "Cost of Farm Programs." *Benefits and Burdens of Rural Development.* Iowa State University, Ames, Iowa, 1970.

BRANDOW, G. E., "Policy for Commercial Agriculture, 1945–71," in L. R. Martin, Ed., *A Survey of Agricultural Economics Literature,* Vol. I. University of Minnesota Press, Minneapolis, 1977, pp. 209–292.

BREIMYER, H. F. "Fifty Years of Federal Marketing Programs." *Journal of Farm Economics* (Nov. 1963) 749–58.

COCHRANE, W. W. *The City Man's Guide to the Farm Problem.* University of Minnesota Press, Minneapolis, 1965.

_____ AND M. E. RYAN. *American Farm Policy, 1948–73.* University of Minnesota Press, Minneapolis, 1976.

DAHL, D. C., and J. W. HAMMOND. "Market and Price Policy." *Market and Price Analysis.* McGraw-Hill Book Company, New York, 1977.

Farm Commodity and Related Programs. U.S. Department of Agriculture. Agriculture Handbook No. 345, March 1976.

Food and Fiber for the Future. Report of the National Advisory Commission on Food and Fiber. U.S. Government Printing Office, Washington, D. C., July 1967.

PAARLBERG, D. *American Farm Policy.* Parts 5 and 6. John Wiley & Sons, Inc. New York, 1964.

RASMUSSEN, W. D., AND G. L. BAKER. "A Short History of Price Support and Adjustment Legislation and Programs for Agriculture, 1933–65." *Agricultural Economics Research* (1966), 69–78.

ROBINSON, K. L. "Commodity Policies and Programs." *Contours of Change.* Yearbook of Agriculture. U.S. Department of Agriculture, 1970, pp. 117–123.

RUTTAN, V. W., et al. *Agricultural Policy in An Affluent Society.* W. W. Norton & Company, Inc. New York, 1969.

TOMEK, G. W., and K. L. ROBINSON. "Government Intervention in Pricing Farm Products," *Agricultural Product Prices.* Cornell University Press, Ithaca, New York, 1972.

TWEETEN, L. G. *Foundations of Farm Policy.* University of Nebraska Press, Lincoln, Neb., 1970.

CHAPTER 22

Food Marketing Regulations

"THE AMERICAN FOOD INDUSTRY has developed under a system in which individual business firms have made virtually all operating and investment decisions within general limits established by public policy . . . the role of government has been to provide certain services and to establish rules to assure that the competitive system operates in the interest of the public and of the industry itself."*

Preview

• This chapter introduces the major laws and regulations influencing the food marketing system.

• Six categories of regulations are discussed: (1) competitive regulations; (2) regulations to control monopolies; (3) trade-facilitating and service regulations; (4) consumer protection regulations; (5) direct food price regulations; and (6) regulations to foster economic and social progress.

• The question of whether, when, and how to regulate marketing activities is discussed.

• An important distinction is drawn between restrictive, facilitating, and permissive market regulations.

• The principal food marketing regulatory agencies are explained.

• The reader is introduced to the following laws:
Sherman Anti-Trust Act
Clayton Act
Federal Trade Commission Act

---

* *Food from Farmer to Consumer,* Report of the National Commission on Food Marketing, Washington, D.C., 1966.

Robinson-Patman Act
Tydings-Miller Act
McGuire Act
Webb-Pomerene Act
Capper-Volstead Act
Agricultural Fair Practice Act
Agricultural Marketing and Bargaining Act
Packers and Stockyards Act
United States Warehouse Act
Produce Agency Act
Perishable Agricultural Commodities Act
Food and Drug Act
Wheeler-Lea Act
Truth-in-Packaging Act
Wholesome Meat Act
Patent Act
Morrill Land-Grant College Act
Hatch Act
Smith-Lever Act
Smith-Hughes Act
Research and Marketing Act

What the appropriate role of government regulation in the food industry should be is a highly controversial topic. Why is public regulation of food markets necessary at all? Is more or less regulation needed in the food industry? Do the benefits of market regulations in the food industry justify their costs? Is regulation improving the food industry, or is the industry over-regulated? These are important food marketing regulation issues.

There has been a rapid growth in the scope of government market regulations in recent years. Many of these newer regulations touch the food industry. In 1976 there were an estimated 77 different federal agencies regulating some aspect of marketing. The newest regulatory missions of the federal government include occupational safety, environmental protection, and energy conservation and development. Each of these regulatory areas has increased the role of government in the market economy. Few food production or marketing decisions today are wholly free from some government regulation.

The food industry is among the most highly regulated of all consumer product industries because of its importance to consumers, farmers, and society in general. Many food industry regulations stem from consumers' concerns with the wholesomeness, quality, and cost of the food supply and from the

453

efforts of farmers and consumers to maintain a workably competitive food marketing system.

Here, food marketing regulations are grouped into 6 classes.

1. Regulations to maintain competition and prevent monopoly.
2. Regulations to control monopoly conditions.
3. Regulations to facilitate trade and provide public services.
4. Regulations to protect consumers.
5. Regulations to directly affect food prices.
6. Regulations to foster economic and social progress.

ISSUES IN MARKET REGULATION

The statement, "There are too many (or too few) food marketing regulations" is guaranteed to start an argument. Everyone has their own opinion on the question of the need or justification for market regulations. Those opposing regulations point to their inhibiting effects on innovation, efficiency, and competition, as well as to the costs of regulations, which are borne either by food firms (in the form of lower profits) or by consumers (in the form of higher prices). Those who are pro-regulations emphasize the need to "harness" private profit-seeking efforts to the public interest and to protect firms and consumers from anticompetitive market practices.

Few people are opposed in principle to *all* government intervention in food markets. Most would agree that an orderly and dynamic economy requires a set of rules that are devised and enforced by society through the instrument of government. But most people would also agree that too much regulation can stifle the profit seeking and independence of decision-making which is so vital to the decentralized free enterprise system. Marketing policy by the public sector seeks to achieve a level of regulation which fosters an innovative, efficient, and progressive food marketing system that serves the public interest. These are not necessarily conflicting objectives, but in practice, the balance between them has been difficult to maintain.

Regulation is perhaps a misnomer for government involvement in food markets. This involvement may be restrictive, permissive, or facilitating. There is a tendency to associate public laws and regulations with restrictions: do not monopolize, do not advertise deceptively, do not fix prices, do not discriminate between buyers, and the like. These kinds of regulations do restrict market freedoms.

Government laws and policies can be permissive, however. For example, this is true when government permits farmers to sell their farm products and bargain collectively for price—acts that might otherwise be considered restraints of trade. Permissive or enabling legislation may also encourage farmers to restrict farm product supplies in order to raise farm prices. This would not be permitted for nonfarm food marketing firms.

Facilitative market regulations, such as grades and standards, regulation of public food markets, and the market news service, increase the efficiency of the food marketing machinery. These services are made equally available to all, and they have none of the compulsory features of restrictive regulations. Perhaps the largest food regulatory program of all—the meat inspection program, which insures the wholesomeness of red meat and poultry products—should be classified as a facilitating market regulation.

Decisions regarding regulations are usually not so simple as to regulate or not to regulate, or, to have free markets or unfettered markets. Often, the freedom of one group must be limited in order to increase the freedom of others. Frequently, regulations also must subordinate the private interest to the public interest. And, of course, there are difficult political choices to be made when regulations benefit one group at the expense of another. As a result, market regulatory policy in the food industry represents a blend of objectives, and usually is never wholly satisfactory to either industry, consumers, or society.

Differences between the intent and the actual effect of food marketing regulations are another problem. Some food marketing regulations appear to have the opposite effect from that intended. For example, regulations designed to protect the owners of small grocery stores from the impact of chainstores in the 1930's appear to have hastened the demise of the smaller stores. Similarly, restrictions on horizontal integration of food marketing firms in the 1950's and 1960's seem to have led to vertical integration and to conglomerates. There is by no means any assurance that a food marketing regulation will have only the intended effects. There is also some concern that the agencies authorized to enforce food marketing regulations may, by altering the nature of a law, adversely affect its regulatory function.

Many food marketing regulations attempt to mold the industry along the lines of perfect competition. Valuable as the perfectly competitive model is, it is increasingly considered an inadequate criterion for judging food industry performance. No market can attain the perfectly competitive conditions, and it is doubtful that consumers would prefer these markets to the imperfectly competitive markets of real life.

REGULATIONS TO MAINTAIN AND POLICE COMPETITION

The rationale for maintaining workably competitive food markets is straightforward. The essence of competitive markets is the free interaction of buyers and sellers in arriving at mutually advantageous trades. The prices determined by these trades then allocate resources and products to their highest-valued uses, and reward producers in proportion to their productive contribution. Business practices that interfere with this freedom to buy and sell, that artifically raise prices by restricting output, or that insulate a company from the discipline of the competitive marketplace violate these objectives and reduce market efficiency. Although these business practices may be profitable for one firm or for whole industries, they are not conducive to the welfare of society as a whole.

The fundamental economic proposition of the United States from its beginning has been that the desired economic organization should be operated primarily by individual, private, competitive enterprises. Out of this organization would come the maximum economic good for all. Throughout the first hundred years or so of our history, it was assumed that such business organization was normal and automatic if government would just let things alone. However, with the price decline and economic troubles that followed the Civil War, public pressure forced investigation into charges of monopoly and collusion. A Congressional investigation into charges of collusion among the large meat packers was in part responsible for the Sherman Anti-Trust Act. This act, which was passed in 1890, became the cornerstone of federal anti-monopoly policy. It stated that "every contract, combination in the form of trust or otherwise, or conspiracy in restraint of trade or commerce among the several states, or with foreign nations is hereby declared to be illegal."

It was not enough, however, simply to declare actions illegal. The subsequent history of legislation in this area has been largely to determine what are "undesirable" or "unfair" methods of competition. Both the Clayton Act (1914) and the Federal Trade Commission Act (1914) spell out how firms should and should not compete in order to maintain competition.

Agricultural marketing firms have frequently been the target of government antitrust actions. In 1892 the government attempted to dissolve the American Sugar Refining Company, which owned 90 per cent of the industry's producing capacity. A 1911 antitrust suit divided the America Tobacco Company into four separate firms. A 1920 antitrust suit stripped meatpackers of their ownership and control of stockyard facilities and prevented packers from engaging in other sectors of food processing and distribution. More recent antitrust activity in the food industry has been directed toward mergers which might lessen market competition.

In 1936 the Robinson-Patman Act attempted to establish rules against price discrimination. Equal treatment must be given to all buyers unless the discounts can be shown to be derived from economies in manufacture, sale, or delivery. The intent of this law was to prevent large concerns from using their market power to secure unfair price advantage over their competitors. The food industry has played a major role in the establishment and interpretation of the Robinson-Patman Act. A 1930's investigation that found food processors making discriminatory price concessions to food chains was a major reason for the 1936 law. Between 1950 and 1965 there were more than 200 cases charging violation of the Robinson-Patman Act by food industry firms. Fluid milk processors, feed and grain manufacturers, fruit and vegetable processors, bakeries, and grocery retailers are frequently indicted—and sometimes convicted—of violating this act.

With the development of large-scale retailing, the cry arose to protect the small retailer. Many states passed so-called fair trade acts which permitted manufacturers to control the retail selling prices of their products. In this way the large retailer was not permitted to undersell the smaller retailer if he wished to continue handling the manufacturer's products. These state regulations were made legal in interstate commerce by the Tydings-Miller Act (1937). This urge to protect the small operator has also resulted in the regulation of selling margins for many products. With the growing practice of the food retailer to use pricing of various items and product lines as a competition weapon, the question of below-cost selling is a major issue. Now, however, it is not so much the question of protecting small retailers but rather of protecting specialized processors against the power of the possible discriminatory actions of the large retailing firms. Many states prohibit the selling of products below "cost." In 1951 a court held that resale price maintenance as then practiced was illegal. Movement was quickly underway in Congress to repair the damage. The McGuire Act (1952) restored the legality of resale price maintenance.

Mergers among lines of business have occurred increasingly in recent years. A business merger may be a method by which one firm absorbs its competition and, therefore, can secure more market power. On the other hand, a business merger may be a way in which two relatively weak firms can join together to become more effectively competitive with other more powerful firms. A blanket prohibition of mergers under these conditions would prevent the desirable along with the undesirable developments. A 1950 amendment to the 1914 Clayton Act declared illegal any merger—whether horizontal, vertical, or conglomerate—which tends to substantially lessen competition or to create a monopoly. This law has been frequently used in challenging food industry mergers, especially in dairy processing and food retailing.

The food industry has been the subject of considerable unfair trade practices regulations. Court records shows numerous charges of price-fixing, boycotting, exclusive dealing arrangements, and predatory pricing practices by food firms. A large number of price-fixing cases, for example, have been brought against the dairy and bakery industries by government agencies.

When one studies the trends in interpretation of the regulations in this area of maintaining and policing competition, it becomes obvious that there is considerable confusion as to what is desired. Monopoly is illegal. But a business does not run around with a sign on it saying, "I am a Monopoly!" Both the Robinson-Patman Act and the resale price maintenance acts have protected the "little fellow" as a way of maintaining competition. The resale price maintenance laws seem to take the position that *numbers* of business establishments are the key to desired competition. Developments in this regulatory area are of real importance to agricultural marketing and can have an important effect on costs.

The legal activities in this general area sharply point up our uncertainty as to the answer to some critical questions. Effective competition requires that several firms offer competing alternatives to consumers. But how many firms are enough? Optimum technological or operational efficiency may require firms of great size. How much cost in operational efficiency must we pay to have desirable economic efficiency in this system?

REGULATIONS TO CONTROL OR OFFSET MONOPOLY CONDITIONS

In some areas of the economy it is felt that vigorous competition is not desirable. This is particularly true for public utilities, such as light, power, and telephone, and in other industries such as public transportation. The large, fixed investments in these industries mean that competitive duplication would be very costly. For these industries, the attempt has been made to stimulate the results of competition through public regulation. It was toward this end that the Interstate Commerce and Federal Communications Commissions were established. Such commissions have been given regulatory powers, the most important of which is the supervisory power over rates charged.

In still other areas of the economy, Congress has recognized that weak and disorganized groups must do business with strong and concentrated industries. Or, in some cases, small and disorganized businesses are at the mercy of marketing forces, with wasteful or disruptive consequences to the public. In these instances Congress has attempted to create "power balance" by granting organizing privileges that would otherwise be in violation of antitrust laws. The Webb-Pomerene Act legalized monopolies in the export trade. The Capper-Volstead Act recognized the legal rights of farmers to act together cooperatively. The Agricultural Marketing Agreement Act (1937) provided that producers and handlers could band together to promote orderly marketing of their products. Under the provisions of this latter law have developed the federally supervised milk markets and the various fruit and vegetable marketing orders which regulate the amounts to be offered for sale.

More recently, such legislation as the Agricultural Fair Practice Act of 1967 and the Agricultural Marketing and Bargaining Act of 1969 ensures the right of producers to join together in a cooperative bargaining association. Handlers must be willing to negotiate with these groups. Producers are protected against discrimination from handlers.

The balance between preventing unfair competition and monopoly and controlling or creating a counterbalancing monopoly is a delicate one indeed. The problems of adequate and intelligent enforcement of regulations in the former area are great. The danger in the latter area is that of creating monopolistic power that may become more vicious than the situation it was intended to balance.

In recent years, many have advocated that cooperatives take a more active part in the marketing of food. However, court decisions in the early 1960's found some cooperative merger and acquisition activities as being in violation of the antitrust statutes. Associations that are attempting to bargain collectively for farmers outside of the marketing order structure also have some doubts as to whether the necessary legal authority exists.

REGULATIONS TO FACILITATE TRADE AND PROVIDE SERVICES

The facilitating marketing functions are standardization, financing, risk-bearing, and market intelligence. Because these influence the overall efficiency of the food marketing process, they are frequently provided by government agencies at public expense.

The Packers and Stockyards Act (1921) sets up the supervisory machinery to control marketing practices and charges on terminal livestock markets. The United States Warehouse Act (1916) provides for the licensing and supervision of warehouses and their operations. The Produce Agency Act (1927) attacks fraudulent practices of commission agents and brokers. The Perishable Agricultural Commodities Act (1930) provides for the licensing of commission men, dealers, and brokers handling fresh fruits and vegetables. All of these laws have attempted to establish standards of practice and operation of markets and men operating in these markets.

Many laws have been passed affecting product handling. Laws regulating weights and measures of containers have aimed for uniformity in this important area. There also have been a series of acts which established the authority of the United States Department of Agriculture to study and promulgate standards and grades for agricultural commodities.

Legislation has established the market news service and the various grading and inspection services. Another series of laws has sanctioned the collection and dissemination of statistics of various commodities and the agricultural census.

Much federal legislation can affect only those commodities that enter into interstate commerce. Therefore, in most of these fields states have evolved counterpart legislation to cover trading within the several states.

REGULATIONS TO PROTECT THE CONSUMER

There is recognition today that in a modern, complex society the consumer cannot possibly be expected to have complete knowledge about all choices and purchases. Regulations in this area generally strive to assure adequate and accurate information so that consumers can make informed decisions and protect themselves from products and practices that might be harmful.

The principal regulations in this area were initiated by the Federal Food and Drug Act (1906, expanded 1938) along with the related laws of the states. Generally the purpose of these laws is to prevent shipments of adulterated or misbranded foods, drugs, and cosmetics. The administrator of the act also has the power to establish minimum quality and fill of container for most packaged goods. The law provides for labeling of contents.

The increased use of chemicals in food production and processing has led to several amendments to the original Food and Drug Act. The Pesticide Chemical Amendment (1954) sets tolerance levels for pesticide residue on food after harvest. The Delaney clause to the Food and Drug Act (1958) prohibits adding to food any substance which has been shown to cause cancer in man or animal. Cyclamates were banned as food additives under the Delaney clause. The FDA Color Additives Act (1960) controls coloring agents which might be used in food processing.

The Wheeler-Lea Act (1935) sets up a code of ethics for advertising. It makes false and deceptive advertising an unfair method of competition and thereby illegal. The Meat Inspection Act (1907) authorizes inspection of animals, meats, and packing establishments to assure that products will be fit for human food. More recent legislation extended inspection to poultry products and processing plants. Also, individual state and local governmental units have set up required health standards for milk and milk processing and for various slaughtering and food processing facilities.

Recently there has been added emphasis on providing factual information about products for consumers. Legislation such as the Truth in Packaging Act, the Wholesome Meat Act, and the Motor Vehicle Safety Act have all been designed to provide the consumer with more information and otherwise protect him from deception and danger.

There has been increased pressure on food processors and retailers to provide a unit price, as well as more nutritional information, on food packages. *Unit prices* are prices stated in a common denominator, such as costs per ounce or cents per quart. This is designed to help consumers make "best buy" comparisons. *Nutritional labeling* is an attempt to focus consumer's attention on the nutritional values and costs of alternative foods. In 1973, the Food and Drug Administration initiated a program whereby food processors declare the calorie, protein, carbohydrate, and fat content of their products, along with the percentage of the U.S. recommended daily allowances of protein and seven vitamins and minerals that the product provides. The labeling requirements are voluntary, but become mandatory if any nutritional claims are made for the product.

To a great extent it is because of these kinds of laws that the consumer can depend upon the weight, volume, and content labels of the food he

460

buys. He can learn the fiber content of his clothes. He can have some assurances that in this age of new chemicals, someone is watching out for his health and well-being.

The dividing line between protector and dictator is a fine one. The intent of these laws has been to protect the consumer from fraud and danger which he could not reasonably detect for himself, and to give him knowledge upon which to make wise decisions. There is always the danger that such regulations may be administered in such a way as to actually make the choice for the consumers. Such interpretation may stifle change and initiative if industry must serve the administrator instead of the consumer. In the late 1950's this problem was brought sharply into focus by an amendment to the Pure Food and Drug Act. This amendment permitted no tolerance limits at all in certain areas of contamination. Because in many instances laboratory tests are not always completely accurate or above argument, the enforcement of this provision has brought cries of anguish from producers and industry groups. With the increasing use of all kinds of chemicals (whose residue may be harmful) in the production process, the problems in this area of regulation are growing.

With the increasing product differentiation and branding in the food industry, there again have arisen proposals to regulate further advertising and other merchandising practices. There is some opinion that advertising, though not overtly dishonest, often goes beyond acceptability and good taste. The proliferation of different package sizes—often making it very difficult for the average consumer to make reasoned choices—has led to proposals for standardization and limitation of this merchandising practice.

Are consumers really being protected, or is the progress of technological change being unnecessarily handicapped? Should it be the role of these regulations to decide what is best? Or should regulations provide the basis for informed consumer action and then leave the decision up to the consumer? The controversy over what to do about cigarettes illustrates this issue. With the establishment of the strong possibility of a connection between cigarette smoking and lung cancer, many wished to prohibit the manufacture of cigarettes. The "warning and information" approach, however, was taken. Cigarette manufacture was not prohibited, but appropriate warning labels must appear on the product. Beginning in 1971, advertising of cigarettes on television was banned because of their potential health hazard. In days when the composition of our food is increasingly complex, these questions become more difficult to answer.

Consumerism—or the consumer movement—is a wide range of government, business, and consumer activities designed to foster and protect the consumer's rights to safety, to information, to choose freely, and to be heard.[1] Legal protection of these rights for the food consumer dates back to two 1906

---

[1] John F. Kennedy, *Special Message on Protecting the Consumer Interest,* March 15, 1962.

laws—the Food and Drug Act and the Meat Inspection Act. Since then, the food industry has served as a proving ground for the consumer movement in the areas of advertising, labeling, packaging, product safety, and other consumer concerns.

The 1960's and 1970's consumer movement broadened consumer legislation and action programs. Legislation in the areas of truth-in-packaging, nutritional labeling, open-code dating, and unit pricing signaled a concern for the food consumers' economic interest in the quality of food markets as well as the wholesomeness and safety of foods. Consumers have also organized to press their demands on the food industry. The meat boycotts of 1967 and 1972 were examples of collective market behavior that attempted to reinforce consumers' political actions.

Today's consumer expects the food industry to function efficiently and honestly. The citizen-consumer also expects to have a voice in public policy decisions affecting food prices and food distribution. As a result, the "farm policy question" has been broadened to the "food policy question." Food consumers also have rising expectations for the food industry. These may or may not be realistic, feasible, or economical, but they cannot be ignored.

Concerns with the rising consumer movement, boycotts, and consumer support for increased regulation of the food industry have prompted the industry to study the nature and level of the food consumers' dissatisfaction. The study of consumer satisfaction and dissatisfaction is still in its infancy, and the results of studies should be interpreted carefully. Satisfaction is a complex attitude; moreover, it is unlikely that consumers ever are fully satisfied with any industry or product. Changes in satisfaction, however, are indicators that can be helpful to food producers and marketing firms.

According to most surveys during the 1970's, food prices were the dominant consumer concern. For example, a 1973 Department of Agriculture-sponsored survey suggested that 94 per cent of Americans thought food prices should be lower.[2] Equally as significant, 91 per cent of the respondents wanted to see food quality improved. A 1976 nationwide opinion poll indicated that 85 per cent of consumers were unhappy with food prices, 50 per cent were dissatisfied with the overall quality and nutritional value of food, and 85 per cent were unhappy with the trend toward sales of food in convenience packages and with fewer foods available in bulk, unprocessed forms. However, 85 per cent of these consumers were generally satisfied with the variety and availability of food.[3]

In another Department of Agriculture survey in the spring of 1974, consumers expressed general satisfaction with the food they buy and with the stores

---

[2] *The PACER Study,* conducted by Response Analysis Corp., sponsored by the USDA's Office of Communication, 1973.

[3] *Agricultural Council of America Consumer Survey,* the Agricultural Council, Washington, D.C., 1977.

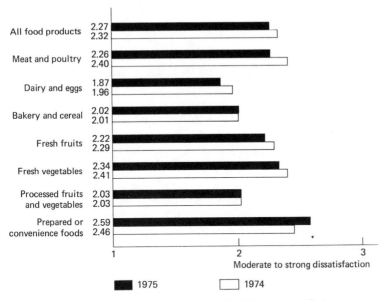

Based on a 5-point scale: 1= always satisfied; 5 = never satisfied.

Figure 22–1. Average level of consumer dissatisfaction with food products. (U.S. Department of Agriculture)

where it is purchased. However, there was considerable dissatisfaction with convenience foods, as well as criticism of food processor advertising.[4] Figure 22-1 shows the trends in the food consumer's degree of satisfaction between 1974 and 1975. Attitudes toward prices dominated these trends.

Consumer satisfaction with the food industry in general and with specific food products can affect farmers and food marketing firms. Dissatisfaction may trigger boycotts, substitutions of one food for another, and, most importantly, consumer support for government intervention in food markets. Intervention may take the form of price controls, restrictions on industry marketing programs, advertising and labeling controls, import-export control policies, and even profit controls. In a 1977 poll, 45 per cent of the polled consumers wanted to see the food manufacturing industry investigated or changed— more than any other industry.[5] It seems likely that the demands of the consumer movement will continue to put pressure on the food industry to make certain that the marketing concept is more fully implemented.

---

[4] C. R. Handy, and M. Pfaff, *Consumer Satisfaction with Food Products and Marketing Service,* USDA, Agricultural Economic Report No. 281, March 1975.

[5] *Consumerism at the Crossroads,* poll by Louis Harris and Associates, sponsored by the Marketing Science Institute, Harvard University, 1977.

REGULATIONS TO DIRECTLY AFFECT FOOD PRICES

Government can influence farm and food prices in many ways. Government regulation of public utilities has led to direct control of rates and prices. Railroad rates, public utility charges, livestock yardage, and numerous other prices and fees are regulated by government. The rationale for intervention in the pricing system is that monopolies can be permitted only if there is assurance that they operate in the public interest. But there is some concern today that government price regulations may in some cases protect inefficient firms and result in higher prices than would be the case without government regulations.

Most farm price and income policies also directly or indirectly influence food prices. Food price supports, supply control, import-export, and domestic demand-expansion programs, such as the Food Stamp program, fall into this category. These programs, of course, may have other objectives and effects outside of and in addition to their impacts on food prices.

There have been periodic attempts of government to directly control food prices through price control or freeze programs. The United States experienced food and other product price controls in World War I (1917–1918), World War II (1941–1946), the Korean conflict (1950–1953), and during the 1971–1973 period. These were periods of rapid price inflation when the government felt an obligation to intervene directly in prices. The 1941–1946 price controls were also accompanied by food rationing. During these periods, retail food prices and marketing margins were "frozen" or controlled whereas farm prices were free to vary. Of course, a retail price freeze influences the derived farm price.

The government's responsibility and ability to directly regulate food prices is a highly debatable point. Control of food prices is an awesome economic power. Because prices allocate resources and influence all food industry decisions, there are significant market consequences of price regulation.

REGULATIONS TO FOSTER ECONOMIC AND SOCIAL PROGRESS

Each group that pressures for preferential legislation generally justifies its actions as being necessary for economic and social progress. Usually such laws fit better into one of our categories. However, there have been legislative developments that have addressed themselves specifically to the general purpose of "holding the carrot in front of the horse" so that our economy will have the urge to move forward.

Patent and copyright laws give the innovator a monopoly for a period of time so that he may reap personal gain from his efforts. Such an incentive system, which has a long history in English law, was recognized by our

Constitution and definitely set forth in the original patent act of 1790. The original intent was to give to the innovator the right of monopoly exploitation for seventeen years, after which the innovation was to become available to the public for general use. Such incentive for gain has no doubt fostered development. But as with other regulations, abuse is possible. Through legal manipulations, protection can be extended well beyond the statutory seventeen years. There is record of one inventor successfully maintaining his exclusive rights for fifty-three years. It is also possible that patent and copyright privileges are being used today to prevent someone else from working in given fields and making discoveries that might destroy the current business power of the firms involved. Such actions, of course, do not encourage progress but retard it. With increasing food processing and more synthetic products, patent and copyright provisions are of growing importance in the marketing of farm products. The challenge is how to furnish incentive for the continuing parade of new and better things and methods without, at the same time, preventing the active search for improvement by anyone in any area of endeavor.

Another very important group of laws is that providing for public support of education and research. In 1862 Congress established the Department of Agriculture. The Morrill Land-Grant College Act (1862) provided the basis for our extensive system of government-supported higher education. This was followed by the Hatch Act (1887), which provided for the establishment of agricultural experiment stations in conjunction with the land-grant colleges.

In 1914 the Smith-Lever Act broadened the educational system in agriculture by establishing the agricultural extension system. Now, through a widespread system of county agents and various types of trained specialists, the findings of the experiment stations are quickly brought to the farmers' attention. This act was followed in a few years by the Smith-Hughes Act, which provided federal support for teaching vocational agriculture in the public schools. The resulting agricultural research-educational team today is the envy of the world.

This educational and research structure has been augmented by a long series of laws making monies available for research in specific areas. Early work was aimed at farm production problems. However, the Research and Marketing Act of 1946 laid the groundwork for a broad research attack on marketing problems. One very pertinent contribution of this legislation has been to expand the horizons of agricultural marketing research and extension beyond the point of first sale. The complete producer-to-consumer area is now recognized as the field in which to work. Official recognition has been given to the fact that the actions of food processors, wholesalers, and retailers are the business of those who are concerned with agricultural marketing. To a large degree the improvements in marketing will depend upon research progress in this enlarged area of study.

Governmental agricultural research is carried on at about 400 field locations, including federal field stations and laboratories and cooperative work at the individual state experiment stations. The states maintain about 325 research centers, including experiment stations and substations. Together the federal and state governments employ over 10,000 agricultural research scientists. The general framework for financing agricultural research consists of the states matching the federal appropriations.

THE REGULATORY AGENCIES

Regulations affecting the food industry are administered by several federal, state, and local agencies. The U.S. Department of Agriculture has been assigned dual regulatory and service roles in the food industry and attempts to serve farmers, food marketing firms, and consumers equally well. The United States Department of Agriculture administers the food grading and inspection programs as well as such laws as the Packers and Stockyards Act, the Warehouse Act, the Produce Agency Act, and the Perishable Agricultural Commodities Act. This department is also involved in farm price support and income programs, and has the responsibility for the food stamp, the school lunch, and milk programs. The laws authorizing agricultural production and marketing research, and the adult education/extension programs, are also the province of the Department of Agriculture.

The Justice Department and the Federal Trade Commission have responsibility for the laws regulating competitive practices in the food industry. Anticompetitive mergers, unfair trade practices, price-fixing, and deceptive advertising are the concerns of these agencies. The Food and Drug Administration is responsible for insuring the safety and wholesomeness of the food supply. The Commodity Futures Trading Commission is the newest member of the food regulatory team, with responsibility for insuring fair trading and orderly growth of the commodity futures market.

Numerous other federal agencies affect food marketing firms and activities in a less direct manner. The Interstate Commerce Commission, the Internal Revenue Service, the Federal Energy Agency, the Environmental Protection Agency, the Federal Communications Commission, the Federal Power Commission, the Occupational Safety and Health Administration, the Securities and Exchange Commission, and the National Highway Traffic Safety Administration all play a role in today's food industry. Consider the effects of a 55 mph speed limit, energy rationing and higher fuel costs, waste water effluent limitations, or the changing tax structure on food marketing.

At the state and local levels, public health agencies, state departments of agriculture, and other agencies oversee a vast number of food marketing programs ranging from grocery store sanitation to commodity promotion programs. The growing number of state and city food regulations is adding to the complexity of the food marketing process. Most state and local regulations follow federal laws, but some local regulations erect trade barriers and artificial restrictions on interstate commerce in food products.

THE FUTURE OF FOOD MARKETING REGULATIONS

We can now return to the initial questions of the where, the what, and the how much of regulation. Careful, unbiased thought brings the conclusion that there is a place for government regulations and laws. Often it is not the intent of regulations, but their enforcement and administration, which causes trouble. The role of government is not passive or static. Nor does the fact that certain laws are on the books make them currently good or adequate laws. A progressive economy is one of change. Legislation once considered vital may no longer be useful. New developments may bring about the need for new regulations even in fields where such actions were once considered improper.

Increasingly, those interested in the performance of agricultural markets must give attention to the proper role of government. At one time agricultural marketing was considered to operate under nearly perfect competitive conditions. However, this is no longer a realistic assumption. We have seen the large-scale enterprises that exist in the processing industries. We have noted the rapid development of large and powerful retailing organizations. We have discussed the implications of more direct marketing channels and integration for the bargaining power of farmers and other participants in the functions of marketing.

How many firms are enough? What trade practices should be allowed? How much protection for individuals and firms is needed? Questions like these are ones that workers in agricultural marketing now find very pertinent. The trend, no doubt, will be toward increasing the area of public influence and regulation through governmental action. The real challenge is to find the "proper" solution among the many alternatives that are always available.

SUMMARY

Food marketing is a highly regulated industry. Food marketing regulations attempt to regulate competition and monopolistic conditions, facilitate trade, protect consumers, directly influence food prices, and foster economic and social progress. These regulations may be restrictive, permissive, or facilitating. The food marketing regulatory environment undergoes continual change in the search for the appropriate blend of regulations that will achieve public and private objectives. Although many food marketing regulations restrict freedoms, others provide valuable services for farmers, food marketing firms, and consumers. An overall evaluation of food marketing regulations requires consideration of both their costs and benefits.

QUESTIONS FOR DISCUSSION

1. Why is it necessary for government to establish basic "rules" for orderly economic and marketing activity?

2. Businessmen frequently complain that there are too many government regulations to comply with, and that these add unnecessarily to the price of food. Comment on this charge.

3. Give an example of a restrictive, a permissive, and a facilitating food marketing law.

4. Comment on the observation that no government regulations would be necessary if businessmen were honest and concerned with the public welfare.

5. Give an example of a food marketing law that has unintended effects in addition to its stated goals.

6. Comment on the feasibility and desirability of regulating all food marketing firms so that they are perfectly competitive.

7. Why has the food marketing system so often been charged by government agencies with monopolistic and anticompetitive practices?

8. Discuss the merits of alternative consumer protection measures for cigarette smoking and for cyclamates.

9. Economists generally argue that direct price controls on food products will not be successful. Why then have they been used during periods of wartime?

10. Do you think there will be more or fewer food marketing regulations in the future?

SELECTED REFERENCES

BREIMYER, H. F. "Market Regulation and the Public Welfare." *Agricultural Marketing* (June 1966), 14–15.

CAMPBELL, R. R. *Food Safety Regulation.* American Enterprise Institute, Hoover Policy Studies, Washington, D.C., Aug. 1974.

CRAWFORD, C. W. "The Long Fight for Pure Foods." *1954 Yearbook of Agriculture.* U.S. Department of Agriculture, pp. 211–220.

"Economic Regulation of the Food Industry," and "Conclusions on Needed Changes In Public Policies, Statutes and Government Services." *Food from Farmer to Consumer,* Report of the National Commission of Food Marketing, Washington, D.C., 1966.

GNAUCK, B. G., AND D. C. DAHL. *Government Regulation of the Farm Supply Industries.* University of Minnesota, Agricultural Economics Bulletin No. 492, 1970.

HANDY, C. R., AND M. PFAFF. *Consumer Satisfaction with Food Products and Marketing Services.* United States Department of Agriculture, Agricultural Economics Research No. 281, March 1975.

PADBERG, D. I. "Consumer Protection for a Modern Industrialized Food System." American Journal of Agricultural Economics (Dec. 1970) 821–28.

POSNER, R. A. "Theories of Economic Regulation." *Bell Journal of Economic and Management Science* (Autumn 1974), 335–58.

SCHUCK, P. S. "Why Regulation Fails." *Harpers* (Sept. 1975), 16–29.

SCHULTZE, C. L. "The Public Use of Private Interest." *Harpers* (May 1977), 43–62.

WEIDENBAUM, M. L. *Government-Mandated Price Increases.* Domestic Affairs Study No. 28. American Enterprise Institute, Washingon, D.C., Feb. 1975.

PART VI

Commodity Marketing

CHAPTER 23

Livestock and Meat Marketing

"To FUNCTION WELL, the livestock marketing system must do a number of things efficiently in each of its phases: livestock must be assembled, transported, and bought and sold with minimal delay, movement and cost; livestock must be converted into many kinds of meat and meat products at the lowest possible cost; timely marketing information must be made available to help buyers and sellers channel meat to consumers in an orderly manner; human health must be safeguarded; and consumer demand must be reflected through the entire system to enable producers to correctly plan their production and marketing."*

Preview

• This chapter examines one of the most complex food products and marketing channels—the livestock economy.

• You will see that the line between farming and marketing of livestock has become blurred by the growth of large-scale cattle feeding operations. These protein conversion operations are hybrid farming and marketing activities.

• The chapter emphasizes the diversity of market conditions and alternatives at each level of the livestock-meat economy—feeders, meat packers, wholesalers, and retailers.

• Attention is given to the key trends that have shaped the modern livestock economy: specialization, decentralization, consumption trends, grading, integration, and central meat processing.

• The discussion of alternative meat wholesaling patterns highlights a key

---

* Willis E. Anthony and William C. Motes, *Agricultural Markets in Change,* U.S. Department of Agriculture, Agricultural Economic Report No. 95, July 1966.

conflict between operational efficiency and consumer satisfaction in the meat industry.

- Key terms and concepts:

boxed beef

carcass weight and grading

central meat processing

direct sales

feeder animals

feedlots

yardage

Livestock is produced on many of the nation's farms and ranches. In 1975–1976 there were 1.9 million cattle producers, 680,000 farm with hogs, and 130,000 farms and ranches with sheep. In all, about one-fourth of all United States farms are classified as primarily livestock operations, the largest single class of specialized agriculture. The $19 billion farm receipts from the sale of cattle and calves in 1975 was greater than receipts for any other commodity.

Here we are concerned with the red meat animals—cattle, calves, hogs, sheep, and lambs. This is one of the most complex sectors of the food industry. Ranchers and farmers, feeders, meat packers, processors, wholesalers, and

Table 23-1. Most Important Changes In The Livestock and Meat Industries, 1876–1976.

	RANKED BY PRIORITY
Most important livestock developments	1. Increased direct marketing, use of auctions, less dependence on terminal markets. 2. Large-scale cattle feeding. 3. Improved transportation. 4. Grading. 5. Improved market information. 6. Improved volume and quality.
Most important meat industry developments	1. Centralized cutting, processing, and prepackaging. 2. Supermarket and chainstore growth. 3. Improved transportation and refrigeration. 4. Grading and inspection. 5. Decentralization of meat business. 6. Improved quality and volume.

Source: E. Uvacek, Jr., "Yesterday's Lessons—Tomorrow's Foundation," *Beginning a New Century of Marketing,* 1976 Livestock Marketing Congress Papers, Livestock Merchandising Institute, Kansas City, Missouri, 1977. Reprinted by permission.

retailers are interrelated through a complex chain of markets involving a large number of marketing activities, functions, and institutions.

It is very difficult to draw a line between farming and marketing in the combined feed-livestock sector of the food industry. Livestock are protein converters, transforming vegetable protein into animal protein. These "protein factories" are a form of food processing. Moreover, livestock feeding can be viewed as an alternative way for the grain farmer to market grain. In this sense, the grain-livestock farm, so common in the corn belt states, is in reality a very sophisticated farming and marketing protein-conversion operation which is integrated both horizontally and vertically.

The red meat livestock segment of the food industry has undergone substantial change over the years and continues to change. Table 23-1 indicates the results of a 1976 survey of the livestock industry leaders' opinions of the most important changes in the livestock producing and red meat industry in the 1876–1976 period. As indicated, decentralization, specialized cattle feeding, the growth of supermarkets and chainstores, and improved transportation, grading, market information, and product quality have been important trends in this industry.

LIVESTOCK PRODUCTION

Because livestock are the largest consumers of domestic feedgrains, animal and grain production are closely linked. The principal livestock producing area is concentrated in the central, corn belt states, as shown in Table 23-2. Its comparative advantage in producing feedgrains also gives this area a comparative advantage in cattle and hog production. Because feed costs are

Table 23-2. Livestock Marketing By Regions, 1976–1977.

	PER CENT OF LIVESTOCK SOLD		
REGION	CATTLE AND CALVES	HOGS	SHEEP AND LAMBS
East Coast	12%	12	4
North Central (corn belt)	41	77	25
South Central	30	9	21
Mountain	11	1	38
West Coast	6	1	12
U.S. Total	100%	100%	100%

Source: U.S. Department of Agriculture.

475

a primary factor in livestock production, there is a direct relationship between grain and livestock production. A short feedgrain crop with high grain prices leads producers to cut back on livestock production. And an abundant grain harvest and low feedgrain prices encourage expansion of livestock production.

Another important characteristic of livestock production is the diversity of producing units. There are a large number of very small producers and a few very large ranches and livestock feeding operations. Enterprise specialization also varies widely. Many producers specialize in either beef, pork, or sheep production. Some combine these enterprises with feedgrain production, others do not. There are other producers who view the livestock enterprise as an income supplement, and use it to occupy excess labor, buildings, or other resources. This diversity of producing units has contributed to the difficulty of organizing livestock producers for collective market actions.

As a result of the long production periods, and because of the tendency to adjust future production to current prices, livestock production is subject to output and price cycles. Farmers and ranchers periodically produce too much livestock to get what they consider to be reasonable prices, and livestock prices are frequently below the cost of production.

Other characteristics of livestock influence their prices and marketing patterns. Livestock and meat products are homogeneous and therefore difficult to brand. Farm animals are also bulky and expensive to transport. Finally, livestock is a moderately perishable commodity. However, meat can be "stored" on the hoof, and livestock sales can be deferred to some extent. By varying the finish and weights of livestock, the producer has alternatives to immediate sale. However, there are limits to these options because when deferred sales eventually come to market, there may be weight and age price discounts.

GROWTH OF SPECIALIZED FEEDLOTS

Prior to the 1950's, most cattle production took place on diversified crop-livestock farms in the corn belt or on western ranges. However, as a result of the rapid growth in demand for fed beef, and economies of size in cattle feeding, large, specialized cattle feedlots developed in the 1950's, 1960's, and 1970's. These are located principally in the Southwestern, Pacific, Western and Mountain corn belt regions. Owners of these feeding operations purchase grain and feeder animals for finishing to market weights. Feedlots are highly specialized protein conversion factories, with only vestigial ties to traditional farming. They represent a de-integration of the grain-livestock farm because the activities of breeding, grain production, and livestock feeding are kept entirely separate.

Cattle feedlots are a highly concentrated segment of the livestock industry. In 1975–1976 some 1,540 cattle feedlots, with a capacity of 1,000 head or more, accounted for only 1 per cent of all feeding operations but 53 per cent of all the fed cattle that were marketed. The remaining 47 per cent of cattle were fed and marketed by 132,000 other farmers and ranchers. This sales concentration varies, however. Although more than 90 per cent of the fed cattle marketed in Oklahoma, Texas, Arizona, and California came from these 1,000+ head feedlots, less than 10 per cent of the fed cattle in Indiana, Illinois, and Iowa originated in these large feedlots.

New markets have developed in the livestock industry as a result of the growth of the commercial feedlot. These markets facilitate the transfer of feeder animals and feedgrains to the feedlots. For example, the western ranges traditionally served as the source of feeder animals for the corn belt. However, in recent years southern states have become important sources of feeder livestock, particularly for the western feedlots. Today, feeder animals move in a clockwise pattern: southern feeder animals are trucked to southwestern feedlots and northwestern range feeders move to corn-belt states. At the same time, feedgrains are moved to the Southwestern states, where insufficient grain is produced.

Thus, entirely new marketing patterns have developed with the growth of commercial feedlots. Moreover, new marketing agencies, such as the feeder animal auction, also have grown. These newer markets present a new set of marketing problems: grading, price discovery, marketing efficiency, and the like.

LIVESTOCK PRODUCTS AND MEAT CONSUMPTION

The consumption of red meats varies considerably by species. As shown in Table 23-3, total red meat consumption increased from 167 pounds to 190 pounds per capita between 1965 and 1976. However, this gain of 23 pounds was solely the result of growth in beef demand as the consumption of veal and lamb fell slightly, and as pork consumption fluctuated without trend.

The reasons for red meat consumption trends lie in the income elasticities of the meats, changes in tastes and preferences associated with sociodemographic trends of consumers, and changing livestock production. Whatever the reasons, these trends have had a major influence on the prices of cattle, hogs, and sheep.

Livestock at the farm level represent a complex bundle of consumer products. As indicated in Table 23-4, about two thirds of the wholesale value of livestock is sold as fresh meat. Canned and processed meats constitute another 27 per cent of wholesale value, and by-products represent another 4 per cent of this value.

Even a fresh meat carcass is in reality a bundle of consumer products, each with different values. A steer is not all steak, as shown in Figure 23-

Table 23-3. Meat Production and Consumption per Person, 1965–1976.

	PRODUCTION (MILLIONS OF POUNDS)					PER CAPITA CONSUMPTION (POUNDS)				
YEAR	BEEF	VEAL	LAMB AND MUTTON	PORK	TOTAL	BEEF	VEAL	LAMB AND MUTTON	PORK	TOTAL
1965	18,727	1,020	651	11,141	31,539	99.5	5.2	3.7	58.7	167.1
1966	19,726	910	650	11,339	32,625	104.2	4.6	4.0	58.1	170.9
1967	20,219	792	646	12,581	34,238	106.5	3.8	3.9	64.1	178.3
1968	20,880	734	602	13,064	35,280	109.7	3.6	3.7	66.2	183.2
1969	21,158	673	550	12,955	35,336	110.8	3.3	3.4	65.0	182.5
1970	21,685	588	551	13,438	36,262	113.7	2.9	3.3	66.4	186.3
1971	21,902	546	555	14,792	37,795	113.0	2.7	3.1	73.0	191.8
1972	22,419	459	543	13,640	37,061	116.1	2.2	3.3	67.4	189.0
1973	21,277	357	514	12,751	34,899	109.6	1.8	2.7	61.6	175.7
1974	23,138	486	465	13,805	37,894	116.8	2.3	2.3	66.6	188.0
1975	23,976	873	410	11,503	36,762	120.1	4.2	2.0	54.8	181.1
1976	25,775	785	375	12,050	38,985	128.0	3.7	1.8	56.5	190.0

Source: U.S. Department of Agriculture.

Table 23-4. Sales of Meat Packers and Processors, 1972.

PRODUCTS	PER CENT OF DOLLAR SALES	
Fresh meats	64%	
Beef		45
Pork		17
Veal, lamb, mutton		2
Processed meats	27	
Sausage, noncanned meats		13
Processed, cured pork		10
Canned meats		4
Meat by-products	4	
Hides, pelts		2
Lard		1
Other		1
Miscellaneous products	5	
Total	100%	
	($25,533,000,000)	

Source: *U.S. Census of Manufacturers, 1972,* Bureau of the Census, 1972.

1. A 1,000 pound steer typically dresses out ιo a 620 pound carcass. From this, we get about 540 pounds of retail meats. In recent years about 40 per cent of this meat has gone into the making of lower-priced hamburger and 60 per cent into higher-valued cuts.

LIVESTOCK ASSEMBLY OPERATIONS

Livestock are usually purchased for one of three reasons: (1) for breeding herds; (2) for placement in feedlots; or (3) for immediate slaughter. The term *livestock assembly* refers to bringing together animals for any of these purposes. There are several livestock assembling agencies:

LOCAL COOPERATIVE ASSOCIATIONS

Local cooperative associations originally functioned largely as shipping agencies which collected the small lots from farmers and shipped them forward to terminal markets in carload lots. In recent years some have taken on a broader service and often merchandise their livestock directly to packers and other buyers.

COUNTRY DEALERS

Country dealers are independent operators who buy and sell livestock for a profit. They usually buy livestock from the farmer and then resell to packers

479

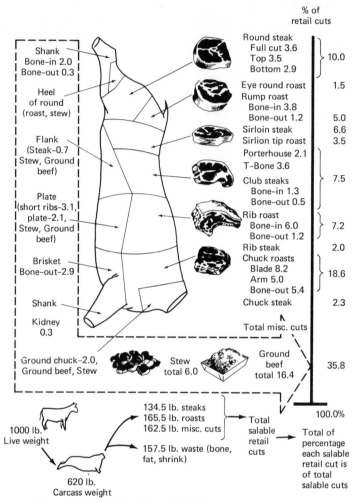

% of
retail cuts

Round steak
Full cut 3.6
Top 3.5   } 10.0
Bottom 2.9

Eye round roast   1.5
Rump roast
Bone-in 3.8
Bone-out 1.2   5.0

Sirloin steak   6.6
Sirlion tip roast   3.5

Porterhouse 2.1
T–Bone 3.6

Club steaks   } 7.5
Bone-in 1.3
Bone-out 0.5

Rib roast
Bone-in 6.0   } 7.2
Bone-out 1.2

Rib steak   2.0

Chuck roasts
Blade 8.2
Arm 5.0   } 18.6
Bone-out 5.4

Chuck steak   2.3

Total misc. cuts

Ground
beef
total 16.4   35.8

100.0%

Shank
Bone-in 2.0
Bone-out 0.3

Heel
of round
(roast, stew)

Flank
(Steak–0.7
Stew, Ground
beef)

Plate
(short ribs–3.1,
plate–2.1,
Stew, Ground
beef)

Brisket
Bone-out–2.9

Shank

Kidney
0.3

Ground chuck–2.0,
Ground beef, Stew

Stew
total 6.0

1000 lb.
Live weight

134.5 lb. steaks
165.5 lb. roasts   } Total
162.5 lb. misc. cuts   salable
                          retail
157.5 lb. waste (bone,   cuts
fat, shrink)

Total of
percentage
each salable
retail cut is
of total
salable cuts

620 lb.
Carcass weight

Figure 23–1. Retail beef cuts. (U.S. Department of Agriculture)

or some other market agency. Some have established places of business and maintain a small yard. Others merely operate a truck and pick up the livestock from the farmer.

AUCTIONS

Livestock are offered for public sale on the auction basis. Some auctions operate as a primary outlet and source for feeder livestock and breeding animals. Others are used as an outlet for fat livestock and are patronized by packers, dealers, and other types of buyers.

CONCENTRATION YARDS

Concentration yards are often referred to as "local markets" and may be operated by independent or cooperative owners or by packing companies to buy livestock. Very often it is difficult to make a clear distinction between such outlets and the country dealer who maintains yard facilities and operates on a large scale.

TERMINAL PUBLIC MARKETS

Terminal public markets are large central markets where livestock are received and cared for and where the privileges of buying and selling are available to all who may wish to use them. The yard facilities are owned by a stockyard company. This organization is often referred to as operating a "livestock hotel." It does not enter into the buying and selling of the livestock, but merely furnishes the physical facilities for which it receives payment in the form of *yardage fees.*

The farmer normally consigns his livestock to commission men who then act as the farmer's selling agent. These men receive the commission charges as payment for their work. Commission organizations may be either privately or cooperatively owned. Very often the private commission companies are organized in what are usually called livestock exchanges. These organizations attempt to self-police the practices used and carry on other activities of mutual concern to their members.

PACKING PLANTS

Some packing plants are located near the large terminal yards and secure most of their livestock through those facilities. Others, either in the production area or at the central markets, may maintain their own buying yards at the plant itself or within the production area. Still others purchase their livestock from dealers, concentration yards, and auctions.

RETAIL MEAT DEALERS

In some instances retailers buy and slaughter their own livestock. In recent years such operations often have occurred in conjunction with the operation of frozen food lockers.

FARMERS

The sale of livestock from one farmer to another is an important outlet, especially for feeding and breeding stock.

DECENTRALIZATION IN THE LIVESTOCK AND MEAT PACKING INDUSTRIES

Probably the most important trend shaping livestock marketing channels in the past one hundred years has been decentralization. This involved the growth in direct sales from producers to meat packers, and the shift of packing plants from the terminal markets to livestock producing areas.

Growth and Decline of Terminal Markets

During the early development of the livestock industry, railroads dominated the transportation picture. This encouraged the development of large packing centers at such railroad centers as Cincinnati, Chicago, St. Louis, and Omaha. The cooperative shipping associations and the large livestock yards grew out of this situation. Because freight rates were higher for less-than-carload lots, the shipping association furnished a means by which farmers, each with a few head of livestock, could assemble a carload to be shipped at one time. At the "end of the line," large terminal markets grew to serve the packers.

Soon after World War I these yards came under government supervision with the passage of the Packers and Stockyards Act. The object of this act was to assure the maintenance of competition and fair dealings. Among other things, the act provided for general supervision of the buying and selling practices of firms operating on the market. In 1958 the Packers and Stockyards Act was amended to extend its coverage to any agency handling interstate livestock. This extension of supervisory coverage was necessary to keep pace with the changing patterns of marketing

These markets reached their peak in 1922, when there were 78 major livestock terminals. Many meat packers built their plants adjacent to these markets. By 1975, the number of terminal livestock markets had declined to 30.

Direct Marketing and Decentralization

Since 1923, livestock terminal markets have declined in importance. Live-stock sales made directly between the producer and packer, without using the services of terminal market facilities, are called *direct sales.* Because this shifts the point of livestock pricing from centralized terminal markets to numerous country points, direct sales are termed *decentralized marketing.*

The livestock decentralization trend is shown in Table 23-5. Between 1923 and 1976, meat packers' cattle purchases from terminal markets declined from 89 per cent to 12 per cent of all purchases. Similar trends are evident for hogs and sheep. Decentralized market channels are represented by packer purchases from producing area auction markets and from direct or country dealers. There is some evidence that the livestock decentralization trend had run its course by 1973. In the early 1970's, meat packers' purchases of hogs from terminals stabilized at 16–17 per cent, and from 1973 to 1975 meat packers' cattle purchases from terminal markets actually increased.

Direct sales and some technological improvements in meat packing and processing plants encouraged meat packers to move their plants from terminal

Table 23-5. Distribution of Packer Livestock Purchases by Market Outlet, Selected Years, 1923–1976.

PER CENT OF TOTAL MARKETINGS

	TERMINAL			AUCTIONS			DIRECT OR COUNTRY DEALERS*		
YEAR	CATTLE	HOGS	SHEEP AND LAMBS	CATTLE	HOGS	SHEEP AND LAMBS	CATTLE	HOGS	SHEEP AND LAMBS
1923	89%	76	85				10	24	14
1930	88	59	84				11	40	15
1940	75	46	63				24	53	36
1950	74	39	57				25	60	42
1960	45	30	35	15	8	10	38	61	54
1961	42	29	36	19	11	10	38	59	52
1962	42	29	35	18	11	15	38	59	49
1963	39	26	30	17	12	14	43	60	56
1964	36	23	28	18	13	13	44	63	57
1965	34	23	25	20	13	12	45	62	62
1966	31	22	21	19	15	13	49	62	64
1967	28	18	19	18	15	16	53	62	64
1968	24	19	18	18	14	15	57	66	66
1969	21	18	16	17	13	13	61	67	70
1970	18	17	15	16	14	12	65	68	72
1971	15	16	13	15	13	12	68	69	74
1972	13	16	13	14	13	12	72	70	74
1973	11	17	12	15	12	14	73	70	73
1974	13	17	11	16	12	13	69	70	75
1975	14	16	10	19	12	15	65	71	74
1976	12	17	9	20	11	15	66	71	75

* Includes auctions, direct or country dealers, and other outlets for 1923–1950. Auction market purchases were not significant until about 1940.
Source: Packers and Stockyards Administration, U.S. Department of Agriculture, P & SA Research Report No. 2, May 1973; P & SA *Resume,* December 24, 1976, December 23, 1977.

markets to livestock producing areas. This decentralization of meat packing facilities was largely completed by the 1970's.

Reasons for Change in Livestock Assembly

The basic reasons for the general change to more direct marketing channels are treated in Chapter 12. The particular reasons for the beginning of this development in livestock marketing in the 1920's, and its continuation, are summarized as follows:

1. The expansion of the corn and livestock production into the northwestern sections of the country placed the production areas still farther from the consuming areas.

2. The freight rate structure favored the shipment of meat over the shipment of live animals. This was particularly true when the saving in shipping weight of carcasses compared to live animals was considered. The continued improvement in refrigeration made it increasingly possible to take advantage of this saving.

3. Originally, lower wage rates encouraged the growth of small local packers in the production area. Later, the national packers also established new plants, both to take advantage of these economies and to meet the local competition in the area.

4. The development of the motor truck, along with improved roads, greatly encouraged local marketing. The availability of this kind of transportation reduced the dependence upon the railroads. This fact, plus the farmer's long-standing distrust of the central market, made him favor markets closer to home.

5. The recent development of much larger farm production units has increased the feasibility for packers to send their buyers directly to the farmer to acquire livestock.

Centralized Versus Decentralized Marketing

It is not possible to say that centralized marketing is either superior or inferior to decentralized marketing. Both marketing arrangements have advantages and disadvantages; and each appeals to various buyers and sellers of livestock for different reasons. The long-existing trend toward decentralization suggests that there may be some advantages, and or preferences, for this marketing channel. However, the recent slowing of the trend toward decentralization may indicate that both types of markets have equal, but different, advantages for producers and meat packers.

Table 23-6 shows the regional variations in farmers' costs of marketing livestock through terminal markets, country dealers, and auction markets in 1966. The market channel and regional cost variations are caused by

Table 23-6. Costs of Marketing Livestock Through Alternative Agencies, By Regions, 1966.

REGION	COST PER ANIMAL UNIT[1]		
	TERMINAL MARKETS[2]	COUNTRY DEALERS	AUCTION MARKETS
Northeast mid-Atlantic	$5.40	12.83	3.61
Southeast	2.79	5.79	2.30
South Central	2.94	9.00	3.97
East North Central	3.13	4.78	3.40
West North Central	2.87	6.95	2.18
Southwest	1.86	2.19	1.77
Mountain	1.10	12.07	1.39
Pacific	1.99	5.58	4.19
U.S. Average	2.76	6.24	2.45

[1] One animal unit is one head of cattle, 2 calves, 3 hogs, or 5 sheep/lambs.
[2] Includes commission firm fees.

Source: D. B. Agnew, *Cost of Marketing U.S. Livestock Through Dealers and Public Agencies,* U.S. Department of Agriculture, Marketing Research Report No. 998, June 1973, p. 14.

the different services and charges for the alternatives. There are indications these cost differences narrowed in the 1970's. In 1975 the cost of livestock marketing at terminals was estimated at $3.59 per head whereas auction market charges were $3.67 per head.[1]

Each producer and packer chooses the most advantageous market channel, based on needs, preferences, and economic returns. Their choices will reflect prices, marketing costs, and net returns of the two alternatives, and neither high prices nor low marketing costs alone determine what that choice will be. The important thing is that all buyers and sellers are free to choose among real alternatives.

Nevertheless, there are several reasons why many farmers have preferred direct sales to terminal market sales. Direct sales usually require fewer marketing services and therefore fewer out-of-pocket marketing expenses for farmers. Also farmers sometimes feel that in direct sales there is less shrinkage, and that direct sales are more convenient. In decentralized marketing farmers maintain physical control over livestock until they are priced and sold, and this, too, probably contributes to the preference of many for this marketing channel.

Even so, many farmers continue to use terminal markets. In some cases this may be because they have no choice. But small producers frequently need and value the assembly and other services provided by terminal markets.

_____
[1] *Packers and Stockyards Resume,* U.S. Department of Agriculture, December 24, 1976, p. 39.

Many farmers contend that competition is more vigorous in the terminal markets. It is true that there may be more buyers and sellers physically present at the terminal markets; however, modern communication networks link all local and terminal markets today.

Pricing efficiency in decentralized livestock markets is a legitimate concern. Decentralization has intensified the market information problem for livestock producers. Collecting and disseminating useful market news for price discovery at the numerous decentralized markets is a problem. It is difficult for the USDA Market News Service to cover these widely scattered markets and to gather accurate, voluntary information from traders.

MEAT PACKING AND PROCESSING

The meat packing industry is a disassembling industry. Whereas other manufacturers combine simple raw materials into a complex, composite product, meat packers break down a complex raw product—livestock—into its constituent parts. This reverse manufacturing process nevertheless adds form utility to livestock products.

The meat packing industry is composed of slaughter houses, where livestock is slaughtered and red meat is further processed, and specialized meat processors which do not slaughter but manufacture sausage, luncheon meats, and other prepared products. The combination slaughter-processors tend to be larger than the specialized meat processors and have experienced more rapid sales growth as a result of the increased demand for fresh beef. About 95 per cent of meat packing companies are single-plant firms; only a few companies own multiple packing plants.

There were over 6,000 livestock slaughtering plants in the United States on March 1, 1977.[2] Many of these plants were quite small, but some were quite large. For example, plants slaughtering 50,000 or more head of cattle per year accounted for 13 per cent of the number of plants but 83 per cent of all cattle slaughtered. Plants slaughtering less than 1,000 head of cattle per year represented 50 per cent of all plants, but less than 1 per cent of cattle slaughter.

All meat sold across state lines must be slaughtered under the supervision of federal inspectors. This is not a form of quality grading; rather, it insures that animals are disease-free, fit for human consumption, and that the plant meets sanitary requirements. The 1967 Wholesome Meat Act required all intrastate meat inspection programs to equal or exceed the federal standards. By 1975, more than 90 per cent of all cattle, 94 per cent of hogs, and 96 per cent of sheep and lambs were slaughtered under federal inspection.

---

[2] *Livestock Slaughter, Annual Summary,* U.S. Department of Agriculture, Statistical Reporting Service, Annual.

Table 23-7. Concentration of Livestock Slaughter By The Largest Meat Packers, 1950–1970.

SPECIES AND RANK OF FIRM	PER CENT OF LIVESTOCK SLAUGHTER					
	1950	1954	1958	1962	1966	1970
Cattle:						
Largest 4 firms	51%	45	35	29	27	24
5th through 10th	8	10	10	10	12	14
Largest 10	60	55	46	39	39	38
Calves:						
Largest 4 firms	58	59	49	39	45	32
5th through 10th	12	11	13	16	17	24
Largest 10	70	71	63	56	63	56
Sheep:						
Largest 4 firms	69	68	64	58	65	56
5th through 10th	15	16	17	17	20	20
Largest 10	85	84	81	76	85	76
Hogs:						
Largest 4 firms	48	48	41	39	39	34
5th through 10th	22	23	23	21	17	21
Largest 10	70	71	64	60	56	55

Source: *Decentralization in the Livestock Slaughter Industry,* U.S. Department of Agriculture, Agricultural Economic Report No. 83, Supplement, April 1966; Packers and Stockyards Administration.

The two most important trends influencing the meat packing business have been specialization and decentralization. The older plants which served centralized markets were very large, and slaughtered hogs, cattle, and sheep, and also processed various meat products. With decentralization of the packing industry to producing areas, newly built plants tend to specialize in slaughtering only one species of animal, and processing is done in separate plants.

Decentralization of the meat packing industry also provided the opportunity for new firms to enter the business. As a result, there has been a decline in livestock purchases by the larger packers. As shown in Table 23-7, the slaughter livestock market shares of the largest packers declined over the 1950–1970 period. Despite this national trend of deconcentration, however, market concentration remains relatively high in many local markets. For example, in 1970, the four largest meat packers purchased 66 per cent of Indiana steers and heifers, 86 per cent of Wisconsin steers and heifers, and 72 per cent of Oklahoma steers and heifers.[3]

Meat packers have not integrated forward into retailing operations. However, there has been backward integration of meat packers into livestock

[3] Aspelin, A., G. Engleman, "National Oligopoly and Local Oligopsony in the Meat Packing Industry," U.S. Department of Agriculture, Packers and Stockyards Administration, 1972.

487

feeding. This takes the form of packer ownership of feedlots, or custom feeding by feedlots under contract to meat packers. Over the 1954–1976 period, some 5 to 8 per cent of fed cattle slaughtered were fed by, or on contract for, meat packers. The feeding of lambs by packers increased from 4 per cent in 1962 to 17 per cent in 1976. Less than 0.5 per cent of hogs are fed by packers.[4] Cattle feeding by packers is more prevalent in the West than elsewhere. Meat packers integrate into feeding operations in order to control product quantity and quality and to reduce procurement costs. Farmers and independent feedlot operators are concerned that this integration provides packers with market power over livestock prices.

MEAT WHOLESALING AND RETAILING

As a result of the chainstore and supermarket movements, integrated retail chainstore organizations are the dominant meat merchandisers today. Most fresh and processed meats move directly from packers and meat processors to chainstore warehouses and then to retail stores. The role of the independent meat wholesaler has accordingly declined, although independent meat wholesalers and jobbers still serve smaller retailers and the away-from-home food market.

There is considerable variation in the ways that beef is being wholesaled by meat packers to food retail operations. Traditionally, packers delivered fresh carcasses direct to retail stores, where the final retail cuts and products were prepared. However, many chainstores have set up a central meat cutting, processing, and fabrication facility for serving several area stores. In this case, the packer ships directly to the central meat cutting facility, and the chainstore then distributes the meat products to individual grocery stores. Some retailers have shifted all butcher operations to these central processing plants; others maintain store butchers. In still another variation, referred to as *boxed beef,* packers break down the carcass into primal cuts (e.g., rounds, loins), subprimal cuts (e.g., top rounds, bottom rounds), or even final retail cuts, then ship these, in frozen form, to either chainstore warehouses or directly to retail stores.

Central meat processing by chainstores seems to result in substantial operational economies. Although centralization offers both labor and material savings, there are problems nevertheless. Labor unions have attempted to prevent central meat processing, and some consumers have balked at the loss of personal butcher service in the retail store. And there are problems in maintaining meat condition ("bloom"), as the distance between central cutting

---

[4] *Packers and Stockyards Resume,* U.S. Department of Agriculture, Packers and Stockyards Administration, Annual issue, December

and the retail store increases. Freezing red meats is necessary if the retail cutting operation is pushed back to the meat packer. This too has met with some consumer resistance. Therefore, the operational economies of boxed beef must be balanced against its impact on consumer acceptance and satisfaction.

STANDARDIZATION AND GRADING OF LIVESTOCK AND MEAT

One of the weaknesses of the livestock marketing system has been the lack of objective standards for grading livestock and meat. As a result of this weakness, the price mechanism works imperfectly in transferring consumer desires to producers. Often resources have been poorly allocated in producing a product which does not have the highest consumer satisfaction. The decline in the value of lard and the agitation for the so-called meat-type hogs illustrates this problem.

Difference Between Live and Carcass Value

Most of the livestock in this country is sold live on the basis of buyer-seller estimates of quality. It was suspected for some time that there is a significant difference in the live estimated value and the actual value of the dressed carcass. To a considerable extent this difference is of only academic interest to packers but it should not be to producers. The packer's interest is that the total amount paid for all livestock is in line with the total of all livestock. He can and may ignore the variation in carcass value between animals and lots of animals if he averages out satisfactorily. The producer may be content to ignore the value errors made within his market lot, but certainly not between his lots and others. The total amount paid for his livestock should be in line with the slaughter value of his animals.

Research has established fairly conclusively that there are substantial differences between hogs and cattle of the same weight, both in dressing percentage and other measurements of carcass value. It also has been established that there is often a substantial difference between the live prices paid and the carcass values of animals.

Carcass Weight and Grade Selling

To some, these research findings mean that livestock should be sold on the basis of *carcass weight and grade*. The bargaining for price is in terms of the weight and grade as finally determined after slaughter. Payment is made on the basis of the prearranged price for the various qualities and weights of carcasses. Arguments for and against live selling and carcass grade selling may be summarized as follows:

Against Live Selling

1. Consumer wants are not reflected accurately and quickly to producer. Makes for inefficient use of resources in production.
2. Farmer now paid on basis of averages. Producers of high consumer-value livestock get less than carcass value; producers of poor livestock get more.
3. Bruise and disease losses shared by all producers.
4. Price and market information now are inaccurate.

For Carcass-Grade Selling

1. Consumer wants are more accurately and quickly reflected to producer. Encourages farmer to produce what is wanted most.
2. Farmer paid for what his product is really worth. Good producers would get high prices; poor producers, lower prices.
3. Losses more nearly assessed against those who deserve them.
4. Market information would be more specific and mean more to producers.

There is considerable debate over objective standards for the carcass itself. Who is to be entrusted to do the grading, and how to handle the shrink allowances if the animal must be transported long distances before slaughter are major points of issue for both packers and farmers. Most of such buying is done by packers operating in the production area and securing livestock direct at the plants. With the increasing decentralization of the packing industry such operations become more feasible.

The selling of livestock on a carcass weight and grade basis is increasing but is still not widely practiced. As shown in Table 23-8, 23 per cent of cattle, 11 per cent of hogs, and 10 per cent of sheep and lambs were sold by producers on a carcass weight and grade basis in 1976. Larger packers

Table 23-8. Meat Packer Purchases of Livestock on a Carcass Weight and Grade Basis, 1965–1976.

	PER CENT OF PURCHASES ON A CARCASS WEIGHT AND GRADE BASIS		
YEAR	CATTLE	HOGS	SHEEP, LAMB
1965	11%	3	5
1970	19	5	10
1975	24	9	11
1976	23	11	10

Source: *Packers and Stockyards Resume,* U.S. Department of Agriculture, Packers and Stockyards Administration, December 24, 1976, December 23, 1977.

are more likely to use carcass weight and grade pricing, and corn belt packers use this purchasing system more frequently than other packers.

Livestock feeders also have a problem in evaluating the potential of feeder animals for further finishing. There are feeder livestock grades, but they are not widely used. Determining the value of feeder animals requires a special talent.

Because of the producers' distrust of the meat packers' grading methods, and the length of time it takes to price livestock, carcass weight and grading sales will probably continue to grow slowly. An alternative has been to improve live-weight pricing procedures. For example, it has been established that the weight, dressing percentage, and fat-back thickness account for a large percentage of the variation in hog carcass value. There is reason to believe that livestock salesmen and buyers, who are trained to give attention to these factors instead of the more conventional standards, can improve their estimate of live carcass value. New federal standards for grading live animals have attempted to reflect these factors. An improvement in the ability to judge the live animals accurately would of course accomplish many of the advantages of carcass-grade selling without incurring the disadvantage of a change in selling methods.

Meat Grading

The development of more widely accepted and objective federal meat grades presents a complex problem. Though federal inspection is mandatory for a large portion of our meat supply, the use of federal meat grades is optional. Many packers have developed their own grades and standards, and only about 50 per cent of cattle slaughtered in 1975 were federally graded as prime, choice, good, and so on.

Since July 1962, there has been a dual livestock grading system: a *quality grade,* which indicates tenderness, flavor, and juiciness, and a *yield grade,* which indicates the cutability, or expected yield, of the carcass. In February 1976, the U.S. Department of Agriculture revised its beef grading standards; it moved the grade boundaries, and required that all carcasses graded be rated for both quality and yield.

The problem of federal meat grading lies in the voluntary nature of the grades and the battle for market power between national packers and retail chainstore organizations. Large chains prefer federal grades because they help them in securing their needs for large volumes of uniform products. Smaller packers also usually favor uniform federal grading because it permits them to sell to these chain buyers on an equal footing with larger packers. Large packers, however, see such grades as a direct competition with their own efforts to grade and differentiate their products—by which they attempt to secure merchandising acceptance from consumers and thereby offset the market pressure of the chains.

LIVESTOCK MARKETING PROBLEMS

The many changes discussed give rise to several problem areas in the marketing of livestock. We might list some of them as follows:

1. *How can farmers be stimulated to assume a more active role in the selling of their livestock?* With the increase of direct marketing and the decreasing use of commission men, effective selling depends more and more on the farmer himself. There is ample evidence, however, that farmers often act from habit or bias instead of from informed judgment.

2. *How can adequate market news and supervision be provided?* With more and more buying points in the countryside, the established systems of collecting market news and supervision of the terminal markets becomes less usable and effective.

3. *Can a grading system be evolved that will permit an efficient transmission of consumer desires to farmers?* The inadequacies of the present methods of grading livestock are amply demonstrated. However, improvement in useful grades and standards has been slow.

4. *How many livestock markets are enough?* There is ample evidence that high costs are incurred when volume is too low at a buying point. The increased preference for direct marketing raises the dilemma of enough markets for effective competition but not too many for adequate volume and low cost of operation.

5. *How will pricing and competition fare in the structural changes in meat packing and distribution taking place?* In the past, antitrust activity in the meat packing industry was great. Does the declining power of the meat packers and the increasing power of the retailer decrease or increase the historic problem? How big must a packer be to obtain a low-cost, efficient operation?

6. *How much integration should there be in livestock marketing?* A few chain stores own packing houses. Some also operate their own feedlots. Some livestock contractual arrangements are in existence. What is the future of this type of market coordination?

7. *How can the livestock industry improve the demand for its products?* Beef demand is shifting rightward with rising income, but pork consumption is not expanding and lamb consumption is declining. Livestock producers sponsor and finance demand expansion and market development programs. How effective are these? What is the future demand for red meats?

8. *What is America's comparative advantage in red meat production?* The United States' comparative advantage in feedgrains and in large acreage suitable for grazing appear to give it a comparative advantage in livestock production. However, United States red meat imports—principally beef and veal, but also pork and lamb—more than doubled between 1960 and 1975. This occurred despite a 1964 law which limited the growth of red meat imports. What is the world market potential for United States red meat exports?

SUMMARY

The feed-livestock sector of the food industry is a complex set of markets, activities, products, and marketing functions. It is an integrated production and marketing system, ranging from almost perfectly competitive feeder animal production to highly concentrated feedlots and to imperfectly competitive livestock slaughter and meat processing firms. The chief trends in livestock production and marketing have been geographic and plant specialization, the development of large-scale feeding operations, decentralization of the meat packing industry, and central meat processing by retail organizations. Each of these has left its imprint on livestock marketing channels. The major problems in livestock marketing are pricing efficiency in integrated, decentralized markets, changing red meat consumption trends, methods of livestock grading and pricing, and meat imports.

QUESTIONS FOR DISCUSSION

1. How does livestock feeding differ from other farming activities?

2. Why are so many different types of marketing agencies involved in livestock assembly?

3. Why do you think the livestock decentralization trend may have stabilized in the 1970's?

4. What is the significance of the statement that livestock are protein-conversion factories and alternative grain markets?

5. Some groups have called for a reduction in the feeding of grain to livestock so that this food would be available for the hungry world. Examine this suggestion.

6. Examine the controversies that surrounded the 1976 change in federal beef grades. What were the issues, and how were they resolved?

7. Frequently it is suggested that decentralization was responsible for the decline in the market concentration ratio of meat packers over the 1950–1976 period. Explain this.

8. Why do you think farmers and packers have not accepted carcass weight and grade selling more rapidly?

9. How do you think livestock will be produced, and meat marketed, in the future?

SELECTED REFERENCES

AGNEW, D. B. *Cost of Marketing U.S. Livestock Through Dealers and Public Agencies.* U.S. Department of Agriculture. Marketing Research Report No. 998, June 1973.
—— *Improvements in Grades of Hogs Slaughtered from 1960–61 to 1967–68.* U.S. Department of Agriculture. Marketing Research Report No. 849, May 1969.
ANTHONY, W. E. *Decentralization in the Livestock Slaughter Industry.* U.S. Depart-

ment of Agriculture. Agricultural Economic Report No. 83, Supplement, April 1966.

ARMSTRONG, J. *Cattle and Beef: Buying, Selling, and Pricing.* Cooperative Extension Service, Purdue University, May 1968.

BREIMYER, H. F. *Demand and Prices for Meat—Factors Influencing Their Historical Development.* U.S. Department of Agriculture. Technical Bulletin No. 1253, 1961.

CROM, R. J. *Marketing Aids for the Cattle Feeder.* U.S.Department of Agriculture. Marketing Research Report No. 819, June 1968.

DUEWER, L. A., AND T. L. CRAWFORD. *Alternative Retail Beef-Handling Systems.* U.S. Department of Agriculture. ERS-661, July 1977.

Effects of Changes in Vertical Coordination on Pork Production and Prices. U.S. Department of Agriculture. Agricultural Economic Report No. 303, Aug. 1975.

Financial Facts About the Meat Packing Industry. American Meat Institute, Washington, D.C., Annual.

"Livestock and Meat." *Market Structure of the Food Industries.* U.S. Department of Agriculture. Marketing Research Report No. 971, Sept. 1972.

The Lamb Industry: An Economic Study of Marketing Structure, Practices, and Problems. U.S. Department of Agriculture. Packers and Stockyards Administration No. 2, 1973.

Livestock and Meat Statistics. U.S. Department of Agriculture. Statistical Bulletin No. 522, Annual supplement.

"Livestock Marketing." *Agricultural Markets in Change.* U.S. Department of Agriculture. Agricultural Economic Report No. 95, July 1966.

Long-Range Adjustments in the Livestock and Meat Industry: Implications and Alternatives. Ohio State Agricultural Research Bulletin No. 1037, March 1970.

McCOY, J. H. *Livestock and Meat Marketing.* AVI Publishing Company, Westport, Conn., 1972.

Meat Facts, a Statistical Summary About America's Largest Food Industry. American Meat Institute, Washington, D.C., Annual.

NELSON, K. E. *Economic Effects of the 1976 Beef Grade Change.* U.S. Department of Agriculture. Technical Bulletin No. 1570, June 1977.

Organization and Competition in the Livestock and Meat Industry. Technical Study No. 1, The National Commission on Food Marketing, Washington, D.C., July 1966.

Packers and Stockyards Administration. *Annual Reports.* U.S. Department of Agriculture.

Price-Quality Relationships for Selected Retail Cuts of Pork. U.S. Department of Agriculture. Agricultural Economics Report No. 245, 1973.

Structural Changes of the Federally Inspected Livestock Slaughter Industry, 1950–62. U.S. Department of Agriculture. Agricultural Economic Report No. 83, 1966.

TYLER, W. E. "Yield Grading Makes Sense—and Dollars." *Agricultural Marketing,* Nov. 1969.

UVACEK, E., AND D. L. WILSON. *Livestock Terminal Markets in the U.S.* U.S. Department of Agriculture. Marketing Research Report No. 299, 1959.

VOIZ, M. D., AND J. M. MARSDER. *Centralized Processing of Fresh Meat for Retail Stores.* U.S. Department of Agriculture. Marketing Research Report No. 628, 1963.

WILLIAMS, W. F., AND T. T. STOUT. *Economics of the Livestock-Meat Industry.* Macmillan Publishing Co. Inc., New York, 1964.

CHAPTER 24

Milk and Dairy Product Marketing

"Over the past 100 years, a complex pricing system has evolved to deal with the problems of coordinating, pricing, and distributing milk. All the various government and private institutions making up the system are designed to work together to insure that the public gets the milk it wants, while the dairy farmer gets the returns he needs to stay in business."*

Preview

• This chapter examines the marketing system for milk and processed dairy products.

• The numerous regulations governing the quality, pricing, and marketing of milk are reviewed. The dairy industry is shown to be one of the most highly regulated food industries.

• The complex of factors influencing milk pricing is studied, including the federal price support programs, federal and state milk marketing orders, classified and blend pricing, dairy product import policies, dairy cooperatives, and competitive pricing arrangements.

• The expanding—and sometimes controversial—role of dairy cooperatives in milk assembly markets and farm price negotiations is examined.

• The dairy processing industry is shown to be oligopolistic with moderate levels of market concentration. Food retail integration into milk processing is seen as a new competitive development in the processing market.

• Trends in dairy product consumption are studied.

---

* A. C. Manchester, *Milk Pricing*, U.S. Department of Agriculture, Agricultural Economic Report No. 315, November 1975.

- Key terms and concepts:

  blend price   milkshed
  bulk handling   Minnesota-Wisconsin milk price
  classified pricing

The dairy industry illustrates a number of food marketing trends, issues, and principles. It is one of the most highly regulated of all the food industries. Also, it has experienced considerable horizontal and vertical integration in recent years. We will emphasize here the very complex pricing arrangements that have evolved for dairy products, and the role of farmer cooperatives, marketing orders, and the government price support program for milk.

MILK PRODUCTION AND USE

Dairy farming accounted for 11 per cent of cash farm sales over the years 1974–1976. As in other segments of agriculture, increased specialization and commercialization of dairy farms have altered traditional production and marketing patterns. Total milk production generally increased from 1924 to 1964. However, as shown in Figure 24-1, the output trend was generally

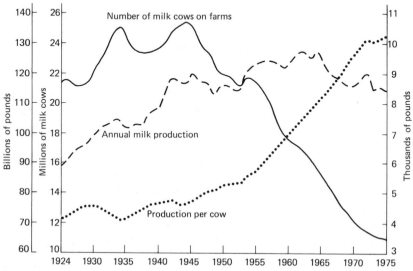

Figure 24–1. Number of milk cows, milk production per cow, and annual U.S. milk production 1924–1975. (U.S. Department of Agriculture)

downward over the 1964–1975 period because the number of dairy cows declined faster than the rate of growth in milk output per cow.

The sideline dairy enterprise on the general farm, and the small dairy farm, are disappearing; they are being replaced by larger, more specialized dairy operations. In the late 1950's, there were nearly 2 million dairy farms with an average herd size of less than 20 cows. By 1977 there were only 400,000 dairy farms, producing only slightly less milk, with herds averaging over 30 cows. Herds of 300 or more cows are common in the South and the West. Milk production is geographically concentrated. In 1975 nearly 50 per cent of all milk in the United States was produced on farms located in the Northeastern and the Great Lakes states. Wisconsin, the leading dairy state, produces twice as much milk as any other state. California, New York, Minnesota, and Pennsylvania are other leading dairy states.

Although the seasonality of milk production is less than it used to be, milk output still varies over the year. Production peaks in the late spring and reaches a low in the fall. Milk consumption, on the other hand, is fairly stable year-round. Just the opposite problem occurs in the shorter run. Cows produce milk every day, whereas consumers purchase most of their milk at the end of the week. Coordinating milk supplies with demand is therefore a difficult marketing task.

Farmers have several options in the use of their milk: (1) feed it to calves; (2) consume it in the farm household; (3) separate it into skim milk and cream and sell the cream only; (4) retail the milk directly to consumers; and (5) sell the whole milk to dairy processors. Over time, important changes have occurred in farmers' use of these marketing alternatives. Today, less than 1 per cent of milk is retailed direct from the farm to consumers. Milk used on the farms where it is produced declined from 25 per cent of total milk production in 1929 to 4 per cent in 1975. In the 1920's about one third of all milk was separated on-farm and only the cream sold, but today there is little on-farm separation. As a result of these trends, 95 per cent of milk produced on farms today enters the commercial marketing channels as whole milk.

PRODUCTS AND CONSUMPTION

The principal milk products are fluid milk and processed dairy products. Fluid products include whole milk, skim and low-fat milk, cream, half-and-half, and such products as flavored milk, eggnog, yogurt, and dips. The processed dairy products are cheese, butter, ice cream, cottage cheese, nonfat dry milk, and evaporated and condensed milk. In recent years, about 45 per cent of all farm milk has been sold to consumers in fluid form and 55 per cent in processed forms.

Per capita consumption of total milk products has been declining since reaching a peak of 409 retail pounds in 1942. By 1975, per capita consumption of milk products had fallen to 348 pounds. This consisted of 200 pounds of whole milk, 85 pounds of low-fat milk, 28 pounds of ice cream, sherbert, and ice milk, 14 pounds of cheese, 8 pounds of evaporated and condensed milk, 6 pounds of dry-milk products, and 5 pounds of butter.

Various dairy products have had different consumption trends in recent years, as shown in Figure 24-2. Low-fat fluid milk, cheese, sherbert, and ice milk were the principal growth products over the 1966–1976 period. Consumption of fluid whole milk, butter, cream, nonfat dry milk, and evaporated and condensed milk declined over this period. These consumption trends reflected the availability and relative prices of dairy product substitutes and changes in consumers' food preferences.

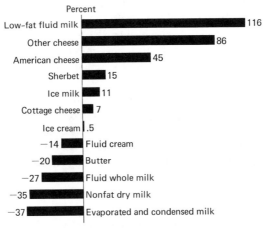

Figure 24–2. Changes in per capita dairy product sales, 1966–1976. (U.S. Department of Agriculture)

These demand trends vividly illustrate the dynamic nature of consumer food preferences. Many in the dairy industry assumed there were no good substitutes for dairy products. Although this may be true from a nutritional standpoint, consumers have made economic substitutions: coffee, tea, and soft drinks for milk; margerine for butter; and coffee whitener for cream. All foods are vulnerable to this kind of competitive market erosion.

COUNTRY ASSEMBLY OF MILK

At one time, the country assembly of milk was performed by trucks picking up cans of milk from individual farms for delivery to local milk plants.

This was a costly phase of milk marketing, because each truck picked up only a small amount of milk for each mile traveled. This farm milk assembly operation was revolutionized by the development of bulk milk handling systems. Milk producers installed large cooling tanks on the farms for receiving the milk from the milking machines. The milk is then pumped directly into tank trucks. The bulk milk delivery system eliminated the laborious loading and unloading of milk cans at the farm and at the dairy plant. It also permitted the accumulation of larger amounts of milk at the farm, which could be picked up every-other-day instead of daily. Because of the large investment in bulk milk handling equipment, an added push was given to the trend toward larger dairy farms and processors.

Improvements in transportation facilities and milk handling methods also have enlarged the procurement area of dairy processing plants. Once, milk markets 30 to 40 miles apart were separate markets. Today, bulk milk moves as far as 2,000 miles, and packaged milk may move 200 miles to market. This development has brought geographically isolated dairy farmers and processors into closer competitive contact. Milk prices and policies in one market are now influenced by potential competition from other markets.

Farmer dairy cooperatives dominate in the production and assembly of farm milk. In 1975, 88 per cent of all dairy farmers in federal market order areas belonged to dairy marketing cooperatives. These cooperatives perform numerous marketing activities, including serving as the sole bargaining agent for members in negotiating prices with dairy processors. They also perform quality control functions, sell dairy supplies, and manage surplus milk supplies. Many cooperatives operate pick-up routes and some operate dairy processing plants.

The number of dairy cooperatives declined from 1,928 in 1950 to 1,100 in 1968, whereas the volume of business per cooperative increased fourfold. This resulted from the consolidation of many small, local dairy cooperatives into large, regional cooperatives. Moreover, during the 1960's many of the dairy co-ops pooled their marketing efforts and became even larger federations of regional cooperatives which coordinate milk marketing efforts over larger areas. The major federations of dairy cooperatives in 1970 are illustrated in Figure 24-3.

MILK PRICING

The farm price of milk is influenced by several factors, including: (1) the cost of production and domestic supply of milk; (2) the consumer demand for milk in its various product forms; (3) the federal government dairy price support programs; (4) federal and state milk marketing orders; (5) dairy farmer cooperatives; and (6) dairy product import policies. No one of these

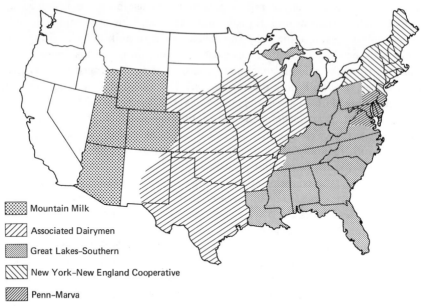

Mountain Milk

Associated Dairymen

Great Lakes–Southern

New York–New England Cooperative

Penn–Marva

Figure 24–3. The main cooperative milk marketing federations, 1970. (*Survey of Bargaining Developments in Midwest Fluid Milk Markets,* Purdue University Department of Agricultural Economics, 1970)

dominates in the pricing of farm milk. Each contributes in some measure to the complex milk pricing process.

Milk Grades and Classifications

There are two grades of farm milk—fluid Grade A and manufacturing Grade B. Grade A milk meets strict sanitary standards and is eligible for sale to the consumer as beverage milk. Grade B milk meets somewhat lower standards, which are acceptable because it undergoes processing at higher temperatures than pasteurized fluid milk. Although Grade B milk can only be used in making processed dairy products, such as cheese and butter, Grade A milk can be, and is, used to produce either fluid products or processed dairy products. In recent years, approximately 80 per cent of the nation's milk supply has met Grade A standards, but only 55 per cent has been sold as fluid products. This routing of Grade A milk into processed dairy products provides a "market bridge" between the prices of milk used for fluid and processed dairy products.

Milk has different values in its various uses. Milk that is used for fluid products has a higher value than the milk used for processed dairy products. There are two reasons for this. First, the retail price of fluid products is higher because it costs more to market highly perishable and bulky fluid milk than it does to market the processed forms of milk, such as cheese and butter. Second, the elasticity of demand is lower for fluid products than for processed dairy products. This provides an incentive for the industry to allocate some of the Grade A milk to processing uses. This legal form of price discrimination results in a higher price for fluid products and a lower price for processed products than would be the case if milk supplies were divided equally between the two uses. Because of these milk-value differentials at the retail level, milk dealers can pay higher prices to farmers for milk used in fluid products than for milk processed into cheese, butter, and other products.

A classified pricing scheme is used to insure that these milk-value differentials are transmitted to farmers. Grade A milk used for fluid products is labeled "Class I" and is priced higher than "Class II" Grade A milk, which is used in making processed dairy products. For example, during the 1966–1974 years, milk dealers paid dairy farmers an average of $7.21 per cwt. for Class I milk, while the average Class II farm price was $4.93. The farm price of Grade B milk is usually identical to the Class II Grade A price, because both are used in producing processed dairy products.

The Dairy Price Support Program

The federal dairy price support program provides the foundation price for all milk used in making processed dairy products. Under the provisions of the Agricultural Act of 1949, the Secretary of Agriculture is required to support the farm price of manufacturing milk at a level between 80 and 90 per cent of the parity milk price. The Department of Agriculture's Commodity Credit Corporation offers to purchase butter, American cheese, and nonfat dry milk at prices that will return the designated support price to farmers for Grade B milk. Because of the market bridge formed by the use of Class II fluid milk in processed products, this dairy support price program also influences the price of Grade A milk. The products purchased by the federal government to support the farm price of milk may be either stored or diverted to noncompeting markets.

The CCC support price is only a minimum price, and the farm price of manufacturing grade milk is free to move higher when supply and demand conditions warrant. The farm price of manufacturing milk is frequently above the support price, as a result of competitive bidding by milk dealers and processors for the available supply. The commonly used measure of the competitively determined farm price of manufacturing grade milk is the price of such milk in Minnesota and Wisconsin, an area where over 50 per cent of all Grade B milk is produced, and where there are several hundred dairy processing plants actively competing for farmers' milk. Because processed dairy products compete in national markets, the Minnesota-Wisconsin area tends to set the price for manufacturing grade milk in the other states.

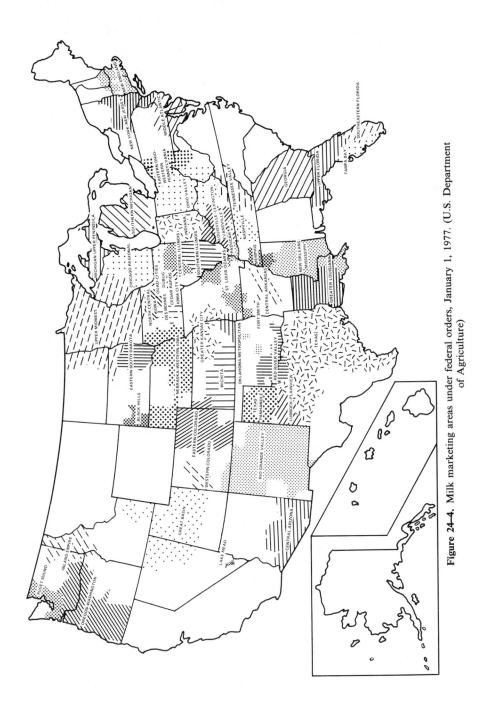

Figure 24-4. Milk marketing areas under federal orders, January 1, 1977. (U.S. Department of Agriculture)

The Federal Milk Marketing Order Program

The farm price of Grade A milk is influenced by both the dairy price support program and federal milk marketing orders. The most important provisions of these orders are those which regulate the minimum prices that dealers must pay farmers for Class I and Class II Grade A milk.

The federal milk marketing order program is authorized by the Agricultural Marketing Agreement Act of 1937. Under this legislation, producers in a designated area of milk production and consumption—known as a *milkshed*—may petition the Secretary of Agriculture to issue a market order governing the pricing of milk in the area. In most cases, two thirds of the producers in the area must approve the terms of the order in a referendum before it is implemented. Each order is administered by a market administrator appointed by the Secretary of Agriculture. The 61 federal milk marketing order areas in effect in 1977 are shown in Figure 24-4. In recent years, about 80 per cent of all Grade A milk and 63 per cent of all milk have been marketed under the provisions of federal milk marketing orders.

Federal milk marketing provisions affect two important pricing decisions: (1) what are the appropriate Class I and Class II prices? and (2) how will the farmers' return, or average, of these prices be determined? The Class II market order price is always at or near the Minnesota-Wisconsin base price for manufacturing grade milk. Manufacturers located elsewhere cannot pay more than this price for Class II milk and remain competitive with processed products shipped from Wisconsin and Minnesota. Thus, the area of greatest surplus and lowest price tends to set the national farm price of Class II milk.

The Class I market order price is determined by adding a Class I differential to the Class II milk price in each market order area. In the 1960's, the Class I differential for each area was established as 15 cents per hundredweight per 100 miles from Eau Claire, Wisconsin, the focal point of the surplus-producing area. This differential represented the cost of transporting bulk milk from the surplus area to each market order area until 1974, when transportation costs increased to about 20 cents per hundredweight.

This procedure for calculating the Class I differential serves two purposes. First, it provides for automatic adjustments in Class I and Class II prices as supply and demand conditions for milk change. If prices were set solely on the basis of administrator decisions or hearings, problems could arise in obtaining timely adjustments to changing market conditions. Second, the Class I differential results in a national milk price structure which conforms fairly well to that which would be expected in a perfectly competitive market. Prices are lowest in the region of greatest surplus, and prices are higher in more distant markets reflecting transportation costs and local supply and demand conditions. The 1975 structure of Class I prices is illustrated in Figure 24-5.

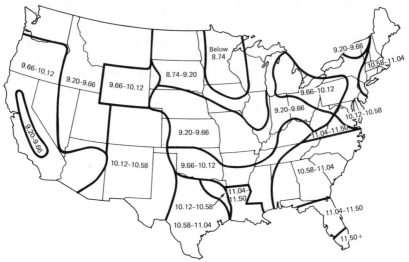

Figure 24–5. 1975 price structure for milk, based on dealers' prices, 3.5 percent butterfat, fluid use. (U.S. Department of Agriculture)

There is still the problem of determining the farmer's price of milk in each market, where some milk is priced at the Class I level and other milk at the Class II level. Under the terms of federal milk marketing orders, the farmer is paid a *blend price* for milk, regardless of how dealers use that milk. The blend price is a weighted average of the Class I and Class II price of milk in each market area. For example, if 70 per cent of the area's fluid grade milk is used for fluid products at a Class I price of $9.36/cwt (the 1975 U.S. price) whereas 30 per cent of the area's milk is processed at a Class II price of $7.65, each producer in the area would receive a blend price of:

$$70\% \times \$9.36 = \$6.55$$
$$+30\% \times \$7.65 = \underline{\$2.30}$$
$$100\% \text{ Blend Price} = \$8.85$$

In this way, no individual producer will gain or lose because of the way his milk is used. It is evident that the blend price may change, either because of a change in the prices of Class I and Class II milk, or because of a change in the use of milk within the market order area.

One of the major pricing problems is to arrive at an effective incentive plan that will encourage a more uniform seasonal pattern of milk production. Markets that have a great amount of seasonality are continually faced with "surplus" milk which must be sold through lower-valued outlets. Marketing orders usually provide for some system of payment that will encourage farmers to produce milk on a more uniform year-round basis.

Included in market orders are one or more of three provisions which provide an incentive for producers to produce more milk in the fall and less in the spring. First, the Minnesota-Wisconsin milk price is higher in the fall than in the spring, reflecting overall supply-demand conditions. Thus, Class I and Class II prices follow a seasonal pattern, serving to encourage relatively greater production in the fall. In addition, the percentage of milk used in Class I is higher in the fall, which increases the blend price relative to the spring. Second, some orders contain base-excess plan provisions. Under these provisions a producer establishes a base during the three to six months of lowest deliveries. During the surplus season (spring), milk produced in excess of this amount receives a lower price than the base milk. In markets using this plan, the price received by producers depends not only on the utilization of milk in the market, but also upon their pattern of deliveries. Third, some orders contain a take-out and pay-back plan. Deductions are made from the blend price during three to five months in the spring, and these monies are added back to the blend price during three to five months in the fall.

Federal milk marketing orders do not directly provide for controls on milk production or the uses of milk. However, Class I and II prices and the dairy price support levels do influence the prices of milk and ultimately affect producers' supply decisions and milk handlers' use decisions. Nor do federal orders set wholesale and retail prices of milk and dairy products, although these are clearly influenced by the farm prices of milk. There are some state marketing orders operating in addition to, or in conjunction with, federal milk marketing orders, and these regulate wholesale and retail fluid milk prices. Only about 4 per cent of the Grade A milk sold in the United States is not covered by either a federal or state milk marketing order.

Cooperatives' Role in Milk Pricing

In recent years, dairy farmer cooperatives have become more active bargaining agents for their members. They have increasingly assumed the tasks of coordinating milk supplies and the procurement activities of milk handlers. In doing so, they have increased their bargaining power and frequently negotiated prices above the minimums specified in the federal market orders. There were over-order prices in 35 per cent of the nation's milk market areas in 1964, 60 per cent in 1971, and 90 per cent in 1975. From 1965 to 1973, these price premiums for Class I milk averaged 20 to 40 cents per hundredweight over order minimums.

The Secretary of Agriculture is required to administer the federal milk marketing order program in the public interest, and has the authority to take action against dairy cooperatives which unduly enhance milk prices.

In many cases, it appears that the over-order prices simply cover the costs of the increased marketing services being performed by dairy cooperatives. However, it is possible that dairy cooperatives have successfully altered the balance of market power in farm milk markets and are now extracting higher prices from dairy processors—and consumers.

The Role of Imports

Only processed dairy products are imported into the United States. Normally, imports amount to only about 1 per cent of total domestic production (milk-equivalent). However, dairy product imports are of concern because the entire United States structure of milk prices is based on the price of Grade B milk, and dairy imports influence the domestic price support program. With a fixed Class I price differential, and the Class II price tied to the price of Grade B milk, any change in the supply and price of processed dairy products is quickly transmitted to fluid milk prices. Moreover, if the federal price support program raises the price of processed products above that in other countries, imports into the United States will increase and part of the price subsidy will go to foreign dairy product manufacturers. Because of these conditions, U.S. dairy product imports are limited through the use of quotas and tariffs.

Rationale for the Milk Pricing System

The student may wonder why such an elaborate and complex system of milk pricing is needed. Is it necessary and desirable for the government to regulate milk prices this closely? Why is milk given such special attention?

Several explanations are usually given. First, milk has always been considered a special and necessary food; and the supply and price of milk are very much a public-interest matter. Second, there has been public concern for the competitive position of the dairy farmer in areas where the perishability of milk gives buyers a strong negotiating position. Finally, it has been felt that special pricing arrangements are necessary to coordinate milk supply with demand in both the short and the long run. Trends in the dairy industry have raised serious questions about many of these assumptions, and about the need for continuing the special treatment of milk prices.

It is probably true that the price support program, milk marketing orders, and dairy cooperatives have raised the farm and retail prices of milk above the levels that would exist in their absence. However, these programs have also contributed to the stability of the milk market and to orderly marketing. Moreover, consumer prices of dairy products do not seem to be out of line with other prices. Table 24-1 shows that dairy product prices in general, and fluid milk prices in particular, increased less rapidly than "all retail

Table 24-1. Retail Prices of Dairy Products, 1950–1976.

	ALL CONSUMER PRICES	ALL FOODS	DAIRY PRODUCTS	FLUID MILK, GROCERY	BUTTER	CHEESE, AMERICAN PROCESS	ICE CREAM	EVAPORATED MILK	MARGARINE, COLORED
					1967 = 100				
1950	72.1	74.5	72.6	71.9	83.4	65.0	102.9	71.9	100.0
1955	80.2	81.6	80.2	81.1	81.5	72.4	98.5	77.6	93.7
1960	88.7	88.0	88.4	91.1	86.7	76.2	100.7	89.7	88.6
1965	94.5	94.4	90.0	90.3	89.4	85.5	95.4	89.7	97.2
1966	97.2	99.1	95.8	96.1	97.3	95.8	97.6	94.2	99.7
1967	100.0	100.0	100.0	100.0	100.0	100.0	100.0	100.0	100.0
1968	104.2	103.6	103.3	104.1	100.8	102.1	99.8	102.0	98.6
1969	109.8	108.9	106.7	107.0	102.1	107.7	100.5	105.2	98.3
1970	116.3	114.9	111.8	111.6	104.5	115.6	104.8	111.9	106.0
1971	121.3	118.4	115.3	114.6	105.8	121.0	106.2	118.6	116.0
1972	125.3	123.5	117.1	116.3	105.3	124.7	106.5	120.0	117.6
1973	133.1	141.4	127.9	127.3	110.7	138.5	113.1	134.3	133.4
1974	147.7	161.7	151.9	152.5	114.1	167.9	133.3	172.2	204.9
1975	161.2	175.4	156.6	152.7	124.2	175.8	151.6	183.9	224.6
1976	169.8	180.7	168.9	160.4	152.6	198.1	157.9	203.9	188.0

Source: U.S. Bureau of Labor Statistics.

food prices" and "all consumer prices" over the 1950–1976 years. By this comparison, the dairy industry has performed reasonably well for consumers.

FLUID MILK CHANNELS

Fluid milk marketing methods have changed considerably over the years. In the 1930's, over 75 per cent of all milk was home delivered, seven days per week in quart-sized glass containers. During World War II, as an economy measure, delivery was cut to every other day. In the 1950's, only 50 per cent of milk was delivered to the home, three times per week, and disposable containers were introduced. By the 1970's, 90 per cent of all fluid milk was sold in grocery stores, most milk containers were disposable, and a wide variety of container sizes was available. These trends illustrate how more efficient marketing techniques tend to displace less efficient ones. Home delivery of milk is more costly than sales through stores, and there are economies to marketing milk in larger packages. These trends are shown in Figure 24-6.

Fluid milk processing is characterized as an oligopolistic industry. Most of the major cities are served by a few national and regional dairy firms and a larger number of smaller dairies. Cooperatives process perhaps 10 to 12 per cent of all fluid milk. Market concentration of dairy companies is not high on a national basis, although concentration often is high in local markets. As shown in Table 24-2, the largest four national dairy firms accounted for 19 per cent of fluid milk product sales in 1970, down from 26 per cent of sales in 1958.

The number of fluid milk bottling plants declined rapidly—from 8,527 in 1948 to 2,080 in 1971. There are substantial economies of size in fluid milk processing and distribution, and the decrease in the number of plants was the result of dairy company mergers and plant consolidations. Typically, the pattern has been for larger dairy companies to buy smaller ones, or for the smaller dairies to discontinue operations altogether.

Merger activity in the dairy industry has been a public policy issue. Between 1951 and 1955, the largest eight dairy processors bought an average of 71 dairy companies each year. This acquisition rate slowed to 27 mergers per year between 1956 and 1961, and to only four mergers per year in the 1962–1974 period, the result of Federal Trade Commission challenges to dairy industry mergers on the grounds that they lessened competition in the industry. Blocked from growing via the horizontal integration route, the dairy companies entered into conglomerate mergers in the 1960's. By 1974, Borden received only 24 per cent of its gross sales from dairy products, Foremost only 22 per cent, and Kraftco only 50 per cent.

Most dairy companies perform their own distribution functions. These include milk delivery to grocery stores, restaurants, institutions, and home

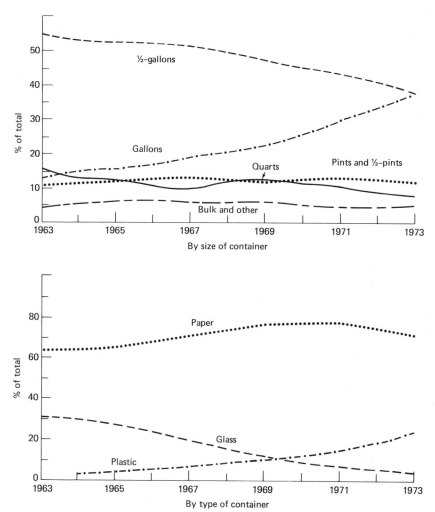

Figure 24–6. Fluid milk product sales by size and type of container, 1963–1973. (U.S. Department of Agriculture)

delivery routes. There are also a few independent distributors who pick up milk at the dairy plant dock for delivery to retailers, schools, or homes. Competition is keen for these accounts. Packaged milk is largely an undifferentiated product, therefore dealers compete on the basis of price and services. Generally, retail chainstores prefer to do business with the larger dairies that can service an entire chainstore division with central delivery and billing. Small dairies service independent retailers, the institutional market, and home delivery routes.

In recent years, food retailers have integrated vertically into milk processing

Table 24-2. Market Share of the Largest Dairy Companies, 1958 and 1970.

COMPANY	SHARE OF FLUID MILK PRODUCT SALES	
	1958	1970
Borden	9.2%	6.3%
Kraftco	8.9	6.3
Foremost	4.3	2.6
Beatrice	3.4	3.6
Top Four Firms	25.8	18.8
Carnation	2.3	2.0
Arden	1.4	1.1
Fairmont	0.9	1.9
Pet	0.6	1.3
Southland	N.A.	2.2
Safeway	N.A.	2.2
Dairylea Cooperative	—	2.1
Top Eight Firms	31.0	27.3

Source: R. C. Parker, *Economic Report of the Dairy Industry,* Staff Report to the Federal Trade Commission, Washington, D.C., March 1973.

and branding. Retailers are now important milk packagers. As shown in Table 24-3, integrated chainstores were the only segment of the dairy industry to increase plant numbers and milk market share over the 1964–1970 period. Retailers packaged perhaps 20 per cent of all fluid milk in 1975. A related development has been the trend toward packaging milk under the retail chainstore's label. Many dairies resisted this, fearing it would undermine their own branding efforts. And the threat that retailers might operate their own

Table 24-3. Ownership of Fluid Milk Plants, 1964–1971.

PLANT OWNERSHIP	NUMBER OF PLANTS		PER CENT OF FLUID-MILK PRODUCTION	
	1964	1971	1964	1971
National firm	264	188	27%	23%
Regional firm	71	60	5	8
Local firm	3,444	1,601	54	47
Cooperative	267	168	10	11
Integrated chainstore	57	63	4	11
Total	4,103	2,080	100	100

Source: A. C. Manchester, *Market Structure, Institutions and Performance in the Fluid Milk Industry,* U.S. Department of Agriculture, Agricultural Economic Report No. 248, January 1974, p. 4.

fluid milk plants encouraged many dairies to engage in private labeling of milk—an example of market power on the part of the chainstores.

These trends in fluid milk distribution have greatly altered the competitive environment of the dairy industry. No longer are milk markets and companies geographically isolated. Where once a small community may have had only one source of milk, it may now find two or three national giants competing against one another. The small, family dairy plant has been displaced by larger, more efficient operations. And even the national dairies find themselves in competition with the chainstore organizations. In such cases, it is not easy to judge whether, overall, competition has increased or decreased, or whether all the trends have been a desirable gain for society in general.

PROCESSED DAIRY PRODUCT CHANNELS

Processed dairy products, such as cheese and butter, are less bulky and perishable than fluid milk. This means they can be produced near areas of concentrated milk production and shipped to markets farther away than fluid products. Minnesota and Wisconsin are the major surplus producers of milk; they annually account for about 44 per cent of U.S. butter production, 51 per cent of cheese production, and 42 per cent of nonfat dry milk production. Processed dairy products can be stored for considerable periods of time, and this influences their marketing and pricing patterns.

Historically, butter was the largest single outlet for farm milk not used in fluid form. Over the 1960–1965 years, twice as much milk was used to produce butter as was used for making cheese. However, because of diverging consumption trends for butter and cheese, cheese was a more important outlet for milk than was butter in the 1972–1977 period.

Dairy processing plants may be independent proprietorships, cooperatives, or corporately owned by multi-plant national and regional dairy companies. The large dairy companies produce a broad range of products, and the small companies usually manufacture a limited product line. Some dairy plants produce more than one product, but many butter and cheese plants and condensories tend to specialize in one product.

Because of plant closings, mergers, and consolidations, there has been a marked decline in the number of plants manufacturing dairy products, as shown in Table 24-4. The technological developments in dairy processing— which sharply reduced costs along with increasing volumes— are propelling the trend toward fewer and larger dairy processing plants. As a result of this trend, the share of butter production accounted for by the four largest processors increased from 11 per cent in 1963 to 45 per cent in 1972. The four-firm market concentration ratio for other dairy products did not change significantly over this period, and in 1972 was 44 per cent for cheese, 41

511

Table 24-4. Number of Plants Manufacturing Selected Dairy Products, 1940–1974.

	NUMBER OF PLANTS			
TYPE OF PLANT	1940	1950	1960	1974
Butter	4,692	3,060	1,659	389
Cheese	2,856	2,158	1,419	862
Cottage cheese	1,783	1,571	1,370	409
Ice cream	4,191	3,269	1,950	1,239
Evaporated milk	142	145	72	32
Nonfat dry milk	273	459	442	159

Source: *Production of Manufactured Dairy Products,* U.S. Department of Agriculture, Statistical Reporting Service, Annual.

per cent for canned and evaporated milk, and 29 per cent for ice cream. These concentration levels are higher than for fluid milk processing.

Processed dairy product marketing channels have undergone decentralization, like so many other food industries. Earlier, cheese and butter were shipped by processors to central terminal markets where wholesalers and jobbers sold the products to retailers. The large meat packers were once major cheese and butter wholesalers. Ice cream was made locally and distributed through ice cream parlors in earlier years. The chainstore and supermarket revolutions, along with the growth of large, national dairy companies, altered these market channels and encouraged more direct sales. Today, supermarkets are the chief outlet for processed dairy products, and dairy processors ship directly to chainstore warehouses or to individual retail stores. Decentralization and direct sales have favored the growth of large, full-line dairy companies.

Despite this decentralization, central markets still serve as important price-discovery points for cheese and butter. Direct sales of butter are frequently negotiated based on price quotations of the Chicago and New York Mercantile Exchanges. The National Cheese Exchange Inc., in Green Bay, Wisconsin, serves as the wholesale price discovery market for American cheese. Concern with the price discovery process has grown as direct sales have increased and as less of the supply passes through these central markets. The price of nonfat dry milk tends to rest on the CCC support price because the government has purchased from 25 to 40 per cent of this product in recent years.

Marketing contracts are widely used throughout the dairy product distribution channel. In addition to the contracts that dairy farmers sign with cooperatives, and the full-supply contracts in force between cooperatives and processors, butter and cheese are normally sold under contracts which specify what the basis of pricing is, and who pays the shipping costs. Processors also compete aggressively for dairy product sales contracts with schools and government installations. There are, in addition, cooperative sales agencies, such as Land O' Lakes, which has marketing contracts with some one hundred member cooperatives for distributing their butter and cheese under a common label. These contracts facilitate the orderly marketing of dairy products, but they also displace open market trading arrangements.

SUMMARY

The dairy industry is undergoing substantial changes in market organization. Declining numbers and increasing sizes of dairy farms, changing consumer preferences for various dairy products, a tendency toward fewer but larger dairy product handlers and processors, chainstore integration into dairy processing, decentralized marketing, and increased cooperative activity in assembly markets have all altered the marketing patterns and competitive environment of the dairy industry. Product quality and price regulations make the dairy industry one of the most highly regulated food sectors. Farm milk prices—and indirectly, consumer prices—are influenced by a complex system of competitive and regulatory arrangements, including federal price supports and classified market order prices. Dairy product retail prices have not increased as fast as other food products in recent years. Dairy farmer cooperatives have assumed most of the assembly market functions and also play an important role in negotiating farm milk prices.

QUESTIONS FOR DISCUSSION

1. What effect has the declining number of dairy farms and dairy cows and the increasing milk output per cow had on the milk marketing machinery?

2. Which sociodemographic trends in consumer markets explain the trends in dairy product consumption?

3. Investigate the market development efforts of the American Dairy Association. What affect do you think these programs have had on dairy product consumption?

4. What are some of the reasons why dairy cooperatives integrated into milk assembly markets? Did dairy processors resist this integration? Why or why not?

5. Explain how the dairy industry can improve profits by adopting a two-price system for milk at the retail level. Why is a classified pricing system needed at the farm level to transmit these price differentials to farmers? Why is a blend price used to insure that all farmers receive the same price within a market area?

6. Use a supply and demand graph to show the effect of the dairy price support program on farm prices of milk when (a) competitive forces would result in a farm price below the support level; and (b) milk processors bid the price of milk above the support level.

7. Under what conditions will the classified blend price promote a higher farm price of milk than would occur if processors paid farmers a simple average of the Class I and Class II milk prices?

8. What factors govern the decision of how much milk will be sold as fluid products and how much will be processed into dairy products?

9. Analyze operational and pricing efficiency trends in the dairy industry.

REFERENCES

The Cheese Industry. U.S. Department of Agriculture, Agricultural Economic Report No. 294, July 1975.

"Dairy Products." *Market Structure of the Food Industries.* U.S. Department of Agriculture. Marketing Research Report No. 971. Sept. 1972, pp. 21–36.

FALLERT, R. F. *A Survey of Central Milk Programs in Midwestern Food Chains.* U.S. Department of Agriculture. Marketing Research Report No. 944, Dec., 1971.

JONES, J. L. *Homemakers' Opinions About Dairy Products and Imitations: A Nationwide Survey.* U.S. Department of Agriculture. Marketing Research Report No. 995, May 1973.

"The Impact of Dairy Imports on the U.S. Dairy Industry." *The Dairy Situation.* U.S. Department of Agriculture, March 1975, pp. 31–35.

JONES, W. W. *Economics of Butter Production and Marketing.* U.S. Department of Agriculture. Agricultural Economic Report No. 365, March 1977.

KNUTSON, R. D. *Cooperative Bargaining Developments in the Dairy Industry, 1960–1970.* U.S. Department of Agriculture. Farmer Cooperative Research Report No. 19, Aug. 1971.

MANCHESTER, A. C. *Market Structure, Institutions, and Performance in the Fluid Milk Industry.* U.S. Department of Agriculture. Agricultural Economic Report No. 248, Jan. 1974.

——— *Milk Pricing.* U.S. Department of Agriculture. Agricultural Economic Report No. 315, Nov. 1975.

——— *Sales of Fluid Milk Products, 1954–72.* U.S. Department of Agriculture. Marketing Research Report No. 997, June 1973.

MATHIS, A. G., AND D. FRAVEL. *Governments' Role in Pricing Fluid Milk in the U.S.* U.S. Department of Agriculture. Agricultural Economic Report No. 152, Dec. 1968.

MILLER, J. J., AND R. R. MILLER. "Changes in Number and Size of Dairy Plants." *The Dairy Situation.* U.S. Department of Agriculture, July 1974, pp. 28–34.

Organization and Competition in the Dairy Industry. Technical Study No. 3, The National Commission on Food Marketing, Washington, D.C., June 1967.

PARKER, R. C. *Economic Report on the Dairy Industry.* Staff Report to the Federal Trade Commission, Washington, D.C., March 1973.

Questions and Answers on Federal Milk Marketing Orders. U.S. Department of Agriculture. Agricultural Marketing Service No. 559, rev. June 1974.

SHAW, C. N., AND S. G. LEVING. *Government's Role in Pricing Fluid Milk in the U.S.* U.S. Department of Agriculture. Agricultural Economic Report No. 397, March 1978.

WILLIAMS, S. W., ET. AL. *Organization in the Midwest Dairy Industries.* Iowa State University Press, Ames, Iowa, 1970.

CHAPTER 25

Poultry and Egg Marketing

"INTEGRATED OPERATIONS have accounted for increasingly larger proportions of production and marketing of poultry and eggs over the past 15 years. These operations are most common in chicken, but are gaining in turkeys and market eggs. Eggs and poultry now typically move through shorter and more direct marketing channels. Increasingly, direct movement from packing plants to retailers is bypassing wholesale distributors."*

Preview

- This chapter examines the major trends in poultry and egg production and marketing which affect the marketing machinery: concentration of production, specialization, integration, and decentralization.
- Operational and pricing efficiency are evaluated in the poultry industry, including trends in production costs, industry market development efforts, pricing trends, and the relationship of prices to costs.
- Poultry and egg consumption trends are reviewed and related to price changes and shifts in supply and demand curves.
- The variety, motives, and initiators of integration in the poultry industry are identified. Special attention is given to the rise of the integrated input supply-producer-processor and distributor of poultry and eggs.
- The price discovery problem in the poultry industry is examined, and industry proposals are reviewed.

---

* *Market Structure of the Food Industries,* U.S. Department of Agriculture, Marketing Research Report No. 971, September 1972.

515

- Key terms and concepts:
  base price quotations   egg breakers
  broilers   ready-to-cook (RTC)

The poultry industry is made up of three segments—eggs, chickens, and turkeys. Although these are three distinct commodities, they have had similar production and marketing trends in recent years. Poultry products accounted for 7 per cent of consumer food expenditures and total farm sales for the 1974–1976 period. In the same years, chicken accounted for 45 per cent of poultry farm sales, eggs 44 per cent, and turkeys 11 per cent.

The popular images of a few chickens scratching in the barnyard and the farmer's wife earning "egg money," are quite obsolete today. The poultry industry is considered one of the most industrialized sectors of agriculture. Modern poultry production units and methods resemble an assembly line, factory-type operation rather than the traditional, land-based agriculture. The industry is one of large, specialized and highly integrated firms. Production and processing are automated and mechanized for maximum operational efficiency. The boundary line between farming and marketing activities has largely been obscured by integration and decentralization. More than any other development, industrialization has shaped the contemporary marketing channels and processes of the poultry industry.

PRODUCTION PATTERNS

Growth and specialization have been the hallmarks of the poultry industry's development. The 1940–1975 expansion in poultry and egg production is traced in Table 25-1. The production of chickens, broilers, and turkeys tripled

Table 25-1. Poultry Production 1940–1975.

	MILLION POUNDS			EGGS (MILLION)
	CHICKENS	BROILERS	TURKEYS	
1940	2,158	413	502	39,707
1950	2,310	1,945	817	58,954
1960	1,346	6,017	2,202	61,602
1970	1,197	10,819	2,184	70,312
1975	1,060	11,034	2,278	64,362

Source: U.S. Department of Agriculture, *Agricultural Statistics,* annual.

516

between 1950 and 1975. Egg production advanced 19 per cent over this period. *Broilers* is the trade term for the young chickens, grown solely for meat, that are usually sold in retail stores today. They are also known as "fryers." As is evident in Table 25-1, the growth in chicken production has been in broilers. The output of farm chickens, a by-product of the egg-laying flock, has declined. The development of separate meat-type and egg-laying chickens is an example of specialization in the poultry industry.

The growth in poultry output, as shown in Table 25-1, was caused by both an increase in demand and improved efficiency in poultry production. The supply curve shifted down and rightward with cost-reducing and yield-increasing improvements in poultry production technology following World War II. For example, the amount of feed needed to produce 1 pound of broiler meat fell from 4 pounds in 1948 to 2.1 pounds in 1972–1974. The amount of feed required to produce 1 dozen eggs fell from 7.2 pounds in 1948 to 4.1 pounds in 1973–1974. Shorter growing periods and lower mortality rates also increased the productive efficiency and output of poultry and eggs over the 1945–1975 period.

These production efficiencies generally favored larger operations and encouraged the growth of more specialized poultry producing units. As a result, although poultry and eggs are still produced on a large number of diversified farms, the bulk of the production is now concentrated in the hands of fewer and larger producers. The number of farms producing meat-type chickens fell from 42,000 in 1959 to 33,000 in 1974, whereas the average size of a flock increased from 34,000 to 72,000 birds. The number of turkey producers fell from 86,700 in 1959 to 5,400 in 1969, and the average flock size increased from 952 to 19,000 birds. The average number of eggs sold per egg farm doubled between 1964 and 1970.[1] The multi-thousand bird egg and chicken factory is a reality which influences the marketing of poultry products today.

There also has been a shift in the geographic location of poultry production. As shown in Table 25-2, production has shifted from the northern to the southern and western states. Labor and energy costs, milder weather, and surplus labor were factors in this shift. In the 1971–1976 period, ten states accounted for 84 per cent of all broiler production, and three of these— Arkansas, Georgia, and Alabama—produced 44 per cent of all broilers. The DelMarVa (Delaware-Maryland-Virginia) area is one of concentrated broiler production. California and Minnesota produce about one third of U.S. turkeys. Egg production is more geographically dispersed but is growing more rapidly in the South and in the West than in the northern states.

The seasonality of poultry supplies has been reduced as confinement production has become concentrated in fewer hands and as the industry has shifted to warmer states. Figure 25-1 shows that egg and broiler output still peak in the spring, and that turkey production is predictably highest

---

[1] *Census of Agriculture* and U.S. Department of Agriculture estimates.

517

Table 25-2. Geographic Location of Poultry Production, 1959–1969.

	PER CENT OF PRODUCTION					
	BROILERS		TURKEYS		EGGS	
REGION	1959	1969	1959	1969	1959	1969
North Atlantic	9%	6%	4%	3%	17%	14%
North Central	8	3	50	42	44	28
South	78	87	23	32	26	42
Mountain-Pacific	5	4	23	23	13	16
U.S.	100%	100%	100%	100%	100%	100%

Source: *U.S. Census of Agriculture.*

in the fall. These seasonal patterns are caused by the biological characteristics of poultry and the seasonality of demand. However, large-scale broiler production in the South has reduced the seasonal variability of broiler production and prices. Seasonal egg production and price variations also are less pronounced than formerly. This has affected the need for the storage marketing function and the capacity utilization of poultry processing plants.

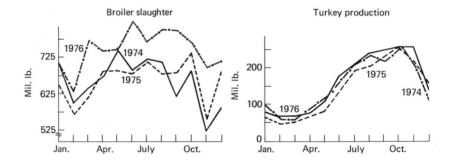

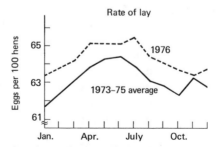

Figure 25-1. Seasonal poultry and egg production. (U.S. Department of Agriculture)

POULTRY PRODUCTS, CONSUMPTION, AND PRICES

Poultry is marketed in a variety of product forms and convenience states. Prior to World War II, most poultry was sold to consumers in the live or the New York dressed state (only blood and feathers removed). By 1975, most broilers and turkeys were marketed as eviscerated ice-packed or frozen ready-to-cook (RTC) poultry. This product is available with varying degrees of built-in maid service: whole birds, cut-up birds, poultry parts, and self-basting poultry. This product diversity contributes to consumer satisfaction, but it also increases the complexity and cost of the marketing process.

Most poultry is marketed in the unprocessed state, but about 10 per cent of eggs and chicken and 25 per cent of turkeys were further-processed in the 1973–1975 period. Eggs are processed—by firms called "breakers"—into dried, frozen, and liquid egg products. These are used as ingredients by food processors in baby foods, noodles, bakery mixes, scrambled egg mixes, mayonnaise, ice cream, and numerous other products. Further-processed turkey and chicken products include breaded and precooked parts, TV dinners, poultry rolls and roasts, soups, and pot pies.

Product Characteristics

The perishability and homogeneity of chicken and eggs are key factors in their marketing. As only a limited amount of these products are processed and stored, most of the supply has a relatively short shelf-life. This requires special transportation and merchandising facilities for marketing poultry. Perhaps 2 to 3 per cent of poultry and eggs are lost in the marketing channel because of spoilage and breakage. The perishability of poultry products also results in an urgency to market them which limits producers' and handlers' flexibility. Birds must be sold when they reach the proper market weight and maturity; and eggs, when they are fresh, regardless of market conditions and prices. Errors in the supply-demand balance are expensive.

Traditionally, poultry products were considered relatively homogeneous and undifferentiated products at both the farm and retail levels. However, branding and brand advertising are now rather common for eggs and further-processed poultry products. And in the 1960's and 1970's, there has been a trend toward more branding and packer advertising of broilers and turkeys. An estimated 40 per cent of broilers were branded by packers in 1976. Through brand advertising, large poultry firms are attempting to build consumer loyalty in order to remove their products from the generic category.

Market Development

The poultry industry has sponsored market development and demand-expansion programs. The growth of the processed egg product industry and

Table 25-3. Poultry Consumption and Prices, 1946–1975.

YEARS	CHICKEN			TURKEY			EGGS		
	FARM PRICE (¢/LB)	RETAIL PRICE (¢/LB)	PER CAPITA CONSUMPTION (POUNDS)	FARM PRICE (¢/LB)	RETAIL PRICE (¢/LB)	PER CAPITA CONSUMPTION (POUNDS)	FARM PRICE (¢/LB)	RETAIL PRICE (¢/LB)	PER CAPITA CONSUMPTION (POUNDS)
1946–50	$.32	$.60	19	.36	NA	3	.40	.70	47
1951–55	.27	.57	21	.33	NA	5	.41	.65	47
1956–60	.18	.44	26	.25	NA	6	.37	.56	44
1961–65	.14	.38	30	.21	NA	7	.34	.55	40
1966–70	.14	.40	37	.21	.51	8	.38	.55	39
1971–75	.20	.52	41	.30	.66	9	.42	.68	37

Source: U.S. Department of Agriculture.

the development of further-processed poultry meat products are examples. The development and promotion of year-round turkey products is another example. The rapid growth of the fast-food chicken industry has also influenced poultry markets. The hotel-restaurant-institutional (HRI) market accounted for perhaps 25 per cent of all broiler sales in 1975. The industry's recognition that consumers desired a younger, smaller, and more tender chicken than was produced as a by-product of the egg-laying flock, and the resulting expansion of the broiler industry, is a classic example of the marketing concept and industry market development. Under the provisions of the 1974 Egg Research and Consumer Information Act, the industry established the American Egg Board to carry out an industry-financed, coordinated program of research, consumer education, and promotion to improve and develop markets for eggs and egg products.

Broilers play an important competitive role in food retail markets. They are among the most frequently "specialed" retail food items—grocers use them for low-pricing strategies in order to attract store patronage. This aggressive price competition and merchandising has no doubt also increased chicken consumption.

Prices and Consumption

The poultry industry provides a dramatic illustration of how food production efficiency gains are passed on to consumers under highly competitive market conditions. As shown in Table 25-3, farm and retail prices of poultry and eggs fell from 1946 to the mid-1960's. These declining prices resulted from the rightward-shifting farm supply curve and from a competitive market environment which transmitted those lower farm costs and prices to consumers in the form of increased supplies and lower retail prices. Even though increased feed costs and inflation halted the decline in broiler, egg, and turkey prices in the late 1960's, the 1971–1975 retail prices of these products were still below their 1946–1950 levels. Few products can match this price record.

Table 25-3 also shows consumption of poultry and eggs over the 1946–1975 period. Per capita consumption of chicken and broilers doubled and turkey tripled during these years. This was a result of declining prices and rightward-shifting demand curves caused by increases in income, more eating out, the development of new products, and the declining price of chicken and turkey relative to other protein sources. These rightward shifts in the demand curve were strong enough to sustain increased per capita consumption of broilers and turkeys over the 1966–1975 period, despite rising retail prices.

Per capita egg consumption did not respond to falling prices and rising income in the same fashion over the 1946–1975 period. Instead, egg consumption has declined steadily from the 1951–1952 peak of 49 pounds per capita. This trend has been attributed to changed attitudes toward breakfast, diet

521

and health considerations, and a basic change in the food preferences of an urbanized population.

INTEGRATION IN THE POULTRY INDUSTRY

The poultry industry provides excellent examples of developing, and nearly complete, integration of farm production and marketing activities. Vertical coordination of the sequential poultry markets—from input suppliers through retailers—is highly developed in this industry. Integration has progressed to the point where large, multi-function producer-packer-processor-distributor firms are the dominant force in poultry and egg production and marketing. These firms may be independents, cooperatives, subsidiaries of feed manufacturers, meat packers, retailers, or affiliates of conglomerate corporations. The multiple activities of integrated poultry and egg firms are illustrated in Table 25-4.

Multi-purpose firms represent the third stage of integration in the poultry industry. Prior to the 1930's, poultry production was a highly integrated operation, combining a breeding flock, a hatchery, grain farming and feed mixing, growing, and delivery services. In the 1930's and 1940's, specialized breeding, hatchery, feed mixing, and packing operations evolved. In the 1950's and 1960's, these separate operations were recombined to form the modern, highly integrated poultry production and marketing firm. At each of these phases there were corresponding adjustments in the marketing machinery.

Several forces fueled the integration of poultry and egg production and marketing. First, new cost-reducing production technologies encouraged

Table 25-4. Activities of Vertically Integrated Poultry and Egg Firms, 1973–1975.

INTEGRATED ACTIVITIES	PER CENT OF PLANTS WITH INTEGRATED ACTIVITIES			
	SHELL EGGS	EGG BREAKERS	BROILER PACKING	TURKEY PACKING
Grain production	6%	0	0	0
Hatcheries	14	1	28	8
Pullet or replacement rearing	21	3	0	0
Breeder flocks	0	0	0	6
Feed mills	34	2	29	10
Own production	67	11	19	10
Contract production	27	3	34	13

Source: G. B. Rogers, et al., "Marketing and Integration in the Poultry and Egg Industries," *Poultry and Egg Situation,* U.S. Department of Agriculture, pp. 39–43.

larger poultry producing units, the expansion of industry capacity, and the use of supervisory management for standardized production tasks. Because increased poultry production means an expanding market for feed, feed manufacturers financed producers by supplying capital for building houses, buying equipment, chickens, and feed. Eventually, feed manufacturers developed contracts which assisted growers in expanding output and in marketing the finished products. Independent packers and wholesalers also entered into production arrangements in order to control quality and assure adequate supplies for efficient plant operation. Large producers also found it necessary to integrate into packing and distributing in order to assure markets for their products. Interestingly, many of the national feed companies that initiated this integration process in the 1940's and 1950's discontinued their poultry operations in the 1970's.

The three types of production-marketing integration prevalent in the poultry industry are shown in Table 25-5. It is apparent that vertical integration of production and marketing has progressed further for broilers than for turkeys and eggs, but the trend is upward for all three commodities. In the case of owner integration, the producing and marketing firms are one and the same. This form of integration has been more important for eggs than for broilers and turkeys. In contract marketing, the producing and marketing

Table 25-5. Vertical Integration In The Poultry Industry, 1955–1970.

	PER CENT OF OUTPUT				
ITEM AND YEAR	OWNER-INTEGRATED ENTERPRISES	CONTRACT PRODUCTION	CONTRACT MARKETING	NON-INTEGRATED	TOTAL
Broilers:					
1955	2%	87	1	10	100%
1960	5	90	1	4	100
1965	5	90	2	3	100
1970	7	90	2	1	100
Turkeys:					
1955	4	21	11	64	100
1960	4	30	16	50	100
1965	8	35	13	46	100
1970	12	42	18	38	100
Market eggs:					
1955	2	1	12	85	100
1960	6	7	13	74	100
1965	13	18	13	56	100
1970	20	20	15	45	100

Source: *Market Structure of the Food Industries,* U.S. Department of Agriculture, Marketing Research Report No. 971, September 1972, p. 38.

firms retain their separate identities, but producers enter into contracts with distributors who specify outlets, timing of delivery, and quality of products. Cooperatives typically use marketing contracts to integrate poultry production and marketing. In 1972, cooperatives handled 16 per cent of market eggs, 18 per cent of turkeys, and 6 per cent of broilers.

Contract production, the dominant form of integration for broilers and turkeys, calls for the producer to grow the birds for the distributor—under closely supervised conditions and for a guaranteed return. For most poultry production contracts, the integrator supplies some inputs (chicks, feed, medication, field supervision) and the grower provides other inputs (housing, water, fuel, labor, and so on). The grower's return is not tied directly to the market price; it is a specified return (such as 5 to 7 cents per bird) plus incentive premiums for superior feed-conversion efficiency. Thus, growers bear less price risk under contract production arrangement than under nonintegrated or contract marketing arrangements. But in return for this, the grower loses considerable freedom of production and marketing decisions.

POULTRY AND EGG MARKETING CHANNELS

Decentralization and direct sales have proceeded hand in hand with the integration of the poultry market channels. As shown in Table 25-6, more than 75 per cent of poultry and eggs moved directly from packing plants to retail buyers in 1970, a significant increase from the 1960 levels.

Integration and decentralization have closed up or shortened the poultry and egg marketing channels. Products may move the entire length of the channel without changing hands or entering into open market trading arrangements. Most of the assembly and wholesale distribution marketing functions

Table 25-6. Direct Marketing In The Poultry and Egg Industries, 1953–1970.

	PER CENT OF SALES MOVING DIRECT FROM PACKING PLANT TO RETAIL OR INSTITUTIONS		
	SHELL EGGS	BROILERS	TURKEYS
1953	22%	40%	47%
1960	26	51	57
1965	55	58	62
1970	78	75	72

Source: *Market Structure of the Food Industries,* Marketing Research Report No. 971, U.S. Department of Agriculture, September 1972, p. 38.

have been assumed by the integrated poultry production and marketing firms. This has reduced the role and numbers of country buyers, independent merchants, wholesalers, brokers, and jobbers. Economies of size, increased density of geographic production, and continuing integration are further reducing the number of poultry marketing firms and increasing their sizes. There is widespread concern for the competitive effects of these trends on the poultry industry.

Egg Channels and Agencies

The shift in market flows of eggs is shown in Figure 25-2. Most eggs are sold in fresh form to retail stores or to institutional buyers. Smaller portions go to breakers (10 per cent); are used in hatcheries (6 per cent); are consumed on-farm (1 per cent); and are exported (less than 1 per cent).

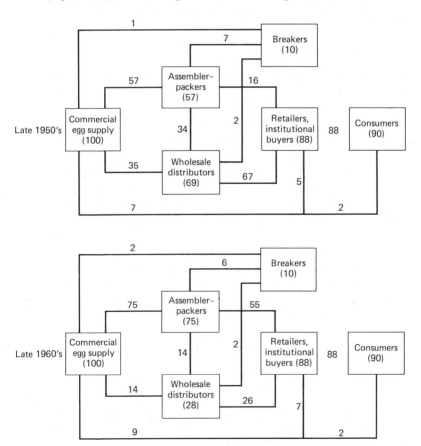

Figure 25-2. Movement of eggs through domestic marketing channels, 1960–1970. The numbers show percentages, excluding use for hatching, export, and consumption on the farm. (U.S. Department of Agriculture)

The increased role of the assembler-packer is evident in Figure 25-2. In the late 1950's, independent wholesaler-distributors made 67 per cent of the sales to retail buyers. By the late 1960's, integrated assembler-packer-distributors accounted for 55 per cent of sales to retail buyers. The integrated egg packing firm also shifted the location of the grading and cartoning operations from the central terminal markets, where they were performed by wholesalers, to country packing plants.

Precise estimates of the number of egg packing and processing plants are not available. However, there are significant economies of size in egg packing and distributing, and the number of plants is probably declining while plant size is growing. The U.S. Department of Agriculture estimated that the number of large egg packing plants—collectively accounting for about 40 per cent of all eggs marketed—declined from 689 in 1965 to 401 plants in 1971.[2] This department also estimated that one hundred egg breaking plants accounted for 80 per cent of processed egg products in 1970.[3]

Poultry Meat Channels and Agencies

Poultry processing firms also have become larger and more specialized, and the slaughter-packing operations have moved from consumption centers to production areas. The broiler marketing channel is illustrated in Figure 25-3. Much of this channel is integrated by the slaughter-packing-distributing firms. The U.S. Department of Agriculture estimates that the number of firms slaughtering broilers fell from 201 in 1964 to 154 in 1975.[4] The number of turkey processing plants is estimated to have fallen from 281 in 1962 to 163 in 1972.[5] The number of federally inspected plants purchasing poultry for further processing, however, increased from 444 in 1964 to 635 in 1970.[6]

Market concentration is not high in the poultry and egg industries. The largest four poultry dressing firms accounted for 17 per cent of total industry sales in 1972, and the largest four poultry and egg processing companies produced 23 per cent of that industry's sales.[7] The four-firm market concentration ratio for broiler packing was stable at 18 per cent from 1964 to 1975.[8] The market concentration ratio for turkey slaughtering plants is rising and stood at 30 per cent in 1968.[9]

---

[2] *Market Structure of the Food Industries,* U.S. Department of Agriculture, Marketing Research Report No. 971, September 1972, p. 39.

[3] Ibid.

[4] V. W. Benson and T. J. Witzig, *The Chicken Broiler Industry, Structure, Practices, and Costs,* U.S. Department of Agriculture, Agricultural Economic Report No. 381, August 1977, p. 13.

[5] W. W. Gallimore and R. J. Irvin, *The Turkey Industry: Structure, Practices, and Costs,* U.S. Department of Agriculture, Marketing Research Report No. 1000, June 1973, p. 15.

[6] *Market Structure of the Food Industries,* op. cit., p. 45.

[7] *U.S. Census of Manufacturing: 1972,* U.S. Bureau of the Census.

[8] *The Chicken Broiler Industry,* op. cit., p. 13.

[9] *The Turkey Industry,* op. cit., p. 17.

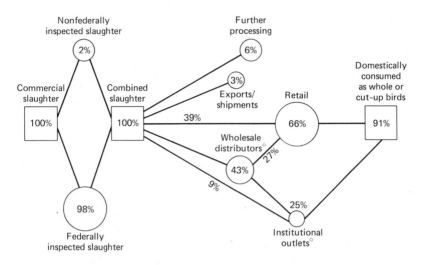

△ Includes company-owned distributors of processors and other firms.
○ Includes fast-food outlets, restaurants, schools, and other institutions.

Figure 25-3. Major marketing channels for ready-to-cook broilers, 1975. (U.S. Department of Agriculture)

INDUSTRY PROBLEMS

The poultry industry is experiencing many marketing problems, including quality control problems, market stability problems, and price discovery problems.

Quality Problems

Because of the perishable nature of the product, egg quality and grading have been a concern for the industry. Poor handling by producers and marketing agencies can result in loss of freshness and quality as eggs move through the marketing channels. Better handling techniques and refrigeration have improved egg quality. Mass merchandisers require consistent quality, and many egg production contracts contain quality control provisions. There is evidence of a trend toward production of a higher quality egg product today. Quality preservation and the control of microorganisms may take several forms for poultry meat. In 1975, 55 per cent of broilers were ice-packed, 28 per cent were chill-packed, and 14 per cent were packed in CO_2.[10] Controlling Salmonella organisms is a persistent problem in egg processing.

About 63 per cent of turkeys, 37 per cent of chickens, and 28 per cent

---

[10] *The Chicken Broiler Industry,* op. cit., p. 41.

of eggs are sold at retail on the basis of federal grades.[11] The difference between Grade A and Grade B poultry depends upon appearance, finish, and meatiness. The age of the bird also is a factor in tenderness. Although age is not a grading factor, this information is legally required on all poultry labels. Eggs are graded for quality and size, on the basis of albumen thickness (as measured by the height of the yolk and white) and shell condition. Egg grades include U.S. Grade AA or Extra Fancy, Grade A, and Grade B. Sizes are U.S. Jumbo, Extra Large, Large, Medium, Small, and Peewee. "Undergrades" are used in egg breaking operations. Mass scanning and sampling techniques have replaced the costly method of hand candling eggs to evaluate their interior quality. There is controversy over whether the egg quality standards reflect consumer preferences. Some studies have shown that consumers cannot discriminate between egg grades in blind tests or are unwilling to pay premium prices for the higher quality grades. There also is concern that grading terminology may be confusing to consumers; for example, a consumer might easily believe that Large, Grade A eggs are the top grade.

There has been an expansion of laws and regulations affecting quality control in the poultry industry. Federal inspection for wholesomeness and safety is mandatory for interstate poultry sales, and state inspection programs must be equal to the federal standards. The Egg Product Inspection Act of 1970 brought egg processing plants under federal inspection. Uniform federal-state grades for shell eggs were adopted in 1972.

Price Cycles and Profits

Like the cattle and hog enterprises, the poultry industries experience cyclical expansions and contractions in output. The resulting price cycles are much shorter than for cattle and hogs because of the shorter biological time period needed to alter the industry's productive capacity. Poultry and egg price cycles are caused by a relatively elastic supply curve and the tendency for producers to base future production plans on current prices. The poultry price cycles are illustrated in Figure 25-4. Contrary to expectations, production concentration, geographic specialization of the industry, and integration have not eliminated the boom-and-bust cycles of the poultry industry. The cycles persist, resulting in considerable risk and income instability for the industry. This instability and risk have encouraged growers to enter into production contracts.

Nor have specialization and integration successfully raised poultry and egg prices significantly above costs of production and marketing. On the contrary, the price-cost record of the poultry industry resembles that expected

---

[11] *Perspectives on Federal Retail Food Grading,* United States Congress, Office of Technology Assessment, June 1977, p. 31.

of a perfectly competitive industry. As shown in Table 25-7, during the 1960–1976 period farm prices hovered near break-even costs of production, and wholesale prices varied—positively and negatively—around processor costs. Occasional periods of profits stimulate production and are quickly followed by years of below-cost prices. This is not the profit situation that would be expected of a monopolistic industry.

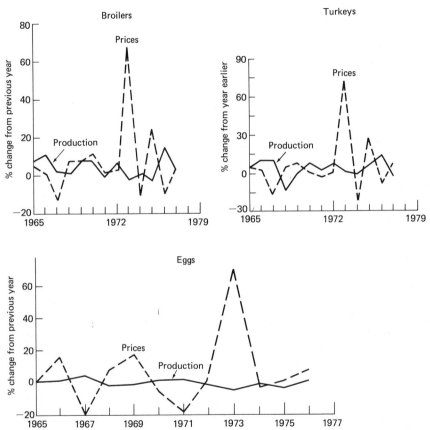

Figure 25-4. Poultry and egg cycles: changes in production and farm prices. (U.S. Department of Agriculture)

From time to time, the poultry industry has considered various ways to control supplies, eliminate the price cycles, and stabilize profits. Marketing orders and agreements, market quotas, mandatory and voluntary supply controls, bargaining associations, two-price systems, and price supports have all been considered and rejected by the industry.

Table 25-7. Costs, Prices, and Net Returns To Firms Producing and Marketing Broilers, 1960–1976.

YEAR	FARM LEVEL (¢/LB)			PROCESSOR-WHOLESALER (¢/LB)		
	PRODUCTION COSTS	FARM PRICE	NET FARM RETURN	ASSEMBLY, PROCESSING, HAULING COSTS	WHOLESALE PRICE	PROCESSOR NET RETURN
1960	15.7¢	16.9	1.2	28.4	29.9	1.5
1961	15.1	13.9	−1.2	27.4	26.1	−1.3
1962	14.8	15.2	0.4	26.8	28.0	1.2
1963	14.8	14.6	−0.2	26.6	27.2	0.6
1964	14.5	14.2	−0.3	26.0	25.4	−0.6
1965	14.5	15.0	0.5	26.3	26.4	0.1
1966	14.7	15.3	0.6	26.8	27.6	0.8
1967	14.1	13.3	−0.8	26.2	25.2	−1.0
1968	13.5	14.2	0.7	25.7	27.2	1.5
1969	13.8	15.2	1.4	26.5	29.1	2.6
1970	14.2	13.5	−0.7	27.1	26.4	−0.7
1971	14.3	13.8	−0.5	27.6	27.2	−0.4
1972	14.3	14.3	0	28.2	28.2	0
1973	22.1	24.2	2.1	39.8	42.4	2.6
1974	22.0	21.8	−0.2	40.1	38.0	−2.1
1975	21.3	26.2	4.9	39.5	45.2	5.7
1976	21.3	23.2	1.9	42.1	40.2	−1.9

Source: *Poultry and Egg Situation*, U.S. Department of Agriculture, Quarterly.

Pricing Problems

Integration and decentralization have complicated the price discovery process for poultry and eggs. Historically, the poultry industry has used a base price quotation procedure. Prices are discovered in the large centralized terminal markets such as New York, Los Angeles, Boston, and Chicago, where it is assumed that supply and demand are fully represented. These cash price quotations are reported to the trade by both private and public agencies. Prices at other points in the marketing channel are then determined by applying premiums and discounts to these base prices. Base price quotation systems are rapid, low-cost methods of price discovery.

Over time, with integration and decentralization, much of the poultry and egg supplies have bypassed these terminal markets. Daily cash trading of eggs at New York and Chicago was terminated in March 1970, removing two major base price quotation points. As a result, there is concern that base prices discovered at central markets no longer fully reflect demand and supply and therefore are not adequate guides to pricing elsewhere in the marketing channel. However, trade practices change slowly and many prices in the poultry and egg industry are still tied to central terminal market quotations.

Alternative price discovery mechanisms are being experimented with in the poultry industry. One alternative is to shift the base price quotation to another level of the market. For example, because most broilers are produced under contract and not traded in open markets, in 1965 the U.S. Department of Agriculture Market News Service discontinued quoting the price of live birds at farm level and began publishing a nine-city average price for RTC broilers delivered to consuming markets in truck-load lots. A National Egg Pricing System Study Committee was formed in the late 1960's to examine the "egg pricing problem" and to make recommendations to the industry. One proposal was to develop an electronic egg exchange. This computerized system would consider all offers and bids of buyers and sellers and attempt to arrive at a market-clearing price. Another proposal was that of "committee pricing"; set up a committee, composed of industry and government representatives, who would periodically analyze all market information and suggest a market-clearing price.

SUMMARY

The poultry and egg marketing channels and processes continue to be shaped by the forces of production concentration, integration, and decentralization. The industry is in the advanced stage of industrialization, as well as coordination of production and marketing. Integration extends from the input supply industries to wholesale distribution. Open market negotiating and pricing are rapidly disappearing. Nevertheless, this industry exhibits a relatively high degree of operational and pricing efficiency. The products are available in a wide variety of forms. The growth of broiler production illustrates the consumer-orientation of the industry. Operational efficiencies in production have been passed on to consumers in the form of increased supplies and falling retail prices. And competitive conditions keep farm and wholesale prices near costs of production and marketing. Major industry problems are production and price instability, quality control, and price discovery in integrated, decentralized markets.

QUESTIONS FOR DISCUSSION

1. What are the reasons for increased concentration of poultry production and marketing? Would you expect this concentration to continue?

2. Discuss the meaning of the word *industrialization* in agriculture and in the poultry industry. Why is this term used to describe the evolution of the poultry industry? What are the pros and cons of industrialized agriculture?

3. If chicken and turkey demand have been shifting rightward as a result of income and other factors, what must happen to the supply curve to result in falling retail prices? If egg demand has also been shifting rightward with income and population growth, how do you explain falling prices and per capita consumption?

4. After reading some current trade reports on the broiler industry, identify the major integrated producer-distributors. Which are conglomerate corporations, cooperatives, feed manufacturers, or meat packers? Do the same for eggs.

5. Why does the poultry industry need a base price quotation for price discovery? How would you recommend that prices be discovered in this industry?

6. Examine pricing efficiency in the poultry industry, including responsiveness to consumer demand, relationship of farm and retail prices and profits. How do you explain this performance record?

7. What recommendation would you make to the egg industry in order to halt the decline in consumption and improve prices?

8. What is the farmer's share for poultry and eggs? Does the share indicate profit levels in poultry production?

9. Why do you think integration in the poultry industry is more often the contract variety rather than the ownership variety?

SELECTED REFERENCES

BENSON, V. W. *The Chicken Broiler Industry: Structure, Practices, and Costs.* U.S. Department of Agriculture. Agricultural Economic Report No. 381, Aug. 1977.

BREIMYER, H. F. "Vertical Integration in Broilers," in his *Individual Freedom and the Economic Organization of Agriculture.* University of Illinois Press, Urbana, Ill., 1965, pp. 205–224.

CATHCART, W. E. "Changes in the Egg Industry and Projections For 1980." *Poultry and Egg Situation.* U.S. Department of Agriculture, June 1970.

Egg Marketing Report, A Team Study. U.S. Department of Agriculture, Sept. 1972.

FABER, F. L. *The Egg Products Industry: Structure, Practices, and Costs.* U.S. Department of Agriculture, Marketing Research Report No. 917, Feb. 1971.

GALLIMORE, W. W. *Contracting and Other Integrating Arrangements in the Turkey Industry.* U.S. Department of Agriculture, Marketing Research Report No. 734. Nov. 1965.

———— AND R. J. IRVIN. *The Turkey Industry: Structure, Practices, and Costs.* U.S. Department of Agriculture, Marketing Research Report No. 1000, June 1973.

———— AND J. G. VERTREES. *A Comparison of Returns to Poultry Growers Under Contract and Operating Independently.* U.S. Department of Agriculture, Marketing Research Report No. 814, Feb. 1968.

KNOTT, E. M. *Homemakers' Opinions About and Preferences for Broiler-Fryers, and Turkeys.* U.S. Department of Agriculture, Marketing Research Report No. 760, July 1966.

PEDERSON, J. R., AND F. L. FABER. *Major Marketing Channels for Shell Eggs in 18 Metropolitan Areas.* U.S. Department of Agriculture, ERS-219, 1965.

"Poultry and Eggs." *Market Structure of the Food Industries.* U.S. Department of Agriculture, Marketing Research Report No. 971, Sept. 1972, pp. 37–50.

Progress Reports of the National Egg Pricing System Study Committee. New Jersey Department of Agriculture, May 20, 1970; April 17, 1972.

ROGERS, G. B. "Changes in Marketing Costs and Price Spreads." *Poultry and Egg Situation* (Aug. 1977), 23–25.

———— "Costs and Returns for Poultry and Eggs, 1955–75." *Poultry and Egg Situation.* U.S. Department of Agriculture, June 1976.

———— "Marketing Channels for Eggs." *The Marketing and Transportation Situation.* U.S. Department of Agriculture, May 1973.

———— *Price Spreads, Costs, and Productivity in Poultry and Egg Marketing, 1955–74.* U.S. Department of Agriculture, Agricultural Economic Report No. 326, Feb. 1976.

———— *Vertical and Horizontal Integration in the Market Egg Industry, 1955–69.* U.S. Department of Agriculture, ERS-477, May 1971.

———— AND R. M. CONLOGUE. *Economic Characteristics of and Changes in the Market Egg Industry.* U.S. Department of Agriculture, Marketing Research Report No. 877, April 1970.

———— et. al. "Marketing and Integration in the Poultry and Egg Industries. *Poultry and Egg Situation* (June 1977), 39–43.

———— AND R. J. IRVIN. "Changes of Location and Flock Size in Poultry Production." *Poultry and Egg Situation* (Nov. 1972), 19–22.

———— AND R. J. IRVIN. *Interregional Movements of Eggs and Poultry, 1955–75.* U.S. Department of Agriculture, Statistical Bulletin No. 565, March 1977.

———— AND L. A. VOSS. *Pricing Systems for Eggs.* U.S. Department of Agriculture. Marketing Research Report No. 850, May 1969.

———— AND L. A. VOSS, Ed. *Readings on Egg Pricing.* College of Agriculture, University of Missouri, Columbia, Mo., Dec. 1971.

CHAPTER 26

Grain Marketing

"THE FLOW OF GRAIN through the marketing channels from the producer to the consumer has been continually changing over time. Increased grain supplies and changing demand for grain and grain products have been largely responsible for altering the marketing system."*

Preview

• This chapter examines the major dimensions of grain and soybean markets—decisions, marketing agencies, and marketing functions.

• Farm grain markets are characterized as being almost perfectly competitive and are interrelated with the livestock enterprise. These markets are contrasted with imperfectly competitive grain and oilseed manufacturing markets and grain mill and vegetable-oil processing markets.

• The major developments influencing these markets are decentralization, integration, growth of the mixed-feed industry, increased export demand, and growth of on-farm storage facilities.

• Special attention is given to the development of subterminal grain elevators in country areas and to the growth of direct farmer sales to processors and terminal elevators.

• Farmers' grain storage options and sales options are reviewed and analyzed.

• Key terms and concepts:

basis pricing	deferred pricing
blending	dockage
carryover	grain balance sheet
cash grain commission merchant	grain bank
country elevator	grain conditioning

---

* Carl J. Vosloh, Jr., *Agricultural Markets in Change,* U.S. Department of Agriculture, Agricultural Economic Report No. 95, July 1966.

grain merchandising
subterminal elevator
terminal elevator

test weight
to arrive, on track sales

The principal food grains of the United States are wheat, rice, and rye. The feedgrains—corn, oats, barley, and grain sorghums—are grown for livestock feed. The soybean is actually an oilseed, not a grain, but is included here because soybeans are marketed much like the grains. Although most of the nation's grain and soybeans are produced in the Central states, some food grains and feedgrains are produced in every state, and indeed, in every nation. This geographic dispersion produces a complex grain marketing channel.

The most important developments influencing grain marketing over the past fifty years have been (1) the sheer growth in volume of grain and oilseeds to be marketed; (2) changed harvesting and farm storage technology, which have influenced the flow-to-market of supplies; (3) the increase in off-farm sales of grain and growth of the commercial mixed-feed industry; (4) government price and income policies influencing grain production, storage, and returns; and (5) in the 1970's, the increased importance of grain export markets.

GRAIN PRODUCTION AND USES

The sources of supply and uses of wheat, corn, and soybeans are summarized (in balance-sheet format) in Table 26-1. These grain balance sheets are constructed so that the total supply exactly matches (or balances) total use during the marketing year (harvest to harvest).

As shown in Table 26-1, imports are not an important source of U.S. supplies of corn, wheat, or soybeans. The United States has a comparative advantage in producing these commodities, and is largely self-sufficient. For the 1974–1976 marketing years, stocks carried over from the previous years were a significant supplement to domestic production. Table 26-1 also shows that these commodity supplies were divided differently among their various uses: livestock feed, food, exports, and ending stocks.

Product Uses

Corn is grown in every state, but production is concentrated in the corn belt, stretching from Iowa to Ohio. About 1 per cent of U.S. corn acreage

Table 26-1. U.S. Commodity Balance Sheets, Wheat, Corn, and Soybeans, 1974–1976.

	PER CENT OF TOTAL BUSHELS: 1974–1976 AVERAGE		
	WHEAT	CORN	SOYBEANS
Supply sources:			
Carryover of previous years	19%	7%	13%
Domestic harvest	81	93	87
Imports	*	*	0
Total supply	100%	100%	100%
(billion bushels)	(2.5)	(6.0)	(1.5)
Uses:			
Livestock, feed	7%	57	}55
Food, industrial, seed	22	8	
Exports	42	25	33
Ending stocks	29	10	12
Total use	100%	100%	100%

* Less than 0.5 per cent.

Source: U.S. Department of Agriculture. Commodity balance sheets are published annually in *Agricultural Outlook,* U.S. Department of Agriculture.

is used for sweet corn and popcorn. But most corn is grown for livestock feed. In recent years, more than 55 per cent of the corn crop has been fed to domestic animals, and another 25 per cent has been exported. An additional 5 per cent of the corn crop is processed by wet millers into starches for further processing into corn syrup, confections, beer, sauces, and industrial products. The numerous wet-milled corn products are shown in Table 26-2. Another 3 per cent of the corn crop has been used by dry millers in the preparation of corn meal.

Corn, grain sorghum, oats, and barley are the major U.S. feedgrains. In the 1974–1976 marketing years, 87 per cent of these crops were fed to livestock. Frequently, these are fed on the farm where they are produced, or are sold directly to another farmer. In other cases, these feedgrains are purchased by mixed-feed manufacturers and then resold to farmers and livestock feeders.

The U.S. wheat crop principally is consumed as a domestic food grain, or is exported. Wheat may, however, be fed to livestock when supplies are abundant and prices are low.

Each special class of wheat has particular food uses. The hard, red spring and winter wheats, which are grown in the Great Plains area, are used largely in the bread industry. The soft, red winter and white wheats, which are grown in the eastern part of the North Central region and in the Pacific

Table 26-2. Wet-Milled Corn Products.

	FOODS	INDUSTRIAL	LIVESTOCK FEED	BREWING
Corn starch	baking powder confections desserts gravies sauces	(dextrins) adhesives ceramics inks metal castings paints textiles	corn-gluten meal	ale beer
Corn syrup	bakery products canned fruits confections food sauces frozen fruits frozen desserts ice cream jellies preserves table syrups	leather tanning paper pharmaceuticals textiles tobacco curing		
Corn sugar	baby foods bakery goods canned fruits condensed milk frozen fruits	chemicals pharmaceuticals	mixed rations	
Crude corn oil	bakery products condiments confections margarine salad dressings table oils	leather tanning paints soaps synthetic rubber textile sizings varnishes	corn-oil meal	
Steepwater concentrates		pharmaceuticals		

Source: *Grains: Production, Processing, Marketing.* ©1973, 1977. Board of Trade of the City of Chicago, p. 120. Reprinted by permission.

Northwest, are used in pastries, crackers, biscuits, and cakes. Durum wheat, grown chiefly in North Dakota, is the wheat used by spaghetti manufacturers.

Soybeans are grown in the Midwest, and America accounts for about 80 per cent of world production. More than one third of the U.S. soybean crop is exported, and soybeans are the nation's leading farm product dollar-earner abroad. Soybeans are probably the most versatile agricultural commodity. They are crushed for their oil and meal, and the myriad resulting products are shown in Figure 26-1.

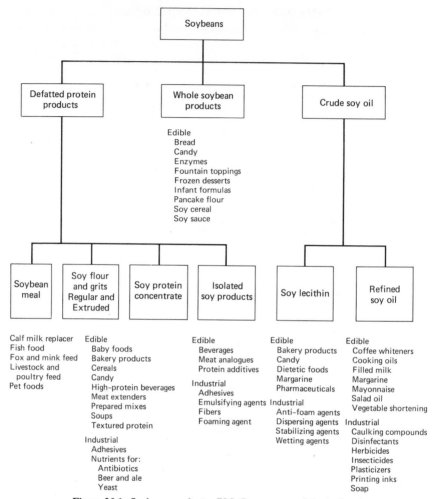

Figure 26-1. Soybean products. (U.S. Department of Agriculture)

Product and Production Characteristics

The grains and oilseeds serve as raw materials for conversion into higher-valued products. This conversion adds form utility and can take place on the farm, as in livestock feeding, in the food processing sector, as in the case of flour or wet-corn milling, or in the household, where flour, shortening, and sugars are combined in order to bake a cake. This dependence upon further-processing results in a relatively low farmer's share for these commodities and a loss of their farm identity in the marketing process.

Farm level grain markets probably come closer to perfect competition than any other food or farm market. There are a large number of relatively small producers; the product is reasonably homogeneous; movement into and out of production is fluid; and market information is quite good. As a consequence, grain farmers encounter all the problems of perfect competitors: price-taking status, no supply control, prices above or below costs of production in the short run, and no effective market power.

The effects of weather, disease, and other uncontrollable factors in grain production also complicate farmer efforts to control supply and influence prices. The acreage planted to the various grains does not vary markedly from year to year, but production does. This is largely because of the weather and its effect on yields. Production is also highly seasonal. Most of the corn is harvested during October through November. The entire crops of wheat, oats, and rye are harvested during the relatively short period of June through September. The soybean crop is harvested during the early fall months.

In contrast to the seasonal nature of production, there is a fairly constant demand throughout the year for animal and human food. Somewhere in the marketing channel, then, must be the facilities for huge amounts of seasonal storage.

The unpredictable nature of production also means that some stocks must be carried over from one year to another. This is necessary if there is to be any stability of supplies of food and feed from year to year. If the harvest is a bumper one, the season-end carryover will be large. If the harvest is small, the carryover will be much reduced. Such carryovers are the safety factors that protect dependent industries from violent, feast-and-famine fluctuations.

The various grains and oilseeds have markedly different demand trends. The demand for feedgrains and soybeans has expanded rapidly with the growth in meat consumption, both domestically and worldwide. Food grain products, on the other hand, generally have a low income elasticity and have experienced less rapid growth in demand. Soybean demand also has benefited from the consumer trend of substituting vegetable oils for animal oils.

THE MARKETING CHANNELS

The geographic dispersion of production, the large number of producers, the interrelationship with the livestock economy, and the high degree of processing involved all contribute to a long and complex grain marketing channel. The corn marketing channel is shown in Figure 26-2. The chief agencies in this channel are farmers—as buyers and sellers—elevators, commission merchants, brokers, processors and millers, exporters, and the grain exchanges.

539

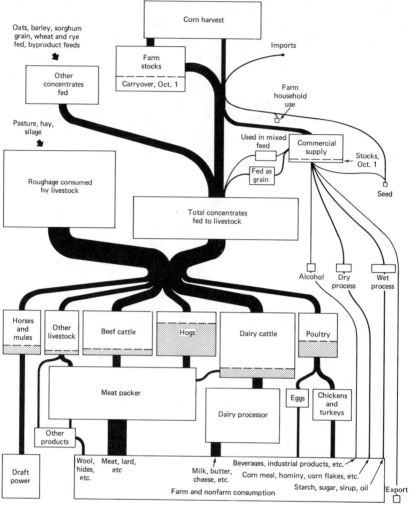

Figure 26-2. Movement of corn from production to consumption. (U.S. Department of Agriculture)

Farmers and Country Elevators

Farmers have three general marketing alternatives for their grain: (1) feed to on-farm livestock or sell to other farmers for feed; (2) sell the grain to the commercial market system at harvest; or (3) store the grain—on-farm or off-farm—for later sale. There are many variations of these alternatives.

As shown in Table 26-3, farmers feed about one-quarter of the major feedgrains on the farm where they are produced. Over the 1963–1975 period, there was a substantial decline in the share of corn used on the farm of

Table 26-3. Percentage of Grain Used on Farms and Sold From Farms, 1963–1975.

GRAIN	USED ON-FARM		SOLD FROM FARMS		TOTAL	
	1963	1975	1963	1975	1963	1975
Oats	32%	38%	68%	62%	100%	100%
Barley	28	27	72	73	100	100
Corn	53	26	47	64	100	100
Rye	18	25	82	75	100	100
Sorghum	23	23	77	77	100	100
Wheat	5	5	95	95	100	100

Source: U.S. Department of Agriculture, *Agricultural Statistics.*

origin. This reflects continuing trends toward farmer purchase of complete feeds from feed manufacturers and specialization of the livestock and cash grain operations.

Farmers also have several alternatives for off-farm grain sales. Besides selling to other farmers, they may sell to elevators, dealers, processors, and even itinerant truckers. However, farmers sell most of their grain to the local country elevator. These elevators (so named because the grain must be conveyed, or elevated, to the top of bins for storage and gravity flow) are scattered throughout grain producing areas, usually along railroads. North Central farmer 1971 grain sales to country elevators and other agencies are shown in Table 26-4.

Table 26-4. Farmer Grain Sales Through Various Outlets, North Central States, 1971.

PURCHASING OUTLETS	PER CENT OF TOTAL SALES		
	CORN	SOYBEANS	WHEAT
Country elevators	70%	79%	80%
Terminal and subterminal elevators	10	12	11
Grain processors	4	5	2
Other farmers	3	0.5	1
Truckers	3	0.5	1
Others	10	3	5
Total	100%	100%	100%

Source: L. D. Hill, "Vertical Coordination Between Farmers and Grain Elevators," in *Coordination and Exchange in Agricultural Subsectors,* North Central Regional Research Publication, No. 228, January 1976, p. 44. Reprinted by permission.

Country elevators fall into three general classes according to their ownership and organization. The independent elevators are under the operational control of their individual owners. Cooperative or farmer-owned elevators are owned and operated cooperatively by the farmers of the area. They may either be organized singly or in state-wide groups. The third type is the line elevator. This is a group of elevators owned and operated from a central headquarters as a chain. Such chains may be owned either by grain companies or millers and processors who use them to secure supplies directly for their manufacturing operations. The ownership of elevators will vary from area to area. In some areas, cooperative elevators predominate. In other areas the line elevator is predominant.

Many studies have been made of the costs of elevator operations. Nearly all have found that operating costs per bushel handled tend to decline with increasing volume. Increased volume for an elevator can be obtained in two principal ways. One is to add other business lines to that of grain handling. The other is to consolidate elevators in order to obtain a larger trade area. The great majority of elevators have taken on various sideline enterprises to boost their volume and offset the highly seasonal nature of their grain operations. The income from these other enterprises may equal or surpass that received from the handling of grain alone. The most common sideline is the feed business. In addition, coal, seeds, implements, building materials, petroleum, and farm supplies are common sales departments. In some communities the elevator is not only the outlet for grain but also the principal source of general farm supplies.

In a great many areas, the elevator is the "general store" for farm supplies. This combination nature of elevators is one of the complicating factors of this phase of grain marketing. Some elevators may pay high prices for grain, but make up the difference by selling their feed, fertilizer, and other supplies at higher prices. Others may choose to pay low prices for grain but sell their other goods to farm customers cheaper—their method of competing for the farmer's business. These practices may reduce the pricing efficiency of the grain marketing system.

Increased volume can be obtained by the consolidation of existing elevators. Much of the present locational pattern was established back in the era of horse-drawn transportation, poor roads, and poor communication, and the supply area of many elevators is small. As is the case in other considerations, the number of firms that will provide an adequate volume for low-cost operation must be balanced against the industry structure that will assure effective competition. The modern farmer, however, with his telephone, daily newspaper, and radio, has a communication network that covers a larger area than was available to his grandfather. With his truck he can sell his grain over a wider area. Some reasonable consolidation seems possible without sacrificing an effectively competitive situation. Here again, the multipurpose nature of the elevator as both buyer of the farmer's grain and seller of the farmer's feed and supplies complicates the issue. Although consolidation and reduction in the number of elevators might be advantageous from the viewpoint of efficient grain marketing, fewer elevators located further from the farm might increase the farmer's costs of acquiring his supplies.

Most country elevator operators sell their grain to firms located at a terminal market and ship it to the designated terminal elevators. Grain may be consigned to commission merchants on the market for sale or it may be sold on *to-arrive* or *on-track* bids. If the grain is consigned to commission merchants, the elevator ships the grain to the terminal and takes the price secured by the commission merchant, much the same as with the use of livestock commission men in the livestock yards. In selling on a "to-arrive" basis, the price and the shipment details are agreed upon in advance of delivery. When sold "on-track, country point," the price is agreed upon for grain in cars at the local elevator. The buyer of the grain takes title to the grain at the country elevator and arranges and pays for the cost of transportation.

Terminal Elevators

Terminal elevators are located in the major grain marketing centers such as Chicago, Minneapolis, Fort Worth, Kansas City, and St. Louis and at the major ports, such as New Orleans, the Texas Gulf ports, and Baltimore. Like country elevators, terminal elevators may be operated independently, by farmer cooperatives or by integrated grain marketing companies. The principal distinctions between country elevators and terminal elevators are their location, their size, and their sources of grain. Terminal elevators are located at major grain trading centers, not in the country; they are usually much larger than country elevators (up to 30 million bushel storage capacity); and terminal elevators receive some grain directly from farmers, but most of their grain is purchased from the country elevators.

Terminal elevators also do much more grain storage than country elevators. Terminal operators often hold grain for considerable periods of time. These operators are small-margin, large-volume handlers, and price fluctuations might easily turn profits into losses. Therefore, hedging insurance often is very desirable to them.

Cash Grain Commission Merchants

The representative of the country elevator operator in the terminal market is the cash grain commission merchant. For a fixed charge the cash grain merchant will accept the responsibility of selling the grain. The principal job of the commission merchant is to seek out interested buyers. Because these merchants on most markets must all charge the same commission, they compete for grain consignments on the basis of service they can render to the elevator operator. They specialize in the analysis of market information for their clients. They also take charge of any arrangements that must be made with the buyer of the grain.

The commission merchant also handles the grain sold "on-track" or "to-arrive." In handling the "on-track" and "to-arrive" sales, the merchants make a practice of sending out bids to the elevator operators at the close of the market day. In many cases, this is in the form of postal card bids; in others, private wire and telephone are used to contact the local elevator.

In soybean marketing the interior carlot dealer is also an important intermediary between the country elevator and the soybean processor. Unlike the commission merchant, the carlot dealer takes title to the soybeans. However, he does not take physical possession of the soybeans, but directs and helps finance their movement to the processor.

Processors and Millers

There are two stages to processing feedgrains. Flour, rice, corn, and oilseed millers first refine or mill basic farm commodities. Their output is then further processed into consumer products by breakfast cereal manufacturers, bakers, distillers, cooking-oil manufacturers, and others.

The buyers of grain differ widely in their wants and desires. Flour millers desire wheat of a specific gluten or protein content, depending upon whether they are producing bread or cake flours. The grains desired for breakfast foods may differ. Corn processors and maltsters look for special characteristics.

Some processors maintain their own buyers on large terminal markets and purchase their supplies from the cash grain commission merchants. Others may retain the services of brokers who buy grain wherever it can be obtained. Still others have built up their own large country buying operations and operate line elevators in the grain belt. In this latter situation they not only protect their supply position but also control the handling and moving of grain throughout the marketing channel. In some instances processors who need a special type of grain for their operations have, through their research departments, developed their own strains and handling practices. Then they contract directly with farmers to grow this grain under their supervision for their own exclusive use. Here, then, is still another example of integration developing between the farmer and the marketing system.

Changing Grain Marketing Patterns

A form of decentralization has been altering grain marketing patterns. Many grain processors and soybean oil mills have located their plants in rural areas, and larger country elevators—called *subterminals*—have assumed many of the terminal marketing functions. As a result, farmers are increasingly selling directly to processors or to subterminal elevators, who in turn sell directly for export or to processors. These sales bypass the traditional terminal elevators and the cash grain commission merchants. The prepared feed industry must also be considered decentralized because most feed manufacturing is done at country points, often at the country elevator.

Overall, grain market decentralization has probably been encouraged by farmers. It has provided increased local marketing alternatives to the country elevator. Moreover, although pricing efficiency remains imperfect in grain markets, it is not likely that decentralization has adversely affected pricing efficiency in country markets. On the other hand, there is evidence of increased operational efficiencies from consolidation of country elevators, subterminal elevator operations, and direct sales by farmers to processors.

Other changes in grain marketing relate to the growth of on-farm storage, the substitution of truck for rail transport, the growth of port facilities to meet export demand, and increasing use of grain and soybean futures contracts for managing market risks.

COUNTRY GRAIN BUYING AND MERCHANDISING

Country and subterminal elevators purchase grain from farmers in several ways. Outright purchase at harvest or from the farmer's storage is the most common type of transaction. Elevators also contract for price in advance of delivery, accept grain from the farmer with the price to be set at a later date *(deferred pricing),* and arrange sales for the farmer without actually taking possession of the grain. In 1974 it was estimated that about 40 per cent of farmers' grain transactions involved same-day pricing and delivery, 50 per cent of the transactions involved forward or advance-price contracts, and 10 per cent of the sales involved pricing after delivery was made.[1]

Many elevator operators use *basis pricing* in quoting grain prices to farmers. A basis price is an offer price stated in terms of a "nearby" futures price. For example, an elevator may quote a November 10 cash price to the farmer of "20 cents under," meaning that the cash price is 20 cents less than the Chicago December futures price. This basis of 20 cents would be set in such a way as to cover elevator handling, transportation costs, and desired profit. Basis pricing is sometimes preferred by farmers and elevators owners because the basis will change less frequently than cash prices.

Elevator operators must buy their grain from producers in such a manner that when they sell it they have an adequate margin to cover their costs and result in some net return. Margins taken by elevators vary widely. The price realized by a farmer for his grain is a combination of the quoted price of the elevator plus the grade of grain delivered. Elevators sell grain on the

---

[1] R. G. Heifner, et al., *The U.S. Cash Grain Trade in 1974: Participants, Transactions and Information Sources,* U.S. Department of Agriculture, Agricultural Economic Report No. 386, September 1977, p. 29.

basis of official federal grades but buy very little on that basis from farmers. Instead, each elevator operator devises his own system of dockage—usually based on weight and moisture. Some elevator owners have been known to follow a system of high-quoted prices plus a heavy dockage program. Others have used under-docking and over-grading instead of price as a competitive weapon. This is very similar to the difference in sorting methods used by livestock buyers.

Farmers must evaluate both quoted prices and buying practices before selling their grain. Once an outlet is chosen, the farmer cannot be sure it will remain the most advantageous. Prices quoted to farmers in a particular county may vary substantially, and no single elevator owner will consistently pay the high or low price.

Grain merchandising is the term used to describe the marketing activities of elevator operators and other grain handlers. Grain merchandising decisions include when to sell, where to sell, how to sell, quality improvements, and pricing the grain. In addition to their buying and selling margin, elevator owners and other grain merchandisers frequently can profit from storage, conditioning, and blending of grain. Storage profits are earned by correctly anticipating seasonal price rises or unusual market developments. *Grain conditioning* refers to the improvement of the quality and value of grain through cleaning, separating, or drying. *Blending* refers to mixing different lots of grain in a way that raises the grade and value of the total lot.

GRAIN GRADING

The 1916 U.S. Grain Standards Act established grain quality grades and requires that these grades be used for grain moving in interstate commerce. Most grain sold off-farm is federally graded. Prior to 1977, grain graders were independent operators licensed by the U.S. Department of Agriculture and paid by the users of grading services. A 1976 Amendment to the Grain Standards Act, however, established a new Federal Grain Inspection Service, and graders are now U.S. government employees.

Whenever grain arrives in a large terminal market, a sample is drawn and graded. Grain grades range from the highest grade, Number 1, down through Number 5 and sample grade. There is also a division into classes and subclasses for each kind of grain. For example, Class I of wheat consists of hard, red spring wheat. This is further divided into the subclasses of Dark Northern Spring, Northern Spring, and Red Spring. Within each class the requirements for the various grades are set up.

Though the factors considered in grades differ somewhat from one grain to another, in general the following factors are used to determine the grade of a given class of grain: (1) test weight—a volume measure of kernel plumpness; (2) moisture content; (3) foreign material or dockage, such as dirt, broken kernels, or weed seeds; and (4) damaged kernels resulting from fermentating, frost, fungus, mold, insects, or other conditions.

Each grade has minimum or maximum limits for these quality standards. Failure to meet any one of the requirements will reduce the grade. The variation possible within a given grade explains why different carloads of the same grade of grain sell at slightly different prices at the same location and time. Different processors have different requirements. One processor who was particular not about damage but about moisture content might pay more for a particular carload than for another. Moreover, some processors may watch for certain factors, such as protein content in wheat, that have not yet been incorporated into official grading standards.

Because the grade of grain is determined by a combination of different factors, each of which can vary within limits, handlers can mix or blend grain in order to raise the grade. For example, suppose two loads of grain were received. One was graded Number 2 because of its moisture content, but it met all other requirements of Number 1 grain. The other load was graded Number 3 because of excessive cracked kernels and foreign material but in all other aspects it met the requirements for Number 2 grain. Through the proper mixing or blendings of these two loads of Number 2 and Number 3 grain, it might be possible to secure two loads (or nearly so) of grain that would grade Number 2. This would be possible because one load was low in the grade factors in which the other load was high. Country elevators sometimes blend grain, and terminal elevators usually do.

The development of satisfactory grain grading standards presents a continual problem. For example, the oil content of soybeans, which is a major determinant of their value, is not currently included in official standards. Research has shown that the oil content of soybeans may vary considerably, and when graded by present standards, price errors in relation to actual value may occur.

Despite their limitations, grain grades make substantial contributions to the marketing process. They increase the homogeneity of grain lots, facilitate efficient buyer and seller transactions, and differentiate between higher- and lower-valued products.

GRAIN STORAGE

One of the principal marketing decisions of the grain producer is whether to sell at harvest time or to store for sale at a later date. If it is decided to store the grain, the next question is where it should be stored.

In answering the question of whether to store, the farmer must balance the costs of storing the grain against the possible gains from a rise in price later in the season. Two factors besides the normal seasonal price rise must be considered. One of these is the possibility of taking advantage of the government price-support programs. The nonrecourse loan removes much of the uncertainty about the relationship of the current price to a possible future price. If the market price of grain at harvest time is enough below the available loan rate to offset storage costs, there is very little to lose and much to gain by storing under government loan. The other consideration is the outlook for the general movement of prices during the storage period. If the general price level is expected to move downward, sales at harvest may be much more attractive to the producer than if the general level is expected to move upward.

Another important question for the farmer is *where* to store the grain. On-farm storage capacity has expanded rapidly in recent years. It was estimated that there was about as much on-farm grain storage capacity in 1977— 6.2 billion bushels—as there was off-farm storage capacity of elevators and processors.[2] During 1972–1975, stocks held on- and off-farm following harvest time (shown in Table 26-5) also confirm this 50:50 distribution of storage capacity.

Table 26-5. Grain and Soybean Stock Positions, 1972–1975.

| | | PER CENT OF STOCKS HELD, 1972–1975 AVERAGE | | |
COMMODITY	DATE	ON-FARM	OFF-FARM	TOTAL
Wheat	October 1	41%	59%	100%
Corn	January 1	74%	26%	100%
Soybeans	January 1	49%	51%	100%

Source: *Agricultural Statistics,* U.S. Department of Agriculture, annual.

The growth of on-farm grain storage is a form of vertical integration for farmers. It provides them with marketing flexibility, gives them additional opportunities for earning conditioning and storage profits, and, overall, increases the farmer's role in the grain marketing process. The 1977 farm bill further stimulated the construction of on-farm grain storage facilities through lower interest rate loans and provisions for a farmer-held grain reserve.

It is not possible to make a blanket prescription about whether farmers should store their grain, or whether it should be stored on-farm or off-farm. These decisions depend upon numerous factors, including the availability of on- and off-farm storage facilities, price expectations, feeding opportunities, and attitudes toward price risk. These will vary for each farmer. Farmers

---

[2] "Storage and Transportation," *Agricultural Outlook,* U.S. Department of Agriculture, August 1977, p. 13.

can use storage hedges to shift the price risks of storage to others if they choose to store. Moreover, storage hedges can help farmers earn carrying charges and thus permit the use of on-farm facilities year after year regardless of price expectations.

For on-farm storage, producers face a number of costs. There are certain fixed costs that must be met whether grain is stored or not. These include the depreciation, maintenance, insurance, taxes, and interest on the capital invested in the available storage facilities and equipment. Then there are several variable costs that will occur only if grain is stored. These will include the costs of shrinkage and loss from damage, insurance and taxes on the grain, any expense of treating or conditioning the grain, and the cost of the labor and transportation expenses resulting from the storage operation. Against these costs of farm storage must be weighed the cost of hiring an elevator to store the grain.

Farmers without storage facilities can rent or hire storage space from elevators. One form of this is the *grain bank.* Farmers deposit grain to be dried and stored until they need it for animal feed. As the grain is needed the farmer "withdraws" grain as he would money from his checking account. His withdrawal is of the same quality he deposited, although it need not be specifically the same grain. The farmer then pays for the storage and handling services. The grain bank is often tied to the elevator's feed mixing and milling services.

Elevator storage availability and charges vary widely. There is some evidence of operational efficiencies for subterminal storage. It was estimated that the average cost of handling and storing a bushel of grain for one year in 1972–1973 was 19.2 cents for subterminals, 21.5 cents for country elevators, and 27.8 cents for port terminals.[3] However, these average costs differed considerably by regions and companies, so care must be exercised in generalizing about the "best" place to store grain.

STRUCTURE AND COMPETITION IN THE GRAIN AND OILSEED PRODUCT INDUSTRIES

The major grain and oilseed products are bread, bakery products, breakfast cereals, vegetable oils, and mixed animal feeds. Market structure and competitive behavior differ substantially in these industries. Firms producing and selling these products tend toward oligopoly and monopolistic competition. With the exception of the livestock feed industries—but including the pet food industry—marketing costs are relatively high, and the farmer's share is lower than in most other food industries.

Timeliness is the key to marketing costs in the bread and soft bakery

[3] A. G. Schienbein, *Cost of Storing and Handling Grain in Commercial Elevators, 1970–71, and Projections For 1972–73,* U.S. Department of Agriculture, ERS-501, March 1972, p. 3.

goods industries. These products are extremely perishable, and consumers place a high value on freshness. Although older products can be picked up and sold at low-priced outlets, there is a high "stale loss" in these businesses. In order to insure freshness, bakers have traditionally operated relatively expensive store-door routes, with delivery direct to grocery stores. More recently, however, corporate and affiliated chainstores have achieved some operational efficiencies by substituting direct warehouse purchases and shipments for the driver-salesman method of procurement. Frozen bakery products also offer some potential for reducing baked goods' marketing costs. In contrast, the significant increase in the number of bread varieties—some bakers sell over forty kinds of breads—has probably sacrificed some economics of standardization and size in bread baking.

The bakery, cracker, and breakfast cereal industries are good examples of industries that practice a high degree of product differentiation along with large consumer advertising programs. A Saturday morning spent watching television will demonstrate the large advertising efforts that go into the merchandising of the newest "most delicious and crunchy" cereal. Advertising expenses tend to be higher for cereal manufacturers than for other grain processors. Nonprice competition is widely used in the merchandising of these products.

Table 26-6. Number of Companies and Market Concentration of the Grain and Oilseed Processing Industries, 1963–1972.

INDUSTRY	NUMBER OF COMPANIES		PER CENT OF SALES BY FOUR LARGEST FIRMS	
	1963	1972	1963	1972
Breakfast cereals	35	34	86	90
Blended, prepared flour	140	115	70	68
Wet-corn milling	49	26	71	63
Cookies, crackers	286	257	59	59
Soybean oil mills	68	54	50	54
Malt beverages	171	108	34	52
Pet foods	NA	147	NA	51
Distilled liquors	70	76	58	47
Shortening, cooking oil	65	64	42	44
Rice milling	62	48	44	43
Cottonseed oil mills	115	74	41	43
Macaroni, spaghetti	207	179	31	38
Flour, meal	510	340	35	33
Bread, cakes	4339	2800	23	29
Prepared animal feeds	—	1579	—	23

Source: U.S. Census of Manufacturers, U.S. Bureau of the Census.

As in other food industries, there has been a decline in the number and an increase in the average size of firms, as shown in Table 26-6. Mergers, business failures, and growth to attain economies of size have all been factors in these trends. Both relatively high and low levels of market concentration can be found for these products. The most concentrated food industry is found in breakfast cereals (90 per cent of sales by the four largest firms in 1972). However, there are also relatively low levels of concentration—animal feeds, breads, cakes, flour, and meal. And over the 1963–1972 period, there were industries marked by both increasing and decreasing concentration.

Vertical integration has been prevalent in the grain and oilseed industries. Chainstores have integrated into baking and bakery product wholesaling. Most oilseed refining facilities are owned by manufacturers of shortening, salad and cooking oils, and margerine. Processors increasingly are using farm contracts to insure quantity and the desired quality of grains. There are frequent combinations of soybean processing and livestock feed manufacturing. Feed manufacturers and dealers have also integrated into livestock production as a way to increase markets for their products.

SUMMARY

The grain marketing channel is a complex one, involving long distances, interrelated livestock marketing decisions, and numerous farmer choices. Feedgrains, food grains, and oilseeds undergo more form transformation in the marketing process than most other agricultural commodities. The major markets are livestock feeding, consumer food products, and exports. The nearly perfect competitive nature of farm grain markets contrasts with the imperfectly competitive milling and processing industries. Several developments have changed grain marketing patterns, including decentralization and the growth of subterminal elevators, expansion of the commercial mixed feed industries, and increased on-farm storage facilities. By and large, these developments have expanded markets for these products and increased farmers' marketing alternatives.

QUESTIONS FOR DISCUSSION

1. Discuss farmer's alternative grain storage facilities and sales outlets. What factors influence farmers' decisions?

2. Examine and explain the trend in grain farmers' use of the futures market.

3. How might grain and oilseed farmers escape from their nearly perfectly competitive markets?

4. What were the issues and results of the great wheat referendum of May 1963? What was the meaning of this vote for wheat supply controls?

551

5. The breakfast cereal sector is one of the most criticized segments of the food industry. Examine these criticisms of the market performance of this sector.

6. What are the major demand trends for the products discussed in this chapter?

7. How is the decision to build on-farm storage facilities different from the decision to use that facility?

SELECTED REFERENCES

EILAND, J. C. AND T. F. MORIAK. *Market Patterns for U.S. Rice, 1971–72.* U.S. Department of Agriculture. ERS-528, Aug. 1973.

Grains: Processing, Production, Marketing. Board of Trade of the City of Chicago, 1973.

"Grains Used for Food," "Fats and Oils," in *Market Structure of the Food Industries.* U.S. Department of Agriculture, Marketing Research Report No. 971, Sept. 1972, pp. 51–59; 76–83.

HEID, W. G. *Changing Grain Channels,* ERS-39, U.S. Department of Agriculture, 1961.

—— *Changes in the Market Structure of the Breakfast Food Industry.* U.S. Department of Agriculture. Marketing Research Report No. 623, 1963.

HEID, W. G., JR., AND M. N. LEATH. *U.S. Barley Industry.* U.S. Department of Agriculture. Agricultural Economic Report No. 395, Feb. 1978.

HEIFNER, R. G. *Hedging Potential in Grain Storage and Livestock Feeding.* U.S. Department of Agriculture, Agricultural Economics Report No. 238, Jan. 1973.

—— et al. *The U.S. Cash Grain Trade in 1974: Participants, Transactions, and Information Sources.* U.S. Department of Agriculture, Agricultural Economic Report No. 386, Sept. 1977.

HILL, L. D. *Farmers' Grain Marketing Patterns in the North Central Region.* North Central Regional Research Publication No. 231, University of Illinois, Agricultural Experiment Station, circa 1976.

KROMER, G. W. "Growth in U.S. Soybean Processing Capacity." *Fats and Oils Situation.* U.S. Department of Agriculture, Nov. 1965, pp. 43–49.

—— "Trends in U.S. Corn Oil Production and Use." *Fats and Oils Situation.* U.S. Department of Agriculture, Nov. 1966, pp. 21–28.

Marketing Grain, Proceedings of the NCM-30 Grain Marketing Symposium. North Central Regional Research Publication No. 176, Purdue University, Jan. 1968.

"Marketing Oilseeds and Oilseed Products," and "Grain Marketing."*Agricultural Markets in Change.* U.S. Deparment of Agriculture, Agricultural Economic Report No. 95, July 1966.

MOORE, J. R., AND R. G. WALSH, Eds. "The Baking Industry," "The Soybean Processing Industry," "The Grain Procurement Industry," and "The Mixed Feed Industry." *Market Structure of the Agricultural Industries.* Iowa State University Press, Ames, Iowa, 1966.

Organization and Competition in the Milling and Baking Industries. National Commission on Food Marketing, Technical Study No. 5, Washington, D.C., July 1966.

"U.S. Soybean Economy in the 1980's. *Fats and Oils Situation.* U.S. Department of Agriculture, April 1973.

VOSLOH, C. J., JR. *Costs and Economies of Scale in Feed Manufacturing.* U.S. Department of Agriculture, Marketing Research Report No. 815, March 1968.

—— *Structure of the Feed Manufacturing Industry, 1975.* U.S. Department of Agriculture, Statistical Bulletin No. 596, Feb. 1978.

CHAPTER 27

Cotton and Textile Marketing

"THE DOMESTIC COTTON INDUSTRY is undergoing rapid and significant changes that are placing a severe strain on an old and tradition-bound marketing system."*

Preview

• This chapter examines cotton production and consumption patterns and market organization of the cotton-textile-apparel industry.

• The effects of the changing geographic location of cotton production and cotton consumption trends on the cotton industry are investigated.

• Decentralization and integration of the cotton distribution channel are reviewed.

• The changing government price support program for cotton is traced over the 1948–1975 period.

• The U.S. cotton import-export balance is examined.

• Some selected cotton marketing problems are discussed.

• Key terms and concepts:

cotton gin   equalization payment
cotton lint or fiber

---

* *Cotton,* National Cotton Marketing Study Committee Report, U.S. Department of Agriculture, August 1975.

553

From colonial days to the nineteenth-century era of "King Cotton," cotton has been a key U.S. agricultural commodity. Its relative importance has declined over time as America's agricultural commodity base has become more diversified; but cotton still accounted for 3 per cent of United States cash farm receipts in the 1974–1976 period. It remains one of the world's major raw materials, and the United States is the world's largest consumer, as well as the leading exporter, of cotton.

The cotton industry is experiencing several changes in market organization and marketing trends, including erosion of markets by man-made fibers and worldwide competition, changes in the geographic location of cotton production, decentralization and integration, and a more market-oriented government policy.

COTTON PRODUCTION

From the end of the Civil War to 1926, U.S. cotton plantings grew from 8 million acres to 45 million acres. Cotton yields were stable at 175–200 pounds per acre over this period, and total cotton production was at an all-time high of 17 million 480-pound bales in 1926. By the 1948–1953 period, cotton plantings had declined to 24 million acres and total production had fallen to 14 million bales. From this level, cotton plantings declined to 11 million acres in 1973–1975. However, as shown in Figure 27-1, total cotton production fluctuated without trend over this latter period between 8 and 16 million bales as yields reached 1 bale per acre in the 1971–1976 period.

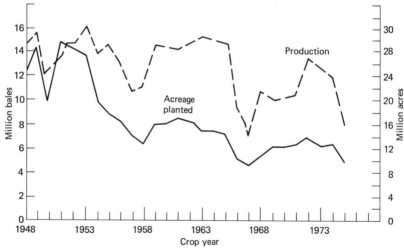

Figure 27-1. U.S. acreage and production of cotton, 1948–1975. (U.S. Department of Agriculture)

The cotton belt stretches across the southern, southwestern and far western tier of states. In recent years cotton production has moved westward. The southeastern states produced 16 per cent of all U.S. cotton in 1964, but only 10 per cent in 1975. In 1976 Texas and California were the two leading cotton producing states, accounting for 45 per cent of total U.S. production. Other major cotton states are Mississippi, Arizona, Arkansas, Louisiana, and Alabama. Cotton is among the three largest cash crops for Arizona, California, Mississippi, and Texas. Cotton yields on the irrigated lands of Arizona and California are almost double the yields of other states.

Cotton production is characterized by many small farms; there are some 500,000 cotton farmers. Under the federal price support program each cotton producer has an acreage allotment. In 1969, the average cotton allotment was 40 acres, but the allotment was above 100 acres in the Southwest and below 35 acres for the southeastern states.

CONSUMPTION TRENDS

The U.S. cotton industry has been confronted with a declining consumption trend. Consumption of all fibers fluctuated around 40 pounds per capita from 1945 to 1964, and increased to 60 pounds in 1975, as shown in Figure 27-2. However, over these years cotton's fiber market share was slowly eroded by synthetic, man-made fibers. Per capita consumption of cotton fell from 23 pounds to 16 pounds between 1964 and 1974. And cotton's share of the U.S. fiber market fell from 84 per cent in 1930 to 31 per cent in 1976.

This competitive market erosion occurred in all three of cotton's end-product uses. Cotton held 63 per cent of the clothing market in 1964, but only 37 per cent in 1974; cotton's share of the household furnishings market (upholstery, carpets, drapes) fell from 57 per cent to 24 per cent between 1964 and 1974; cotton's share of the industrial fiber market fell from 28 per cent to 22 per cent over this period. As one example, cotton accounted for 96 per cent of all tire fibers in 1939 but only 2 per cent in 1963.

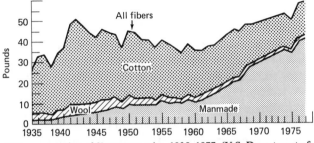

Figure 27-2. U.S. consumption of fibers per capita, 1935–1977. (U.S. Department of Agriculture)

There were many reasons for this loss of cotton's market. Changes in the availability and relative prices of substitutes were major factors. When it was developed in 1930, rayon was priced five times higher than cotton. By 1945, mass production techniques had pushed the price of rayon below the price of cotton. Other market-erosion factors were wartime shortages of cotton, government price support programs for cotton, and changes in consumers' fabric preferences.

One cotton product is running counter to the declining consumption trend. Per capita consumption of cotton denim—for dungarees, blue jeans, and casual clothing—grew from 1.3 pounds in 1965 to 3.1 pounds in 1976. Denim's share of the United States fabric market leaped from only 3 per cent in 1970 to 16 per cent in 1977. This growth was not sufficient to offset other cotton market losses, but it is a vivid illustration of the dynamic role that changes in consumer lifestyles can have on the demand for farm products.

COTTON INDUSTRY STRUCTURE

The cotton plant produces two marketable products—fiber (lint) and the cottonseed. The cotton fiber is the more valuable component, representing 85 to 90 per cent of the farm value of cotton. Cottonseed oil and meal compete with other edible vegetable oils and animal feeds.

The cotton fiber-textile-apparel marketing chain is shown in Figure 27-3. In the early 1970's, this chain was comprised of some 500,000 cotton farmers, 3,200 cotton gins (which separate the cotton fiber and seed), 650 cotton warehouses, 7,200 textile mills, 24,400 apparel and household textile manufacturers, and thousands of wholesalers, exporters, and retailers of cotton products. As cotton and cotton products move from farm to retail levels, these marketing agencies' product lines become more diverse.

Assembly Markets

Cotton gins and interior cotton warehouses are scattered throughout the cotton belt. Raw cotton is a bulky product, so the ginning takes place in country markets near cotton production. Cotton gins may be privately owned or cooperatively operated. They do not usually buy the cotton from farmers, but rather render a service to farmers for a fee. Cotton farmers normally retain ownership of the cotton until it is sold to a textile mill or exported. Farmer cotton ginning costs increased from $16.78 per bale in 1964–1965 to $41.16 per bale in 1975–1976.

Some gin owners grow their own cotton, and cooperative gins are another example of vertical integration of cotton production and assembly market activities. There is also a trend toward forward contracting of cotton between

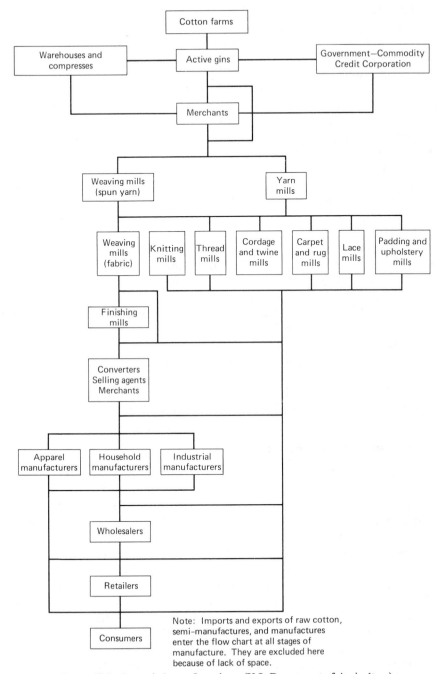

Figure 27-3. Cotton industry flow chart. (U.S. Department of Agriculture)

farmers and textile mills. Perhaps one third of cotton is now grown under contract to buyers.

After ginning, cotton is frequently stored for considerable periods of time awaiting sale. Because cotton is a bulky and expensive commodity to store, many warehouses also operate compressors. These compress cotton bales from the 12 pounds per cubic foot density as it leaves the gin to 23 pounds per cubic foot for cotton to be stored, and to 33 pounds per cubic foot for cotton to be exported. This compression has somewhat the same effect on the costs of storing and transporting cotton that processing and concentration have on perishable, bulky foods.

In some years, the government's Commodity Credit Corporation has been an important assembly market buyer of cotton. This agency assumes title to cotton when market prices are near the loan rate and farmers default on their nonrecourse government loans. CCC cotton stocks are stored in public warehouses.

A few cotton trading centers, strategically situated throughout the cotton belt, play a key role in cotton marketing. Cities such as Memphis, Dallas, Little Rock, Fresno, Lubbock, and Montgomery have large-scale facilities for storing and merchandising cotton and have concentrations of cotton merchants. Trading is carried on under the rules of the local cotton exchange serving these market areas. These "spot markets" serve as focal points for the discovery of cotton prices.

There are a variety of merchant wholesalers and brokers which link the cotton assembly markets with textile mill buyers and with exporters. The role of these middlemen has declined somewhat as more mills have bought directly from cotton producers and cotton cooperatives.

Textile and Clothing Manufacturing

The textile/apparel complex is made up of three types of firms: (1) textile mills which spin yarns and weave cloth; (2) finishing mills which bleach, dye, print, and prepare fabric for apparel makers; and (3) garment cutters and household manufacturers who make the final consumer products. Many companies specialize in one of these operations; others combine various phases of spinning, weaving, finishing, fabricating, and even wholesaling and retailing of textile products.

The textile/apparel industry presents an interesting example of how the changing location of agricultural production can influence the marketing channel. Producers of finished apparel and household textile products are principally located in the northeastern United States, the historical center of the American textile industry. Most of the 655 textile finishing plants are located in a one-half square mile of New York City! Domestic cotton mills, on the other hand, are principally located in the southeast—the early center of cotton production. However, over 50 per cent of the cotton crop is now produced in the West and the Southwest. Hence, the geographic location of the textile industry has not caught up with changing cotton production patterns, and there has been a lenghtening of the cotton-textile distribution channel.

As in most manufacturing industries, there has been a decline in the number of textile plants and companies and a corresponding growth in firm size. The number of textile manufacturing plants fell from 7,700 in 1958 to 7,200 in 1972, whereas average plant sales grew from $1.6 million dollars to $3.9 million. In 1972, the market share of the four largest textile firms varied— 20 per cent of the tufted carpet and rug industry, 31 per cent of cotton weaving sales, and 78 per cent of the woven carpet and rug industry. Market concentration appears to be higher in the man-made fiber industry than in cotton fibers.

Cottonseed Processing

Cottonseed is a bulky product with a low value, so cottonseed oil mills are generally located in cotton producing areas. Ginners usually purchase cottonseed from farmers and many ginners operate their own processing facilities. Cottonseed is processed into oil, cakes or meal, and hulls, all of which have commercial value.

Cottonseed oil and meal compete with soybeans as sources of edible vegetable oils and animal feeds. The soybean crushing industry has grown more rapidly than the cottonseed processing industry, but both have benefited from the substitution of vegetable fats for animal fats in the consumer's diet. The number of cottonseed oil mills fell from 286 in 1954 to 150 plants in 1967, and average plant sales rose from $2.1 to $2.7 million. The market share of the four largest cottonseed processing companies increased from 41 to 43 per cent between 1963 and 1972.

COTTON TRADE

Cotton is a key U.S. export commodity. One third of America's cotton crop was exported in the 1971–1977 years. U.S. cotton is sold to Western Europe, Canada, Japan, and India. Ports such as Houston, Galveston, Los Angeles, and San Francisco are the major gateways for American cotton exports.

World production of cotton has been expanding more rapidly than the rate of growth in the United States production. In 1968 the United States accounted for 20 per cent of world cotton production, but only 15 per cent in 1975. In the 1950's and early 1960's, high cotton price supports reduced U.S. cotton exports. However, changes in the cotton price support programs in 1966 resulted in a rise in the United States share of cotton exports—from 17 per cent in 1968 to 19 per cent in 1975.

U.S. cotton textile imports grew more rapidly over the 1960–1975 period than exports, as shown in Figure 27-4. The major cotton exporters to the United States are the United Arab Republic, Egypt, India, Mexico, and Peru. U.S. textile imports are limited under the terms of the 1962 International Textile Agreement and the 1974 Multi-Fiber Arrangement of the General Agreement on Tariffs and Trade.

Increased production of synthetic fibers has been a worldwide trend. Between 1947–1949 and 1962–1963 world synthetic fiber production increased by 300 per cent whereas cotton production grew by only 70 per cent. Thus, U.S. cotton has faced three competitive challenges: competition from domestic as well as foreign man-made fibers, and competition from foreign cotton producers.

Figure 27-4. U.S. cotton textile trade, 1960–1975. (U.S. Department of Agriculture)

COTTON MARKETING MARGINS AND PRICES

Because considerable value must be added to raw farm cotton to make it useful to consumers, the farmer receives a relatively small share of the consumer's cotton dollar. As shown in Figure 27-5, the farmer's share of the retail cotton product declined from 14 per cent in 1962 to 8 per cent in 1967. This share varies by products; farmers receive only 6 per cent of the retail price of a cotton shirt. Manufacturing and retailing activities take the largest share of the cotton dollar—62 per cent in 1967. As with food products, labor is the largest marketing cost, representing more than 50 per cent of the spread between retail cotton product prices and the farm value of cotton.

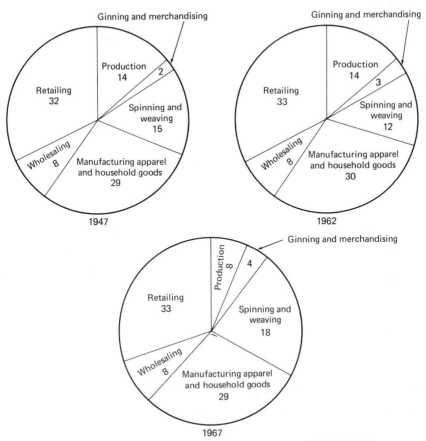

Figure 27-5. Distribution of the consumer's cotton dollar, 1947–1967. (U.S. Department of Agriculture)

The U.S. farm price of cotton is influenced by domestic and international trends in demand; cotton production, supply and stocks; and the federal cotton price support program. The Commodity Credit Corporation supports the farm price of cotton through a nonrecourse loan program. Since 1967 this program has been supplemented with a target price-deficiency payment program for cotton producers.

The cotton industry's experience with the federal farm price support program illustrates the complexity—and sometimes unintended effects—of government intervention in the farm pricing process. Figure 27-6 shows that the market price of cotton closely followed the Commodity Credit Corporation's loan rate or support level over the 1948–1966 period. Cotton prices were supported at the 27 to 35-cents per pound level at a time of declining domestic demand for U.S. cotton and falling world cotton prices. The result

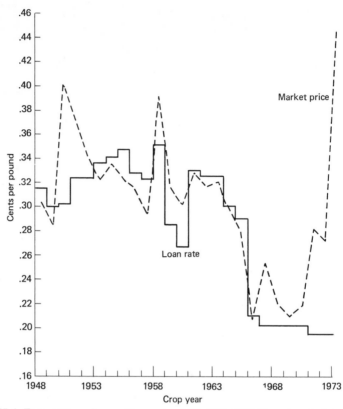

Figure 27-6. Farm cotton prices and loan rates, 1948–1973. (U.S. Department of Agriculture)

was that, not only did U.S. farmers receive higher prices than they otherwise would have, but cotton and cotton products lost their competitive position in world markets. Nevertheless, in order to encourage cotton exports, the U.S. government granted a subsidy to cotton exporters, amounting to the difference between the United States "supported" price and the competitive world price. This, however, put American textile mills, which were paying the higher support price for U.S. cotton, at a competitive disadvantage in world markets. To correct this situation, the American government granted another subsidy, called the *equalization payment,* to domestic cotton users— again, the difference between the United States and the world price of cotton.

In 1966, government intervention in cotton pricing was reduced. The cotton loan rate was dropped to world price levels, and the export subsidy and equalization payments were no longer necessary. Cotton farmers were given deficiency payments to support their incomes. The effect of this market orientation policy on cotton prices is shown in Figure 27-6. Cotton prices moved above support levels in 1967 and remained there for the 1967–1977 period.

At the same time, the United States' share of world cotton exports rose, cotton stock levels fell, and the CCC was no longer the major market outlet for U.S. cotton.

PROBLEMS IN COTTON MARKETING

The cotton industry has undergone considerable change in recent years at all market levels. New production patterns, improved ginning and textile manufacturing technologies, and altered marketing practices have all influenced the marketing of cotton. Associated with these changes have been adjustments in the market organization and in the competitive environment.

Declining demand is at the heart of the cotton marketing problem. Changes in government price support programs affecting the competitive position of cotton in domestic and international markets, research into new cotton products, and cotton promotion programs are directed toward improving the cotton demand picture. The Cotton Research and Promotion Act of 1966 authorized a producer-sponsored cotton research and promotion program. Voluntary contributions of one dollar per bale by producers amounted to $11 million for this purpose in 1974–1975. The Agricultural Act of 1973 also authorized the CCC to donate $3 million per year to the cotton research program. A Cotton Board composed of twenty producers administers the cotton research and promotion program. One research priority of this program is to develop a durable-press 100 per cent cotton fabric. This would help to offset the technological development which gave man-made fibers a competitive edge over cotton.

A 1975 cotton industry study committee pointed out several problem areas where cotton marketing might be improved.[1] One area of concern was that it is increasingly difficult to discover cotton prices in the spot markets. Even though less and less of the cotton is passing through them (as a result of direct mill purchases), these markets still serve as the basis for pricing cotton throughout the marketing channel. There was also some concern for the effects of cotton contracts (between producers and cotton buyers) on the open market competitive processes.

Cotton grades and standards were also singled out as a cotton marketing problem. U.S. Department of Agriculture cotton grading is provided as a free service to producers through Cotton Classing Offices in the cotton belt. Cotton quality standards are based on staple length and grade. These standards do not capture all the properties of cotton which affect mill operating costs, nor do they fully reflect the value of cotton for different uses, especially in the newer textile technologies. Improved means of evaluating cotton quality for better pricing efficiency are needed. The trend toward greater mechanical

---

[1] *National Cotton Marketing Study Committee Report,* U.S. Department of Agriculture, August 1975.

harvesting has also presented problems in cotton quality. Additional seed cotton conditioning and cleaning equipment has been installed in gins to handle the roughly harvested crop. Mechanical harvesting frequently causes problems of cotton's spinnability, particularly in the newer mills.

Other changes needed in cotton marketing include: (1) the development of automatic samplers and higher-density compressors; (2) improved cotton warehouse facilities and handling methods; (3) improved baling techniques to control bale contamination, broken bands, and weather damage; and (4) improved transportation facilities to efficiently transport cotton.

SUMMARY

Cotton marketing patterns are changing as a result of shifts in regional production, competition from synthetic fibers and from other nations which produce cotton and cotton products, the growth of contract integration and of cotton cooperative selling activities, and direct mill purchases of cotton. The declining demand trend dominates the cotton marketing problem. Cotton exports are important to the U.S. economy. Cotton prices rose significantly in the 1967–1975 period as the industry moved from a government price support orientation to a market orientation.

QUESTIONS FOR DISCUSSION

1. What are the reasons for the shift of United States cotton production from the southeast to the West? What has happened to the land formerly used to grow cotton in the South?

2. Based on Figures 27-1 and 27-6, what affect did the 1967 reduction in government cotton loan rates have on production in the short run? In the long run?

3. What market development strategies could the cotton industry have used in the past fifty years to prevent declining consumption of cotton?

4. Using a supply and demand diagram, show the effect of the government loan program on farm prices of cotton prior to 1967 and after 1967.

SELECTED REFERENCES

BARLOWE, R. G., AND J. R. DONALD. "The Cotton Fiber-Textile-Apparel Complex: Structure and Outlook for the 1970's." *Cotton Situation.* U.S. Department of Agriculture, July 1970, pp. 10–23.

CABLE, C. C., JR. "Marketing Cotton and Cotton Textiles," in *Agricultural Markets in Change.* Agricultural Economic Report No. 95, July 1966, pp. 112–149.

The Classification of Cotton. U.S. Department of Agriculture, Miscellaneous Publication No. 310, 1965.

CORKERN, R. S. "Some Recent Trends in the Domestic Marketing System for Textile Fibers and Products." *Cotton and Wool Situation.* U.S. Department of Agriculture, Dec. 1975, pp. 34–40.

DONALD, J. R., F. LOWENSTEIN, AND M. S. SIMON. *The Demand for Textile Fibers in the U.S.* U.S. Department of Agriculture, Technical Bulletin No. 1301, 1963.

HOWELL, L. D. *The American Textile Industry-Competition, Structure, Facilities, Costs.* U.S. Department of Agriculture, Agricultural Economic Report No. 58, 1964.

National Cotton Marketing Study Committee Report. U.S. Department of Agriculture, Aug. 1975.

Statistics on Cotton and Related Data, 1920–1973. U.S. Department of Agriculture, Statistical Bulletin No. 535, annual supplements.

U.S. Textile Fiber Demand-Price Elasticities in Major End-Use Markets. U.S. Department of Agriculture, Technical Bulletin No. 1500, Sept. 1974.

CHAPTER 28

Tobacco and Tobacco Product Marketing

"THE SETTING OF THE TOBACCO INDUSTRY in 1973 is the result of changing conditions, both inside and outside the industry, that have taken place over many years. Many of the forces that have caused tobacco firms to make adjustments have not run their course, and new forces are appearing on the horizon."*

Preview

• This chapter reviews the market structure and problems of the tobacco industry.

• The unique role that tobacco plays in the domestic and world economy is highlighted.

• The factors affecting tobacco demand—health issues, prices, legal restrictions, and taxes—are examined. The public-versus-private choice dilemma of the tobacco industry is discussed.

• The major features of the tobacco marketing channel—large numbers of small growers, local auction markets, and oligopolistic tobacco product manufacturers—are examined.

• There is discussion of the tobacco acreage allotment and price support programs.

• Some tobacco marketing problems are reviewed.

• Key terms and concepts:

cooperative stabilization corporations	tobacco allotment
	tobacco class
pinhookers	tobacco curing

---

* Robert H. Miller, "Tobacco and Tobacco Products Consumption for 1985," 25th National Tobacco Workers Conference, Hamilton, Ontario, Canada, August 9, 1973.

Tobacco is a controversial United States farm commodity. Since its introduction to the civilized world over four hundred years ago, it has been under constant attack. Though tobacco consumption has fallen somewhat in recent years, the commodity has shown a remarkable resiliency, despite legislation and zealots. Here, we will not pass judgment on the health issue connected with tobacco; we will merely review the effect of this controversy on the marketing of the commodity.

There can be no doubt that tobacco is an important farm and consumer product. Between 1974 and 1976, consumers spent $15 to $17 billion for tobacco, about 1.5 per cent of their disposable income. Perhaps 40 per cent of the adult population and 17 per cent of youths smoke tobacco today. Tobacco is the fifth largest cash crop, just behind corn, soybeans, wheat, and cotton, and it accounts for from 4 to 5 per cent of total United States cash farm receipts. Some 500,000 farm families depend upon tobacco for a significant part of their livelihood. Tobacco is also important to the American economy. In 1975, tobacco taxes generated almost $6 billion of federal, state, and local tax receipts. In addition, tobacco has contributed about $1 billion per year to the U.S. trade balance of payments.

TOBACCO PRODUCTION

There are six major classes of tobacco grown in the United States. However, two of these, burley and flue-cured, account for about 90–95 per cent of total production. These tobaccos are chiefly used in making cigarettes, the largest tobacco product. Cigarettes normally contain 40–45 per cent flue-cured tobacco, 30–35 per cent burley tobacco, and the rest is oriental tobacco. Other classes are Maryland (primarily a cigarette tobacco); fire-cured (used for making snuff, plug, twist, cigar, and smoking tobacco); and air-cured (for cigarettes and cigars). In curing, the green tobacco leaves are hung in barns and dried by metal flues, open fire, or by air circulation. In addition to curing the tobacco, the heat produces sugar, which gives the leaves a sweet taste.

Tobacco is grown in 23 states, but the six southeastern states of North Carolina, Kentucky, South Carolina, Virginia, Georgia, and Tennessee account for 90 per cent of all U.S. tobacco production. For North Carolina, Kentucky, and South Carolina, tobacco is the leading agricultural commodity, accounting for 33 per cent of cash farm receipts in North Carolina and 30 per cent of receipts in Kentucky. As shown in Table 28-1, the importance of tobacco declined in all of the major producing states over the 1966–1970 to 1974–1976 period.

Tobacco is produced on several hundred thousand small farms. It is a labor-intensive commodity that requires up to 300 man-hours of labor per acre, compared to 3 man-hours per acre for wheat. As a result, the average

Table 28-1. Importance of Tobacco Farming, By States, 1966–
1976.

STATE	TOBACCO'S PERCENTAGE OF FARM CASH RECEIPTS	
	1966–1970	1974–1976
North Carolina	38%	33%
Kentucky	35	30
South Carolina	23	21
Virginia	16	15
Tennessee	13	12
Georgia	8	7
U.S.	2.8	2.4

Source: U.S. Department of Agriculture.

tobacco farm unit is only 2.7 acres and has been declining in size. This means that the marketing system must accommodate small quantities of product from numerous producers. There are specialized tobacco farms, but usually tobacco is grown along with other crops.

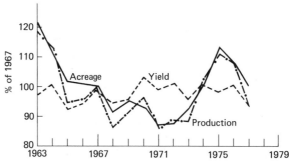

Figure 28-1. Tobacco acreage, yield, and production, 1963–1977. (U.S. Department of Agriculture)

As shown in Figure 28-1, tobacco acreage and production trended downward from 1963 to 1971, increased from 1971 to 1975, and returned to 1963 levels in 1976–1977. Yields did not change appreciably over this period. During this time, tobacco acreage and production were restricted by government price support programs.

TOBACCO CONSUMPTION

Tobacco has a unique demand situation. Because its use is apparently governed by habit, the price elasticity of demand for smokers is quite low ("essential" products normally have inelastic demands). But for the nonsmoking population there is *no demand* for tobacco, presumably at any price. What is more, the alleged health hazards of tobacco to both users and nonusers make smoking a public health issue. In such cases, the private decisions of consumers are frequently overridden by public decisions.

The relative importance of various tobacco products has changed over the years. In the 1920's, cigarettes accounted for only 23 per cent of tobacco use; pipe tobacco, cigars, and snuff accounted for the remainder. In 1975, cigarettes accounted for 80 per cent of domestic tobacco use.

The United States is the largest user of tobacco in the world, whether measured in total quantity, value, or in per capita terms. With 6 per cent of the world's population, the United States consumes nearly one sixth of the world's tobacco. Per capita consumption of tobacco products in America peaked at 13 pounds in 1952, as shown in Figure 28-2. Consumption then trended downward over the 1952–1975 period. This declining consumption trend was related to health considerations, rising tobacco prices, antismoking laws and regulations, and declining production of tobacco under government supply control programs.

Cigarette smoking declined from 1965 to 1970, following the 1964 Surgeon General's Report on Smoking and Health and the 1966 law requiring a warning label on cigarette packages. However, annual per capita consumption of cigarettes grew from 3,985 in 1970 to 4,121 in 1975. This occurred despite a 1970 change in the package health warning (from "may be hazardous to your health" to "is dangerous to your health"); a 1971 ban on radio and television cigarette advertising; and a large-scale antismoking advertising cam-

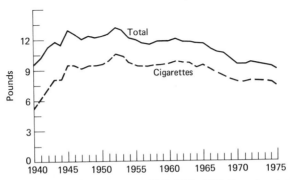

Figure 28-2. Tobacco consumption per person, 1940–1975. (U.S. Department of Agriculture)

paign. Clearly, the demand for cigarettes is a strong one! The 1972 Surgeon General's Report broadened the attack on cigarette smoking by indicating that high concentrations of carbon monoxide—such as in smoke-filled rooms and automobiles—pose a health hazard to smokers and nonsmokers alike. Beginning with Arizona in 1973, thirty states have enacted laws banning smoking in certain public places.

The tobacco industry has responded to these attacks in various ways. There have been denials that cigarettes are health hazards; increased research in order to find a "tobaccoless" cigarette; and the development of "safer" cigarettes (filter-tip, lower nicotine and tar).

It is interesting that the demand for tobacco per se did not increase over the 1971–1977 period, despite increased cigarette production, as shown in Figure 28-3. This was the result of the switch to filter-tip cigarettes, which have a shorter tobacco column, a reduction in cigarette circumference, and new technological developments which permit the use of tobacco stems and midribs in cigarettes. Nor did tobacco farmers benefit significantly from the record high consumer tobacco expenditures of $16.5 billion in 1976 because much of this was a tobacco tax. Farmers receive only 8 per cent of the retail tobacco dollar.

The future of U.S. tobacco consumption—and production—are difficult to predict—unless tobacco is made illegal. The industry appears to have survived the worst publicity any agricultural product has ever received. And there was evidence that cigarette smoking had stabilized among the adult population in the mid 1970's. However, there is still a large discrepancy between public attitudes toward smoking and actual behavior. Public Health Service surveys in the mid-1970's indicated that six out of ten smokers had tried to give up smoking, with various degrees of success, and more than

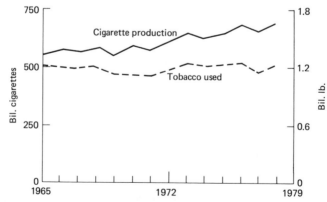

Figure 28-3. Cigarette production and amount of tobacco used, 1965–1978. (U.S. Department of Agriculture)

half of all smokers would like to see smoking allowed in fewer places. These attitudes suggest that further changes may take place in the consumption of tobacco.

MARKETING CHANNELS AND METHODS

The tobacco distribution channel is shown in Figure 28-4. In 1975 this channel consisted of 865 auction houses, 200 tobacco production factories, 2,000 tobacco wholesalers, and over 220,000 retail tobacco outlets.

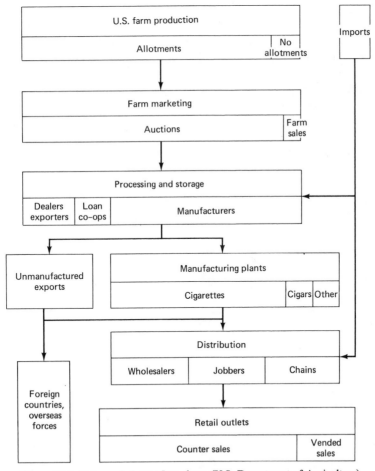

Figure 28-4. Tobacco industry flow chart. (U.S. Department of Agriculture)

Farm Tobacco Markets

About 98 per cent of United States tobacco is auctioned at 865 sales warehouses in 175 markets scattered throughout the tobacco belt. These markets
are shown in Figure 28-5. These auction markets have changed little since
the first one was organized in Danville, Georgia, in 1863. The sales warehouses

Figure 28-5. Tobacco auction markets and producing areas. (U.S. Department of Agriculture)

are one-story buildings, usually well lighted with skylights, and sometimes have as much as 100,000 square feet or more of unobstructed floor space. Sales warehouses are located in the major production areas so that most of the tobacco to be sold is usually brought in by the farmers themselves. The tobacco is weighed and tagged and displayed on the floor in round piles with the stem end out. Before the sale the tobacco is graded by a federal grader.

Sales are conducted according to a prearranged schedule which permits buyers to move among the several warehouses in a given market area. Small markets with only two or three sales warehouses may have only one group of buyers, whereas a larger market may have several sets of buyers who work simultaneously. Buyers include representatives of tobacco manufacturing and exporting companies and speculators (pinhookers). The sale is conducted as the auctioneer moves about the various piles of tobacco on display in the warehouse.

To the uninitiated observer sales are a scene of utter confusion. One can scarcely tell auctioneer from buyer from warehouseman, and it is almost impossible to determine who bought which pile of tobacco for what price. The owner may "no sale" any basket and place it elsewhere in the warehouse, remove it to another warehouse, hold it for later sale, or take out a nonrecourse loan from the Commodity Credit Corporation.

The sales dates vary with production areas. The Georgia-Florida markets open first, usually in mid-July, and continue through most of August. Markets in South Carolina open a week or so later and continue through October. North Carolina markets follow and conduct sales through November. Burley and fire-cured markets operate from December to February or March. Southern Maryland markets begin sales in May and continue through the summer months. Thus some type of tobacco is being sold nearly every month in the year.

Cooperative associations do not make up a separate type of market organization, but function largely as farmers' representatives in conjunction with the auction system. Tobacco cooperatives have a long and turbulent history. By 1923 almost half of the nation's tobacco was marketed through various cooperative associations. But the movement declined, and by 1930 only about 2 per cent of the production was marketed by cooperative organizations. At the present time *cooperative stabilization corporations* perform the storage functions in connection with the government loan programs, which are the mechanism of price supports.

Tobacco, as delivered to the market by farmers, is in a semiperishable condition because of high moisture content. Except for certain cigar types, aging and fermentation occur after leaving the farm. Sometimes a period of two or three years is necessary for the complete fermentation process to take place. This situation means that almost 80 per cent of the current available supply of tobacco is carried over from one season to the next in storage.

573

Prior to storage, tobacco is cleaned, reclassified, and redried to obtain the moisture necessary for fermentation. The weight loss from cleaning, redrying, aging, and stemming is such that the manufacturer's net yield is about two thirds of the farm sales weight.

Tobacco Product Manufacturing

Tobacco product manufacturing is subject to substantial economies of scale and is a highly concentrated industry. In 1972 the four largest tobacco companies accounted for 84 per cent of total cigarette sales. The number of plants making cigarettes declined from 19 in 1958 to 12 in 1972, but these 12 plants accounted for 88 per cent of the total value-added by all tobacco manufacturing plants. Cigarette plants are concentrated in North Carolina, Virginia, and Kentucky. Most of the 40 cigar plants are located in Pennsylvania and Florida.

Cigarette manufacturing is an excellent example of oligopoly—a few firms produce and sell nearly all the U.S. cigarette output. Competition tends to focus on product differentiation, such as length, product image, filters, and the like, rather than on prices. There were 20 leading brands of cigarettes in the 1950's. In the 1960's about one new brand was introduced each year, and there were 120 brands and brand variations available by 1970. Mass-media advertising is used to build brand preferences. Cigarette manufacturers represented 1 per cent of all advertising dollars spent during 1970–1974, and advertising costs account for about 13 per cent of the cigarette marketing bill. The major cigarette manufacturers are shown in Table 28-2.

Table 28-2. Cigarette Sales and Advertising, Top 10 Brands, 1976.

| | | SALES | | ADVERTISING |
| | | BILLION CIGARETTES | PER CENT OF TOTAL | EXPENDITURE PER CARTON |
BRAND	COMPANY			
Marlboro	Phillip Morris	94.2	15%	6.7¢
Winston	Reynolds	90.1	14	6.8
Kool	Brown & Williamson	60.7	10	7.5
Salem	Reynolds	52.6	9	9.4
Pall Mall	American Tobacco	46.8	8	5.3
Kent	P. Lorillard	27.8	4	16.3
Benson & Hedges	Phillip Morris	26.2	4	10.7
Camel	Reynolds	26.0	4	5.1
Tareyton	American Tobacco	16.5	3	8.8
Vantage	Reynolds	14.3	2	28.0
Top 10 as a per cent of total			73%	

Source: *Advertising Age* and John C. Maxwell, Jr., December 26, 1977, pp. 38–9. Reprinted by permission.

Reconstituted tobacco sheets represent an example of efficient technological change in the tobacco industry. These sheets use tobacco stems, scrap, and dust which were formerly discarded; these cost about one fifth of the price of tobacco leaf. Since the mid-1950's, reconstituted tobacco sheets have replaced most of the natural binder in cigars, and have also permitted total cigarette production to rise although the amount of domestic leaf used in cigarettes has remained unchanged.

TOBACCO TRADE

The United States is the world's largest producer and exporter of tobacco and one of the largest tobacco importers. Of the $11.7 billion world tobacco crop in 1975, the U.S. crop accounted for $2.2 billion; the second largest producer, the People's Republic of China, accounted for $2.1 billion. Over the 1974–1975 period, the United States represented 18 per cent of world tobacco production but 25 per cent of tobacco exports. In recent years about 35 per cent of the U.S. tobacco crop has been exported, with cigarettes accounting for 92 per cent of these exports. In 1975, the United States exported $1.3 billion of tobacco and imported $300 million of tobacco, for a net $1 billion contribution to the balance of trade.

As shown in Figure 28-6, the United Kingdom (the world's largest tobacco importer), Western Europe, and the Far Pacific are the leading export markets for American tobacco. Turkey, Greece, and Yugoslavia are the leading sources of U.S. tobacco imports.

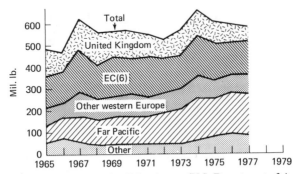

Figure 28-6. Export markets for U.S. tobacco. (U.S. Department of Agriculture)

SUPPLY CONTROL AND PRICE SUPPORT PROGRAMS

Federal tobacco price support programs have existed since the early 1930's. These programs have been designed to maintain tobacco supplies in line with demand, to promote the orderly marketing of tobacco, and to support and stabilize farm prices. The principal components of the program are producer supply controls and a nonrecourse loan program. The two are related: tobacco growers agree to restrict production in return for guaranteed minimum prices of tobacco.

In the original 1938–1940 supply control program, each tobacco grower was allotted a share of the national acreage which would result in a reasonable balance of supply and demand. Predictably, these acreage allotments encouraged farmers to boost yields, and tobacco yields increased rapidly in the 1950's and early 1960's. As a result, a poundage allotment was added to the acreage allotment in 1965 for burley and flue-cured tobacco. This slowed yield increases, forced farmers' attentions on quality rather than quantity, and provided more effective tobacco supply control.

In 1977 there were 537,000 tobacco allotments. This number is greater than the number of tobacco farms because some farmers are permitted to grow more than one type of tobacco. Average allotments for the various types of tobacco are shown in Table 28-3. Producers are legally bound to abide by these allotments, and actual production has been quite near the national target allotment. Each annual allotment is determined by the Secretary of Agriculture.

Under the terms of the CCC nonrecourse tobacco loan program, the Secretary of Agriculture also establishes a support price for each grade of tobacco. If the auction bid is below this price, the tobacco can be delivered to the

Table 28-3. U.S. Tobacco Allotments, by Kinds of Tobacco, 1972.

KINDS	ALLOTMENTS	ACREAGE ALLOTTED	POUNDAGE ALLOTTED	AVERAGE SIZE OF ALLOTMENT
			Million	
	Number	*Acres*	*Pounds*	*Acres*
Flue-cured (11–14)[1]	192,792	[2]645,631	1,197	[3]6,210
Burley (31)[4]	298,107	[2]—	683	[3]2,291
Va. fire-cured	5,150	11,159	—	2.17
Ky.-Tenn. fire-cured (22–23)	14,834	32,708	—	2.20
Dark air-cured (35–36)	19,601	13,203	—	.67
Va. sun-cured (37)	853	1,568	—	1.84
Cigar binder (51–52)	—	[2]—	—	—
Cigar filter and binder (42–44, 53–55)	5,752	19,453	—	3.38
Total	537,089	723,722	—	—

[1] Acreage poundage with national average yield goal of 1,854 pounds per acre. [2] Acreage allotments terminated. [3] Pounds. [4] Poundage quota.

Source: U.S. Department of Agriculture.

local cooperative association, which pays the farmer the loan support price. The cooperative is authorized by CCC to purchase, handle, and eventually market the tobacco. In most years, the cooperative has been able to market the tobacco at a price sufficient to repay the CCC loan rate; therefore the program has been self-financing.

The tobacco support price averaged 90 per cent of parity from 1942 to 1956, fell to 87 per cent of parity in 1960, and averaged 65 per cent of parity in the early 1970's. However, the dollar support price rose from 56¢/pound in 1960–1966 to $1.00/pound in 1975–1976. Market prices followed these support prices quite closely over the 1965–1977 period, as shown in Figure 28-7.

The tobacco allotment and price support programs frequently have been criticized. The following are some of the chief criticisms. Allotments of any kind on an historical basis tend to freeze production patterns, limit entry and freedoms, and provide profits to allotment holders. Tobacco land prices are more affected by the land's allotment than its fertility and productivity. There can be no guarantee that the allotments will be held by the most

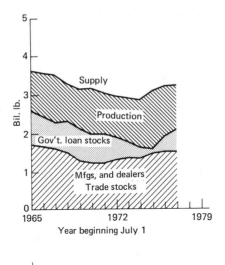

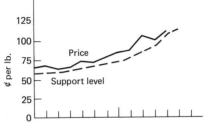

Figure 28-7. Supply and prices of flue-cured tobacco, 1965–1977. (U.S. Department of Agriculture)

efficient producers, although they are transferable and are sold. There is also concern that the price support program has kept U.S. tobacco prices above world levels and thus eroded the competitive position of American tobacco in world markets.

The tobacco program, however, has proved to be popular with growers. Except in 1939, they have overwhelmingly voted for the allotments in triennial referendums, sometimes approving them by 90 per cent of all growers. Apparently tobacco growers consider the sacrifice of production freedoms to be a small price to pay for the price supports.

TOBACCO MARKETING PROBLEMS

The public-health issue overshadows all other tobacco marketing problems. The possibility of legislation which would restrict tobacco use, and changes in consumer attitudes toward tobacco, create considerable uncertainty for the industry. Additional industry shocks may be forthcoming. It appears that, rightly or wrongly, demand for tobacco would continue strong if consumers are given a free choice, but there is no guarantee of this freedom in the case of tobacco.

The very substantial differences in the sizes and numbers of tobacco growers and tobacco product manufacturers is another source of industry concern. The large numbers of relatively small tobacco producers selling in open auction markets represents a situation quite close to perfect competition. Tobacco manufacturing, however, is among the most concentrated, oligopolistic industries. The resulting imbalance of market power has consequences for tobacco prices and other terms of trade. The federal government frequently has applied the antitrust laws to the tobacco industry. The most famous case was the 1911 dissolution of the American Tobacco Company (which had accounted for 90 per cent of industry sales) into four firms: American Tobacco Co., R. J. Reynolds Tobacco Co., Liggett and Meyers, and P. Lorillard Co.

The large number of tobacco sellers in relation to buyers presents problems concerning the fair allocation of sales opportunities among growers and tobacco-producing areas. There have been charges of preferential treatment of some growers. In the 1960's, many growers engaged in extensive tobacco shipping when they were unable to sell their tobacco at local markets as rapidly as they would have liked. As a result, in 1974 the industry adopted a program whereby each grower designates a sales warehouse, within a 100 mile radius of his county, where his tobacco will be sold. The Flue-Cured Tobacco Advisory Committee then sets opening dates, sales schedules, and sales opportunities for each market area. This program has reduced cross-state tobacco shipment costs, provided more equitable treatment for all producers, and has generally resulted in more orderly tobacco marketing.

The farmer's share of the retail tobacco dollar is quite low compared with

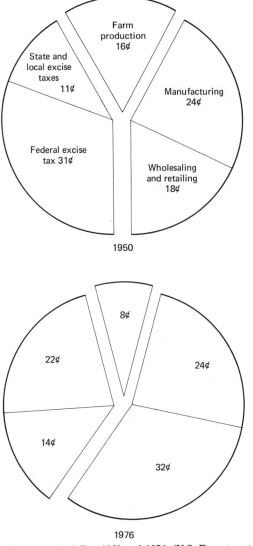

Figure 28-8. The tobacco user's dollar, 1950 and 1976. (U.S. Department of Agriculture)

other agricultural commodities. As shown in Figure 28-8, it fell from 16 per cent in 1950 to 8 per cent in 1976. This means that farmers receive only a small share of increased retail tobacco prices, and farm tobacco prices are less important to retail prices than the manufacturing and marketing activities. The large share of the tobacco dollar which goes for taxes is also apparent in Figure 28-8. In 1976, federal, state, and local taxes accounted for 36 percent of the tobacco dollar.

Tobacco quality continues to be an industry problem. Currently, there

579

are 140 grades of flue-cured tobacco and 106 grades of burley. Weather conditions cause wide variations in the proportion of each year's crop falling into the various grade categories. In recent years, loan rates have been adjusted to give above-average prices for the tobacco grades that are in strongest demand. Mechanical harvesting of tobacco—and less leaf handling by farm workers—has increased the amount of foreign matter on tobacco, thereby reducing its value to manufacturers. As a result, in 1977 tobacco grades were revised, imposing more stringent regulations regarding the presence of foreign matter.

SUMMARY

The tobacco industry is facing a serious consumption problem because of the public health issues regarding smoking. The tobacco issue is complicated by the large number of producers involved, the strategic role tobacco plays in the economy of some states, the contribution tobacco taxes make to federal, state, and local treasuries, and the critical position of tobacco in the United States trade picture. Tobacco is marketed at open auctions in the tobacco belt. Almost perfectly competitive producers face strong oligopolistic buyer-manufacturers in these markets. Tobacco prices are supported by a producer acreage and poundage allotment program and a nonrecourse loan price support program. Tobacco stabilization cooperatives and industry advisory committees play strategic roles in tobacco marketing.

QUESTIONS FOR DISCUSSION

1. How does tobacco consumption differ from the consumption of other agricultural commodities? What is a *habit?* And how do *habits* differ from *preferences?*

2. How will the public weigh the economic benefits of the tobacco industry (taxes, trade, farm income, etc.) against the "costs" of smoking? How do the notions of "risk" and "consumer sovereignty" enter into this policy area?

3. Why is tobacco produced on such small farms—2.7 acres per farm, on the average? How does this affect farm marketing?

4. Why haven't farmer cooperatives been more successful in marketing tobacco? What unique role do cooperatives play in tobacco marketing?

5. Why do you think there is little integration of tobacco-product manufacturers into tobacco production?

6. How might tobacco farmers increase their share of the retail tobacco dollar?

SELECTED REFERENCES

Annual Report on Tobacco Statistics, 1976. U.S. Department of Agriculture. Agricultural Marketing Service, April 1977.

BORDEAUX, A. F., JR., AND R. H. BRANNON, Ed. *Social and Economic Issues Confronting the Tobacco Industry in the Seventies.* Center for Developmental Change, University of Kentucky, Lexington, Ky., Feb. 1972.

BRADEN, J. D. "Changes in Marketing, Processing, and Use of Tobacco." *Tobacco Situation.* U.S. Department of Agriculture, March 1970, pp. 49–55.

"Facts About Flue-Cured Tobacco Grade Standards." U.S. Department of Agriculture. Agricultural Marketing Service, Publication No. 573, May 1977.

HALL, R. "Economic Importance of the U.S. Tobacco Industry." *Tobacco Situation.* U.S. Department of Agriculture, Dec. 1976, pp. 30–35.

MILLER, R. H. "Government Actions Relating to Smoking and Health, 1964–1974." *Tobacco Situation.* U.S. Department of Agriculture, June 1974, pp. 33.

_____ "Tobacco Price Support Programs." *Tobacco Situation.* U.S. Department of Agriculture, June 1975, pp. 33–36.

Report of the Tobacco Marketing Systems Study Committee. U.S. Department of Agriculture. Agricultural Stabilization and Conservation Service, July 1973.

Tobacco in the U.S. U.S. Department of Agriculture. Miscellaneous Publication No. 867, Jan. 1973.

"Tobacco Marketing." *Agricultural Markets in Change.* U.S. Department of Agriculture. Agricultural Economic Report No. 95, July 1966, pp. 382–395.

Glossary

ACREAGE CONTROLS—A provision of many farm programs which attempts to reduce farm output by limiting the acreage that farmers plant.

ADVERTISING—Nonpersonal sales presentations addressed to large numbers of consumers.

ADVERTISING-TO-SALES RATIO—A firm's or industry's advertising expenditure expressed as a per cent of its sales; a measure of the importance of advertising to the firm's or industry's marketing effort.

AFFILIATED CHAINSTORE—A contractually integrated retail and wholesale operation; the affiliate can be either a wholesaler firm which is cooperatively owned by independent retailers or a wholesaler-sponsored retail chain.

AGENT MIDDLEMAN—A food marketing firm that represents buyers and sellers in the marketplace; agents do not take title to goods for their own account and may not physically handle the food products.

AGRIBUSINESS—The sum total of all institutions, firms, and activities involved in the commercial production and marketing of food.

AGRICULTURAL ADJUSTMENT ACT (OF 1933 AND 1938)—Early farm legislation that contained the first provisions designed to aid farmers through supply control, government purchase programs, and orderly marketing tools.

AGRICULTURAL EXEMPTION—A clause of the Interstate Commerce Act that exempts from Interstate Commerce Commission regulations motor carriers transporting raw agricultural commodities.

AGRICULTURAL (FARM) STRUCTURE—Refers to the number, size, ownership, specialization, and other characteristics of farming.

AGRICULTURAL PRODUCTIVITY—Refers to operational efficiency in farming; usually measured by the ratio of farm output to farm inputs.

AGRICULTURAL SUBSTITUTE—A product that is manufactured from farm commodities but which is a substitute for a traditional farm food product (e.g., corn-oil margarine or soy-protein steaks).

AGRICULTURAL TRADE DEVELOPMENT AND ASSISTANCE ACT OF 1954—Also known as the "food for peace" program, or PL-480; the federal pro-

583

gram designed to increase United States farm product exports by selling commodities on low-interest loans, exchanging commodities for local currencies, or donating commodities to needy countries.

AGRICULTURAL TREADMILL—Refers to the situation in which farmers find themselves, after having been encouraged to adopt new output-increasing and cost-reducing production technologies, producing food at a lower price with no increase in profits.

ANALOG, FOOD—A food product that resembles, and is a substitute for, a traditional farm food product (e.g., a steak made out of soybean meal, with a plastic bone).

ASSEMBLY MARKET; ASSEMBLERS—Markets and firms that consolidate the produce of individual farms and prepare it for the marketing process.

ASSORTING—The process of accumulating a heterogeneous set of products from homogeneous lots.

AUCTION MARKET—A production-area wholesale market that sells farm products to buyers on an auction basis.

AWAY-FROM-HOME FOOD MARKET—The market where consumers buy food away from home; includes restaurants, cafeterias, hotels, motels, and other food service operations.

BACKHAUL—Freight that a carrier hauls in returning to its point of origin; without a backhaul, a truck or train must run empty when returning to its departure point.

BALANCE OF TRADE—The value of a nation's exports less its imports.

BALANCE SHEET, COMMODITY—A commodity table showing the sources of supply and the uses of products, with total supply equal to total use.

BARGAINED PRICES—Prices arrived at by joint interaction of a group of buyers and sellers.

BARGAINING ASSOCIATION—A farm cooperative having as its principal function the influencing of farm prices and other terms of trade.

BARGAINING POWER—A form of market power denoting the relative strength of buyers and sellers in influencing the terms of exchange in a transaction.

BASE PRICE QUOTATION—A price that is discovered in a central market and which serves as a base point for pricing elsewhere in the marketing channel.

BASIS—The difference between a cash price and any futures price.

BASIS PRICING—A price quotation technique whereby the current cash price of a commodity is described by indicating the basis; for example, "30 cents under" would indicate a \$2.70/bu. cash price if the futures price were \$3.00.

BATTLE OF THE BRANDS—The competitive rivalry between food processors' nationally advertised brands and the unadvertised (private) brand products of food wholesalers and retailers.

BEAR—A trader who anticipates falling prices.

BEHAVIORAL SYSTEM—A set of related marketing institutions and functions, their goal being the solution of marketing problems.

BID PRICE—The price buyers offer to sellers.

BIOLOGICAL LAG—The time period necessary for a changed production decision to influence market supplies, owing to the biological nature of agricultural products.

BLEND MILK PRICE—The farmer's price of milk as determined by a weighted average of Class I and Class II milk prices.

BLENDING—A grain marketing strategy whereby two different qualities of grain are blended in such a way as to raise the total value of both lots.

BOXED BEEF—Beef that is sold by the meatpacker in primal, subprimal, or final retail cuts rather than as a carcass; this beef is usually frozen and boxed for shipping convenience.

BOYCOTT, CONSUMER—A group tactic whereby a number of consumers refuse to purchase a product (as in the 1967 and 1972 meat boycotts) in an attempt to influence the price or to influence other market conditions.

BRAND—Any name, sign, symbol, design, and so on, used to identify the products of one firm and set them apart from competitors' offerings.

BREAKER—An egg processor who makes dried, frozen, and liquid egg products.

BROILER—A young meat-type chicken; also called *fryers.*

BROKER—An agent middleman who facilitates trades but does not usually physically handle food products; usually paid a set service fee by buyers and sellers.

BULK HANDLING—Any procedure that permits handling a large concentration of products rather than small lots.

BULL—A trader who anticipates rising prices.

BUSINESS CYCLE—Periodic expansions and contractions in the real value of gross national product, often accompanied by periods of rising and falling price levels.

BUYER'S MARKET—A market situation wherein a surplus of products provides buyers some advantage in price bargaining with sellers.

CAPPER-VOLSTEAD ACT (1922)—The federal law that sanctions and encourages agricultural cooperatives to serve as instruments for maintaining reasonable competition in the marketing and purchasing of agricultural products and supplies.

CARCASS WEIGHT AND GRADING—An alternative to pricing live farm animals; in carcass weight and grading, the final value of the animal is determined after slaughter and cut-out.

CARRYOVER STOCKS—Supplies of commodities left over from one marketing season to the next.

CARTEL—An association of firms that attempts to regulate industry output and prices through mutual agreement.

CENTRAL MEAT PROCESSING—The movement of the meat cutting and processing operations to a central point (usually a retail chain warehouse) in the meat distribution channel.

CHAINSTORE—Usually defined as a set of 11 or more related grocery stores, operating under a similar name.

CHAINSTORE MOVEMENT—A trend toward combining retail stores into a single firm, one which also operates food wholesaling facilities.

CHANNEL CAPTAIN—A dominant member of an industry who assumes responsibility for the coordination of all members' decisions in the marketing process.

CLASS FREIGHT RATE—A common freight rate that applies to a class of products.

CLASSIFIED MILK PRICING—The system whereby farmers receive a higher price for Grade A milk used in producing fluid milk products than for milk used in making processed dairy products.

CLAYTON ACT (1914)—A supplement to the 1890 Sherman Antitrust Act; this act further identified market activities considered to be monopolistic and in restraint of trade.

COMMISSION MAN, MERCHANT—An agent middleman who physically handles products for buyers and sellers and is paid a percentage of the selling price for his services.

COMMODITY BALANCE SHEET—See Balance sheet, commodity.

COMMODITY CREDIT CORPORATION (CCC)—The government agency that buys, sells, and stores farm commodities in connection with federal farm price and income support programs.

COMMODITY EXCHANGE—The marketplace where cash commodities and futures contracts are traded.

COMMODITY FUTURES TRADING COMMISSION—The federal agency responsible for regulating futures trading in the United States.

COMMON CARRIER—Any regulated transportation firm that offers its services to all shippers at a fee and which follows scheduled routes.

COMPARATIVE ADVANTAGE—The relative efficiency of producing one commodity as compared with producing another.

COMPETITIVE FRINGE—The small firms in an industry that account for a relatively small share of total industry sales but which nevertheless furnish competition for the dominant core firms.

COMPLEMENTARY IMPORT—An imported product that does not compete directly with domestically produced products of the importing nation; also known as a *noncompetitive import.*

COMPLEMENTARY PRODUCTS—Products that are usually consumed together (e.g., ham and eggs).

CONGLOMERATION—The combining of unlike kinds of economic activities into a single firm; also known as *diversification.*

CONSUMER—The ultimate buyer and user of food products; firms that buy products for resale rather than for direct consumption are referred to as *middlemen* or *market intermediaries.*

CONSUMER BOYCOTT—See Boycott, consumer.

CONSUMER FRANCHISE—Refers to consumer loyalty to a brand or to a store as a result of past experiences or promotional efforts.

CONSUMER NEED—The difference between an actual and desired state of being for a consumer.

CONSUMER SOVEREIGNTY—The proposition that ultimately the consumer should, or does, direct all production and market activities in the economy.

CONSUMER WANT—Goods or services purchased by consumers and therefore presumed to be satisfying in some sense; wants may be physiological or sociopsychological; most products (e.g., food) are purchased to satisfy both wants and needs.

CONSUMERISM—A wide range of government, business, and consumer activities designed to assist and protect consumers and to foster consumer rights and responsibilities.

CONSUMPTION PATTERN—The set of products that consumers purchase, as well as the processes by which these products are produced and prepared for use.

CONTRACT CARRIER—A transport carrier that deals with a few customers and does not offer its services to the general public.

CONTRACT INTEGRATION—An agreement between two independent firms on a mutually profitable venture.

CONTRACT MATURITY—The time at which the futures contract promise is due; usually seven to eight trading days before the end of the month designated for maturity.

CONVENIENCE FOOD—A product that reduces the time, effort, or ingredients required of the consumer in home preparation; for example, frozen orange juice is a convenience form of beverage orange juice; convenience foods are said to have "built-in maid service."

CONVENIENCE STORE—A neighborhood, limited-line food retail outlet.

COOPERATIVE—A business voluntarily owned and controlled by its member-patrons and operated for them on a nonprofit or cost basis.

COOPERATIVE PATRON—A member of a cooperative who uses the co-op's services.

CORNER—A situation where a single buyer or seller holds a large share of the outstanding long or short positions in the cash and futures markets, and therefore can influence to his advantage prices in these markets.

CORPORATE CHAINSTORE—A fully integrated wholesale-retail firm operating under a single corporate identity; e.g., A & P, Kroger, or Safeway.

CORPORATE FARM—Any farm organized under corporate law as compared to a proprietorship or a partnership. Family farms may or may not be corporations; some corporate farms are owned by food marketing firms or nonfood firms.

COST-PRICE SQUEEZE—A situation wherein price levels are persistently equal to, or even occasionally below, costs of production.

COUNTERVAILING POWER—A market power position that nullifies another position in the market; for example, farmers might gain countervailing power against imperfectly competitive buyers by selling, as a single agent, through cooperatives.

CROSS ELASTICITY OF DEMAND—The relationship of quantity demanded for one commodity to a price change for another commodity.

CROSS-SUBSIDIZATION—The practice of using the profits from one industry to subsidize aggressive price competition in another.

DECENTRALIZATION—A market trend that has replaced central market trading by direct sales of farmers to buyers in production areas; also refers to the movement of food processing plants from cities to farm production areas.

DEFERRED PRICING—A price that is determined sometime after the product has been transferred from the seller to the buyer.

DEFICIENCY PAYMENT—A direct price supplement paid to farmers by the government; in the 1973 and 1977 farm bills, the deficiency payment was the difference between the market price the farmer receives and the target or support price.

DEMAND—A schedule of the quantities of products which consumers will buy at alternative prices.

DEMAND EXPANSION—A marketing effort that seeks to shift the demand curve for a product or industry to the right so that more can be sold at the same price, or so that a higher price can be obtained for a given quantity of sales.

DE-MARKETING—A marketing strategy used to reduce consumer demand for a product in order to bring the demand to a level that can be supplied.

DEMOGRAPHY—The study of human populations—numbers of people, where they live, how they live, and their characteristics.

DEPRESSION—A period of time when the real value of the gross national product declines, as in the 1930 depression.

DERIVED DEMAND—The relationship of a demand schedule at one market level to a schedule at another market level; for example, the farm demand for hogs is derived (or results from) the consumer demand for pork chops.

DIFFERENTIATED MARKETING—The practice whereby firms develop separate marketing programs for different target consumer groups.

DIFFERENTIATED PRODUCTS—Products which, in the eyes of consumers, have significant differences, because of either price, quality, advertising, or other characteristics.

DIRECT BUYING—The practice whereby food marketing firms purchase directly from farmers or shipping-point markets rather than from terminal markets.

588

DIRECT SALE—A farm sale to buyers which does not go through, or use, the facilities of an intermediate market or marketing agency.

DIVERSIFICATION—Refers to performing more than one unrelated market activity; the opposite of *specialization.*

DIVERSION PRIVILEGE—Permission for a shipper to divert a product to an alternative destination while enroute.

DOCKAGE—Extraneous material found in grain, such as dirt, weed seeds, other grains or broken kernels.

DOMINANT CORE—The largest firms in the industry, those which account for a significant share of industry sales.

DUMPING—The practice of pricing products for sale in foreign markets at prices considerably below the selling price in the domestic market.

ECONOMIES OF SCALE OR SIZE—A situation wherein efficiency gains accrue from increasing the size of operations; for example, large food processors may have lower average unit costs than smaller processors.

EFFECTIVE DEMAND—Consumer needs and wants backed up by purchasing power or a willingness to sacrifice money for products.

EFFICIENCY—A ratio of market output (satisfaction) to marketing input (cost of resources); an increase in this ratio represents improved efficiency, a decrease denotes reduced efficiency.

ELEVATOR—A marketing facility for purchasing and storing grain and for mixing animal feeds; many elevators also sell farm supplies.

ENGEL'S LAW—A tendency for the share of a family's (or nation's) income spent for food to fall as income rises. This suggests that the income elasticity of food is lower than that of other products.

ENTREPRENEUR—An individual or firm that commits resources to productive activities in pursuit of a profit; a risk-taker and profit-seeker.

EQUALIZATION PAYMENT—A government payment to United States cotton users representing the difference between the United States and the world price of cotton.

EQUILIBRIUM PRICE—That market price at which the quantity supplied is equal to the quantity demanded; also called the *market clearing price.*

EQUITY FINANCING—Borrowing money (usually working capital) by pledging the value of a product in storage or in production as collateral for a loan.

EXCHANGE—An economic process by which two traders voluntarily arrive at a mutually advantageous bargain.

EXCHANGE RATE—The rate at which one nation's currency can be exchanged for other currencies.

EXEMPT CARRIER—A motor vehicle that hauls raw agricultural commodities and is therefore exempt from Interstate Commerce Commission regulations.

EXTENDER, FOOD—A product that can be added to a traditional food to expand its volume (e.g., "Hamburger Helper").

FAMILY FARM—A farm enterprise in which the owner-operator supplies most of the land, capital, and labor (himself and/or his family); any farm using less than 1.5 man-years of total labor.

FAMILY LIFE CYCLE—The stages families pass through; described in terms of adult ages, number and ages of children, income, and so forth.

FARM MARKETING PLAN—See Marketing plan, farm.

FARM PROBLEM—A complex set of problems associated with agriculture's perfectly competitive structure, the inelastic demand for food, and the high ratio of fixed-to-variable costs. The farm problem is usually expressed as instability of farm prices and incomes, periodically declining farm prices, and low farm incomes relative to nonfarm incomes.

FARM-RETAIL PRICE SPREAD—The difference between the retail price of a food product and the farm value of an equivalent quantity of food sold by farmers.

FARM SPECIALIZATION—Any specialization of production activity on the farm, either by commodity, processes, personnel, or geography.

FARMER COOPERATIVE SERVICE—The branch of the U.S. Department of Agriculture with responsibility for fostering agricultural cooperatives.

FARMER-DIRECT SALES—Farm sales of produce made directly to consumers, without the use of traditional middlemen; the farm roadside market is an example.

FARMER MARKET POWER PROBLEM—Problems associated with the relative bargaining power of farmers and their suppliers and buyers.

FARMER'S SHARE—The farm value of food expressed as a percentage of its retail price.

FAST-FOOD INDUSTRY—A restaurant segment of the away-from-home food market; it emphasizes standardized menus, rapid service, and minimum table service.

FED BEEF—Beef produced from cattle that have been finished on grain rations, as compared with grass-fed or range cattle.

FEDERAL TRADE COMMISSION—An independent federal regulatory agency with broad powers over commerce, including the regulation of competition, trade practices, and mergers.

FEEDER ANIMALS—Livestock bought for the purpose of finishing to market weights.

FEEDLOT—A specialized form of farming which involves the feeding of livestock, under confined conditions, to market weights.

FINANCING—Financial support for a business activity when current receipts are not always equal to expenses, as in the financing of a food canner's inventory of canned goods.

FINISH—A term referring to the final quality of a farm product.

FIXED COSTS—Those costs that do not vary as a firm's output changes, such as overhead, insurance, and depreciation.

590

F.O.B.—Abbreviation for "free on board"; an FOB factory price is a price quotation that does not include shipping charges.

FOOD ANALOG—See Analog, food.

FOOD AND DRUG ACT (1906)—A federal law regulating the healthfulness and wholesomeness of the food supply.

FOOD EXTENDER—See Extender, food.

FOOD MARKETING SYSTEM—The collection of product channels, middlemen, and business activities involved in the physical and economic transfer of food from producers to consumers.

FOOD RESERVES—Food stocks that are held in order to balance supplies with demand over the long run, or to even out supplies between countries.

FOOD SHARE OF INCOME—The percentage of consumers' income (usually after-tax income) used for the purchase of food.

FOOD STAMP PROGRAM—A publicly supported food program which attempts to increase the food purchasing power and dietary adequacy of certain groups of people; food stamps are a form of currency and can be used only to purchase food.

FOODWAY—A society's behavior pattern of producing, selling, buying, sharing, and consuming food.

FORM UTILITY—The value added to basic commodities when they are converted into finished products.

FORMULA PRICING—A pricing technique whereby an individual transaction is priced according to an agreed-upon basis; for example, much wholesale meat is priced "at the market," as indicated by a privately collected market price quotation.

FORWARD PRICE CONTRACT—A contract farmers may enter into, prior to the harvesting of a crop, which fixes the price in advance.

FORWARD PRICING—Any technique that permits a seller or buyer to fix the price of a commodity prior to the actual physical exchange.

FREE MARKET—A marketplace with minimum direct involvement of government in market decisions.

FREE-RIDER PROBLEM—A problem common to any group effort where each person must make some sacrifice so that the total group will benefit. Unless the benefits can be restricted to only those making the sacrifice, individuals will have no incentive to cooperate, but may nevertheless enjoy a "free ride" on the group.

FREE STOCKS—Commodity stocks held by farmers or the trade, rather than by government.

FREIGHT FORWARDER—A wholesaler who specializes in aggregating small lots of products into larger shipments in order to benefit from more favorable rates.

FUNCTION, MARKETING—A specialized business activity necessary to the food marketing process.

FUTURES CONTRACT—A legal contract certifying agreement to either make or take delivery of a commodity in the future at a specified price.

FUTURES MARKET—The arena for exchanging futures market contracts; consists of all traders, the trading exchanges, and all attendant trading operations.

FUTURES PRICE—The current price offered for future delivery of a commodity.

GATEKEEPER—Any firm that controls a strategic resource in the food marketing system, such as shelf-space in retail stores, a sales force, or any other key marketing variable.

GENERAL-LINE WHOLESALER—A wholesaler offering a reasonably complete assortment of products to retailers, as opposed to a limited-line wholesaler.

GENERIC—A word used to describe a general class of products, such as meats, vegetables, or grains.

GENERIC ADVERTISING—Advertising that attempts to alter the demand for an entire class of products, for example, all meat or all beef.

GOVERNMENT PURCHASE PROGRAM—A government program intended to raise farm prices by purchasing and storing agricultural commodities; these commodities may be sold later, diverted to other markets, or destroyed.

GRADING—The sorting of unlike lots of the same product into uniform categories, according to quality standards.

GRAIN BANK—An elevator service to farmers who lack on-farm storage space for their grain, which is to be fed to their livestock; farmers deposit grain with the elevator and withdraw it as needed over the marketing year.

GRAIN MERCHANDISING—General term referring to the marketing activities of grain handlers, including timing of buying and selling, grain conditioning, storage, and grain blending.

GROSS FARM INCOME—The total value received by farmers from sales of products, government payments, the value of farm products consumed on-farm, the rental value of farm dwellings, and other farm-related income.

GROSS MARGIN—The difference between the price a firm pays for products and the price it charges its customers; it is also termed *gross profit,* and may be expressed as a percentage of the firm's selling price.

HEDGE—A risk-management, profit-oriented marketing tool involving the temporary substitution of a futures market transaction for a cash transaction; involves equal and opposite positions on the cash and futures markets.

HEDGER—A handler of an agricultural commodity who prefers to speculate on a basis change rather than on cash price changes.

HOMOGENEITY OF PRODUCTS—A characteristic of a set of products denoting that, in the eyes of traders, they are perfect substitutes for each other.

HORIZONTAL INTEGRATION—Combining similar marketing functions and decisions at the same market level into a single firm; for example, one food processor buying another food processing company.

HRI MARKET—The hotel, restaurant, and institutional market for food.

IMPORT QUOTA—A restriction on the amount of a specific category of goods that may be imported into a country.

INCOME ELASTICITY—The responsiveness of food consumption (measured in quantity or expenditures) to changes in consumers' income.

INDEPENDENT RETAILER—Any retailer who is not formally affiliated with other retailers or a food wholesaling operation.

INFERIOR GOOD—A product for which there is an inverse relationship between consumer's income and consumption; i.e., consumption declines as income rises; sometimes referred to as "poor people's products."

INFLATION—A persistent and general rise in the price level which reduces consumers' purchasing power.

INNOVATION—A new product, a new business technique, or a new way of doing things.

INPUT INDUSTRY—Also called the farm supply industry; the industry includes markets that supply resources for farm production, such as chemicals, seeds, feed, energy, and other farm supplies. In this book it is considered part of the food marketing system. Farmers procure production supplies from the input markets.

INPUT-OUTPUT SYSTEM—Any activity that transforms resources into more valuable products; the production process is an input-output system.

INTEGRATION—The consolidation under a single management of previously independent marketing functions and decisions.

INSTITUTION, MARKETING—Any public or private entity involved in the marketing process: an individual business, a corporation or group of firms, a government agency, or the legal system.

INTEGRATOR—A firm that takes the initiative in integrating the production and marketing processes.

INTENTIONS REPORT—A report on the expected future behavior of farmers.

INTERREGIONAL COMPETITION—Rivalry between two areas or markets, e.g., oranges from Florida and oranges from California.

INTERSTATE COMMERCE COMMISSION (ICC)—The federal regulatory agency that has authority over freight rates, transportation routes, and other facets of the nation's transportation system.

JOBBER—A wholesaler of foods; synonymous with *distributor* and *wholesaler*.

LAW OF DEMAND—An economic principle which states that, everything else being equal, consumers can be expected to buy more of a product as its price falls and less as its price rises.

LAW OF MARKET AREAS (LOMA)—An economic principle which holds that the boundary between two markets or sellers is a locus of points such that the final selling prices, including plant price plus transportation costs, are equal for all sellers.

LAW OF ONE PRICE (LOOP)—A marketing principle which holds that, under perfectly competitive market conditions, all prices within a market will be uniform after the costs of adding place, time, and form utility are taken into consideration.

LAW OF SUPPLY—An economic principle suggesting that, everything else being equal, producers will offer to sell more of a product at a higher price than at a lower price.

LENGTH OF RUN—A period of time during which production, marketing, and consumption decisions are influenced; the proportion of fixed and variable costs, as well as the decision-makers' ability—and willingness—to alter decisions, will vary during the length of run.

LEVERAGE—The ability to control a large amount of money with a small amount of funds.

LOAN RATE—The price the government is willing to loan the farmer for his commodities under the terms of a nonrecourse storage loan.

LONG—A trader who has purchased a futures contract.

LONG HEDGE—A hedge that initially is established by buying in the futures market.

LOSS LEADER—A product priced at less than the seller's cost, in the hopes of attracting into the store customers who will then purchase more profitably priced merchandise.

MANUFACTURER'S SALES BRANCH—An establishment operated by a processor or manufacturer which serves as a wholesale outlet for a market territory.

MARGIN—The amount of ernest money that must be posted with a broker when a futures commodity position is first taken (buy or sell).

MARKET—An arena for organizing and facilitating business activities and for answering the economic questions: What to produce? How much to produce? How to produce? and How to distribute production? It may be defined by a location, a product, a time, a group of consumers, or a level of the marketing system.

MARKET CONCENTRATION—A measure of the dominance of large firms over an industry or market; dominance is measured by the share of total sales made by a few of the largest companies.

MARKET CONDUCT—The manner in which firms within an industry adjust prices, output, product quality, and promotional efforts in response to competitive pressures.

MARKET DEVELOPMENT—Marketing activities and efforts designed to enhance the value of food products to consumers and in the process expand sales and profits.

MARKET INFORMATION—Any form of information which is relevant to a market decision.

MARKET INTELLIGENCE—Any market information that is relevant to decisions made by firms; a marketing function.

MARKET NEWS—Descriptive information on current market conditions, including prices, stocks, demand, and so on.

MARKET PERFORMANCE—The economic results that market participants (farmers, consumers, middlemen) and society expect from the food marketing system.

MARKET POWER—The ability to influence advantageously markets, market behavior, or market results.

MARKET RISK—The possibility of loss—through product deterioration in quantity or quality or value change—while a product is being produced or marketed.

MARKET SEGMENTATION—The marketing technique of developing separate products and marketing programs to appeal to different consumer classes.

MARKET STRUCTURE—The environmental characteristics of an industry which influence the behavior of firms in the marketplace: size and number of firms, product differentiation, barriers to firm entry, and so on.

MARKET TONE—A market news term referring to the general attitude of buyers and sellers toward prevailing prices.

MARKETABLE SURPLUS—The production of an individual or a society which exceeds that needed or desired for personal consumption; this surplus is then available for sale to other individuals or countries.

MARKETING—The performance of all business activities involved in the flow of food products and services from the point of initial agricultural production until they are in the hands of consumers; a value-adding process which adds time, form, place, and possession utility to farm commodities; the study of exchange processes and relationships.

MARKETING AGREEMENT—A self-help farmer marketing tool which permits farmers and handlers of farm commodities to enter into agreements about how products will be marketed.

MARKETING BILL—The total dollar expenditures going to food marketing firms to pay for all marketing activities.

MARKETING BOARD—A marketing agency granted wide powers over the production and marketing of a commodity.

MARKETING CHANNELS—Alternative routes of product flows from producers to consumers.

MARKETING CONCEPT—A management philosophy which holds that all company planning begins with an analysis of consumer wants, and that all company decisions should be based upon the profitable satisfaction of consumer wants.

MARKETING FUNCTION—See Function, marketing.

MARKETING INSTITUTION—See Institution, marketing.

MARKETING MACHINERY—A synonym for the food marketing system.

MARKETING MARGIN—The portion of the consumers' food dollar paid to food marketing firms for their services and value-adding activities; the "price" of all food marketing activities.

MARKETING MIX—The unique way in which a firm or industry combines its price, promotion, product, and distribution channel strategies to appeal to consumers.

MARKETING MYOPIA—A term referring to the tendency of some firms to define their business too narrowly in terms of a specific product; for example, a dairy firm may define its business as *dairy products* or, more broadly, as *fluid beverages.*

MARKETING ORDER—A legally binding instrument which specifies how a particular farm product shall be marketed; the purpose of an order is to foster orderly marketing of the commodity over time, form, and space.

MARKETING PLAN, FARM—A set of objectives, strategies, and tactics which guide a farmer's production and marketing decisions.

MARKETING PROCESS—The sequence of events and actions that coordinate the flow of food and the value-adding activities in the food marketing system.

MARKETING STRATEGY—A procedure used to achieve a market goal; for example, one grocery store may use the strategy of low prices to attract consumers; another might employ the strategy of high quality.

MERCHANT MIDDLEMAN—A food marketing firm that provides a variety of marketing functions, including taking title to products.

MERCHANT WHOLESALER—A wholesaling middleman who physically handles and takes title to products.

MERGER—The combining of the assets of two independent firms into a single company.

MIDDLEMAN—A person or business firm operating between producers and consumers and performing marketing functions; a term frequently used to describe the nonfarm firms in the food industry; food processors, wholesalers, and retailers are middlemen.

MIDDLEMAN BIAS—A commonly held attitude that middlemen are not productive, and that they frequently exploit the farmers and consumers with whom they deal.

MILKSHED—A designated geographic area of milk production and consumption.

MINNESOTA-WISCONSIN MILK PRICE—The price of Grade B milk used for manufacturing purposes in Minnesota and Wisconsin.

MIX PRICING—A pricing tactic of multi-product retailers whereby each product is assigned a different gross profit, thus attempting to differentiate one retail chain store from others.

MONOPOLISTIC COMPETITION—A competitive situation wherein a relatively large number of firms sell products that are slightly differentiated.

MONOPOLY—A market situation where there is only one seller of a product, and where there are no close substitutes for the product.

MONOPSONY—A firm that is the only buyer of a product.

NET FARM INCOME—Net profit from farming operations; gross farm income less the costs of farm production expenses.

NONRECOURSE STORAGE LOAN—A government price support program that allows the farmer to store his commodities at harvest and use them as collateral for a loan; the farmer may redeem the commodities later by paying back the loan, or keep the loan by forfeiting the commodities to the government.

NORMAL GOOD—A product with a positive income elasticity; consumption increases with income.

NORMAL PROFIT—A profit level or return to resources only equal to that which they could earn in other uses.

NUTRITIONAL LABELING—Labels that provide consumers with information about products' nutritional values.

OFFER PRICE—A seller's asking price.

OLIGOPOLY—A market situation with relatively few sellers who are mutually interdependent in their marketing activities; some food processing industries are oligopolistic.

OLIGOPSONY—A competitive situation where there are a few large buyers of a product.

ONE-STOP SHOPPING—The tendency for some consumers to purchase all desired products from one store in one trip.

OPEN-CODE DATING—Food labels providing consumers with information on when food was processed and packaged, when it should be sold or withdrawn from the market, or when the product is no longer acceptable for sale.

OPERATIONAL EFFICIENCY—A change in the market efficiency ratio caused by a change in the costs of performing the marketing functions.

OPPONENT-GAIN BARGAINING POWER—Bargaining power gained by offering another market party compensation.

OPPONENT-PAIN BARGAINING POWER—Bargaining power gained through threat or coercion of another market party.

ORDERLY MARKETING—Coordination of the total supply of a commodity over time, form, and spatial markets, in such a way as to achieve sellers' market objectives.

OUTLOOK—A forecast of future market events, such as supplies, prices, and so on.

OWNERSHIP INTEGRATION—A complete combination of the assets of two firms; the same as a merger.

PARASITIC ADVERTISING—Advertising by one group which takes sales away from another group. For example, beef advertisements may reduce pork sales; orange advertisements may reduce apple sales.

PARITY—A concept that attempts to define a "fair price" for farmers such that farm products have a purchasing power equivalent to that which they had in an earlier period.

PARITY RATIO—The ratio of farm prices received to farm prices paid; a 100 per cent parity price would be a farm price which gives a commodity the same purchasing power it had in a base year (usually 1910–1914).

PATRONAGE REFUND—The earnings of a cooperative which are paid to member-patrons, either in the form of stock or cash.

PER CAPITA FOOD CONSUMPTION—The average quantity of food eaten per person within a time period, usually a year; usually calculated by dividing the total food available for consumption by the population figures.

PERFECT COMPETITION—A market situation wherein there are so many firms that no single one of them has a significant influence on price; other prevailing conditions are homogeneous products, ease of new firms' entry into the market, and perfect market information; also termed *pure competition* and *atomistic competition.*

PERFECT HEDGE—A hedge in which the profit and losses from the cash and futures markets are exactly equal.

PHYSICAL DISTRIBUTION—Refers to all physical market activities (such as transportation, warehousing, materials handling, inventory control, and so on) involved in moving products from producer to consumer.

PINHOOKER—A speculator in tobacco prices.

PLACE UTILITY—Also referred to as *spatial utility;* the value added to products by moving them in space to make them more valuable to users, usually by transportation.

POINT-OF-PURCHASE ADVERTISING—An advertising message to which consumers are exposed in the store, such as shelf labels or store banners.

POSSESSION UTILITY—The value added to products by transferring title from sellers to buyers; also referred to as *ownership utility.*

PRE-HARVEST HEDGE—A hedge that is in effect prior to the harvesting of a commodity.

PRICE CEILING—A legally imposed price which is below the equilbrium price level.

PRICE CYCLE—Regular, periodic fluctuations in prices resulting from changes in production.

PRICE DISCOVERY—The processes by which buyers and sellers attempt to arrive at the equilibrium price consistent with supply and demand conditions.

PRICE DISCRIMINATION—A marketing technique which allocates the total supply of a commodity to alternative elasticity markets in a way that will maximize total seller returns.

PRICE ELASTICITY—The relationship of changes in quantity supplied, or demanded, to price changes.

PRICE FLOOR—A legally imposed price which is above the equilibrium price level.

PRICE-TAKER—Any firm that cannot influence the general level of commodity prices by altering the quantity produced; price-takers are often called "quantity adjusters" because their chief decision is to adjust output to a given price; perfectly competitive firms are price-takers.

PRICE WAR—A price-cutting situation wherein firms attempt to rival each other in lowering prices.

PRICING EFFICIENCY—Refers to the capability of prices to allocate resources efficiently and in accordance with consumer preferences.

PRINCIPLE OF COMPARATIVE ADVANTAGE—An economic principle which holds that economic gains are to be had, in the form of reduced costs of production and/or increased standards of living, if, under free trade conditions, each nation will specialize in and export those products it can produce relatively most efficiently, by virtue of its resource endowment, and import commodities for which it has a comparative disadvantage.

PRIVATE LABEL—A brand used exclusively by a wholesaler or retailer, and usually not widely advertised.

PRIVATE TREATY—A market agreement arrived at by a buyer and seller in private negotiations.

PRODUCT—A bundle of physical, service, and symbolic attributes which satisfies consumer wants and needs.

PRODUCT BUNDLE OF ATTRIBUTES—All of the physical characteristics and socio-psychological values that consumers associate with a product.

PRODUCT DIFFERENTIATION—See Differentiated products.

PRODUCT LIFE CYCLE—A set of stages that most new products pass through; these include the development stage, the introductory stage, the growth stage, the mature stage, and the declining sales stage.

PRODUCTION—The process of adding value to resources; an input-output process. Production is not restricted to farming, because value also is added to food in the food marketing system.

PROTECTIONISM—Government trade policies that limit the volume of trade in order to protect domestic industries from international competition.

PSYCHOLOGICAL LAG—The time period necessary to convince producers or consumers that changed economic conditions warrant a change in market behavior.

PUBLIC FOOD PROGRAM—Publicly supported programs that attempt to increase the demand for food, improve the level of the diet, or otherwise influence food consumption; examples are the food stamp program, the school milk program, and so on.

PUBLIC LAW-480—The 1954 Agricultural Trade Development and Assistance Act that authorizes shipment of United States food to foreign countries under special conditions; also known at the "food for peace" program.

QUALITY—A property of a product relating to its usefulness, desirability, and value to customers.

QUALITY STANDARDS—Commonly agreed upon yardsticks for measuring differences in product quality.

QUOTA—A trade restriction on the quantity of products which may be imported into a country; a protectionist trade device.

REAL PRICE—The current price of a commodity, adjusted for its change in purchasing power over time; for example, today's real price of corn in 1970 dollars is the current price of corn divided by the current index of all prices (1970 = 100).

RELATIVE PRICE—The price of one product stated in terms of another; a ratio of two prices.

RESALE PRICE MAINTENANCE (FAIR TRADE)—Laws that permit manufacturers to set and enforce the retail prices at which their products are sold.

RESERVATION DEMAND—The "demand" of a seller for his own product, either for current use or for storage and later sale; a farmer, for example, may reserve part of his production for later sale by storing at harvest time.

RESIDUAL-INCOME CLAIMANT—A firm that has little control over prices received, or income, in the marketplace, and accepts whatever payment is offered for services.

RESOURCE ALLOCATION—An economic term that refers to the shifting of resources between alternative uses.

RESOURCE ENDOWMENT—A nation's, firm's, or individual's unique set of productive resources, including land, labor, capital, and management skills.

RISK-BEARING—A marketing function performed by any firm that is subjected to price or quality change risks.

ROADSIDE MARKET—A food marketing system in which farmers sell directly to consumers, thereby transferring the food marketing functions to consumers and farmers.

ROBINSON-PATMAN ACT (1936)—A federal law that prohibits certain kinds of price discrimination among buyers and sellers.

RTC—Ready-to-cook; refers to a broiler or turkey marketed as eviscerated, with blood, feathers removed.

SALES BRANCH—A manufacturer's establishment that serves as a warehouse and sales office for a particular territory.

SCRATCH FOOD—A form of food that requires considerable preparation on the part of consumers before it can be eaten; a "scratch" cake is one made by formulating the basic ingredients in the home, as opposed to a ready-to-bake cake.

SEASONAL PRICE VARIATION—A regular price variation occurring within a marketing season.

SEASONAL STOCKS—Stocks of commodities held to balance out supply and demand over a marketing season when production is not continuous over the season.

SELLER'S MARKET—A market situation wherein a shortage of products provides sellers some advantage in bargaining for prices with buyers.

SET-ASIDE—A supply control provision of some farm programs which entails farmers withdrawing some acreage from production, either voluntarily or on a required basis.

SHERMAN ANTI-TRUST ACT (1890)—A federal law prohibiting restraint of trade and monopolistic practices.

SHORT—A trader who sells a futures market contract.

SHORT HEDGE—A hedge that is initially established by selling in the futures market.

SHRINKAGE—The loss in physical volume or weight of a commodity while it is being held or marketed.

SOCIAL CAPITAL—The societal resources that are available to facilitate food marketing, such as the transportation, legal, and communication systems.

SORTING—The process of classifying a mixed lot of produce into homogeneous categories, as in the grading of farm products.

SPECIALITY FOOD STORE—A food retail store with a limited and specialized product line; for example, a dairy store, a bakery, or a fruit and vegetable store.

SPECIALIZATION—A fundamental economic activity whereby division of labor and concentration of effort on a single task increases efficiency and output.

SPECULATIVE MIDDLEMAN—A marketing firm specializing in the risk-bearing marketing function; an individual who profits from uncertain changes in food prices.

SPECULATIVE STOCKS—Inventories of commodities held in anticipation of a future price rise.

SPECULATOR—A trader who holds a market position in anticipation of a favorable price movement.

SPOT PRICE—The cash price offered for immediate delivery.

STANDARDIZATION—The grouping of unlike items into uniform lots on the basis of qualitative criteria, such as a food grade.

STATE TRADING MONOPOLY—A trading agency granted a government monopoly in foreign sales or purchases of agricultural commodities.

STICKY MARKETING MARGIN—Refers to the fact that the dollar marketing margin does not adjust to changing farm and retail food prices.

STOCKHOLDERS' EQUITY—The total financial interest that stockholders have in a firm; also called *net worth.*

STORAGE HEDGE—A hedge that is in effect during the time period when a commodity is stored.

SUBSECTOR ANALYSIS—An approach to studying the food marketing process; in this method the entire set of institutions and relationships involved in transforming basic resources into satisfying food products is examined.

SUBSTITUTE PRODUCTS—Products that, in the eyes of buyers, have some characteristics and utilities in common (e.g., apples and oranges).

SUBTERMINAL ELEVATOR—A large grain elevator located in producing areas; the owner buys directly from farmers and sells directly to exporters or grain processors.

SUPERMARKET—A large-scale, departmentalized retail store with a variety of merchandise which usually is operated on a self-service basis.

SUPERMARKET MOVEMENT—A trend toward replacing small, neighborhood high-service food retail stores with large, departmentalized, self-service grocery stores.

SUPPLEMENTARY IMPORT—An imported product that competes directly with a domestically produced product; also referred to as a *competitive import.*

SUPPLY—The quantity of product which producers are willing to produce and sell at alternative price levels.

SUPPLY CONTROL—Any attempt to reduce marketable supplies by restricting either production or flow-to-market; involves shifting the supply curve leftward or preventing rightward shifts.

SUPPORT PRICE—A price level above the equilibrium supply and demand point; support prices are used by government to increase farm prices or farm incomes.

SYNTHETIC FOOD/FIBER—A food or fiber produced from a nonagricultural raw material, for example, a nondairy coffee creamer, a synthetic orange juice, an imitation shoe leather, or a man-made fiber.

TARGET PRICE—A support price level set by government.

TARIFF—A government tax on imported products which has the effect of reducing imports and increasing the consumer prices of imported products; a protectionist trade device.

TECHNOLOGY—The machinery, state-of-the-arts, and level of ingenuity which determine the efficiency and output of any productive process.

TERMINAL MARKET—A central wholesale market, usually located at the terminus of a transportation line in an area of high population.

TEXAS HEDGE—Not a true hedge; involves either short or long positions in both the cash and futures markets.

THIN MARKET—A market in which so little volume is traded that it is questionable whether the supply and demand forces are adequately represented.

TIME UTILITY—The value added to products by changing their time of availability to users, usually through storage operations.

TRADER—A general term for a buyer or seller; one who engages in buying and selling for a profit.

TRADING STAMPS—A form of store promotion widely used by grocery retailers in the 1960's and still used by some; the number of trading stamps given to customers depends upon the cash amount spent in the store; stamps can be traded for merchandise or for cash.

TRANSACTIONS COSTS—Those costs incurred by buyer-seller search, negotiation, and contract-enforcement activities.

TRANSIT PRIVILEGE—Permission for a shipper to halt the movement of a product for processing or handling and then continue shipment to its destination, at a through-rate.

TRANSPORTATION MODE—A means of transportation, such as rail, truck, or water.

TRUTH-IN-PACKAGING—A 1967 federal law (the Fair Packaging and Labeling Act) which attempts to facilitate consumer comparisons of grocery products by standardizing package sizes and label nomenclature (e.g., reducing the number of "Jumbo" sizes).

UNIT PRICING—Comparative pricing of items in standard units of measurement, for example, cents per ounce or dollars per pound.

UNIT TRAIN—Entire trains carrying a single commodity with a single point of origin and point of destination.

UNITED STATES WAREHOUSE ACT—A federal law that regulates public warehouses.

UTILITY—A characteristic of goods and services which describes their want-satisfying power for consumers; economists differentiate between form, time, place, and possession utility.

VALUE-ADDED—The difference between the cost of goods purchased by a firm and the price for which it sells those goods; this difference represents the value-added by the productive activities of the firm.

VARIABLE COSTS—Those costs of the firm which change when output changes, for example, raw material costs, wages, and so on.

VARIABLE-PRICE MERCHANDISING—A retail pricing strategy whereby selective price reductions are used to attract consumers to the store.

VERTICAL INTEGRATION—Combining vertically related marketing functions and decisions into a single firm.

VERTICAL MARKET COORDINATION—The process of directing and harmonizing the several interrelated and sequential decisions involved in producing and marketing farm and food products.

WAREHOUSE FOOD OUTLET—A discount supermarket that offers lower prices and less services than traditional supermarkets.

WEAK SELLER—A seller of a product who has little bargaining power or influence on price, either because of product perishability, lack of control over supply, or other factors.

WEBB-POMERENE ACT (1918)—A federal law authorizing monopolies in the export trade.

WHEEL OF RETAILING—A theory that retailing passes through alternating cycles of low service, low prices and high service, high prices.

WHOLESALE-SPONSORED CHAINSTORE—A set of retail food stores which are supplied by a single wholesaler.

WORKABLE COMPETITION—A set of market performance criteria which represent a compromise between perfect competition and the real world of competitive imperfections.

WORKING STOCKS—The stock levels necessary for the marketing system to function efficiently at full capacity and without supply disruptions; also referred to as *pipeline stocks.*

YARDAGE—Fees charged by livestock merchants and marketing organizations for services to buyers and sellers.

YIELD GRADE—A livestock grading term that refers to the meat yield of the carcass.

Index

A

Act to Regulate Commerce, 18
Adaptive behavior, 35
Administered prices, 179
Affiliated retail chainstore, 118
Agent middlemen, 29–30
Agribusiness, 9
Agricultural Act of 1949, 501, 563
Agricultural Adjustment Act, 317, 442, 445
Agricultural Fair Practice Act (of 1967), 458
Agricultural Fair Practices Act (of 1968), 325
Agricultural inputs, 62, 67
Agricultural Marketing Act, 366, 441
Agricultural Marketing and Bargaining Act, 458
Agricultural Marketing Agreement Act, 317, 442, 458, 502
Agricultural structure, 51–56
Agricultural substitutes and synthetics, 305
Agricultural Trade Development and Assistance Act (P.L. 480), 143, 443
Agricultural treadmill, 443
Alternative transportation modes, 382–385, 390
    Amtrak, 387
American Agricultural Marketing Association, 281, 324
American Egg Board, 520
American Farm Bureau, 281
American Farm Bureau Federation, 324
Analog, 306
Assorting, 13, 14
Away-from-home food market, 89–90

B

Bargained prices, 179
Bargaining association, 317, 324–326, 529

Bargaining power, 311–317, 326, 327, 332
Base price quotations, 531
Basis, 419, 420, 421, 423, 426, 429, 430, 431
    Local harvest basis, 426
Basis pricing, 545
Battle of the brands, 97, 105
Bears and bulls, 418, 419, 429
Behavioral system, 22, 34–36, 45
Bid and offer prices, 335
Biological and psychological lag, 207, 212–214, 218
Blending, 546
Blend price, 504–505
Boxed beef, 488
Brands, 94, 96, 97
Brand advertising, 299, 308
Brand label, 116
Brand loyalty, 94
Broker, 30, 109, 256, 259, 431, 525
Broilers, 517, 519, 520, 523, 524, 531
Bulk milk handling, 499
Bundle of attributes, 144
Business cycle, 208–211
Buyers' market, 160
Buying function, 24

C

Capper-Volstead Act, 272, 279, 288, 325, 458
Carcass weight and grading, 489–491
Car-lot receivers, 30
Carrying charges, 424, 425
Carryover, 539
Carryover stocks, 398, 409
Cash grain commission merchant, 543–544
Cartel, 189
Centralized marketing, 259

605

Centralized plants, 102
Central meat processing, 488
Chainstore movement, 115–119, 122, 126
Chicago Board of Trade, 17, 414, 428
Chicago Mercantile Exchange, 414
Channel captains, 123, 126
Class, commodity rates, 386
Classified pricing, 501
Clayton Act, 456, 457
Commission agents, 109
Commission man, 10, 30, 34, 104, 259
Commodity Credit Corporation (CCC), 402,
    442, 448, 501, 558, 563, 573, 576, 577
Commodity Exchange Act, 18, 432
Commodity Exchange Authority (CEA), 432
Commodity Futures Trading Commission
    (CFTC), 432, 466
  Commodity Futures Act, 432
Common carriers, 388
Communications system, 35
Competitive food markets, 185
  brand competition, 185
  firm competition, 185
  functional competition, 185
  horizontal competition, 185
  institutional competition, 185
  interregional competition, 185
  price-nonprice competition, 185
  product competition, 185
  vertical competition, 185
Competitive fringe, 96, 104
Competitive imperfections, sources of, 191–193
Competitive imports, 140
Complementary imports, 139
Complementary products, 164
Conglomerate market power, 314
Conglomerates, 262, 455
  cross-subsidization, 262
Conglomeration, 261, 262; (*see also*
    Integration)
Consumer food preferences, 74
Consumer franchise, 94
Consumerism, 461
Consumer sovereignty, 22, 40–42, 45, 297, 370
Contracts, farm-marketing firms, 264
Contract maturity, 418, 420, 421, 431
Controlled labels, 124
Convenience foods, 83, 87, 88
Cooperatives, 276–289, 301, 317, 324, 326, 327,
    331, 441, 512, 577
  dairy cooperatives, 506
  dairy farmer cooperatives, 505

dairy marketing cooperatives, 499
  farmer cooperatives, 543
  tobacco cooperatives, 573
  cooperative corporation, 273
Cooperative groups, 111
Cooperative patron-owner, 272, 283
  patrons, 285, 286
  patron-members, 277, 287
  patron-user, 287
Cooperative stabilization corporations, 573
Corporate chainstores, 118
Corporate farming, 54
Cost of production, 60
Cost-price squeeze, 64, 170, 173, 187, 439, 443
Cotton Board, 563
Cotton classing offices, 563
Cotton Futures Act, 366
Cotton gins, 556
Cotton lint or fiber, 556
Cotton Research and Promotion Act, 310, 563
Countervailing power, 313, 317
County elevator, 541–543, 547
Crop Reporting Board, 335, 337
Cross-elasticity of demand, 164

D

Decentralization, 250, 255–260, 266, 268, 316,
    486–487, 493, 512, 516, 524, 531, 544, 545,
    551, 553, 554
Decentralized marketing, 482, 485
Deferred pricing, 545
Deficiency payment, 448, 562
Delaney clause, 460
Delivery months, 417
Demand curve, 154–155, 160–163, 165, 169,
    180, 207, 208, 294, 322, 520
  derived demand, 155–156
  effective demand, 154
  reservation demand, 156
  see also Law of Demand)
Demand states, 294–296
Demographic trends, 79, 82, 90
Demurrage, 387
Depression, recession, 208, 210
Direct buying (purchasing), 256
Direct sales, 482, 485, 524, 545
Diversification, 250, 252, 254, 255, 315
Diversification trend, 96
Diversion and reconsignment privilege, 387
Division of labor, 32
Division of Foreign Markets, United States
    Department of Agriculture, 18

Dockage, 546
Dominant core, 96

E

Economic price discrimination, 322
Economic (price) risk, 421, 422, 432, 433
Economies of scale, 32, 33
Effective food demand, 84
Efficiency ratio, 37–39
Efficiency–utility conflict, 45
Egg breakers, 519, 525
Egg Product Inspection Act, 528
Egg Research and Consumer Information Act, 301, 520
Elasticity of demand, 163–138
Engel's law, 86
Enterprise specialization, 55
Environmental Protection Agency, 466
Equalization payment, 562
Equilibrium price, 159–160, 162, 173, 174, 195
Equity financing, 428
European Economic Community, 142, 176
Exchange function, 24
Exports, farm product, 135–136, 142, 145
Export market expansion, 142–144
Extender, food, 307

F

Facilitating marketing functions, 24, 25, 27, 459
Facilitative organizations, 29, 31
Family farm, 54, 67
Farm Credit Administration, 288
Farmer's Alliance, 17
Farmer's Holiday movement, 317
Farmer's share, 323–324, 237–240; (*see also* Marketing bill)
Farm-factory, 265
Farm inputs, 62, 67
Farm marketing problem, 63–67
Farm product exports, 135–136, 142, 145
Farm productivity, efficiency, 52
Farm specialization, 54
Federal Communications Commission, 458, 466
Federal Energy Agency, 466
Federal Farm Board, 441, 442
Federal Land Bank Associations, 275
Federal Power Commission, 466
Federal Trade Commission, 221, 254, 466, 508
Federal Trade Commission Act, 456
Feeder animals, 477
Feedlots, 476–477, 488

Fiber market, 555
Financing function, 24, 25, 403
  financing, 412, 459
Fixed costs, 158
Flow-to-market, 320–321, 327
Flue-cured Tobacco Advisory Committee, 578
Food and Drug Act, 460–462
Food and Drug Administration (FDA) 360, 460, 466
Food and Drug Administration Color Additives Act, 460
Food brokers, 111
Food consumption patterns, 74, 82, 85, 90
Food for peace program, 143
Food marketing system, 5–6, 9, 20, 22, 51, 56, 67, 74, 80, 87, 89, 121
Food processing costs, 102
Food product bundle, 90
Food-related social problems, 89
Food reserve, 396, 398, 409
Food Stamp program, 464
Foodways, 74–75
Formula prices, 179
Form utility, 10, 87, 93, 105, 252, 538
Forward pricing, 415, 428
Four P's (4P's), 294
Free-rider problem, 64, 302, 323
Free stocks, 403
Freight forwarder, 388
Functional approach, 22, 23–28, 29, 34, 45
Futures contract, 414, 415, 417, 418, 419, 420, 422; (*see also* Forward pricing)
Futures exchanges, 430, 432
Futures market, 409, 414–419, 421–432
Futures prices, 414–430

G

Gatekeepers, 123, 315
Generic advertising, 301, 308
Giantism, 43
Grade labeling, 376
Grading, 363–364, 365, 376, 477
Grain balance sheets, 535
Grain bank, 549
Grain conditioning, 546
Grain Futures Act, 432
Grain merchandising, 546
Grain Standards Act, 366
Gross and net farm income, 210, 211, 216–218
Gross margin, 121, 122

H

Hatch Act, 465
Hedging, hedges, 411, 417, 418, 422, 423, 427,
    428, 429, 430, 431, 433
    short hedge, 424
    long hedge, 424
    Texas hedge, 424
Homogeneous products, 57, 316
Hortizontal integration, 324, 455
Horizontal power, 314, 315
Hotel-restaurant-institutional (HRI) market,
    520

I

Imperfect competition, 313
Imports
    competitive, 140
    complementary, 139
    supplementary, 140
Independent, unaffiliated chainstores, 118
Inelastic demand, 316, 439
Inferior good, 85
Income elasticity, 85
Input–output system, 34–35, 45
Institutional advertising, 299
Institutional approach, 22, 29–34, 45
Integration, 250, 260–268, 316, 516, 522–525,
    528, 531, 544, 553, 554
    conglomerate, 261
    contract, 261, 262, 265, 266
    horizontal, 260, 262
    ownership, 261, 262
    vertical, 260–261, 262
Internal Revenue Service, 466
International Textile Agreement, 560
Interstate Commerce Act, 388
    agricultural commodities exemption clause,
    388, 389
Interstate Commerce Commission (ICC), 18,
    384, 387, 388, 458, 466
Inventory-storage function, 124
Item advertising, 299

J

Jobbers, 30

L

Law of demand, 153–154, 162
    derived demand, 155–156
    effective demand, 154
    reservation demand, 156
Law of market areas, 101
Law of one price, 176, 178, 202, 259

Leverage, 419
Livestock assembly, 479
Livestock grading system, 491
    quality grade, 491
    yield grade, 491
Loan rate, 447
Location decision, 100, 101
Long run, 239
Loss leader, 123, 205

M

Margin, 419
    financial leverage, 419
Market, 9, 14, 174
    geographic, 175–176
    product, 175
    seasonal, 175
Market boundaries, 102, 175–176
Marketable surplus, 14
Market basket, 235, 243
Market concentration, 97, 105, 194
Market corner, 431
Market development, 292, 293, 294, 300
Market information, 330–332, 340–343
Marketing defined, 4–5, 6–7, 19
Marketing agencies, 10, 63, 103, 108, 121, 223,
    224, 267, 297, 301, 313, 322, 337, 368,
    369, 370, 413, 477
Marketing allotments, 319
Marketing bill, 223–227, 229, 230, 239, 242,
    243
    farm-retail spread, 230, 231, 242, 243
    farmer's share, 232–234, 237–240
    profit rates, 227–229
Marketing channels, 4, 5, 34, 43, 108, 111,
    116, 124, 204, 250, 251, 256, 262, 289,
    294, 314, 369, 372, 373, 402, 414, 484,
    485, 497, 512, 519, 531, 558, 563
Marketing concept, 22, 42
Marketing cooperatives, 274, 276, 278, 280,
    324
Marketing contracts, 512, 513
Marketing economics, 60
Marketing efficiency, 477
Marketing efficiency ratio, 37–39, 45
Marketing functions, 5, 23, 27–28, 33, 45, 56,
    64, 87, 93, 108, 112, 113, 119, 121, 242,
    250, 296, 312, 316, 331, 343, 380, 393,
    397, 402, 403, 406, 409, 412, 421
Marketing institution, 29, 32
Marketing machinery, 5, 14, 15, 18, 19, 49,
    51, 55, 56, 331, 522

Marketing margin, 221–223, 226, 230, 231, 237–241, 243
  cost components, 231
  dollar amount, 239
  inflexible 239–240, 243
  percentage, 239
Marketing mix, 294, 302
Marketing plan, 66–67
Marketing profits, 222
Market intelligence, 24, 26, 330, 331, 412, 459
Market news, 330, 331, 332, 334–335, 413
Market news Service, 459
Market order and agreement, 317, 318, 320, 321, 324
Market performance, 36–37, 45
Market power, 311–319, 323, 326, 327
Market research, 330, 331
Market segmentation, 300
Market share, 120
Market situation reports, 334
Market tone, 335
Marshall Plan, 443
McGuire Act, 457
McNary-Haugen Bill, 441
Meat Inspection Act, 460, 462
Mergers, 260
Middleman, 242, 271, 283, 402
  specialized middleman, 388
Middleman bias, 34
Middlemen, 5, 8, 9, 10, 19, 27, 29–34, 222, 365, 414, 558
  merchant middlemen, 29, 30
Milk marketing order, 506
Milkshed, 502
Minnesota-Wisconsin (milk) price, 502, 505
Mix pricing, 122
Monopolistic competition, 188–190, 549
Monopoly, 188–189, 195, 198, 457
  monopoly agencies, 144
Monopsony, 188
Morrill Land-Grant College Act, 465
Motor Vehicle Safety Act, 460
Multi-Fiber Arrangement of the General Agreement on Tariffs and Trade, 560

N

National Agricultural Bargaining Acts, 325
National Agricultural Bargaining Board, 325
National Commission on Food Marketing, 211, 242, 243, 254, 317, 327
National egg pricing system study committee, 531

National Farmers Organization (NFO), 281, 324
National Farm Loan Associations, 281
National Highway Traffic Safety Administration, 466
National Industrial Recovery Act, 442
National Wool Act of 1954, 301, 303
Net worth, 217
Nonrecourse loan, 447, 573, 576, 580
Nontariff trade barriers, 141
Normal good, 85
Nutritional labeling, 460

O

Occupational Safety and Health Administration, 466
Office of Markets, 18
Office of Price Administration, 171
Office of Price Stabilization, 171
Oligopoly/oligopsony, 188–189, 508, 549, 574
Operational efficiency, 22, 38, 40, 93, 102, 105, 254, 259, 325, 332, 389, 390, 403, 406, 430, 458, 516, 532
Operational-pricing efficiency dilemma, 254, 296
Opponent-pain bargaining power, 314–315, 325, 326
Orderly marketing, 318
Outlook, 334

P

Packers and Stockyards Act, 18, 459, 466, 482
Palletized shipping and containerization, 390
Parasitic advertising, 303
Parity, 445
Patent Act, 465
Patronage refund, 272
Perfect competition, 186–188, 190, 194, 195, 313, 363, 455, 538
Perfect hedge, 411, 422, 423
Perishable Agricultural Commodities Act, 459, 466
Pesticide Chemical Amendment, 460
Physical function, 24–25
Place utility, 10, 381
Plant capacity, 99, 102
Plant specialization, 95
Possession utility, 10, 126, 293
Potato Research and Promotion Act, 301
Poundage allotment program, 580
Power system, 35

Pre-harvest hedge, 411, 426, 427, 431, 432, 433
Price ceiling, floor, 171
Price cycles, 212–215
Price determination, 178
Price discovery, 178–179, 316, 477, 486
  administered pricing systems, 179
  bargained prices, 179
  formula pricing systems, 179
  individual, decentralized negotiations, 179
  organized, central markets, 179
  price-discovery process, 430–433
Price discrimination, 322
Price elasticity of demand, 163–164
  elastic demand, 163–165
  inelastic demand, 163–165, 169, 170, 180
Price–margin relationship, 239
Price system, 150–151, 180
  pricing machinery, 151
  fluctuating competitive prices, 151
  relative prices, 152–153
  substitute products, 152
Price takers–price makers, 63, 187, 188, 193, 198, 267, 427
Price wars, 189
Pricing efficiency, 22, 39, 40, 64, 121, 123, 151, 176–179, 204, 205, 239, 242, 254, 259, 260, 266, 268, 297, 486, 532, 542, 545, 563
Principle of comparative advantage, 133–134, 145
Private label, 97, 118, 124
Private treaty negotiations, 179
Process specialization, 55
Processing cooperative, 274, 275
Processing functions, 25, 87
Processors and manufacturers, 28, 31
Produce Agency Act, 459, 466
Product bundle of attributes, 75, 87
Product differentiation, 191, 194, 300, 315, 323
Production, defined, 10
Product innovation, 93, 96
Product life cycle, 94
Product-line advertising, 299
Production Credit Associations, 275, 281
Productivity crisis, 39
Public food programs, 307
Public Health Service, 360
Public Law, 480, 143, 443
Purchasing cooperatives, 274, 278, 280
Pure Food and Drug Act, 461

Q

Quality, of food, 361
Quality control, 57, 314, 365, 374, 408

R

Railroad Revitalization and Regulatory Reform Act, 388
Ready-to-cook (RTC) poultry, 519
  broilers, 531
Real prices, 207
Relative prices, 152–153
Research and Marketing Act, 465
Residual-income claimant, 193
Resource endowment, 132–133
Retailers, 16, 29, 30, 109, 119–126, 251, 254, 264, 298, 300, 406
Retail pricing strategies, 123
Ricardo, David, 133
Risk-bearing, 24, 26, 403, 412, 430, 449, 459
Risk-transfer, 428
Robinson-Patman Act, 456–457
Round turn, 416
Rural Electric Associations, 275, 281

S

Scale economies, 32, 33
Seasonality (seasonal production variability), 59
  seasonality of demand, 518
Seasonal food stocks, 397–8, 409
Seasonal prices, 215
Search and transactions costs, 32, 363
Secretary of Agriculture, 318, 338, 366, 401, 502, 505, 576
Securities and Exchange Commission, 466
Sellers' market, 160
Selling function, 24
Service cooperatives, 274–275, 280
Set-aside policies, 438, 444
Shapiro, Aaron, 317
Sherman Anti-trust Act, 18, 456
Short and long-run, 170, 172–174
Smith-Hughes Act, 465
Smith-Lever Act, 465
Social capital, 13
Soil Conservation and Domestic Allotment act, 442
Sorting, 13, 14, 322
Specialization, 14, 25, 135, 252, 255, 487, 516, 517, 528
  product, 252
  functional, 252
  institutional, 252
Specialization and diversification, 250, 267, 268
Specification buying, 258, 259
Speculative middlemen, 29, 30, 31
Speculative stocks, 398

Speculators, 417–418, 423, 427, 428, 429, 430, 431
Spot and futures prices, 335
Spot price, 414
  spot markets, 563
Standard Container Act, 361
Standardization, 90, 319, 360, 363, 365, 368, 374, 413, 459, 550
Standardization function, 25
Standards, 360, 361, 364, 369–370
Statistical Reporting Service (SRS), 335
Sticky margin, 239, 241, 243
Storage function, 24, 397, 449, 573, 518
Storage hedge, 411, 424–425, 426, 431, 433, 549
Strategies, tactics, 66–67
Substitutability, 164
Subterminal elevator, 541, 544–545, 551
Superior and inferior foods, 85
Supermarket in movement, 115, 119–120, 122, 126
Supplementary imports, 140
Supply analysis, 158
Supply, Law of, 156–159, 163
  supply schedule, 157–158, 159
  supply curve, 157–158, 160–162, 169, 170, 182
Supply control, 64, 315, 322
Supply–elasticity Analysis, 166
Support price, 448, 501, 576, 577
  support price levels, 444
  support prices, 441
Surgeon General's Report, on smoking, 570

T

Target price, 448
Tariffs, 414
Terminal Elevator, 541, 543, 545, 547
Terminal markets, 10, 251, 256, 259, 267, 401, 422, 482, 485, 486, 543
Test weight, 546
Thin markets, 260
Time utility, 10, 397
Tobacco allotments, 576–577
Tobacco class, 567
Tobacco curing, 567
Tobacco sheets, 575
Trade
  aid, 143
  balance of trade, 130–131
  gains from trade, 132
  protectionism, 141–142
  specialization and trade, 132–134

state trading monopolies, 144
trade associations, 31
trade groups, 144, 304, 365
trade protectionism, 141
Transfer of marketing functions, 27
Transit privilege, 387
Transportation Act, 387
Transportation function, 25
Truth-in-Packaging Act, 460
Tydings-Miller Act, 457

U

Union stockyards, 17
United States Bureau of Weights and Measures, 360
United States Department of Agriculture, 288, 361, 362, 432, 459, 465, 466, 526, 563
  Agricultural Marketing Service, 366
  Economic Research Service (ERS), 338
  Farmer Cooperative Service, 288
  Food Safety and Quality Service, 366
  grades, 365, 366, 370, 375, 376
  Information Services, 330, 341, 342
  News Service, 179, 334, 531
United States Department of Justice, 466
United States Grain Standards Act, 546
  Federal Grain Inspection Service, 546
United States Warehouse Act, 401, 459
Unit elasticity, 163, 164
Unit prices, 460
Unit train, 386, 390
Urbanization, 82, 87, 90
Urner-Barry Report, 179
Utilities, 10, 75, 90, 175, 176, 177

V

Value-added, 19
Variable costs, 158
Variable price merchandising, 123
Vertical coordination, 250
Vertical integration, 284, 340, 414, 455, 523, 548, 551, 556
Vertical power, 314, 315
Voluntary chain, 177
Voluntary groups, 111
Voluntary stocks, 399

W

Warehouse Act, 466
Weak seller, 193
Webb-Pomerene Act, 458
Wheat Research and Promotion Act of 1970, 301

Wheeler-Lea Act, 460
Wheel of retailing, 122
Wholesalers, 29, 30, 108–111, 251, 254, 255,
    256, 264, 298, 406
Wholesome Meat Act, 460, 486

Workable competition, 195, 198
Working inventory stocks, 396, 397, 409

Y

Yardage fees, 481